ancient
greek

Gavin Betts
and
Alan Henry

TEACH YOURSELF BOOKS

> ***The authors wish to acknowledge the help of***
> ***George Gellie and Deane Blackman.***

For UK order queries: please contact Bookpoint Ltd, 130 Milton Park, Abingdon, Oxon OX14 4SB. Telephone: (44) 01235 400414, Fax: (44) 01235 400454. Lines are open from 9.00–6.00, Monday to Saturday, with a 24 hour message answering service. Email address: orders@bookpoint.co.uk

For U.S.A. order queries: please contact McGraw-Hill Customer Services, P.O. Box 545, Blacklick, OH 43004-0545, U.S.A. Telephone: 1-800-722-4726. Fax: 1-614-755-5645.

For Canada order queries: please contact McGraw-Hill Ryerson Ltd., 300 Water St, Whitby, Ontario L1N 9B6, Canada. Telephone: 905 430 5000. Fax: 905 430 5020.

Long renowned as the authoritative source for self-guided learning – with more than 30 million copies sold worldwide – the *Teach Yourself* series includes over 200 titles in the fields of languages, crafts, hobbies, business and education.

British Library Cataloguing in Publication Data
A catalogue record for this title is available from The British Library.

Library of Congress Catalog Card Number: On file

First published in UK 1989 by Hodder Headline Plc, 338 Euston Road, London, NW1 3BH.

First published in US 1993 by Contemporary Publishing ,4255 West Touhy Avenue, Lincolnwood (Chicago), Illinois 60646–1975 U.S.A.

This edition published 2001.

The 'Teach Yourself' name and logo are registered trade marks of Hodder & Stoughton Ltd.

Typeset by Transet Limited, Coventry, England.
Printed in Great Britain for Hodder & Stoughton Educational, a division of Hodder Headline Plc, 338 Euston Road, London NW1 3BH by Cox & Wyman Ltd, Reading, Berkshire.

Impression number   10 9 8 7 6 5 4 3 2 1
Year   2005 2004 2003 2002 2001

CONTENTS

INTRODUCTION

How to use this book

ἀρχὴ ἥμιϲυ παντόϲ   *a [good] beginning is half the whole*

On one occasion when giving a speech, Hiero, a Greek ruler in ancient Sicily, was interrupted by complaints about his bad breath. This revelation of what must have been a chronic problem distressed him considerably, and on returning home he reproached his wife for not having told him of it. She indignantly justified herself by saying that she had thought that all adult males smelt as he did. To depend on a virtuous spouse to correct such faults has obvious dangers. If you are relying solely on this book to begin the study of ancient Greek, there are similar pitfalls. Apart from the Key, you will have few checks on your progress, and it will be essential to follow up any doubt, however small, about meanings of words and points of grammar. To be able to do this you must make yourself completely familiar with the arrangement of the book's contents.

We assume that you are acquainted with the basics of traditional English grammar, as this is the framework we use to explain the structure of Greek. You should be familiar with the **parts of speech** (*adjective, adverb, article, conjunction, interjection, noun, preposition, pronoun, verb*) and with the meaning of such terms as *finite, transitive/intransitive, clause, phrase, subject, object,* etc. If these are new to you, you should consult the **Glossary of grammatical terms** on the website http://tyancientgreek.org, or one of the many elementary books on the subject.

The main part of the book consists of twenty-five units. Each consists of either two or three sections. The first is taken up with grammar, the second contains sentences and passages of Greek for reading, while the third section (except in the first unit) is a longer Greek passage for additional reading.

The grammatical sections, which are headed **.1**, are carefully graded over the course of the book in order to set out the basic features of Greek grammar in a systematic and easily digestible way. Each should be mastered before tackling the next. Very often a particular section cannot be understood without a knowledge of what has gone before.

Grammar as a whole can be divided into two parts, one involving the forms which a word can take (e.g. those of a first declension feminine noun, 2.1/2), the other dealing with the ways in which these forms are used to make up phrases and sentences (e.g. the uses of the dative case, 2.1/3*e*). The former we must learn by heart. The latter we can only fully understand when, after learning a general rule, we see, and are able to understand, examples of it in use. Because of the importance of such examples the sentences given to illustrate grammatical rules are nearly always original Greek, and every effort should be made to understand them fully. By reading them carefully every time you revise a unit you will not only come to understand the grammatical point involved but also extend your vocabulary.

To work through the reading exercises with one finger in the corresponding page of the key is **not** recommended, although you should make full use of any help provided by the notes. It is only by analysing the forms of words and patiently working out the construction of clauses and sentences that you will make progress. A full translation of an exercise should be written out and then compared with the key. When you discover you have made a mistake, you must meticulously hunt out the point of grammar concerned and see how you came to be wrong. To help you do this many cross-references have been supplied in all parts of the book (a reference of the form 22.1/2 is for the **grammatical** section (.1) of a unit, but one such as 22.2.2 is to the **reading** section (.2)). Your final step should be to read through the Greek aloud until you are able to translate it without reference to your own version or the key. This will familiarise you with the construction employed and any new vocabulary. Some rote learning of new words is, of course, inevitable. If, however, you go to the trouble of actually memorising some of the many famous phrases and verse passages contained in the reading you will find your grasp on the language extending itself in an enjoyable and rewarding fashion.

Appendices 1–7 give grammatical tables and other information to supplement particular units. **Appendix 8** is on accentuation and should be consulted regularly and mastered over the course of the whole book. **Appendix 9** is added to show how Greek verse was constructed; a knowledge of metre is not necessary for understanding Greek verse but obviously adds to our enjoyment of it.

The section **Principal parts of verbs** complements the vocabulary with information about verbs whose present stem is either not used, or not used in a regular way, to provide the stems of other tenses.

For ease of reference to grammatical points an index is provided.

Extra reading, revision exercises, and other material will be on the website http://tyancientgreek.org .

Abbreviations

a. or acc.	accusative	ind.	indicative
absol.	absolute	indecl.	indeclinable
act.	active	indef.	indefinite
adj.	adjective	indir.	indirect
adv.	adverb	inf.	infinitive
aor.	aorist	interrog.	interrogative
c.	about, approximately	intr.	intransitive
cap.	capital	*l.*	line
cf.	compare	lit.	literally
compar.	comparative	*ll.*	lines
conj.	conjunction	m. or m	masculine
dat.	dative	mid.	middle
ex.	example	n. or n	neuter
f. or f	feminine	n. or nom.	nominative
f.	following	opt.	optative
fut.	future	pass.	passive
gen.	genitive	pers.	person
imp.	imperative	perf.	perfect
impers.	impersonal	pl.	plural
impf.	imperfect	plpf.	pluperfect

poet.	poetical	s.	singular
poss.	possessive	*sc.*	namely
pple.	participle	subj.	subjunctive
prep.	preposition	supl.	superlative
pres.	present	tr.	transitive
pron.	pronoun	trans.	translate
refl.	reflexive	v. or voc.	vocative
rel.	relative	viz	that is to say

Round brackets ( ) contain explanatory material or a literal translation; in the vocabulary round brackets are also used to indicate alternative forms.

Square brackets [ ] are used in translations for words which are required by English idiom but have no equivalent in the Greek original; not all such words are marked in this way. Square brackets are also used to supply missing words.

+ means *in conjunction with, compounded with,* or *followed by.*

< means *is derived from.*

> means *produce(s).*

* marks a word which cannot stand first in a clause or phrase.

\# indicates that the following sentence or passage is verse; in the vocabulary this sign indicates that the word to which it is attached is poetical.

† is explained in the introductory note to the vocabulary.

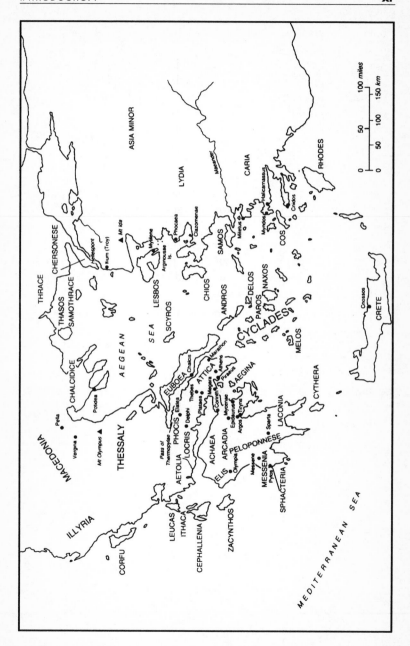

1 | UNIT ONE

1.1 Grammar

1.1/1 The Greek alphabet and its pronunciation

The Greek alphabet consists of twenty-four letters, each with its traditional name. Today it is used in both upper and lower case but in antiquity it existed only in different varieties of capitals. The pronunciation given below does not in every case reflect what we know of the language of fourth-century Athens (the type of Greek described here – see 1.3); because we learn ancient Greek for the purpose of reading, not of communication, we do not need to be as careful about its pronunciation as we would be with a modern language.

	Name	**Pronunciation**
A α	alpha (ἄλφα)	*a* (see below)
B β	bēta (βῆτα)	*b*
Γ γ	gamma (γάμμα)	*g* (as in *game*, never as in *gesture*, but as *n* in *ink* before κ, ξ, χ or another γ; see below)
Δ δ	delta (δέλτα)	*d*
E ε	epsīlon (ἒ ψῑλόν)	short *e* (as in *met*)
Z ζ	zēta (ζῆτα)	*sd* (as in *wisdom*, but represented in English as *z*)
H η	ēta (ἦτα)	long *e* (like *ai* in *fairy*)
Θ θ	thēta (θῆτα)	*th* (as in *thing*; see below)
I ι	iōta (ἰῶτα)	*i* (see below)
K κ	kappa (κάππα)	*k* (but represented in English as *c*)
Λ λ	lambda (λάμβδα)	*l*

M μ	mū (μῦ)	*m*
N ν	nū (νῦ)	*n*
Ξ ξ	xī (ξεῖ)	*x* (as in *axe*)
O o	omicron (ὂ μικρόν)	short *o* (as in *lot*)
Π π	pī (πεῖ)	*p*
P ρ	rhō (ῥῶ)	*r*
C c	sigma (cίγμα)	*s* (as in *sign*)
T τ	tau (ταῦ)	*t*
Υ υ	upsīlon (ὖ ψῑλόν)	*u* (represented in English as *y*, see below)
Φ φ	phī (φεῖ)	*ph* (see below)
X χ	chī (χεῖ)	*ch* (see below)
Ψ ψ	psī (ψεῖ)	*ps* (as in *maps*)
Ω ω	ōmega (ὦ μέγα)	long *o* (like *oa* in *broad*)

In Greek words taken into English and in transcriptions of Greek proper names Greek letters are normally represented by their phonetic equivalent except where indicated above (and in some diphthongs – see note 2).

Consonants

The normal English pronunciation is recommended where no example is given. To distinguish between κ and χ the latter is pronounced as the *ch* in the Scottish pronunciation of *loch*. The letters ζ, ξ, ψ are double consonants and the equivalents of cδ, κc, πc respectively, for which they must always be used: e.g. when c is added to the stem γυπ– we must write γῦψ, never γῦπc (5.1/1). The letters θ, φ, χ are **not** double consonants; the pronunciation given above is that normally used today but in the Greek of our period they were pronounced as *t, p, k* with an accompanying emission of breath (i.e. something like these consonants in English when initial. Compare the difference between the English and French pronunciation of the *P* in *Paris*).

Examples of the second pronunciation of γ are: cπόγγος (spóngos) *sponge*, Cφίγξ (Sphinx) *Sphinx*, ἔλεγχος (élenchos) *scrutiny*.

The form of sigma given above (which dates from the Roman period) is, for reasons of convenience, the one increasingly used in modern editions. The traditional forms of lower case sigma, which date from the Middle Ages, are σ when initial or medial, ς when final, e.g σύστασις (cύcταcιc) *composition.* The traditional upper case version is Σ. All three forms occur in Σωσιγένης (Cωcιγένης) *Sosigenes.*

Vowels

All Greek vowels have a long and short pronunciation. These pronunciations have separate symbols in the case of ε/η and ο/ω. The other vowels have both values but only one symbol. In works of reference, but not in normal printed texts, the two values of these vowels are distinguished by marking the long form with a bar above (macron), ᾱ, ῑ, ῡ. They are pronounced:

ᾱ as in *father*

α (i.e. short *a*) as in a shortened version of ᾱ, like *u* in *but*, never as in *sat* (this sound did not exist in Greek).

ῑ as *ee* in *need*

ι as *i* in *sit* (or, more accurately, as in French *petit*).

ῡ as in French *sûr*

υ as in French *tu*

Diphthongs

Greek had two types of diphthongs:

(i) where both elements are written normally and pronounced as follows:

αι as *ai* in *aisle*   οι as *oi* in *oil*

αυ as *ow* in *cow*   ου as *oo* in *cool*

ει as *ei* in *rein*   υι as *we*

ευ/ηυ as *eu* in *feud*

When any of these combinations is not to be taken as a diphthong, the second element is marked with a diaeresis (¨): βοΐ (bo–í), Λαΐc (La–ís).

(ii) where the long vowels ᾱ, η, ω are combined with an iota. This iota is placed **below** the vowel (**iota subscript**), not after it: ᾳ, ῃ, ῳ.[1] For convenience these diphthongs are always pronounced as simple ᾱ, η, ω.

Breathings

Every word beginning with a vowel or diphthong has a rough (῾) or smooth (᾿) breathing. A rough breathing denotes an initial *h*, a smooth

---

[1] The iota is, however, placed **after** the long vowel when the latter is in upper case. The only common examples is Ἅιδης *Hades.*

breathing (which is something of a superfluity) the absence of initial *h*: ἡμέρᾱ (hēmérā) *day*, ἀγαθός (agathós) *good*. A breathing is placed over the second element of a category (i) diphthong: αἴνιγμα (aínigma) *riddle*; Αἰσχύλος (Aischúlos) *Aeschylus*; but when an initial vowel which does not form part of a diphthong is in upper case the breathing is placed in front: Ὅμηρος (Hómēros) *Homer*. Words beginning with υ always have a rough breathing ὓς (hūs) *pig*; ὕψος (húpsos) *height*. Initial ρ is also always given a rough breathing because it was pronounced *rh*: ῥυθμός (rhuthmós) *rhythm*.

Notes

1 In the grammar and reference sections long α, ι, υ are marked ᾱ, ῑ, ῡ, except in the case of ᾳ, ᾶ, ῖ, ῦ, because iota subscript appears only under long vowels and in the other three cases the circumflex accent (see next subsection) shows that the vowel must be long.

2 The traditional spelling and pronunciation of Greek proper names, and also the form taken by Greek derivatives in English, almost always reflect the Roman system of transliteration: Αἰσχύλος (Aischúlos) *Aéschylus*; Οἰδίπους (Oidípous) *Oédipus*; καταστροφή (katastrophé) *catástrophe*.

3 For marks of punctuation Greek uses the full stop and comma as in English but for colon and semicolon there is only one sign, which is a dot at the top of the line (·). Our semicolon is used as a question mark in Greek (;). Inverted commas and the exclamation mark are not normally used. A capital letter is used at the beginning of a paragraph but not with each new sentence.

1.1/2 Accents

We owe the idea of visually indicating word accent to Aristophanes of Byzantium (not to be confused with the Athenian comic poet), an altruistic scholar of around 200 BC who wished to help foreigners to pronounce Greek correctly. Since the Renaissance, accents have always been employed in printed texts. While not of crucial importance in reading Greek, they are useful in distinguishing certain words and present little difficulty if correctly approached.

Accent in classical Greek was one of **pitch**, not of stress as in English. An English-speaker, when told that ἄνθρωπος *human being* is accented on its first syllable, would naturally pronounce that syllable with a heavier emphasis. A Greek, however, instead of emphasising the α, would have pronounced it at a higher pitch and so given the word what we should consider a somewhat sing-song effect. We do, of course, use pitch in spoken English, but in a totally different way. In the question *you're going to Athens?* the last word has a rising pitch, but in the statement *you're going to Athens* it has a falling pitch.

Classical Greek has three accents:

  ´ **acute**, indicating rising pitch
  ` **grave**, indicating falling pitch
  ˆ **circumflex**, indicating a combined rising and falling pitch (the sign, originally ^, is a combination of an acute and a grave). Because the time taken by this operation was necessarily longer than that indicated by an acute or a grave, it can occur only with long vowels and diphthongs, and only on these do we find a circumflex.

The basic features of Greek accentuation are:

(*a*) nearly every word has an accent, which can be on the final syllable (ποταμός *river*), or the second syllable from the end (ἵππος *horse*), or on the third syllable from the end (ἱπποπόταμος *hippopotamus*). In forms of verbs the position of the accent is nearly always determined by the length of the final syllable (see **Appendix 8**, *b*); with other words whose form can change the accent is generally fixed.

(*b*) an acute or grave accent can stand on a diphthong or long or short vowel, but a circumflex only on a long vowel or diphthong.

(*c*) an acute can stand on the end syllable of a word (πειρᾱτής *pirate*), on the second from the end (μοναρχίᾱ *monarchy*), or on the third from the end (ἀκρόπολις *acropolis*).

(*d*) a grave can stand only on a final syllable, where it automatically replaces an acute when another word follows (ὁ πειρᾱτὴς ἀπάγει τὸν ἱπποπόταμον *the pirate is leading away the hippopotamus*). A final acute is retained, however, before a mark of punctuation (ὦ ποιητά, ἢ πῖθι ἢ ἄπιθι *O poet, either drink or go away*) or when a word so accented is quoted. (For the effect of enclitics see **Appendix 8**, *d*).

(*e*) a circumflex can stand on a final syllable (τῶν ποταμῶν *of the rivers*) and, within certain limitations, on the second from the end (Μυκῆναι *Mycenae*).

The rules for accents are given in **Appendix 8**. These should be referred to and gradually mastered in the course of studying this book. For purposes of pronouncing Greek words, each of the three accents should be treated alike and given a simple stress accent as in English. The old British (and Dutch) habit of imposing the Latin system of accentuation on Greek is to be avoided. This system has prevailed in our pronunciation of nearly all Greek proper names in English. We say *Eurípides* (Εὐρῑπίδης), *Sócrates* (Cωκράτης), *Epidaúrus* (Ἐπίδαυρος) because the Romans, not unreasonably, adapted them in this way to their own language (cf. second note to last subsection). A Roman, however, who did the same in actually speaking Greek (as every educated Roman could), would have been disowned by his friends as an embarrassing ignoramus.

1.2 Exercise

1 Read aloud and transliterate the following names of famous writers: Ἀριστοτέλης, Ἀριστοφάνης, Δημοσθένης, Ἡρόδοτος, Θεόκριτος, Καλλίμαχος, Πίνδαρος, Πλάτων.

2 Read aloud and transliterate the following words and then look up their meaning in the vocabulary:

ἀκμή, ἀνάθεμα, ἀνάλῡσις, ἀντίθεσις, ἄσβεστος, αὐτόματον, ἀφασίᾱ, βάθος, γένεσις, διάγνωσις, δόγμα, δρᾶμα, ζωνή, ἦθος, ἠχώ, ἰδέᾱ, κῑνημα, κλῖμαξ, κόσμος, κρίσις, κῶλον, μέτρον, μίασμα, νέκταρ, νέμεσις, ὀρχήστρᾱ, πάθος, σκηνή, στίγμα, ὕβρις, ὑπόθεσις, χάος, χαρακτήρ, ψῡχή.

3 For practice with capitals read aloud and identify the following proper names (accents are not used when a word is put in upper case):

(a) ἈΓΑΜΕΜΝΩΝ, ἈΧΙΛΛΕΥΣ, ἝΚΤΩΡ, ἙΛΕΝΗ, ὈΔΥΣΣΕΥΣ, ΠΑΤΡΟΚΛΟΣ, ΠΗΝΕΛΟΠΕΙΑ.

(b) ἈΘΗΝΑΙ, ἌΡΓΟΣ, ΘΗΒΑΙ, ΚΟΡΙΝΘΟΣ, ΣΠΑΡΤΗ, ΚΡΗΤΗ, ῬΟΔΟΣ, ΣΑΜΟΣ.

1.3 Excursus - The different forms of Greek

Greek is a member of the Indo-European family of languages, as are English, French, German and most European languages. The original Indo-European speakers lived in what is now western Russia but migration began at an early date, possibly soon after 3000 BC. The groups which we would now call Greek originally came to Greece at different times during the period 2000–1000 BC. They have lived there ever since and preserved their identity despite invasions and long periods of foreign domination. Greek settlements also existed, in some cases for over 2,500 years, in other Mediterranean countries and in Asia Minor.

The earliest records in Greek date from about 1300 BC and are written on clay tablets in a syllabic script called Linear B, which is totally different from the Greek alphabet familiar to us. The latter was taken over, with some modifications, from the Phoenicians at some time before 750–700 BC, the period to which the oldest surviving examples can be assigned.

It is possible that Greek had already split into dialects early in the second millennium BC. Certainly there is unmistakable evidence of different dialects in the oldest works of Greek literature, the *Iliad* and the *Odyssey* of Homer (25.1/1), which must have been composed before 700 BC (their exact date and manner of composition are matters of dispute). From then up to the time of Alexander the Great (died 323 BC) a large quantity of Greek texts survives and proves the existence of five major dialect groups, which show, in some cases, considerable differences from each other. By no means all dialects served as vehicles of literature and we need only concern ourselves with those which were so used. From an early stage Greek literature was clearly divided into different genres (epic, elegiac poetry, choral lyric, etc.), and often a particular dialect became so intimately associated with a literary genre that a tradition was established which sometimes lasted long after the dialect had ceased to be spoken. Some of these associations are mentioned in the following list:

Ionic – the language of the Aegean islands (except those on the southern fringe and Lesbos to the north) and the central area of the west coast of Asia Minor. The latter contained the most important Ionic settlements and it was there that Greek cultural and intellectual life began with Homer and the earliest philosophers. Poets of the 7th and 6th centuries BC established Ionic as the dialect of elegiac and iambic poetry. It was also the original dialect for literary prose and was used by Herodotus (a Dorian by birth) for his *Histories* (4.2.9).

Aeolic – the language of Lesbos and the adjoining Asia Minor coast. It was used by the most famous poetess of antiquity, Sappho (early 6th century BC), and her male contemporary, Alcaeus, for personal lyric poetry. Their initiative was not continued.

Homeric dialect – the language of Homer's *Iliad* and *Odyssey.* This was an artificial dialect which was never the language of a particular area or group, but had been developed over a long period by generations of poets. It was basically an older form of Ionic but with elements from other dialects, chiefly Aeolic. Homer's position as the greatest Greek poet was never disputed in antiquity, and epics which reproduced his language were still being written in the 5th century AD. The Ionic of Elegy, which survived even longer, generally had a Homeric flavour.

Doric – the language of the Peloponnesus (except the central and north-west area), Crete, and other parts of the Greek world. Choral poetry, which was sung by dancing choirs, was originally the creation of Dorians and even when written by non-Doric speakers was always given at least a Doric flavour.

Attic – the language of Athens (historically an offshoot of Ionic). With the rapid political expansion and cultural development of Athens after the final defeat of the Persians by the Greeks (479 BC) Attic became firmly established as a literary dialect despite its late start when compared with Ionic and Aeolic. By the beginning of the 4th century BC Athens had become the main cultural centre of Greece. This was in no small part brought about by the literary masterpieces that had been written and were still being written by Athenians in their own dialect. The Attic of the early and middle period of the 4th century BC, as exemplified in Plato's dialogues and Demosthenes' speeches, has always been taken as the most satisfactory form of Greek for beginners and is the type described in this book. Attic is the language of Tragedy and Comedy (except for their choral odes, which have a tinge of Doric). By the end of the 5th century BC it had superseded Ionic as the language of prose.

The conquests of Alexander (died 323 BC) had important political and linguistic consequences for the Greek world, which he enlarged considerably. Greek culture and civilisation were extended over all lands bordering on the eastern Mediterranean and a lingua franca emerged which, with a few exceptions, gradually replaced the older dialects even in Greece itself. This new language was basically a development of Attic and was called ἡ κοινὴ διάλεκτος *the common dialect* (in English the **koine**). It was the language of the Greek man in the street and for that reason was used by the writers of the New Testament, who wanted to reach as wide an audience as possible. Educated classes, imbued with the prestige of Classical Attic, regarded it as a debased form of Greek, but the koine, apart from the few survivors of the older dialects, had, by the first century of our era, become the living form of the language and is the ancestor of **Modern Greek**. The latter cannot, of course, be understood simply with a knowledge of 4th-century Attic or the koine, but, because of the conservative nature of Greek, which we see at all periods, the changes that have occurred over a period of 2400 years are fewer than those which distinguish Modern English from Anglo-Saxon.

2 | UNIT TWO

For this and all subsequent units extra reading will be found at the Internet website http://tyancientgreek.org

2.1 Grammar

2.1/1 Nouns in Greek

In English the gender of a noun is determined by its meaning; *man* is masculine, *woman* is feminine, *car* is neuter, and when referring to these we would say *he, she, it* respectively. In Greek, however, the gender of a noun is often arbitrary and does not necessarily indicate anything about what it denotes. While, for example, γυνή *woman* is feminine and ἀνήρ *man* is masculine, χώρᾱ *land* is feminine, and λόγος *speech* is masculine, though δῶρον *gift* is, understandably, neuter. More often than not we cannot see why a particular noun has a particular gender. It is, however, generally possible to tell the gender of a noun by its ending in the nominative and genitive singular, and it is also according to these endings that Greek nouns are grouped into three classes, which are called **declensions**. Each declension has a distinctive set of endings which indicate both case and number, just as in English we have *child, child's, children, children's,* though Greek distinguishes more cases. To go through the list of all possible forms of a noun is to **decline** it.

2.1/2 First declension (feminine nouns) and the feminine definite article

Most first declension nouns are feminine (the few masculines are declined slightly differently – 3.1/2). The feminines end in –η or –α. Those in –α change alpha to eta in the genitive and dative singular unless the alpha is preceded by a vowel or ρ. All first declension nouns have the same endings in the plural. The feminine form of the definite article is declined in the same way as the feminines in –η.

SINGULAR

Nominative	ἡ	τῑμ–ή	χώρ–ᾱ	θάλαττ–α
	the	*honour*	*country*	*sea*
Vocative	——	τῑμ–ή	χώρ–ᾱ	θάλαττ–α
Accusative	τήν	τῑμ–ήν	χώρ–ᾱν	θάλαττ–αν
Genitive	τῆc	τῑμ–ῆc	χώρ–ᾱc	θαλάττ–ηc
Dative	τῇ	τῑμ–ῇ	χώρ–ᾳ	θαλάττ–ῃ

PLURAL

Nominative	αἱ	τῑμ–αί	χῶρ–αι	θάλαττ–αι
Vocative	——	τῑμ–αί	χῶρ–αι	θάλαττ–αι
Accusative	τάc	τῑμ–ᾱc	χώρ–ᾱc	θαλάττ–ᾱc
Genitive	τῶν	τῑμ–ῶν	χωρ–ῶν	θαλαττ–ῶν
Dative	ταῖc	τῑμ–αῖc	χώρ–αιc	θαλάττ–αιc

Notes

1 The definite article must agree with the noun it qualifies in number, gender, and case: τῶν τῑμῶν *of the honours,* τὰc χώρᾱc *the countries* (accusative). Contexts where it is used in Greek but not in English are:
   (i) with abstract nouns, ἡ ἀλήθεια *truth*
   (ii) with nouns (usually plural) indicating a general class, αἱ κόραι *girls* (as a class)
   (iii) optionally with proper nouns, with no differences in sense: ἡ Cικελίᾱ or Cικελίᾱ *Sicily,* ἡ Ἀφροδίτη or Ἀφροδίτη *Aphrodite.* In translating a common noun in the singular without the definite article, *a* should be supplied in English: ἡ νίκη *the victory,* but νίκη *a victory.*
2 The final alpha of most nouns ending in –έα, –ία, –ρα is long.
3 Here (and in the second declension) when the final syllable bears an acute in the nominative, as in τῑμή, the accent becomes a circumflex in the genitive and dative (for the technical terms see **Appendix 8**).
4 In the genitive plural all first declension nouns have a circumflex on their final syllable.

2.1/3 Basic uses of cases

In English the only case ending in nouns is that of the genitive (as in *girl's, men's,* etc.). Elsewhere, the function of a noun is shown by its position (the difference in meaning between *the traffic warden hit the driver* and *the driver hit the traffic warden* depends solely on the word order) or by a preposition: *the traffic warden was hit by a car* (here the part played by the car is indicated by the preposition *by*). In Greek, however, the function of a noun is indicated by its **case ending**:

(*a*) The subject of a clause must be put in the **nominative**.

(*b*) When we address a person the **vocative** is used; this is normally preceded by ὦ *O* and followed by a mark of punctuation. For the sake of completeness the vocative is given for such nouns as τῑμή but these forms rarely occur.

(*c*) The direct object of a verb must be put in the **accusative.**

(*d*) The **genitive** can express possession: *Cleon's horse* (in English we can also say the *horse of Cleon*). Another common use of the genitive in Greek is to express separation (20.1/4).

(*e*) With nouns denoting living things the **dative** expresses the indirect object after verbs of saying, giving and the like (24.1/2*a*). In *Socrates gave a drachma to Xanthippe* the direct object is *drachma* (answering the question *gave what?*), which would be put into the accusative δραχμήν; the indirect object is *Xanthippe* (*gave to whom?*), which would be τῇ Ξανθίππῃ with no preposition (we may also say in English *Socrates gave Xanthippe a drachma*). The dative has other uses with nouns denoting living things and can nearly always be translated by *to* or *for*. With inanimate nouns (*Athens, arrow, boat*) different uses are possible and will be treated separately.

The accusative, genitive, and dative, are, for convenience of reference, called the **oblique cases.** They are the cases used after **prepositions**, which perform the same function in Greek as in English, i.e. they define the relation between the word they govern and the rest of the clause in which they are used. In Greek the word governed is always a noun (or noun-equivalent, see 5.1/3) or pronoun (Greek does not say *before now* because *now* is an adverb). With prepositions indicating **motion** and **rest** a pattern can be seen in the case required:

(*f*) Prepositions indicating **motion towards** govern the accusative, e.g.

εἰc τὴν χώρᾱν *into the country,* πρὸc τὴν οἰκίᾱν *towards the house.*

(g) Prepositions indicating **motion away from** govern the genitive, e.g. ἀπὸ τῆc μάχηc *from the battle,* ἐκ Cικελίᾱc *out of Sicily.*

(h) Prepositions indicating **rest** or **fixed position** govern the dative, e.g. ἐν τῇ θαλάττῃ *in the sea.*

All the above prepositions, except πρόc (3.1/5), take only the case shown.

2.1/4 Verbs in Greek

A finite form of a Greek verb (i.e. one that can function as the verb of a clause) is defined in terms of person, number, tense, mood, and voice. **Person** and **number** are determined by the subject of the verb: a finite verb must agree with its subject in person and number (just as in English we cannot say *we is*). First person is the person(s) speaking, i.e. *I* or *we*; second person is the person(s) spoken to, i.e. *you*; third person is the person(s) or thing(s) spoken about, which can be a pronoun (*he, she, it, they*) or a noun. The concept of number is the same as with nouns. **Tense** indicates the time in which the action of the verb takes place. **Mood** tells us something about the nature of the verb's action in a particular context; at the moment we are only concerned with the **indicative** mood, which is used to express facts. **Voice** shows the relation of the subject to the verb. We shall first deal with the **active**, which is the voice used when the subject is the doer of the action.

Auxiliary verbs (*shall/will, have, be* etc.) are used to form most tenses of an English verb (*I shall teach, he has taught, we will be taught*), but in Greek are found only in certain passive forms. Elsewhere, the person, number, tense and voice (and also mood – 14.1/1) are shown by the stem and ending. For example, we can tell by the stem and ending that λύcουcι is third person plural future indicative active of the verb λύω *I loosen,* and therefore means *they will loosen.* It is superfluous to add the Greek for *they* (unless for emphasis), as this is part of the information conveyed by the ending.

Verbs in Greek belong to one of two groups (called **conjugations**). These are distinguished by the ending of the first person singular present indicative active, the form in which Greek verbs are customarily cited[1] (contrast the convention in English of referring to

---

[1] A sub-category called deponents is slightly different – 8.1/2.

a verb by its present infinitive active). Those in –ω (e.g. λΰω) are by far the larger class; the other consists of verbs in –μι, e.g. εἰμί *I am* (3.1/6), δίδωμι *give* (18.1/2).

2.1/5 Present and future indicative active of –ω verbs (and corresponding infinitives)

The present indicative active is formed by taking the present stem (λῦ– i.e. λΰω minus ω) and adding the endings given below. For the future indicative active we make up the future stem by adding sigma to that of the present (i.e. λῦ + c > λῦc–) and we then apply the same endings. These stems are also used for the infinitives.

		PRESENT		FUTURE	
SINGULAR	1	λΰ–ω	*I loosen*	λΰc–ω	*I shall loosen*
	2	λΰ–εις	*you* (s.) *loosen*	λΰc–εις	*you* (s.) *will loosen*
	3	λΰ–ει	*he, she, it loosens*	λΰc–ει	*he, she, it will loosen*
PLURAL	1	λΰ–ομεν	*we loosen*	λΰc–ομεν	*we shall loosen*
	2	λΰ–ετε	*you* (pl.) *loosen*	λΰc–ετε	*you* (pl.) *will loosen*
	3	λΰ–ουcι(ν)	*they loosen*	λΰc–ουcι(ν)	*they will loosen*
INFINITIVE		λΰ–ειν	*to loosen*	λΰc–ειν	*to be going to loosen*

Notes

1 In English we have different forms of the present tense, *I loosen, I am loosening, I do loosen* and so on. There are distinctions in usage between these forms, but as Greek has only one we must decide from the context which English form we should use to translate a Greek verb in the present tense. In one context λΰουcι might mean *they loosen,* in another *they are loosening* or *do they loosen.* Likewise, λΰcω can also mean *I shall be loosening.*

2 The Greek second person singular is always used when addressing one person, the plural when addressing more than one person. Greek has a distinction here which we no longer have in English. Greek does not, however, have familiar and polite forms of the second person as in French, German, and other languages. A slave and master would have addressed each other in the second person singular.

3 It will be noticed that in each form the stem is followed by an o- or e- sound. This indicates the presence of the so-called **thematic vowel** (o or ε), which is most clearly seen in the first and second

persons plural. The same pattern, which marks these tenses as **thematic**, is repeated in the imperfect (4.1/1).

4 The final ν shown in brackets in the ending of the third person plural is called the movable ν. In prose it is used (without brackets) only when a word with this ending is followed by a word beginning with a vowel or diphthong or stands at the end of a clause (its use in verse is freer). It occurs here and in a few other endings.

5 To form the future of πέμπω *send,* the final π of the present stem is combined with c to give πέμψ–ω *I will send.* Other final consonants in present stems will be treated at 6.1/4 and 11.1/3.

2.1/6 Word order and elision

(*a*) Although the order of words within a Greek sentence may often be similar to that of English, Greek word order is generally much less predictable. As mentioned in 2.1/3, there is a close link in English between the order in which words occur and their function. In Greek, however, where the grammatical function of a word is determined by its form, not by its position, word order can be varied much more than in English. This is mainly done to emphasise a particular word or phrase. If in the English sentence *Aphrodite is beautiful* we wished to emphasise *beautiful* we would, in speech, articulate it with greater weight (in writing we could underline it or put it in italics). In Greek the emphasis would be conveyed by a change in the word order; ἡ Ἀφροδῑ́τη ἐcτὶ καλή would become καλή ἐcτιν ἡ Ἀφροδῑ́τη. These differences will be indicated as they occur. Emphasis apart, two further points regarding word order should be noted here:

  (i) Adverbs nearly always precede the word they modify, ταχέωc τρέχει *he runs* (τρέχει) *quickly* (ταχέωc). This particularly applies to the negative οὐ(κ) *not,* οὐκ ἔχω ... *I do not have ...* (οὐκ is the form used before vowels and diphthongs with a smooth breathing; it becomes οὐχ if the following vowel or diphthong has a rough breathing, e.g. οὐχ ὕει *it is not raining*).

  (ii) Just as in English we can say *the land of Aphrodite* or *Aphrodite's land,* so in Greek we have ἡ χώρᾱ τῆc Ἀφροδῑ́τηc and ἡ τῆc Ἀφροδῑ́τηc χώρᾱ (note that the article of χώρᾱ must be retained in the latter).

(*b*) The Greeks disliked the juxtaposition of a final vowel and an initial vowel (e.g. ἀπὸ 'Αθηνῶν *from Athens*). Although tolerated in prose, this is almost totally absent from most forms of verse. In the case of final short vowels (except υ) it is avoided by eliding (i.e. dropping and not pronouncing) α, ε, ι, ο before a word beginning with a vowel or diphthong, e.g. ἀπ' οἰκίᾱς (= ἀπὸ οἰκίᾱς) *from a house*; παρ' 'Αφροδῑ́την (= παρὰ 'Α.) *to Aphrodite*. When the vowel following κ, π, or τ is elided before a word beginning with a rough breathing, these consonants become χ, φ, θ, respectively, e.g. ὑφ' 'Ελένης (= ὑπὸ 'Ε.) *by Helen*. Elision is marked by an apostrophe as shown. It is not always applied in prose texts.[1]

2.2 Greek reading

The *Odyssey* describes the return of the Greek hero Odysseus (in English we sometimes use the Latin form of his name *Ulysses*) to his homeland, Ithaca, after the sack of Troy. At a later stage we shall read some of the original, but now we shall start with a simplified version of Odysseus's landing at Scheria, probably to be identified with the modern Corfu. The scene occurs in the sixth book of the Odyssey.

In reading Greek the following steps should be followed:

(a) Look up each word in the vocabulary and parse it (i.e. define it grammatically; this is particularly necessary with words which vary in form).

(b) Mark all finite verbs as this will indicate the number of clauses.

(c) By observing punctuation and conjunctions used to join clauses, work out where each clause begins and ends.

(d) Take each clause separately and see how each word relates to the finite verb of its clause (subject, object, part of an adverbial phrase, etc.).

(e) See from the conjunctions how the clauses are related to each other and work out the overall meaning of the sentence.

An analysis of sentence 13 will be found in the Key.

1 ὁ 'Οδυσσεὺς ἀπὸ τῆς Τροίας ἥκει, ἀλλὰ ὁ Ποσειδῶν ἐν τῇ Σχερίᾳ τὴν ναῦν (*ship*) διαφθείρει.

2 ὁ 'Οδυσσεὺς ἐκ τῆς θαλάττης φεύγει καὶ ὑπὸ ἐλάᾳ ἑαυτὸν (*himself* acc.) κρύπτει πρὸς τῇ ἀκτῇ.

---

[1] The final αι of verbal endings can be elided in poetry, and occasionally even in prose (example at 21.2.2(xi)).

3 ὄναρ ἡ Ἀθηνᾶ τῇ βασιλείᾳ Ναυσικάᾳ λέγει ὅτι δεῖ (*it is necessary*) τὴν στολὴν ἐν τῇ ἀκτῇ πλύνειν.

4 ἅμα τῇ ἡμέρᾳ ἡ Ναυσικάα τὴν στολὴν ἐκ τῆς οἰκίας ἐν ἁμάξῃ πρὸς τὴν θάλατταν φέρει.

5 ἐν τῇ ἁμάξῃ ἐστὶ (*there is*) καὶ (*also*) ἐδωδὴ τῇ Ναυσικάᾳ καὶ ταῖς ἑταίραις.

6 αἱ κόραι τάχα πλύνουσι τὴν στολὴν πρὸς τῇ ἐλάᾳ οὗ ὁ Ὀδυσσεὺς καθεύδει.

7 ἔπειτα αἱ κόραι τὴν στολὴν ἐπὶ τὴν ἀκτὴν ἐπιβάλλουσιν.

8 λούουσιν ἑαυτὰς (*themselves*) καὶ τὴν ἐδωδὴν ἐσθίουσιν ἣν (*which*) ἐν τῇ ἁμάξῃ ἔχουσιν.

9 ἕως (*while*) ἐν τῇ ἀκτῇ παίζουσιν, ἡ Ναυσικάα σφαῖραν ῥίπτει ἀλλ᾿ ἡ σφαῖρα εἰς δίνην πίπτει.

10 αἱ τῶν κορῶν βοαὶ τὸν Ὀδυσσέα (acc.) ἐγείρουσι καὶ ἐκπλήττουσιν.

11 ὁ Ὀδυσσεὺς θαυμάζει ποῖ τῆς γῆς ἥκει, καὶ ἀπὸ τῆς ἐλάας ἐξαίφνης ἕρπει.

12 τὴν Ναυσικάαν καὶ τὰς ἑταίρας ἐκπλήττει.

13 ἀλλ᾿ ἡ Ναυσικάα ἐν τῇ ἀκτῇ ἀναμένει διότι ἡ Ἀθηνᾶ τὴν ἀνδρείαν εἰς τὴν καρδίαν εἰσβάλλει.

14 ὁ Ὀδυσσεὺς τῇ Ναυσικάᾳ λέγει ὅτι ἀπὸ τῆς Ὠγυγίας ἥκει.

15 ἡ Ναυσικάα ταῖς ἑταίραις λέγει ὅτι δεῖ τῷ Ὀδυσσεῖ (dat.) ἐδωδὴν καὶ στολὴν παρέχειν.

16 τὸν Ὀδυσσέα πρὸς τὴν τοῦ πατρὸς (*of her father*) οἰκίαν ἄγειν ἐθέλει ἀλλὰ τὴν τῶν πολιτῶν (*of the citizens*) αἰτίαν δειμαίνει εἰ βλέπουσιν αὐτὴν (*her*) μετὰ τοῦ Ὀδυσσέως (gen.).

17 ὥστε ἡ Ναυσικάα καὶ αἱ κόραι τὴν στολὴν πάλιν ἐν τῇ ἁμάξῃ πρὸς τὴν οἰκίαν φέρουσιν, ἀλλ᾿ ὁ Ὀδυσσεὺς ἐκτὸς ἀναμένει.

Notes

1 ὁ nom. s. m. of the definite article (3.1/1); Ὀδυσσεύς 3rd declension (11.1/4); ἥκει *has come* (the subject is ὁ Ὀδυσσεύς) the present tense of this verb is to be translated by the perfect tense in English; τὴν ναῦν lit. *the ship,* but we would translate *his ship;* Greek normally does not indicate possession if this is obvious from the context (9.1/5; cf. sentences 4, 5, 12, 13, 15, 16).

2 ὑπὸ ἐλάᾳ *beneath an olive-tree;* as Greek does not have an indefinite article (*a, an* in English) this must be supplied in our translation; cf. below ἐν ἁμάξῃ (4) and σφαῖραν (9).

5 The datives τῇ Ναυσικάᾳ and ταῖς ἑταίραις are to be translated
  for ...

7 ἐπὶ ... ἐπιβάλλουςιν the repetition of ἐπί as a verbal prefix cannot
  be reproduced in English and we would simply say *they throw* ...
  on to the shore.

9 ἀλλ᾽ = ἀλλά (2.1/6*b*).

10 τόν acc. s. m. of the definite article; ἐκπλήττουςιν sc. *him*
   (Odysseus; because the object of the second verb is the same as
   that of the first, no pronoun is needed in Greek).

13 εἰς ... εἰςβάλλει for the repetition of εἰς cf. note on 7.

15 τῷ dat. s. m. of the definite article.

16 τοῦ gen. s. m. of the definite article.

2.2/1 Vocabulary

Individual vocabularies are provided for Units 2-9. Personal names
whose English form is a simple transliteration of the Greek, or close
to it (e.g. Cωκράτης *Socrates*), are not included, but will be found in
the main vocabulary. The meaning given to each word is that
appropriate to its use in the preceding reading; for a fuller range of
meanings the main vocabulary should be consulted. Words already
given in a grammatical table (or earlier vocabulary) are not repeated,
except where a different meaning is involved.

It is normal practice in Greek dictionaries and lists of Greek words to
give the nominative singular of a noun, its genitive (usually in
abbreviated form) and the appropriate nominative singular form of
the article; this information establishes both its declension and gender,
e.g. θάλαττα, -ης, ἡ (note that the accent in the genitive - here θαλάττης
- is not always on the same syllable as in the nominative; see **Appendix
8,** *a*). Verbs are cited in the first person singular present indicative, e.g.
κρύπτω.

ἄγω *lead, bring*	ἀλλά (conj.) *but*
᾽Αθηνᾶ, -ᾶς,[1] ἡ (the goddess)	ἅμα see ἡμέρᾱ
Athena	ἅμαξα, -ης, ἡ *wagon*
αἰτίᾱ, -ᾱς, ἡ *blame, censure*	ἀναμένω *wait, stay*
ἀκτή, -ῆς, ἡ *shore, coast*	ἀνδρείᾱ, -ᾱς, ἡ *courage*

---

[1]᾽Αθηνᾶ, originally ᾽Αθηνάᾱ, has its genitive in -ᾶς, -ᾳ̂ (not -ῆς, -ῇ); cf. ἐλάᾱ, -ᾶς below.

βασίλεια, –ᾱς, ἡ   *princess*
βλέπω   *see*
βοή, –ῆς, ἡ   *shout*
γῆ, –ῆς, ἡ   *land, earth, world*
δειμαίνω (+acc.)   *be afraid of,*
   fear
διαφθείρω   *destroy*
δῑνη, –ης, ἡ   *whirlpool*
διότι (conj.)   *because*
ἐγείρω   *awaken, arouse*
ἐδωδή, –ῆς, ἡ   *food*
ἐθέλω   *be willing, wish*
εἰ (conj.)   *if*
εἰς (prep.+acc.)   *into*
εἰσβάλλω   *throw into, put into*
ἐκ (prep.+gen.)   *out of*
ἐκπλήττω   *strike with panic,*
   frighten
ἐκτός (adv.)   *outside*
ἐλάᾱ, –ᾱς, ἡ   *olive-tree*
ἐν (prep.+dat.)   *in, on*
ἐξαίφνης (adv.)   *suddenly*
ἔπειτα (adv.)   *then, next*
ἐπί (prep.+acc.)   *on to*
ἐπιβάλλω   *throw upon*
ἕρπω   *creep, crawl*
ἐσθίω   *eat*
ἑταίρᾱ, –ᾱς, ἡ   *companion*
   (female)
ἔχω   *have*
ἥκω   *have come*
ἡμέρᾱ, –ᾱς, ἡ   *day*
   ἅμα τῇ ἡμέρᾳ   *at day-break* or
   dawn
θαυμάζω   *wonder*
καθεύδω   *sleep*

καί (conj.)   *and*
καρδίᾱ, –ᾱς, ἡ   *heart*
κόρη, –ης, ἡ   *girl*
κρύπτω   *hide*
λέγω   *say, speak*
λούω   *wash* (the body)
μετά (prep.+gen.)   *along with,*
   (in company) with
οἰκίᾱ, –ᾱς, ἡ   *house*
ὄναρ (adv.)   *in a dream*
ὅτι (conj.)   *that*
οὗ (conj.)   *where*
παίζω   *play*
πάλιν (adv.)   *back*
παρέχω   *provide* (something to
   somebody)
πῑπτω   *fall*
πλῡνω   *wash* (clothes)
ποῖ (interrog. adv.)   *(to) where?*
   ποῖ τῆς γῆς   *where in the world*
πρός (prep.) (+acc.)   *towards, to*
   (+dat.)   *near, beside*
ῥῑπτω   *throw*
στολή, –ῆς, ἡ   *clothes*
σφαῖρα, –ᾱς, ἡ   *ball*
Σχερίᾱ, –ᾱς, ἡ   *Scheria,* the
   land of the Phaeacians
τάχα (adv.)   *quickly*
Τροίᾱ, –ᾱς, ἡ   *Troy*
ὑπό (prep.+dat.)   *beneath*
φέρω   *carry, bring, take*
φεύγω   *flee, run away*
Ὠγυγίᾱ, –ᾱς, ἡ   *Ogygia,* the
   island of Calypso
ὥστε (conj.)   *consequently, so*

3 | UNIT THREE

3.1 Grammar

3.1/1 Second declension and the masculine and neuter definite article

The second declension is divided into two groups: nouns whose nominative singular ends in –oc, which, with a few exceptions, are masculine, and those whose nominative singular ends in –ov, which are all neuter. Both groups have identical endings except for the nominative, vocative, and accusative. For these cases second declension neuter nouns observe the rule which holds for all neuter nouns in Greek:

The vocative and accusative of all neuter nouns are the same as the nominative, both in the singular and in the plural. In the plural the nominative, vocative, and accusative of all neuter nouns end in –α (for an apparent exception see 6.1/1c).

	ὁ ἵππoc *the horse*				τὸ δῶρον *the gift*		
	SINGULAR		PLURAL		SINGULAR		PLURAL	
Nom.	ὁ	ἵππ–oc	oἱ	ἵππ–οι	τὸ	δῶρ–ον	τὰ	δῶρ–α
Voc.	—	ἵππ–ε	—	ἵππ–οι	—	δῶρ–ον	—	δῶρ–α
Acc.	τὸν	ἵππ–ον	τoὺc	ἵππ–ουc	τὸ	δῶρ–ον	τὰ	δῶρ–α
Gen.	τoῦ	ἵππ–ου	τῶν	ἵππ–ων	τoῦ	δώρ–ου	τῶν	δώρ–ων
Dat.	τῷ	ἵππ–ῳ	τoῖc	ἵππ–οιc	τῷ	δώρ–ῳ	τoῖc	δώρ–οιc

Notes

1 Feminine nouns of the second declension are declined in exactly the same way as masculines but they require the feminine form of the definite article (and of adjectives; see below 3.1/3): ἡ νῆcoc *the*

island, τῆc νόcου *of the disease.* Only rarely can they be recognised as feminine by their meaning, e.g. ἡ παρθένοc *the girl.*

2 A finite verb which has a plural **neuter** noun as its subject is almost always *singular*: τὰ δῶρά ἐcτιν ἐν τῇ οἰκίᾳ *the gifts are in the house* (ἐcτί is the 3rd s. pres. ind. of εἰμί *I am* – see below 3.1/6). This curious idiom, which has not been satisfactorily explained, even applies when the neuter noun denotes human beings: τὰ ἀνδράποδα οὐκ ἔcτιν ἐν τῇ ἀγορᾷ *the captives are not in the market place.*

3 In poetry an expanded form of the dative plural of both first and second declensions, –αιcι(ν) –οιcι(ν), often occurs, e.g. τῑμαῖcι(ν), ἵπποιcι(ν) (on the movable ν see 2.1/5 note 4).

3.1/2 First declension (masculine nouns)

These nouns have borrowed the –c of the nominative singular and the –ου ending of the genitive singular from second declension masculines. They are subdivided into those ending in –ᾱc (always preceded by ε, ι or ρ) and those in –ηc.

	νεᾱνίᾱc *young man*		κριτήc *judge*	
	SINGULAR	PLURAL	SINGULAR	PLURAL
Nom.	νεᾱνί–ᾱc	νεᾱνί–αι	κριτ–ήc	κριτ–αί
Voc.	νεᾱνί–ᾱ	νεᾱνί–αι	κριτ–ά	κριτ–αί
Acc.	νεᾱνί–ᾱν	νεᾱνί–ᾱc	κριτ–ήν	κριτ–ᾱc
Gen.	νεᾱνί–ου	νεᾱνι–ῶν	κριτ–οῦ	κριτ–ῶν
Dat.	νεᾱνί–ᾳ	νεᾱνί–αιc	κριτ–ῇ	κριτ–αῖc

Notes

1 Most nouns in this class involve male occupations; cf. also ναύτηc *sailor,* cτρατιώτηc *soldier.*

2 When used with these nouns the definite article (and adjectives) must be masculine.

3 Nouns in -τηc (as well as compounds and names of peoples) have a vocative singular in -α (not -ᾱ). All other nouns in -ηc of this declension have a vocative in -η, e.g. ὦ Ἑρμῆ *O Hermes!* Contrast third declension proper names such as Cωκράτηc (6.1/1c).

4 The patronymic suffixes –ίδηc, –ιάδηc are added to the stem of proper names to mean *son of* (Κρονίδηc *son of* Κρόνοc). In many names these suffixes have lost their original force: Θουκυδίδηc *Thucydides,* Ἀλκιβιάδηc *Alcibiades.*

3.1/3 First and second declension adjectives

Adjectives in English, apart from *this* (pl. *these*) and *that* (pl. *those*), are invariable in form. In Greek, however, adjectives must agree with the nouns they qualify (i.e. go with and describe) in case, number and gender, and consequently they are declined in the same way as nouns, e.g. ὁ κακὸς νόμος *the wicked law,* τὴν καλὴν νἵκην *the fine victory* (acc.), λόγων δεινῶν *of clever speeches.*

The majority of Greek adjectives have their feminine form declined according to the first declension but their masculine and neuter according to the second or third. This latter feature allows us to classify them into first and second declension adjectives and first and third declension adjectives (10.1/3). First and second declension adjectives have, therefore, a feminine in –η (or –ᾱ, when preceded by ε, ι or ρ), a masculine in –ος and a neuter in –ον. καλός *handsome, beautiful, fine* is declined:

	SINGULAR			PLURAL		
	M.	F.	N.	M.	F.	N.
Nom.	καλ–ός	καλ–ή	καλ–όν	καλ–οί	καλ–αί	καλ–ά
Voc.	καλ–έ	καλ–ή	καλ–όν	καλ–οί	καλ–αί	καλ–ά
Acc.	καλ–όν	καλ–ήν	καλ–όν	καλ–ούς	καλ–ᾱς	καλ–ά
Gen.	καλ–οῦ	καλ–ῆς	καλ–οῦ	καλ–ῶν	καλ–ῶν	καλ–ῶν
Dat.	καλ–ῷ	καλ–ῇ	καλ–ῷ	καλ–οῖς	καλ–αῖς	καλ–οῖς

δίκαιος *just* and αἰσχρός *ugly, disgraceful* are declined as follows in the singular:

	M.	F.	N.	M.	F.	N.
Nom.	δίκαι–ος	δικαί–ᾱ	δίκαι–ον	αἰσχρ–ός	αἰσχρ–ά	αἰσχρ–όν
Voc.	δίκαι–ε	δικαί–ᾱ	δίκαι–ον	αἰσχρ–έ	αἰσχρ–ά	αἰσχρ–όν
Acc.	δίκαι–ον	δικαί–ᾱν	δίκαι–ον	αἰσχρ–όν	αἰσχρ–άν	αἰσχρ–όν
Gen.	δικαί–ου	δικαί–ᾱς	δικαί–ου	αἰσχρ–οῦ	αἰσχρ–ᾶς	αἰσχρ–οῦ
Dat.	δικαί–ῳ	δικαί–ᾳ	δικαί–ῳ	αἰσχρ–ῷ	αἰσχρ–ᾷ	αἰσχρ–ῷ

The plural is the same as for καλός.[1]

The way in which these adjectives are given in the vocabulary (and in dictionaries) is καλός, –ή, –όν; δίκαιος, –ᾱ, –ον; αἰσχρός, –ά, –όν.

---

[1] The accent in the genitive plural feminine follows that of the masculine: δικαίων, not δικαιῶν which we would have expected on the analogy of first declension nouns (2.1/2 note 4).

Some adjectives, however, have no separate feminine (the so-called **two termination** adjectives) but employ the –oc forms for masculine and feminine alike. These are nearly all compounds, e.g. εὔλογος *reasonable* (εὖ + λόγος *reason*), ἔμπειρος *experienced* (ἐν + πεῖρα *experience*). Many have the negative ἀ- (or ἀν- before a vowel; cf. English *in-, un-*) e.g. ἄλογος *irrational* (ἀ + λόγος *reason*); ἀνάξιος *unworthy* (ἀν + ἄξιος *worthy*). These adjectives are cited in the form εὔλογος, –ον; ἔμπειρος, –ον. Examples of them in agreement with feminine nouns are: ἡ ἄδικος νῑκη *the unjust victory*, αἱ ἔμπειροι Μοῦσαι *the experienced Muses*.

Two important adjectives, πολύς *much* (pl. *many*), and μέγας *great, big*, show irregularities in the masculine and neuter nominative and accusative singular. Otherwise they are declined exactly as if their nominative singular masculine were πολλ–ός and μεγάλ–ος. So in the singular we find:

	M.	F.	N.	M.	F.	N.
Nom.	**πολύς**	πολλ–ή	**πολύ**	**μέγας**	μεγάλ–η	**μέγα**
Voc.	—	—	—	μεγάλ–ε	μεγάλ–η	**μέγα**
Acc.	**πολύν**	πολλ–ήν	**πολύ**	**μέγαν**	μεγάλ–ην	**μέγα**
Gen.	πολλ–οῦ	πολλ–ῆς	πολλ–οῦ	μεγάλ–ου	μεγάλ–ης	μεγάλ–ου
Dat.	πολλ–ῷ	πολλ–ῇ	πολλ–ῷ	μεγάλ–ῳ	μεγάλ–η	μεγάλ–ῳ

The plural is entirely regular.

Position of adjectives

(a) Where the definite article is absent, the adjective may appear either before or after its noun: εἰς οἰκίᾱν καλήν *into a beautiful house*, περὶ δεινοῦ λόγου *concerning a clever speech*.

(b) When a noun is used with the definite article we have several possibilities. An adjective used as a simple attribute may occupy the same position as in English: ὁ δίκαιος νεᾱνίᾱς *the just young man*. But note that Greek may achieve exactly the same effect by writing ὁ νεᾱνίᾱς ὁ δίκαιος with the article repeated. Both these positions are called **attributive**. Totally different, however, is the case where the adjective appears outside of the article-noun complex, ὁ νεᾱνίᾱς δίκαιος or δίκαιος ὁ νεᾱνίᾱς. In both these positions the adjective is considered as functioning as a predicate, and the meaning is *the young man is just* (on the omission of ἐστί see below 3.1/6). Greek makes great use of this **predicative** position and can have a simple sentence where English would require a complex one. So whereas οἰκίᾱν ἔχει καλήν means *he has a beautiful house,* τὴν οἰκίᾱν ἔχει καλήν or καλὴν ἔχει τὴν οἰκίᾱν means *the house which he has is beautiful, it is a beautiful house which he has* (lit. *beautiful the house he has*).

3.1/4 Adverbs

Most adverbs are formed from adjectives by adding –ωc to the stem. In effect this means changing the final ν of the gen. pl. m. of the adjective to c, e.g. δίκαιος (gen. pl. m. δικαίων) *just,* adv. δικαίως *justly;* ἄδικος (gen. pl. m. ἀδίκων) *unjust,* adv. ἀδίκως *unjustly.*

Unlike in English, adverbs are nearly always placed immediately **before** the word they modify (2.1/6*a*(i)); κακῶς καθεύδουcιν *they sleep badly.* This is frequently a valuable clue in reading Greek.

3.1/5 Prepositions

We have already seen some prepositions which indicate motion or rest (2.1/3*f, g, h*). Many prepositions govern both the accusative and genitive, some the accusative, genitive and dative. There are always differences of meaning involved, e.g. παρά +acc. = *to (wards);* +gen. = *from;* +dat. = *at, beside* (παρά is used for persons, not places, e.g. παρὰ ἐμοί lit. *beside me,* i.e. *at my house,* cf. Fr. *chez moi*). The following are particularly common:

(*a*) with accusative:	διά	*on account of*
	μετά	*after*
	περί	*around* (time, place, or number)
(*b*) with genitive:	ἀντί	*instead of*
	διά	*through, by means of*
	μετά	*(in company) with*
	ὑπέρ	*on behalf of*
	περί	*concerning*

Common idiomatic phrases involving παρά and another preposition κατά are: κατὰ γῆν καὶ κατὰ θάλατταν *by land and sea;* κατὰ/παρὰ τοὺc νόμους *according to/contrary to the laws.*

3.1/6 Present indicative and infinitive of εἰμί *I am*

This verb is irregular in Greek as is its equivalent in other languages. It has little in common with other –μι verbs (18.1/1).

SINGULAR				PLURAL		
	1	εἰμί	*I am*		ἐςμέν	*we are*
	2	εἶ	*you* (s.) *are*		ἐςτέ	*you* (pl.) *are*
	3	ἐςτί(ν)	*he, she, it is*		εἰςί(ν)	*they are*
INFINITIVE		εἶναι	*to be*			

All the above forms are enclitic (see **Appendix 8**, *d*) except εἶ and εἶναι.

εἰμί **never** governs an accusative because it does not express an action inflicted by a subject on an object. What is said about the subject in clauses such as *I am **Aphrodite**, wisdom is a **skill**, the girls are **beautiful*** is put into the **nominative**: εἰμὶ Ἀφροδῑτη, ἡ coφίᾱ τέχνη ἐςτίν, αἱ κόραι εἰςὶ καλαί. In clauses of this nature the appropriate form of εἰμί (usually ἐςτί or εἰςί) is often omitted (cf. above 3.1/3*b*): ἀθάνατος ἡ ψῡχή *the soul [is] immortal*; ἄνθρωπος μέτρον ἁπάντων *a man [is] the measure of all things*. Sometimes the context requires that ἐςτί and εἰςί should be translated by *there is* and *there are* respectively; κόραι ἐν τῇ ἀγορᾷ εἰςιν *there are girls in the agora* (we would not normally say in English *girls are in the agora*).

3.2 Greek reading

An analysis of sentence 10 will be found in the key.

Proverbs and short quotations

By the end of antiquity the Greeks had accumulated an enormous number of proverbs and pithy sayings. Some have no identifiable origin, others are quotations, generally from poets. The following, and those included in future exercises, are nearly always in their original form.

1 οὐκ εἰςὶν οἱ παμπλούςιοι (*the very rich*) ἀγαθοί.
2 ἐρημία μεγάλη ἐςτὶν ἡ μεγάλη πόλις (*city*).
3 ἡ πενία τὰς τέχνας ἐγείρει.
4 νεκρὸς οὐ δάκνει.
5 In these shorter sayings supply εἰςί in (*i*), ἐςτί in the rest: (*i*) πολλοὶ τραπέζης, οὐκ ἀληθείας, φίλοι. (*ii*) ἡ εὐτυχία πολύφιλος.

(*iii*) ὁ ἄνθρωπος πολιτικὸν ζῷον. (*iv*) ἀθάνατος ὁ θάνατος. (*v*) οὐ σχολὴ δούλοις. (*vi*) χωρὶς ὑγιείας ἄβιος βίος. (*vii*) νόσος φιλίας ἡ κολακεία. (*viii*) κακὸς ἀνὴρ (*man*) μακρόβιος.

6# τὰ μεγάλα δῶρα τῆς Τύχης ἔχει φόβον.

7# κακὸν φέρουσι καρπὸν οἱ κακοὶ φίλοι.

8# αὐθαίρετος λύπη ἐστὶν ἡ τέκνων σπορά.

9 δῶρα θεοὺς πείθει.

10 οὔτε συμπόσιον χωρὶς ὁμιλίας οὔτε πλοῦτος χωρὶς ἀρετῆς ἡδονὴν ἔχει.

11 ὁ ἀνεξέταστος βίος οὐ βιωτὸς ἀνθρώπῳ.

12 A fable of Aesop

Aesop was a slave on the island of Samos in the early sixth century BC who composed animal fables. These were at first transmitted orally and became widely known. The collection that survives under Aesop's name seems to have been put into its present form early in the Christian era. The following is an adaptation.

(*i*) πολλοὶ βάτραχοι ἀγγέλους πέμπουσι πρὸς τὸν Κρονίδην διότι μονάρχου χρῇζουσιν.

(*ii*) οἱ ἄγγελοι τῷ Κρονίδῃ ὑπὲρ τῶν βατράχων λέγουσιν· ὦ δίκαιε Κρονίδη, δεσπότης εἶ τῶν θεῶν. ἆρα ἐθέλεις τοῖς βατράχοις δεσπότην παρέχειν;

(*iii*) ὁ Κρονίδης σφόδρα θαυμάζει καὶ μέγα ξύλον εἰς τὴν τῶν βατράχων λίμνην ῥίπτει.

(*iv*) τὸ ξύλον ἐκπλήττει τοὺς βατράχους καὶ ταχέως ἀποτρέχουσιν, ἀλλὰ ὑποπτεύειν ἄρχουσιν ἐπεὶ τὸ ξύλον ἐστὶν ἀκίνητον.

(*v*) ὕστερον τῷ ξύλῳ ἄνευ φόβου ἐπιβαίνουσι καὶ λέγουσιν· ὦ ξένε, ἆρα θεὸς εἶ ἢ ἄνθρωπος ἢ ζῷον;

(*vi*) ἐπεὶ οὐ λέγει οὐδέν, νομίζουσιν ἀνάξιον εἶναι εἰ τοιοῦτον δεσπότην ἔχουσι καὶ ἀγγέλους πάλιν πρὸς τὸν Κρονίδην πέμπουσιν περὶ νέου μονάρχου.

(*vii*) οἱ ἄγγελοι τῷ Κρονίδῃ λέγουσιν· ὦ δέσποτα, δεῖ ἄλλον μόναρχον τοῖς βατράχοις πέμπειν ἐπεὶ ὁ πρῶτός ἐστιν ἀκίνητος καὶ ἀργός.

(*viii*) ὁ τῶν θεῶν δεσπότης ἐν ὀργῇ ἔχει τοὺς βατράχους καὶ μεγάλην ὕδραν πέμπει.

(*ix*) ἡ ὕδρα ἐστὶν ἀπαραίτητος καὶ τοὺς βατράχους ἐσθίει.

(*x*) ὁ μῦθος σαφηνίζει ὅτι δεῖ τοὺς ἀργοὺς δεσπότας φέρειν ἐπεὶ οἱ δραστήριοι δεσπόται ταλαιπωρίας πολλάκις φέρουσιν.

Notes

2 ἡ μεγάλη πόλιϲ the article indicates a general class (2.1/2 note 1); in English we would say *a large city.*

3 With neither noun would we use an article in English (2.1/2 note 1). The same applies in 5 (ii), (iii), (iv), and 7.

6 # indicates that the sentence (or passage) is in verse. Poets often vary normal prose usage (but not in 6, 7, 8). Here (and in 9) a neuter plural subject is followed by a singular verb (3.1/1 note 2).

12 (*ii*) A question which does not involve an interrogative word (*who? how?*, etc.) may be introduced by ἆρα (10.1/2), which has no English equivalent; in such cases, we normally reverse subject and verb (*are you a sailor?* ἆρα ναύτηϲ εἶ;).

   (*iv*) ἄρχουϲιν here *begin.*

   (*v*) τῷ ξύλῳ ... ἐπιβαίνουϲι *they step on to the log,* ἐπιβαίνω here takes the dative (cf. 13.1/2*b*).

   (*vi*) Certain compound negatives (here οὐδέν) **reinforce** a preceding simple negative (οὐ) and the meaning here is *it says nothing at all* (see 7.1/6); ἀνάξιον (neuter) εἶναι εἰ ... lit. [*it*] *to be unworthy if ...,* i.e. *that it is despicable that ...*

   (*viii*) ἐν ὀργῇ ἔχει lit. *has in anger,* i.e. *is angry with.*

   (*x*) Note the pun on the two meanings of φέρω, *endure* and *bring.*

3.2/1 Vocabulary

ἄβιοϲ, –ον *unlivable, intolerable*
ἀγαθόϲ, –ή, –όν *good*
ἄγγελοϲ, –ου, ὁ *messenger*
ἀθάνατοϲ, –ον *immortal*
ἀκῑ́νητοϲ, –ον *motionless*
ἀλήθεια, –ᾱϲ, ἡ *truth*
ἄλλοϲ, –η, –ον *other, another*
ἀνάξιοϲ, –ον *unworthy*
ἀνεξέταϲτοϲ, –ον *without enquiry*
ἄνευ (prep.+gen.) *without*
ἄνθρωποϲ, –ου, ὁ *man, human being*

ἀπαραίτητοϲ, –ον *unmoved by prayer, pitiless*
ἀποτρέχω *run away*
ἆρα (interrog. particle) see note to 12 (ii)
ἀργόϲ, –όν *lazy, idle*
ἀρετή, –ῆϲ, ἡ *excellence, virtue*
ἄρχω *begin*
αὐθαίρετοϲ, –ον *self-chosen, self-inflicted*
βάτραχοϲ, –ου, ὁ *frog*
βίοϲ, –ου, ὁ *life*
βιωτόϲ, –όν *worth living*

δάκνω bite
δεcπότης, -ου, ὁ master
δοῦλος, -ου, ὁ slave
δραστήριος, -ον active
δῶρον, -ου, τό gift
ἐπεί (conj.) since
ἐπιβαίνω (+dat.) step on to
ἐρημίᾱ, -ᾱς, ἡ desert, wilderness
εὐτυχίᾱ, -ᾱς, ἡ good fortune
ζῷον, -ου, τό living being,
  animal
ἤ (conj.) or
ἡδονή, -ῆς, ἡ pleasure
θάνατος, -ου, ὁ death
θεός, -οῦ, ὁ god
κακός, -ή, -όν bad, evil
καρπός, -οῦ, ὁ fruit
κολακείᾱ, -ᾱς, ἡ flattery
Κρονίδης, -ου, ὁ son of Cronos
  (i.e. Zeus)
λίμνη, -ης, ἡ pool, marsh
λύπη, -ης, ἡ grief
μακρόβιος, -ον long-lived
μόναρχος, -ου, ὁ monarch
μῦθος, -ου, ὁ story, fable
νεκρός, -οῦ, ὁ corpse
νέος, -ᾱ, -ον new
νομίζω think, consider
νόcος, -ου, ἡ disease
ξένος, -ου, ὁ stranger
ξύλον, -ου, τό log
ὁμῑλίᾱ, -ᾱς, ἡ company
ὀργή, -ῆς, ἡ anger
  ἐν ὀργῇ ἔχειν (+acc.) be
  angry with
οὐ (οὐκ, οὐχ) no(t) (see 2.1/6a)
οὐδέν (neuter pron.) nothing
οὔτε ... οὔτε neither ... nor
παμπλούcιος, -ον very rich

πείθω persuade
πέμπω send
πενίᾱ, -ᾱς, ἡ poverty
πλοῦτος, -ου, ὁ wealth
πολῑτικός, -ή, -όν political
πολλάκις (adv.) often
πολύφιλος, -ον having many
  friends
πρῶτος, -η, -ον first
cαφηνίζω make clear
cπορά, -ᾱς, ἡ sowing, begetting
cυμπόcιον, -ου, τό drinking
  party
cφόδρα (adv.) very much,
  exceedingly
cχολή, -ῆς, ἡ leisure, rest
ταλαιπωρίᾱ, -ᾱς, ἡ hardship,
  distress
ταχέως (adv.) quickly
τέκνον, -ου, τό child
τέχνη, -ης, ἡ art, craft, skill
τοιοῦτος (adj. 21.1/3) of such a
  kind, such
τράπεζα, -ης, ἡ table
Τύχη, -ης, ἡ Fortune, Chance
ὑγίεια, -ᾱς, ἡ health
ὕδρᾱ, -ᾱς, ἡ hydra, water-
  serpent
ὑποπτεύω suspect, be suspicious
ὕcτερον (adv.) later, afterwards
φέρω bear, bring
φιλίᾱ, -ᾱς, ἡ friendship
φίλος, -η, -ον dear, friendly; as
  a noun friend
φόβος, -ου, ὁ fear
χρήζω (+gen.) be in need of,
  desire
χωρίc (prep.+gen.) without,
  apart from

4 | UNIT FOUR

For this and every third subsequent unit a revision exercise will be found at the Internet website http://tyancientgreek.org

4.1 Grammar

4.1/1 Imperfect indicative active and weak aorist indicative active and infinitive active of –ω verbs

Both the imperfect and the aorist (in the indicative) have reference to the past. The aorist has other moods, which we shall treat later, but the imperfect exists only in the indicative.

The term **weak** aorist is used to distinguish the formation of this tense in λύω (and most other –ω verbs) from that in a minority of –ω verbs which have a **strong** aorist (7.1/1). There is no difference in meaning. The weak aorist is so named because its stem requires a suffix (c added to the present stem), whereas the stem of the strong aorist resembles that of the imperfect in having no suffix. The concept of verbal strength as shown in the presence (weak) or absence (strong) of suffixes is a somewhat whimsical notion of nineteenth-century grammarians.

The aorist stem of λύω is λῡc– (the same as for the future), while the imperfect simply uses that of the present, λῡ–. The **augment** is prefixed to the stem in the indicative of both. This, in λύω and other verbs beginning with a consonant, consists of the vowel ἐ, giving us ἐλῡ– (imperfect), ἐλῡc– (aorist). The two sets of endings have similarities but the vowel immediately following the stem in the aorist is α in five of the six forms, whereas in this position in the imperfect we have the same pattern of o– and e– sounds as in the present (cf. 2.1/5 note 3):

		IMPERFECT	AORIST
SINGULAR	1	ἔλῡ-ον *I was loosening,* *used to loosen*	ἔλῡc-α *I loosened*
	2	ἔλῡ-εc	ἔλῡc-αc
	3	ἔλῡ-ε(ν)	ἔλῡc-ε(ν)
PLURAL	1	ἐλύ-ομεν	ἐλύc-αμεν
	2	ἐλύ-ετε	ἐλύc-ατε
	3	ἔλῡ-ον	ἔλῡc-αν
INFINITIVE		——	λῦc-αι

The imperfect and the aorist indicative both represent actions which occurred in the past, but, whereas the aorist simply tells us that an action took place, e.g. τοὺc νεᾱνίᾱc ἐπαιδεύcαμεν *we educated the young men,* the imperfect tells us that an action was continuous or repeated, e.g. τοὺc νεᾱνίᾱc ἐπαιδεύομεν *we were educating/used to educate the young men* (the choice between continuous action *were educating* and habitual action *used to educate* will depend on the context).[1] In other words, while the aorist indicative views a past action as a simple event, the imperfect indicative views it as a process, either continuous or interrupted (repeated or habitual). The difference between the two usually depends on our perception of the nature of the action or event described. We may, in a particular context, see it simply as something that happened in the past (*it rained last summer*). In another context we may see the same event as something continuous (*it was raining last summer when Socrates visited us*) or repeated (*last summer it used to rain every time I went to the Acropolis*). Naturally, many past actions and events are not normally viewed in more than one way (*Pericles died during the plague*). The term covering distinctions of this sort is **aspect**. We say that, although both these tenses of the indicative describe something that happened in the past, the aorist indicative expresses a momentary aspect, the imperfect a continuous or habitual aspect.

This distinction in the indicative between the imperfect and the aorist also applies in the **infinitive** between the **present** and **aorist**, although there is no specific time reference (but see 8.1/3*a* and 21.1/1 note). The present infinitive is used for an action which is seen as going on, in the process of happening or being repeated. The aorist infinitive is used for an action which is seen simply as an event. Often both are to be

---

[1] The imperfect has two other meanings, which are less common: *began to* (*I began to educate* etc. **inceptive imperfect**) and *tried to* (*I tried to educate* etc. **conative imperfect**).

translated in English simply by a present infinitive: ὁ Ἱππόλυτος τὸν Γλαῦκον ἐκέλευσεν αἰὲν ἀριστεύειν *Hippolytus ordered Glaucus to be always best* (ἀριστεύειν *to be best* present infinitive, because the action is seen as one which is going on and continuing); ἡ Ξανθίππη τὸν δοῦλον ἐκέλευσε κροῦσαι τὴν θύραν *Xanthippe ordered the slave to knock [on] the door* (κροῦσαι aorist infinitive, because Xanthippe envisages a simple (single) act; the present infinitive κρούειν would imply a continual action and require the translation *to keep knocking*).

The imperfect has no infinitive because the present infinitive covers the meaning it would have had (i.e. *to be loosening* in a past context). For similar reasons the imperfect has no moods other than the indicative.

Notes

1 The augment is prefixed to the indicative forms of the three **historic** tenses (the tenses whose indicative describes something in the past, viz imperfect, aorist, pluperfect (16.1/2)); it does **not** occur in the three **primary** tenses (the tenses whose indicative describes something in the present or future, viz present, future, perfect (15.1/1), and future perfect (16.1/4 note 2)). There is also a formal difference between the two categories in the 3rd pl. ind. act. ending. In historic tenses this has a final –ν (e.g. ἔλῦον, ἔλῡσαν), but in primary tenses ends in –ςι(ν) (e.g. λῦουςι(ν), λῦςουςι(ν)).

2 There are two types of augment:

   (i) the **syllabic** augment, as described above, where a verb begins with a consonant. An initial ρ is doubled: ῥῑπτω *throw*, impf. ἔρρῑπτον. This augment is so called because it adds a syllable to the forms where it is used.

   (ii) the **temporal** augment. This variety of the augment is called temporal (Latin **tempus** *time*) because it increases the time taken to pronounce (i.e. it lengthens) an initial vowel according to the following table. Note that α is lengthened to η and that ι, when the second element of a diphthong, becomes subscript. As ι and υ (unlike ε/η and ο/ω) can represent both long and short vowels the temporal augment does not affect the spelling of verbs beginning with them.

$$\alpha > \eta \qquad\qquad \alpha\iota > \eta$$
$$\varepsilon > \eta \qquad\qquad \alpha\upsilon > \eta\upsilon$$
$$\iota > \bar{\iota} \qquad\qquad \varepsilon\iota > \eta$$

$$o > \omega \qquad \varepsilon\upsilon > \eta\upsilon$$
$$\upsilon > \bar{\upsilon} \qquad o\iota > \omega$$

η and ω remain unchanged

Examples are: ἀκούω *hear*, aor. ἤκουςα; ἐλπίζω *hope*, impf. ἤλπιζον; οἰκτίρω *pity*, impf. ᾤκτῑρον; ὠδῑνω *be in labour*, impf. ὤδῑνον (for other examples see **Principal parts of verbs**). A few verbs with initial ε take ει not η, e.g. ἔχω has impf. εἶχον. ει and ευ are often not changed, e.g. εὑρίςκω *find,* impf. εὕριςκον or ηὕριςκον.

3 The endings of the lst s. and 3rd pl. of the imperfect indicative active are the same. The context of a particular form will always make clear which person is meant.

4 Like its present, the imperfect of εἰμί is irregular: ἦ or ἦν, ἦςθα, ἦν, ἦμεν, ἦτε, ἦςαν. This is the only past tense of εἰμί because the act of being was regarded as necessarily extending over a period of time. For all forms of εἰμί see **Appendix 3**.

4.1/2 First and second person pronouns, and αὐτόν, –ήν, –ό

As in English, so in Greek we have pronouns of the first and second persons. These are declined as follows:

	First Person		**Second Person**	
	SINGULAR			
Nom.	ἐγώ	*I*	cύ (also voc.)	*you* (s.)
Acc.	ἐμέ, με	*me*	cέ, ce	*you*
Gen.	ἐμοῦ, μου	*of me*	coῦ, cου	*of you*
Dat.	ἐμοί, μοι	*to/for me*	coί, coι	*to/for you*
	PLURAL			
Nom.	ἡμεῖς	*we*	ὑμεῖς (also voc.)	*you* (pl.)
Acc.	ἡμᾶς	*us*	ὑμᾶς	*you*
Gen.	ἡμῶν	*of us*	ὑμῶν	*of you*
Dat.	ἡμῖν	*to/for us*	ὑμῖν	*to/for you*

The unaccented forms με, μου, μοι, ce, cου, coι are unemphatic and enclitic **Appendix 8**, *d*): διώκει με ἡ 'Αcπαcίᾱ *Aspasia is chasing me.* The other forms are emphatic: οὐ cέ, ἀλλὰ ἐμὲ διώκει ἡ 'Αcπαcίᾱ *it's me, not you, that Aspasia is chasing* (lit. *Aspasia is chasing not you but me*). With prepositions the emphatic forms are used, e.g. μετὰ coῦ *with you,* except for πρός: πρός με *towards me.* Since the endings of verbs indicate the person involved, the nominative forms will occur only where emphasis is required.

Likewise, in the third person there is no need in Greek for an unemphatic form of the pronoun in the nominative since this too is supplied by the personal endings of the verb: λέγει *he/she/it speaks* (the gender of the subject will be clear from the context). The oblique cases (2.1/3), however, are supplied by αὐτόν, -ήν, -ό *him, her, it* (the nominative has another meaning – 9.1/3), which is declined exactly like the corresponding forms of καλός (3.1/3) except that the neuter accusative singular is αὐτό: ἡ Ἀσπασίᾱ ἐχθὲς ἐδίωκεν αὐτόν *Aspasia was chasing him yesterday.* In the plural, whereas English has only one form (*them*), Greek distinguishes between the genders: m. αὐτούς, f. αὐτάς, n. αὐτά etc. (for the emphatic third person pronouns, see 9.1/1).

Note

The possessive genitive of the **unemphatic** personal pronoun is placed after the noun which it qualifies, εἰς τὴν οἰκίᾱν μου *into my house* (lit. *into the house of me*); ἐκ τῆς οἰκίᾱς αὐτῶν *from their house* (lit. *from the house of them*). For the position of the genitive of the **emphatic** personal pronouns see 9.1/5.

4.1/3 Connecting particles

A fundamental feature of Greek is the ubiquitous occurrence of particles. These are short, indeclinable words, many of which are **postpositive**, i.e. they cannot occur as first word in the phrase or sentence where they are used (these we shall mark here and in the vocabulary with an asterisk). Those such as καί *and* and ἀλλά *but,* which are not postpositive, are also called conjunctions.

Particles have two basic functions:

(*a*) to act as connectives linking grammatical elements of equal weight (words with words, phrases with phrases, sentences with sentences)

(*b*) to add shades of tone, colour, or emphasis to individual words, phrases, or sentences, which in English would simply be conveyed by a variation in the tone or emphasis of the voice.

Here we will concentrate mainly on connectives. Other particles will be explained as they occur in the reading and at 13.1/3.

With very few well-defined exceptions, every sentence in Greek is connected to the preceding sentence by a connecting particle. The commonest of these is δέ* *and,* which is regularly used to connect a string of sentences where in English we would avoid any connecting word at all. In English it would be considered very bad style to begin sentence after sentence with *and,* but in Greek it is totally natural and acceptable. δέ* is also translatable as *but,* but when so used it denotes only a slight contrast: ὁ Ἀχιλλεὺς ἦν ἐν τῇ ϲκηνῇ· ὁ δὲ Πάτροκλοϲ ἔφερεν οἶνον *Achilles was in the tent but* (or *and*) *Patroclus was bringing wine.* A strongly contrasting *but* is expressed by ἀλλά, e.g. οὐ βραδέωϲ ἀλλὰ ταχέωϲ οἱ βάρβαροι ἡμᾶϲ ἐδίωκον *the barbarians were chasing us not slowly but quickly.* Note also γάρ* *for, as,* which introduces the **reason** for what goes before, οὐ μένομεν· οἱ γὰρ βάρβαροι ἡμᾶϲ διώκουϲιν *we are not staying as the barbarians are chasing us.* Similarly οὖν* *therefore, so,* introduces the **result** of what goes before, οἱ βάρβαροι ἡμᾶϲ διώκουϲιν· ταχέωϲ οὖν τρέχομεν *the barbarians are chasing us; therefore we are running quickly.*

καί *and* is frequently used as a simple conjunction connecting words, clauses or sentences, ἡμεῖϲ καὶ ὑμεῖϲ *you and we* (Greek gives precedence to the 1st person, English is more polite). καὶ ... καί is used to express *both ... and* καὶ ἡ Ἀφροδίτη καὶ ὁ Διόνῡϲοϲ *both Aphrodite and Dionysos,* and the same sense can also be conveyed by τε* ... καί, but since τε* is postpositive (and enclitic; see **Appendix 8**, *d*), the above phrase would become ἥ τε Ἀφροδίτη καὶ ὁ Διόνῡϲοϲ. Less commonly τε* is used by itself as the equivalent of δέ or καί to connect a sentence to a preceding sentence.

καί may also be used **adverbially** in the sense *also, even, actually,* καὶ ϲύ, τέκνον *even you* (or *you too*), *[my] child*; τὸν βάρβαρον καὶ ἐδιώκομεν *we were actually chasing the barbarian.* In this usage καί stands immediately before the word it modifies. The negative of adverbial καί is οὐδέ, *not even,* e.g. οὐδὲ ὁ οἶνοϲ ἀγαθόϲ *not even the wine [is] good.* (As a conjunction οὐδέ also means *nor, and ... not*).

One of the most important combinations of particles is that of μέν* followed at a distance by δέ*. μέν*, however, does **not** connect its own word group with anything preceding. For convenience, it is normally translated in dictionaries by *on the one hand,* which is somewhat too emphatic since μέν* simply introduces the first of a parallel pair of

balanced or contrasted items. When we see μέν* we know to look
ahead to find the corresponding δέ*. This tendency to place words in
a formally balanced structure is fundamental to Greek. Any page of a
Greek author will contain at least one μέν* ... δέ*.

We may think of the pair as meaning *on the one hand ... and/but on the
other hand,* but in most cases such a translation would be heavy or
clumsy. Thus Cωκράτης μὲν λέγει ἐν τῇ ἀγορᾷ, ἐγὼ δὲ βαδίζω μετὰ τῆς
'Αcπαcίᾱc should not be translated by *Socrates on the one hand is
speaking in the agora, but I on the other hand am walking with Aspasia*
but by *Socrates is speaking ... but I am walking ...* or *whereas Socrates
is speaking ... I am walking ...*

The two elements balanced by μέν* ... δέ* must always be structurally
parallel and the words they follow must be of equal grammatical
weight. These can be nouns and pronouns (as above), or adverbs, e.g.
εὖ μὲν λέγει, κακῶc δὲ πράττει *he speaks **well** but acts **badly**,* or verbs
e.g. λέγει μὲν εὖ, πράττει δὲ κακῶc *he **speaks** well but **acts** badly*; here
the change in the elements contrasted has meant that the adverbs εὖ
and κακῶc have been placed after the words they qualify (cf. 2.1/6).
Other parts of speech can also be contrasted in this way.

4.2 Greek reading

An analysis of sentence 5 will be found in the Key.

1 αἱ μὲν ἡδοναὶ θνηταί, αἱ δ' ἀρεταὶ ἀθάνατοι.
2 ἄρτον οὐκ εἶχεν ὁ πτωχὸc καὶ τυρὸν ἠγόραζεν.
3 μιcθὸc ἀρετῆc ἔπαινοc, κακίαc δὲ ψόγοc.
4# δεινοὶ πλέκειν τοι μηχανὰc Αἰγύπτιοι.
5 τοῖc μὲν δούλοιc ἡ ἀνάγκη νόμοc, τοῖc δὲ ἐλευθέροιc ἀνθρώποιc ὁ
  νόμοc ἀνάγκη.
6 πάλαι ποτ' ἦcαν ἄλκιμοι Μιλήcιοι.
7 ἀετὸc μυίαc οὐ θηρεύει.
8 **Futility**
  (*i*) εἰc οὐρανὸν πτύειc. (*ii*) ἐξ ἄμμου cχοινίον πλέκειc. (*iii*)
  θάλατταν cπείρειc. (*iv*) ἵππον εἰc πεδίον διδάcκειc τρέχειν. (*v*)
  κατόπιν ἑορτῆc ἥκειc. (*vi*) νεκρὸν μαcτίζειc. (*vii*) ὄνον κείρειc.
  (*viii*) πρὸ τῆc νίκηc τὸ ἐγκώμιον ᾄδειc. (*ix*) πρὸc κέντρα λακτίζειc.
  (*x*) τὰc μηχανὰc μετὰ τὸν πόλεμον κομίζειc.

9   The fall of Croesus

Herodotus (fifth century BC) is the earliest surviving Greek historian
and has been called the father of history. The subject of his work is
the rise of the Persian empire and its fateful clash with the Greek
world which culminated in the unsuccessful invasion of Greece in 480-
479 BC. The following passage is based on Herodotus' description of
the subjugation of Lydia (see map on p. xi), which brought the
Persians into contact with the Greeks of the Asia Minor coast.

ὁ δὲ Κροῖcoc ὁ τῶν Λυδῶν βαcιλεὺc (king) τὴν τῶν Περcῶν ἀρχὴν
διαφθείρειν ἤθελεν· κατὰ γὰρ τὸ ἐν Δελφοῖc χρηcτήριον ἀρχὴν
μεγάλην ἔμελλε παῦcαι. ἀλλὰ τέλος τὴν μὲν ἑαυτοῦ (his own) ἀρχὴν
ἔπαυcεν, τὴν δὲ τῶν Περcῶν οὔ. μετὰ δὲ τὴν τῶν Περcῶν νίκην ὁ Κῦρος
ὁ τῶν Περcῶν βαcιλεὺc τὸν Κροῖcον ἐπὶ πυρὰν μεγάλην ἀνεβίβαcεν 5
(made ... go up). ὁ δὲ Κροῖcoc τοὺc λόγουc τοὺc τοῦ Cόλωνoc (of
Solon) τοῦ ᾿Αθηναίου ἐφρόντιζεν· οὐδεὶc (no-one) τῶν ἀνθρώπων
ὄλβιος πρὸ τοῦ θανάτου. ἥcυχος οὖν ἔμενε τὴν τελευτήν· ἀλλὰ ὁ
Κῦρος, διότι ὁ Κροῖcoc καὶ ὅcιος ἦν καὶ ἀγαθός, ἐκέλευcε μὲν τοὺc
cτρατιώταc ἀπὸ τῆc πυρᾶc αὐτὸν καταβιβάcαι (to bring down), ἔλεξε 10
(spoke) δὲ ὧδε· ὦ Κροῖcε, τίc (who?) cε ἀνθρώπων ἔπειcε (persuaded)
πολέμιον ἀντὶ φίλου ἐπὶ τὴν γῆν μου cτρατεῦcαι; ὁ δὲ Κροῖcoc, ὦ
Κῦρε, ἔφη (said), ἐγὼ μὲν ἐπὶ cὲ ἐcτράτευcα, ὁ δὲ θεὸc ὁ ἐν Δελφοῖc
ἔπειcέ με cτρατεῦcαι. οὐ γάρ εἰμι ἀνόητος οὐδὲ ἐθέλω τὸν πόλεμον
ἔχειν ἀντὶ τῆc εἰρήνηc. ἐν μὲν γὰρ τῇ εἰρήνῃ οἱ νεανίαι τοὺc γεραιοὺc 15
(the old) θάπτουcιν, ἐν δὲ τῷ πολέμῳ οἱ γεραιοὶ τοὺc νεανίαc. ἀλλὰ
τοῦτο (lit. this thing) φίλον ἦν τοῖc θεοῖc. ὁ οὖν Κῦρος αὐτὸν ἔλυcε καὶ
ἐγγὺc καθεῖcεν (made ... sit). ὁ δὲ Κροῖcoc αὖθιc ἔλεξεν· ὦ Κῦρε, τί
(what?) πράττουcιν οἱ cτρατιῶταί cου; τὴν πόλιν (city) cου, ἔφη ὁ
Κῦρος, ἁρπάζουcι καὶ τὸν πλοῦτόν cου ἐκφέρουcιν. οὐχ ἁρπάζουcι 20
τὴν πόλιν μου, ἔφη ὁ Κροῖcoc, οὐδὲ τὸν πλοῦτον· οὐδὲν (nothing) γὰρ
ἐμοί ἐcτιν. ἀλλὰ cὲ ἄγουcί τε καὶ φέρουcιν. μετὰ δὲ τοῦτο φίλοc ἦν
αὐτῷ. τὴν γὰρ coφίαν αὐτοῦ ἐν τιμῇ εἶχεν ὁ Κῦρος.

Notes

1   The appropriate part of εἰμί is to be supplied (also in 3, 4, 5).
2   Cheese (τῡρόc) would have been a luxury to the poor.
3   Take μιcθόc with the genitives ἀρετῆc and κακίαc; normal prose
    usage would require ὁ μιcθόc but the definite article is often
    omitted in proverbs and in verse.
4   τοι is a particle conveying emphasis, commonly employed in
    proverbs; it is not to be translated, since in English we would
    convey the emphasis by tone of voice; μηχανᾱ́c here used

metaphorically *devices, ways and means* (in 8(*x*) below the word is used concretely).

6 Miletus, the city of the Μιλήϲιοι, flourished in the seventh and sixth centuries BC; in later times it became symbolic of past greatness; Μιλήϲιοι does not have an article as this is optional with proper nouns (2.1/2(iii)).

8 (*x*) μηχαναί are here *engines of war* (siege weapons and the like).

9 *l*.1 δέ connects this passage with what precedes in the original and need not be translated. *1.2* Δελφοί is a plural place name. There are many such names in Greek (Ἀθῆναι *Athens*, Θῆβαι *Thebes*). *l*.3 ἔμελλε *was destined to, was going to*. *l*.6 Solon was an Athenian statesman who had visited Croesus and, in conversation with him, had enunciated the very Greek sentiment *Call no man happy before he dies* (only then can a true and full judgement be made). *ll.*7f. ἐφρόντιζεν *began to ponder* inceptive imperfect (4.1/1 footnote); οὐδεὶϲ ... θανάτου are Solon's actual words (inverted commas are not normally used in printing Greek – 1.1/1 note 3); ἥϲυχος translate by an adverb *quietly* (Greek often uses an adjective where English would have an adverb). *l*.11 Take τίϲ ... ἀνθρώπων together. *l*.12 Take πολέμιον with ϲε, *[as an] enemy* (Greek does not here need an equivalent to the English *as*). *l*.17 τοῦτο refers to what has happened to Croesus; φίλον +dat. *dear to, pleasing to*. *l*.20 οὐχ 2.1/6*a*(i). *l*.22 ἄγουϲί τε καὶ φέρουϲιν lit. *are both driving and carrying*, i.e. *are plundering and carrying off* (a set expression; the τε need not be translated) but here translate simply by *plunder*.

4.2/1 Vocabulary

ἀγοράζω *buy*	ἀπό (prep.+gen.) *from, away from*
ἄγω καὶ φέρω *plunder*	
ᾄδω *sing*	ἁρπάζω *seize, plunder, snatch*
ἀετός, –οῦ, ὁ *eagle*	ἄρτος, –ου, ὁ *bread*
Ἀθηναῖος, –ᾱ, –ον *Athenian*	ἀρχή, –ῆϲ, ἡ *empire*
Αἰγύπτιος, –ᾱ, –ον *Egyptian*	αὖθιϲ (adv.) *again*
ἄλκιμος, –ον *brave*	γάρ* (connecting particle) *for, as*
ἄμμος, –ου, ἡ *sand*	
ἀνάγκη, –ηϲ, ἡ *necessity*	δεινόϲ, –ή, –όν *clever at* (+inf.)
ἀνόητοϲ –ον *foolish*	Δελφοί, –ῶν, οἱ *Delphi*
ἀντί (prep.+gen.) *instead of*	διδάϲκω *teach*

ἐγγύς (adv.) *near, nearby*
ἐγκώμιον, –ου, τό *victory-song*
ἐθέλω *am willing, wish*
εἰρήνη, –ης, ἡ *peace*
ἐκφέρω *carry out*
ἐλεύθερος, –ᾱ, –ον *free*
ἐξ = ἐκ
ἑορτή, –ῆς, ἡ *feast*
ἔπαινος, –ου, ὁ *praise*
ἐπί (prep.+acc.) *on to, to,
   against*
ἥσυχος, –η, –ον *quiet, peaceful*
θάπτω *bury*
θηρεύω *hunt*
θνητός, –ή, –όν *mortal*
ἵππος, –ου, ὁ *horse*
κακίᾱ, –ᾱς, ἡ *wickedness*
κατά (prep.+acc.) *according to*
κατόπιν (+gen.) *after*
κείρω *cut* (the hair), *shear*
κελεύω *order*
κέντρον, –ου, τό *goad*
κομίζω *bring*
λακτίζω *kick*
λόγος, –ου, ὁ *word*
Λῡδός, –οῦ, ὁ *Lydian*
μαστίζω *whip, flog*
μέλλω *be destined to*
μένω *wait (for)*
μετά (prep.+acc.) *after*
μηχανή, –ῆς, ἡ *engine of war;
   device*
Μῑλήσιος, –ᾱ, –ον *of Miletus,
   Milesian*
μισθός, –οῦ, ὁ *pay, reward*
μυῖα, –ᾱς, ἡ *fly*
νῑκη, –ης, ἡ *victory*
νόμος, –ου, ὁ *law*

ὄλβιος, –ᾱ, –ον *happy*
ὄνος, –ου, ὁ/ἡ *ass*
ὅσιος, –ᾱ, –ον *pious, devout*
οὐδέ (conj.) *and not, nor*
οὖν* (particle) *therefore, so,
   then*
οὐρανός, –οῦ, ὁ *sky*
πάλαι (adv.) *long ago*
παύω (tr.) *stop, put an end to*
πεδίον, –ου, τό *plain*
Πέρσης, –ου, ὁ *Persian*
πλέκω *plait; devise, contrive*
πολέμιος, –ᾱ, –ον *hostile,
   enemy*
πόλεμος, –ου, ὁ *war*
ποτέ* *once*
πρᾱττω *do*
πρό (prep.+gen.) *before*
πτύω *spit*
πτωχός, –οῦ, ὁ *beggar*
πυρᾱ, –ᾶς, ἡ *funeral pyre*
σοφίᾱ, –ᾱς, ἡ *wisdom*
σπείρω *sow* (with seed)
στρατεύω *make an expedition*
στρατιώτης, –ου, ὁ *soldier*
σχοινίον, –ου, τό *little rope*
τε* ... καί/τε* *both ... and*
τελευτή, –ῆς, ἡ *end, death*
τέλος (adv.) *in the end, finally*
τῑμή, –ῆς, ἡ *respect*
τοι* see note on 4
τρέχω *run*
τῡρός, –οῦ, ὁ *cheese*
φροντίζω *think about, ponder*
χρηστήριον, –ου, τό *oracle*
ψόγος, –ου, ὁ *blame*
ὧδε (adv.) *thus, as follows*

5 | UNIT FIVE

5.1 Grammar

5.1/1 Third declension – consonant stem nouns (1)

The third declension contains nouns of all three genders. They are divided into two classes, those with stems ending in a consonant and those with stems ending in a vowel or diphthong. Within the various sub-groups of each class masculine and feminine nouns have the same case endings but neuters always follow the rule previously given (3.1/1) for the nominative, vocative and accusative (not every sub-group has each gender). The gender of a third declension noun is only sometimes predictable from its ending.

With all consonant stem nouns we discover the stem by subtracting –oc from the genitive singular (e.g. γύψ *vulture,* gen. γῦπός, stem γῦπ–) and the other case endings are added to this. As the stem is modified, occasionally beyond recognition, in the nominative singular, both nominative and genitive singular must be learnt.

(*a*) *Stems in* κ, γ, χ *(palatals),* π, β, φ *(labials), and* τ, δ, θ *(dentals)*
The declension of regular masculine and feminine nouns with stems ending in these consonants is given below. Masculine and feminine nouns in these sub-groups have a nominative singular in c, which combines with, or replaces, the final consonant of the stem as follows:

κ/γ/χ + c > ξ; π/β/φ + c > ψ; τ/δ/θ + c > c

The same changes occur before the dative plural ending –cι (which can take a movable ν; cf. 2.1/5 note 4); they also occur in verbs with similar stems (6.1/4).

	φύλαξ (m)	γύψ (m)	ἔρωc (m)	πατρίc (f)
	guard	*vulture*	*love*	*native land*
stem	φυλακ–	γῡπ–	ἐρωτ–	πατριδ–

SINGULAR

N.V.	φύλαξ	γύψ	ἔρωc	πατρίc (*v.* πατρί)
Acc.	φύλακ–α	γῦπ–α	ἔρωτ–α	πατρίδ–α
Gen.	φύλακ–οc	γῦπ–όc	ἔρωτ–οc	πατρίδ–οc
Dat.	φύλακ–ι	γῦπ–ί	ἔρωτ–ι	πατρίδ–ι

PLURAL

N.V.	φύλακ–εc	γῦπ–εc	ἔρωτ–εc	πατρίδ–εc
Acc.	φύλακ–αc	γῦπ–αc	ἔρωτ–αc	πατρίδ–αc
Gen.	φυλάκ–ων	γῦπ–ῶν	ἐρώτ–ων	πατρίδ–ων
Dat.	φύλαξι(ν)	γῦψί(ν)	ἔρω–cι(ν)	πατρί–cι(ν)

Within these sub-groups the only neuters are those with a τ stem. The vast majority of these have a nominative singular in –μα and a genitive in –ματοc. Of the others some have a sigma in the nominative singular (as κέραc), some do not (e.g. ἧπαρ, ἥπατοc *liver*).

	cῶμα (n) *body*		κέραc (n) *horn*	
stem	cωματ–		κερᾱτ–	

	SINGULAR	PLURAL	SINGULAR	PLURAL
N.V.	cῶμα	cώματ–α	κέραc	κέρᾱτ–α
Acc.	cῶμα	cώματ–α	κέραc	κέρᾱτ–α
Gen.	cώματ–οc	cωμάτ–ων	κέρᾱτ–οc	κερᾱτ–ων
Dat.	cώματ–ι	cώμα–cι(ν)	κέρᾱτ–ι	κέρᾱ–cι(ν)

(b) Stems in ντ (all masculine)

These have a nominative singular in –ᾱc or –ων. Unlike nouns of the preceding sub-groups (except πατρίc), they have a separate vocative singular, which is formed by dropping τ from the stem. Their dative plural has the change ντ + c > c, with lengthening of the preceding α and o to ᾱ and ου (not ω) respectively. This lengthening occurs to compensate for the reduction of three consonants to one.

	γίγᾱc (m) *giant*		λέων (m) *lion*	
stem	γιγαντ–		λεοντ–	
	SINGULAR	PLURAL	SINGULAR	PURAL
Nom.	γίγᾱc	γίγαντ–ec	λέων	λέοντ–ec
Voc.	γίγαν	γίγαντ–ec	λέον	λέοντ–ec
Acc.	γίγαντ–α	γίγαντ–αc	λέοντ–α	λέοντ–αc
Gen.	γίγαντ–οc	γιγάντ–ων	λέοντ–οc	λεόντ–ων
Dat.	γίγαντ–ι	γίγᾱcι(ν)	λέοντ–ι	λέουcι(ν)

Notes

1 Some nouns with these stems are slightly irregular, mostly in the nominative singular. The most common are:

γόνυ	γόνατος (n)	*knee*
γυνή	γυναικός (f)	*woman* (voc. s. γύναι)
θρίξ	τριχός (f)	*hair* (dat. pl. θριξί(ν)
νύξ	νυκτός (f)	*night* (dat. pl. νυξί(ν))
ὀδούς	ὀδόντος (m)	*tooth*
οὐc	ὠτός (n)	*ear*
παῖc	παιδός (m or f)	*child* (voc. sing. παῖ)
πούc	ποδός (m)	*foot*
ὕδωρ	ὕδατος (n)	*water*

2 Stems in ιδ which are **not** accented on the ι have –ιν, not –ιδα, in the acc. s., e.g. ἔρις, ἔριδος (f) *strife*, acc. ἔριν. This also applies to χάρις, χάριτος (f) *favour*, acc. χάριν and ὄρνῑς, ὄρνῑθος (m. or f.) *bird*, acc. ὄρνιν.

3 Third declension monosyllables are accented on their ending in the genitive and dative, both singular and plural (see γῦψ above).

5.1/2 Contracted verbs

Unlike verbs with stems ending in ι and υ (ἐcθίω *eat*, λύω *loosen*), verbs whose stems end in α, ε and ο contract their stem vowel with the initial vowel of the endings in the present and imperfect. A consonantal suffix is used to form the stem of the other tenses (e.g. c in the future and aorist – see note 2). Examples of contracted verbs are: τῑμά–ω *honour*, ποιέ–ω *do, make*, δηλό–ω *make clear, show*. Since all three types contract their stem vowels and the –ω of the lst s. pres. ind. act. to –ῶ (τῑμῶ, ποιῶ, δηλῶ), these verbs are always cited in vocabulary lists in their **uncontracted** form to make identification immediately

obvious. For the rules governing the accentuation of contracted verbs
see **Appendix 8**, *b*(i). Paradigms for the three types are given in
Appendix 2. As the endings involved are the same as for λΰω, it is the
rules for contraction which are our principal concern here:

(*a*) **Stems in α** (*model* τῑμάω)

α + an e-sound (ε, η) > ᾱ: ἐτίμᾱ (ἐτίμα–ε)

α + an o-sound (ο, ου, ω) > ω: τῑμῶσι (τῑμά–ουσι); τῑμῶμεν
(τῑμά–ομεν)

α + an ι- diphthong (ει, ῃ, οι) obeys the above rules but retains the
iota as a subscript in the contracted form: τῑμᾷ (τῑμά–ει)

The combinations of α + η/ῃ/οι occur in forms not yet treated.

(*b*) **Stems in ε** (*model* ποιέω)

ε + ε > ει: ποιεῖτε (ποιέ–ετε)

ε + ο > ου: ἐποίουν (ἐποίε–ον)

ε disappears before a long vowel or diphthong: ποιῶ (ποιέ–ω);
ποιοῦσι (ποιέ–ουσι).

(*c*) **Stems in ο** (*model* δηλόω)

ο + ε/ο/ου > ου: ἐδήλου (ἐδήλο–ε); δηλοῦμεν (δηλό–ομεν); δηλοῦσι
(δηλό–ουσι)

ο + η/ω > ω: δηλῶ (δηλό–ω)

ο + an ι–diphthong (ει, οι, ῃ) > οι: δηλοῖ (δηλό–ει)

The combinations ο + η/οι/ῃ occur in forms not yet treated.

The above contractions, which cover all forms of contracted verbs,
also occur in other parts of speech, e.g. the noun νοῦς (< νόος; 6.1/2).
Contraction was a regular feature of Attic Greek but was not as
rigorously applied in other dialects.

Notes

1 The present infinitives of α– and ο–stems contract to –ᾶν and –ουν
respectively, **not** –ᾷν and –οιν. This is because the –ειν of the pres.
inf. act. of uncontracted –ω verbs (e.g. λΰ–ειν) is itself a
contraction of ε + εν. With –αω and –οω verbs we therefore have
the double contractions α + ε + εν > ᾱ + εν > ᾶν; ο + ε + εν > ου
+ εν > ουν, which give us τῑμᾶν, δηλοῦν.

2 All tenses other than the present and imperfect are formed by
lengthening the stem vowel and proceeding exactly as with
uncontracted verbs (α > η (except after ε, ι, ρ where we have α >
ᾱ); ε > η; ο > ω). The fut. ind. act. of the model verbs is τῑμήσω,

ποιήσω, δηλώσω and the aor. ind. act. ἔτῑμησα, ἐποίησα, ἐδήλωσα. However, γελάω *laugh* does not lengthen its α: fut. γελάσομαι (8.1/1 note 1) aor. ἐγέλασα. Likewise, καλέω *call* and τελέω *complete* do not lengthen their ε in the aorist: ἐκάλεσα, ἐτέλεσα; their future is, rather confusingly, the same as their present, καλῶ, τελῶ, because the expected καλέσω, τελέσω lost the intervocalic c and contraction resulted (cf. 6.1/1*c*).

3   A contracted future also occurs in most verbs in –ίζω (6.1/4*b*) and all verbs with stems in λ, μ, ν, ρ (11.1/3). Nearly all such futures have a stem in ε (i.e. the contraction is –ῶ, –εῖc, –εῖ, etc., exactly as the present of ποιέω). A few have a stem in α, as ἐλαύνω *drive,* fut. stem ἐλα– giving ἐλῶ, ἐλᾷc, ἐλᾷ, etc., exactly as the present of τῑμάω.

4   ζάω *be alive* contracts to η where other –άω verbs have ᾱ: pres. ind. act. ζῶ, ζῇc, ζῇ, ζῶμεν, ζῆτε, ζῶcι(ν), inf. ζῆν; impf. ind. act. ἔζων, ἔζης, ἔζη, ἐζῶμεν, ἐζῆτε, ἔζων. So also πεινάω *be hungry* and διψάω *be thirsty.*

5   Most disyllabic verbs in –εω (as δέω *need,* πλέω *sail,* πνέω *breathe,* ῥέω *flow*) contract only when ε is followed by ε. The pres. ind. act. of πλέω is πλέω, πλεῖc, πλεῖ, πλέομεν, πλεῖτε, πλέουcι(ν); impf. ἔπλεον, ἔπλεις, ἔπλει, ἐπλέομεν, ἐπλεῖτε, ἔπλεον. The 3rd s. act. of δέω *need,* pres. δεῖ, impf. ἔδει, is used impersonally in the sense of *it is/was necessary* (examples have already occurred in the reading exercises). It is construed with the **accusative** of the person involved and an infinitive: δεῖ με ἐν τῇ οἰκίᾳ μένειν, *it is necessary for me to remain in the house,* i.e. *I must remain ...*

6   There is **no** movable ν in the 3rd s. of the impf. ind. act. of contracted verbs.

5.1/3 Further uses of the definite article

In English we can, to a limited degree, use the definite article with an adjective to form a noun-equivalent: *only the good die young; only the brave deserve the fair.* In Greek, however, the definite article can be used to create a noun-equivalent out of virtually any part of speech (adjective, adverb, prepositional phrase, infinitive) to which it is prefixed: ὁ cοφός *the wise [man];* ἡ cοφή *the wise [woman];* οἱ τότε *the then [men],* i.e. *the men of that time;* οἱ νῦν *the now [men],* i.e. *the men of today;* οἱ ἐν τῇ οἰκίᾳ *the [men] in the house* (the last three examples can also mean *the [people]* ..., as Greek uses the masculine article to refer to mixed groups). The neuter singular article is used with adjectives to express abstractions: τὸ καλόν *beauty,* τὸ αἰσχρόν *ugliness.* When prefixed to an infinitive (**articular infinitive,** i.e. article + infinitive) it forms an equivalent of verbal nouns in English: τὸ λέγειν *the [act of] speaking, speech;* τὸ φεύγειν *the [act of] fleeing, flight.* Each of these noun-equivalents functions exactly like any normal noun, and the case of the article (and of an accompanying adjective) varies according to a particular context: φέρω τὸν κακόν *I am carrying the cowardly [man];* περὶ τοῦ παιδεύειν ἔλεγεν *he was speaking about the [act of] educating,* i.e. *about education;* ἐδιώκομεν τοὺς ἐν τῇ νήσῳ *we were chasing the [men] in the island.*

Another very common type of noun-phrase consists of the neuter plural of the definite article followed by a genitive. Here the article may be translated in a wide variety of ways. Thus τὰ τῶν Ἀθηναίων (lit. *the [things] of the Athenians*) can mean *the property/situation/ condition/fortunes/interests,* etc., *of the Athenians;* τὰ ἐν τῇ Ῥώμῃ *the things/events/circumstances,* etc. *in Rome.* The context must determine the most appropriate rendering.

The article can also be used as a third person pronoun when combined with the particles μέν* ... δέ; ὁ μὲν ... ὁ δέ *the one ... the other (one man ... another);* οἱ μὲν ... οἱ δέ *some ... others:* ὁ μὲν διώκει τὴν δόξαν, ὁ δὲ τὸ ἀργύριον *one man chases fame, another money;* οἱ μὲν ἀπέθνῃσκον, οἱ δὲ ἔφευγον *some were dying, others running away.* ὁ δέ *but/and he* (and οἱ δέ, etc.) when used by itself refers to someone mentioned in the preceding sentence other than its subject: ὁ Σωκράτης ἐκέλευσε τὴν Ξανθίππην κροῦσαι τὴν μυῖαν· ἡ δὲ οὐκ ἤθελεν *Socrates ordered Xanthippe to swat the fly but she refused* (lit. *was not willing*). This use of the article is a survival from an earlier stage in Greek when it was employed solely as a third person pronoun (cf. 25.1/3*a*)

We have already met three usages of the article in Greek where there is no corresponding article in English (2.1/2 note 1). There is also one important instance where the reverse holds true, viz where the noun or adjective is predicative. Thus, when Thucydides (6.2.11) is telling us that originally the Athenians called the Acropolis simply 'the polis', he writes καλεῖται (3rd s. pres. ind. passive) ἡ Ἀκρόπολις ἔτι πόλις *the Acropolis is still called 'the polis',* but there is no article with πόλις. In

such sentences, therefore, there should be no doubt as to which word
is the subject and which is the complement.

Notes

1 Adjectives without the definite article can also be used as nouns
but they then have an indefinite sense: ἐν τῷ πολέμῳ πολλοὶ κακὰ
ἔφερον *in the war many [people] were suffering hardships* (*lit. bad
things*). When used indefinitely in the singular an adjective is
normally accompanied by the indefinite pronoun τις (10.1/1).

2 In expressions such as Ἀλκιβιάδης ὁ Κλεινίου *Alcibiades, [son]
of Cleinias* the article is followed by the genitive and the word for
son or daughter is omitted (cf.24.1/1a). As Greeks, both male and
female, had only one name, the name of a person's father is often
given in this way to achieve greater precision.

5.2 Greek reading

1 ὁ χρόνος παιδεύει τοὺς σοφούς.
2 πόλλ᾽ ἔχει σιωπὴ καλά.
3# πόλλ᾽ ἔστιν ἀνθρώποισιν, ὦ ξένοι, κακά.
4# οὐ δεῖ φέρειν τὰ πρόσθεν ἐν μνήμῃ κακά.
5 Supply ἐστί in the following: (*i*) καλὸν ἡσυχία. (*ii*) χαλεπὰ τὰ
καλά. (*iii*) μέτρον ἄριστον. (*iv*) μέγα βιβλίον μέγα κακόν. (*v*)
κοινὰ τὰ τῶν φίλων. (*vi*) κοινὸς Ἑρμῆς. (*vii*) μικρὸν κακὸν μέγα
ἀγαθόν. (*viii*) ἄλλα ἄλλοις καλά. (*ix*) ἡ γλῶττα πολλῶν αἰτία
κακῶν. (*x*) χαλεπὸν τὸ ποιεῖν, τὸ δὲ κελεῦσαι ῥᾴδιον. (*xi*)#
κακὸν τὸ μεθύειν πημονῆς λυτήριον. (*xii*) παθήματα μαθήματα.
(*xiii*) κακοῦ κόρακος κακὸν ᾠόν. (*xiv*) πιστὸν γῆ, ἄπιστον
θάλαττα. (*xv*) κἂν μύρμηκι χολή.
6 (*i*) δεῖ γαμεῖν ἐκ τῶν ὁμοίων. (*ii*) μῶρος μῶρα λέγει. (*iii*) ἔξω
πηλοῦ τὸν πόδα ἔχεις. (*iv*) ζεῖ χύτρα, ζῇ φιλία. (*v*) λέοντα ξυρεῖς.
(*vi*) πρὸς σῆμα μητρυιᾶς κλαίεις.
7# φεῦ φεῦ, τὰ μεγάλα μεγάλα καὶ πάσχει κακά.
8# ὄνου χρείαν ἐλέγχει τραχύτης ὁδοῦ.
9# ἄνθρωπός ἐστι πνεῦμα καὶ σκιὰ μόνον.
10# τύχη τέχνην ὤρθωσεν, οὐ τέχνη τύχην.
11# πολλῶν τὰ χρήματ᾽ αἴτι᾽ ἀνθρώποις κακῶν.
12# γύναι, γυναιξὶ κόσμον ἡ σιγὴ φέρει.

13# καλὸν δὲ καὶ γέροντι μανθάνειν σοφά.
14 οἱ ᾿Αθηναῖοι Θουκυδίδην τὸν ᾿Ολόρου ἔπεμψαν πρὸς τὸν
   στρατηγὸν τῶν ἐν Θρᾴκῃ.
15 οὔτε παρὰ νεκροῦ ὁμιλίαν οὔτε παρὰ φιλαργύρου χάριν δεῖ ζητεῖν.
16# ἱκανὸν τὸ νικᾶν ἐcτι τοῖc ἐλευθεροῖc.
17# κἂν τοῖc ἀγροίκοιc ἐcτὶ παιδείαc ἔρωc.
18 ὁ λύκοc τὴν τρίχα, οὐ τὴν γνώμην, ἀλλάττει.
19# τὰ χρήματ᾿ ἀνθρώποιcιν εὑρίcκει φίλουc.
20 φαῦλοc κριτὴc καλοῦ πράγματοc ὄχλοc.
21 **The Egyptians and their crocodiles** (from Herodotus)
   τοῖc μὲν οὖν τῶν Αἰγυπτίων ἱεροί εἰcιν οἱ κροκόδιλοι, τοῖc δ᾿ οὔ,
   ἀλλ᾿ ἅτε πολεμίουc περιέπουcιν. οἱ δὲ περί τε Θήβαc καὶ τὴν
   Μοίρεωc (*of Moeris*) λίμνην cφόδρα νομίζουcιν αὐτοὺc εἶναι
   ἱερούc. ἕνα (*one*) δὲ ἑκάτεροι τρέφουcι κροκόδιλον καὶ
   διδάcκουcιν, ἀρτήματα δὲ λίθινα χυτὰ εἰc τὰ ὦτα ἐμβάλλουcι καὶ 5
   ἀμφιδέαc περὶ τοὺc ἐμπροcθίουc πόδαc καὶ cιτία ἀπότακτα
   παρέχουcι καὶ ἱερεῖα. ἕωc μὲν οὖν ζῶcιν οἱ κροκόδιλοι μάλ᾿ εὖ
   πάcχουcιν, μετὰ δὲ τὸν θάνατον ταριχεύουcιν αὐτοὺc οἱ
   Αἰγύπτιοι καὶ θάπτουcιν ἐν ἱεραῖc θήκαιc. ἀλλ᾿ οἱ περὶ
   ᾿Ελεφαντίνην πόλιν (*city*) καὶ ἐcθίουcιν αὐτούc· οὐ γὰρ 10
   νομίζουcιν ἱεροὺc εἶναι.

Notes

2 πόλλ᾿ = πολλά (also in 3) 2.1/6*b*.
3 ἀνθρώποιcιν dat. pl.; –οιcιν is the longer form of the ending (3.1/1
   note 3).
4 Take τὰ πρόcθεν ... κακά together and ἐν μνήμῃ with φέρειν;
   dislocations of this sort are common in verse.
5 (*i*) καλόν is neuter because the meaning is *a fair [thing]*; we would
   have expected the definite article with ἡcυχία (2.1/1 note 1) – see
   note on 4.2.3. (*iv*) here, and in some of the following proverbs, it
   is necessary to decide which is subject and which is predicate, i.e.
   is a big book a big evil? or *is a big evil a big book?* Obviously the
   former is what is meant. (*vi*) An appeal to share in the luck that
   another is enjoying (e.g. in finding a coin in the street); Hermes, as
   god of luck, shares, or should share, his blessings equally. (*viii*)
   ἄλλα ἄλλοιc ... lit. *other [things] ... to other [people]*, i.e. *different
   [things] ... to different people.* (*xiv*) πιcτόν, ἄπιcτον cf. καλόν in (*i*).
   (*xv*) κἂν = καὶ ἐν (crasis 11.1/5); καί here means *even* (4.1/3).

6 (*iv*) ζεῖ < ζέω *boil*, ζῇ < ζάω *live* (the latter is irregular – 5.1/2 note 4).

7 Prose order would be τὰ μεγάλα καὶ πάσχει μεγάλα κακά; καὶ is here adverbial *also* (4.1/3); take the second μεγάλα with κακά.

10 Translate ὤρθωσεν by a present; the aorist is often used to express general truths, particularly in proverbs (so-called **gnomic aorist**; cf. *faint heart never won fair lady*).

11 Supply ἐcτί (and also in 13 and 20); χρήματ᾽ αἰτί᾽ both have an elided α; the plural of χρῆμα *thing* here means *money* (a very common use).

13 δέ cf. note on 4.2.9 (there are many examples of such connectives at the beginning of verse and prose extracts in subsequent reading exercises); καί *even* 4.1/3.

14 τὸν Ὀλόρου 5.1/3 note 2.

17 κἄν see above on 5 (*xv*).

19 χρήματ(α) see on 11; ἀνθρώποιcιν see note on 3.

20 Only the sense can indicate which noun is subject and which predicate (cf. note on 5(*iv*)).

21 *ll.*1f. τοῖc μὲν ... τοῖc δέ *for some ... for others* (5.1/3); οὖν connects this passage with what goes before in the original context (cf. 13 above); ἅτε πολεμίουc *as enemies*; Θῆβαι *Thebes* not to be confused with the city of the same name in Greece. *l.*4 Take ἕνα (m. acc. of εἷc (7.1/5)) with κροκόδιλον; ἑκάτεροι *each of the two* (i.e. those around Thebes and those around the swamp of Moeris). *l.*7 οὖν *therefore, so* shows that what follows is a consequence of what was said in the previous sentence, while μέν functions with the δέ of the next line to contrast ἕωc ζῶcιν ... with μετὰ τὸν θάνατον ...

5.2/1 Vocabulary

ἄγροικος, –ον *from the country, rustic, boorish*

αἰτίᾱ, –ᾱc, ἡ *cause*

ἀλλάττω *change* (tr.)

ἀμφιδέᾱ, –ᾱc, ἡ *bracelet, anklet*

ἄπιcτος, –ον *untrustworthy*

ἀπότακτος, –ον *set apart for special use*

ἄρισtος, –η, –ον *best*

ἄρτημα, –ατος, τό *ear-ring*

ἅτε (particle) *as if, as*

βιβλίον, –ου, τό *book*

γαμέω *marry*

γέρων, –οντος, ὁ *old man*

γλῶττα, –ης, ἡ   *tongue*

γνώμη, –ης, ἡ   *mind*

γυνή, –αικός, ἡ   *woman*

διδάσκω   *teach, train*

ἑκάτερος, –ᾱ –ον   *each* (of two)

ἐλέγχω   *test*

Ἐλεφαντίνη, –ης, ἡ   *Elephantine*
  (city in Egypt)

ἐμβάλλω   *put in*

ἐμπρόσθιος, –ον   *(in) front*

ἔξω (+gen.)   *outside*

εὖ (adv.)   *well*

εὑρίσκω   *find; get*

ἕως (conj.)   *while*

ζάω   *be alive, live, pass one's life*

ζέω   *boil*

ζητέω   *look for, seek* (+acc.)

ἡσυχίᾱ, –ᾱς, ἡ   *peace, quiet*

Θῆβαι, –ῶν, αἱ   *Thebes* (city in
  Egypt)

θήκη, –ης, ἡ   *tomb*

Θρᾴκη, –ης, ἡ   *Thrace*

θρίξ, τριχός, ἡ   *hair*

ἱερεῖα, –ων, τά   *offerings*

ἱερός, –ά, –όν   *sacred, holy*

ἱκανός, –ή, –όν   *sufficient*

κλαίω   *weep*

κοινός, –ή, –όν   *common, shared*

κόραξ, –ακος, ὁ   *crow*

κόσμος, –ου, ὁ   *decoration*

κροκόδῑλος, –ου, ὁ   *crocodile*

λίθινος, –η, –ον (χυτός)   *made
  of glass*

λύκος, –ου, ὁ   *wolf*

λυτήριον, –ου, τό   *remedy*

μάθημα, –ατος, τό   *lesson*

μάλα (adv.)   *very*

μανθάνω   *learn*

μεθύω   *be drunk*

μέτρον, –ου, τό   *measure, due
  measure, moderation*

μητρυιά, –ᾶς, ἡ   *step-mother*

μικρός, –ά, –όν   *small*

μνήμη, –ης, ἡ   *memory*

μόνον (adv.)   *only, merely*

μύρμηξ, –ηκος, ὁ   *ant*

μῶρος, –ᾱ, –ον   *stupid, foolish*

νικάω   *win*

ξυρέω   *shave*

ὁδός, –οῦ, ἡ   *road*

ὅμοιος, –ᾱ, –ον   *like*

ὀρθόω   *guide*

οὖς, ὠτός, τό   *ear*

ὄχλος, –ου, ὁ   *crowd, mob*

πάθημα –ατος, τό   *suffering,
  misfortune*

παιδείᾱ, –ᾱς, ἡ   *education,
  culture*

παιδεύω   *teach, educate*

παρά (prep.) (+gen.)   *from*

πάσχω   *suffer*
  εὖ πάσχω *be well treated*

περί (prep.) (+acc.)   *around*

περιέπω   *treat*

πηλός, –οῦ, ὁ   *mud*

πημονή, –ῆς, ἡ   *woe, misery*

πιστός, –ή, –όν   *trustworthy*

πνεῦμα, –ατος, τό   *breath*

ποιέω   *make, do*

πολέμιος, –ᾱ, –ον   *hostile, enemy*

πούς, ποδός, ὁ   *foot*

πρᾶγμα, –ατος, τό   *thing, matter*

πρός (prep.) (+acc.)   *to, towards;
  on, at*

πρόσθεν (adv.)   *previously*

ῥᾴδιος, –ᾱ, –ον   *easy*

cῆμα, -ατος, τό   tomb
cιγή, -ῆc, ἡ   silence
cῑτία, -ων, τά   provisions, food
cιωπή, -ῆc, ἡ   silence
cκιᾱ, -ᾱc, ἡ   shadow
cοφόc, -ή, -όν   wise, clever
cτρατηγόc, -οῦ, ὁ   general,
   commander
ταριχεύω   embalm, mummify
τραχύτηc, -ητοc, ἡ   roughness
τρέφω   rear
φαῦλοc, -ον (also -η, -ον)   poor,
   inadequate
φεῦ (interjection)   alas!

φιλάργυροc, -ον   avaricious,
   miserly
χαλεπόc, -ή, -όν   difficult, hard
χάρις, -ιτοc (acc. χάριν), ἡ
   favour
χολή, -ῆc, ἡ   bile; anger
χρείᾱ, -ᾱc, ἡ   use, serviceability
χρῆμα, -ατοc, τό   thing; (pl.)
   money
χρόνοc, -ου, ὁ   time
χυτόc, -ή, -όν   melted (with
   λίθινος, made of glass)
χύτρᾱ, -ᾱc, ἡ   pot
ᾠόν, -οῦ, τό   egg

6 | UNIT SIX

6.1 Grammar

6.1/1 Third declension – consonant stem nouns (2)

(a) *Stems in ν (masculine and, rarely, feminine)*

These stems nearly all have a nominative singular in –ην or –ων with a genitive –ενοc/–ηνοc or –ονοc/–ωνοc. There is no rule to determine whether a particular word has a long or short vowel in its stem. Those with a short vowel do not lengthen it in the dative plural because here we have ν + c > c, not ντ + c > c (cf. 5.1/1*b*).

	λιμήν (m)	μήν (m)	δαίμων (m or f)	ἀγών (m)
	harbour	*month*	*divine being*	*contest*
stem	λιμεν–	μην–	δαιμον–	ἀγων–
SINGULAR				
Nom.	λιμήν	μήν	δαίμων	ἀγών
Voc.	λιμήν	μήν	δαῖμον	ἀγών
Acc.	λιμέν–α	μῆν–α	δαίμον–α	ἀγῶν–α
Gen.	λιμέν–οc	μην–όc	δαίμον–οc	ἀγῶν–οc
Dat.	λιμέν–ι	μην–ί	δαίμον–ι	ἀγῶν–ι
PLURAL				
N.V.	λιμέν–εc	μῆν–εc	δαίμον–εc	ἀγῶν–εc
Acc.	λιμέν–αc	μῆν–αc	δαίμον–αc	ἀγῶν–αc
Gen.	λιμέν–ων	μην–ῶν	δαιμόν–ων	ἀγών–ων
Dat.	λιμέ–cι(ν)	μη–cί(ν)	δαίμο–cι(ν)	ἀγῶ–cι(ν)

Notes

1 There are a few such nouns in –ῑc, –ῑνοc, e.g. ῥίc, ῥῑνόc (f) *nose*; δελφῑ́c, –ῖνοc (m) *dolphin*.

2   The vocative singular of ν–stems is the same as the nominative
    when the nominative is accented on the final syllable (so λιμήν,
    but δαῖμον).
3   κύων, κυνός (m or f) *dog* has an irregular stem κυν–.

(*b*) *Stems in* ρ (*mainly masculine*)

The majority have a nom. s. –ηρ, gen. –ηρος or nom. s. –ωρ, gen.
–ορος. Four nouns with a nom. s. in –ηρ form a special sub-group
and are declined alike: πατήρ *father*, μήτηρ *mother*, θυγάτηρ
daughter, γαστήρ (f) *stomach*. Also given below is the slightly
irregular ἀνήρ *man, male*. Of these nouns only those in –ηρ, –ηρος
do not have a distinct vocative singular (cῶτερ from cωτήρ, –ῆρος
(m) *saviour* is an exception).

	θήρ (m) *wild beast*	ῥήτωρ (m) *speaker*	πατήρ (m) *father*	ἀνήρ (m) *man*
stem	θηρ–	ῥητορ–	πατ(ε)ρ–	ἀνδρ–
SINGULAR				
Nom.	θήρ	ῥήτωρ	πατήρ	ἀνήρ
Voc.	θήρ	ῥῆτορ	πάτερ	ἄνερ
Acc.	θῆρ–α	ῥήτορ–α	πατέρ–α	ἄνδρ–α
Gen.	θηρ–ός	ῥήτορ–ος	πατρ–ός	ἀνδρ–ός
Dat.	θηρ–ί	ῥήτορ–ι	πατρ–ί	ἀνδρ–ί
PLURAL				
N.V.	θῆρες	ῥήτορ–ες	πατέρ–ες	ἄνδρ–ες
Acc.	θῆρ–ας	ῥήτορ–ας	πατέρ–ας	ἄνδρ–ας
Gen.	θηρ–ῶν	ῥητόρ–ων	πατέρ–ων	ἀνδρ–ῶν
Dat.	θηρ–cί(ν)	ῥήτορ–cι(ν)	πατρά–cι(ν)	ἀνδράcι(ν)

A few nouns with stems in ρ do not have a nom. s. in –ηρ/–ωρ. Of
these, χείρ, χειρός (f) *hand* (stem χειρ–) can also have a stem χερ–,
which is the more usual in the dat. pl., viz χερcί(ν); ἔαρ (n) (the season
of) *spring* has gen. ἦρος, dat. ἦρι; πῦρ (n) *fire* has gen. πυρός, dat. πυρί
(see also 13.1/1*c*).

(*c*) *Stems in* εc (*neuters in* –οc, *masculine proper names in* –ηc)

Neuters in –οc, as γένοc, γένουc *race, clan* (stem γενεc–), form a large
class. They appear to be irregular because they were affected by a
sound change at an earlier stage of Greek whereby intervocal sigma

was lost and in Attic the two previously separated vowels were contracted (in Homeric Greek and other dialects the uncontracted forms survived).

	SINGULAR		PLURAL	
N.V.	γένοc		γένη	(<γένε(c)–α)
Acc.	γένοc		γένη	
Gen.	γένουc	(<γένε(c)–οc)	γενῶν	(<γενέ(c)–ων)
Dat.	γένει	(<γένε(c)–ι)	γένεcι (ν)	(<γένε(c)–cι)

Many masculine proper names are compounds with a stem in εc because their second element is a neuter noun of this type, e.g. Διογένης (γένοc), Cωκράτης (κράτοc), 'Αριστοτέλης (τέλοc). These must be distinguished from first declension masculine proper names in –ης (see 3.1/2 notes 3 and 4). A complication arises with proper names containing the neuter κλέοc *fame* as their second element (e.g. Περικλῆc, 'Ηρακλῆc, Θεμιcτοκλῆc) since a further contraction is required in the nom. voc. and dat. because of the additional ε in the stem (κλεεc–). Compare the declensions of Cωκράτης and Περικλῆc:

Nom.	Cωκράτης		Περικλῆc	(<κλέης)
Voc.	Cώκρατες		Περίκλεις	(<κλεες)
Acc.	Cωκράτη	(<–ε(c)α)	Περικλέᾱ	(<κλέε(c)α)
Gen.	Cωκράτους	(<–ε(c)οc)	Περικλέους	(<–κλέε(c)οc)
Dat.	Cωκράτει	(<–ε(c)ι)	Περικλεῖ	(<–κλέε(c)ι)

The acc. Περικλέᾱ has a final ᾱ (not η as in γένη) because of the preceding ε (cf. ἀργυρᾶ < –εᾱ, 6.1/2). One noun in –ης which belongs here but is not a masculine proper noun is τριήρης (f) *trireme.* (singular as for Cωκράτης, plural n.v.a. τριήρεις, gen. τριήρων, dat. τριήρεcι(ν)).

6.1/2 Second declension contracted nouns and first and second declension contracted adjectives

The few second declension masculine nouns in –οοc and neuters in –εον are contracted in Attic according to the rules given for contracted verbs (5.1/2; on ε + α, which does not occur in verbs, see below). The uncontracted forms, which are regular, occur in other dialects. Examples are:

	νόος *mind*		ὀστέον *bone*	
	Contracted (Attic)	Uncontracted (non-Attic)	Contracted Attic)	Uncontracted (non-Attic)
SINGULAR				
Nom.	νοῦς	νό-ος	ὀστοῦν	ὀστέ-ον
Voc.	νοῦ	νό-ε	ὀστοῦν	ὀστέ-ον
Acc.	νοῦν	νό-ον	ὀστοῦν	ὀστέ-ον
Gen.	νοῦ	νό-ου	ὀστοῦ	ὀστέ-ου
Dat.	νῷ	νό-ῳ	ὀστῷ	ὀστέ-ῳ
PLURAL				
Nom.	νοῖ	νό-οι	ὀστᾶ	ὀστέ-α
Voc.	νοῖ	νό-οι	ὀστᾶ	ὀστέ-α
Acc.	νοῦς	νό-ους	ὀστᾶ	ὀστέ-α
Gen.	νῶν	νό-ων	ὀστῶν	ὀστέ-ων
Dat.	νοῖς	νό-οις	ὀστοῖς	ὀστέ-οις

In the nom. voc. acc. pl. of neuters ε + ᾰ produces ᾱ on the analogy of the α–ending of normal second declension neuters (cf. χρῡσᾶ below).

Like νοῦς are declined ῥοῦς *stream,* πλοῦς *voyage,* and compounds of the latter such as περίπλους *circumnavigation.*

Most first and second declension contracted adjectives are formed with –εος, –εα, –εον, e.g. χρῡσοῦς (< χρύσεος) *golden,* which is declined:

SINGULAR	M.		F.		N.	
N.V.	χρῡσοῦς	(–εος)	χρῡσῆ	(–έᾱ)	χρῡσοῦν	(–εον)
Acc.	χρῡσοῦν	(–εον)	χρῡσῆν	(–έᾱν)	χρῡσοῦν	(–εον)
Gen.	χρῡσοῦ	(–έου)	χρῡσῆς	(–έᾱς)	χρῡσοῦ	(–έου)
Dat.	χρῡσῷ	(–έῳ)	χρῡσῇ	(–έᾳ)	χρῡσῷ	(–έῳ)
PLURAL						
N.V.	χρῡσοῖ	(–εοι)	χρῡσαῖ	(–εαι)	χρῡσᾶ	(–εα)
Acc.	χρῡσοῦς	(–έους)	χρῡσᾶς	(–έᾱς)	χρῡσᾶ	(–εα)
Gen.	χρῡσῶν	(–έων)	χρῡσῶν	(–έων)	χρῡσῶν	(–έων)
Dat.	χρῡσοῖς	(–έοις)	χρῡσαῖς	(–έαις)	χρῡσοῖς	(–έοις)

In the feminine singular ε + ᾱ > η, except where ε is preceded by ε, ι, or ρ, e.g. ἀργυροῦς (–εος), –ᾶ (–έᾱ), –οῦν, (–εον) *[made of] silver,* whose feminine singular is: nom. ἀργυρᾶ, acc. ἀργυρᾶν, gen. ἀργυρᾶς, dat. ἀργυρᾷ (here ε + ᾱ > ᾱ).

ἁπλοῦς, -ῆ, -οῦν *simple* is contracted from ἁπλόος but follows χρῡσοῦς completely, even in the feminine.

6.1/3 Compound verbs formed with prepositional prefixes

Many verbs form compounds by prefixing one, or sometimes more than one, preposition (e.g. ἐπιβαίνω, 3.2.12(*v*)). This involves important sound changes when certain vowels and consonants are juxtaposed:

(*a*) With the exception of περί and πρό, prepositions ending in a vowel drop this vowel (by elision) when compounded with a verb which begins with a vowel or diphthong: ἀπάγω (ἀπό+ἄγω) *lead away*, παρέχω (παρά+ἔχω) *provide*, but προάγω *lead forward*, περιάγω *lead round*.

(*b*) When, owing to the elision of the final vowel of the preposition, π, τ, or κ are brought into contact with an initial aspirated vowel or diphthong, these consonants must themselves adopt their aspirated forms, φ, θ and χ: ἀφαιρέω (ἀπό+αἱρέω) *take away*; καθαιρέω (κατά+αἱρέω) *destroy*.

(*c*) When compounded with a verb beginning with a vowel or diphthong, ἐκ becomes ἐξ: ἐξάγω (ἐκ+ἄγω) *lead out*; ἐξαιρέω (ἐκ+αἱρέω) *take out*.

(*d*) When compounded with a verb beginning with a consonant, the ν of ἐν and cύν is assimilated as follows:

ν before π, β, φ, ψ and μ becomes μ: cυμβουλεύω (cυν+βουλεύω) *advise*

ν before γ, κ, χ, and ξ becomes nasal γ: ἐγγράφω (ἐν+γράφω) *write in/on*

ν before λ becomes λ: cυλλαμβάνω (cυν+λαμβάνω) *gather together*

ν of cύν is dropped before c: cυcτρατεύω (cυν+cτρατεύω) *join in an expedition*.

(*e*) When a verb compounded with a preposition is used in a tense which requires the augment, the augment comes between the preposition and the verb, **not** in front of the preposition: προc–ἔ–βαλλον (<προcβάλλω) *I was attacking*. If the insertion of the augment results in the clash of two vowels, e.g. κατα + ἐ–γίγνωcκον the same process as in (*a*) above will apply: so κατεγίγνωσκον (<καταγιγνώσκω) *I was condemning*. In these circumstances πρό normally contracts with the augment προὔβαλλον[1] (<προβάλλω; the expected form would be προέβαλλον) *I was putting forward*; προὔπεμπον (<προπέμπω) *I was escorting* (the contracted diphthong is generally indicated by a sign identical with a smooth breathing (11.1/5*b*)).

(*f*) The assimilation of ἐν and cύν described in (*d*) is blocked by the syllabic augment in the augmented tenses; thus cυμβουλεύω but cυνεβούλευον.

Notes

1 The meaning of a compound verb is not always predictable from its constituent parts (cf. above παρέχω). Prepositions may retain their normal meanings (as ἀπάγω, ἐγγράφω) but some have acquired a special sense, e.g. μεταγιγνώσκω *change one's mind* (from γιγνώσκω *know*) where μετα– conveys the idea of change.

2 In the augmented tenses of compound verbs the accent never goes further back than the augment, even when the last syllable is short: παρεῖχον *they were providing*; παρῆcαν *they were present* ; cf. **Appendix 8**, *b*(vi).

3 Greek has a few compound verbs which contain no prepositional element: οἰκοδομέω *build a house* (οἶκος *house*); ναυμαχέω *fight with ships* (ναῦc *ship*). These compounds are augmented at the beginning, **not** between the two elements (ᾠκοδόμηcα, ἐναυμάχηcα).

6.1/4 –ω verbs with stems in palatals, labials, dentals

The sound changes shown by nouns with these stems (5.1/*l*) also occur in the corresponding verbs when c is added to form the future or weak aorist. Some resemble λύω in having a simple present stem to which this c can be attached. Others, far more numerous, have a suffix in their present stem which is not kept elsewhere.

(*a*) *Verbs of the above type with no suffix in the present stem*

πλέκω	*plait*	fut.	πλέξω	aor.	ἔπλεξα
πέμπω	*send*	fut.	πέμψω	aor.	ἔπεμψα
πείθω	*persuade*	fut.	πείcω	aor.	ἔπειcα

---

[1]On this type of contraction, which is called crasis, see 11.1/5.

(b) Verbs with a suffix in the present stem

At a very early stage in its development Greek possessed a consonant which was pronounced as the *y* in the English *yes*. This sound no longer existed in the form Greek had taken by the time of the introduction of the alphabet. It had occurred in words inherited from Indo-European (1.3) and had also served as a suffix to form the present stem of many –ω verbs whose primitive or original stem ended in a consonant. In this function it combined with the preceding consonant. The combinations which concern us here are κ/γ/χ + *y* > ττ; π/β/φ +*y* > πτ; τ/δ/θ + *y* > ζ. As this suffix (and others – see below) was only used to form the present stem, the future and weak aorist are formed by applying c to the original stem. Examples are (the original stem is given in brackets):

PALATALS

φυλάττω	guard	(φυλακ–)	fut.	φυλάξω	aor.	ἐφύλαξα
ἀλλάττω	change	(ἀλλαγ–)	fut.	ἀλλάξω	aor.	ἤλλαξα

LABIALS

κόπτω	cut	(κοπ–)	fut.	κόψω	aor.	ἔκοψα
βλάπτω	harm	(βλαβ–)	fut.	βλάψω	aor.	ἔβλαψα
κρύπτω	hide	(κρυφ–)	fut.	κρύψω	aor.	ἔκρυψα

DENTALS

φράζω	tell	(φραδ–)	fut.	φράσω	aor.	ἔφρασα

The original stem can be seen in cognate words (e.g. φυλακή *act of guarding*, βλάβη *damage*). It need not be memorised as these verbs follow the above patterns. An exception is a few verbs in –ζω which are palatals, not dentals, as e.g. cφάζω *slaughter* (cφαγ–) fut. cφάξω, aor. ἔcφαξα (cf. cφαγή *[act of] slaughtering*).

All dental-stem verbs in –ίζω of more than two syllables have a future in –ιέω (originally –ιέcω; cf. 5.1/2 note 3), which always contracts to –ιῶ: νομίζω *think,* fut. νομιῶ, νομιεῖc, νομιεῖ, etc., but κτίζω *found, build,* fut. κτίcω. A few verbs in –ίζω are palatals: μαcτίζω *whip* (stem μαcτιγ–), fut. μαcτίξω, aor. ἐμάcτιξα.

Of the other present stem suffixes belonging here we may mention cκ (as in διδάcκω (<διδαχ + cκ–ω) *teach,* fut. διδάξω, etc.) and αν. The latter is often accompanied by a nasal infix (i.e. a nasal inserted before the final consonant of the root); neither αν nor the infix occur outside the present stem, e.g. λαμβάνω *take,* aor. stem λαβ– (in λα–μ–β–άν–ω the nasal infix takes the form of the labial nasal μ before the following labial; cf. μα–ν–θ–άν–ω *learn*, aor. stem μαθ; λα–γ–χ–άν–ω *obtain*, aor. stem λαχ–; see 7.1/1).

6.2 Greek reading

1   *As well as translating the following give the 1st s. present indicative of each verb:*
     (*i*) οἱ φύλακες τοὺς Πέρσας ἐφύλαξαν. (*ii*) ἆρα ἔκρυψας τὸν χρυσοῦν ἵππον; (*iii*) οἱ Ἀθηναῖοι καὶ οἱ Λακεδαιμόνιοι συνεστράτευσαν. (*iv*) πολλὰ ἐν τῇ πέτρᾳ ἐνέγραψεν. (*v*) οἱ δαίμονες πολλὰ καὶ μεγάλα πράξουσιν. (*vi*) ὁ Σωκράτης ἡμᾶς ἐδίδαξεν. (*vii*) τὴν οἰκίαν τοῦ Περικλέους ἔβλαψαν. (*viii*) ἐν τῷ λιμένι ἐναυμαχήσαμεν.
2# κάτοπτρον εἴδους χαλκός ἐστ’, οἶνος δὲ νοῦ.
3# χεὶρ χεῖρα νίπτει, δάκτυλοι δὲ δακτύλους.
4   ἡ μὲν φωνή ἐστιν ἀργυρᾶ, ἡ δὲ σιγὴ χρυσῆ.
5# ὦ δαῖμον, ὡς οὐκ ἔστ’ ἀποστροφὴ βροτοῖς
     τῶν ἐμφύτων τε καὶ θεηλάτων κακῶν.
6   **Further futility**
     (*i*) εἰς ὕδωρ γράφεις. (*ii*) εἰς ψάμμον οἰκοδομεῖς. (*iii*) γλαῦκ’ Ἀθήναζε (*sc.* φέρεις). (*iv*) κύματα μετρεῖς. (*v*) ὄρνιθος γάλα ζητεῖς. (*vi*) σίδηρον πλεῖν διδάσκεις. (*vii*) ἡλίῳ φῶς δανείζεις. (*viii*) βατράχοις οἰνοχοεῖς. (*ix*) τὸν ἀέρα τύπτεις. (*x*) ἐλέφαντα ἐκ μυίας ποιεῖ.
7   **Other short proverbs and aphorisms**
     (*i*) ψυχῆς μέγας χαλινός ἐστιν ὁ νοῦς (*ii*) Ἕλληνες ἀεὶ παῖδες, γέρων δὲ Ἕλλην οὐκ ἔστιν. (*iii*)# εἰσὶ μητρὶ παῖδες ἄγκυραι βίου. (*iv*) οἴκοι λέοντες, ἐν μάχῃ δ’ ἀλώπεκες. (*v*) νοῦς ὁρᾷ καὶ νοῦς ἀκούει. (*vi*) μακραὶ τυράννων χεῖρες. (*vii*) ψεύδεσιν Ἄρης φίλος. (*viii*) Ἑλλὰς Ἑλλάδος αἱ Ἀθῆναι. (*ix*) τέττιγι μέλιτταν συγκρίνεις. (*x*) χαλεπὸν θυγάτηρ κτῆμα.
8   τὸ μὲν πῦρ ὁ ἄνεμος, τὸν δὲ ἔρωτα ἡ συνήθεια ἐκκαίει.
9   κατὰ τὸν Σωκράτη οὐδεὶς ἑκουσίως ἁμαρτάνει.
10 οὐ μετανοεῖν ἀλλὰ προνοεῖν χρὴ τὸν ἄνδρα τὸν σοφόν.
11 **The siege of Melos**
     Thucydides, the other great historian of the fifth century BC, wrote a history of the Peloponnesian War, which was fought

between Athens and Sparta (the major power in the Peloponnese) from 431 BC to 404 BC, when Athens fell. Melos was an island in the southern Aegean whose desire to stay neutral was brutally suppressed by the Athenians.

καὶ οἱ μὲν Ἀθηναίων πρέσβεις (*ambassadors*) ἀνεχώρησαν εἰς τὸ στράτευμα, οἱ δὲ στρατηγοὶ περιετείχισαν τοὺς Μηλίους. καὶ ὕστερον φυλακὴ μὲν ὀλίγη τῶν συμμάχων ἐκεῖ παρέμενε καὶ ἐπολιόρκει τὸ χωρίον, οἱ δὲ ἄλλοι στρατιῶται καὶ κατὰ γῆν καὶ κατὰ θάλατταν ἀνεχώρησαν. ἔπειτα δὲ οἱ Μήλιοι τὸ 5 περιτείχισμα ἀνέσπασαν τῶν Ἀθηναίων, ἐπειδὴ παρῆσαν οὐ πολλοὶ τῶν φυλάκων. ἀλλὰ στρατιὰν ὕστερον ἐκ τῶν Ἀθηνῶν ἄλλην ἐξέπεμψαν οἱ Ἀθηναῖοι, καὶ κατὰ κράτος ἤδη ἐπολιόρκουν. προδοσία δὲ ἦν ἐν τοῖς Μηλίοις καὶ συνεχώρησαν τοῖς Ἀθηναίοις. οἱ δὲ ἔσφαξαν Μηλίων τοὺς ἄνδρας, παῖδας δὲ 10 καὶ γυναῖκας ἠνδραπόδισαν. καὶ ὕστερον ἀποίκους πολλοὺς ἐξέπεμψαν καὶ τὸ χωρίον ᾤκισαν.

Notes

1 (*v*) πολλὰ καὶ μεγάλα lit. *many and great [things]* but translate *many great [things]* ; when πολύς in the plural is combined with another adjective καί is regularly inserted between the two.
2 Greek mirrors were made of polished bronze or silver.
5 Take ἀποστροφή with the genitives in the next line. *l.*2 Take κακῶν as a noun and ἐμφύτων and θεηλάτων as adjectives; καί can be translated here by *and* or *or* because the evils are not necessarily both *innate* and *sent by the gods*.
6 (*iii*) The Acropolis at Athens was notorious as a haunt of small brown owls, the bird which was adopted as the Athenian emblem.
7 (*ii*) This remark of an Egyptian priest to the Athenian statesman Solon implicitly contrasts the age of Greek civilisation with that of the Egyptians. (*iv*) A phrase of abuse, not a sentence; foxes were symbolic of a low cunning devoid of courage. (*viii*) The Athenians liked to regard themselves as the quintessence of Greekness. (*x*) The patriarchal nature of most Greek societies meant that sons were more highly valued than daughters.
11 *ll.*3f. Translate the imperfects παρέμενε and ἐπολιόρκει by *stayed* and *besieged* (Greek prefers to regard both events as extending over a period of time than as single actions - 4.1/1). *l.*8 ἐξέπεμψαν

< ἐκπέμπω (6.1/3); κατὰ κράτος lit. *in accordance with [their full]
strength*, i.e. *energetically*. *ll.*10f. παῖδας καὶ γυναῖκας the regular
order in Greek for *women and children*; ἠνδραπόδισαν <
ἀνδραποδίζω (4.1/1 note 2(ii)).

6.2/1 Vocabulary

ἄγκῡρα, –ᾱς, ἡ *anchor*
ἀεί (adv.) *always*
ἀήρ, –έρος, ὁ *air*
'Ἀθήναζε (adv.) *to Athens*
'Ἀθῆναι, –ῶν, αἱ *Athens*
ἀκούω *hear*
ἀλώπηξ, –εκος, ἡ *fox*
ἁμαρτάνω *err, do wrong*
ἀνασπάω *pull down*
ἀναχωρέω *withdraw, retreat,
  retire*
ἀνδραποδίζω *enslave*
ἄνεμος, –ου, ὁ *wind*
ἀνήρ, ἀνδρός, ὁ *man*
ἄποικος, –ου, ὁ *settler, colonist*
ἀποστροφή, –ῆς, ἡ *turning away
  from, escape*
ἀργυροῦς, –ᾶ, –οῦν *made of
  silver, silver*
'Ἄρης, –ου, ὁ *Ares* (god of war)
βλάπτω *damage*
βροτός, –οῦ, ὁ *mortal man*
γάλα, –ακτος, τό *milk*
γλαῦξ, –αυκός, ἡ *owl*
γράφω *write*
δαίμων, –ονος, ὁ *god*
δάκτυλος, –ου, ὁ *finger*
δανείζω *lend*
ἐγγράφω *write in/on, inscribe*
εἶδος, –ους, τό *appearance*
ἐκεῖ (adv.) *there*

ἐκκαίω *kindle*
ἑκουσίως (adv.) *willingly*
ἐκπέμπω *send out*
ἐλέφᾱς, –αντος, ὁ *elephant*
Ἑλλάς, –άδος, ἡ *Greece*
Ἕλλην, –ηνος, ὁ *a Greek*
ἔμφυτος, –ον *inborn, innate*
ἐπειδή (conj.) *when*
ἤδη (adv.) *now*
ἥλιος, –ου, ὁ *sun*
θεήλατος, –ον *sent by the gods*
θυγάτηρ, –τρός, ἡ *daughter*
κάτοπτρον, –ου, τό *mirror*
κράτος –ους, τό *strength, power*
κτῆμα, –ατος, τό *(a) possession*
κῦμα, –ατος, τό *wave*
Λακεδαιμόνιος, –ου, ὁ
  Lacedaemonian, Spartan
μακρός, –ά, –όν *long*
μάχη, –ης, ἡ *battle, fight*
μέλιττα, –ης, ἡ *bee*
μετανοέω *think afterwards,
  change one's mind, repent*
μετρέω *measure*
Μήλιοι, –ων, οἱ *Melians*
μήτηρ, –τρός, ἡ *mother*
ναυμαχέω *fight a sea battle*
νίπτω *wash*
οἰκίζω *colonise*
οἰκοδομέω *build a house*
οἴκοι (adv.) *at home*

οἶνος, –ου, ὁ   wine
οἰνοχοέω   pour wine
ὀλίγος, –η, –ον   small
ὁράω   see
ὄρνῑς, –ῑθος, ὁ/ἡ   bird
οὐδείς   no one (7.1/5a)
παῖς, παιδός, ὁ/ἡ   child
παραμένω   remain
πάρειμι (παρά+εἰμί)   be present
περιτειχίζω   build a wall round
περιτείχισμα, –ατος, τό
   blockading wall
πέτρᾱ, –ᾱς, ἡ   rock
πλέω   sail
πολιορκέω   besiege
προδοσίᾱ, –ᾱς, ἡ   treachery
προνοέω   think beforehand
πῦρ, πυρός, τό   fire
σίδηρος, –ου, ὁ   iron
στράτευμα, –ατος, τό   army
στρατιᾱ, –ᾱς, ἡ   army
συγκρῑνω   compare (something
   with something, acc. and dat.)
συγχωρέω   yield to (+dat.)
σύμμαχος, –ου, ὁ   ally
συνήθεια, –ᾱς, ἡ   acquaintance,
   intimacy

συστρατεύω   join an expedition,
   fight alongside
σφάζω   slaughter
τέττιξ, –ῑγος, ὁ   cicada,
   grasshopper
τύπτω   hit, beat
τύραννος, –ου, ὁ   absolute ruler;
   tyrant
ὕδωρ, –ατος, τό   water
φυλακή, –ῆς, ἡ   guard, garrison
φύλαξ, –ακος, ὁ   guard
φυλάττω   guard
φωνή, –ῆς, ἡ   voice, speech
φῶς, φωτός, τό   light
χαλινός, –οῦ, ὁ   bit (for a
   horse's bridle)
χαλκός, –οῦ, ὁ   bronze
χείρ, χειρός, ἡ   hand
χρή   it is necessary
χωρίον, –ου, τό   place
ψάμμος, –ου, ἡ   sand
ψεῦδος, –ους, τό   falsehood, lie
ψῡχή, –ῆς, ἡ   soul
ὡς (exclamatory adv.)   how ...!

7 | UNIT SEVEN

7.1 Grammar

7.1/1 Strong aorist indicative and infinitive active of –ω verbs

We have seen at 4.1/1 that –ω verbs have either a weak or a strong aorist and that the distinction between the two is solely one of form. The indicative of the strong aorist has the same endings as the imperfect; the infinitive has the same ending as the present (as do all other parts). As the strong aorist takes no suffix its stem must necessarily undergo some internal modification to differentiate it from that of the present. Any suffix attached to the latter is dropped (cf. 6.1/4b), and ει is reduced to ι, and ευ to υ. Some strong aorist stems are simply irregular and must be learnt.

The following list of the most common verbs with a strong aorist shows examples of each type. The present infinitive and the imperfect indicative are included for comparison.

PRESENT INDICATIVE	IMPERFECT INDICATIVE	AORIST INDICATIVE	PRESENT INFINITIVE	AORIST INFINITIVE
ἄγω *lead, bring*	ἦγον	ἤγαγον	ἄγειν	ἀγαγεῖν
αἱρέω *take, capture*	ᾕρουν	εἷλον (stem ἑλ–)	αἱρεῖν	ἑλεῖν
βάλλω *throw*	ἔβαλλον	ἔβαλον	βάλλειν	βαλεῖν
εὑρίσκω *find*	εὕρισκον (or ηὕ–)	εὗρον (or ηὗ–)	εὑρίσκειν	εὑρεῖν
ἔχω *have*	εἶχον	ἔσχον	ἔχειν	σχεῖν
λαγχάνω *obtain*	ἐλάγχανον	ἔλαχον	λαγχάνειν	λαχεῖν
λαμβάνω *take*	ἐλάμβανον	ἔλαβον	λαμβάνειν	λαβεῖν

λέγω *say*	ἔλεγον	εἶπον	λέγειν	εἰπεῖν
		(stem εἰπ-)		
λείπω *leave*	ἔλειπον	ἔλιπον	λείπειν	λιπεῖν
μανθάνω *learn*	ἐμάνθανον	ἔμαθον	μανθάνειν	μαθεῖν
ὁράω *see*	ἑώρων	εἶδον	ὁρᾶν	ἰδεῖν
		(stem ἰδ-)		
πάσχω *suffer*	ἔπασχον	ἔπαθον	πάσχειν	παθεῖν
πίπτω *fall*	ἔπῑπτον	ἔπεσον	πίπτειν	πεσεῖν
τυγχάνω *happen*	ἐτύγχανον	ἔτυχον	τυγχάνειν	τυχεῖν
φέρω *carry*	ἔφερον	ἤνεγκον	φέρειν	ἐνεγκεῖν
φεύγω *flee*	ἔφευγον	ἔφυγον	φεύγειν	φυγεῖν

Notes

1 The ending of the strong aorist infinitive active always has a circumflex accent.

2 The aorists of αἱρέω, λέγω, ὁράω, φέρω come from roots entirely different from their presents (cf. English *go/went*). The unaugmented aorist stems of the first three (ἑλ-, εἰπ-, ἰδ-) require particular attention. εἶπον and ἤνεγκον quite irregularly take the **weak** aorist endings in the 2nd. s. and pl.: εἶπας, εἴπατε; ἤνεγκας, ἠνέγκατε. We may sympathize with the Greeks who found εἶπον too complicated and gave λέγω a regular weak aorist ἔλεξα (good Attic but not as common). The strong aorist ἦλθον *I came/went* likewise has a present tense from another root. This verb is peculiar in having an active aorist but a deponent present (ἔρχομαι 8.1/2).

3 By this stage you should be confident enough to consult the table of **Principal parts of verbs**, which sets out the principal parts of important verbs which have some irregularity. A normal transitive verb in Greek has six principal parts and from these all possible forms can be deduced (see next note for the only exceptions). These parts are:

 (i) lst s. present indicative active (λύω; 2.1/5)
 (ii) lst s. future indicative active (λύσω; 2.1/5)
 (iii) lst s. aorist indicative active (ἔλῡσα; 4.1/1; for strong aorist see above)
 (iv) lst s. perfect indicative active (λέλυκα; 15.1/1)
 (v) lst s. perfect indicative middle and passive (λέλυμαι; 16.1/3)
 (vi) lst s. aorist indicative passive (ἐλύθην; 11.1/1).

This list is not as formidable as it might seem at first sight as some verbs do not exist in every possible part, while many (such as λύω) are completely regular and all their principal parts can be deduced from their present stem. Do not, at this stage, try to digest the **Principal parts of verbs** (in any case, we have not yet dealt with principal parts (iv) - (vi)), but familiarise yourself with its arrangement and get into the habit of using it. When individual principal parts are wildly irregular (e.g. εἶπον), they are given separate entries in the **Vocabulary**.

4 A few verbs have an imperfect which cannot be predicted from their present stem. Thus ὁράω > ἑώρων, with both syllabic and temporal augment; ἔχω > εἶχον (the original form of ἔχω was cέχω with an imperfect ἔcεχον, which lost its intervocalic sigma (6.1/1c) and then contracted ε+ε to ει (5.1/2b)).

7.1/2 φημί *say* (see also **Appendix 3**)

This irregular –μι verb (2.1/4) is inflected as follows in the present and imperfect:

		PRESENT	IMPERFECT
SINGULAR	1	φημί	ἔφην
	2	φῄc	ἔφηcθα or ἔφηc
	3	φηcί (ν)	ἔφη
PLURAL	1	φαμέν	ἔφαμεν
	2	φατέ	ἔφατε
	3	φαcί (ν)	ἔφαcαν
INFINITIVE		φάναι	

Notes

1 All the forms of the present indicative are enclitic (**Appendix 8**) except the second person singular (cf. εἰμί, 3.1/6).

2 The imperfect regularly has an aorist meaning, *I said*.

3 φημί, not λέγω, is regularly used in the direct quotation of conversations (i.e. **direct speech** – see next subsection). When so used, φημί does not appear until after the beginning of the quotation: δοκεῖc, ἔφη, ὦ Cώκρατεc, εὖ λέγειν *"You seem," he said, "to be speaking well, Socrates."*

4 The φη/φα alternation in the forms of this verb is explained at 19.1/1.

7.1/3 Indirect speech

When we wish to report what someone has said (or thought, etc.) we may do this in one of two ways. We may either give his exact words (cf. 7.1/2 note 3): *"Justice is the advantage of the stronger,"* said *Thrasymachus*; or we may grammatically subordinate the speaker's words to a verb of saying (or thinking, etc.): *Thrasymachus said that justice was the advantage of the stronger.* The first form is called **direct speech,** the second **indirect** (or **reported**) **speech.**

Since speech may be conveniently divided into statement, question and command, we therefore have three corresponding forms of indirect speech:

(*a*) **Indirect statement**: *He said that he was happy.* (Direct *I am happy.*)
(*b*) **Indirect question**: *We asked if he was happy.* (Direct *Are you happy?*)
(*c*) **Indirect command**: *I told him to cheer up.* (Direct *Cheer up!*)

These examples show the adjustments in pronouns that are nearly always necessary in English. Greek does the same but does not, as we shall see, make the **tense** adjustments required by English in (*a*) and (*b*).

7.1/4 Indirect command

For this construction Greek, like English, uses an infinitive after a verb of ordering: ἐκέλευσε τὸν παῖδα τὰ γράμματα μαθεῖν *he ordered the boy to learn [his] letters.* If the infinitive is negated, the negative μή, not οὐ, is used: ὁ νόμος ἡμᾶς κελεύει μὴ ἀδικεῖν *the law orders us not to do wrong.*

The two adverbs of negation, μή and οὐ, are always to be translated by *no/not* but have quite distinct uses (see 7.1/6). The rule here is that μή is always used to negate an infinitive except in indirect statement (8.1/3).

The tense of the infinitive is a matter of aspect (4.1/1). In the above examples μαθεῖν simply conveys that the learning is to be done, whereas ἀδικεῖν indicates that we are not to do wrong on any occasion.

7.1/5 Numerals (see also Appendix 7)

There are three types of numeral:

(*a*) **Cardinals** (in English *one, two, three, four,* etc.)

In Greek, as in English, these function as adjectives. The numbers *one* to *four* are declined as follows:

	εἷc *one*			δύο *two*
	M.	F.	N.	M.F.N.
Nom.	εἷc	μία	ἕν	δύο
Acc.	ἕνα	μίαν	ἕν	δύο
Gen.	ἑνόc	μιᾶc	ἑνόc	δυοῖν
Dat.	ἑνί	μιᾷ	ἑνί	δυοῖν

	τρεῖc *three*		τέτταρεc *four*	
	M. & F.	N.	M. & F.	N.
Nom.	τρεῖc	τρία	τέτταρεc	τέτταρα
Acc.	τρεῖc	τρία	τέτταραc	τέτταρα
Gen.	τριῶν	τριῶν	τεττάρων	τεττάρων
Dat.	τρισί(ν)	τρισί(ν)	τέτταρσι(ν)	τέτταρσι(ν)

So, e.g. ἐκ μιᾶc νήcου *out of one island,* εἰc τέτταραc οἰκίαc *into four houses.*

The numbers *five* to *one hundred* are indeclinable (i.e. have no variable inflections), except when they contain any of the numbers *one* to *four* (e.g. εἴκοcι τέτταρεc *twenty-four,* where τέτταρεc would alter its ending as required: εἴκοcι τέτταρα ἔργα *twenty-four tasks*). The words for *two hundred, three hundred,* etc. follow the plural of καλόc (3.1/3): so διᾱκόcιοι, –αι, –α, *two hundred*; τριcχίλιοι, –αι, –α *three thousand.*

(*b*) **Ordinals** (in English, *first, second, third,* etc.)

These also are first and second declension adjectives (3.1/3), e.g. ἡ πρώτη γυνή *the first woman.*

(*c*) **Numeral adverbs** (in English, *once, twice, three times,* etc.)

All except ἅπαξ *once,* δίc *twice,* τρίc *three times,* end in –άκιc (cf. πολλάκιc *often,* lit. *many times*).

Notes

1 Like εἷc is declined the pronoun οὐδείc (<οὐδέ + εἷc *not even one*), οὐδεμία, οὐδέν, gen. οὐδενόc, οὐδεμιᾶc, οὐδενόc *no-one, nobody, none.* The neuter οὐδέν means *nothing,* but is often used adverbially in the sense *in no respect, not at all* (20.1/5). οὐδείc can also be used as an adjective meaning *no,* e.g. οὐδεμία γυνή *no woman.*

2 Compound numbers over twenty are expressed by putting the smaller number first with καί (δύο καὶ εἴκοσι *two and twenty*), or the larger number first without καί (εἴκοσι δύο *twenty-two*).

7.1/6 Negatives

Unlike English, Greek has two negatives οὐ (οὐκ, οὐχ, 2.1/6a(i)) and μή, and although we translate both by *not* their uses are quite distinct. These involve many constructions not yet described (for a summary see 24.1/2). We may, however, note:

(*a*) οὐ is used to negate statements and so is the negative used with a verb in the indicative in main clauses (examples at 3.2.1, 3.2.4 etc.)

(*b*) μή is the negative used with infinitives except in indirect statement (see above 7.1/4 and 8.1/3*a*).

(*c*) For every compound of οὐ (e.g. οὐδέ, οὐδείς) there is a corresponding compound of μή (e.g. μηδέ, μηδείς). The latter are used, where appropriate, in constructions otherwise requiring μή.

We have already seen at 3.2.12(*vi*) (see note) that the compound negative οὐδείς reinforces a simple preceding negative (οὐ λέγει οὐδέν *he says nothing*). However, when the order is reversed and a compound negative precedes a simple negative the two cancel each other to give a strong affirmative: οὐδεὶς οὐκ ἔπαθεν *no-one did not suffer,* i.e. *everyone suffered.*

7.1/7 Phrases expressing time and space

Many temporal phrases in English contain a preposition, e.g. *on Wednesday, for six days* (but cf. *I will see you next week*). In three types of temporal phrase of this sort Greek simply uses a particular case, provided that the noun involved signifies some period, point, or division of time (*dawn, day, winter, year,* etc.):

(*a*) *Time how long* is expressed by the **accusative**:

ἐννέα ἔτη οἱ Ἀχαιοὶ πρὸ τῆς   *For nine years the Achaeans were*
Τροίᾱς ἐστρατοπέδευον.   *encamped before Troy.*

(*b*) *Time when* is expressed by the **dative**:

δεκάτῳ ἔτει ἱερὸν Ἴλιον   *In the tenth year they sacked*
ἐπόρθησαν.   *holy Ilium* (the definite article
     is generally omitted before
     ordinal numerals in this
     construction).

(c) *Time within which* is expressed by the **genitive**:

τριῶν ἡμερῶν ἔπλευςε Μενέλᾱος εἰς τὴν Ἑλλάδα.	*Within three days Menelaus sailed to Greece.*
εἴκοςι ἐτῶν Ὀδυςςεὺς τὴν Ἰθάκην οὐκ εἶδεν.	*For (i.e. within the space of) twenty years Odysseus did not see Ithaca.*
τέλος εἰς τὴν πατρίδα νυκτὸς ἐνόςτηςεν.	*Finally he returned to [his] native land by night.*

With nouns which do not indicate a period, point, or division of time (e.g. *war* as in *during the war*) a preposition is generally used (e.g. διά + gen.).

(d) *Spatial extent* is expressed by the **accusative** (this use is similar to (a) above:

ἀπέχει τῆς Τροίᾱς ἡ Ἰθάκη πολλοὺς ςταδίους.	*Ithaca is many stades distant from Troy.*
οἱ ςτρατιῶται διὰ τοῦ πεδίου ἐβάδιςαν ςταθμοὺς τέτταρας.	*The soldiers walked four stages through the plain.*

7.2 Greek reading

1 ἡ παροιμία ἡμᾶς κελεύει μὴ κινεῖν ἀκίνητα.
2# εὑρεῖν τὸ δίκαιον πανταχῶς οὐ ῥάδιον.
3 ὁ δὲ Ἰςχόμαχος εἶπεν, ὦ Cώκρατες, χειμῶνος μὲν τὴν οἰκίαν δεῖ εὐήλιον εἶναι, τοῦ δὲ θέρους εὔςκιον.
4 οὐκ ἔχομεν οὔτε ὅπλα οὔτε ἵππους.
5# οὐδὲν ἕρπει ψεῦδος εἰς μῆκος χρόνου.
6 μίαν μὲν οὖν ἡμέραν οἱ Ἀθηναῖοι αὐτοῦ ἐςτρατοπέδευςαν· τῇ δὲ ὑςτεραίᾳ Ἀλκιβιάδης ἐκκληςίαν ἐποίηςε καὶ ἐκέλευςεν αὐτοὺς καὶ ναυμαχεῖν καὶ πεζομαχεῖν καὶ τειχομαχεῖν. οὐ γὰρ ἔςτιν, ἔφη, χρήματα ἡμῖν, τοῖς δὲ πολεμίοις ἄφθονα.
7 οὐδεὶς ἀνθρώπων οὐκ ἀποθνῄςκει.
8 **Proverbs**
   (*i*) μία χελιδὼν ἔαρ οὐ ποιεῖ. (*ii*) δὶς παῖδες οἱ γέροντες. (*iii*) ἐν δυοῖν τρία βλέπεις. (*iv*) εἷς ἀνὴρ οὐδεὶς ἀνήρ. (*v*) μία ἡμέρα ςοφὸν οὐ ποιεῖ. (*vi*) ἡ γλῶττα πολλοὺς εἰς ὄλεθρον ἤγαγεν. (*vii*) ἐν πολέμῳ οὐκ ἔνεςτι δὶς ἁμαρτεῖν. (*viii*) ἐξ ὀνύχων τὸν λέοντα ἔνεςτι μαθεῖν.

9 ὁ Κῦρος ἦλθε διὰ τῆς Λυδίας σταθμοὺς τρεῖς παρασάγγας δύο καὶ εἴκοσι ἐπὶ τὸν Μαίανδρον ποταμόν. τὸ δὲ εὖρος αὐτοῦ ἦν δύο πλέθρα.

10 ὁ κόσμος σκηνή, ὁ βίος πάροδος· ἦλθες, εἶδες, ἀπῆλθες.

11 εἶπέ τις (*someone*) τῷ Cωκράτει, κακῶς ὁ Μεγακλῆς σε λέγει· ὁ δέ, καλῶς γάρ, ἔφη, λέγειν οὐκ ἔμαθεν.

12 A sea battle

Thucydides did not finish his history of the Peloponnesian war but his account was taken up and completed by Xenophon, a versatile writer whose life straddled the fifth and fourth centuries BC. The battle described by him below took place in 406 BC.

εἶχε δὲ τὸ δεξιὸν κέρας τῶν Πελοποννησίων Καλλικρατίδας. Ἕρμων δὲ ὁ κυβερνήτης, καλόν ἐστιν, ἔφη, ἀποπλεῦσαι· αἱ γὰρ τριήρεις τῶν Ἀθηναίων μάλα ἰσχυραί εἰσιν. ἀλλὰ Καλλικρατίδας, αἰσχρόν ἐστιν, ἔφη, τὸ φεύγειν. ἐναυμάχησαν δὲ αἱ τριήρεις χρόνον πολύν, πρῶτον μὲν ἀθρόαι, ἔπειτα δὲ 5 σποράδες. ἐπεὶ δὲ Καλλικρατίδας τε ἀπέπεσεν εἰς τὴν θάλατταν καὶ ἀπέθανε καὶ Πρωτόμαχος ὁ Ἀθηναῖος καὶ οἱ μετ' αὐτοῦ τῷ δεξιῷ τὸ εὐώνυμον ἐνίκησαν, ἐντεῦθεν φυγὴ ἦν τῶν Πελοποννησίων εἴς τε Χίον καὶ Φώκαιαν· οἱ δὲ Ἀθηναῖοι πάλιν εἰς τὰς Ἀργινούσας κατέπλευσαν. τῶν μὲν οὖν Ἀθηναίων 10 τριήρεις πέντε καὶ εἴκοσι κατέδυσαν οἱ Λακεδαιμόνιοι, τῶν δὲ Πελοποννησίων Λακωνικὰς μὲν ἐννέα οἱ Ἀθηναῖοι, τῶν δὲ ἄλλων συμμάχων ὡς ἑξήκοντα.

13 A troublesome visitor

In Athenian courts litigants were obliged to conduct their own cases, but they could use speeches written for them by professional writers. The following comes from such a speech composed by Lysias some time after 394 BC for a middle-aged homosexual defending himself against a charge of assault brought against him by a fellow Athenian, Simon, who was his rival for the affection of a young slave.

ἐπεὶ γὰρ ἐπὶ τὴν οἰκίαν μου τῆς νυκτὸς ἦλθεν ὁ Cίμων, ἐξέκοψε τὰς θύρας καὶ εἰσῆλθεν εἰς τὴν γυναικωνῖτιν, οὗ ἦσαν ἥ τ' ἀδελφή μου καὶ αἱ ἀδελφιδαῖ. πρῶτον μὲν οὖν οἱ ἐν τῇ οἰκίᾳ ἐκέλευσαν αὐτὸν ἀπελθεῖν, ὁ δ' οὐκ ἤθελεν. ἔπειτα δὲ ἐξέωσαν βίᾳ. ἀλλ' ἐξηῦρεν οὗ ἐδειπνοῦμεν καὶ πρᾶγμα σφόδρα ἄτοπον καὶ 5

ἄπιϲτον ἐποίηϲεν. ἐξεκάλεϲε γάρ με ἔνδοθεν, καὶ ἐπειδὴ
τάχιϲτα ἐξῆλθον, εὐθύϲ με τύπτειν ἐπεχείρηϲεν· ἐπειδὴ δὲ αὐτὸν
ἀπέωϲα, ἔβαλλέ με λίθοιϲ καὶ ἐμοῦ μὲν ἁμαρτάνει,
Ἀριϲτόκριτον δὲ ἔβαλε λίθῳ καὶ ϲυντρίβει τὸ μέτωπον.

Notes

2 Supply ἐϲτί; τὸ δίκαιον (*what is*) *right* (5.1/3)

3 χειμῶνοϲ, τοῦ θέρουϲ the definite article can be omitted in such
expressions; τὴν οἰκίᾱν indicates a general class (hence the
definite article, 2.1/2 note 1) – trans. *a house*.

5 οὐδέν is here an adjective with ψεῦδοϲ; trans. *no falsehood* (cf.
οὐδείϲ in 8(*iv*)).

6 *l.*1 αὐτοῦ adv. *there, in that place* (**not** the gen. sing. m. or n. of
αὐτόϲ). *ll.*3-4 οὐ ... ἔϲτιν ... ἡμῖν lit. *there is not to us,* i.e. *we do not
have.*

8 (*vi*) The aorist is gnomic and should be translated by a present
(see note on 5.2.10).

9 παραϲάγγαϲ δύο καὶ εἴκοϲι (*22 parasangs*) is in apposition to
ϲταθμοὺϲ τρεῖϲ (*three days' march*) and explains how far Cyrus
marched in three days; αὐτοῦ gen. sing. m. of αὐτόϲ (referring
back to τὸν Μαίανδρον).

10 Gnomic aorists (see note on 8 above).

11 κακῶϲ λέγω + acc. *speak ill of, malign, abuse;* ὁ δέ *and he* (i.e.
Socrates) 5.1/3; γάρ Socrates' reply sarcastically explains M's
action and in English would be introduced by *yes, for he ...* (see
24.1/1) or *well, he ...*; καλῶϲ λέγω can mean either *speak well of*
or *speak properly* (κακῶϲ λέγω by itself can also mean *speak
badly*) – Socrates is punning on the two senses.

12 *l.*1 εἶχε *had* i.e. *commanded;* the first δέ connects this sentence
with the preceding one in the original context and need not be
translated (cf. the beginning of 4.2.9); Καλλικρατίδᾱϲ (nom. s.; =
Attic –ίδηϲ – 3.1/2 note 3) was a Spartan and his name has the
non-Attic (and non-Ionic) form of the patronymic suffix. *l.*3
τριήρειϲ 6.1/1c. *ll.*6 ff. ϲποράδεϲ nom. pl. f. (this is a third
declension adj., 10.1/4a) *scattered* (agreeing with τριήρειϲ);
Καλλικρατίδᾱϲ τε ... καὶ Πρωτόμαχοϲ ... lit. *both Callicratidas ...
and Protomachus ...* Greek is fond of linking clauses with
particles such as τε ... καὶ (cf. 4.1/3 and ἄγουϲί τε καὶ φέρουϲιν
in *l.*22 of 4.2.9) but in English we would not translate τε; notice

that between this τε ... καί another καί occurs to join ἀπέπεcεν
(< ἀποπίπτω) and ἀπέθανε (< ἀποθνήcκω) but it is the second καί
which picks up τε because the two elements, which must be
parallel, are *Callicratidas* and *Protomachus and those with him*;
τῷ δεξιῷ *with their right [wing]* dat. of instrument (11.1/2). *l.*13
ἄλλων cannot here be translated *other* because the allies referred
to are allies of the Spartans; the meaning is *of their allies as well*
(cf. ᾿Αθῆναι καὶ αἱ ἄλλαι νῆcοι *Athens and the islands as well* **not**
Athens and the other islands because Athens is not an island); ὡc
here *about* (22.1/1*a*(vii)).

13 *l.*2 τὰc θύρᾱc i.e. the two leaves of the door at the house entrance;
γυναικωνῖτιν in an Athenian house the women had separate
quarters; ἤ τ᾿ ... καί the τε need not be translated (cf. *l.*5 of
previous passage). *l.*3 μέν is balanced by δέ after ἔπειτα, and οὖν
connects this sentence with the previous one (neither word would
have an equivalent in idiomatic English). *l.*4 ἐξέωcαν < ἐξωθέω
(the temporal augment in the aorist of this verb is irregular, cf.
4.1/1 note 2(ii). *ll.*8f. ἀπέωcα < ἀπωθέω; ἔβαλλε *started to pelt*
inceptive use of the imperfect (4.1/1 footnote); λίθοιc *with stones*
(dat. of instrument, 11.1/2); ἁμαρτάνει ... cυντρῖβει Greek often
uses the present tense in narrative for vividness (vivid present);
translate with the English simple past (*missed... gashed*); take
ἐμοῦ (*l.*8) with ἁμαρτάνει *missed me* (ἁμαρτάνω is followed by
the gen., 13.1/2*a*(iv)).

7.2/1 Vocabulary

ἀδελφή, –ῆc, ἡ   *sister*
ἀδελφιδῆ, –ῆc, ἡ   *niece*
ἀθρόοc, –ᾱ, –ον   *all together, all
at once, in a body*
αἰcχρόc, –ά, –όν   *shameful,
disgraceful*
ἀκῑ́νητοc, –ον   *motionless,
immovable*
ἁμαρτάνω   *make a mistake;*
(+gen.) *miss*
ἀπέθανον aor. of ἀποθνήcκω
die, be killed

ἀπῆλθον aor. of ἀπέρχομαι   *go
away, depart*
ἀποπίπτω (aor. ἀπέπεcον)   *fall
overboard*
ἄπιcτοc, –ον   *incredible*
ἀποπλέω (aor. ἀπέπλευcα)   *sail
away*
ἀπωθέω (aor. ἀπέωcα)   *push
away*
᾿Αργινοῦcαι, –ῶν, αἱ
Arginousae (islands)
ἄτοποc, –ον   *extraordinary*

αὐτοῦ (adv.) *there, in that place*
ἄφθονος, -ον *abundant, plentiful*
βάλλω *pelt*
βία, -ᾱς, ἡ *force, violence*
βίος, -ου, ὁ *life*
γυναικωνῖτις, -ιδος, ἡ *women's apartments*
δειπνέω *dine*
δεξιός, -ά, -όν *on the right hand*
διά (prep.+gen.) *through, across*
δίκαιος, -ᾱ, -ον *just*
δίς (adv.) *twice*
ἔαρ, ἦρος, τό *(the season of) spring*
εἶδον aor. of ὁράω *see, look at*
εἴκοσι(ν) (indecl. adj.) *twenty*
εἶπον aor. of λέγω *say*
εἰσῆλθον aor. of εἰσέρχομαι *enter*
ἐκκαλέω *call (someone) out*
ἐκκλησίᾱ, -ᾱς, ἡ *assembly*
ἐκκόπτω *knock out*
ἔνδοθεν (adv.) *from inside*
ἔνεστι (impers.) *it is possible*
ἐννέα (indecl. adj.) *nine*
ἐντεῦθεν (adv.) *thereupon*
ἐξευρίσκω *find out, discover*
ἐξήκοντα (indecl. adj.) *60*
ἐξῆλθον aor. of ἐξέρχομαι *come out*
ἐξωθέω (aor. ἐξέωσα) *push out*
ἐπεί (conj.) *when*
ἐπειδὴ τάχιστα *as soon as*
ἐπί (prep.+acc.) *to*
ἐπιχειρέω *attempt, take in hand*
ἕρπω *spread*

εὐήλιος, -ον *sunny, with a sunny aspect*
εὐθύς (adv.) *at once, straightaway*
εὖρος, -ους, τό *breadth*
εὔσκιος, -ον *well-shaded*
εὐώνυμος, -ον *left, on the left hand*
ἤγαγον aor. of ἄγω *lead, bring*
ἦλθον aor. of ἔρχομαι *go, come*
θέρος, -ους, τό *summer*
θύρᾱ, -ᾱς, ἡ *door*
ἰχῡρός, -ά, -όν *powerful, strong*
κακῶς/καλῶς (+acc.) λέγω *speak ill/well (of)* (see note on 11)
καταδύω *make to sink, sink* (tr.)
καταπλέω *sail back*
κέρας, -ατος, τό *wing of a fleet*
κῑνέω *move*
κόσμος, -ου, ὁ *world*
κυβερνήτης, -ου, ὁ *helmsman*
Λακωνικός, -ή, -όν *Laconian, Spartan*
λίθος, -ου, ὁ *stone*
Λῡδίᾱ, -ᾱς, ἡ *Lydia* (territory in west of Asia Minor)
Μαίανδρος, -ου, ὁ *Maeander* (river in Phrygia)
μέτωπον, -ου, τό *forehead*
μῆκος, -ους, τό *length*
νύξ, νυκτός, ἡ *night*
ὄλεθρος, -ου, ὁ *destruction*
ὄνυξ, -υχος, ὁ *claw*
ὅπλα, -ων, τά *weapons, arms*
οὗ (conj.) *where*
πανταχῶς (adv.) *in all ways, altogether*

παρασάγγης, –ου, ὁ   *parasang* (a Persian measure of distance of about 30 stades [= c. 6 km.])

πάροδος, –ου, ὁ   *passage, entrance*

παροιμίᾱ, –ᾱς, ἡ   *proverb*

πεζομαχέω   *fight on land*

Πελοποννήσιοι, –ων, οἱ   *Peloponnesians*

πέντε (indecl. adj.)   *five*

πλέθρον, –ου, τό   *plethron* (c. 30 metres)

ποταμός, –οῦ, ὁ   *river*

ϲκηνή, –ῆϲ, ἡ   *stage* (in theatre)

ϲποράϲ, –άδοϲ (adj.)   *scattered*

ϲταθμόϲ, –οῦ, ὁ   *day's march*

ϲτρατοπεδεύω   *make camp, encamp*

ϲυντρῑβω   *smash, gash*

τειχομαχέω   *fight against walls/fortifications*

τριήρης, –ουϲ, ἡ   *trireme*

ὑϲτεραῖοϲ, –ᾱ, –ον   *following, next* τῇ ὑϲτεραίᾳ *on the following day*

φυγή, –ῆϲ, ἡ   *flight*

Φώκαια, –ᾱϲ, ἡ   *Phocaea* (city in Asia Minor)

χειμών, –ῶνοϲ, ὁ   *winter*

χελῑδών, –όνοϲ, ἡ   *swallow*

Χίοϲ, –ου, ἡ   *Chios* (island and city in the Aegean Sea)

UNIT EIGHT

8.1 Grammar

8.1/1 Middle and passive voices

In a clause where the verb is active the subject is the doer (*the man bit the dog; Alcibiades is running through the agora*). There may or may not be an object, depending on whether the verb is transitive or intransitive. In a clause with a passive verb the subject is the sufferer (*the dog was bitten by the man; the Athenians were defeated in Sicily*). The agent or instrument (11.1/2) may or may not be specified. The active and passive voices are used in Greek in much the same way as in English. Greek, however, has a third voice, the **middle**. This has no English equivalent because the meanings it conveys are expressed in English in different ways. These meanings are:

(*a*) to do something to oneself, e.g. λούομαι *I wash myself, I wash* (intr.); παύομαι *I stop myself, I cease, stop* (intr.)

(*b*) to do something for oneself, for one's own advantage, e.g. κομίζω (act.) *carry, convey*, κομίζομαι (mid.) *I convey for myself, recover*:

ἑκατὸν δραχμᾶς ἐκομίσατο.   *He recovered a hundred drachmas.*

(*c*) to cause something to be done (one's own advantage is always involved):

διδάσκομαι τοὺς παῖδας τὴν   *I am having [my] children taught*
τῶν Ἑλλήνων γλῶτταν.   *the language of the Greeks.*

Of these three uses (*a*) is restricted to verbs with an appropriate meaning, (*b*) is very common, (*c*) is somewhat rare. Very often a verb when used in the middle voice in sense (*b*) acquires a special meaning, e.g. λύω *loosen, free,* λύομαι (mid.) *free* (someone) *for one's own advantage, ransom*; αἱρέω *take, seize,* αἱρέομαι *take for oneself, choose.*

As will be seen in **Appendix 1**, the forms of the middle and passive indicative are identical in the present and imperfect (and also in the perfect and pluperfect – 16.1/3). This does not create ambiguity as the context of a particular verb normally shows its voice. The future and aorist passive differ in form from the middle and will be treated separately in 11.1/1. With regard to the forms of the indicative of the present middle and passive, the imperfect middle and passive, the future middle and the aorist middle, which can now be learnt (see p.277f.), we should note that:

(*d*) in each case the stem is the same as for the active, and the link vowel between the stem and the ending proper (which is more easily distinguishable in these forms) is ο/ε in the present, imperfect (and strong aorist) and future, but α in the weak aorist (on –ω of the 2nd s., see below).

(*e*) in each tense the 2nd s. ending has undergone contraction. The present and future ending was originally –εcαι, the imperfect –εco and the aorist –αco. With the loss of intervocal c (cf. 6.1/1*c*) these became η (or ει), ου, ω respectively (we have already met the second and third contractions with contracted verbs – 5.1/2).

(*f*) when allowance has been made for the 2nd s., the endings, except for the 1st pl. and 2nd pl. which do not vary, fall into two classes. For the primary tenses they are –μαι, –cαι, –ται, –νται and for the historic –μην, –co, –το, –ντο (cf. 4.1/1 note 1).

(*g*) the endings of the strong aorist indicative middle are the same as those of the imperfect: αἰcθάνομαι *perceive,* impf. ἠcθανόμην, aor. ἠcθόμην; and the infinitive ending of the strong aorist is the same as that of the present: αἰcθάνεcθαι (pres.), αἰcθέcθαι (aor.).

Notes

1 Many common verbs have, for no perceptible reason, their future in the middle voice, not the active, e.g. ἀκούω *hear,* ἀκούcομαι; βοάω *shout,* βοήcομαι; διώκω *pursue,* διώξομαι; μανθάνω *learn,* μαθήcομαι. These are verbs which would not otherwise have had reason to be used in the middle. For other examples see **Principal parts of verbs**.

2   εἰμί *be* also has a future middle, which is formed with the stem ἐc–: ἔcομαι, ἔcει (–ῃ), ἔcται, ἐcόμεθα, ἔcεcθε, ἔcονται. The original form of the 3rd s., ἔcεται, occurs in dialects other than Attic.

3   Contracted verbs form their present and imperfect middle/passive according to the rules given at 5.1/2 (see **Appendix 2**).

4   In Indo-European (1.3) there were only active and middle voices. In Greek the passive use of the middle led to the development of separate forms in the future and aorist, but even in Attic we occasionally meet the future middle used in a passive sense.

8.1/2 Deponent verbs

A linguistic peculiarity for which English offers no parallel is deponent verbs, which are **middle or passive in form** but **active in meaning**. They may be transitive (as κτάομαι *acquire*) or intransitive (as πορεύομαι *march*). In some cases the meaning of a deponent exemplifies one of the uses of the middle voice (κτάομαι originally meant *procure for oneself*), but elsewhere (as ἕπομαι *follow*) no explanation seems possible, although these verbs are among the most commonly used in Greek.

As we have seen in the previous subsection, the forms of the middle and passive voices differ only in the future and aorist. This divergence allows a classification of deponents into two groups:

(*a*) **middle deponents**, whose future and aorist are middle in form, as αἰνίττομαι *speak in riddles,* fut. αἰνίξομαι, aor. ἠνιξάμην. This is the larger group

(*b*) **passive deponents**, whose aorist is passive in form. Nearly all passive deponents, however, have a middle, not passive, future. For the aorist passive and examples of passive deponents see 11.1/1.

Examples of deponents in use are: ἀπὸ τῶν ᾿Αθηνῶν ἔρχονται *they are coming from Athens* (ἔρχομαι *come, go*; for the aorist of this verb see 7.1/1 note 2); τὸ ἆθλον δέχομαι *I accept the prize* (δέχομαι *accept, receive*).

A very common deponent is γίγνομαι, which has the basic meanings *be born, become, happen*. In many contexts, however, English requires a more specific word: ἀνὴρ ἀγαθὸς ἐγένετο *he showed himself a brave man* (lit. *he became a brave man*); νὺξ ἐγένετο *night fell*.

8.1/3 Indirect statement

In English we can say, with the same meaning, *he considers that I am clever* or *he considers me to be clever.* Both constructions, a noun clause introduced by *that* or an infinitive phrase without *that,* have their equivalents in Greek, but, unlike English, Greek shows a distinct preference for the infinitive construction after most verbs of **saying, thinking** and the like (for verbs of **knowing** and **perceiving**, see 15.1/2*a*): νομίζω, οἴομαι both *think, consider*; φάσκω *state, declare*; ἡγέομαι *consider.* The first three are used almost exclusively with the infinitive construction.

(*a*) *Infinitive construction*

In this form there is no introductory word (like ὅτι *that* in the other construction – see below (*b*)) and the finite verb of the original statement is changed to the infinitive of the same tense (the present infinitive represents both the present and the imperfect indicative of the direct form). If the subject of the finite verb of the original direct statement is the same as the subject of the verb of saying or thinking introducing the indirect statement, it remains in the nominative, as do any words agreeing with it (**nominative and infinitive**). Such sentences are of the type *Xerxes said that he was master.* Since in the original direct statement (δεσπότης εἰμί *I am master*) there is no need to state the subject explicitly (except for emphasis: ἐγώ εἰμι δεσπότης *I am master*), so too the subject of the infinitive is normally not expressed: Ξέρξης ἔφη δεσπότης εἶναι. When the two subjects are not identical, the subject of the infinitive is put into the accusative (**accusative and infinitive**): ὁ σατράπης ἔφη Ξέρξην εἶναι δεσπότην *the satrap said that Xerxes was master* (lit. *Xerxes to be master*; original Ξέρξης ἐστὶ δεσπότης *Xerxes is master*). If the direct statement was negated, the same negative, οὐ (see 7.1/6), will appear with the infinitive. Further examples are:

ἡ Ἀσπασίᾱ νομίζει καλὴ εἶναι.   *Aspasia thinks that she is beautiful* (original καλή εἰμι *I am beautiful*).

ὁ Περικλῆς ἐνόμιζε τὴν Ἀσπασίᾱν καλὴν εἶναι.   *Pericles used to think that Aspasia was beautiful* (original ἡ Ἀσπασίᾱ ἐστὶ καλή *Aspasia is beautiful*).

ἡγοῦμαι τὴν Ἀσπασίᾱν οὐκ
εἶναι αἰςχρᾱν.

*I consider that Aspasia is not
ugly* (original ἡ Ἀσπασίᾱ οὐκ
ἔςτιν αἰςχρᾱ. *Aspasia is not
ugly*).

ὁ Cωκράτης ἔφη τὴν γυναῖκα
χιτῶνα κτήςεςθαι.

*Socrates said [his] wife would
get a chiton* (original ἡ γυνὴ
χιτῶνα κτήςεται lit. *the wife
will get a chiton*).

ὑποπτεύω τὴν Ξανθίππην πέντε
χιτῶνας ἐχθὲς κτήςαςθαι.

*I suspect that Xanthippe got five
chitons yesterday* (original ἡ
Ξανθίππη πέντε χιτῶνας ἐχθὲς
ἐκτήςατο *Xanthippe got five
chitons yesterday*).

Notes

1   It is only in this construction that the distinction between the
present and aorist infinitives is one of time, **not** aspect (cf. 4.1/1).
In the last example κτήςαςθαι means literally *to have got*. If we
were to substitute the present infinitive κτᾶςθαι *to be getting* (and
eliminate ἐχθές) the meaning would be *I suspect that Xanthippe is
getting...* (original ἡ Ξανθίππη κτᾶται ...).

2   Since, in the accusative and infinitive construction, the infinitive of
a transitive verb has both its subject and its object in the
accusative, there is obviously a possibility of ambiguity. When
confronted with cέ φημι Ῥωμαίους νῑκήςειν (the reply of the
Delphic priestess to Pyrrhus of Epirus) one might well wonder
whether the meaning was *I say that you will conquer the Romans*
or *I say that the Romans will conquer you*. Normal Greeks left such
equivocation to oracles.

3   φημί tends to occupy an unemphatic position and so, unlike in
English, does not precede the indirect statement which it reports:
Πέρςης ἔφη εἶναι *he said he was a Persian* (cf. 7.1/2 note 3).

4   οὐ φημι means *I say that ... not, I deny*: οὐκ ἔφη Πέρςης εἶναι *he
denied he was a Persian*; it **never** means *I do not say that...*, which
would require a different verb, e.g. οὐ λέγω ὅτι ... (on ὅτι see (*b*)
below).

5   Verbs of **hoping** (ἐλπίζω), **promising** (ὑπιςχνέομαι), **swearing**
(ὄμνῡμι 20.1/1), **threatening** (ἀπειλέω) and the like regularly take
the infinitive construction. When these verbs have a future

reference, as they generally do, they can be construed with the future infinitive (a present or aorist infinitive is also possible): ἐλπίζω νῑκήσειν ἐν τῇ μάχῃ *I hope to conquer in the battle.* For a negative hope of this sort the negative μή, not οὐ, is used because the original is really not a statement but a wish (wishes are always negated by μή – 21.1/1): ἐλπίζω τοὺς Λακεδαιμονίους μὴ καύσειν τὸν ἐμὸν ἀγρόν *I hope the Spartans won't burn my farm* (original *may the Spartans not burn my farm!*). This use of μή is extended to verbs of promising, swearing and threatening.

(b) *Construction with finite verb*

Indirect statements in Greek may also be expressed by a noun-clause introduced by ὅτι or ὡς, *that.* Insofar as these two conjunctions can be differentiated, ὅτι is used to introduce a fact, whereas ὡς tends to convey the suggestion that the reporter considers the statement as a mere opinion, an allegation, or as untrue. As in the infinitive construction, the tense of the direct speech is retained in the indirect form even after a main verb which is in the past; in such cases we make a tense adjustment in English (see the second, third and fourth examples below).

This is the regular construction after λέγω *say* (but see note 1) and certain other verbs. Examples are:

λέγει ὡς ὑβριστής εἰμι.	*He claims that I am insolent.*
εἶπον ὅτι ὁ Κῦρος διώκει.	*They said that Cyrus was pursuing* (original *Cyrus is pursuing*).
ἀπεκρίναντο ὅτι στρατὸν πέμψουσιν.	*They replied that they would send an army* (original *we will send an army*).
εἴπομεν ὅτι ὁ Περικλῆς ταῦτα οὐ ποιήσει.	*We said that Pericles would not do this* (original *Pericles will not do this*).

Notes

1 For the impersonal English construction *it is said that ...* Greek uses a personal construction with the infinitive: ὁ Σωκράτης λέγεται τοὺς νέους βλάψαι *it is said that Socrates harmed the young* (lit. *Socrates is said to have harmed ...*).

2 Occasionally even a **direct** quote is introduced by ὅτι: εἶπον ὅτι ἑτοῖμοί ἐcμεν *they said, 'We are ready'.*

3 For the change of mood which may occur after a historic main verb see 14.1/4*d*.

8.1/4 Third declension nouns – stems in ι and υ

These stems differ from those in consonants (5.1/1, 6.1/1) in having ν, not α, as the acc. s. ending for masculine and feminine nouns.

Stems in ι consist of a large number of feminines (including many abstract nouns, mostly in –cιc, e.g. φύcιc *nature),* a few masculines, but no neuters in normal use. All are declined alike, with the odd anomaly that the original ι of the stem has been lost in most forms. The –εωc of the gen. s. was originally –ηοc (as occurs in Homer); the quantity of the two vowels was interchanged but the original accent was retained, i.e. πόληοc > πόλεωc. This accent was extended by analogy to the genitive plural.

Masculine and feminine υ stems are divided into two sub-groups, both very small. The declension of the first (πῆχυc) is very close to πόλιc, of the second (ἰχθῦc) to consonantal stems. ἄcτυ, the only neuter, follows πῆχυc in the genitive and dative.

	πόλιc (f)	πῆχυc (m)	ἄcτυ (n)	ἰχθῦc (m)
	city	*forearm*	*city*	*fish*
SINGULAR				
Nom.	πόλιc	πῆχυc	ἄcτυ	ἰχθῦc
Voc.	πόλι	πῆχυ	ἄcτυ	ἰχθῦ
Acc.	πόλιν	πῆχυν	ἄcτυ	ἰχθῦν
Gen.	πόλεωc	πήχεωc	ἄcτεωc	ἰχθύοc
Dat.	πόλει	πήχει	ἄcτει	ἰχθύϊ
PLURAL				
N.V.	πόλειc	πήχειc	ἄcτη (<εα)	ἰχθύεc
Acc.	πόλειc	πήχειc	ἄcτη (<εα)	ἰχθῦc
Gen.	πόλεων	πήχεων	ἄcτεων	ἰχθύων
Dat.	πόλεcι(ν)	πήχεcι(ν)	ἄcτεcι(ν)	ἰχθύcι(ν)

The normal word for *city* is πόλιc. ἄcτυ means *city, town* as opposed to the country.

Note

πρέcβυc, which follows πῆχυc, is a poetical word for *old man* (prose uses γέρων or πρεcβύτηc). Its plural πρέcβειc, however, is the normal prose word for *ambassadors* (the singular *ambassador* is supplied by πρεcβευτήc).

8.2 Greek reading

1 ὁ θεὸc καὶ ἡ φύcιc οὐδὲν μάτην ποιοῦcιν.

2# φύcιν πονηρὰν μεταβαλεῖν οὐ ῥᾴδιον.

3# πόλειc ὅλαc ἠφάνιcε διαβολὴ κακή.

4 Ἰηcοῦc Χριcτὸc Θεοῦ Υἱὸc Cωτήρ (*the name of an early Christian symbol is concealed in the initial letters of this formula*).

5 ὁ χρυcὸc οὐ μιαίνεται.

6 οἴεcθε ἄλλουc τὴν Ἑλλάδα cώcειν, ὑμεῖc δ' ἀποδράcεcθαι;

7 ἐκ τοῦ ἐcορᾶν γίγνεται ἀνθρώποιc ἐρᾶν.

8# ἀρετῆc βέβαιαί εἰcιν αἱ κτήcειc μόνηc.

9# φεῦ φεῦ, παλαιὸc αἶνοc ὡc καλῶc ἔχει·
γέροντεc οὐδέν ἐcμεν ἄλλο πλὴν ψόφοc
καὶ cχῆμ', ὀνείρων δ' ἕρπομεν μιμήματα,
νοῦc δ' οὐκ ἔνεcτιν, οἰόμεcθα δ' εὖ φρονεῖν.

10 ἐλέφαc μῦν οὐ δάκνει.

11 ἀταλαίπωροc τοῖc πολλοῖc ἡ ζήτηcιc τῆc ἀληθείαc καὶ ἐπὶ τὰ ἕτοιμα μᾶλλον τρέπονται.

12 οἱ Λακεδαιμόνιοι κήρυκα ἔπεμψαν καὶ τοὺc νεκροὺc διεκομίcαντο.

13 διὰ τὸ θαυμάζειν οἱ ἄνθρωποι καὶ νῦν καὶ τὸ πρῶτον ἤρξαντο φιλοcοφεῖν.

14 ὤδινεν ὄροc, εἶτα μῦν ἔτεκεν.

15# πολλῶν ὁ λιμὸc γίγνεται διδάcκαλοc.

16 οἱ Cκύθαι οὐ λούονται ὕδατι.

17 A Greek translation of the Old Testament was prepared at Alexandria in the third century BC. Legend tells us that the version acquired its name of *Septuagint* (Latin **septuaginta** *seventy*) from the number of those involved, of whom thirty knew Greek but not Hebrew, thirty Hebrew but not Greek, while the remaining ten were administrators with no knowledge of either. This calumny probably arose from the colloquial nature

of its language. The following are well-known passages.

(*i*) ἐν ἀρχῇ ἐποίησεν ὁ θεὸς τὸν οὐρανὸν καὶ τὴν γῆν. ἡ δὲ γῆ ἦν
ἀόρατος καὶ ἀκατασκεύαστος, καὶ σκότος ἐπάνω τῆς ἀβύσσου,
καὶ πνεῦμα τοῦ θεοῦ ἐπεφέρετο ἐπάνω τοῦ ὕδατος. καὶ εἶπεν ὁ
θεός, γεννηθήτω (lit. *let ... be born*) φῶς. καὶ ἐγένετο φῶς. καὶ
εἶδεν ὁ θεὸς τὸ φῶς ὅτι καλόν. καὶ διεχώρισεν ὁ θεὸς ἀνὰ μέσον 5
τοῦ φωτὸς καὶ ἀνὰ μέσον τοῦ σκότους. καὶ ἐκάλεσεν ὁ θεὸς τὸ
φῶς ἡμέραν καὶ τὸ σκότος ἐκάλεσεν νύκτα.

(*ii*) ἐπέστρεψα καὶ εἶδον ὑπὸ τὸν ἥλιον ὅτι οὐ τοῖς κούφοις ὁ
δρόμος, καὶ οὐ τοῖς δυνατοῖς ὁ πόλεμος, καὶ οὐ τοῖς σοφοῖς
ἄρτος, καὶ οὐ τοῖς συνετοῖς πλοῦτος.

18   **Crime does not pay**

Hegestratus, a rascally owner-captain, had hired his ship to an
Athenian who wished to import grain from Syracuse. After the
grain had been loaded, Hegestratus, with Zenothemis, an
accomplice in crime, went round Syracuse borrowing money
against the cargo as though it were his. This type of loan
(bottomry) was made to enable merchants to cover costs of
transportation by sea, and was not recoverable if the ship sank.

Ζηνόθεμις δ᾿ ἀδίκημα κακὸν μεθ᾿ Ἡγεστράτου συνεσκευάσατο.
χρήματα γὰρ ἐν ταῖς Συρακούσαις ἐδανείζοντο. ὡς δὲ
ἐλάμβανον τὰ χρήματα, οἴκαδε ἀπέστελλον εἰς τὴν Μασσαλίαν,
καὶ οὐδὲν εἰς τὸ πλοῖον εἰσέφερον. ἐπειδὴ δὲ ἦσαν αἱ συγγραφαὶ
ἀποδοῦναι (*to repay*) τὰ χρήματα μετὰ τὸν τοῦ πλοίου 5
κατάπλουν, καταδῦσαι ἐβουλεύσαντο τὸ πλοῖον· ἐβούλοντο γὰρ
τοὺς δανειστὰς ἀποστερῆσαι. ὁ μὲν οὖν Ἡγέστρατος, ὡς ἀπὸ τῆς
γῆς ἀπῆραν δυοῖν ἢ τριῶν ἡμερῶν πλοῦν, τῆς νυκτὸς διέκοπτε
τοῦ πλοίου τὸ ἔδαφος, ὁ δὲ Ζηνόθεμις ἄνω μετὰ τῶν ἄλλων
ἐπιβατῶν διέτριβεν. ἀλλὰ ἐπεὶ ψόφος ἐγένετο, αἰσθάνονται οἱ ἐν 10
τῷ πλοίῳ ὅτι κακόν τι (*some mischief*) κάτω γίγνεται, καὶ
βοηθοῦσιν. ὡς δ᾿ ἡλίσκετο ὁ Ἡγέστρατος καὶ κακῶς πείσεσθαι
ὑπελάμβανε, φεύγει καὶ πηδᾷ εἰς τὴν θάλατταν. οὕτως οὖν,
ὥσπερ ἄξιος ἦν, κακὸς κακῶς ἀπέθανεν.

Notes

2 ῥᾴδιον (*sc.* ἐστί) *it is easy* – when impersonal expressions involve
an adjective the neuter singular form is used.

3 ἠφάνιcε < ἀφανίζω (4.1/1 note 2(ii)), the aorist is gnomic (see note on 5.2.10).

6 ἄλλουc ... cώcειν acc. and inf., ὑμεῖc ... ἀποδρᾶcεcθαι nom. and inf.; ἀποδρᾶcεcθαι < ἀποδιδράcκω, which has a middle future (8.1/1 note 1).

7 ἐρᾶν is the subject of γίγνεται.

8 κτήcειc should be translated by a singular.

9 *l*.1 *how right the old saying is* (ὡc is exclamatory, 22.1/1*a*(ii)); Greek uses ἔχω + an adverb (here καλῶc) to express a state where English has the verb *to be* + an adjective. *l*.3 μιμήματα is in apposition to the understood subject of ἕρπομεν *we crawl [along] [as] copies ...* *l*.4 –μεcθα (in οἰόμεcθα) is an alternative ending used in verse for –μεθα (1st pl.) of the middle and passive; εὖ φρονεῖν *think rightly* i.e. *be sane, be of right mind.*

11 τοῖc πολλοῖc lit. *for the many,* i.e. *for the majority, for most people*; τρέπονται lit. *they turn themselves* (use (*a*) of the middle in 8.1/1). Whereas the English verb *turn* can be either transitive (*I turned my car towards him*) or intransitive (*I turned towards him*), τρέπω in the active is transitive only (i.e. must be always followed by an object), and the middle (τρέπομαι lit. *I turn myself,* i.e. *I turn*) is employed for the intransitive use of the English *turn*. Here we would translate *they turn*.

12 διεκομίcαντο could represent use (*b*) or (*c*) as given in 8.1/1.

14 ὤδῑνεν impf. (or aor.) of ὠδῑνω (4.1/1 note 2(ii)).

16 λούονται *wash*; just as with τρέπω and *turn* (above 11), λούω is transitive only, whereas *wash* in English can be transitive (*I washed the baby five times*) or intransitive (*I washed five times*).

17 (*i*) *l*.1 ἐν ἀρχῇ the absence of the article gives the phrase a poetical ring. *ll*.5f. εἶδεν ... τὸ φῶc ὅτι καλόν lit. *saw the light that [it was] beautiful.* i.e. *saw that the light was ...;* ἀνὰ μέcον (+ gen. *between*) need only be translated once.

(*ii*) ἐπέcτρεψα *I turned* (unlike τρέπω this verb can be either transitive or intransitive in the active mood) – the author, who was of a rather pessimistic nature, *turned* from one depressing observation to another; ὑπὸ τὸν ἥλιον i.e. here on earth.

18 *l*.1 cυνεcκευάcατο < cυcκευάζομαι (6.1/3). *ll*.2ff. ὡc *when, as* as also in *ll*.7 and 12 below (22.1/1*b*(iv)); ἐλάμβανον ... ἀπέcτελλον ... εἰcέφερον the imperfect indicates that they did these things on

several occasions. *l*.4 αἱ cυγγραφαί *the contracts* – the infinitive phrase beginning with ἀποδοῦναι defines them. *l*.8 ἀπῆραν < ἀπαίρω *sail away*; πλοῦν acc. of extent (7.1/6*d*); διέκοπτε *began to cut through*; (inceptive imperfect, 4.1/1 footnote). *ll*.10ff. αἰcθάνονται ... γίγνεται ... βοηθοῦcιν vivid presents (cf. note on 7.2.13 *l*.8); ἡλίcκετο ... ὑπελάμβανε imperfect because these two actions were going on when Hegestratus escaped; the two following verbs are in the vivid present, which is more commonly used in main clauses than in subordinate clauses.

8.2/1 Vocabulary

ἄβυccoc, -ου, ἡ *abyss*
ἀδίκημα, -ατος, τό *crime, wrong*
αἶνος, -ου, ὁ *tale, story*
αἰcθάνομαι *perceive, notice, realise*
ἀκαταcκεύαcτος, -ον *unformed*
ἁλίcκομαι *be caught*
ἀνὰ μέcον see note on 17(*i*)
ἄνω (adv.) *above, up above*
ἄξιος, -ᾱ, -ον *deserving*
ἀόρᾱτος, -ον *unseen, invisible*
ἀπαίρω (aor. ἀπῆρα) *sail away, depart*
ἀποδιδράcκω (fut. -δρᾱcομαι) *run away, escape*
ἀποcτέλλω *send, send away*
ἀποcτερέω *rob, defraud*
ἄρχομαι (mid.) *begin* (of something continued by oneself)
ἀταλαίπωρος, -ον *without taking pains, not painstaking*
ἀφανίζω *make unseen, wipe out, destroy*
βέβαιος, -ᾱ, -ον *secure*
βοηθέω *(run to) help*

βουλεύω *plan, resolve*; (mid.) *plot*
βούλομαι *wish, want*
γίγνομαι *become, be, happen, take place*
δανείζω *lend*; (mid.) *borrow*
δανειcτής, -οῦ, ὁ *creditor*
διά (prep.+acc.) *because of, on account of*
διαβολή, -ῆc, ἡ *slander*
διακομίζομαι (mid.) *carry across*
διακόπτω *cut through*
διατρῑβω *pass* (time)
διαχωρίζω *separate, divide*
διδάcκαλος, -ου, ὁ *teacher*
δρόμος, -ου, ὁ *race*
δυνατός, -ή, -όν *strong*
ἔδαφος, -ους, τό *bottom*
εἰcφέρω *bring/carry into*
εἶτα (adv.) *then, next*
ἔνειμι *be in*
ἐπάνω (+gen.) *upon*
ἐπιβάτης, -ου, ὁ *passenger*
ἐπιcτρέφω *turn about*
ἐπιφέρομαι *move* (intr.)

ἐράω   *love, desire passionately*

ἐcοράω (= εἰcοράω)   *behold, look at*

ἕτοιμος, –η, –ον   *ready, ready to hand*

ζήτηcιc, –εωc, ἡ   *search, inquiry*

Ἰηcοῦc, –οῦ, ὁ   *Jesus*

καλέω   *call, name*

καλῶc ἔχω   *be right*

κατάπλουc, –ου, ὁ   *arrival in port*

κάτω (adv.)   *below, down*

κῆρυξ, –υκοc, ὁ   *herald*

κοῦφος, –η, –ον   *light, nimble*

κτῆcιc, –εωc, ἡ   *possession*

λαμβάνω   *take, get*

λῑμόc, –οῦ, ὁ   *hunger, famine*

λούω *wash* (the body); (mid.) *wash oneself*

μᾶλλον   *rather*

Μαccαλίᾱ, –ᾱc, ἡ   *Marseilles*

μάτην (adv.)   *in vain; without reason*

μεταβάλλω   *change, alter* (tr. and intr.)

μιαίνω   *stain, pollute*

μῑμημα, –ατοc, τό   *imitation*

μόνος, –η, –ον   *alone, only*

μῦc, μυός, ὁ   *mouse*

νῦν (adv.)   *now*

οἴκαδε (adv.)   *homewards*

οἴομαι (also οἶμαι)   *think*

ὅλοc, –η, –ον   *whole, complete*

ὄνειρος, –ου, ὁ   *dream*

ὄροc, –ουc, τό   *mountain*

οὕτωc (adv.)   *thus, in this way*

παλαιόc, –ά, –όν   *ancient, (of) old*

πάcχω (fut. πείcεcθαι)   *experience, be treated*

πηδάω   *leap, jump*

πλήν (adv.)   *but, except*

πλοῖον, –ου, τό   *vessel, ship*

πλοῦc, –οῦ, ὁ   *sailing, voyage*

πόλιc, –εωc, ἡ   *city, city-state*

πονηρόc, –ά, –όν   *wicked, bad*

cκότοc, –ουc, τό   *darkness*

Cκύθηc, –ου, ὁ   *Scythian*

cυγγραφαί, –ῶν, αἱ   *contract, bond*

cυνετόc, –ή, –όν   *intelligent*

Cυρᾱκοῦcαι, –ῶν, αἱ   *Syracuse*

cυcκευάζομαι   *contrive, concoct*

cχῆμα, –ατοc, τό   *form, shape, appearance*

cῴζω   *save, keep safe*

cωτήρ, –ῆροc, ὁ   *saviour*

τίκτω (aor. ἔτεκον)   *give birth to*

τρέπομαι see note on 11

υἱόc, –οῦ, ὁ   *son*

ὑπό (prep.+acc.)   *under*

ὑπολαμβάνω   *assume*

φιλοcοφέω   *pursue/study philosophy*

φρονέω   *think*

  εὖ φρονέω   *be sane*

φύcιc, –εωc, ἡ   *nature/Nature*

χρῡcόc, –οῦ, ὁ   *gold*

ψόφος, –ου, ὁ   *noise*

ὠδῑνω   *be in labour* (of childbirth)

ὡc see notes to 9 and 18

ὥcπερ (conj.)   *as*

9 | UNIT NINE

9.1 Grammar

9.1/1 Demonstrative Pronouns

Demonstratives in Greek draw our attention to persons and things and are used not only as pronouns but also as adjectives. The English *this* and *that* have similar functions although their use as pronouns is restricted; *this* in *this temple* is an adjective, *that* in *I do not like that* is a pronoun. Greek has three demonstratives, each with a special shade of meaning. The basic differences between them when used as adjectives are:

ὅδε *this near me* (the speaker); normally to be translated *this*;

οὗτος *this* or *that near you* (the person spoken to); normally to be translated *this* or *that*;

ἐκεῖνος *that over there* (i.e. away from both speaker and person spoken to); normally to be translated *that*.

When used as pronouns ὅδε will literally mean *this man near me*, οὗτος *this* or *that man near you*, ἐκεῖνος *that man over there*, but the first can generally be translated by *this man*, the third by *that man*, while the translation of οὗτος by *this man* or *that man* will depend on the context.

ὅδε is simply a compound of the definite article and –δε. In this combination even the unaccented forms of the article bear an accent: ὅδε, ἥδε, οἵδε, αἵδε (cf. 2.1/2; 3.1/1). ἐκεῖνος is declined as a first and second declension adjective (3.1/3), except that the neuter nom. and acc. s. is ἐκεῖνο (for other words with this ending -o see 9.1/3). οὗτος is similarly declined but the first syllable undergoes changes according to the following rules:

(a) an initial vowel with a rough breathing occurs in the same forms as in the definite article (2.1/2, 3.1/1)
(b) an initial τ occurs in the same forms as in the definite article
(c) where the ending contains α or η the diphthong of the first syllable changes from ου to αυ.

	SINGULAR			PLURAL		
	M.	F.	N.	M.	F.	N.
Nom.	οὗτος	αὕτη	τοῦτο	οὗτοι	αὗται	ταῦτα
Acc.	τοῦτον	ταύτην	τοῦτο	τούτους	ταύτᾱς	ταῦτα
Gen.	τούτου	ταύτης	τούτου	τούτων	τούτων	τούτων
Dat.	τούτῳ	ταύτῃ	τούτῳ	τούτοις	ταύταις	τούτοις

In prose, when a demonstrative is used as an adjective, the noun which it qualifies must retain the definite article and the demonstrative must appear in the predicative position (3.1/3b): ἐκεῖνος ὁ νεᾱνίᾱς *that young man*; ἡ γυνὴ ἥδε *this woman*.

Notes

1 In certain contexts οὗτος refers to what precedes, ὅδε to what follows: ταῦτα ἔλεξεν *he said this* (as already reported), but τάδε ἔλεξεν *he spoke as follows*.
2 ἐκεῖνος ... οὗτος can mean *the former ... the latter*.

9.1/2 The relative pronoun ὅς and adjectival clauses

Adjectival clauses qualify nouns or pronouns, and so perform the same function as adjectives. They are introduced by a relative pronoun, which in English is *who, which* etc.

*I am the man **who** dedicated a bronze tripod at Delphi.*
*The tripod **which** you dedicated is inferior.*

An adjectival clause normally has an antecedent, i.e. a noun or pronoun to which the clause refers and which it qualifies (in the above examples *man* and *tripod*). In English the forms of the relative pronoun are not interchangeable but are influenced by the antecedent (*the man which* or *the tripod who* are clearly impossible). Further, we cannot say *I know the man whom visited Delos* because, although *man,* the antecedent of the adjectival clause, is the object of *know* (and so would be in the accusative in Greek), the relative pronoun is the subject of the clause it introduces and must take the nominative form *who,* not the accusative form *whom.* The same holds for Greek, where the rule is **a relative pronoun takes its number and gender from its antecedent but its case from the function it performs in its own clause** (but see note 2 below). Greek cannot, moreover, omit the relative pronoun as we so often do in English (*the man Apollo cursed cannot come into my house;* Greek must say *the man whom*).

The normal relative pronoun in Greek is ὅc, which is declined as a first and second declension adjective (3.1/3) except that the neuter s. nom. and acc. is ὅ without ν (for other words with this ending see 9.1/3):

	SINGULAR			PLURAL		
	M.	F.	N.	M.	F.	N.
Nom.	ὅc	ἥ	ὅ	οἵ	αἵ	ἅ
Acc.	ὅν	ἥν	ὅ	οὕc	ἅc	ἅ
Gen.	οὗ	ἧc	οὗ	ὧν	ὧν	ὧν
Dat.	ᾧ	ᾗ	ᾧ	οἷc	αἷc	οἷc

Unlike *who, which* etc. in English, which can also be used as interrogatives (*which is your tripod?*), the Greek relative pronoun has no other functions in prose. Examples of adjectival clauses are:

Θάνατον εἰcορῶ ὃc Ἄλκηcτιν εἰc Ἅιδου δόμον μέλλει κατάξειν.	*I see Death who is going to* (μέλλει) *take Alcestis down to the house of Hades.*
ὁρᾷc τὸν μόρον τοῦ Ἀκταίωνος ὃν οἱ κύνεc οὓc ἐθρέψατο διεcπάcαντο.	*You know* (lit. *see*) *the fate of Actaeon whom the dogs whom he [had] reared tore apart.*
οἱ cτρατιῶται οἷc ταῦτα εἶπε Ξενοφῶν ἐπανῆλθον πρὸc τοὺc Πέρcᾱc.	*The soldiers to whom Xenophon said this* (lit. *these things*) *returned to the Persians.*

Notes

1 The antecedent of an adjectival clause, if a pronoun, is often omitted: ὃν οἱ θεοὶ φιλοῦcιν ἀποθνήcκει νέος *[he] whom the gods love dies young.*

2 Contrary to the rule given above, the Greek relative pronoun is often put into the same case as its antecedent. This quite illogical attraction is most frequent when a relative pronoun in the accusative case has an antecedent in the genitive or dative: ἤγαγεν cτρατὸν ἀπὸ τῶν πόλεων ὧν (for ἅc) ἔπειcεν *he led an army from*

the cities which he [had] persuaded. Sometimes the antecedent, if a pronoun, is omitted (cf. note l); ἐπαινῶ cε ἐφ' οἷc (for ἐπὶ τούτοιc ἃ) λέγειc *I praise you for what you are saying.*

3　Sometimes when both the relative and its antecedent are in the accusative the latter is put into the adjectival clause: οὐκ ἀπεκρύπτετο ἣν εἶχε γνώμην *he did not conceal the opinion which he had* (= τὴν γνώμην ἣν εἶχε); here the relative is used as an adjective.

9.1/3 αὐτόc and its uses

*For the terms **attributive position** and **predicative position** see 3.1/3b.*

αὐτόc is a pronoun which, like demonstratives (9.1/1), is also used as an adjective. αὐτόc is declined like καλόc (3.1/3) except that in the neuter its nom. and acc. s. is αὐτό (the expected αὐτόν only occurs in ταὐτόν – see below). The –ο ending for the nom. and acc. neuter singular also occurs in the definite article (τό), the relative pronoun (ὅ), τοῦτο, ἐκεῖνο (9.1/1), and ἄλλο *other.* αὐτόc is used in three ways:

(*a*)　as an **emphasising adjective** meaning *self.* Greek has no separate words corresponding to the English emphatic *myself, yourself* etc. (as opposed to the **reflexive** *myself, yourself* etc., see 9.1/4) and instead uses αὐτόc for all persons. When used with a noun it stands in the **predicative** position: αὐτὸc ὁ ἀνήρ *the man himself,* περὶ τῆc γυναικὸc αὐτῆc *concerning the woman herself.* αὐτόc can also be used by itself in the nominative and agree with the understood subject: αὐτὸc ἥκειc *you yourself have come.*

Two idioms involving this use of αὐτόc are:

(i)　with ordinal numbers: πρεcβευτὴc ἦλθε δέκατοc αὐτόc *he came as ambassador with nine others* (lit. *himself the tenth*).

(ii)　with a dative to express the idea of accompaniment (23.1/2*k*), especially in connection with the loss or destruction of something; τῶν τριήρων μίαν κατέδυcαν αὐτοῖc ἀνδράcιν *they sank one of the triremes crew and all* (lit. *[with] men themselves*).

(*b*)　ὁ αὐτόc means *the same.* In the **attributive** position (i.e. between the article and the noun) αὐτόc **always** has this meaning: τοὺc αὐτοὺc δεcπότᾱc εἴχομεν, *we had the same masters*; ἐγὼ μὲν ὁ αὐτόc εἰμι, ὑμεῖc δὲ μεταβάλλετε, *I am the same, [it is] you [who]* *change. The same as* is expressed either by ὁ αὐτὸς καί or, more commonly, by ὁ αὐτός and the dative:

τὰ αὐτὰ φρονεῖ ἐμοί *he thinks the same as I do*; τὰ αὐτὰ καὶ ὁ
'Αλκιβιάδης πείθουσιν, *they give the same advice as Alcibiades* (lit.
they persuade the same [things] ...).

In this use αὐτός may coalesce with those parts of the article ending in a vowel (**crasis** – ll.1/5), and where this is possible both contracted and uncontracted forms are found in normal use. The following table shows all possible variations.

SINGULAR

	M.	F.	N.
Nom.	ὁ αὐτός, αὑτός	ἡ αὐτή, αὑτή	τὸ αὐτό, ταὐτό, ταὐτόν
Acc.	τὸν αὐτόν	τὴν αὐτήν	τὸ αὐτό, ταὐτό, ταὐτόν
Gen.	τοῦ αὐτοῦ, ταὐτοῦ	τῆς αὐτῆς	τοῦ αὐτοῦ, ταὐτοῦ
Dat.	τῷ αὐτῷ, ταὐτῷ	τῇ αὐτῇ, ταὐτῇ	τῷ αὐτῷ, ταὐτῷ

PLURAL

Nom.	οἱ αὐτοί, αὑτοί	αἱ αὐταί, αὑταί	τὰ αὐτά, ταὐτά
Acc.	τοὺς αὐτούς	τὰς αὐτάς	τὰ αὐτά, ταὐτά
Gen.	τῶν αὐτῶν	τῶν αὐτῶν	τῶν αὐτῶν
Dat.	τοῖς αὐτοῖς	ταῖς αὐταῖς	τοῖς αὐτοῖς

The alternative neuter in –ον occurs only in the contracted form.

The shorter forms bear a confusing resemblance to the corresponding parts of οὗτος, e.g. αὑτή *the same woman*, αὕτη *this/that woman*; ταὐτά *the same things*, ταῦτα *these/those things*. The accent will always show which word is involved.

(*c*) The **oblique cases** (2.1/3) of αὐτός are used to **express the personal pronoun of the third person**, *him, her, it, them* (4.1/2). In this use αὐτόν, αὐτήν etc. are unemphatic and postpositive (just as are με, σε, etc., cf. 4.1/2): ἐκέλευσαν αὐτὴν μένειν *they ordered her to remain.* As an **emphatic** third person pronoun, Greek uses the demonstratives οὗτος or ἐκεῖνος:

οὗτος μὲν τοὺς 'Αθηναίους   *He likes the Athenians, but she*
   φιλεῖ, αὕτη δὲ τοὺς   *likes the Spartans.*
   Λακεδαιμονίους.
ἐκεῖνον φιλοῦμεν.   *We like him.*

Greek has no word which functions as an unemphatic third person pronoun in the nominative since the verbal inflections themselves already indicate the person involved.

To illustrate all three principal uses of αὐτόc learn the following sentence:

ὁ cτρατηγὸc αὐτὸc τῷ αὐτῷ   *The general himself killed them*
ξίφει αὐτοὺc ἔcφαξεν.   *with the same sword.*

9.1/4 Reflexive and reciprocal pronouns

(*a*) A **reflexive pronoun** is one which refers back to the subject of a sentence or clause, as in the sentence *he killed himself.* In English all reflexive pronouns end in -*self* (*myself, yourself, himself, themselves,* etc.) and are to be carefully distinguished from the emphatic adjectives of the same form, e.g. *he himself killed the soldier.*

In the singular the reflexives of the first and second persons are formed by joining the stems of the personal pronouns (4.1/2) to the appropriate parts of αὐτόc; in the plural the two components are written and declined separately. The normal third person reflexive is formed from the stem of the indirect third person reflexive ἑ (see below) and αὐτόc. Reflexive pronouns can occur only in the oblique cases and the possibility of a neuter exists only in the direct third person forms.

	First Person		**Second Person**	
	M.	F.	M.	F.
	SINGULAR			
Acc.	ἐμαυτόν	ἐμαυτήν	cεαυτόν, cαυτόν	cεαυτήν, cαυτήν
Gen.	ἐμαυτοῦ	ἐμαυτῆc	cεαυτοῦ, cαυτοῦ	cεαυτῆc, cαυτῆc
Dat.	ἐμαυτῷ	ἐμαυτῇ	cεαυτῷ, cαυτῷ	cεαυτῇ, cαυτῇ
	PLURAL			
Acc.	ἡμᾶc αὐτούc	ἡμᾶc αὐτάc	ὑμᾶc αὐτούc	ὑμᾶc αὐτάc
Gen.	ἡμῶν αὐτῶν	ἡμῶν αὐτῶν	ὑμῶν αὐτῶν	ὑμῶν αὐτῶν
Dat.	ἡμῖν αὐτοῖc	ἡμῖν αὐταῖc	ὑμῖν αὐτοῖc	ὑμῖν αὐταῖc

	Third Person Direct			**Indirect**
	M.	F.	N.	M. & F.
	SINGULAR			
Acc.	ἑαυτόν, αὑτόν	ἑαυτήν, αὑτήν	ἑαυτό, αὑτό	ἑ
Gen.	ἑαυτοῦ, αὑτοῦ	ἑαυτῆς, αὑτῆς	ἑαυτοῦ, αὑτοῦ	οὑ
Dat.	ἑαυτῷ, αὑτῷ	ἑαυτῇ, αὑτῇ	ἑαυτῷ, αὑτῷ	οἱ
	PLURAL			
Acc.	ἑαυτούς, αὑτούς	ἑαυτᾶς, αὑτᾶς	ἑαυτά, αὑτά	σφᾶς
Gen.	ἑαυτῶν, αὑτῶν	ἑαυτῶν, αὑτῶν	ἑαυτῶν, αὑτῶν	σφῶν
Dat.	ἑαυτοῖς, αὑτοῖς	ἑαυταῖς, αὑταῖς	ἑαυτοῖς, αὑτοῖς	σφίσι(ν)

The contracted forms of the second and third person reflexives are more common than the uncontracted ones; ἑ, οὑ and οἱ are usually enclitic.

Examples of these pronouns in use are:

βούλομαι ἐμαυτὸν μὲν ἀποκτείνειν, ὑμᾶς δ' οὔ.	*I want to kill myself, not you.*
ἑαυτοὺς μὲν φιλοῦσιν οἱ κακοί, τοὺς δ' ἄλλους οἱ ἀγαθοί.	*Wicked people love themselves, good people [love] others.*
ὁρᾷς σαυτὸν ἐν τῷ κατόπτρῳ.	*You see yourself in the mirror.*

The third person **direct** reflexive is used as above. The third person **indirect** reflexive is used only in subordinate constructions referring back to the subject of the main clause: κελεύουσιν ἡμᾶς κοινῇ μετὰ σφῶν πολεμεῖν *they urge us to make war in common with them* (ἡμᾶς is the subject of the infinitive πολεμεῖν but σφῶν refers back to the subject of the main verb, κελεύουσιν). Direct reflexive forms are, however, often substituted, Ὀρέστης ἔπεισεν τοὺς Ἀθηναίους ἑαυτὸν κατάγειν *Orestes persuaded the Athenians to restore him(self).*

(*b*) For **reciprocal** action the reflexive pronoun can be used: ἡμῖν αὐτοῖς διαλεξόμεθα *we shall converse with ourselves,* i.e. *each other.* Greek does, however, have a special reciprocal pronoun which was formed by doubling the stem of ἄλλος *other*: ἀλλήλους, ἀλλήλᾱς, ἄλληλα *one another, each other.* It is declined like καλός (3.1/3) except that its meaning excludes a nominative case and a singular number. With ἀλλήλους no ambiguity is possible: ἀλλήλους σφάζουςιν *they are killing each other.* It is used for all three persons.

9.1/5 Possessive adjectives and pronouns

Possessive adjectives are of two types in English, attributive (*my, your, his, her, its; our, your, their,* which occur in phrases such as *my house*) and predicative (*mine, yours, his, hers; ours, yours, theirs,* which occur in clauses such as *the house is mine*). Greek has similar possessive adjectives for the first and second persons only, and these may be used either attributively or predicatively. For the third person it uses the genitive of the personal and demonstrative pronouns. Significantly, however, where the context leaves no doubt as to who the possessor is and there is no need for emphasis, the definite article alone suffices in Greek: ὠφέληςα τόν πατέρα *I helped my father;* εὖ ἐποίηςε τὴν πόλιν *he benefited his city* (cf. note on 2.1.1). In these cases no personal pronoun or possessive adjective is employed. In cases where it is desirable to clarify the reference, Greek proceeds as follows:

(*a*) Where no emphasis is intended the genitive of the unemphatic personal pronouns (μου, cου, αὐτοῦ, αὐτῆς; ἡμῶν, ὑμῶν, αὐτῶν) is employed in the **predicative** position:

φιλεῖ τὴν μητέρα μου *he loves my mother* (lit. *the mother of me*); εἰς τὴν οἰκίᾱν αὐτοῦ εἰςήλθομεν *we entered his house* (*the house of him*); θαυμάζω τὸ κάλλος αὐτῆς *I admire her beauty* (*the beauty of her*).

(*b*) Where some degree of emphasis is desired:

(i) For the first and second persons Greek uses the adjectives ἐμός, –ή, –όν (*my, mine*); cός, cή, cόν (*your* when referring to one person); ἡμέτερος, –ᾱ, –ον (*our*); ὑμέτερος, –ᾱ, –ον (*your* when referring to more than one person), in the **attributive** position:

εἰς τὰς ὑμετέρᾱς οἰκίᾱς ἦλθον *they went into **your** houses;* ὁ cός, Αἰςχίνη, κοινωνός, οὐχ ὁ ἐμός *your partner, Aeschines, not **mine**.*

Note carefully that Greek requires both the definite article and the possessive adjective.[1]

---

[1] But contrast ὁ ἐμὸς δοῦλος *my slave* and ἐμὸς ὁ δοῦλος (or ὁ δοῦλος ἐμός) *the slave [is] mine* (predicative). The latter has **no** article immediately before the possessive.

(ii) For the third person Greek uses the genitive of a demonstrative pronoun, e.g. τούτου *of this/that man*; ἐκείνης *of that woman,* again in the **attributive** position:

περὶ τῶν τούτου λόγων *concerning **his** words*; ἀφικνοῦνται παρ' Ἀριαῖον καὶ τὴν ἐκείνου στρατιάν *they come up to Ariaeus and **his** army.*

(*c*) When a **reflexive** sense is involved (i.e. when the reference is to the subject of the clause to which the noun-group containing the possessive belongs), the genitive of the reflexive pronouns is used, again in the **attributive** position:

τὸν ἐμαυτοῦ ἀδελφὸν ἔπεμψα *I sent my own brother*; τὴν ἑαυτοῦ γυναῖκα ὑβρίζει *he misuses his own wife*; ἀγαπῶσι τοὺς ἑαυτῶν ἵππους *they love their own horses.*

In less emphatic contexts, however, the ordinary first and second person possessives, ἐμός, σός, ἡμέτερος, ὑμέτερος (above *b*(i)), may also be used:

τοὺς ὑμετέρους παῖδας ἀγαπᾶτε *you love your children.*

9.2 Greek reading

1# καλὸν τὸ θνῄσκειν οἷς ὕβριν τὸ ζῆν φέρει.

2 ὁ σοφὸς ἐν αὐτῷ περιφέρει τὴν οὐσίαν.

3# καρτερὸς ἐν πολέμοις Τιμόκριτος οὗ τόδε σῆμα·
   Ἄρης δ' οὐκ ἀγαθῶν φείδεται, ἀλλὰ κακῶν.

4 ὁ Κλέων οὐκ ἔφη αὐτὸς ἀλλ' ἐκεῖνον στρατηγεῖν.

5 οἱ αὐτοὶ περὶ τῶν αὐτῶν τοῖς αὐτοῖς τὰ αὐτά (*sc.* λέγουσιν).

6 τὸ ἐμὸν ἐμοὶ λέγεις ὄναρ.

7 ἔπειτα ἐκεῖνος ὁ ἀνὴρ εἶπεν, ἀλλ' εἰ ἄλλου δεῖ πρὸς τούτοις οἷς λέγει Ξενοφῶν, αὐτίκα ἔξεστι ποιεῖν. μετὰ δὲ ταῦτα Ξενοφῶν εἶπε τάδε· δῆλον ὅτι πορεύεσθαι ἡμᾶς δεῖ ὅπου ἕξομεν τὰ ἐπιτήδεια· ἀκούω δὲ κώμας εἶναι καλὰς αἳ εἴκοσι στάδια ἀπέχουσιν.

8 ὁ φίλος ἐστὶν ἄλλος αὐτός.

9 φιλοσοφίαν πρῶτος ὠνόμασε Πυθαγόρας καὶ ἑαυτὸν φιλόσοφον.

10 παραβαλεῖν δεῖ αὐτοὺς παρ' ἀλλήλους· οὕτω γὰρ σκεψόμεθα εἰ διοίσουσιν ἀλλήλων.

11 ἀπίστως ἔχουσι πρὸς αὐτοὺς οἱ Ἕλληνες.

12 The Persian empire was founded in the sixth century BC by Cyrus the Great (died 530 BC). His achievements were such that in the following century Xenophon (7.2.6) wrote an account of his life (the earliest surviving biography). The following is an extract.

μετὰ δὲ δεῖπνον ἐπήρετο ὁ Κῦρος, ὦ Τιγράνη, ποῦ δὴ ἐκεῖνός ἐστιν ὁ ἀνὴρ ὃς cυνεθήρα ἡμῖν; cὺ γάρ μοι μάλα ἐδόκεις θαυμάζειν αὐτόν. ἐφόνευcεν αὐτὸν, ἔφη, οὗτος ὁ ἐμὸς πατήρ. διαφθείρειν γὰρ αὐτὸν ἔφη ἐμέ. καίτοι, ὦ Κῦρε, καλὸς κἀγαθὸς ἐκεῖνος ἦν· ὅτε γὰρ ἀποθνῄcκειν ἔμελλε προcεκάλεcέ με καὶ 5 εἶπε, οὐ δεῖ cέ, ὦ Τιγράνη, χαλεπαίνειν ὅτι ὁ cὸc πατὴρ ἀποκτείνει με· οὐ γὰρ διὰ κακόνοιαν τοῦτο ποιεῖ, ἀλλὰ δι' ἄγνοιαν· ἃ δὲ δι' ἄγνοιαν οἱ ἄνθρωποι ἐξαμαρτάνουcιν, ἀκούcια ταῦτ' ἔγωγε νομίζω.

13 Δημοcθένης δέ, ὃς ἑώρα τοὺς Λακεδαιμονίους μέλλειν προcβάλλειν πλοίοιc τε ἅμα καὶ πεζῷ, παρεcκευάζετο καὶ αὐτός, καὶ τὰc τριήρειc αἳ περιῆcαν αὐτῷ ἀνέcπαcε ὑπὸ τὸ τείχιcμα, καὶ τοὺc ναύταc ἐξ αὐτῶν ὥπλιcεν ἀcπίcι φαύλαιc καὶ οἰcυΐναιc ταῖc πολλαῖc· οὐ γὰρ ἦν ὅπλα ἐν χωρίῳ ἐρήμῳ 5 πορίcαcθαι, ἀλλὰ καὶ ταῦτα ἐκ λῃcτρικῆc Μεccηνίων τριακοντέρου καὶ κέλητοc ἔλαβον, οἳ παρεγίγνοντο. ὁπλῖταί τε τῶν Μεccηνίων τούτων ὡc τετταράκοντα ἐγένοντο. τοὺc μὲν οὖν πολλοὺc τῶν cτρατιωτῶν ἐπὶ τὰ ἐχυρὰ τοῦ χωρίου πρὸc τὴν ἤπειρον ἔταξε, αὐτὸc δὲ ἀπελέξατο ἑξήκοντα ὁπλίταc καὶ 10 τοξόταc ὀλίγουc καὶ ἐχώρει ἔξω τοῦ τείχουc ἐπὶ τὴν θάλατταν, ᾗ μάλιcτα ἐκείνουc προcεδέχετο πειράcεcθαι ἀποβαίνειν. κατὰ τοῦτο οὖν πρὸc αὐτὴν τὴν θάλατταν ἔταξε τοὺc ὁπλίταc.

Notes

1 τὸ θνῄcκειν (supply ἐcτί) and τὸ ζῆν are both articular infinitives (5.1/3); understand τούτοιc as the antecedent of οἷc.

3 Translate πολέμοιc by a singular; supply ἦν with Τῑμόκριτοc and ἐcτί with cῆμα. *l*.2 φείδεται *is sparing of, spares* takes the genitive (cf. 13.1/2).

4 οὐκ ἔφη 8.1/3*a* note 4; after ἔφη we have a combination of a nominative (αὐτόc) + infinitive and accusative (ἐκεῖνον) + infinitive (8.1/3*a*).

7 *l*.1 δεῖ + gen. *there is need of* (21.1/4*b* and note 3); both ἄλλου (*another thing*) and τούτοιc (*those things*) are neuter; οἷc (= ἅ) has

been attracted into the case of its antecedent (τούτοις) – 9.1/2 note
2. *l*.2 ἔξεστι an impersonal verb (cf. δεῖ, χρή) meaning *it is possible*
(21.1/4*a*). *l*.3 δῆλον supply ἐστί, [*it is*] *clear*; ἕξομεν (note rough
breathing) fut. of ἔχω.

10 As this sentence comes from a conversation we can supply ἡμᾶς
(*us*, i.e. the speaker and his audience) with δεῖ.

11 ἀπίςτως ἔχουςι = ἄπιςτοί εἰςι (cf. note on 8.2.9).

12 *l*.1 ἐπήρετο < ἐπερωτάω. *ll*.3f. οὗτος ὁ ἐμὸς πατήρ *my father here*;
we must tell from the context that αὐτόν is the subject of
διαφθείρειν and ἐμέ its object; καλὸς κἀγαθός (= καὶ ἀγαθός) a set
expression meaning *fine fellow, gentleman* (cf.13.3(ii) *l*.14). *l*.6
οὐ δεῖ cέ ... i.e. *you must not* ... *ll*.8f. The relative clause ἃ ...
precedes its antecedent ταῦτ'(α); νομίζω here has the acc. and inf.
construction (8.1/3*a*) but the inf. εἶναι is understood.

13 *l*.2 πλοίοις ... πεζῷ dat. of instrument (11.1/2) lit. *with both ships
and infantry at the same time* (ἅμα, which is here an adverb). *l*.3
αὐτῷ (*to/for him*) is dative with περιῆςαν (< περίειμι). *ll*.4f. ἀςπίςι
... πολλαῖς lit. *with shields* (dat. of instrument – see above) *inferior
and the many made of wickerwork*, i.e *inferior shields mostly made
of wickerwork* (οἱ πολλοί can mean *the majority* as it does in *ll*.8f.);
ἦν = ἐξῆν *it was possible* (ἔστι used in the sense of the impersonal
ἔξεστι (21.1/4*a*) is common). *ll*.6f. Μεccηνίων, which is to be taken
with both τριακοντέρου and κέλητος in the sense *belonging to
[some] Messenians,* is the antecedent of οἵ. *l*.9 τὰ ἐχυρά *the strong
[points]; πρός towards, i.e. facing. l.*11 ᾗ is here the relative adverb
where, not the relative pronoun. *ll*.12f. ἐκείνους i.e. the enemy;
κατὰ τοῦτο *at this [point]* (κατά is used here of *place where*); πρὸς
... τὴν θάλατταν Greek regularly uses prepositions appropriate to
motion towards (πρός + acc., εἰς, etc.) with verbs logically
requiring a preposition indicating **position at**, when some previous
motion is to be understood (Demosthenes must have moved his
troops **to** the seaside before drawing them up there). Consequently
πρὸς ... τὴν θάλατταν must be translated *by the sea*. This **pregnant**
use of prepositions is so termed because the idea of motion
towards is implied by (i.e. contained within) the preposition.

9.2/1 Vocabulary

ἀγαθός, -ή, -όν brave
ἄγνοια, -ᾱς, ἡ ignorance
ἄκούςιος, -ον against the will, involuntary
ἀλλήλους, -ᾱς, -α (reciprocal pron.) each other, one another (9.1/4b)
ἅμα (adv.) at the same time
ἀνασπάω (aor. -έςπαςα) haul up
ἀπέχω be distant
ἀπίςτως ἔχω be mistrustful
ἀποβαίνω land
ἀποκτείνω kill
ἀπολέγομαι pick out
ἀσπίς, -ίδος, ἡ shield
αὐτίκα (adv.) at once, immediately
δεῖ (impers.) it is necessary (+ acc. and infin.); there is a need of (+ gen.)
δεῖπνον, -ου, τό dinner
δή * (particle) indeed, certainly
δῆλος, -η, -ον clear, obvious
διαφέρω (fut. διοίςω) differ from (+gen.)
διαφθείρω corrupt
δοκέω seem
ἔγωγε (= ἐγώ + γε, 13.1/3b) I at least; I for my part
εἴκοςι(ν) (indecl. adj.) twenty
ἔλαβον aor. of λαμβάνω take
ἐξαμαρτάνω do wrong
ἔξεςτι (impers.) it is possible
ἐξήκοντα (indecl. adj.) 60
ἐπερωτάω (aor. ἐπηρόμην) ask (a question)

ἐπιτήδεια, -ων, τά necessities of life, provisions
ἔρημος, -ον empty, deserted
ἐχυρός, -ά, -όν strong, secure
ἑώρα 3rd s. impf. of ὁράω see
ᾗ (adv.) where
ἤπειρος, -ου, ἡ mainland
θνῄσκω die
καίτοι (particle) and yet, however
κακόνοια, -ᾱς, ἡ malice
κακός, -ή, -όν cowardly
καλὸς κἀγαθός see note on 12
καρτερός, -ά, -όν strong, mighty
κέλης, -ητος, ὁ fast-sailing ship, pinnace
κώμη, -ης, ἡ village
λῃςτρικός, -ή, -όν belonging to pirates
μάλιςτα especially
μέλλω be about to
Μεςςήνιος, -ᾱ, -ον Messenian
ναύτης, -ου, ὁ sailor
οἰςύϊνος, -η, -ον made of osier/wickerwork
ὄναρ, τό (nom. and acc. only) dream
ὀνομάζω call, name
ὁπλίζω equip, arm
ὁπλῑ́της, -ου, ὁ hoplite
ὅπου (relative adv.) where
ὅτε (conj.) when
οὐςίᾱ, -ᾱς, ἡ property, substance
οὕτω another form of οὕτως
παραβάλλω compare

παραγίγνομαι *be present*
παρασκευάζω *prepare, equip;*
  (mid.) *make one's preparations*
πεζός, -ή, -όν *on foot*
  πεζοί *infantry*
πειράομαι *try*
περίειμι *survive, remain*
περιφέρω *carry round*
πορεύομαι *march, journey*
πορίζομαι *procure*
πρός (prep.+dat.) *in addition to*
προσβάλλω *attack*
προσδέχομαι *expect*
προσκαλέω *summon*
ποῦ; (adv.) *where?*
σκέπτομαι *examine, consider*
στάδιον, -ου, τό *stade* (c. 200
  metres)
στρατηγέω *be general*
συνθηράω *hunt with* (+ dat.)

τάττω *station, draw up, post*
τείχισμα, -ατος, τό *fort*
τεῖχος, -ους, τό *wall*
τετταράκοντα (indecl. numeral)
  forty
τοξότης, -ου, ὁ *archer*
τριᾱκόντερος, -ου, ἡ *thirty-*
  oared ship
ὕβρις, -εως, ἡ *insult,*
  humiliation
φαῦλος, -ον (also -η, -ον)
  cheap, of poor quality
φείδομαι *spare* (+ gen.)
φιλοσοφίᾱ, -ᾱς, ἡ *philosophy*
φιλόσοφος, -ου, ὁ *philosopher*
φονεύω *murder, slay*
χαλεπαίνω *be angry*
χωρέω *go*
ὡς (adv.+numerals) *about,*
  nearly

10 | UNIT TEN

10.1 Grammar

10.1/1 Interrogative τίϲ and indefinite τιϲ

The interrogative and indefinite pronouns belong to the third declension and have identical forms except for the accent. The interrogative pronoun τίϲ *who?*, τί *what?* is easily identifiable, since it always retains an acute accent on the first syllable (see **Appendix 8**, note 2). The indefinite pronoun τιϲ *someone, anyone,* τι *something, anything,* is enclitic and postpositive.

		Interrogative		Indefinite	
		M. & F.	N.	M. & F.	N.
SINGULAR	*Nom.*	τίϲ	τί	τιϲ	τι
	Acc.	τίνα	τί	τινά	τι
	Gen.	τίνοϲ, τοῦ	τίνοϲ, τοῦ	τινόϲ, του	τινόϲ, του
	Dat.	τίνι, τῷ	τίνι, τῷ	τινί, τῳ	τινί, τῳ
PLURAL	*Nom.*	τίνεϲ	τίνα	τινέϲ	τινά
	Acc.	τίναϲ	τίνα	τινάϲ	τινά
	Gen.	τίνων	τίνων	τινῶν	τινῶν
	Dat.	τίϲι(ν)	τίϲι(ν)	τιϲί(ν)	τιϲί(ν)

In the genitive and dative singular the shorter forms coincide with the corresponding masculine and neuter forms of the definite article (3.1/1; the indefinite forms have no accent). Both the interrogative and the indefinite pronouns may also be used as adjectives: τίϲ (τίϲ ἀνήρ) τοῦτο ἐποίηϲεν; *who (what man) did this?* λέγει τιϲ τοῦτο *someone says this*; κλέπτηϲ τιϲ τοῦτο ἐποίηϲεν *some thief did this.* Used in this way, indefinite τιϲ is often little more than the equivalent of the English indefinite article.

Notes

1 The acc. sing. neuter τί (or, more fully, διὰ τί, lit. *on account of what?*) means *why* (cf. 20.1/5).

2 ἄττα, which is **not** enclitic, sometimes replaces the indefinite neuter pl. τινά.

10.1/2 Questions, direct and indirect

(a) Direct questions

Direct questions are those which are directly asked of someone else. In Greek, as in English, they are, where appropriate, introduced by an interrogative pronoun or adjective (10.1/1) or adverb (e.g. πότε *when?*). Where there is no interrogative word and English uses inversion (*are you sick?*) Greek, as we have seen (e.g. 3.2.12(ii)), uses the interrogative particle ἆρα (ἆρα νοσεῖς;), which has no English equivalent. However, a question of this sort may simply be indicated by a different tone of voice without ἆρα: ταῦτα εἶπας; *you said this?* (lit. *these things*).

This latter type of direct question may also be framed in such a way as to invite (but not necessarily receive) a negative answer: *you didn't say this, did you?* or *surely you didn't say this?* In Greek such a question is prefixed with μῶν (<μὴ οὖν) or μή: μῶν (or μὴ) ταῦτα εἶπας; We may also invite a positive answer by saying *you did say this, didn't you?* or *surely you said this?* In Greek we begin with ἆρα οὐ (ἆρ' οὐ) or οὐ: ἆρα οὐ ταῦτα εἶπας;

For alternative questions Greek uses as an introductory word for which English has no equivalent, πότερον or πότερα (there is no distinction between the two[1]): πότερον ταῦτα εἶπας ἢ ἐκεῖνα *did you say this or that?* (lit. *these things or those things*). As with ἆρα, the introductory word can be omitted.

(b) Indirect questions

Indirect questions are another form of indirect speech (7.1/3) and are expressed in Greek by a subordinate clause, just as in English: ἐρωτᾷ εἰ Περικλῆς πρὸς τὸν Πειραιᾶ ἦλθεν *he is asking if Pericles went to Piraeus* (direct question: ἆρα Περικλῆς πρὸς τὸν Πειραιᾶ ἦλθεν; *did Pericles go to Piraeus?*).

---

[1] They are respectively the n. acc. s. and n. acc. pl. of πότερος *which (of two)?* The accusative is here used adverbially (20.1/5).

The Greek interrogative pronouns, adjectives and adverbs, which, where appropriate, introduce questions, can have a direct form (τίς, πότε, ποῦ, etc.) or an indirect form:

DIRECT	INDIRECT	DIRECT	INDIRECT
τίς; *who?, which?*	ὅςτις	ποῦ; *(at) where?*	ὅπου
ποῖος; *of what kind?*	ὁποῖος	ποῖ; *(to) where?*	ὅποι
πόςος; *how big?, how much?* pl. *how many?*	ὁπόςος	πόθεν; *from where?*	ὁπόθεν
		πότε; *when?*	ὁπότε
πότερος; *which (of two)?*	ὁπότερος	πῶς; *how?*	ὅπως

The forms ending in –ος are declined as first and second declension adjectives (3.1/3); for the declension of ὅςτις see note 1.

The difference between direct and indirect forms is one of use, not meaning. The indirect are used in indirect questions only, as ἐρωτᾷ ὅςτις εἶ *he is asking who you are* (but see also note 2). The direct forms can be used in direct questions (τίς εἶ; *who are you?*) or in indirect ones (ἐρωτᾷ τίς εἶ *he is asking who you are*). When used in the latter context they give a touch of immediacy and vividness.

Where the original question begins with ἆρα (ἆρα εὐωχεῖ; *are you holding a party?*) or has no interrogative word at all (εὐωχεῖ;) the indirect version is introduced by εἰ *if/whether*: ἐρωτᾷ εἰ εὐωχεῖ *he is asking if* (or *whether*) *you are holding a party*).

As in indirect statements (8.1/3), the tense of the original direct question is retained in the indirect form.[1] As will be seen in the third example below, an indirect question is not always preceded by a verb of asking.

τούτων ἕκαστον ἠρόμην εἴ τινές εἰςι μάρτυρες.	*I asked each of them if there were any witnesses* (direct: ἆρα μάρτυρές τινές εἰςιν; *Are there any witnesses?*)
ὁ κῆρυξ ἠρώτᾱ τίς (or ὅςτις) ἀγορεύειν βούλεται.	*The herald used to ask who wanted to speak* (direct: τίς ἀγορεύειν βούλεται;).
οὐ δεῖ σε εἰπεῖν πόςους (or ὁπόςους) πόνους ἔχεις.	*You don't have to say how many troubles you have* (implying a direct question πόςους πόνους ἔχω; in the mind of the person addressed).

---

[1] For the change of mood which may occur after an introductory historic verb, see 14.1/4d.

Notes

1 ὅϲτιϲ is a combination of the relative pronoun ὅϲ (9.1/2) and the indefinite τιϲ (10.1/1). There are some alternative forms:

		M.	F.	N.
SINGULAR	Nom.	ὅϲτιϲ	ἥτιϲ	ὅτι
	Acc.	ὅντινα	ἥντινα	ὅτι
	Gen.	οὗτινοϲ, ὅτου	ἧϲτινοϲ	οὗτινοϲ, ὅτου
	Dat.	ᾧτινι, ὅτῳ	ᾗτινι	ᾧτινι, ὅτῳ
PLURAL	Nom.	οἵτινεϲ	αἵτινεϲ	ἅτινα, ἅττα
	Acc.	οὕϲτιναϲ	ἅϲτιναϲ	ἅτινα, ἅττα
	Gen.	ὧντινων, ὅτων	ὧντινων, ὅτων	ὧντινων, ὅτων
	Dat.	οἷϲτιϲι(ν), ὅτοιϲ	αἷϲτιϲι(ν)	οἷϲτιϲι(ν), ὅτοιϲ

The neuter singular ὅτι is sometimes printed ὅ τι in modern texts to avoid confusion with the conjunction ὅτι *that, because*. This distinction is not employed in this book; the context should show which is being used.

2 The indirect interrogative ὅϲτιϲ is also used as an **indefinite relative** with the meaning *whoever*; ὅϲτιϲ γαμεῖ πονηράν, μῶρόϲ ἐϲτιν *whoever marries an evil woman is stupid.* The other indirect interrogatives are similarly used (ὅπου *wherever*, etc). For ὅπωϲ, which has additional meanings, see the **Vocabulary**.

3 Just as the interrogative τίϲ becomes, with a change in accentuation, the indefinite τιϲ (10.1/1), so some other direct interrogatives can be converted to indefinite pronouns and adverbs. Very common are που *somewhere*, ποτέ *at some time, once*, πωϲ *somehow* (all enclitic).

10.1/3 First and third declension adjectives

The masculine and neuter of adjectives in this category belong to the third declension, but their feminine to the first. There are two types:

(*a*) *Stems in* υ

In this large class the nom. s. ends in –ύϲ, –εῖα, –ύ (always so accented). ἡδύϲ *sweet* is declined:

	SINGULAR			PLURAL		
	M.	F.	N.	M.	F.	N.
Nom.	ἡδύς	ἡδεῖα	ἡδύ	ἡδεῖς	ἡδεῖαι	ἡδέα
Voc.	ἡδύ	ἡδεῖα	ἡδύ	ἡδεῖς	ἡδεῖαι	ἡδέα
Acc.	ἡδύν	ἡδεῖαν	ἡδύ	ἡδεῖς	ἡδείᾱς	ἡδέα
Gen.	ἡδέος	ἡδείᾱς	ἡδέος	ἡδέων	ἡδειῶν	ἡδέων
Dat.	ἡδεῖ	ἡδείᾳ	ἡδεῖ	ἡδέσι(ν)	ἡδείαις	ἡδέσι(ν)

(b) Stems in ντ

This class contains only a few adjectives but very many participles
(12.1/1). The ντ of the stem is lost in all feminine forms and in the
masculine and neuter dat. pl. (cf. γίγᾱς 5.1/1*b*). πᾶς *all* is declined:

	SINGULAR			PLURAL		
	M.	F.	N.	M.	F.	N.
N.V.	πᾶς	πᾶσα	πᾶν	πάντες	πᾶσαι	πάντα
Acc.	πάντα	πᾶσαν	πᾶν	πάντας	πάσᾱς	πάντα
Gen.	παντός	πάσης	παντός	πάντων	πᾱσῶν	πάντων
Dat.	παντί	πάσῃ	παντί	πᾶσι(ν)	πάσαις	πᾶσι(ν)

Like πᾶς are declined its emphatic forms ἅπᾱς and σύμπᾱς (which we
must also translate by *all*). The only other adjectives in this group end
in –εις (gen. –εντος), –εσσα, –εν, e.g. χαρίεις, χαρίεσσα, χαρίεν
graceful, gen. s. χαρίεντος, χαριέσσης, χαρίεντος, dat. pl. χαρίεσι(ν),
χαριέσσαις, χαρίεσι(ν).

Notes

1 In the predicative position πᾶς means *all*: περὶ πάντας τοὺς θεοὺς
   ἀσεβοῦσιν *they commit impiety with respect to all the gods.* In the
   attributive position it means *whole*: ἡ πᾶσα Σικελίᾱ *the whole of
   Sicily.* Without the article it means *every* in the singular, but *all* in
   the plural: πᾶσα πόλις *every city*; πάντες πολῖται *all citizens.*
2 μέλᾱς, μέλαινα, μέλαν *black* has a stem in ν (not ντ); gen. s.
   μέλανος, μελαίνης, μέλανος; dat. pl. μέλασι(ν), μελαίναις,
   μέλασι(ν). Exactly similar is τάλᾱς *miserable.*

10.1/4 Third declension adjectives

These adjectives are declined wholly within the third declension and
fall into two groups. In both, the masculine and feminine have the
same form.

(a) Stems in ον

These are declined like δαίμων (6.1/1*a*), except that the nom. voc. and acc. neuter ends in –ον in the singular and –ονα in the plural. An example is ἄφρων *senseless*:

	SINGULAR		PLURAL	
	M. & F.	N.	M. & F.	N.
Nom.	ἄφρων	ἄφρον	ἄφρον–ες	ἄφρον–α
Voc.	ἄφρον	ἄφρον	ἄφρον–ες	ἄφρον–α
Acc.	ἄφρον–α	ἄφρον	ἄφρον–ας	ἄφρον–α
Gen.	ἄφρον–ος	ἄφρον–ος	ἀφρόν–ων	ἀφρόν–ων
Dat.	ἄφρον–ι	ἄφρον–ι	ἄφρο–σι(ν)	ἄφρο–σι(ν)

Comparative adjectives in –ων (17.1/2*b*) are similarly declined.

(b) Stems in εc

These belong to the same type as neuter nouns in εc (6.1/1*c*). This is most obvious in the genitive and dative, where we find similar endings. ἀληθής *true* (stem ἀληθεc–) is declined:

	SINGULAR		PLURAL	
	M. & F.	N.	M. & F.	N.
Nom.	ἀληθής	ἀληθές	ἀληθεῖc	ἀληθῆ
Voc.	ἀληθές	ἀληθές	ἀληθεῖc	ἀληθῆ
Acc.	ἀληθῆ	ἀληθές	ἀληθεῖc	ἀληθῆ
Gen.	ἀληθοῦc	ἀληθοῦc	ἀληθῶν	ἀληθῶν
Dat.	ἀληθεῖ	ἀληθεῖ	ἀληθέcι(ν)	ἀληθέcι(ν)

ἀληθῆ, ἀληθεῖc are contractions of ἀληθέ(c)α, ἀληθέ(c)εc. ἀληθεῖc as acc. pl. (m. and f.) is irregular; we would have expected ἀληθῆc (< –ε(c)αc). The n. pl. nom. voc. and acc. ἀληθῆ are only an apparent exception to the rule given at 3.1/1 (cf. γένοc: pl. γένη < γένεc–α, 6.1/1*c*).

The few adjectives with other stems are mostly compounds whose second element is a third declension noun, e.g. εὔχαρις (εὖ + χάρις) *charming*, stem εὐχαριτ–; εὔελπις (εὖ + ἐλπίc) *hopeful*, stem εὐελπιδ–.

10.2 Greek reading

1# παχεῖα γαστὴρ λεπτὸν οὐ τίκτει νόον.
2# ὡς ἡδὺ τὴν θάλατταν ἀπὸ τῆς γῆς ὁρᾶν.
3# ὁ χρόνος ἅπαντα τοῖσιν ὕστερον φράσει.

4   ἡ εὐδαιμονία ἐστὶν ἐνέργειά τις τῆς ψυχῆς.
5   ὦ Μένανδρε καὶ βίε, πότερος ἄρ' ὑμῶν πότερον ἀπεμιμήcατο;
6# τίς δ' οἶδεν (*knows*) εἰ τὸ ζῆν μέν ἐcτι κατθανεῖν,
    τὸ κατθανεῖν δὲ ζῆν κάτω νομίζεται;
7   ὁ βίος βραχύς, ἡ δὲ τέχνη μακρή, ὁ δὲ καιρὸς ὀξύς, ἡ δὲ πεῖρα
    cφαλερή, ἡ δὲ κρίcιc χαλεπή.
8   cύντομος ἡ πονηρία, βραδεῖα ἡ ἀρετή.
9   ὅπου εὖ πράττει τις, ἐνταῦθα πατρίc.
10# ὅcτιc δὲ θνητῶν βούλεται δυcώνυμον
    εἰc γῆραc ἐλθεῖν, οὐ λογίζεται καλῶc·
    μακρὸc γὰρ αἰὼν μυρίουc τίκτει πόνουc·
11# ὡc ἡδὺ δούλοιc δεcπόταc χρηcτοὺc λαβεῖν
    καὶ δεcπόταιcι δοῦλον εὐμενῆ δόμοιc.
12# ἅπαντ' ἐπαχθῆ πλὴν θεοῖcι κοιρανεῖν·
    ἐλεύθεροc γὰρ οὔτιc ἐcτὶ πλὴν Διόc.
13 οἱ ἀμαθεῖc ὥcπερ ἐν πελάγει καὶ νυκτὶ φέρονται ἐν τῷ βίῳ.
14 ἡ γυνὴ ἔφη ὅτι αὐτάρκηc κόcμοc μοι ἡ τοῦ ἀνδρὸc ἀρετή.
15# ὅπου τιc ἀλγεῖ, κεῖcε καὶ τὸν νοῦν ἔχει.
16 **Other proverbs**
    (*i*) μιcῶ μνήμονα cυμπότην. (*ii*) δυcμενὴc ὁ τῶν γειτόνων
    ὀφθαλμόc. (*iii*) τὸν ἀτυχῆ καὶ πρόβατον δάκνει. (*iv*) ἀνὴρ ἄτεχνοc
    τοῖc πᾶcίν ἐcτι δοῦλοc. (*v*) γλυκὺc ἀπείρῳ πόλεμοc. (*vi*) χρόνῳ τὰ
    πάντα κρίνεται. (*vii*) ἐν νυκτὶ λαμπρόc, ἐν φάει δ' ἀνωφελήc. (*viii*)
    ἀλλήλαc νίπτουcι χεῖρεc. (*ix*) ὑπὸ παντὶ λίθῳ cκόρπιοc
    καθεύδει. (*x*) ῥάδια πάντα θεῷ. (*xi*) ἅπαc ἐχῖνοc τραχύc. (*xii*) ὃν
    ἡ τύχη μέλανα γράψει τοῦτον ὁ πᾶc χρόνοc οὐ δύναται λευκάναι.
17 **Stories about Diogenes**
    The Greeks were fond of short, pithy anecdotes ending in a *bon
    mot*. Diogenes, the philosopher of the fourth century BC whose
    eccentric lifestyle made him a tourist attraction in the Athens of
    his day, is the subject of a large collection.
    (*i*)   ὁ Διογένηc ᾔτει ποτὲ ἀνδριάντα· ἐρωτηθεὶc (*having been
            asked*) δὲ διὰ τί τοῦτο ποιεῖ, μελετῶ, εἶπεν, ἀποτυγχάνειν.
    (*ii*) ἐρωτηθεὶc ποῖον οἶνον ἡδέωc πίνει, ἔφη, τὸν ἀλλότριον.
    (*iii*) φιλάργυρον ᾔτει· ὅτε δὲ ἐβράδυνεν, ὁ Διογένηc, ἄνθρωπε,
            εἶπεν, εἰc τροφήν cε αἰτῶ, οὐκ εἰc ταφήν.
    (*iv*) ἐρωτηθεὶc πόθεν ἐcτίν, κοcμοπολίτηc, ἔφη.
    (*v*)   ὅτε εἶπέ τιc κακὸν εἶναι τὸ ζῆν, οὐ τὸ ζῆν, ἔφη, ἀλλὰ τὸ
            κακῶc ζῆν.

Notes

1 The uncontracted νόον (= νοῦν, 6.1/2) shows that this is Ionic Greek (1.3).

3 τοῖσιν = τοῖς (3.1/1 note 3).

5 Menander was famous for his faithful representation of everyday life; πότερος ἄρ' lit. *which of you two then ...?* (ἄρ' = ἄρα an inferential particle which must be distinguished from ἆρα, 10.1/2*a*).

6 κατθανεῖν shortened form of καταθανεῖν (aor. inf. act. of καταθνήσκειν). *l.*2 δέ is postponed for metrical reasons (prose order would be τὸ δὲ κατθανεῖν); κάτω *below* i.e. in Hades.

7 The well-known aphorism of Hippocrates, the famous doctor of the 5th century BC. He wrote in Ionic Greek and the η of μακρή and cφαλερή would be ᾱ in Attic. By τέχνη Hippocrates meant the art of medicine.

9 ὅπου here (and in 15 below) is the relative adverb *where,* not the indirect interrogative.

10 Take δυcώνυμον with γῆρας *old age* (acc. s., 13.1/1*b*(iii)).

11 *l.*2 λαβεῖν is to be understood; δεcπόταιcι has the longer form of the dat. pl. ending (3.1/1 note 3; cf. θεοῖcι in the next sentence); δόμοιc dat. without preposition to express *place where* (23.1/2*n*) – translate by a singular.

12 κοιρανεῖν here takes the dative, not the genitive as is normal after verbs of ruling (13.1/2*a*); Διός gen. of Ζεύς (11.1/4)

14 For ὅτι introducing a **direct** statement see 8.1/3*b* note 2.

16 (*iv*) τοῖc πᾶcιν the article is added for emphasis (as also in (*vi*)). (*vi*) χρόνῳ *by time* dat. of instrument (11.1/2); τὰ πάντα cf. (*iv*) above. (*vii*) A phrase of abuse, not a sentence (cf. 6.2.7 (iv)). (*xii*) Although ὅν comes first, its antecedent is τοῦτον; δύναται *is able* from δύναμαι (on verbs with –αμαι instead of –ομαι see 19.1/3*b*).

17 (*i*) ᾔτει (< αἰτέω) *was begging [alms from]* + acc.; ποιεῖ on the tense see 10.1/2*b* (this also applies to πῑνει (*ii*) and ἐcτίν (*iv*)). (*ii*) with τὸν ἀλλότριον supply ἡδέως πῑνω. (*iii*) ᾔτει see (*i*); εἰc *with regard to,* i.e. *for.*

10.3 Extra reading

From this point extra reading will be included with certain units.

Because it will consist of longer passages it will necessarily be somewhat harder than the other exercises. If you do not feel confident enough to tackle it when working your way through the book for the first time, it may conveniently be left until later.

The wisdom of Socrates

Socrates (469–399 BC) was to philosophy what Herodotus was to history. Previous thinkers had speculated on the physical nature of the world, but Socrates was the first to concern himself with moral and ethical problems. His uncompromising pursuit of truth made him so unpopular with his fellow citizens at Athens that, when he was brought to trial on a trumped-up charge of corrupting the young, he was convicted and executed. The following is from his defence in court, as reported by his pupil Plato; here Socrates explains the origin of his reputation (ὄνομα) for exceptional wisdom, which, he claims, is unjustified.

ἐγὼ γάρ, ὦ ἄνδρες Ἀθηναῖοι, δι᾽ οὐδὲν ἄλλ᾽ ἢ διὰ σοφίαν τινὰ τοῦτο τὸ ὄνομα ἔχω. ποίαν δὴ σοφίαν ταύτην; ἥπερ ἐστὶν ἴσως ἀνθρωπίνη σοφία· τῷ ὄντι γὰρ κινδυνεύω ταύτην εἶναι σοφός. οὗτοι δέ, οὓς ἄρτι ἔλεγον, δαιμονίαν τινὰ σοφίαν σοφοί εἰσιν, ἣν οὐκ ἔχω διηγεῖσθαι· οὐ γὰρ δὴ ἔγωγε αὐτὴν ἐπίσταμαι, ἀλλ᾽ ὅστις φησί, ψεύδεταί τε καὶ ἐπὶ διαβολῇ 5 τῇ ἐμῇ λέγει. καὶ ἐλπίζω ὑμᾶς, ὦ ἄνδρες Ἀθηναῖοι, μὴ θορυβήσειν μοι, μηδ᾽ εἰ δοκῶ τι ὑμῖν μέγα λέγειν· οὐ γὰρ ἐμὸν ἐρῶ τὸν λόγον ὃν λέγω, ἀλλ᾽ εἰς ἀξιόπιστόν τινα ἀνοίσω. τῆς γὰρ ἐμῆς, εἰ δή τίς ἐστι σοφία καὶ οἵα, μάρτυρα ὑμῖν παρέξομαι τὸν θεὸν τὸν ἐν Δελφοῖς. γνώριμος γάρ που ὑμῖν ἦν Χαιρεφῶν. οὗτος ἐμός τε ἑταῖρος ἦν ἐκ νέου καὶ ὑμῶν τῷ 10 πλήθει. καὶ εὔγνωστον ὑμῖν ἐστιν οἷος ἦν Χαιρεφῶν, ὡς παντάπασι σφοδρός. καὶ δή ποτε καὶ εἰς Δελφοὺς ἦλθε καὶ ἐτόλμησε μαντεύεσθαι, εἴ τίς ἐστι σοφώτερος ἢ (wiser than) ἐγώ. ἀνεῖλεν οὖν ἡ Πυθία οὐδένα σοφώτερον εἶναι.

Notes

l.1 ἄλλ᾽ = ἄλλο; ἤ than. l.2 ποίαν etc. supply λέγω; ἥπερ [the one] which, the suffix περ is added to the relative pronoun for emphasis. l.3 τῷ ὄντι in reality, really (12.1/1 note 1); ταύτην (sc. τὴν σοφίαν) accusative of respect (20.1/5) with σοφός, lit. wise in respect of this [wisdom], i.e. possessed of this wisdom – the same construction occurs with σοφοί (l.4). l.4 οὐκ ἔχω I am not able. ll.5f. ἔγωγε cf. 9.2.12 l.9;

ἐπίϲταμαι has –αμαι instead of –ομαι (19.1/3*b*); φηϲί *sc. that this is so*; ἐπί *with a view to*, i.e *to arouse*; διαβολῇ τῇ ἐμῇ not *my prejudice* but *prejudice against me*; this use of the possessive adjective is the same as that of the objective genitive (23.1/1*c*). *l.*6 μή is used after ἐλπίζω (8.1/3*a* note 5) and consequently we also have μηδ'(ε) (7.1/6*c*), which here means *not even,* but, as we would not normally repeat the negative in such a construction in English, simply translate by *even*; θορυβήϲειν μοι lit. *to be going to make a noise for me*, i.e. *to be going to interrupt me. l.*7 ἐμόν predicative with τὸν λόγον, lit. *not [as] mine shall I tell the story which I am telling. ll.*8f. ἀνοίϲω < ἀναφέρω; τῆϲ ... ἐμῆϲ (*sc.* ϲοφίᾱϲ) with μάρτυρα *a witness of my [wisdom]*; εἰ ... οἵᾱ two indirect questions to be taken with μάρτυρα *[as to] whether it is some sort of* (τιϲ) *wisdom and what sort of [wisdom it is]* (the indefinite τιϲ has an acute accent because of the following ἐϲτιν (see **Appendix 8**, *d*(ix)); it is **not** the interrogative τίϲ); τὸν θεόν, i.e. Apollo. *ll.*10ff. που *I suppose, think,* the original meaning, which is also common, is *somewhere* (10.1/2*b* note 3); τε ... καί (*both ... and* but trans. simply by *and*) joins ἐμόϲ and ὑμῶν; ἐκ νέου lit. *from [being] young*, i.e. *from youth*; ὑμῶν τῷ πλήθει lit. *to the people of you,* i.e. to the [Athenian] democracy (to be taken with ἑταῖροϲ, which may be here translated by one word and by another word with ἐμόϲ); ὡϲ ... ϲφοδρόϲ *how [he was] completely impetuous* Chaerephon had died before the trial (hence ἦν in the previous clause). *l.*12 καὶ δή *and indeed, and as a matter of fact*; ποτε καί ... *once even/actually* (*he actually went to Delphi once*). *l.*13 ἀνεῖλεν < ἀναιρέω.

11 | UNIT ELEVEN

11.1 Grammar

11.1/1 Root aorist, aorist passive and future passive

A few –ω verbs form their aorist active by adding endings directly to their basic stem or root without a suffix (such as c in the weak aorist – 4.1/1) or a link vowel (such as o/ε of the strong aorist endings – 7.1/1). The roots of all such verbs end in the long vowels ᾱ, η, ῡ or ω, and the endings applied to form the root aorist are –ν, –c, –, –μεν, –τε, –cαν. As an example we may take the aorist of βαίνω *go* (root βη–).

	SINGULAR	PLURAL
1	ἔβην *I went*	ἔβημεν
2	ἔβης	ἔβητε
3	ἔβη	ἔβηcαν
INFINITIVE	βῆναι	

Some other common verbs with root aorists are given below. Note that the form of the root cannot be predicted from the present stem.

	PRESENT STEM	ROOT	ROOT AORIST
(ἀπο) διδράcκω[1] *run away*	διδραcκ–	δρᾱ–	–έδρᾱν
φύω *cause to grow, produce*	φυ–	φῡ–	ἔφῡν
γιγνώcκω *get to know*	γιγνωcκ–	γνω–	ἔγνων
βιόω *live*	βιο–	βιω–	ἐβίων

φύω also has a regularly formed weak aorist active: ἔφῡcα. In such cases where a verb has two sets of aorist active forms, the root aorist

---

[1] This verb occurs only in compounds.

is intransitive: ἔφῦν (*I grew* intr.); and the weak aorist transitive: ἔφῦσα (*I caused to grow, I produced*); cf. καταδύω *cause to sink*; κατέδῦσα *I caused to sink*, κατέδῦν *I sank.*[1] Examples are:

αἱ τρίχες ἔρρεον ἃς πρὶν ἔφῦσε τὸ φάρμακον.	*The hairs fell out which the drug previously made grow.*
ἐλάα ἐντὸς τῆς αὐλῆς ἔφῦ.	*An olive tree grew inside the courtyard.*

Another important verb with two aorists and a similar distinction between them is ἵστημι (19.1/1).

Only a few verbs, however, have a root aorist with an active meaning. Elsewhere the root aorist has developed a passive meaning and is normally classified as an aorist passive. An example is πνῑ́γω *strangle, choke* (tr.), which, like φύω, has a weak aorist ἔπνῑξα *I strangled, choked* (tr., e.g. ἐχθὲς ἔπνῑξα τὸν τοῦ γείτονος κύνα *yesterday I choked the neighbour's dog*) and what is really a root aorist ἐπνίγην *I choked* (intr., e.g. ὁ σὸς κύων, ἔφην, ἐπνίγη ἐν τῷ τοῦ πυρὸς καπνῷ *"Your dog," I said, "choked in the smoke of the fire"*). The original contrast between the transitive and intransitive aorists in verbs of this sort developed into one of active/passive, and forms such as ἐπνίγην were used in contexts where they must be interpreted as passive (ὁ ἐμὸς κύων, ἔφη, οὐκ ἐπνίγη καπνῷ *"My dog," he said, "was not choked by smoke"* – on this use of the dative see 11.1/2 below). Consequently, most root aorists in –ην, (but not in –ᾱν, ῦν, or, with one exception, –ων) which could be interpreted as passive came to be so regarded and classified. This could not happen with intransitive verbs, such as βαίνω, whose meaning precludes any passive sense.

The total number of aorist passives in –ην is also small, but they formed the model for the vast majority of transitive verbs, where a special aorist passive stem was created by attaching the suffix θη to the root.[2] To this were added the same endings as for the root aorist. For this reason **all** aorist passive endings are of the **active** type; the aorist passive **never** has the passive endings of the other historic tenses (–μην, –σο, –το etc. 4.1/1 note 1).

The aorist passive indicative (and corresponding infinitive) of λύω will be found in **Appendix 1**. This tense is included in the principal parts of

---

[1] In these verbs the 3rd plural of the root aorist and of the weak aorist active are identical: ἔφῦσαν (from ἔφῦ-σαν or ἔφῦς-αν).
[2] The η of the suffix undergoes change in some forms other than the indicative, e.g. the aor. pass. pple. λυθείς (12.1/1).

verbs which show some irregularity (7.1/1 note 3) as the form it takes is not always predictable. We may, however, note:

(a) Most verbs whose present stem ends in a vowel or diphthong form their aorist passive stem regularly. In a few cases the suffix is enlarged to cθη on the analogy of dental stems (see below), e.g. ἠκούcθην *I was heard* (ἀκούω); ἐκελεύcθην *I was ordered* (κελεύω). In regular contracted verbs the final vowel of the present stem is lengthened in the same way as in the aorist active (5.1/2 note 2), e.g. ἐτῑμήθην (τῑμάω); ἐποιήθην (ποιέω); ἐδηλώθην (δηλόω).

(b) In palatal and labial stems (6.1/4b) final κ and γ become χ, final π and β become φ (i.e. they are assimilated to the following θ by becoming aspirates), e.g. ἐφυλάχθην *I was guarded* (φυλάττω, stem φυλακ–); ἐπέμφθην *I was sent* (πέμπω, stem πεμπ–). In dental stems the final consonant becomes c, e.g. ἐπείcθην *I was persuaded* (πείθω, stem πειθ–).

Occasionally (and unpredictably) a verb has a root aorist passive, e.g. ἐπνίγην (see above); ἐκόπην *I was cut* (κόπτω), sometimes both, e.g. ἐβλάβην, ἐβλάφθην *I was hurt* (βλάπτω; there is no difference in meaning).

The stem of the **future passive** is that of the aorist passive with an added c (λυθηc–, τῑμηθηc–, κοπηc–). The endings are those of the present middle and passive: λυθήcομαι *I shall be loosened*; τῑμηθήcομαι *I shall be honoured*; κοπήcομαι *I shall be cut*. For the full future passive of λύω see **Appendix 1.**

Note

As mentioned in 8.1/2 some deponents are classified as **passive** because their aorist is passive, not middle, in form (most, however, have a **middle future**). Among the most common passive deponents are:

βούλομαι *wish*; fut. βουλήcομαι; aor. ἐβουλήθην
δύναμαι *be able*; fut. δυνήcομαι; aor. ἐδυνήθην
πορεύομαι *march*; fut. πορεύcομαι; aor. ἐπορεύθην

In the future and aorist of the first two η is inserted. δύναμαι has –αμαι, –αcαι, –αται etc., not –ομαι –ῃ, –εται etc. in the present (see 19.1/3b).

The difference between middle and passive deponents is simply one of **form**; both are active in **meaning**.

11.1/2 Agent and instrument

In English we can say *the policeman was hit by a demonstrator* and *the policeman was hit by a placard* but Greek makes a distinction between agent (*demonstrator*) and instrument (*placard*). An agent is a living being and agency is normally expressed by ὑπό with the genitive. An instrument is nearly always inanimate and the construction used for it is the dative without a preposition (examples have already occurred at 7.2.13 *l.*8, 9.2.13 *l.*2, 10.2.16(vi); in English we use either *by* or *with*: Ἀσπασίᾱ με τύπτει μήλοις *Aspasia is hitting me with apples* (instrument); ἡ Τροίᾱ ὑπὸ τῶν Ἑλλήνων ἐπορθήθη *Troy was sacked by the Greeks* (agent).

11.1/3 –ω verbs with stems in λ, μ, ν, ρ

Most verbs with these stems originally formed their present with a *y* suffix (6.1/4*b*). This combined with a preceding λ to give λλ, but disappeared after μ, ν, ρ, although, by way of compensation, a preceding ε, ι, υ was lengthened and a preceding α became αι. The future of these verbs is of the contracted type (–ῶ < –έω; 5.1/2 note 3); where a *y* suffix has been used in the present the future reverts to the original stem. In the weak aorist (which occurs in all common verbs of this group, except βάλλω *throw*) the sigma is dropped and the preceding vowel lengthened (note that here we have α > η except after vowels and ρ, where α becomes ᾱ; also, ε becomes ει). The following table shows the different possibilities:

PRESENT			FUTURE	AORIST
βάλλω	throw	(< βάλ–*y* ω)	βαλῶ	ἔβαλον
στέλλω	send	(< στέλ–*y* ω)	στελῶ	ἔστειλα
νέμω	apportion	(no *y* suffix)	νεμῶ	ἔνειμα
μένω	wait	(no *y* suffix)	μενῶ	ἔμεινα
σημαίνω	indicate	(< σημάν–*y* ω)	σημανῶ	ἐσήμηνα
μιαίνω	stain	(< μιάν–*y* ω)	μιανῶ	ἐμίᾱνα
αἰσχύνω	dishonour	(< αἰσχύν–*y* ω)	αἰσχυνῶ	ᾔσχῡνα
αἴρω	lift	(< ἄρ–*y* ω)	ἀρῶ	ἦρα
οἰκτίρω	pity	(< οἰκτίρ–*y* ω)	οἰκτιρῶ	ᾤκτῑρα

For the principal parts of ἐλαύνω *drive* and φέρω *carry*, which are irregular, see **Principal parts of verbs.**

The aorist passive of verbs in –αίνω and –ύνω ends in –άνθην and –ύνθην, e.g. ἐcημάνθην (cημαίνω); ἠcχύνθην (αἰcχῦνω). Likewise, we have ἤρθην from αἴρω, but the other verbs listed above which have an aorist passive are irregular.

11.1/4 Third declension nouns – stems in ευ, αυ, ου

A large number of masculine nouns end in –εύc (always so accented). Most common nouns of this type involve male occupations, e.g. ἱερεύc *priest,* ἱππεύc *horseman.* The names of some Homeric heroes are also of this type, as Ὀδυccεύc, Ἀχιλλεύc. The genitive and dative singular endings are the same as for stems in ι (8.1/4).

The only examples of stems in αυ and ου are those given below:

	βαcιλεύc (m)	ναῦc (f)	γραῦc (f)	βοῦc (m or f)
	king	*ship*	*old woman*	*ox, cow*
SINGULAR				
Nom.	βαcιλεύ–c	ναῦ–c	γραῦ–c	βοῦ–c
Voc.	βαcιλεῦ	ναῦ	γραῦ	βοῦ
Acc.	βαcιλέ–ᾱ	ναῦ–ν	γραῦ–ν	βοῦ–ν
Gen.	βαcιλέ–ωc	νε–ώc	γρᾱ–όc	βο–όc
Dat.	βαcιλεῖ	νη–ΐ	γρᾱ–ΐ	βο–ΐ
PLURAL				
N.V.	βαcιλῆc (or –εῖc)	νῆ–εc	γρᾶ–εc	βόεc
Acc.	βαcιλέ–ᾱc	ναῦc	γραῦc	βοῦc
Gen.	βαcιλέ–ων	νε–ῶν	γρᾱ–ῶν	βο–ῶν
Dat.	βαcιλεῦ–cι(ν)	ναυ–cί(ν)	γραυ–cί(ν)	βου–cί(ν)

Note also Ζεύc *Zeus,* which is irregular: voc. Ζεῦ, acc. Δία, gen. Διόc, dat. Διί (in poetry there is an alternative stem, Ζην–, for the oblique cases, giving Ζῆνα, Ζηνόc, Ζηνί).

11.1/5 Crasis

Crasis (κρᾶcιc *mixing, blending*) is the contraction of a vowel or diphthong at the end of one word with a vowel or diphthong at the beginning of the following word. It is found chiefly in poetry but is not uncommon in the orators. Only a very small number of words occur as the first element of crasis, viz the relevant parts of the definite article, καί and a few others. Examples we have already met are κἄν (= καὶ ἐν 5.2.17) and αὑτός (= ὁ αὐτός), ταὐτοῦ etc. (9.1/3*b*). In all such cases elision (2.1/6*b*), even if theoretically possible, is never used in preference to crasis. The rules for crasis are:

(*a*) The first word loses its accent, if any.

(*b*) A vowel (always long) or diphthong resulting from crasis is marked with ' (technically called **coronis** but identical in form with a smooth breathing), e.g. τοὔνομα (τὸ ὄνομα). When the second word begins with a rough breathing, a consonant preceding it in crasis (always κ or τ) is aspirated, e.g. θοἰμάτιον (τὸ ἱμάτιον). When, however, the first word is simply an aspirated vowel or diphthong (ὁ, οἱ, etc.), the rough breathing is kept in crasis, e.g. οὑν (ὁ ἐν).

(*c*) The rules that apply for internal contraction in verbs (5.1/2) are generally followed, as in the above examples. There are, however, some combinations which do not occur in verbs, as well as some exceptions. We should note:

   (i) When the definite article is combined with a word beginning with α, this α is always kept, e.g. ἅνθρωπος (ὁ ἄνθρωπος), αὑτός (ὁ αὐτός, 9.1/3*b*).

   (ii) The αι of καί is dropped in certain combinations, e.g. κοὐ (καὶ οὐ), χἠ (καὶ ἡ).

11.2 Greek reading

1   ἡ τυραννὶς ἀδικίας μήτηρ ἔφυ.
2   ἀεὶ εὖ πίπτουσιν οἱ Διὸς κύβοι.
3# ἔστι τι κἀν κακοῖσιν ἡδονῆς μέτρον.
4# κοὐκ ἐμὸς ὁ μῦθος, ἀλλ᾽ ἐμῆς μητρὸς πάρα,
    ὡς οὐρανός τε γαῖά τ᾽ ἦν μορφὴ μία·
    ἐπεὶ δ᾽ ἐχωρίσθησαν ἀλλήλων δίχα
    τίκτουσι πάντα κἀνέδωκαν (*sent up*) εἰς φάος
    δένδρη, πετεινά, θῆρας, οὕς θ᾽ ἅλμη τρέφει   5
    γένος τε θνητῶν.
5# κακὸν τὸ κεύθειν κοὐ πρὸς ἀνδρὸς εὐγενοῦς.
6   εἶπέ τις τῷ Σωκράτει, θάνατον σοῦ κατέγνωσαν οἱ Ἀθηναῖοι, ὁ δὲ εἶπεν, κἀκείνων ἡ φύσις (*sc.* θάνατον καταγιγνώσκει).
7   ἅμαξα τὸν βοῦν ἕλκει.

8 **Advanced futility**

(*i*) γραῦς χορεύει. (*ii*) τυφλῷ κάτοπτρον χαρίζῃ. (*iii*) ἄνεμον δικτύῳ θηρᾷς. (*iv*) λίθοις τὸν ἥλιον βάλλεις. (*v*) καλεῖ χελώνη τοὺς βοῦς βραδύποδας. (*vi*) σπόγγῳ πάτταλον κρούεις. (*vii*) πάτταλον ἐξέκρουσας παττάλῳ. (*viii*) τὴν ἀμίδα σανδάλῳ ἐπιφράττεις. (*ix*) οἴνῳ οἶνον ἐξελαύνεις. (*x*) αὐτὸς τὴν σαυτοῦ θύραν κρούεις λίθῳ.

9# πᾶσιν γὰρ ἀνθρώποισιν, οὐχ ἡμῖν μόνον,
ἢ καὶ παραυτίκ' ἢ χρόνῳ δαίμων βίον
ἔσφηλε, κοὐδεὶς διὰ τέλους εὐδαιμονεῖ.

10# Odysseus explains to Neoptolemus that they must obtain the bow of Philoctetes if Troy is to be captured.

τούτων γὰρ οὐδὲν ἀλγυνεῖ μ'· εἰ δ' ἐργάσῃ
μὴ ταῦτα, λύπην πᾶσιν Ἀργείοις βαλεῖς.
εἰ γὰρ τὰ τοῦδε τόξα μὴ ληφθήσεται,
οὐκ ἔστι (= ἔξεστι) πέρσαι σοι τὸ Δαρδάνου πέδον.

11 In 525 BC Egypt was conquered and permanently occupied by the Persians, whose power in the eastern Mediterranean continued to increase until their unsuccessful invasion of Greece (480-479 BC). The subsequent rise of Athens encouraged the Athenians to invade Egypt (c.461 BC), with disastrous results, as Thucydides tells us in the introduction to his history.

οὕτω μὲν τὰ τῶν Ἑλλήνων πράγματα ἐφθάρη· καὶ ὀλίγοι ἀπὸ πολλῶν διὰ τῆς Λιβύης ἐς Κυρήνην ἐπορεύθησαν καὶ ἐσώθησαν, οἱ δὲ πλεῖστοι ἀπέθανον. Αἴγυπτος δὲ πάλιν ὑπὸ βασιλέα ἐγένετο πλὴν Ἀμυρταίου τοῦ ἐν τοῖς ἕλεσι βασιλέως· τοῦτον δὲ διὰ μέγεθός τε τοῦ ἕλους οὐκ ἐδύναντο ἑλεῖν καὶ ἅμα σφόδρα 5 μάχιμοί εἰσιν οἱ ἕλειοι. Ἰνάρως δὲ ὁ Λιβύων βασιλεύς, ὃς τὰ πάντα ἔπραξε περὶ τῆς Αἰγύπτου, προδοσίᾳ ἐλήφθη καὶ ἀνεσταυρώθη. ἐκ δὲ τῶν Ἀθηνῶν καὶ τῆς ἄλλης ξυμμαχίδος πεντήκοντα τριήρεις διάδοχοι ἔπλευσαν ἐς Αἴγυπτον καὶ ἔσχον κατὰ τὸ Μενδήσιον κέρας. ἀλλ' αὐτοῖς ἔκ τε γῆς ἐπέπεσον πεζοὶ 10 καὶ ἐκ θαλάσσης Φοινίκων ναυτικὸν καὶ διέφθειραν τὰς πολλὰς τῶν νεῶν. τὰ οὖν κατὰ τὴν μεγάλην στρατείαν Ἀθηναίων καὶ τῶν ξυμμάχων ἐς Αἴγυπτον οὕτως ἐτελεύτησεν.

12 Euxitheos and Herodes were fellow passengers on a voyage to Thrace. In the process of changing ships at Lesbos, Herodes disappeared and Euxitheos was subsequently charged with his

murder. His speech of defence was written by Antiphon.

ἐπειδὴ δὲ μετεξέβημεν εἰς τὸ ἕτερον πλοῖον, ἐπίνομεν. καὶ
φανερὸν μέν ἐστιν ὅτι ὁ Ἡρώδης ἐξέβη ἐκ τοῦ πλοίου καὶ οὐκ
εἰσέβη πάλιν· ἐγὼ δὲ τὸ παράπαν οὐκ ἐξέβην ἐκ τοῦ πλοίου τῆς
νυκτὸς ἐκείνης. τῇ δὲ ὑστεραίᾳ, ἐπειδὴ ἀφανὴς ἦν ὁ ἀνήρ,
ἐζητεῖτο οὐδέν τι μᾶλλον ὑπὸ τῶν ἄλλων ἢ καὶ ὑπ' ἐμοῦ· καὶ εἴ 5
τῳ τῶν ἄλλων ἐδόκει δεινὸν εἶναι, καὶ ἐμοὶ ὁμοίως. καὶ εἴς τε
τὴν Μυτιλήνην ἐγὼ αἴτιος ἢ πεμφθῆναι ἄγγελον, καὶ ἐπεὶ ἄλλος
οὐδεὶς ἤθελε βαδίζειν, οὔτε τῶν ἀπὸ τοῦ πλοίου οὔτε τῶν αὐτοῦ
τοῦ Ἡρώδου ἑταίρων, ἐγὼ τὸν ἀκόλουθον τὸν ἐμαυτοῦ πέμπειν
ἕτοιμος ἦ. ἐπειδὴ δὲ ὁ ἀνὴρ οὔτε ἐν τῇ Μυτιλήνῃ ἐφαίνετο οὔτ' 10
ἄλλοθι οὐδαμοῦ, πλοῦς τε ἡμῖν ἐγίγνετο, καὶ τἆλλ' ἀνήγετο
πλοῖα ἅπαντα, ᾠχόμην κἀγώ.

Notes

1 ἔφῦ < φύω (11.1/1) the primary meaning of this root aorist is *was
born* but often, as here, it has the present sense *is*.

2 Διός gen. of Ζεύς (11.1/4).

3 τι with μέτρον; κακοῖσιν = κακοῖς (3.1/1 note 1).

4 *l*.1 κοὐκ = καὶ οὐκ (11.1/5); πάρα some disyllabic prepositions can,
in verse, be placed after the noun they govern, cf. δίχα in *l*.3; when
they are normally accented on the final syllable (as with παρά, but
not with δίχα), the accent is then thrown back on to the first
syllable. *l*.2 With a double subject (οὐρανός and γαῖα) the verb
sometimes agrees only with the nearer, hence ἦν; τε ... τ(ε) lit. *both
... and* but simply trans. by *and. l*.4 τίκτουσι vivid present, trans.
brought forth (τίκτω can be used of either parent); κἀνέδωκαν = καὶ
ἀνέδωκαν (ἔδωκαν is the 3rd pl. aor. ind. act. of δίδωμι *give,* 18.1/2
note 3). *l*.5 δένδρη acc. pl. of δένδρον (13.1/1*c*); οὕς an antecedent
meaning *creatures* is to be understood; θ' i.e. τε; after the ε is elided,
τ' becomes θ' because of the rough breathing of ἅλμη.

6 καταγιγνώσκω *condemn* takes the gen. of the person condemned
and the accusative of what he is condemned to (23.1/1*k*(i));
κἀκείνων = καὶ ἐκείνων.

8 (*iv*) λίθοις instrumental dat. (11.1/2); βάλλεις here *pelt.* (*vii*)
ἐξέκρουσας < ἐκκρούω.

9 *l*.1 The datives should be translated by *for. l*.2 καί is here adverbial
and emphasises the following word but need not be translated;

βίον English idiom requires the plural. *l*.3 ἔcφηλε gnomic aorist (see note on 5.2.10); cφάλλω *trip up, cause to fall* (as in wrestling) is here (and often elsewhere) used metaphorically; κούδείc = καὶ ούδείc.

10 The future tense in εἰ clauses (*l*.1 ἐργάcῃ and *l*.3 ληφθήcεται) is to be translated into English by a present; μή (as in *ll*.2 and 3) is the negative used in εἰ clauses (18.1/4) but in *l*.2 it is somewhat unusually placed after the verb it negates (cf. 2.1/6*a*(i)). *l*.3 Translate τὰ τόξα by a singular (the plural is often used for the singular in verse). *l*.4 On ἔcτι = ἔξεcτι see 21.1/4 note 1.

11 Thucydides uses the non-Attic spelling cc for ττ (*l*.11 θαλάccηc), the old Attic form ξύν (ξυμ– etc. in compounds) for the normal cύν (*l*.8 ξυμμαχίδοc, *l*.13 ξυμμάχων), and the old Attic ἐc for εἰc (*ll*.2, 9, 13). *l*.1 ἔφθάρη < φθείρω. *l*.3 ὑπό lit. *under*, i.e. *under the control of*; βαcιλέᾱ at this period the Persian king was a figure of supreme importance and the Greeks referred to him simply as βαcιλεύc. *l*.5 τε ... καί join the two reasons why Amyrtaeus could not be captured and in English we would supply *because* after ἅμα. *ll*.6f. τὰ πάντα see note on 10.2.16(*iv*); ἐλήφθη < λαμβάνω. *ll*.9f. διάδοχοι lit. *[as] relieving*, i.e. *as a relieving force*; ἔcχον *put in*; τὸ Μενδήcιον κέραc the north-east arm of the Nile delta; take αὐτοῖc with ἐπέπεcον (< ἐπιπῑπτω), lit. *fell upon them. ll.*11f. τὰc πολλάc *the majority of, most of*; τὰ ... κατὰ τὴν ... cf. 5.1/3, lit. *the [things] with respect to the ...*

12 *l*.1 Translate μετεξέβημεν (< μετεκβαίνω) by a pluperfect *had transferred* (16.1/2); ἐπῑνομεν *we began to drink* (inceptive imperfect 4.1/1). *l*.3 τὸ παράπαν οὐκ *not ... at all*; the adverb παράπαν is converted by τό to a noun equivalent (4.1/4), which functions here as an accusative of respect (20.1/5), lit. *[with respect to] the altogether. l*.5 οὐδέν τι μᾶλλον ὑπό ... ἢ ... ὑπό, lit. *nothing more by ... than by* (οὐδέν τι *not at all* is also an accusative of respect). *ll*.6ff. τῳ = τινι (indefinite, 10.1/1); the καί of καὶ εἴc τε joins this sentence to the preceding one; τε is to be taken with the καί before ἐπεί (*l*.7) and the two link ἐγὼ αἴτιος ἢ ... with ἐγὼ ... ἕτοιμος ἦ; τε ... καί literally mean *both ... and* but translate here *not only ... but also* to give the necessary emphasis; πεμφθῆναι ἄγγελον accusative and infinitive (8.1/3*a*) after αἴτιος ἦ. *l*.8 οὔτε ... οὔτε continue the preceding negative οὐδείc, lit. *no-one ... neither*

from ... nor of, but in English we would say *either ... or* (the rule given at 7.1/6 does not apply because οὔτε ... οὔτε do not negate the verb of this clause; cf. 10.3 *ll.*6f.). *ll.*10ff. ἐπειδή is followed by three clauses with the second joined to the first by τε (*l.*11) and the third to the second by καί (*l.*11); πλοῦϲ *[the time for] sailing;* ἐγίγνετο, lit. *was coming into being,* i.e *was starting;* τἆλλ᾽ = τὰ ἄλλα; ἀνήγετο impf. of ἀνάγομαι; κἀγώ = καὶ ἐγώ (11.1/5).

12 | UNIT TWELVE

12.1 Grammar

12.1/1 Participles

Participles are those parts of verbs which function as adjectives. They
have tense (*killing* is present, *going to kill* future) and voice (*killing* is
active, *being killed* passive). In Greek there are participles for all three
voices in the present, future, and aorist (and also the perfect, 15.1/1)
and they use the same stem as the corresponding indicatives (but the
augment is dropped in the aorist). For the sake of completeness the
following table includes perfect participles, which can be ignored until
we treat these in 16.1/4.

ACTIVE

Present	m. λΰ–ων (gen. λΰ–οντος), f. λΰ–ουσα, n. λῦ–ον *loosening*
Future	m. λΰc–ων (gen. λΰc–οντος), f. λΰc–ουσα, n. λῦc–ον *going to loosen, about to loosen*
Aorist	m. λΰc–ᾱc (gen. λΰc–αντος), f. λΰc–ᾱcα, n. λῦc–αν *having loosened, after loosening*
Perfect	m. λελυκ–ώc (gen. λελυκ–ότος), f. λελυκ–υῖα, n. λελυκ–όc (*in a state of*) *having loosened*

MIDDLE

Present	λῦ–όμενος, –ομένη, –όμενον *ransoming*
Future	λῦc–όμενος, –ομένη, –όμενον *going to ransom, about to ransom*
Aorist	λῦc–άμενος, –αμένη, –άμενον *having ransomed, after ransoming*
Perfect	λελυ–μένος, –μένη, –μένον (*in a state of*) *having ransomed*

PASSIVE

Present	λῦ–όμενος, –ομένη, –όμενον *being loosened*

Future	λυθης-όμενος, –ομένη, –όμενον *going to be loosened, about to be loosened*
Aorist	m. λυθ–είς (gen. λυθ–έντος), f. λυθεῖcα, n. λυθέν *having been loosened, after being loosened*
Perfect	λελυ–μένος, –μένη, –μένον *(in a state of) having been loosened*

All active participles, together with that of the aorist passive, are declined like first and third declension adjectives (10.1/3). The declension of the aorist active participle is identical with that of πᾶc (10.1/3*b*). The present active and aorist passive are declined as follows:

SINGULAR

	M.	F.	N.	M.	F.	N.
N.V.	λῡ́ων	λῡ́ουcα	λῦον	λυθείc	λυθεῖcα	λυθέν
Acc.	λῡ́οντα	λῡ́ουcαν	λῦον	λυθέντα	λυθεῖcαν	λυθέν
Gen.	λῡ́οντοc	λῡούcηc	λῡ́οντοc	λυθέντοc	λυθείcηc	λυθέντοc
Dat.	λῡ́οντι	λῡούcῃ	λῡ́οντι	λυθέντι	λυθείcῃ	λυθέντι

PLURAL

	M.	F.	N.	M.	F.	N.
N.V.	λῡ́οντεc	λῡ́ουcαι	λῡ́οντα	λυθέντεc	λυθεῖcαι	λυθέντα
Acc.	λῡ́ονταc	λῡούcᾱc	λῡ́οντα	λυθέντας	λυθείcᾱc	λυθέντα
Gen.	λῡόντων	λῡουcῶν	λῡόντων	λυθέντων	λυθειcῶν	λυθέντων
Dat.	λῡ́ουcι(ν)	λῡούcαιc	λῡ́ουcι(ν)	λυθεῖcι(ν)	λυθείcαιc	λυθεῖcι(ν)

The future active participle follows λῡ́ων. All middle participles and that of the future passive follow καλόc (3.1/3). The present (and perfect) participle passive has the same form as the middle.

The meanings given above for the present and aorist participles simply reflect the temporal distinction between their corresponding indicatives: λῡ́ων *loosening*, λῡ́cᾱc *having loosened*. This difference of time occurs in a sentence such as ἐργαζόμενοι μὲν ἠρίcτων, ἐργαcάμενοι δὲ ἐδείπνουν *they used to have breakfast while they were working* (lit. *working*), *but used to dine after they finished work* (lit. *having worked*), but the distinction is sometimes one of aspect (4.1/1), i.e. the present participle conveys the idea of continuation, the aorist of simple occurrence. An aorist participle so used can denote an action which happens **at the same time** as that of the finite verb of its clause (**coincidental** use), e.g. εὖ ἐποίηcαc ἀναμνήcᾱc με *you did well to remind me* (lit. *reminding*, not *having reminded*); ὑπολαβὼν ἔφη *he said in reply* (lit. *replying*, not *having replied*).

Notes

1 The present participle of εἰμί (*I am*) is ὤν, οὖσα, ὄν *being*; gen. s. ὄντος, οὔσης, ὄντος; dat. pl. οὖσι(ν), οὔσαις, οὖσι(ν). Its future participle is ἐσόμενος, –η, –ον (cf. 8.1/1 note 2); it has no others. The idiomatic expression τὸ ὄν (lit. *the [really] existing [thing]*) has the meaning *reality*; τῷ ὄντι is used in the sense *in reality, in truth* (on this use of the dative see 23.1/2*j*).

2 In tenses where they differ from λύω, contracted verbs, verbs with a contracted future, and verbs with stems in λ, μ, ν, ρ form their participles according to the rules already given for those tenses, e.g. the future active and aorist active participles of στέλλω are στελῶν (<ἐ + ων), στελοῦσα (< ἐ + ουσα), στελοῦν (< ἐ + ον) and στείλ–ᾱς, –ᾱσα, –αν.

3 Strong aorists take the participial endings of the present (cf. 7.1/1), e.g. active λαβών, –οῦσα, –όν;[1] middle λαβόμενος (< λαμβάνω).

4 The participles of root aorists are similar to those of the weak aorist active or the aorist passive, as the following examples show:
   (*i*) ἔγνων (γιγνώσκω): m. γνούς (gen. γνόντος), f. γνοῦσα, n. γνόν.
   (*ii*) ἔφῡν (φύω): m. φῡς (gen. φύντος), f. φῦσα, n. φύν.
   (*iii*) –ἐδρᾱν (–διδράσκω, which occurs only in compounds): m. –δρᾱς (gen. –δράντος), f. –δρᾶσα, n. –δράν.
   (*iv*) ἐπνίγην (πνῑγω): m. πνιγείς (gen. πνιγέντος), f. πνιγεῖσα, n. πνιγέν.
   (*v*) ἔβην (βαίνω) follows –ἐδρᾱν: m. βᾱς (gen. βάντος), f. βᾶσα, n. βάν (cf. ἔστην 19.1/1).

12.1/2 Uses of participles

(*a*) A participle in Greek can often be rendered by the same in English, but Greek regularly uses a participle and finite verb where English would more naturally have two verbs joined by *and*: τοῦτο ποιήσᾱς ἀπῆλθεν *he did this and went away* (lit. *having done this he went away*). In many other cases a subordinate clause should be used to translate a participle. The negative, when required, varies as indicated. When used within a clause participles are used to express:

(i) The **temporal relation** between two actions (negated by οὐ)

---

[1] Unlike the present active participle, the strong aorist active participle is always accented on the first syllable of its ending, hence λαμβάνων (pres.) but λαβών (aor.).

ἀφικόμενοι εἰς τὰς ᾿Αθήνᾱς   *When they arrived* (lit. *having*
ἔλεξαν τάδε.   *arrived*) *at Athens, they spoke*
                               as follows.

Sometimes the temporal relation is made more precise by
qualifying the participle with adverbs such ἅμα *together with*,
εὐθύς *immediately*, μεταξύ *in the middle of*:

μεταξὺ θύων ληκύθιον   *Did he lose his little oil-flask*
ἀπώλεσεν;   *while* (lit. *in the middle of*)
                               sacrificing? (on ἀπώλεσεν see
                               20.1/1 note 2).

ἅμα φεύγοντες τοὺς   *While* (lit. *together with, at the*
῞Ελληνας ἐτίτρωσκον.   *same time as*) *fleeing they kept*
                               wounding the Greeks.

ἄγων *leading*, ἔχων *having*, φέρων *carrying* are often to be
translated simply by *with*: ἦλθεν ἔχων ξίφος *he came with a sword*
(lit. *having a sword*).

(ii) **Cause** (negated by οὐ)
A participle used in this sense is often preceded by ἅτε *because* for
a reason the writer or speaker sees as valid, or by ὡς *as* for a
reason he does not vouch for. ὡς (which has many other uses –
22.1/1) here, and elsewhere, marks what follows as the subjective
opinion of the person described and must often by translated by
thinking that, on the grounds that. ἅτε is used only with phrases
(with or without a participle):

ὁ Κῦρος, ἅτε τὸν χρῡσὸν   *Cyrus hired mercenaries because*
ἔχων πάντα, ἐπικούρους   *he had all the gold.*
ἐμισθώσατο.

ὁ βασιλεὺς τοὺς Πέρσᾱς   *The king imprisoned the Persians*
εἶρξεν ὡς κατασκόπους   *on the ground that they were*
ὄντας.   *spies.*

οὐχ ἡγεμόνας ἔχων πλανᾷ   *Because you have no guides you*
ἀνὰ τὰ ὄρη.   *are wandering over the*
                               mountains.

(iii) **Concession** (negated by οὐ)
The participle is often preceded by καίπερ *although*, which, like
ἅτε, is used only with phrases:

ταῦτα φέρειν ἀνάγκη   *It is necessary* (lit. *[there is]*
καίπερ ὄντα δύσφορα.   *necessity) to endure these things*
                                 although they are (lit. *although*
                                 being) hard to bear.
δόξω γυναῖκα, καίπερ οὐκ   *I shall seem to have [my] wife,*
ἔχων, ἔχειν.   *although I do not have [her]*
                                 (lit. *although not having*).

καί and καὶ ταῦτα (*and that [too]*) are used as equivalents of
καίπερ:

ἐν τῇ Ἰλιάδι οἱ ἥρωες ἰχθῦς   *In the Iliad the heroes do not eat*
οὐκ ἐσθίουσι καὶ ταῦτα   *fish although they are* (lit. *and*
ἐπὶ τῇ θαλάττῃ ὄντες.   *that being) by the sea.*

(iv) **Condition** (negated by **μή**, as in conditional clauses, 18.1/5)
No introductory word is required: ἁμαρτήσῃ μὴ δρᾱσᾱς τάδε *you
will make a mistake if you do not do this* (lit. *not having done these
things*).

(v) **Purpose** (negated by **οὐ**)
With verbs of motion a future participle can be used by itself:
ἥκομεν τοὺς σοὺς ἄθλους, Προμηθεῦ, ὀψόμενοι (< ὁράω) *we have
come to see your ordeals, Prometheus.* Elsewhere the future
participle is preceded by ὡς (cf. (ii) above; in both cases ὡς
presents the attitude of the subject of the participle): συλλαμβάνει
Κῦρον ὡς ἀποκτενῶν *he seizes Cyrus in order to kill [him].* In these
examples English uses an infinitive phrase to express purpose (for
clauses expressing purpose see 14.1/4c(i)).

(vi) **Noun equivalent**
If preceded by the definite article, adjectives may function as
nouns, as ὁ κακός *the evil man* (5.1/3). Since participles are
adjectives, they can be treated in the same way. οἱ μανθάνοντες
literally means *the learning [ones]* and, depending on the context,
could be translated *those who are learning* or (*the*) *learners* (in
English the article is dropped if a general class is meant – 2.1/2
note 1):

ὡς ἡδὺ λεύσσειν τὸ φῶς τοῖς   *How sweet [it is] both for those*
τε καλῶς πράττουσι καὶ   *who are faring well and for*
τοῖς δυστυχοῦσιν.   *those who are unfortunate to*
                                  look upon the light (i.e. *be alive*).

This use is negated by μή if a general class meant, but by οὐ if the reference is to a specific person or group:

οἱ μὴ εὐτυχοῦντες   lit. *the [class of] people who are not fortunate*, i.e. *the unfortunate*;

οἱ οὐκ εὐτυχοῦντες   *those [particular] people who are not fortunate.*

(*b*) Genitive absolute

This construction (*absolute* here means *independent*), in its simplest form, involves a noun or pronoun and a participle which are both in the genitive case and which stand apart from (i.e. are **grammatically** independent of) the rest of the sentence; there is, of course, a connection in **sense** as otherwise there would be no point in putting the two together. We have an absolute construction (the nominative absolute) in English. Although it is a little clumsy, we can say *the Persians having sailed away, Miltiades returned to Athens.* In Greek this becomes τῶν Περςῶν ἀποπλευςάντων, ὁ Μιλτιάδης ἐπανῆλθεν εἰς τὰς ᾿Αθήνᾱς. The genitive absolute is employed in uses (i) - (iv) as detailed above and can be accompanied by ἅτε, ὡς, καίπερ when appropriate. It is negated by οὐ except when it expresses a condition (above (iv)).

ταῦτ᾽ ἐπρᾱ́χθη Κόνωνος ϲτρατηγοῦντος.	*These things were done when Conon was general* (lit. *Conon being general*) **(temporal relation).**
ἅτε πυκνοῦ ὄντος τοῦ ἄλϲουϲ οὐκ εἶδον οἱ ἐντὸς τοὺς ἐκτόϲ.	*Because the grove was thick those inside did not see those outside* (lit. *inasmuch as the grove being thick*) **(cause).**
ἀποπλεῖ οἴκαδε καίπερ μέϲου χειμῶνος ὄντος.	*He sails home although it is midwinter* (lit. *although [it] being midwinter*) **(concession).**
ἀνέβη ἐπὶ τὰ ὄρη τῶν πολεμίων οὐ κωλυόντων.	*He went up on to the mountains as the enemy did not prevent [him]* (lit. *the enemy not preventing*) **(cause, hence οὐ).**

ὡς ἡδὺ τὸ ζῆν μὴ φθονούσης   *How sweet [is] life if fortune is*
τῆς τύχης.   *not jealous* (lit. *fortune not*
    being jealous) (**condition**,
    hence μή).

12.2 Greek reading

1# ἀνὴρ ὁ φεύγων καὶ πάλιν μαχήσεται.
2 ἄρκτου παρούσης οὐ δεῖ ἴχνη ζητεῖν.
3# λίαν φιλῶν σεαυτὸν οὐχ ἕξεις φίλον.
4 ἑαυτὸν οὐ τρέφων κύνας τρέφει.
5# ὁ μὴ γαμῶν ἄνθρωπος οὐκ ἔχει κακά.
6 καπνὸν φεύγων εἰς τὸ πῦρ ἐνέπεσες.
7 ἀνὴρ φεύγων οὐ μένει λύρας κτύπον.
8 οἱ κύνες ἅπαξ δὴ καυθέντες λέγονται φοβεῖσθαι τὸ πῦρ.
9# θάψων γὰρ ἥκω Καίσαρ᾽, οὐκ ἐπαινέσων.
10 οὐδεὶς πεινῶν καλὰ ᾄδει.
11 ἄγροικός εἰμι τὴν σκάφην σκάφην λέγων;
12 ὁ δηχθεὶς ὑπὸ ὄφεως καὶ σχοινίον φοβεῖται.
13# ὁ γραμμάτων ἄπειρος οὐ βλέπει βλέπων.
14 χαλεπόν ἐστι πρὸς γαστέρα λέγειν ὦτα οὐκ ἔχουσαν.
15# ΠΡΟΜΗΘΕΥΣ
    δέρκῃ θέαμα, τόνδε τὸν Διὸς φίλον,
    οἵαις ὑπ᾽ αὐτοῦ πημοναῖσι κάμπτομαι.
    ΩΚΕΑΝΟΣ
    ὁρῶ, Προμηθεῦ, καὶ παραινέσαι γέ σοι
    θέλω τὰ λῷστα καίπερ ὄντι ποικίλῳ.
16 ὁ Κῦρος ἐντεῦθεν ἐξελαύνει διὰ τῆς Λυκαονίας σταθμοὺς πέντε,
    παρασάγγας τριάκοντα, ταύτην δὲ τὴν χώραν ἐπέτρεψε
    διαρπάσαι τοῖς Ἕλλησιν ὡς πολεμίαν οὖσαν.
17# Ἡσιόδου ποτὲ βίβλον ἐμαῖς ὑπὸ χερσὶν ἑλίσσων
    Πύρρην ἐξαπίνης εἶδον ἐπερχομένην·
    βίβλον δὲ ῥίψας ἐπὶ γῆν χερί, τοῦτ᾽ ἐβόησα·
    ἔργα τί μοι παρέχεις, ὦ γέρον Ἡσίοδε;
18# In this fragment from a lost play of Euripides the leader of a
    band of mystics greets Minos, the king of Cnossus in Crete,
    whose wife, Pasiphae, after an unfortunate experience with a
    bull, will give birth to the Minotaur.

Φοινικογενοῦς τέκνον Εὐρώπης
καὶ τοῦ μεγάλου Ζηνός, ἀνάccων
Κρήτης ἑκατομπτολιέθρου,
ἥκω ζαθέουc ναοὺc προλιπών...
ἁγνὸν δὲ βίον τείνομεν ἐξ οὗ   5
Διὸc Ἰδαίου μύcτηc γενόμην (= ἔγεν–),
καὶ νυκτιπόλου Ζαγρέωc βούτηc
τὰc ὠμοφάγουc δαῖταc τελέcαc
μητρί τ᾽ ὀρείᾳ δᾷδαc ἀναcχὼν
μετὰ Κουρήτων,   10
βάκχοc ἐκλήθην ὁcιωθείc.

Notes

2   ἄρκτου παρούcηc gen. absolute (12.1/2*b*).
3   φιλῶν < φιλέων (pres. pple. m. nom. s. of φιλέω).
5   μή because a general class is meant (12.1/2*a*(vi)).
6   ἐνέπεcεc < ἐμπίπτω.
8   δή emphasises ἅπαξ.
9   A translation of a line of Shakespeare, not a piece of original
     Greek; θάψων, ἐπαινέcων 12.1/2*a*(v).
10   καλά (n. pl.) trans. by an adverb.
13   βλέπων is used here concessively, *[though] seeing.*
14   ὦτα < οὖc
15   *l.*1 τόνδε τὸν Διὸc φίλον *this friend of Zeus* (i.e me, Prometheus)
     is in appositon to θέᾱμα (lit. *spectacle*). *l.*2 οἵαιc (with πημοναῖc)
     lit. *with what sort of* dat. of instrument (11.1/2). *l.*3 παραινέω
     takes the dative (13.1/2*b*(i)); γε (lit. *at any rate* (13.1/3*b*) need not
     be translated.
16   ἐξελαύνει vivid present (see note on 7.2.13*l.*8); on the relation
     between cταθμούc and παραcάγγαc see note on 7.2.9.
17   Hesiod, an early poet, wrote the Ἔργα καὶ Ἡμέραι (traditionally
     translated *Works and Days* but the real meaning is *Fields and
     Days [for ploughing them]*), which is the book referred to here. *l.*1
     Books in antiquity were written on papyrus rolls and the reader
     kept his hands on top of a roll to manipulate it (hence ἐμαῖc ὑπὸ
     χερcίν *under my hands*). *l.*2 ἐπερχομένην *coming* (for this use of a
     participle see 15.1/2). *l.*4 ἔργα here *troubles,* but trans. by a
     singular – the author is punning on the title of the book he is
     reading (and wilfully misinterpreting the sense of ἔργα).

18 Europa, the daughter of Agenor, king of Tyre in Phoenicia (hence Φοινικογενής) was carried off by Zeus to Crete after the latter had taken the form of a bull (not related to the bull loved by Pasiphae); she subsequently gave birth to Minos. *ll.* 1f. τέκνον vocative – with it we must take ἀνάccων; the m. pple. (ἀνάccων) is used because τέκνον, although neuter, refers to a male being, viz Minos – slight violations of strict grammatical agreement on this pattern are not rare (agreement according to the sense); Ζηνός see 11.1/4; ἀνάccω *be king of, rule over* takes the genitive (13.1/2*a*(i)). *l.* 4 προλιπών < προλείπω. *l.* 5 τείνομεν lit. *we lead* but as ἐξ οὗ (*from what [time]*, i.e. *since*) follows, English idiom requires *have led*. *l.* 6 Διός see 11.1/4. *l.* 7 νυκτιπόλου Ζαγρέωc βούτηc *[as] a herdsman of night-roaming Zagreus*. *l.* 8 ὠμοφάγουc δαῖταc *meals of raw flesh* were a regular feature of Dionysiac orgies (the beast was torn apart by the participants). *l.* 9 μητρὶ ὀρείᾳ, i.e. Cybele, another divinity worshipped with nightly orgies. *l.* 11 ἐκλήθην < καλέω.

12.3 Extra reading

Epigrams

For the Greeks an epigram was a short poem of two to twelve lines (we have already met examples at 9.2.3 and 12.2.17). The genre formed a sub-division of elegiac poetry because it was written in the elegiac metre (see **Appendix 9**; particular metres had, from an early stage in Greek literature, become the hallmarks of most poetical genres). Authors of epigrams used, although not very consistently, forms of words from Ionic and Homeric Greek (examples in 1, 3, 4, 8, 9). There was virtually no restriction on subject matter.

1# χρυcὸν ἀνὴρ εὑρὼν ἔλιπεν βρόχον· αὐτὰρ ὁ χρυcὸν
    ὃν λίπεν οὐχ εὑρὼν ἦψεν ὃν εὗρε βρόχον.
2# ἡ Κύπρις τὴν Κύπριν ἐνὶ Κνίδῳ εἶπεν ἰδοῦcα,
    φεῦ, φεῦ, ποῦ γυμνὴν εἶδέ με Πραξιτέληc;
3# πάντεc μὲν Κίλικεc κακοὶ ἀνέρεc· ἐν δὲ Κίλιξιν
    εἷc ἀγαθὸc Κινύρηc, καὶ Κινύρηc δὲ Κίλιξ.
4# εἴcιδεν Ἀντίοχοc τὴν Λυcιμάχου ποτὲ τύλην
    κοὐκέτι τὴν τύλην εἴcιδε Λυcίμαχοc.

5# εἴκοσι γεννήσας ὁ ζωγράφος Εὔτυχος υἱοὺς
     οὐδ' ἀπὸ τῶν τέκνων οὐδὲν ὅμοιον ἔχει.
6# ἡ τὰ ῥόδα, ῥοδόεσσαν ἔχεις χάριν· ἀλλὰ τί πωλεῖς,
     σαυτήν, ἢ τὰ ῥόδα, ἠὲ συναμφότερα;
7# τὴν ψυχήν, 'Αγάθωνα φιλῶν, ἐπὶ χείλεσιν ἔσχον·
     ἦλθε γὰρ ἡ τλήμων ὡς διαβησομένη.
8# ἡ σοβαρὸν γελάσασα καθ' Ἑλλάδος, ἡ τὸν ἐραστῶν
     ἑσμὸν ἐπὶ προθύροις Λαῒς ἔχουσα νέων,
     τῇ Παφίῃ τὸ κάτοπτρον· ἐπεὶ τοίη μὲν ὁρᾶσθαι
     οὐκ ἐθέλω, οἵη δ' ἦν πάρος οὐ δύναμαι.
9# *They told me, Heraclitus, they told me you were dead* ...
     εἶπέ τις, Ἡράκλειτε, τεὸν μόρον, ἐς δέ με δάκρυ
     ἤγαγεν, ἐμνήσθην δ' ὁσσάκις ἀμφότεροι
     ἥλιον ἐν λέσχῃ κατεδύσαμεν· ἀλλὰ σὺ μέν που,
     ξεῖν' 'Αλικαρνησεῦ, τετράπαλαι σποδιή·
     αἱ δὲ τεαὶ ζώουσιν ἀηδόνες, ἧσιν ὁ πάντων   5
     ἁρπακτὴς 'Αίδης οὐκ ἐπὶ χεῖρα βαλεῖ.

Notes

1 λίπεν = ἔλιπεν (aorist of λείπω) in Homer the augment is optional
   in the imperfect and aorist, and unaugmented forms of these
   tenses are often found in literary genres which use features of
   Homeric language, cf. below 4.
2 Κύπρις another name for Aphrodite because of her association
   with Cyprus (Κύπρος).
3 ἀνέρες (Homeric) = ἄνδρες.
4 εἴσιδεν = εἰσεῖδεν (< εἰσοράω) the augment is dropped as in λίπεν
   (above 1); κοὐκέτι = καὶ οὐκέτι (11.1/5).
5 Eutychus apparently was a bad painter with an unfaithful wife;
   οὐδ'(ὲ) *not even,* but trans. *even* (cf. 11.2.12 *l.*8).
6 ἡ τὰ ῥόδα (*sc.* ἔχουσα) *[you] the [woman having,* i.e. *with*
   (12.1/2a(i))*] the roses* a concise form of address towards someone
   whose name the speaker does not know.
7 *l.*1 φιλῶν *kissing* (despite some restrictions, male homosexuality
   was common in Greek society, cf. 7.2.13). *l.*2 As the future
   participle is used by itself to express purpose (12.1/2a(v)) ὡς
   διαβησομένη means *thinking that it was going to cross over* (i.e. *with
   the idea of...* cf. 12.1/2a(ii)).

8   Lais (4th century BC), a beautiful courtesan now past her prime, dedicates her mirror to Aphrodite because she has no further use for it. The epigram consists of a single sentence and a main verb meaning *I dedicate* is to be supplied (the first two lines are in apposition to *I*, i.e. *I, the one who...*). *l.*1 coβαρόν the n. acc. s. of the adjective is used adverbially, trans. *haughtily*; καθ', i.e. κατά with elision and aspiration before the following initial aspirate; καθ' Ἑλλάδoc lit. (*laughing*) *against Greece*, i.e. *at Greece*. *l.*2 Trans. προθύροιc as singular (the plural is often used for the singular in verse); take νέων (< νέοc) with ἐραcτῶν in the previous line. *l.*3 τῇ Παφίῃ i.e. to Aphrodite, whose temple at Paphos in Cyprus was famous; τοίη (= Attic τοιαύτη (21.1/3)) *of such a sort [as I am now]*, translate simply by *as I am now*; ὁρᾶcθαι middle voice *see myself* (8.1/1a). *l.*4 οἵη (= Attic οἵα) ... ἦν πάροc lit. *of what sort I was before*, trans. *as I was before*; with δύναμαι (on deponents in –αμαι see 19.1/3b) supply ὁρᾶcθαι from the previous line.

9   An epigram of Callimachus (3rd century BC), well known in its English translation (see **Appendix 9**). The person addressed is not the philosopher Heraclitus. *l.*1 τεόc is the Homeric form of cóc (cf. τεαί in *l.*5). *l.*2 ἐμνήcθην (aor. of μέμνημαι 19.1/3b) *I remembered*. *l.*3 *We sank the sun in conversation*, i.e. *we talked into the night*. *l.*5 ζώουcιν Homeric for ζῶcιν (< ζάω); Heraclitus' nightingales were his poems, which, ironically, have not survived; ᾗcιν = αἷcιν (i.e. αἷc) – the dat. is governed by ἐπὶ ... βαλεῖ, *on to which*. *l.*6 ἐπὶ χεῖρα βαλεῖ = χεῖρα ἐπιβαλεῖ; in Homer when the first element of a compound verb (as ἐπιβάλλω) is a prepositional prefix (here ἐπί), it can be separated from the verbal element (here βάλλω) by one or more words (**tmesis** lit. *a cutting*).

13 | UNIT THIRTEEN

13.1 Grammar

13.1/1 Oddities of declension

As we have now covered all regular nouns and adjectives, a few remaining oddities can be conveniently listed here. Only a very small number of nouns exist in each group.

(*a*) *Attic declension*

This subdivision of the second declension contains nouns which in Attic (and sometimes Ionic) end in –ωc, but which in other dialects preserve the original –oc. Hence Homeric νᾱόc (m) *temple* became first νηόc (in Attic ᾱ >η except after a vowel or ρ) and then νεώc (cf. the gen. s. of πόλιc, 8.1/4). νεώc is declined:

	SINGULAR	PLURAL
N.V.	νεώc	νεῴ
Acc.	νεών	νεώc
Gen.	νεώ	νεών
Dat.	νεῴ	νεῴc

Other nouns of this class are λεώc (m; Homeric λᾱόc) *people,* Μενέλεωc (Homeric Μενέλᾱοc) *Menelaus,* λαγώc (m) *hare,* ἕωc (f) *dawn* (singular only; the accusative is ἕω). The adjective ἵλεωc *propitious* also belongs here (m.f. ἵλεωc, n. ἵλεων; n. pl. ἵλεα). The masculine and neuter of πλέωc *full* follow ἵλεωc but its feminine, πλέᾱ, follows δικαίᾱ (3.1/3).

(*b*) *Third declension nouns in –ωc, –ω, and –αc*

 (i) ἥρωc (m) *hero* is declined:

	SINGULAR	PLURAL
N. V.	ἥρως	ἥρω–ες
Acc.	ἥρω–α or ἥρω	ἥρω–ας
Gen.	ἥρω–ος	ἡρώ–ων
Dat.	ἥρω–ι or ἥρῳ	ἥρω–cι(ν)

Similarly declined are δμώς (m) *slave* and Τρῶες (m. pl.) *Trojans.* αἰδώς (f) *shame* is irregular: *n. v.* αἰδώς; *acc.* αἰδῶ; *gen.* αἰδοῦς; *dat.* αἰδοῖ (no plural).

(ii) πειθώ (f) *persuasion* has affinities with αἰδώς and is declined: *n.* πειθώ; *v.* πειθοῖ; *acc.* πειθώ; *gen.* πειθοῦς; *dat.* πειθοῖ (no plural). So also ἠχώ (f) *echo* and women's names such as Cαπφώ and Καλυψώ.

(iii) In addition to neuter dental stems with a nominative in –ας (as κέρας *horn, gen.* κέρατος, 5.1/1*a*), there are a few neuter nouns in –ας whose declension is parallel to neuters in –ος (6.1/1*c*, i.e. contraction has taken place after the loss of intervocalic sigma). γέρας (n) *prize* is declined:

	SINGULAR		PLURAL	
N. V.	γέρας		γέρᾱ	(<α(c)–α)
Acc.	γέρας		γέρᾱ	
Gen.	γέρως	(<α(c)–ος)	γερῶν	(<ά(c)–ων)
Dat.	γέραι	(<α(c)–ι)	γέρασι(ν)	(< α(c)–cι)

Similarly declined are γῆρας *old age,* κρέας *meat,* and also κέρας when it means *wing of an army* (cf. 5.1/1*a*).

(c) Nouns declined in two ways

In English *brothers* and *brethren* are both plural forms of *brother,* even though we attach a broader meaning to the second. In Greek, anomalies of this sort sometimes reflect dialectal differences (as, e.g., between Homeric and Attic Greek), but some examples exist entirely within Attic. These may involve alternative forms (as in υἱός), or an apparent irregularity (as in δένδρον). The main examples are:

δάκρυον, –ου (n) *tear;* alternative n.v.a. in the singular: δάκρυ (as in 12.3.9 *l.*1).

δένδρον, –ου (n) *tree* has an irregular dat. pl. δένδρεσι(ν). δένδρε(α) in 13.2.22 *l.*2 is the Homeric and old Ionic form of the n.v.a. plural, which can be contracted to δένδρη (11.2.4 *l.*5).

πῦρ, πυρός (n) *fire* (6.1/1*b*); the plural πυρά is second declension (πυρῶν, πυροῖς) and means *watch-fires.*

cῖτoc, –ου (m) *grain* (i.e. wheat or barley); the plural is neuter: cῖτα.

υἱóc, –οῦ (m) *son* can be declined in the second declension throughout but also has the following third declension forms from an original nom. s. υἱύc (declined like ἡδύc – 10.1/3): gen. s. υἱέοc; dat. s. υἱεῖ; nom. and acc. pl. υἱεῖc; gen. pl. υἱέων; dat. pl. υἱέcι(ν).

13.1/2 Verbs used with the genitive or dative

A transitive verb is defined as one that can be followed by the accusative case. Both the Greek πέμπω and the English *send* are transitive, and in the sentences Περικλῆc δῶρον ἔπεμψεν and *Pericles sent a gift* both δῶρον and *gift* are direct objects and therefore accusative. We might at first assume that if a verb is transitive in English its Greek equivalent will be the same. However, although this is true for the greater number of verbs, there are some which are transitive in one language but intransitive in the other.

The verb δειπνέω (*dine*) is transitive in Greek and so we can say ἄρτον δειπνῶ *I am dining [on] bread*, but we cannot say in English *I dine bread* because *dine* is an intransitive verb and must be followed by a preposition, not a direct object (in *I am dining on bread, bread* is accusative after the preposition *on*). Similarly, there are verbs which are transitive in English but not in Greek, but, whereas in English the logical object of an intransitive verb is preceded by a preposition (*dine on bread*), in Greek it is put into the genitive or dative. Greek verbs of this type can, to a large extent, be classified according to their meaning. The following are the main groups:

(*a*) *Verbs followed by the genitive* (see also 23.1/1*k*)

 (i) Verbs of **ruling**, e.g. ἄρχω *rule*; κρατέω lit. *have power* (κράτοc) *over*; βαcιλεύω lit. *be king* (βαcιλεύc) *of* (all three are normally translated by *rule*):

ἐν ἀμφιάλῳ Ἰθάκῃ βαcιλεύcει Ἀχαιῶν.	*He will rule the Achaeans in sea-girt Ithaca.*

 (ii) Verbs of **desiring, needing, caring for**, e.g. ἐπιθυμέω *desire*; ἐράω *love, desire* (sexually); δέομαι *need*; ἐπιμελέομαι *care for*:

οὐκ ἐρᾷ ἀδελφὸς ἀδελφῆς   *A brother does not desire his*
οὐδὲ πατὴρ θυγατρός.   *sister, nor a father his*
                              daughter.

(iii) Verbs of **perceiving, remembering, forgetting,** e.g. αἰcθάνομαι
      perceive (also + acc.); πυνθάνομαι *ascertain* (+ acc. of thing
      ascertained and gen. of informant); ἀκούω *hear, listen to* (+
      acc. of thing heard, gen. of person heard); μέμνημαι (19.1/3*a*)
      remember; ἐπιλανθάνομαι *forget* (also + acc.):

      ταῦτα Κίρκης ἤκουσα   *I heard this from Circe* (but
                               Κίρκης ἤκουσα *I heard* (or
                               listened to) *Circe*).

(iv) Verbs of **reaching, obtaining, missing,** e.g. τυγχάνω *hit the*
      mark, succeed, obtain; ἁμαρτάνω *miss, fail to achieve*:

      τίνος πότμου ἔτυχεν;   *What fate did he meet* (lit.
                               obtain)?

      τῶν ἐλπίδων ἡμάρτομεν   *We did not realize* (lit. *missed*)
                               our hopes.

(v) Verbs of **sharing,** e.g. μετέχω *share, have a share in*:

      πάντες οἱ πολῖται   *All the citizens take part in*
      μετέχουcι τῆς ἑορτῆς   (lit. *share*) *the festival.*

(*b*) *Verbs followed by the dative*

(i) Verbs indicating that **the subject is asserting himself in some**
     way over someone else, e.g. παραινέω *advise*; βοηθέω (*run to*)
     help, assist; ὀργίζομαι *become angry with*; ἀπειλέω *threaten*;
     φθονέω *feel ill-will against, grudge*:

     φθονεῖν φαcι μητρυιᾶc   *They say that step-mothers feel*
     τέκνοιc.   *ill-will against their children.*

(ii) Verbs indicating that **the subject is submitting himself in some**
     way to somebody else, e.g. πείθομαι (middle of πείθω) *obey*;
     πιcτεύω *trust*; εἴκω *yield*:

     πατρὶ πείθεcθαι χρὴ τέκνα. *Children must obey their father.*

(iii) Verbs indicating **association of some sort,** e.g. ἕπομαι *follow*;
      ἐντυγχάνω *fall in with*; ἀπαντάω *meet*; πλησιάζω *approach,*
      associate with; μάχομαι *fight*; χράομαι *associate with* (people),
      use (things):

οὐδεὶς ἔτι ἡμῖν μάχεται.   *No-one is fighting us any longer.*
τῷ δεσπότῃ ἑσπόμην   *I followed my master.*
  (< ἕπομαι)

(iv) Verbs indicating **likeness**, e.g. ὁμοιόομαι, ἔοικα (19.1/3*a*) both
be like, resemble: οὐ χρή σε ὁμοιοῦσθαι κακοῖς *you should not
be like bad men.*

Not all verbs which, by virtue of their meaning, we would expect to
belong to these groups do in fact take the genitive or dative, e.g. φιλέω
love and ὠφελέω *help* both take the accusative (we would have expected
the genitive and dative respectively). Some of the verbs listed above
(e.g. ἐπιλανθάνομαι) also take the accusative with no difference in
meaning. Full details will be found in the vocabulary.

13.1/3 Further particles

The fundamental importance of particles (see 4.1/3) should now be
clear. Their use, especially as connectives, has been widely illustrated
in the reading exercises, and we have now met ἀλλά *but*; ἄρα* *then, so*;
γάρ* *for, as*; δέ* *and, but*; δήπου* *I presume, I should hope, doubtless*;
καί *and, even*; οὐδέ *and not, nor, not even*; οὖν* *therefore, so, then*; τοι*
in truth, be assured, you know; and που* *perhaps, I suppose*; as well as
the combinations μέν*... δέ* *on the one hand ... and/ but on the other
hand*, τε*... καί and καὶ... καί *both ... and*, and καὶ δή* *and moreover*.
Some other particles of common occurrence are listed below:

(*a*) Particles with a **connective** function

δῆτα*: (i) in answers, particularly emphatic negative answers, οὐ δῆτα
         no indeed.
         (ii) in questions, πῶς δῆτα; *how then?*, τί δῆτα; *what* (or *why*)
         then?, e.g. τί δῆτά με ζῆν δεῖ; *why then* (or *in that case*) *should
         I live ?*

μήν* may be used (like δῆτα) to enliven a question, often in
combination with ἀλλά, e.g. ἀλλὰ τί μὴν δοκεῖς; *but* (or *well*) *what then
do you think?* By itself, τί μήν; has the meaning *of course*:

A. μισθωτῷ μᾶλλον   A. *Do they entrust the horses to*
   ἐπιτρέπουσιν ἢ σοὶ τοὺς   *a hireling rather than to you ?*
   ἵππους;

B. ἀλλὰ τί μήν;   B. *But of course* (lit. *But what
                               then* sc.*if not that?*).

τοίνυν*: the temporal adverb νῦν (so accented) means *now, at present*. Unaccented νυν* is an inferential particle, *now* in the sense *then, therefore*, especially with imperatives (17.1/1): cπεῦδέ νυν *hurry up then*. τοίνυν, a strengthened form of νυν, likewise has a transitional or inferential force, *now then, furthermore, well now*, e.g. ἐπειδὴ τοίνυν ἐποιήcατο τὴν εἰρήνην ἡ πόλιc ... *well now, since the city made peace* ...

(*b*) Particles which do not connect but convey **shades of tone, colour or emphasis**

γε* is an intensive and restrictive particle which affects the preceding word. Its literal meaning is *at least, at any rate, certainly, indeed*, e.g. ἔγωγε[1] *I for my part* (examples have already occurred at 9.2.12 *l.*9 and 10.3 *l.*5), but in English we would often simply use an emphatic tone of voice rather than an equivalent word, e.g. οἵδε κρινοῦcί γε εἰ χρή cε μίμνειν *they shall **judge** if you are to remain*; cυγχωρεῖc τοῦτό γε καὶ cύ *even you admit **this***. It is also extremely common in replies to previous remarks, especially to questions, and is often to be rendered as *yes*:

A. ἆρα cτενάζει;   A. *Is he groaning?*
B. κλαίει γε.   B. *Yes, he is weeping.*

A. κενὸν τόδ᾽ ἄγγοc ἢ cτέγει τι;   A. *[Is] this vessel empty, or does it hold something?*
B. cά γ᾽ ἔνδυτα.   B. *Yes, your garments.*

Sometimes it re-enforces a negative and must be translated by *no*:

A. ἔcτι τιc λόγοc;   A. *Is there some explanation?*
B. οὐδείc γε.   B. *No, none.*

(On ways of saying *yes* and *no* in Greek see 24.1/1).

δή* emphasises the preceding word. *Indeed, certainly* are only approximate translations; the force of the particle would normally be conveyed to the hearer in English by the loudness of the voice or some accompanying emphatic gesture. δή is particularly common with adjectives or adverbs, e.g. ἅπαντεc δή *absolutely everyone*; μόνοc δή *quite alone*; πολλάκιc δή *very often*. It may also convey irony or sarcasm, Cωκράτηc ὁ coφὸc δή *Socrates the **wise*** (the tone of voice in English will indicate whether *wise* is complimentary or ironical).

---

[1] ἐγώ and γε are combined to form one word (with a different accent). Cf. below μέντοι (μέν + τοι), καίτοι (καί + τοι).

(c) Frequent combinations of particles

καὶ δή*: as well as being used as a lively connective, *and moreover* (e.g. καὶ δὴ τὸ μέγιστον *and moreover the principal point*) καὶ δή is common in replies to a command:

A. οὔκουν ἐπείξει τῷδε δεσμὰ περιβαλεῖν;	*A. Hasten then to cast fetters round this fellow.* (lit. *won't you hasten ...?*)
B. καὶ δὴ πρόχειρα ψάλια.	*B. There you are* (lit. *actually indeed*), *the chains [are] ready to hand.*

It is also used in making assumptions: καὶ δὴ πολέμιοί εἰσιν *and suppose they are hostile.* Note that καὶ δὴ καί means *and especially, and in particular*; in this combination the stress is laid on the word following the second καί:

καὶ δὴ καὶ τότε ἅμ᾿ ἡμέρᾳ συνελέγημεν.	*And on that particular occasion* (lit. *and then in particular*) *we gathered at dawn.*

Combinations with οὖν

(i) οὐκοῦν is merely a synonym for οὖν*, *therefore, accordingly, well then*:

ἢ τοὺς ἀμύνεσθαι κελεύοντας πόλεμον ποιεῖν φήσομεν; οὐκοῦν ὑπόλοιπον δουλεύειν.	*Or shall we say that those who urge [us] to defend ourselves are making war? Then* (or *in that case*) *it remains [for us] to be slaves.*

It is to be distinguished from οὔκουν (so accented), in which the negative retains its full force:

οὔκουν, Προμηθεῦ, τοῦτο γιγνώσκεις, ὅτι ὀργῆς νοσούσης εἰσὶν ἰατροὶ λόγοι;	*Do you not know this then, Prometheus, that when a temperament is sick* (lit. *a temperament being sick* gen. absolute, 12.1/2b) *there are words [to act as] healers?* (see also the example given in (c) above).

(ii) δ᾿ οὖν has a resumptive force, *be that as it may*, used in dismissing a subject:

εἰ δὴ δίκαια ποιήσω,   *If indeed I shall do what is*
οὐ γιγνώϲκω· αἱρήϲομαι   *right* (lit. *just things*) *I do not*
δ᾽ οὖν ὑμᾶϲ.   *know; however that may be,*
                             I shall choose you.

(iii) μὲν οὖν: this combination sometimes has no other force than the
value of its two constituent parts (μέν looking forward to δέ,
and οὖν *therefore*), but it can also be used to correct a previous
statement, with the sense *no, on the contrary*:

A. ἢ ϲὺ οὐδὲν ἡγῇ   *A. Or do you think that the*
πράττειν τὸν γραμματιστήν;   *schoolmaster does nothing?*
B. ἔγωγε ἡγοῦμαι μὲν οὖν.   *B. On the contrary, I do think*
                             (*sc. that he does something*).

Combinations with τοι*

(i) καίτοι means *and yet, however*: καίτοι τί φημι; *and yet what am I
saying?*
(ii) μέντοι* is used either to emphasise, e.g. A. ἐγώ; B. ϲὺ μέντοι. *A.
Me ?* (lit. *I*) B. *Yes, you*; or in an adversative sense, *however, yet*,
often with an added γε: οὐ μέντοι οἵ γε Ϲκύθαι ταύτῃ εἰϲέβαλον
yet the Scythians did not invade by this route.

Other uses of particles will be explained as they occur in the reading.

13.2 Greek reading

1# καλόν γε γαστρὸϲ κἀπιθυμίαϲ κρατεῖν.
2#   τῷ γήρᾳ φιλεῖ
χὠ νοῦϲ ὁμαρτεῖν καὶ τὸ βουλεύειν ἃ δεῖ.
3 τοῦτό τοι τἀνδρεῖον, ἡ προμηθία.
4# πανταχοῦ γε πατρὶϲ ἡ βόϲκουϲα γῆ.
5# ϲοφόν γέ τοί τι πρὸϲ τὸ βουλεύειν ἔχει
τὸ γῆραϲ, ὡϲ δὴ πόλλ᾽ ἰδόν τε καὶ παθόν.
6# ὦ τλῆμον ἀρετή, λόγοϲ ἄρ᾽ ἦϲθ᾽· ἐγὼ δέ ϲε
ὡϲ ἔργον ἤϲκουν· ϲὺ δ᾽ ἄρ᾽ ἐδούλευεϲ τύχῃ.
7# πατὴρ μὲν ἡμῖν Οἰδίπουϲ ὁ Λαΐου,
ἔτικτε δ᾽ Ἰοκάϲτη με, παῖϲ Μενοικέωϲ·
καλεῖ δὲ Πολυνείκη με Θηβαῖοϲ λεώϲ.
8# οὐκ ἔϲτι Πειθοῦϲ ἱερὸν ἄλλο πλὴν λόγοϲ,
καὶ βωμὸϲ αὐτῆϲ ἔϲτ᾽ ἐν ἀνθρώπου φύϲει.

9 ὁ δύο λαγὼς διώκων οὐδέτερον καταλαμβάνει.

10 ὁ Κῦρος ἅτε παῖς ὢν καὶ φιλόκαλος καὶ φιλότιμος ἥδετο τῇ στολῇ.

11 ἀνάγκῃ οὐδὲ οἱ θεοὶ μάχονται.

12 κακὸν ἀναγκαῖον τὸ πείθεϲθαι γαϲτρί.

13 τὴν Χάρυβδιν ἐκφυγὼν τῇ Ϲκύλλῃ περιέπεϲεϲ.

14 ὄνος πεινῶν οὐ φροντίζει ῥοπάλου.

15# τοῦ ζῆν γὰρ οὐδεὶς ὡς ὁ γηράϲκων ἐρᾷ.

16# μόνος θεῶν θάνατος οὐ δώρων ἐρᾷ.

17# ὁ μηδὲν ἀδικῶν οὐδενὸς δεῖται νόμου.

18 τέτταρας δακτύλους θανάτου οἱ πλέοντες ἀπέχουσιν.

19 ἦρος χρῄζεις ἐπειδὴ παλαιὸν χιτῶνα ἔχεις.

20 Γοργὼ ἡ Λάκαινα, ἐρωτηθεῖϲα ὑπό τινος ᾿Αττικῆϲ, διὰ τί ὑμεῖϲ ἄρχετε μόναι τῶν ἀνδρῶν αἱ Λάκαιναι; ὅτι, ἔφη, καὶ τίκτομεν μόναι ἄνδρας.

21 **A noteworthy pun**

᾿Αντιϲθένηϲ ὁ φιλόϲοφοϲ, πρὸς μειράκιόν τι μέλλον φοιτᾶν παρὰ αὐτὸν καὶ πυθόμενον τίνων αὐτῷ δεῖ, ἔφη, βιβλίου καινοῦ καὶ γραφείου καινοῦ καὶ πινακιδίου καινοῦ, τὸν νοῦν παρεμφαίνων.

22# ἡ γῆ μέλαινα πίνει,
πίνει δὲ δένδρε᾿ αὐτήν·
πίνει θάλασσα κρουνούϲ,
ὁ δ᾿ ἥλιος θάλαϲϲαν,
τὸν δ᾿ ἥλιον ϲελήνη.   5
τί μοι μάχεϲθ᾿, ἑταῖροι,
καὐτῷ θέλοντι πίνειν;

Notes

1 κἀπιθῡμίᾱϲ = καὶ ἐπιθῡμίᾱϲ (11.1/5).

2 φιλέω + infinitive *be accustomed to*; φιλεῖ is singular because it agrees with the closer of the two subjects; χὠ = καὶ ὁ (11.1/5); ἃ δεῖ is the object of βουλεύειν.

3 The subject τοῦτο (*sc.* ἐϲτί) anticipates ἡ προμηθίᾱ; τἀνδρεῖον = τὸ ἀνδρεῖον (11.1/5).

5 Take ϲοφόν ... τι together as the object of ἔχει (the subject is τὸ γῆρας); ὡϲ + participle to give a supposed reason (12.1/2*a*(ii)); πόλλ᾿ i.e. πολλά; ἰδόν < ὁράω; παθόν < πάϲχω (both aorist participles are neuter nom. s. agreeing with γῆρας).

6 ἀρετή *virtue* was the philosophical ideal of the Stoics. These lines,
   whose exact source is unknown, were the last words of the Roman
   Brutus before committing suicide; ἄρ' = ἄρα (distinguish from
   ἀρα); ἦσθ'= ἦσθα; ὡς *as* (22.1/1a(i)).

7 *l*.1 ἡμῖν trans. by a singular (royal plural – Polyneices in fact
   continues in the singular). *l*.2 ἔτικτε trans. as though aorist, *bore*
   (τίκτω is used idiomatically to mean *be parent of*).

9 λαγώς acc. pl. (13.1/1a).

12 τὸ πείθεσθαι is the subject; κακόν is used as a noun *an evil*.

15 ὡς *as* (cf. 6 above).

17 μηδέν, not οὐδέν, because a general class is meant (12.1/2a(vi)), lit.
   the [person] doing wrong not at all (adverbial acc., 20.1/5), i.e.
   those who do no wrong.

18 τέτταρας δακτύλους acc. of extent of space (7.1/7d); the width of
   four fingers was the normal thickness of the sides of an ancient
   ship.

19 ἦρος < ἔαρ (6.1/1b).

20 Spartan men prided themselves on manly virtues; they were not,
   however, male chauvinists, as the story shows; ὅτι *because.*

21 μέλλον acc. n. s. of the pres. act. pple. of μέλλω (here *intend*), to
   be taken with μειράκιον; δεῖ *there is need of* + gen. of thing
   needed and dat. of the person in need (cf. 21.1/4b and note 3); in
   Antisthenes' reply the genitives depend on an understood δεῖ (i.e.
   you need ...).

22 A poem in imitation of Anacreon (22.3). It is written in Ionic
   Greek as is shown by the forms θάλασσα and θέλοντι. *l*.1 The
   prose order would be ἡ μέλαινα γῆ. *l*.2 πῑνει i.e. *draws nourishment
   from*; δένδρε' i.e. δένδρεα. *l*.6 μάχεσθ' i.e. μάχεσθε. *l*.7 καὐτῷ = καὶ
   αὐτῷ.

13.3 Extra reading

Plato (c. 429–347 BC)

All Plato's philosophical writings (except the *Apology*) are in the form
of discussions and arguments which are supposed to have taken place
on a particular occasion between various contemporaries. For this
reason they are called dialogues, but we have no way of telling where

factual reporting stops and Plato's imagination (or his desire to expound his own ideas) begins. Some dialogues are in simple dramatic form, whereas in others the conversation is reported by one of the characters (the second extract is an example of the former, the first of the latter). In all his dialogues (except the *Laws*) Plato introduces his master, Socrates (8.2.13), as a protagonist, but nowhere does he introduce himself.

(*i*) ΣΩΚΡΑΤΗΣ

ἐπορευόμην μὲν ἐξ Ἀκαδημείας εὐθὺ Λυκείου τὴν ἔξω τείχους ὑπ᾽ αὐτὸ τὸ τεῖχος· ἐπειδὴ δ᾽ ἐγενόμην κατὰ τὴν πυλίδα ᾗ ἡ Πάνοπος κρήνη, ἐνταῦθα συνέτυχον Ἱπποθάλει τε τῷ Ἱερωνύμου καὶ Κτησίππῳ τῷ Παιανιεῖ καὶ ἄλλοις μετὰ τούτων νεανίσκοις. καί με προσιόντα (*approaching*) ὁ Ἱπποθάλης ἰδών, ὦ Σώκρατες, ἔφη, ποῖ δὴ πορεύῃ καὶ πόθεν;   5
ἐξ Ἀκαδημείας, ἦν δ᾽ ἐγώ, πορεύομαι εὐθὺ Λυκείου.
δεῦρο δή, ἦ δ᾽ ὅς, εὐθὺ ἡμῶν. οὐ παραβάλλεις; ἄξιον μέντοι.
ποῖ, ἔφην ἐγώ, λέγεις, καὶ παρὰ τίνας τοὺς ὑμᾶς;
δεῦρο, ἔφη, δείξας (*showing*) μοι ἐν τῷ καταντικρὺ τοῦ τείχους περίβολόν τέ τινα καὶ θύραν. διατρίβομεν δέ, ἦ δ᾽ ὅς, αὐτόθι ἡμεῖς τε 10
αὐτοὶ καὶ ἄλλοι πάνυ πολλοὶ καὶ καλοί.
ἔστιν δὲ δὴ τί τοῦτο, καὶ τίς ἡ διατριβή;
παλαίστρα, ἔφη, νέα· ἡ δὲ διατριβὴ τὰ πολλὰ ἐν λόγοις ὧν σε μετέχειν ἐθέλομεν.
καλῶς γε, ἦν δ᾽ ἐγώ, ποιοῦντες· διδάσκει δὲ τίς αὐτόθι;   15
σὸς ἑταῖρός γε, ἦ δ᾽ ὅς, καὶ ἐπαινέτης, Μίκκος.
μὰ Δία, ἦν δ᾽ ἐγώ, οὐ φαῦλός γε ἀνήρ, ἀλλ᾽ ἱκανὸς σοφιστής.
βούλει οὖν ἕπεσθαι, ἔφη, καὶ ὁρᾶν τοὺς ὄντας αὐτόθι;

(*ii*) ΕΥΚΛΕΙΔΗΣ – ΤΕΡΨΙΩΝ

ΕΥ. ἄρτι, ὦ Τερψίων, ἢ πάλαι ἐξ ἀγροῦ;
ΤΕΡ. ἐπιεικῶς πάλαι. καὶ σέ γε ἐζήτουν κατ᾽ ἀγορὰν καὶ ἐθαύμαζον ὅτι οὐχ οἷός τ᾽ ἦ εὑρεῖν.
ΕΥ. οὐ γὰρ ἦ κατὰ πόλιν.
ΤΕΡ. ποῦ μήν;   5
ΕΥ. εἰς λιμένα καταβαίνων Θεαιτήτῳ ἐνέτυχον φερομένῳ ἐκ Κορίνθου ἀπὸ τοῦ στρατοπέδου Ἀθήναζε.
ΤΕΡ. πότερον ζῶντι ἢ οὔ;
ΕΥ. ζῶντι καὶ μάλα μόλις· χαλεπῶς μὲν γὰρ ἔχει καὶ ὑπὸ τραυμάτων τινῶν, μᾶλλον μὴν αὐτὸν αἱρεῖ τὸ νόσημα τὸ ἐν τῷ στρατεύματι.   10
ΤΕΡ. μῶν ἡ δυσεντερία;

ΕΥ. ναί.

ΤΕΡ. οἷον ἄνδρα λέγεις ἐν κινδύνῳ εἶναι.

ΕΥ. καλόν τε καὶ ἀγαθόν, ὦ Τερψίων, ἐπεί τοι καὶ νῦν ἤκουόν τινων
μάλα ἐγκωμιαζόντων αὐτὸν περὶ τὴν μάχην.   15

ΤΕΡ. καὶ οὐδέν γ' ἄτοπον. ἀτὰρ πῶς οὐκ αὐτοῦ Μεγαροῖ κατέλυεν;

ΕΥ. ἠπείγετο οἴκαδε· ἐπεὶ ἔγωγ' ἐδεόμην καὶ συνεβούλευον, ἀλλ' οὐκ
ἤθελεν. καὶ δῆτα προπέμψας αὐτόν, ἀνεμνήσθην καὶ ἐθαύμασα
Σωκράτους ὡς μαντικῶς ἄλλα τε δὴ εἶπε καὶ περὶ τούτου. δοκεῖ γάρ
μοι ὀλίγον πρὸ τοῦ θανάτου ἐντυχεῖν αὐτῷ μειρακίῳ ὄντι, καὶ   20
συγγενόμενός τε καὶ διαλεχθεὶς πάνυ ἀγασθῆναι αὐτοῦ τὴν φύσιν.

Notes

(i)

The speaker is Socrates, who is going from the Academy, a park with
sporting facilities (i.e. a γυμνάσιον) lying north-west of ancient
Athens, to the Lyceum, a similar establishment to the east. The road
between the two skirted the north wall. *l.*1 τὴν ἔξω τείχους *sc.* ὁδόν
on/along the [road] outside the wall, this use of the accusative without
a preposition is classified as an acc. of spatial extent (7.1/7d). *l.*2 ᾗ
where (*sc.* ἐστί). *l.*3 Παιανιεῖ (< Παιανεύς) an adjective meaning *of the
deme Paeania*; as the Athenians had only one personal name (cf. 5.1/3
note 2) they were officially distinguished by the *deme* (local
administrative unit) to which they belonged. *l.*6 ἦν δ' ἐγώ *said I* a
stereotyped formula, often used by Plato, which employs the nearly
defunct verb ἠμί *say* (18.1/1a) (δ' is part of the formula and should not
be translated). *l.*7 δεῦρο often used as an order *[come] over here*; ἦ δ'
ὅς *said he* the same formula as above but in its third person singular
version (the use of the relative ὅς as a demonstrative pronoun is
archaic). *l.*8 λέγεις *do you mean*; παρὰ τίνας τοὺς ὑμᾶς *sc.* ὄντας *to
whom the [group of] you being [am I to come]?* i.e. *who are you to
whom*, etc. *l.*9 δείξας *showing* coincidental use of aor. pple. (12.1/1).
*l.*12 Supply ἐστί with ἡ διατριβή. *l.*13 τὰ πολλά lit. *for the many
[times]*, i.e. *usually* (adverbial acc. 20.1/5); ὧν has λόγοις as its
antecedent and is governed by μετέχειν, which takes the genitive of
what is shared (13.1/2a(v)). *l.*15 καλῶς γε ... ποιοῦντες (*sc.* ἐθέλετε, to
be supplied from ἐθέλομεν in the previous line) *doing well at any rate
[you wish this]*, an expression of gratitude for their invitation.

(*ii*)

The speakers are Eucleides and Terpsion. *l.*1 *sc.* ἦλθες the omission is typical of Plato's colloquial style. *l.*3 οἷός τ᾽ εἰμί an idiom meaning *I am able* (τ᾽ is not to be translated; on οἷος see 21.1/3). *l.*4 Terpsion has not been able to find Eucleides in the agora; in English the latter's reply would be *No, you couldn't, for I was not in the city,* but Greek omits the words *No, you couldn't* (which confirm the previous statement) and simply gives the reason *for I was not,* etc. (24.1/1). *l.*8 πότερον introduces two alternative questions (10.1/2*a*) but is not to be translated; with ζῶντι supply ἐνέτυχες from ἐνέτυχον in *l.*6. *l.*9 ἔχω + adv. to express a state (cf. note on 8.2.9 *l.*1). *l.*10 μήν has an adversative sense (*but*) and balances the preceding μέν; the combination gives a stronger contrast than μέν ... δέ. *l.*11 μῶν (10.1/2*a*) in his anxiety Terpsion is hoping for a negative answer. *l.*13 οἷον ... exclamatory *what a man ...!* (21.1/3). *l.*14 The Athenian male ideal was summed up in the phrase καλὸς κἀγαθός (here slightly varied), which can be translated *gentleman* (cf. 9.2.12 *l.*4). *l.*17 ἐπεί *since* introduces proof for the fact that Theaetetus was hurrying home, and governs the following three finite verbs; we would omit it in English; ἐδεόμην καὶ συνεβούλευον i.e. *him to stay. l.*18 καὶ δῆτα *in fact* (lit. *and indeed* but more emphatic than καὶ δή); translate προπέμψας by a finite verb and supply *and* before the next clause. *l.*19 Σωκράτους is genitive with ἀνεμνήσθην and ἐθαύμασα, lit. *remembered and admired Socrates, how prophetically he spoke ...* but English idiom requires *how prophetically Socrates spoke ...* (where appropriate, Greek often anticipates the subject of an indirect question in this way); ἄλλα τε ... καὶ περὶ τούτου lit. *both other [things] and about him,* i.e. *in particular about him;* ἄλλος τε καί is often used in the sense *particularly, especially;* δοκεῖ the subject is *he* (i.e. Socrates). *l.*21 διαλεχθείς < διαλέγομαι; ἀγασθῆναι < ἄγαμαι.

14 | UNIT FOURTEEN

14.1 Grammar

14.1/1 Moods of the Greek verb

Mood is a characteristic of all finite forms[1] of the Greek verb (i.e. those that can stand alone in a clause). Up to now we have dealt only with the indicative, the mood used for facts. There are three other moods, the imperative, which expresses commands (17.1/1), and the subjunctive and optative. In a main clause the subjunctive can express the will of the subject, e.g. λύϲωμεν (aor. subj. act.) τοὺϲ δούλουϲ *let us free the slaves*, while the optative can express the wish of the speaker, e.g. μὴ γένοιτο (aor. opt. mid.) *may it not happen!* These uses illustrate, in part, an original distinction between what is **willed** or **expected** (subjunctive) and what is **desired** or considered **possible** (optative), but the functions of both moods have been expanded to such a degree that neither can be brought under a single definition.

In English we still possess some single-word subjunctive forms (*be that as it may*; *if I were you*) but the optative disappeared in the Germanic branch of Indo-European (1.3) before the evolution of English. Apart from the few relics of the subjunctive, we use auxiliary verbs (*let, may, would*, etc.) for uses covered by these moods in Greek.

The subjunctive and optative exist in the present and aorist (and perfect, 16.1/4 note 1). There is also a future optative, but **no** future subjunctive. The distinction between the present and aorist forms of these moods is one of aspect (4.1/1) **not** time (for an exception see 14.1/4*d*). As with infinitives, the present subjunctive or optative is used

---

[1] The non-finite forms of verbs (i.e. participles and infinitives) are not considered as belonging to any mood.

for an action which is seen as going on, in the process of happening, or being repeated; the aorist subjunctive or optative is used for an action which is seen as a single event (cf. 4.1/1).

14.1/2 Subjunctive mood

For complete table of λύω *see* **Appendix 1**.

The subjunctive has only one set of endings, which are applied to the present and aorist stems (the latter without the augment). The endings are formed by lengthening all the initial short vowels (even when the first element of a diphthong) of the present indicative endings:

Active: –ω, –ῃς, –ῃ, –ωμεν, –ητε, –ωσι(ν).
Middle and passive: –ωμαι, –ῃ, –ηται, –ωμεθα, –ησθε, –ωνται.

Note that ει becomes η but in ου > ω (3rd pl. act.) the second element of the diphthong disappears. As the aorist passive takes active endings (11.1/1), for the aorist passive subjunctive of λύω we have λυθῶ,[1] λυθῇς etc.

In the present subjunctive of contracted verbs the rules of contraction apply as for the indicative (5.1/2). Paradigms will be found in **Appendix 2**.

The endings for the subjunctive are classified as **primary** (4.1/1 note 1 and 8.1/1*f*; we have –σι(ν) in the 3rd pl. act., –μαι in the 1st s. mid./pass., etc.). This classification is relevant to the use of the subjunctive in certain subordinate clauses (14.1/4*c*).

Notes

1 The indicative and subjunctive coincide in a few forms, e.g. λύω, τιμῶ, τιμᾷς.
2 Strong aorists and root aorists have the normal subjunctive endings (i.e. –ω, –ῃς, –ῃ etc.), except for a few root aorists in –ων, which have –ω, –ῳς, –ῳ, –ωμεν, –ωτε, –ωσι(ν). An example is ἔγνων (γιγνώσκω), subj. γνῶ, γνῷς, γνῷ, γνῶμεν, γνῶτε, γνῶσι(ν); cf. the present and aorist subjunctive active of δίδωμι (18.1/2 note 1).
3 The subjunctive of εἰμί is identical with the endings of the present subjunctive of λύω, viz ὦ, ῇς, ῇ, ὦμεν, ἦτε, ὦσι(ν).

---

[1] The aorist passive subjunctive is always accented with a circumflex on the first syllable of the ending (the circumflex indicates contraction, λυθῶ < λυθέω etc.).

14.1/3 Optative mood

For complete table of λύω *see* **Appendix 1**.

The optative, like the subjunctive, uses the same stems as the indicative, but its endings show some variety between tenses. For λύω and other uncontracted –ω verbs we have:

(*a*) **Present and future active:** –οιμι, –οις, –οι, –οιμεν, –οιτε, –οιεν; e.g. λύοιμι, λύοις etc. (present); λύσοιμι, λύσοις, etc. (future).

(*b*) **Present and future, middle and passive:** –οιμην, –οιο, –οιτο, –οιμεθα, –οισθε, –οιντο; e.g. λυοίμην (pres. mid./pass.), λυσοίμην (fut. mid.), λυθησοίμην (fut. pass.).

(*c*) **Weak aorist active:** –αιμι, –ειας (or –αις), –ειε(ν) (or –αι), –αιμεν, –αιτε, –ειαν (or –αιεν); e.g. λύσαιμι, λύσειας, etc. The bracketed forms are less common.

(*d*) **Weak aorist middle:** –αιμην, –αιο, –αιτο, –αιμεθα, –αισθε, –αιντο; e.g. λυσαίμην, λύσαιο, etc.

(*e*) In the **aorist passive** the final η of the stem is dropped (λυθη > λυθ) and to this are added: –ειην, –ειης, –ειη, –ειμεν, –ειτε, –ειεν; e.g. λυθείην, λυθείης, etc.

Contracted –ω verbs have different endings for the singular of the present optative active: –οιην, –οιης, –οιη. These, and the other present endings, contract according to the rules given at 5.1/2 (for paradigms see **Appendix 2**).

Present active	Present middle/passive
τῑμῴην (τῑμα–οίην), τῑμῴης, etc.	τῑμῴμην (τῑμα–οίμην), τῑμῷο, etc.
ποιοίην (ποιε–οίην), ποιοίης, etc.	ποιοίμην (ποιε–οίμην, ποιοῖο, etc.
δηλοίην (δηλο–οίην), δηλοίης, etc.	δηλοίμην (δηλο–οίμην), δηλοῖο, etc.

In the future, aorist, and perfect of contracted verbs the optative is formed by taking the appropriate stem and adding the normal endings.

The endings of the optative are classified as **historic** (4.1/1 note 1 and 8.1/1*f*; we have –ν in the 3rd pl. act., –μην in the 1st s. mid./pass., etc.). This classification is relevant to the use of the optative in certain subordinate clauses (14.1/4*c*).

Notes

1 The optative of the strong aorist has the same endings as the present; e.g. the aorist optative active of μανθάνω is μάθοιμι,

μάθοις, μάθοι, μάθοιμεν, μάθοιτε, μάθοιεν.
2   The root aorist ἔβην (βαίνω) has an optative βαίην, βαίης, βαίη,
    βαῖμεν, βαῖτε, βαῖεν (cf. the optative of –ἐδρᾶν which is –δραίην,
    –δραίης, etc.) but other root aorists in –ην have an optative in
    –ειην, –ειης, etc., just as that of the aorist passive. The optative of
    root aorists in –ων has the endings –οιην, –οιης, etc., and so from
    ἔγνων (γιγνώσκω) we have γνοίην, γνοίης, γνοίη, γνοῖμεν, γνοῖτε,
    γνοῖεν. The optative of root aorists in –υν is extremely rare.
3   The present optative of εἰμί is εἴην, εἴης, εἴη, εἶμεν, εἶτε, εἶεν.
    The future optative is ἐσοίμην, ἔσοιο, ἔσοιτο, etc.

14.1/4 Uses of the subjunctive and optative

The subjunctive and optative complement each other in several types
of subordinate clauses, but in main clauses their uses are quite distinct.

(a) Subjunctive in main clauses

(i) The **jussive** subjunctive (negated by μή) is used for giving orders
    but, because we also have the imperative (17.1/1), its use is limited.
    In the first person plural (the singular is possible but not as
    common) it expresses self-exhortation or self-encouragement: μή,
    πρὸς θεῶν, μαινώμεθα *in the name of* (πρός) *the gods, let us not be
    mad!* The use of the second and third persons of the jussive
    subjunctive complements the imperative mood in the aorist. Both
    are treated at 17.1/1.
(ii) The **deliberative** subjunctive (negated by μή) is used exclusively in
    questions and indicates the uncertainty of the speaker about the
    future and what must be done (in English we use the verb *to be*
    followed by an infinitive):

    εἴπωμεν ἢ σῑγῶμεν;   *Are we to speak or keep silent?*
    ποῖ φύγω μητρὸς χέρας;   *Where am I to escape my
                                mother's hands?*

(b) Optative in main clauses

The two uses of the optative in main clauses, to express a future wish
and to express a future potential, are complemented by the indicative,
which is used for both constructions in the present and past. For this
reason we shall treat all forms of wishes at 21.1/1, of conditions at
18.1/5 and of potentials at 19.1/2.

*(c) **Subordinate clauses where the subjunctive and optative complement each other***

In three types of subordinate clause the subjunctive is used after a main verb in a primary tense (4.1/1 note 1), the optative after a main verb in a historic tense. This reflects the fact that the subjunctive has primary endings (14.1/2) and the optative has historic endings (14.1/3).

In uses (i) and (ii) both subjunctive and optative can be literally translated by *may* or *might*. In (iii) both are to be translated by an indicative in English:

(i) **Purpose clauses** (negated by μή)

These can be introduced by ἵνα or ὅπως (both conjunctions meaning *in order that, so that*). The negative is μή, but a negated purpose clause can also be introduced by μή alone.

> ἀποφεύγομεν ἵνα (or ὅπως) οἱ   *We are fleeing so that the*
> βάρβαροι μὴ ἕλωσιν ἡμᾶς.   *barbarians may not capture us.*
> ἀπεφύγομεν ἵνα (or ὅπως) οἱ   *We fled so that the barbarians*
> βάρβαροι μὴ ἕλοιεν ἡμᾶς.   *might not capture us.*

In both cases ἵνα/ὅπως ... μή could be replaced by μή at the beginning of the purpose clause (μὴ οἱ βάρβαροι ἕλωσιν/ ἕλοιεν ἡμᾶς).

The subjunctive is often retained after a historic main verb, as this was regarded as producing a vivid effect (cf. vivid present, see note on 7.2.13 *l.*8). The second of the above examples would then become: ἀπεφύγομεν ἵνα (or ὅπως) οἱ βάρβαροι μὴ ἕλωσιν ἡμᾶς. As English has no way of bringing out the force of the subjunctive here, we must translate as previously.

(ii) **Noun clauses after verbs of fearing** (negated by οὐ)

The most common verb meaning *to fear* is φοβέομαι, which functions as a passive deponent with a middle future (11.1/1 note; it is not a true deponent as we also have an active φοβέω *terrify*). φοβέομαι and other verbs of fearing can be followed by a noun in the accusative: τὸν λέοντα φοβοῦμαι *I fear* (or *am afraid of*) *the lion*. They may also be followed by a clause which performs the same function as a noun (and hence is called a noun clause): *I am afraid that the lion may eat me.* Most (but not all) clauses of this sort have reference to a time subsequent to that of the main verb and in Greek are introduced by μή, which here, and elsewhere when used as a conjunction, can be literally translated by *lest*. The verb in the μή clause is put into the subjunctive after a main verb in a primary tense or into the optative after a main verb in a historic tense. As with purpose clauses, the subjunctive can be retained after a historic tense for a vivid effect.

φοβοῦμαι μὴ ὁ λέων με φάγῃ.   *I am afraid that* (lit. *lest*) *the*
                                 lion may (or *will*) *eat me.*
ἐφοβήθην μὴ ὁ λέων με   *I was afraid that the lion might*
   φάγοι (or φάγῃ).   (or *would*) *eat me.*

If the μή clause is negated, the negative is οὐ:

ὁ λέων φοβεῖται μὴ τροφὴν   *The lion is afraid that he may*
   οὐχ εὕρῃ.   *not find food.*

The noun clause can also have reference to the same time as, or a time anterior to, the verb of fearing. Here μή is followed by the indicative because what is feared either is happening or has happened:

φοβοῦμαι μὴ ὁ λέων τὸν   *I am afraid that the lion is now*
   ἐμὸν φίλον νῦν ἐσθίει/τὴν   *eating my friend / ate my wife*
   ἐμὴν γυναῖκα ἐχθὲς ἔφαγεν. *yesterday.*

Where in English a verb of fearing is followed by an infinitive, Greek has the same construction:

αἱ ψύλλαι οὐ φοβοῦνται   *The fleas are not afraid to eat*
   φαγεῖν τὸν λέοντα.   *the lion* (or *of eating the lion*).

(iii) **Indefinite subordinate clauses** (negated by μή)

Certain temporal conjunctions (e.g. ἐπεί, ὅτε) may introduce a subordinate clause referring to the present or past and be followed by the indicative. Greek idiom here is very similar to that of English and we have already met examples (e.g. at 7.2.12). These clauses refer to single definite events. Another type of subordinate clause is that with an indefinite sense and is expressed in English by the addition of *ever*. In *I dislike what he is doing* the subordinate clause refers to a specific thing (viz the thing that he is doing), but in *I dislike whatever he does* the subordinate clause refers to a general class of thing (viz whatever thing he does), and so is called **indefinite.** Such clauses may be adjectival (as above), or adverbial, e.g. *I am going wherever my sister goes* (contrast *I am going to where my sister lives* where the adverbial clause refers to a definite place).

In Greek the construction used for these clauses in **primary sequence** (i.e. when the main verb is in a primary tense) is similar. The particle ἄν, which here[1] is the equivalent of *ever,* is added to the subordinate clause but in addition its verb is put into the subjunctive. ἄν coalesces with certain conjunctions, e.g. ὅταν *whenever* (= ὅτε + ἄν), ἐπειδάν (= ἐπειδή + ἄν) *whenever.* Examples of indefinite clauses in primary sequence are:

ὅταν τις κλέπτῃ, ζημιοῦται. *Whenever anyone steals he is punished.*

πράττουσιν ἃ ἂν βούλωνται. *They do whatever they want [to do].*

Compare the above with the definite relative clause in:

πράττουσιν ἃ βούλονται. *They are doing [the things] which they want [to do].*

Because we can never be completely certain of what is going to happen in the future, the construction of ἄν + subjunctive is very common in subordinate temporal clauses with a future reference (cf.18.1/5). Often English idiom does not require us to translate ἄν:

ἡ Δίκη μάρψει τοὺς κακοὺς *Justice will seize the wicked men*
ὅταν τύχῃ. *when (lit. whenever) she finds [them].*

For indefinite subordinate clauses in **historic sequence** the optative **without** ἄν is used (we do **not** have the option of the primary construction as in (i) and (ii) above):

ὁ Κῦρος ἐθήρευεν ἀπὸ ἵππου *Cyrus used to hunt from*
ὁπότε γυμνάσαι βούλοιτο *horseback whenever (or simply*
ἑαυτὸν καὶ τοὺς ἵππους *when) he wanted to exercise himself and his horses.*

The negative for all indefinite clauses is μή:

ὁ μῶρος γελᾷ καὶ ὅταν τι *Fools laugh (lit. the fool laughs)*
μὴ γέλοιον ᾖ. *even when something is not funny.*

---

[1] ἄν has an entirely different force when used in a main clause (18.1/5).

(*d*) **Optative in indirect speech**
The optative has two further uses in subordinate clauses, one of which
we shall deal with here (for the other see 18.1/5). In indirect speech
which is introduced by a verb in a historic tense (*he said that ...; he
asked if ...* etc.) all finite verbs **may** be put into the optative. There is
no change in sense, and optatives of this sort are translated as
indicatives:

ὁ Κλέανδρος εἶπεν ὅτι Δέξιππον οὐκ ἐπαινοίη (or ind. ἐπαινεῖ).	*Cleander said that he did not* *commend Dexippus* (original: Δέξιππον οὐκ ἐπαινῶ *I do not* *commend Dexippus*).
εἶπεν ὅτι κατίδοι (or κατεῖδε, < καθοράω) στράτευμα.	*He said that he had caught sight* *of an army* (original: κατεῖδον στράτευμα *I caught sight of an* *army*; on the use of the English pluperfect *had caught* see 16.1/2).
Ξενοφῶν οὐκ ἤρετο τί τὸ πάθος εἴη (or ἐστίν).	*Xenophon did not ask what the* *misfortune was* (original: τί ἐστι τὸ πάθος; *what is the* *misfortune?*).

Finite verbs in indirect speech always retain the tense of the original
direct speech (8.1/3*b*), and consequently the distinction between the
present and aorist optative here involves time, **not** aspect, as the above
examples show.

A verb in a future tense in direct speech can be put into the future
optative when reported in historic sequence: εἶπον ὅτι τοῦτο ποιήσοιμι
(or ποιήσω) *I said that I would do this* (original: τοῦτο ποιήσω *I shall do
this*). The future optative has no other uses.

Notes

1   When an adverbial clause of reason (introduced by ὅτι *because,*
    ἐπεί *since,* etc.) occurs after a historic tense its verb is put into the
    optative if the speaker or writer wishes to ascribe a reason or
    motive to the subject of the main verb but does not vouch for it
    himself. This type of expression is called **virtual indirect speech** as
    no verb of saying, thinking, etc. is actually used. The
    subordinating conjunction is to be translated by *on the grounds*

that, thinking/saying that:

οἱ Ἀθηναῖοι τὸν Περικλέα   *The Athenians abused Pericles*
ἐκάκιζον ὅτι ϲτρατηγὸϲ   *on the grounds that, [though]*
ὧν οὐκ ἐπεξάγοι.   *being general, he did not lead*
                                    [them] out.

2   When a deliberative question (τί ποιῶμεν; *what are we to do?*) is reported after a verb in a historic tense its verb may be put into the optative:

ἠποροῦμεν τί (or ὅτι)   *We were at a loss [as to]what*
ποιοῖμεν   *we should do.*

The subjunctive may, however, be retained.

14.2 Greek reading

In addition to translating, define each use of the subjunctive and optative.

1#   ἔνεϲτι γάρ τιϲ καὶ λόγοιϲιν ἡδονή,
      λήθην ὅταν ποιῶϲι τῶν ὄντων κακῶν.

2#   πῶϲ οὖν μάχωμαι θνητὸϲ ὢν θείᾳ τύχῃ;

3#   νοῦν χρὴ θεᾶϲθαι, νοῦν· τί τῆϲ εὐμορφίαϲ
      ὄφελοϲ, ὅταν τιϲ μὴ καλὰϲ φρέναϲ ἔχῃ;

4   ὃϲ ἂν δὶϲ ναυαγήσῃ, μάτην μέμφεται Ποϲειδῶνα.

5   Cωκράτηϲ ἔφη τοὺϲ μὲν πολλοὺϲ ἀνθρώπουϲ ζῆν ἵνα ἐϲθίωϲιν,
    αὐτὸϲ δὲ ἐϲθίειν ἵνα ζῇ.

6   φάγωμεν καὶ πίωμεν· αὔριον γὰρ ἀποθνήϲκομεν.

7#   θεὸϲ αἰτίαν φύει βροτοῖϲ
      ὅταν κακῶϲαι δῶμα παμπήδην θέλῃ.

8#   ὡϲ χαρίεν ἐϲτ᾽ ἄνθρωποϲ ὅταν ἄνθρωποϲ ᾖ.

9#   Α. τίϲ ἐϲτιν οὗτοϲ; Β. ἰατρόϲ. Α. ὡϲ κακῶϲ ἔχει
      ἅπαϲ ἰατρόϲ, ἐὰν κακῶϲ μηδεὶϲ ἔχῃ.

10# ϲφόδρ᾽ ἐϲτὶν ἡμῶν ὁ βίοϲ οἴνῳ προϲφερήϲ·
      ὅταν ᾖ τὸ λοιπὸν μικρόν, ὄξοϲ γίγνεται.

11   οἱ μὲν φοβούμενοι μὴ φύγωϲι πατρίδα καὶ οἱ μέλλοντεϲ μάχεϲθαι
    φοβούμενοι μὴ ἡττηθῶϲιν οὔτε ϲίτου οὔτε ὕπνου δύνανται
    λαγχάνειν διὰ τὸν φόβον· οἱ δὲ ἤδη φυγάδεϲ, ἤδη δὲ ἡττηθέντεϲ
    δύνανται καὶ μᾶλλον τῶν εὐδαιμόνων ἐϲθίειν καὶ καθεύδειν.

12 πίθηκος ὁ πίθηκος κἄν (= καὶ ἐάν) χρυσᾶ ἔχῃ σάνδαλα.
13 ἐφοβήθησαν οἱ Ἕλληνες μὴ προσάγοιεν οἱ Πέρσαι πρὸς τὸ κέρας καὶ περιπτύξαντες ἀμφοτέρωθεν αὐτοὺς κατακόψειαν.
14 ὁ δὲ ἀνήρ, ὃν συνέλαβον, ἐρωτώμενος ποδαπὸς εἴη, Πέρσης μὲν ἔφη εἶναι, πορεύεσθαι δ' ἀπὸ τοῦ Τιριβάζου στρατεύματος ὅπως ἐπιτήδεια λάβοι.
15 ὁ Διογένης, ἰδὼν τοξότην ἀφυῆ, παρὰ τὸν σκοπὸν ἐκάθισεν εἰπών, ἵνα μὴ πληγῶ.
16#   τοῦ θανεῖν ἀπειρίᾳ
    πᾶς τις φοβεῖται φῶς λιπεῖν τόδ' ἡλίου.
17 ἔτρεχέ τις μὴ βρεχθείη καὶ εἰς βόθρον ἀπεπνίγη.
18 ἅμα δὲ τῇ ἡμέρᾳ συνελθόντες οἱ στρατηγοὶ ἐθαύμαζον ὅτι Κῦρος οὔτε ἄλλον πέμποι σημανοῦντα ὅτι χρὴ ποιεῖν, οὔτε αὐτὸς φαίνοιτο. ἔδοξεν οὖν αὐτοῖς συσκευασαμένοις ἃ εἶχον καὶ ἐξοπλισαμένοις ἰέναι (*to go*) εἰς τὸ πρόσθεν. ἤδη δὲ ἐν ὁρμῇ ὄντων, ἅμα ἡλίῳ ἀνέχοντι ἦλθε Προκλῆς ὁ Τευθρανίας ἄρχων 5 καὶ Γλοῦς ὁ Ταμῶ. οὗτοι δὲ εἶπον ὅτι Κῦρος μὲν ἀποθάνοι, Ἀριαῖος δὲ ἐν τῷ σταθμῷ εἴη μετὰ τῶν ἄλλων βαρβάρων καὶ λέγοι ὅτι ταύτην τὴν ἡμέραν περιμενοῖεν αὐτούς.
19 εἴ ποτε τοὺς στρατιώτας εὐτάκτως βαδίζοντας ἴδοι, ἐπῄνεσεν.
20# νόμον φοβηθεὶς οὐ ταραχθήσῃ νόμῳ.

Notes

1 *l*.1 ἔνεστι *is in* is followed by the dat. λόγοισιν. *l*.2 The first two words would be in reverse order in prose; ὄντων (< ὤν) lit. *being,* i.e. *existing.*

3 The pl. φρένες is very often used with the meaning of the singular (here *mind*).

5 τοὺς πολλοὺς ἀνθρώπους *most people, the majority of people* (cf. note on τοῖς πολλοῖς in 8.2.11 and on τὰ πολλά in 13.3(i) *l*.13)

7 φύει here *plant*; βροτοῖς *in mortals* (dat. to express place where, 23.1/2*n*); take παμπήδην with κακῶσαι (*ruin completely*).

8 ὡς exclamatory *how* (also in 9, see 22.1/1*a*(ii)); χαρίεν (n.) lit. *charming thing*; ἄνθρωπος (penultimate word) i.e. *a [real] human being.*

9 A and B hold this conversation on seeing a destitute doctor; A's second remark plays on two possible meanings of κακῶς ἔχω (*a*) *I am destitute,* (*b*) *I am sick* (on ἔχω + adv. to express a state see note on 8.2.9 *l*.1).

11 φεύγω + acc. here means *go/be in exile from* (17.1/5); λαγχάνειν (+ gen., lit. *get*) should be translated *take* (the men spoken of can obtain food and have time for sleep, but their fear prevents them from taking either); δύνανται on deponents in –αμαι see 19.1/3*b*; μᾶλλον + gen. *more than* (genitive of comparison 17.1/4*a*).

13 προσάγω is here used intransitively, *advance*.

14 cυνέλαβον (< cυλλαμβάνω) take as 3rd pl., not as 1st s.

15 εἰπών coincidental use of the aorist pple. (12.1/1); πληγῶ 1st s. aor. subj. pass. of πλήττω.

17 The pass. of βρέχω means *to get wet*; εἰc illustrates the pregnant use of prepositions (see on 9.2.13 *l*.13) – the person must have fallen **into** the hole before drowning **in** it. Consequently εἰc βόθρον is to be translated by *in a hole*.

18 *ll*.2f. πέμποι and φαίνοιτο opt. in indirect speech 14.1/4*d*; cημανοῦντα fut. pple. to express purpose, 12.1/2*a*(v); ὅτι here the indirect interrogative pronoun (10.1/2*b* note 1), trans. *what*; ἔδοξεν (< δοκέω) αὐτοῖc *it seemed good to them*, i.e. *they decided* (21.1/4). *ll*.4f. εἰc τὸ πρόcθεν *to the in front [place]*, i.e. *forward*; ὄντων is the pple. of a genitive absolute in which the subject (αὐτῶν) is omitted, lit. *[they] being already at the point of starting* (ὁρμῇ); ἦλθε is singular because it agrees with the nearer subject (Προκλῆc) only. *l*.6 ὁ Ταμῶ *the son of Tamos* (Ταμώc, which is declined like νεώc 13.1/1*a*), for this use of the definite article see 5.1/3 note 2. *l*.8 περιμενοῖεν the fut. opt. represents a fut. ind. in direct speech (14.1/4*d*).

19 As the optative in itself makes the εἰ clause indefinite (14.1/4*c*(iii)), ποτέ is really superfluous.

20 ταραχθήcῃ 2nd s. fut. ind. pass. of ταράττω.

15 | UNIT FIFTEEN

15.1 Grammar

15.1/1 Perfect indicative active

The perfect tense in both Greek and English expresses a present state resulting from an action in the past. κέκλεικα τὴν θύραν *I have closed the door* means that the door is now closed as a result of my past action of closing it. The aorist ἔκλεισα τὴν θύραν *I closed the door* describes a single past action, but tells us nothing about the present state of the door, not even whether it is still in existence. Because the perfect tense describes a present state it is classified as a **primary** tense (4.1/1 note 1). The perfect is by no means as common as the aorist and does not exist in every Greek verb.

There are two types of the perfect active, called **weak** and **strong**; only in the few verbs with both is there a difference in meaning (see note 2). There is a common set of endings (in the indicative –α, –ας, –εν, –αμεν, –ατε, –ᾱσι(ν)), but, whereas the strong perfect, like the strong aorist, has no suffix, the weak perfect has a suffixed κ which is attached in a way similar to that of the ς of the weak aorist (see below).

The stem of the perfect is normally modified by **reduplication**. Thus if a verb begins with a single consonant (except ρ) or with two consonants of which the second is λ, μ, ν, or ρ, the initial consonant is doubled with the insertion of ε; hence **weak** λέλυκα (λύω) *I have loosened*; πεπίστευκα (πιστεύω) *I have trusted*; κέκλεικα (κλείω) *I have closed*; **strong** γέγραφα (γράφω) *I have written*. When, however, the initial consonant is an aspirate (θ, φ, χ), it is reduplicated in its unaspirated form; τεθήρᾱκα (θηράω) *I have hunted*; πεφόνευκα (φονεύω) *I have murdered*; κεχόρευκα (χορεύω) *I have danced*.

In other cases the perfect stem is not reduplicated but simply augmented by the **temporal augment** (4.1/1 note 2(ii)) for verbs with an initial vowel or diphthong: ἦχα (ἄγω) *I have led*; ᾕρηκα (αἱρέω) *I have captured* (see also note 3); or by the **syllabic augment** (4.1/2 note 2(i)) for verbs beginning with ρ, a double consonant (ζ, ξ, ψ), or two consonants (the second not being λ, μ, ν, ρ): ἔρρῑφα (ῥῑπτω) *I have thrown*; ἐζήτηκα (ζητέω) *I have sought*; ἔκτικα (κτίζω) *I have founded*.

The conjugation of λέλυκα (perf. ind. act. of λύω) will be found in **Appendix 1**. An example of a strong perfect is ἔρρῑφα (ῥῑπτω *throw*), which is conjugated: ἔρρῑφα, ἔρρῑφας, ἔρρῑφε(ν), ἐρρῑφαμεν, ἐρρῑφατε, ἐρρῑφᾱσι(ν).

The weak perfect occurs mostly in:

(*a*) stems ending in vowels or diphthongs. Here the κ suffix is added to the present stem: κέκλεικα (κλείω). As in the aorist, the final vowel of most contracted verbs is lengthened: δεδήλωκα (δηλόω).

(*b*) stems ending in λ and ρ, where the κ suffix must be added to the original stem (i.e. the present stem stripped of any suffix, cf. 11.1./3): ἤγγελκα (ἀγγέλλω, i.e. ἀγγέλ–γω); ἦρκα (αἴρω, i.e. ἄρ–γω).

(*c*) dental stems (6.1/4), where the final dental is lost before the κ suffix: πέπεικα (πείθω); κεκόμικα (κομίζω, stem κομιδ–).

The strong perfect occurs in palatal and labial stems: πέφευγα (φεύγω); γέγραφα (γράφω). Often a final unaspirated consonant is aspirated (i.e. γ/κ > χ; β/π > φ): πέπρᾱχα (πρᾱττω stem πραγ–); τέτριφα (τρῑβω *rub* stem τριβ–). In many strong perfects an ε in the present stem is changed to ο: λέλοιπα (λείπω); πέπομφα (πέμπω). A few verbs with stems in other consonants have a strong perfect, e.g. γέγονα (γίγνομαι – note change in voice; the verb has another perfect γεγένημαι, which has the same meaning as γέγονα). For other examples of all types see **Principal parts of verbs.**

Notes

1 The strong perfect of some otherwise transitive verbs has an intransitive sense: ἐγείρω *I wake* (*somebody*) *up* (tr.), ἐγρήγορα (on this form see below note 3) *I have woken up* (intr.), i.e. *I am awake.*

2 πείθω and πρᾱττω each have both a transitive and an intransitive perfect:
transitive: πέπεικα *I have persuaded*; πέπρᾱχα *I have done.*

intransitive: πέποιθα *I have confidence in* (+ dat.), i.e. *I trust*; πέπρᾱγα *I have fared*.

Note that πέποιθα can be translated by a present tense in English (*I trust*; cf. ἐγρήγορα above). A few other verbs (e.g. ὄλλῡμι, 20.1/1 note 2) follow πείθω and πράττω in having a transitive weak perfect and an intransitive strong perfect.

3   Some verbs which begin with α, ε, ο reduplicate their entire initial syllable in addition to lengthening their original initial vowel:

ἀκήκοα (ἀκούω – the only common verb in a vowel stem which has a strong perfect)

ἐγρήγορα (ἐγείρω – the reduplicated syllable ἐγρ– also contains the ρ of the stem).

4   Many perfects are slightly irregular, e.g. βέβληκα (βάλλω); κέκληκα (καλέω); πέπτωκα (πῑπτω).

15.1/2 Verbs used with participles

In the sentence Περικλέᾱ εἶδον ἐν τῇ ἀγορᾷ βαδίζοντα *I saw Pericles walking in the agora* the participle is not used in any of the ways mentioned in 12.1/2, where participles qualify either the finite verb of their clause or the clause itself. Here βαδίζοντα gives us further information (*I not only saw Pericles – I saw him **walking***; cf. ex. in 12.2.17 *l.*2) and is called a **supplementary participle**. Participles can only be used in this way with verbs whose meaning permits it (as ὁράω in Greek and *see* in English). Most can be classified according to their meaning. With some the accompanying participle may occur in a case other than the accusative.

(*a*)   Verbs of **knowing** and **perceiving**, e.g. ἐπίσταμαι (present tense as for δύναμαι, 19.1/3*b*) *know*; γιγνώσκω *recognise*; ὁράω *see*; αἰσθάνομαι *perceive*; πυνθάνομαι *ascertain*; ἀκούω *hear*; μανθάνω *learn*:

τῶν στρατιωτῶν τις εἶδε Κλέαρχον διελαύνοντα.	*One of the soldiers saw Clearchus riding through.*
ἤκουσαν αὐτοῦ βοῶντος.	*They heard him shouting* (genitive because ἀκούω is followed by the genitive of the person heard – 13.1/2*a*(iii)).

These verbs can also be followed by a noun clause introduced by
ὅτι (8.1/3*b*):

ὁ Δωριεὺς εὖ ἠπίστατο ὅτι   *Dorieus knew well that he*
(αὐτὸς) cχήcει τὴν   *(himself) would obtain the*
βαcιλειᾶν.   *kingship.*

All such ὅτι clauses can, however, be converted to a participial
phrase. When the subject of the participle is the same as the
subject of the finite verb (as in the converted form of this
example), the participle is put into the nominative; the subject
itself will only be expressed if emphasis is required (normally
some form of αὐτός; cf. nominative and infinitive, 8.1/3*a*): ὁ
Δωριεὺς εὖ ἠπίστατο (αὐτὸς) cχήcων τὴν βαcιλειᾶν (the meaning
is the same as above).

When the subject of the participle is **not** the same as that of the
finite verb both the participle and its subject are put into the
accusative:

ἔμαθε τὴν Χερρόνηcον   *He learnt that the Chersonese*
πόλεις ἕνδεκα ἢ δώδεκα   *had eleven or twelve cities*
ἔχουcαν.   (= ὅτι ἡ Χερρόνηcοc ἔχει ...).

Verbs of **knowing** and **learning** can also be followed by an
infinitive, but in the sense of *know/learn how to ...*: ἐπίcταμαι νεῖν
I know how to swim.

(*b*) Verbs of **beginning, stopping, continuing**, e.g. ἄρχομαι (mid.) *begin*
(doing something; the middle is more common than the active in
this use); παύω *stop* (someone doing something); παύομαι (mid.)
stop (doing something oneself); διατελέω *continue*. With such
verbs in English we have sometimes a participle, sometimes an
infinitive.

ὁ ἄνεμος ἐπαύcατο θῦων.   *The wind stopped raging.*
μόνοι Θρᾳκῶν διατελοῦcιν   *Alone of the Thracians they*
ὄντες ἐλεύθεροι.   *continue to be free.*
γελῶντας ἐχθροὺς παύcομεν *With our present journey we will*
τῇ νῦν ὁδῷ.   *stop our enemies laughing.*

ἄρχομαι regularly takes a participle: ἄρξομαι διδάcκων *I shall
begin teaching.* However, as with the English *begin,* an infinitive is
also found: ἤρξαντο οἰκοδομεῖν *they began to build.*

(c) Verbs of **emotion**, e.g. ἥδομαι, χαίρω both *be pleased, take pleasure*; ἄχθομαι *be vexed*; αἰσχύνομαι *be ashamed*:

ἥδομαι ἀκούων coυ φρονίμους   *I am pleased to hear wise words*
   λόγους.   *from you.*
οὐκ αἰσχύνῃ εἰς τοιαῦτα   *Aren't you ashamed at bringing*
   ἄγων τοὺς λόγους;   *the argument to such a point?*
                                             (*lit. to such things*).

αἰσχύνομαι may also be followed by an infinitive in the sense *be ashamed* to do something (and therefore not do it):

αἰσχύνομαί ce προcβλέπειν   *I am ashamed to look at you*
   ἐναντίον.   *straight in the face.*

Verbs of emotion may be followed by ὅτι and a finite verb with the same sense as their use with a participle. The first example above could be ἥδομαι ὅτι ἀκούω ... (lit. *I am pleased that I hear ...*). They are followed by the dative in clauses such as Πηνελοπείᾳ ἄχθομαι *I am annoyed with Penelope*.

(d) φαίνομαι *seem, be seen, be obvious*. Although φαίνομαι with an infinitive has the expected meaning *seem* (to be doing something), with a participle it means the same as δῆλός/φανερός εἰμι + participle, viz *I am obviously* (doing something).

φαίνονται οὐδὲν λέγειν.   *They seem to be speaking*
                                             nonsense (lit. *saying nothing*).
φαίνονται οὐδὲν λέγοντες.   *They are obviously speaking*
                                             nonsense (lit. *they, saying*
                                             nothing, are obvious).

(e) τυγχάνω *chance, happen* (to be doing something, i.e. *by chance I am [doing something]*; there is an etymological connection with τύχη *chance, fortune*). τυγχάνω is often used with a participle to express the idea that something has occurred fortuitously.[1]

ἔτυχε τότε ἐλθών.   *He happened to have come then*
                                             (lit. *he chanced having come*
                                             then).
δηλώcω τὸ πᾶν ὃ παρὰ τοῦδε   *I shall reveal the whole [matter]*
   τυγχάνω μαθών.   *which I happen to have learnt*
                                             from this man.

---

[1] This verb must be distinguished from γίγνομαι, which means *happen* in the sense of *take place* (for its range of meanings see 8.1/2).

(f) λανθάνω *escape the notice of* (+ acc.) and φθάνω *anticipate, be beforehand* can also be accompanied by a participle agreeing with their subject (in this construction they generally, but not always, have an object). As the main idea is contained in the participle, this will become the finite verb of the clause in an idiomatic translation:

πάντας λανθάνει δάκρυα λείβων.	*He sheds tears without anyone knowing* (lit. *he [in] shedding tears escapes the notice of all*).
Μενέλεως ἡμᾶς ἔλαθε παρών.	*Menelaus was present without us knowing* (lit. *Menelaus [in] being present escaped the notice of us*).
ἔφθασαν τὸν χειμῶνα ἀνασπάσαντες τᾱς ναῦς.	*They hauled up their ships before winter* (lit. *they [in] hauling up their ships anticipated the winter*).
ἔφθασαν οἱ Σκύθαι τοὺς Πέρσᾱς ἐπὶ τὴν γέφῡραν ἀφικόμενοι.	*The Scythians arrived at the bridge before the Persians* (lit. *The Scythians [in] arriving at the bridge anticipated the Persians*).

The difference here between the present and aorist participle is one of **aspect**, not of time. A present participle indicates a **condition** or **process** (first and second examples), an aorist participle indicates an **event** (third and fourth examples). Cf. 12.1/1 and, for a similar distinction between the present and aorist infinitive, 4.1/1.

In sentences of this type it is, in fact, immaterial whether λανθάνω /φθάνω appear as the finite verb with an accompanying participle (as above), or as the participle (always aorist; the participle here has no temporal force) with an accompanying finite verb. Thus in the first and third examples we could have, with identical meanings: πάντας λαθὼν δάκρυα λείβει (lit. *escaping the notice of all, he sheds tears*); φθάσαντες οἱ Σκύθαι τοὺς Πέρσᾱς ἐπὶ τὴν γέφῡραν ἀφίκοντο (lit. *the Scythians, anticipating the Persians, arrived at the bridge*).

15.2 Greek reading

1 cποδὸν φεύγων εἰc πῦρ ἐμπέπτωκα.
2 οὐδεὶc λανθάνει θεοὺc πονηρὰ ποιῶν.
3 καρκίνοc ὀρθὰ βαδίζειν οὐ μεμάθηκεν.
4# ἅπαντέc ἐcμεν εἰc τὸ νουθετεῖν cοφοί,
αὐτοὶ δ' ἁμαρτάνοντεc οὐ γιγνώcκομεν.
5 εἴληφεν ἡ παγὶc τὸν μῦν.
6# ἀνὴρ γὰρ ὅcτιc ἥδεται λέγων ἀεί,
ἔλαθεν ἑαυτὸν τοῖc cυνοῦcιν ὢν βαρύc.
7 cκορπίουc βέβρωκεν.
8# ὅcτιc καθ' ἑτέρου δόλια μηχανεύεται,
αὐτὸc καθ' αὑτοῦ λανθάνει ποιῶν.
9 ἔτυχον ἐν τῇ ἀγορᾷ οἱ ὁπλῖται καθεύδοντεc.
10 Μένων δῆλοc ἦν ἐπιθυμῶν πλουτεῖν ἰcχυρῶc.
11 **The crucifixion of Jesus**

παρέλαβον οὖν τὸν Ἰηcοῦν· καὶ βαcτάζων ἑαυτῷ τὸν cταυρὸν
ἐξῆλθεν εἰc τὸν λεγόμενον Κρανίου Τόπον, ὃ λέγεται ἑβραϊcτὶ
Γολγοθα, ὅπου αὐτὸν ἐcταύρωcαν, καὶ μετ' αὐτοῦ ἄλλουc δύο
ἐντεῦθεν καὶ ἐντεῦθεν, μέcον δὲ τὸν Ἰηcοῦν. ἔγραψεν δὲ καὶ
τίτλον ὁ Πιλᾶτοc καὶ ἔθηκεν (*placed [it]*) ἐπὶ τοῦ cταυροῦ, 5
ἸΗCΟΥC Ὁ ΝΑΖΩΡΑΙΟC Ὁ ΒΑCΙΛΕΥC ΤΩΝ ἸΟΥΔΑΙΩΝ.
τοῦτον οὖν τὸν τίτλον πολλοὶ ἀνέγνωcαν τῶν Ἰουδαίων, ὅτι ἐγγὺc
ὁ τόποc τῆc πόλεωc ὅπου ἐcταυρώθη ὁ Ἰηcοῦc. ἔλεγον οὖν τῷ
Πιλάτῳ οἱ ἀρχιερεῖc τῶν Ἰουδαίων, μὴ γράφε (*do not write*), ὁ
βαcιλεὺc τῶν Ἰουδαίων, ἀλλ' ὅτι ἐκεῖνοc εἶπεν, βαcιλεύc εἰμι 10
τῶν Ἰουδαίων. ἀπεκρίθη ὁ Πιλᾶτοc, ὃ γέγραφα γέγραφα.

12 ἑπτὰ ἡμέραc, ἃc ἐπορεύοντο διὰ τῶν Καρδούχων, πάcαc
μαχόμενοι διετέλεcαν.

13 Κλεάρετοc, παρακαλέcαc τοὺc cτρατιώταc, ἦγεν ἐπὶ τὸ χωρίον·
πορευόμενον δ' αὐτὸν ἔφθαcεν ἡμέρα γενομένη.

14 According to Plutarch intellectual pleasures are much superior
to those of the body and therefore our reactions to the former
are much more enthusiastic.

ὁ Ἀρχιμήδηc λουόμενοc, ὥc φαcιν, ἐκ τῆc ὑπερχύcεωc ἐννοήcαc
τὴν τοῦ cτεφάνου μέτρηcιν, οἷον ἔκ τινοc κατοχῆc ἢ ἐπιπνοίαc,
ἐξήλατο βοῶν, εὕρηκα, καὶ τοῦτο πολλάκιc φθεγγόμενοc
ἐβάδιζεν. οὐδενὸc δ' ἀκηκόαμεν οὔτε γαcτριμάργου οὕτωc

περιπαθῶc βοῶντος, βέβρωκα, οὔτε ἐρωτικοῦ, πεφίληκα, μυρίων 5
ἀκολάcτων γενομένων καὶ ὄντων.
15# Α. γεγάμηκε δήπου. Β. τί cὺ λέγεις; ἀληθινῶc
γεγάμηκεν, ὃν ἐγὼ ζῶντα περιπατοῦντά τε
κατέλιπον;
16 τὸ δὲ μέγα τεῖχος ἐπαύσαντο οἰκοδομοῦντες φοβούμενοι μὴ οὐχ
ἱκανὸν εἴη ἀντέχειν.
17# ὁρῶ δὲ τοῖc πολλοῖcιν ἀνθρώποιc ἐγὼ
τίκτουcαν ὕβριν τὴν πάροιθ’ εὐπραξίαν.

Notes

3   ὀρθά acc. n. pl. used adverbially (= ὀρθῶc, cf. 20.1/5).
4   εἰc *with respect to.*
6   ἀνὴρ ... ὅcτιc lit. *whatever man* (ὅcτιc is here the indefinite relative
     – 10.1/2b note 2) but translate *the man who*; ἔλαθεν gnomic aor.;
     translate by present; cυνοῦcι dat. pl. m. of the pres. pple of
     cύνειμι.
9   As the subject is plural ἔτυχον must be 3rd pl.
10   δῆλος ἦν ἐπιθυμῶν lit. *was obvious desiring,* i.e. *it was
     obvious/clear that M. desired.*
11   *l.*3 Γολγοθα has no accent because it is not a Greek word. *l.*4
     ἐντεῦθεν καὶ ἐντεῦθεν lit. *from here and from there,* i.e. *on each
     side. ll.*7f. Take πολλοί with τῶν Ἰουδαίων and ἐγγύc with τῆc
     πόλεωc. *l.*8 ἔλεγον *said* the imperfect is used because the subject
     is an unspecified number of individuals.
13   ἦγεν inceptive imperfect *began to lead.*
14   The famous story of Archimedes’ discovery of the principle of
     displacement (when two bodies of the same weight are
     submerged they will displace the same amount of liquid only if
     they are of identical composition). Using this he was able to
     establish that his patron, Hiero of Syracuse, had been cheated by
     a jeweller who had been commissioned to make a crown of pure
     gold (the crown did not displace the same volume of water as an
     amount of gold of exactly equal weight). *ll.*4f. ἐβάδιζεν impf. to
     express repeated action *went about;* οὐδενὸc ... οὔτε ... οὔτε lit. *of
     no-one ... neither ... nor* but translate *neither of any ... nor of any
     ...;* ἀκηκόαμεν royal (or author’s) plural. *l.*6 ἀκολάcτων the adj.
     (*unrestrained, licentious*) is here used as a noun (*sensualist*).

16 φοβούμενοι μὴ οὐχ ... see 14.1/4*c*(ii).

17 τοῖς πολλοῖς *for the majority* (cf. 8.2.11); ὕβριν is governed by τίκτουσαν, which agrees with εὐπρᾱξίᾱν; πάροιθ'(ε) is an adv. but translate by an adj. *former.*

15.3 Extra reading

Prometheus Bound (1)

This is the first of two passages from the *Prometheus Bound,* a play which has come down under the name of the first great Attic tragedian, Aeschylus (525–456 BC). Its plot, like that of nearly all tragedies, is taken from mythology.

Prometheus, who belonged to an older but minor order of divinities called Titans, had helped Zeus wrestle supreme control of heaven from his father Cronos. At this stage mankind lived in primitive squalor, but Prometheus took pity on them and gave them fire. This he was obliged to steal from heaven as it had been the exclusive possession of the gods. Zeus, incensed by the theft, ordered that Prometheus be fastened to a rock at the ends of the earth. In the following scene, with which the play opens, Zeus' henchman Κράτος (*Might*), who with his fellow lackey Βία (*Violence*) has escorted Prometheus to the rock, tells Hephaestus, the divine blacksmith, to execute Zeus' command.

ΚΡΑΤΟΣ
χθονὸς μὲν εἰς τηλουρὸν ἥκομεν πέδον,
Σκύθην ἐς οἶμον, ἄβροτον εἰς ἐρημίαν.
Ἥφαιστε, σοὶ δὲ χρὴ μέλειν ἐπιστολὰς
ἅς σοι πατὴρ ἐφεῖτο (*enjoined on*), τόνδε πρὸς πέτραις
ὑψηλοκρήμνοις τὸν λεωργὸν ὀχμάσαι   5
ἀδαμαντίνων δεσμῶν ἐν ἀρρήκτοις πέδαις.
τὸ σὸν γὰρ ἄνθος, παντέχνου πυρὸς σέλας,
θνητοῖσι κλέψας ὤπασεν. τοιᾶσδέ τοι
ἁμαρτίας σφε δεῖ θεοῖς δοῦναι (*to give* i.e. *to pay*) δίκην,
ὡς ἂν διδαχθῇ τὴν Διὸς τυραννίδα   10
στέργειν, φιλανθρώπου δὲ παύεσθαι τρόπου.

ῬΦΑΙΣΤΟΣ

Κράτος Βία τε, σφῷν μὲν ἐντολὴ Διὸς
ἔχει τέλος δὴ κοὐδὲν ἐμποδὼν ἔτι,
ἐγὼ δ᾽ ἄτολμός εἰμι συγγενῆ θεὸν
δῆσαι βίᾳ φάραγγι πρὸς δυσχειμέρῳ.   15
πάντως δ᾽ ἀνάγκη τῶνδέ μοι τόλμαν σχεθεῖν·
εὐωριάζειν γὰρ πατρὸς λόγους βαρύ.
τῆς ὀρθοβούλου Θέμιδος αἰπυμῆτα παῖ,
ἄκοντά σ᾽ ἄκων δυσλύτοις χαλκεύμασι
προσπασσαλεύσω τῷδ᾽ ἀπανθρώπῳ πάγῳ,   20
ἵν᾽ οὔτε φωνὴν οὔτε του μορφὴν βροτῶν
ὄψῃ, σταθευτὸς δ᾽ ἡλίου φοίβῃ φλογὶ
χροιᾶς ἀμείψεις ἄνθος· ἀσμένῳ δέ σοι
ἡ ποικιλείμων νὺξ ἀποκρύψει φάος
πάχνην θ᾽ ἑῴαν ἥλιος σκεδᾷ (*will scatter*) πάλιν·   25
ἀεὶ δὲ τοῦ παρόντος ἀχθηδὼν κακοῦ
τρύσει σ᾽, ὁ λωφήσων γὰρ οὐ πέφυκέ πω.

Notes

*ll.*1f. In poetry the demonstrative adjective, as well as the definite
article, can be omitted, and in English we would supply *this* with
πέδον, οἶμον and ἐρημίαν; take Σκύθην with οἶμον and ἄβροτον with
ἐρημίᾱν. *l.*3 δέ is here used idiomatically in a clause following a
vocative and should not be translated; ἐπιστολάς is the subject of
μέλειν (which governs the dative σοί). *l.*4 πατήρ i.e. Zeus, whom
Homer calls *father of gods and men. l.*5 ὀχμάσαι aor. inf., to be taken
after ἐπιστολάς which it explains. *l.*7 ἄνθος *flower* but here
metaphorically *glory, pride*; παντέχνου lit. *[required] for all arts*
because fire was seen as necessary for any technological progress. *ll.*8f.
θνητοῖσι = θνητοῖς (3.1/1 note 3); κλέψας ὤπασεν lit. *having stolen ...
he gave [it]*; τοιᾶσδέ ... ἁμαρτίᾱς gen. with δίκην (*penalty for such a
wrong*); σφε = αὐτόν, i.e. Prometheus. *l.*10 ὡς ἄν + subj. expresses
purpose (= ἵνα + subj. 14.1/4*c*(i)). *l.*11 παύεσθαι is followed by a gen.
(φιλανθρώπου ... τρόπου). *l.*12 σφῷν *for you two* (24.1/4). *l.*13 κοὐδέν =
καὶ οὐδέν (11.1/5). *l.*15 δῆσαι aor. inf. act. of δέω *bind. ll.*16f. Supply
ἐστί with both ἀνάγκη and βαρύ. *l.*19 σ᾽= σε (also in *l.*27); δυσλύτοις
χαλκεύμασι dat. of instrument (11.1/2). *l.*20 τῷδ᾽(ε) ἀπανθρώπῳ πάγῳ
to this ... the dat. is governed by the προσ– of προσπασσαλεύσω. *l.*21
ἵν᾽(α) (+ ind.) *where*; του = τινός (10.1/1). *l.*22 ὄψῃ (< ὁράω) lit. *you will*

see is appropriate to μορφήν but not to φωνήν although it governs both
– trans. *you will perceive.* *l.*23 χροιᾶς ἀμείψεις ἄνθος *you will alter* (i.e.
lose) *the bloom* (lit. *flower*) *of [your] skin* (through constant exposure
to the sun Prometheus' skin will become tanned and rough); ἀсμένῳ ...
соι *for you [being] glad* dat. of reference (24.1/2e). *l.*25 θ' i.e. τε. *l.*27 ὁ
λωφήсων lit. *the [one] going to relieve*; γάρ can be placed after the first
phrase rather than the first word; πέφῡκε (perf. of φύω is always
intransitive) *has been born.*

16 | UNIT SIXTEEN

16.1 Grammar

16.1/1 Phrases and clauses of result

Result in English is usually expressed by a subordinate clause of the type (*he was so poor*) *that he couldn't buy food,* although we may omit *that* and say *he was so poor he couldn't buy food.* In Greek the corresponding conjunction, ὥcτε *that, so that,* is always expressed. As in English, there is usually an anticipatory word in the main clause such as οὕτωc *so, to such an extent;* τοιοῦτοc *of this kind, of such a kind;* τοcοῦτοc *so much,* pl. *so many* (on the declension of the last two see note 1 below).

ὥcτε is usually followed by an **infinitive**, particularly where the result is to be marked as merely contemplated or in prospect and not stressed as a fact (here ὥcτε is to be translated *as* – see first example). Where the subject of the infinitive is the same as the subject of the main verb, it is normally not expressed; where it is different, it is in the accusative (just as in the infinitive construction of indirect statement (8.1/3)). If the infinitive is negated, the negative is μή:

οὕτω cκαιὸc εἶ ὥcτε μὴ δύναcθαι μανθάνειν.	*You are so stupid as not to be able to understand.*
τοcαύτην κραυγὴν ἐποίηcαν ὥcτε τοὺc ταξιάρχουc ἐλθεῖν.	*They made such a din that the taxiarchs came* (i.e. *such a din as to cause the taxiarchs to come*).

ὥcτε + infinitive may also express an **intended** result. The distinction between this and a purpose clause can be tenuous: τοῦτο ποιοῦcιν ὥcτε μὴ ἀποθανεῖν *they are doing this so as not to die.*

ὥϲτε may also be followed by a finite verb in the **indicative** (negated by
οὐ), but only where there is emphasis on the actual occurrence of the
result; so οὕτω ϲκαιὸϲ εἶ ὥϲτε οὐ δύναϲαι μανθάνειν would mean *you
are so stupid that you [actually] cannot understand*; ἐπέπεϲε χιὼν
ἄπλετοϲ ὥϲτε ἀπέκρυψε καὶ τὰ ὅπλα καὶ τοὺϲ ἀνθρώπουϲ *an immense
amount of* (lit. *boundless*) *snow fell so that it [actually] covered both the
weapons and the men.*

Notes

1   τοιοῦτοϲ and τοϲοῦτοϲ are compounds of οὗτοϲ (9.1/1) and are
    inflected in the same way, except that the initial τ which οὗτοϲ has in
    most forms is dropped: τοιοῦτοϲ, τοιαύτη, τοιοῦτο(ν); τοϲοῦτοϲ,
    τοϲαύτη, τοϲοῦτο(ν) (unlike τοῦτο, the neuter s. nom. and acc. can
    end in ν).
2   ὥϲτε may be used to introduce an independent sentence, with much the
    same force as οὖν, i.e. *and so, therefore, consequently*: οὐχ ἧκεν·
    ὥϲτε οἱ Ἕλληνεϲ ἐφρόντιζον *he had not come; consequently, the
    Greeks were worried.*
3   The English phrase *to such a pitch/point/degree of x* is expressed in Greek
    by εἰϲ τοῦτο or εἰϲ τοϲοῦτο(ν) + genitive (cf. 23.1/1d): εἰϲ τοϲοῦτον
    ὕβρεωϲ ἦλθον ὥϲτε ἔπειϲαν ὑμᾶϲ ἐλαύνειν αὐτόν *they reached such
    a pitch of insolence that they persuaded you to drive him out.*
4   ὥϲτε may also be used in the sense *on the condition that* to express a
    condition or proviso: ὑπέϲχοντο ὥϲτε ἐκπλεῖν *they made a promise
    on condition that they should sail away.*

    However, *on condition that* is more usually expressed by ἐφ᾽ ᾧ or ἐφ᾽
    ᾧτε followed by an infinitive or, less frequently, by a future indicative:
    ἐποιήϲαντο εἰρήνην ἐφ᾽ ᾧ   τὰ μακρὰ τείχη καθελόντεϲ τοῖϲ
    Λακεδαιμονίοιϲ ἕπεϲθαι (or ἕψονται) *they made peace on condition
    that after taking down the long walls they would follow the Spartans.*
    Both the infinitive and future indicative in conditions of this type are
    negated by μή.
5   For the use of a comparative + ἢ ὥϲτε, see 17.1/4c.

16.1/2 Pluperfect indicative active

The Greek pluperfect exists only in the indicative mood. It is normally to
be translated by the same tense in English (*I **had washed** before you
came*) but its use is much more restricted (see below).

The pluperfect is a **historic** tense (4.1/1 note 1) and its active stem is formed from that of the perfect active. Where the latter contains reduplication (15.1/1), the pluperfect active stem is formed by adding the augment, e.g.

PERFECT ACTIVE STEM	PLUPERFECT ACTIVE STEM
λελυκ– (λύω)	ἐλελυκ–
γεγραφ– (γράφω)	ἐγεγραφ–
πεπομφ– (πέμπω)	ἐπεπομφ–

Where, however, the perfect active stem is already augmented it is also used for the pluperfect without change, e.g. ἠχ– (ἄγω).

The pluperfect active endings are: –η, –ης, –ει(ν), –εμεν, –ετε, –εϲαν. For the conjugation of ἐλελύκη *I had loosened* see **Appendix 1**.

The pluperfect is the past version of the perfect and thus expresses a state that existed in the past (cf. 15./1):

ἔθυον πρότερον οἱ Πελαϲγοι τοῖϲ θεοῖϲ, ὄνομα δὲ ἐποιοῦντο οὐδενὶ αὐτῶν· οὐ γὰρ ἀκηκόεϲάν πω.	*Formerly the Pelasgians used to sacrifice to the gods but gave a name to none of them; for they had not yet (πω) heard [their names]* (i.e. they were in a state of ignorance about the names of the gods).

The pluperfect is relatively uncommon in Greek. In English we often use the pluperfect in subordinate clauses to denote an action which happened two stages back in the past, e.g. *when the soldiers had assembled, Cyrus spoke as follows* (if we regard Cyrus' speaking as one stage back in the past, then the soldiers' assembling, which happened before Cyrus' speaking, is two stages back in the past). Greek, however, normally regards both actions as single past events and uses two aorists: ἐπεὶ οἱ ϲτρατιῶται ϲυνῆλθον, Κῦροϲ ἔλεξε τάδε (lit. *when the soldiers assembled ...,* which we can also say in English). It would be possible to regard the soldiers as being in a state of having assembled and so justify a Greek pluperfect, but in subordinate clauses of time and reason (and also relative clauses) this is rarely done.

16.1/3 Perfect and pluperfect indicative middle/passive

In both the perfect and pluperfect the middle and passive voices have the same forms.

PERFECT

The stem of the strong perfect active is retained in the middle/passive, but that of the weak perfect active loses its κ. Consequently the distinction between strong and weak perfects is not maintained. As, however, the stem of the perfect middle/passive is not always predictable, the first person perfect indicative middle/passive is included in the principal parts of irregular verbs (7.1/1 note 3 and **Principal parts of verbs**).

When a perfect middle/passive stem ends in a vowel or diphthong[1] (e.g. λελυ–, νενῑκη–) the endings –μαι, –σαι, –ται, –μεθα, –σθε, –νται are added (for the conjugation of λέλυμαι *I have ransomed* (mid.), *I have been loosened* (pass.) see **Appendix 1**).

When a perfect middle/passive stem ends in a consonant, a sound change is necessary in certain cases to assimilate the final consonant of the stem to the initial consonant of the ending. With all consonant stems a succession of three consonants in the second and third plural is avoided; in the second plural the c of the ending (–σθε) is dropped, but in the third plural Attic Greek sidesteps the difficulty by using a two-word periphrasis consisting of the perfect middle /passive participle (see 16.1/4) and the third plural present of εἰμί.

Consonant stems are classified in the same way as for the present tense (6.1/4 and 11.1/3):

(a) *Palatal stems*

The final palatal of the stem appears as γ before –μαι and –μεθα (and –μένοι of the participle), and as κ before –σαι (giving –ξαι) and –ται. In the second pl. κ + σθε > κθε > χθε (the κ is aspirated to assimilate it to θ). From φυλάττω *guard* (perf. mid./pass. stem πεφυλακ–) we have:

	S.		PL.	
	1	πεφύλαγμαι		πεφυλάγμεθα
	2	πεφύλαξαι		πεφύλαχθε
	3	πεφύλακται		πεφυλαγμένοι εἰσί(ν)

---

[1] This occurs only in verbs with a weak perfect active where the κ of the stem is preceded by a vowel or diphthong; the strong perfect ἀκήκοα (ἀκούω) has no passive in Classical Greek.

When these forms are used as passives they mean *I have been guarded, you have been guarded*, etc. When they are used as middles their sense depends on the use of the middle involved in a particular context (8.1/1), i.e. *I have guarded myself* etc., or *I have guarded for myself* etc., or *I have had (something) guarded* etc. The participle used in the third plural varies in gender according to the subject. This applies to all forms of this type.

(*b*) *Labial stems*

The final labial of the stem appears as μ before –μαι and –μεθα (and –μένοι of the participle), and as π before –cαι (giving –ψαι) and –ται. In the second pl. π + cθε > πθε > φθε. From κρύπτω *hide* (perf. mid./pass. stem κεκρυπ–) we have:

s.	1	κέκρυμμαι	PL.	κεκρύμμεθα
	2	κέκρυψαι		κέκρυφθε
	3	κέκρυπται		κεκρυμμένοι εἰcί(ν)

The passive meaning is *I have been hidden*, etc.

(*c*) *Dental stems*

The final dental of the stem becomes c before all endings. In the second person s. and pl. cc > c. From πείθω *persuade* (perf. mid./pass. stem πεπειθ–) we have:

s.	1	πέπειcμαι	PL.	πεπείcμεθα
	2	πέπεικαι		πέπεικθε
	3	πέπεικται		πεπεικμένοι εἰcί(ν)

The passive meaning is *I have been persuaded*, etc.

(*d*) *Stems in* λ, μ, ν, ρ

The final consonant of λ and ρ stems remains unchanged. ἀγγέλλω *announce,* cπείρω *sow* (perf. mid./pass. stems ἠγγελ–, ἔcπαρ–; the α of the latter is irregular) have ἤγγελμαι, ἤγγελcαι etc. and ἔcπαρμαι, ἔcπαρcαι etc. The final consonant of ν stems is dropped in some verbs, but in others becomes c before –μαι, –μεθα, (and –μένοι). From κρῑ́νω *judge,* φαίνω *show* (perf. mid./pass. stems κεκρι–, πεφαν–) we have:

s.	1	κέκριμαι	πέφαcμαι
	2	κέκρικαι	πέφανcαι
	3	κέκριται	πέφανται
PL.	1	κεκρίμεθα	πεφάcμεθα
	2	κέκρικθε	πέφανθε
	3	κεκριμένοι εἰcι(ν)	πεφαcμένοι εἰcί(ν)

The passive meaning is *I have been judged,* etc., *I have been shown,* etc.

-η is added to the few μ stems both in the perfect active and in the perfect middle/passive, e.g. νέμω *apportion,* νενέμηκα (act.), νενέμημαι (mid./pass.), 3 pl. νενέμηνται.

PLUPERFECT

The pluperfect indicative middle/passive uses the perfect middle/passive stem except that the syllabic augment is added when the latter is reduplicated, e.g. ἐλελυ- (λύω), ἐπεφυλακ- (φυλάττω); but ἐσπαρ- (σπείρω) is used for both perfect and pluperfect (cf. 16.1/2). The historic middle/passive endings are –μην, –σο, –το, –μεθα, –σθε, –ντο (cf. 8.1/1*f*). For the conjugation of ἐλελύμην *I had ransomed* (mid.), *I had been loosened* (pass.) see **Appendix 1**. With stems ending in a consonant the same sound changes are involved as with the perfect indicative middle/passive, and the perfect middle/passive participle with ἦσαν is used for the third plural, e.g.

s.			PL.	
	1	ἐπεφυλάγμην		ἐπεφυλάγμεθα
	2	ἐπεφύλαξο		ἐπεφύλαχθε
	3	ἐπεφύλακτο		πεφυλαγμένοι ἦσαν

The passive meaning is *I had been guarded* etc.

Note

Third **plural** endings in –αται (< νται) and –ατο (< ντο) occur in early Attic and other dialects, e.g. πεφυλάχαται (perf. – its passive meaning is *they have been guarded*), ἐπεφυλάχατο (pluperf. – its passive meaning is *they had been guarded*). These endings must be carefully distinguished from third **singular** endings in –ται and –το.

16.1/4 Other parts of the perfect tense

The perfect infinitives and participles are formed from the same stems as the corresponding indicatives (the reduplication or the temporal/syllabic augment of the perfect indicative stem is **not** dropped). The infinitive endings are –έναι (act.) and –σθαι (mid./pass.; with consonantal stems this ending undergoes the same changes as –σθε). The active participle is a first and third declension adjective (10.1/3) in –ώς, –υῖα, –ός (see below), and the middle/passive participle is a first and second declension adjective (3.1/3) in –μένος, –μένη, –μένον.[1] In the following table for

---

[1] The accent of all forms of the perfect middle/passive participle is on the second syllable from the end (paroxytone, see **Appendix 9**, b(*v*)).

λύω, φυλάττω, κρύπτω, πείθω, κρῑνω only the masculine forms of the participles are given.

Infinitives		**Participles**	
ACTIVE	MIDDLE/PASSIVE	ACTIVE	MIDDLE/PASSIVE
λελυκέναι	λελύcθαι	λελυκώc	λελυμένοc
to have loosened	mid. to have ransomed	having loosened	mid. having ransomed
	pass. to have been loosened		pass. having been loosened
πεφυλαχέναι	πεφυλάχθαι	πεφυλαχώc	πεφυλαγμένοc
κεκρυφέναι	κεκρύφθαι	κεκρυφώc	κεκρυμμένοc
πεποιθέναι		πεποιθώc	
πεπεισθαι	πεπεῖcθαι		πεπεισμένοc[1]
πεπεικέναι		πεπεικώc	
κεκρικέναι	κεκρίcθαι	κεκρικώc	κεκριμένοc

The corresponding forms of the aorist are sometimes to be translated in the same way as those of the perfect, but the meanings and uses of the two tenses are quite distinct. The perfect always expresses a state (on the meaning of the aorist see 4.1/1, 12.1/1).

λελυκώc is declined:

	SINGULAR			PLURAL		
	M.	F.	N.	M.	F.	N.
N.V.	λελυκώc	λελυκυῖα	λελυκόc	λελυκότεc	λελυκυῖαι	λελυκότα
Acc.	λελυκότα	λελυκυῖαν	λελυκόc	λελυκόταc	λελυκυίᾱc	λελυκότα
Gen.	λελυκότοc	λελυκυίᾱc	λελυκότοc	λελυκότων	λελυκυιῶν	λελυκότων
Dat.	λελυκότι	λελυκυίᾳ	λελυκότι	λελυκόcι(ν)	λελυκυίαιc	λελυκόcι(ν)

Notes

1 A perfect subjunctive and perfect optative exist but are rare. The active is formed by adding to the active stem the endings –ω, –ῃc, –ῃ, –ωμεν, –ητε, –ωcι(ν) (subj., giving λελύκω etc.) and –οιμι, –οιc, –οι, –οιμεν, –οιτε, –οιεν (opt., giving λελύκοιμι etc.). There are alternative active forms consisting of the perfect active participle and the appropriate part of εἰμί: λελυκὼc ὦ, etc. (subj.); λελυκὼc εἴην etc. (opt.). In the middle/passive the subjunctive and optative follow the latter pattern (subj. λελυμένοc ὦ etc., opt. λελυμένοc εἴην etc.) For tables see **Appendix 1**.

---

[1] On the two perfect stems of πείθω see 15.1/1 note 2.

2 Greek has also a **future perfect** tense, which expresses a future state.
For most verbs it exists only in the passive and is not common. Its
stem is formed by adding c to the perfect middle/passive stem (e.g.
λελῦc–), and to this are added the present middle/passive endings, viz
λελῦcομαι *I shall have been loosened,* λελῦcῃ (–ει), λελῦcεται,
λελῦcόμεθα, λελῦcεcθε, λελῦcονται The future perfect occurs
mostly with verbs whose perfect has a present meaning (19.1/3*a*) and
for this reason is not included in Appendix 1.

16.2 Greek reading

1 ἐπεὶ δὲ ἐπὶ τὰc cκηνὰc ἦλθον, οἱ μὲν ἄλλοι περὶ τὰ ἐπιτήδεια
ἦcαν, cτρατηγοὶ δὲ καὶ λοχαγοὶ cυνῆλθον. καὶ ἐνταῦθα πολλὴ
ἀπορία ἦν. ἔνθεν μὲν γὰρ ὄρη ἦν ὑπερύψηλα, ἔνθεν δὲ ὁ ποταμὸc
τοcοῦτοc ὥcτε μηδὲ τὰ δόρατα ὑπερέχειν πειρωμένοιc τοῦ βάθουc.

2 ὁ Διογένηc, ἐρωτηθεὶc διὰ τί οἱ ἀθληταὶ ἀναίcθητοί εἰcιν, ἔφη ὅτι
κρέαcιν ὑείοιc καὶ βοείοιc ἀνῳκοδόμηνται.

3 γαμεῖν κεκρικότα δεῖ.

4 πάντα τὸν βίον ἐν κινδύνοιc διατελοῦμεν ὄντεc, ὥcτε οἱ περὶ
ἀcφαλείαc διαλεγόμενοι λελήθαcιν αὑτοὺc τὸν πόλεμον εἰc
ἅπαντα τὸν χρόνον καταcκευάζοντεc.

5 κύνα δέρειc δεδαρμένην.

6 οἱ Ποτειδεᾶται προcδεχόμενοι τοὺc Ἀθηναίουc ἐcτρατοπεδεύοντο
πρὸc Ὀλύνθου ἐν τῷ ἰcθμῷ, καὶ ἀγορὰν ἔξω τῆc πόλεωc
ἐπεποίηντο. καὶ cτρατηγὸν μὲν τοῦ πεζοῦ παντὸc οἱ ξύμμαχοι
ᾕρηντο Ἀριcτέα, τῆc δὲ ἵππου Περδίκκαν.

7 ἐπεὶ οἱ βάρβαροι ἐκ τῆc χώραc ἀπῆλθον, οἱ Ἀθηναῖοι τὴν ἑαυτῶν
πόλιν ἀνοικοδομεῖν παρεcκευάζοντο. τῶν γὰρ οἰκιῶν αἱ μὲν
πολλαὶ ἐπεπτώκεcαν, ὀλίγαι δὲ περιῆcαν, ἐν αἷc αὐτοὶ ἐcκήνωcαν
οἱ δυνατοὶ τῶν Περcῶν.

8 εἰc ἠκονημέναc μαχαίραc ἡ αἴξ ἥκει.

9 καὶ τὴν μὲν νύκτα ἐνταῦθα διήγαγον· ἐπεὶ δ᾽ ἡμέρα ὑπέφαινεν,
ἐπορεύοντο cιγῇ cυντεταγμένοι ἐπὶ τοὺc πολεμίουc· καὶ γὰρ
ὁμίχλη ἐγένετο, ὥcτε ἔλαθον ἐγγὺc προcελθόντεc.

10 ἔπειτα δὲ καὶ πρὸc ἅπανταc τοὺc μετὰ Δημοcθένουc ὁμολογία
γίγνεται, ἐφ᾽ ᾧτε μὴ ἀποθανεῖν μηδένα, μήτε βιαίωc, μήτε δεcμοῖc,
μήτε cίτου ἐνδείᾳ.

11 Τιρίβαζοc εἶπεν ὅτι cπείcαcθαι βούλοιτο ἐφ᾽ ᾧ μήτε αὐτὸc τοὺc

Ἕλληνας ἀδικεῖν, μήτ' ἐκείνους καίειν τὰς οἰκίας, λαμβάνειν τε
τὰ ἐπιτήδεια ὧν δέοιντο. ἔδοξε ταῦτα τοῖς ϲτρατηγοῖς καὶ
ἐϲπείϲαντο ἐπὶ τούτοις.

12 οὐδὲ βουλεύεϲθαι ἔτι ὥρα, ὦ Cώκρατες, ἀλλὰ βεβουλεῦϲθαι. μία
δὲ βουλή· τῆϲδε γὰρ τῆϲ νυκτὸϲ πάντα ταῦτα δεῖ πεπρᾶχθαι.

13 οὕτως οὖν οὐ ταὐτόν ἐϲτι θάρϲοϲ τε καὶ ἀνδρεία· ὥϲτε ϲυμβαίνει
τοὺϲ μὲν ἀνδρείουϲ θαρραλέουϲ εἶναι, μὴ μέντοι τούϲ γε
θαρραλέουϲ ἀνδρείουϲ πάνταϲ· θάρϲοϲ μὲν γὰρ καὶ ἀπὸ τέχνηϲ
γίγνεται ἀνθρώποιϲ καὶ ἀπὸ θυμοῦ καὶ ἀπὸ μανίαϲ, ὥϲπερ ἡ
δύναμιϲ, ἀνδρεία δ' ἀπὸ φύϲεωϲ καὶ εὐτροφίαϲ τῶν ψυχῶν 5
γίγνεται.

14 οἱ Λακεδαιμόνιοι τὰϲ ϲπονδὰϲ προτέρουϲ λελυκέναι τοὺϲ
Ἀθηναίουϲ ἡγοῦντο.

15 ἡ αἲξ οὔπω τέτοκεν.

16 Φίλιππος, ὁ πατὴρ τοῦ μεγάλου Ἀλεξάνδρου, φρούριόν τι
βουλόμενοϲ λαβεῖν ὀχυρόν, ὡϲ ἀπήγγειλαν οἱ κατάϲκοποι
χαλεπὸν εἶναι παντάπαϲι καὶ ἀνάλωτον, ἠρώτηϲεν εἰ χαλεπὸν
οὕτως ἐϲτὶν ὥϲτε μηδὲ ὄνον προϲελθεῖν χρυϲίον κομίζοντα.

Notes

1 ἦλθον *had come* (16.1/2); περὶ ... ἦϲαν *were busy with*; πειρωμένοιϲ
τοῦ βάθουϲ lit. *for [them] testing the depth.*

2 ὅτι here *because*; ἀνῳκοδόμηνται < ἀνοικοδομέω.

3 κεκρικότα agrees with ἄνδρα understood, lit. *it is necessary for a
man ...*

4 εἰϲ + acc. is used here instead of the plain acc. for emphasis (cf.
7.1/7a).

6 ᾕρηντο < αἱρέομαι *choose* (18.1/4); ἡ ἵπποϲ *the cavalry.*

7 αἱ πολλαί *the majority, most* (cf. 8.2.11 and 15.2.17); ἐπεπτώκεϲαν
< πίπτω.

8 ἠκονημένᾱϲ < ἀκονάω.

9 ὑπέφαινεν, ἐπορεύοντο inceptive imperfects (*began to ...*).

11 βούλοιτο (and later δέοιντο) opt. in reported speech in historic
sequence (14.1/4d); μήτε ... μήτ' introduce the negated conditions
(*that neither he ... nor they...*); the subject of λαμβάνειν is ἐκείνουϲ
from the previous phrase but note that it is **not** negated; ἔδοξε ταῦτα
these things seemed good.

12 οὐδὲ ... ἔτι ὥρα supply ἐϲτί *nor [is it] still [the] time*; βεβουλεῦϲθαι
i.e. *to have finished deliberating.*

13 *l.*1 ταὐτόν *the same [thing]*; the subject of ἐcτί is θάρcoc and ἀνδρείᾱ (with double subjects the verb may agree with only the nearer one).

14 Take προτέρους with τοὺς Ἀθηναίους, which is the subject of λελυκέναι.

16 ὡc *when*; ἐcτίν present tense because in indirect speech Greek always retains the tense of the original direct speech (7.1/3); Philip cynically implies that any fort can be captured if a sufficient bribe is offered to a potential traitor; προcελθεῖν the infinitive here denotes a **possible** result, *could approach.*

16.3 Extra reading

Heracles

After an attack of madness, Heracles wakes up to find himself tied to a pillar and surrounded by destruction which he himself has unwittingly perpetrated. The passage is from the Ἡρακλῆc of Euripides (485–406 BC), the third of the great Attic tragedians.

ἔμπνους μέν εἰμι καὶ δέδορχ᾽ ἅπερ με δεῖ,
αἰθέρα τε καὶ γῆν τόξα θ᾽ ἡλίου τάδε.
ὡc δ᾽ ἐν κλύδωνι καὶ φρενῶν ταράγματι
πέπτωκα δεινῷ καὶ πνοὰc θερμὰc πνέω
μετάρcι᾽, οὐ βέβαια πλευμόνων ἄπο.   5
ἰδού, τί δεcμοῖc ναῦc ὅπωc ὡρμιcμένοc
νεανίαν θώρακα καὶ βραχίονα
πρὸc ἡμιθραύcτῳ λαΐνῳ τυκίcματι
ἧμαι, νεκροῖcι γείτοναc θάκουc ἔχων;
πτερωτὰ δ᾽ ἔγχη τόξα τ᾽ ἔcπαρται πέδῳ,   10
ἃ πρὶν παραcπίζοντ᾽ ἐμοῖc βραχίοcιν
ἔcῳζε πλευρὰc ἐξ ἐμοῦ τ᾽ ἐcῴζετο.
οὔ που κατῆλθον αὖθιc εἰc Ἅιδου πάλιν,
Εὐρυcθέωc δίαυλον ἐξ Ἅιδου μολών;
ἀλλ᾽ οὔτε Cιcύφειον εἰcορῶ πέτρον   15
Πλούτωνά τ᾽ οὐδὲ cκῆπτρα Δήμητροc κόρηc.
ἔκ τοι πέπληγμαι· ποῦ ποτ᾽ ὢν ἀμηχανῶ;
ὠή, τίc ἐγγὺc ἢ πρόcω φίλων ἐμῶν
δύcγνοιαν ὅcτιc τὴν ἐμὴν ἰάcεται;

Notes

*l.*1 δέδορχ' (= –κα) the perfect here is virtually an emphatic present *I really see*. *ll.*3ff. ὡϲ ... exclamatory, lit. *how I have fallen in a terrible wave* ... i.e. *into what a terrible wave* ...; μετάρϲι'(α) ... βέβαια n. acc. pl. used adverbially (20.1/5), lit. *how* (ὡϲ *l.*3) ... *I breathe warm breaths shallowly, not steadily from my lungs* (Heracles is panting but does not know why); ἄπο on the accent of disyllabic prepositions when they follow the word they govern see note on 11.2.4. *ll.*6f. Take ναῦϲ ὅπωϲ together *like a ship*; ὡμιϲμένοϲ (< ὁρμίζω) *anchored*; νεᾱνίᾱν here used adjectivally in the sense *sturdy* (not *youthful*, Heracles being no longer young); θώρακα καὶ βραχίονα lit. *with respect to chest and arm* this use of the accusative (called *accusative of respect*, 20.1/5) is used to clarify verbs and adjectives; here the accusatives tell where (i.e. with respect to what parts of his body) Heracles is anchored (ὡρμιϲμένοϲ). *l.*9 ἧμαι (19.1/3*b*) *I sit*; θάκουϲ trans. by a singular *seat* (the plural is often used for the singular in verse; cf. τόξα in *l.*10 and ϲκῆπτρα in *l.*16). *l.*10 The *winged weapons* (πτερωτὰ ἔγχη) are arrows; ἔϲπαρται 3rd s. perf. ind. pass. of ϲπείρω. *l.*11 πρίν (here an adverb) *previously, formerly*; παραϲπίζοντ'(α) governs the following dative, lit. *shielding my arms*. *l.*12 ἐξ = ὑπό *by*. *l.*14 Eurystheus was the king of Mycenae for whom Heracles had to complete his twelve labours (one of them, the descent to Hades to bring back Cerberus, is referred to here); Εὐρυϲθέωϲ δίαυλον lit. *the double course* (i.e. the descent and return) *of* (i.e. *prescribed by*) *Eurystheus*; μολών (aor. pple. of βλώϲκω) to be taken with δίαυλον *going [on] the double course* (acc. of spatial extent, 7.1/7*d*). *ll.*15f. Sisyphus was one of the sights of Hades. For his sins on earth he had to push a rock to the top of a hill, but when he reached the summit the rock invariably rolled down and he had to start afresh; οὔτε ... τ'(ε) ... οὐδέ *neither ... or* (lit. *and*) ... *nor yet* (οὐδέ indicates a slight climax). *l.*16 The daughter of Demeter was Persephone, who was the wife of Pluto (= Hades). *l.*17 ἐκ ... πέπληγμαι = ἐκπέπληγμαι (tmesis, see 12.3.9 *l.*6); ποῦ etc. lit. *wherever being am I helpless?* but the emphasis is on ὤν and we must translate *wherever am I in my helplessness?*

17 UNIT SEVENTEEN

17.1 Grammar

17.1/1 Imperative mood: commands and prohibitions

The imperative mood is used for **commands**. In Greek it exists in the present and aorist tenses (and also the perfect – see note 4). The stem used is the same as that of the corresponding indicative. As well as second person imperatives (which we have in English), Greek also has imperatives in the **third** person with the meanings given below.

The imperative of λύω is

Present

		ACTIVE		MIDDLE/PASSIVE	
S.	2	λῦε	*loosen!*	λύου	mid. *ransom!*
					pass. *be loosened!*
	3	λῦέτω	*let him loosen!*	λῦέcθω	mid. *let him ransom!*
					pass. *let him be loosened!*
PL.	2	λύετε	*loosen!*	λύεcθε	mid. *ransom!*
					pass. *be loosened!*
	3	λῦόντων[1]	*let them loosen!*	λῦέcθων	mid. *let them ransom!*
					pass. *let them be loosened!*

Aorist

		ACTIVE	MIDDLE	PASSIVE
S.	2	λῦcον	λῦcαι	λύθητι
	3	λῦcάτω	λῦcάcθω	λυθήτω
PL.	2	λύcατε	λύcαcθε	λύθητε
	3	λῦcάντων	λῦcάcθων	λυθέντων

---

[1] Note that λῦόντων, λῦcάντων, and λυθέντων can also be the gen. pl. of masculine and neuter of the corresponding participles.

The aorist is usually to be translated in the same way as the present but the two are not interchangeable. The difference, as elsewhere, is one of aspect. The present is used for an action which is seen as going on, in the process of happening or being repeated, the aorist for an action which is seen simply as an event. Sometimes this distinction can be brought out in English by using a verbal periphrasis:

κροῦcον (aor.) ἐκείνην τὴν μυῖαν.   *Swat that fly!*

κροῦε (pres.) ἐκείνην τὴν μυῖαν.   *Keep swatting that fly!*

Generally the present imperative is used with verbs which in themselves imply continual action, e.g. cπεῦδε βραδέωc *hasten slowly,* while the aorist imperative is used with verbs which usually (but not necessarily) indicate a single act, e.g. καῦcον πῦρ ἐν τῇ ἑcτίᾳ *light a fire in the hearth.*

Prohibitions (negative commands) are expressed with μή, e.g. μὴ πᾶcι πίcτευε *do not trust everyone*; μηδεὶc τοῦτο ἀγνοείτω *let no-one be unaware of this,* but if the **aorist** aspect is appropriate the mood employed is always the **subjunctive**, not the imperative:

μὴ ἐπὶ δουλείᾱν ἑκὼν ἔλθῃc.   *Do not go willingly to slavery.*

μηδεὶc θαυμάcῃ.   *Let no-one be surprised.*

For the other use of this (jussive) subjunctive see 14.1/4a(i).

To express a very strong prohibition οὐ μή and the future indicative is used, e.g.

τί ποιεῖc; οὐ μὴ καταβήcει.   *What are you doing? You shall (or must) not come down.*

Notes

1. The imperative of the strong aorist has the same endings as the present. From μανθάνω (aor. ἔμαθον) the aor. imp. act is μάθε, μαθέτω, μάθετε, μαθόντων. However, five strong aorist imperatives are irregularly accented on the last syllable in the second person singular: εἰπέ (λέγω), ἐλθέ (ἔρχομαι), εὑρέ (εὑρίcκω), ἰδέ (ὁράω), λαβέ (λαμβάνω).

2. The imperative of the root aorist (11.1/1) follows that of the aorist passive except that the ending for the 2nd s. is –θι, not –τι: from ἔγνων (γιγνώcκω) we have γνῶθι, γνώτω, γνῶτε, γνόντων.

3. The present imperative of contracted verbs is regular but, because of contraction, the 2nd s. forms are easily confused:

Active	τίμᾱ (τίμαε)	ποίει (ποίεε)	δήλου (δήλοε)
Mid./pass.	τιμῶ (τιμάου)	ποιοῦ (ποιέου)	δηλοῦ (δηλόου)

The position of the accent can be important for distinguishing between different forms, e.g. ποίει (imp.), ποιεῖ (ind.).

4   In addition to the present and aorist there is also a perfect imperative. The perfect imperative active consists of the perfect active participle and the imperative of εἰμί (see below note 6), e.g. λελυκὼc ἴcθι (lit. *be in a state of having loosened*); but the perfect imperative middle/passive has single-word forms, e.g. λέλυcο (lit. *be in a state of having been loosened*). This is rare except in verbs whose perfect has a present meaning (19.1/3*a*), e.g. μέμνηcο *remember!* (< μέμνημαι). For these forms of λύω see **Appendix 1**.

5   The **infinitive** is sometimes used instead of the second person imperative, (cf. English *Not to worry*, i.e. *do not worry*): πάντως, ὦ Κριτόβουλε, ἀπαληθεῦσαι πρὸς ἡμᾶς *at any rate, Critobulus, tell the truth to us.*

6   The imperative of εἰμί is ἴcθι *be!*, ἔcτω, ἔcτε, ἔcτων (or ὄντων). ἴcθι is also the 2nd s. imperative active of οἶδα (19.1/3*a*), with the meaning *know!*

7   Some imperatives have a fixed use:

χαῖρε, χαίρετε *hello* or *goodbye* (χαίρω *rejoice*)
ἔρρε, ἔρρετε *be damned! go to hell!* ἐρρέτω *let him/her/it be damned!* (ἔρρω *go to one's harm*)
ἄγε, ἄγετε; φέρε, φέρετε *come on! come now!* (by way of encouragement).

17.1/2 Comparison of adjectives and adverbs

Adjectives (and adverbs) have three degrees: **positive** *bad, sick, wonderful*; **comparative** *worse, sicker, more wonderful*; **superlative** *worst, sickest, most wonderful*. To give the three degrees of an adjective is to **compare** it. Some adjectives in English are compared regularly (*sick, wonderful*), some irregularly (*bad*). The same applies in Greek. By far the greater number of adjectives are compared by the addition of suffixes, and of these Greek has two sets:

(*a*) *Comparative in* –τεροc, *superlative in* –τατοc

In this type both the comparative in –τεροc (f. –τερᾱ, n. –τερον) and the superlative in –τατοc (f. –τατη, n. –τατον) are first and second declension adjectives (3.1/3). All regularly compared adjectives belong here. The way in which –τερος and –τατος are attached to the stem of an adjective depends on the class of its positive form:

(i) First and second declension adjectives (3.1/3) add –οτερος, –οτατος if the last syllable of their stem is long, but –ωτερος, –ωτατος if this is short (the stem is obtained by subtracting –ος from the nom. m. s., e.g. coφóc, stem coφ–). A syllable is long if it contains either a long vowel, or a diphthong, or a short vowel followed by two consonants (the second not being λ, μ, ν, or ρ); a syllable is short if it contains a short vowel followed by a single consonant (for further details see **Appendix 9**). Examples are:

POSITIVE	STEM	COMPARATIVE	SUPERLATIVE
coφóc	coφ–	coφώτερος	coφώτατος
wise		*wiser*	*wisest*
δίκαιος	δικαι–	δικαιότερος	δικαιότατος
just		*more just*	*most just*
ἔρημος	ἐρημ–	ἐρημότερος	ἐρημότατος
desolate		*more desolate*	*most desolate*

Some 1st and 2nd declension adjectives belong to class (*b*) below. A few others belong to class (*a*) but are irregular, e.g. φίλος *dear,* compar. φιλαίτερος, supl. φιλαίτατος or φίλτατος.

(ii) Third declension adjectives (10.1/4) with a stem in ον add –εστερος, –εστατος, e.g. ἄφρων (stem ἀφρον–) *stupid,* ἀφρονέστερος *more stupid,* ἀφρονέστατος *most stupid.* Those with a stem in εσ add –τερος, –τατος, e.g. ἀληθής (stem ἀληθεσ–) *true,* ἀληθέστερος, ἀληθέστατος.

(iii) First and third declension adjectives (10.1/3) in –εις follow χαρίεις, *charming,* χαριέστερος, χαριέστατος. Some in –υς follow γλυκύς, *sweet,* γλυκύτερος, γλυκύτατος but most are irregular (see below).

(b) *Comparative in –(τ)ων, superlative in –ιστος*

This group, which is much smaller, contains irregular adjectives from all classes. The stem of the positive form is sometimes changed for the other degrees of comparison. The following are the most common examples:

POSITIVE		COMPARATIVE	SUPERLATIVE
ἀγαθός	*good*	ἀμείνων	ἄριστος
		βελτίων	βέλτιστος
		κρείττων	κράτιστος

αἰσχρός	*ugly*	αἰσχΐων	αἴσχιστος
ἀλγεινός	*painful*	ἀλγΐων	ἄλγιστος
ἐχθρός	*hostile*	ἐχθΐων	ἔχθιστος
ἡδύς	*sweet*	ἡδΐων	ἥδιστος
κακός	*bad*	κακΐων	κάκιστος
		χείρων	χείριστος
καλός	*beautiful*	καλλΐων	κάλλιστος
μέγας	*great*	μείζων	μέγιστος
ὀλίγος	*small, few*	ἐλᾱ́ττων	ἐλάχιστος
πολύς	*much*	πλείων	πλεῖστος
ῥᾴδιος	*easy*	ῥᾴων	ῥᾷστος
ταχύς	*swift*	θᾱ́ττων	τάχιστος

Two adjectives (ἀγαθός and κακός) are compared in more than one way; κρείττων, κράτιστος (from ἀγαθός) can also mean *stronger, strongest* (cf. κράτος *power*).

Comparatives in this class are declined as third declension adjectives in ον (10.1/4*a*), but with some very important alternative forms (we can ignore the vocative, which is rare), e.g.

	SINGULAR		PLURAL	
	M. & F.	N.	M. & F.	N.
Nom.	μείζων	μεῖζον	μείζονες/μείζους	μείζονα/μείζω
Acc.	μείζονα/μείζω	μεῖζον	μείζονας/μείζους	μείζονα/μείζω
Gen.	μείζονος		μειζόνων	
Dat.	μείζονι		μείζοσι(ν)	

The alternatives are contracted versions of forms without ν (μείζω < μείζοα). The acc. pl. μείζους (< μείζοας) has an irregular contraction (ο + α normally produces ω, as in the singular). It is important to note that the forms in –ους may be **nom**. pl. as well as acc. pl.

πλείων *larger,* (pl.) *more* has a stem πλει– before ω/ου but πλει– or πλε– before ο (but always πλέον):

	SINGULAR		PLURAL	
	M. & F.	N.	M. & F.	N.
Nom.	πλείων	πλέον	πλείονες	πλείονα
			πλέονες	πλέονα
			πλείους	πλείω
Acc.	πλείονα	πλέον	πλείονας	πλείονα
	πλέονα		πλέονας	πλέονα
	πλείω		πλείους	πλείω

Gen.	πλείονος	πλειόνων
	πλέονος	πλεόνων
Dat.	πλείονι	πλείοσι(ν)
	πλέονι	πλέοσι(ν)

Adverbs formed from adjectives (e.g. coφῶc *wisely*) have as their comparative the neuter **singular** nom./acc. of the comparative of the adjective (coφώτερον *more wisely*), and as their superlative the neuter **plural** nom./acc. of the superlative (coφώτατα *most wisely*). Of the few adverbs not formed from adjectives we may note μάλα *very*, μᾶλλον *more*, μάλιστα *most*.

Notes

1 The meaning of some adjectives (e.g. πᾶc *all*) precludes a comparative or superlative.

2 The adverbs μᾶλλον *more* and μάλιστα *most* are sometimes used to compare adjectives: μᾶλλον φίλοc *more dear, dearer*; μάλιστα φίλοc *most dear, dearest*.

3 ἥττων *lesser, weaker, inferior* has no positive. Its superlative (ἥκιστος) is only common as an adverb, ἥκιστα *least of all, not at all*.

17.1/3 Meaning of the comparative and superlative

Comparatives and superlatives in Greek are not always to be understood in the sense *more X* and *most X*. A comparative adjective is sometimes used where no comparison is expressed, and indicates a higher degree than the positive. English here uses *rather* or *too* (cf. also 17.1/4):

ὁ Κῦρος ἦν πολυλογώτερος.	*Cyrus was rather talkative.*
αἱ ἐμαὶ διατριβαὶ ὑμῖν βαρύτεραι γεγόνᾱσι καὶ ἐπιφθονώτεραι.	*My discourses have become too burdensome and odious for you.*

Likewise, the superlative (without the definite article) is often used to express a very high degree:

καί ποτε ὄντος πάγου δεινοτάτου Cωκράτης ἐξῆλθεν ἱμάτιον ἔχων.	*And once when there was a very terrible frost Socrates went out wearing* (lit. *having*) *[only] a cloak.*

As in English, a superlative adjective is preceded by the definite article
when it means *the most X*: ὁ δεινότατος πάγος *the most terrible frost*. The
article is omitted, however, when a superlative adjective is used as a
predicate, e.g. ὁ Cωκράτης cόφωτατος πάντων ἐςτίν *Socrates is wisest of
all* (cf. 5./3).

17.1/4 Constructions involving the comparative and superlative

(*a*) In comparisons in English a comparative adjective or adverb is
followed by *than*. In Greek ἤ *than* (which may elsewhere mean *or*)
is used in the same way:

ἐν τοῖς ὄχλοις πιθανώτεροι οἱ ἀπαίδευτοι ἢ οἱ πεπαιδευμένοι.	*Among crowds the uneducated [are] more persuasive than the educated* (lit. *the having been educated [people]*).
τὸ μὴ εἶναι κρεῖττον ἢ τὸ ζῆν κακῶς.	*Not existing [is] better than living badly.*

ἤ is here a conjunction and what follows must be in the same case as
what precedes. Whereas in English we can nowadays say *Socrates is
wiser than me,* in Greek we must have Cωκράτης cοφώτερός ἐςτιν ἢ
ἐγώ; the first member of the comparison (Cωκράτης) is nominative
and therefore the second member must also be nominative (hence
ἐγώ).

There is, however, another construction, the **genitive of comparison**,
in which the second member of the comparison is put into the
genitive and ἤ is omitted:

ὁ χρῦcὸς κρείττων μῡρίων λόγων βροτοῖς.	*For mortals gold [is] stronger than countless words.*
οὐδὲν cιωπῆς ἐςτι χρηςιμώτερον.	*Nothing is more useful than silence.*

(*b*) A comparative may be accompanied by a dative of **measure of
difference**: κεφαλῇ ἐλάττων *shorter by a head*; μείζων πολλῷ
greater by much, i.e. *much greater.*

(*c*) In sentences of the type *he is too weak to help* ... Greek uses a
comparative adjective followed by ἢ ὥςτε and an infinitive (ὥςτε
here introduces a phrase of result – 16.1/1): μεῖζόν ἐςτι τὸ

κακὸν ἢ ὥστε φέρειν *the evil is too great to bear* (lit. *greater than so as to ...*).

(*d*)   A superlative adjective or adverb is preceded by ὡc or ὅτι (both used here adverbially) for expressions such as ὡc (ὅτι) πλεῖcτοι *as many as possible*; ὡc (ὅτι) τάχιcτα *as quickly as possible*.

17.1/5 Active verbs used in a passive sense

The verb ἀποκτείνω does not occur in the passive. Instead, Greek uses the active forms of ἀποθνήcκω (literally *die*, but in this context *be killed*): οἱ αἰχμάλωτοι ἀπέθανον ὑπὸ τῶν βαρβάρων *the captives were killed by the barbarians*. The passive sense of ἀπέθανον is here made clear by the agent construction ὑπό + gen. (11.1/2). Some indication of this sort is normally present.

Similarly, φεύγω (literally *flee*) and ἐκπίπτω (literally *fall out*) are used as the passive of ἐκβάλλω *banish, send into exile*:

ἐκ Νάξου ἔφυγον πλούcιοί   *Some wealthy men were exiled*
τινεc ὑπὸ τοῦ δήμου.   *from Naxos by the people.*

ἐκ γὰρ τῆc ἄλληc Ἑλλάδοc   *For when the most influential men*
οἱ πολέμῳ ἢ cτάcει   *were driven out of the rest of*
ἐκπίπτοντεc παρ' Ἀθηναίουc   *Greece by war or sedition, they*
οἱ δυνατώτατοι ἀνεχώρουν.   *used to withdraw to the*
                                                      Athenians (lit. *those exiled by*
                                                      war ..., the most influential, ...
                                                      used to ...).

εὖ/κακῶc λέγω (+ acc.) *speak well/badly of* has the passive εὖ/κακῶc ἀκούω *be well/badly spoken of* (lit. *hear well/badly*):

ἐμὲ κακῶc ἀκούcαντα ὑπὸ   *I was deeply grieved when you*
coῦ μεγάλη ἔδακε λύπη.   *spoke badly of me* (lit. *great*
                                                      grief bit me being badly spoken
                                                      of by you).

Likewise, εὖ/κακῶc ποιέω (+ acc.) *treat well/badly* has the passive εὖ/κακῶc πάcχω *be treated well/badly* (lit. *suffer well/badly*): οὐκ ἀεικὲc κακῶc πάcχειν ὑπὸ ἐχθρῶν *[it is] not shameful to be badly treated by enemies*.

17.2 Greek reading

1   A large number of pithy maxims current in antiquity were said to be inscribed on the columns of the temple of Apollo at Delphi. The following is a selection from surviving lists (the columns themselves no longer exist). The most famous are (*v*) and (*x*).

(*i*) ἀδικούμενος διαλλάττου. (*ii*) ἀλλοτρίων ἀπέχου. (*iii*) βραδέως ἐγχείρει. (*iv*) γαμεῖν μέλλε. (*v*) γνῶθι σεαυτόν. (*vi*) γονέας αἰδοῦ. (*vii*) φρόνει θνητά. (*viii*) ἐπὶ νεκρῷ μὴ γέλα. (*ix*) καιρὸν γνῶθι. (*x*) μηδὲν ἄγαν. (*xi*) πίνων μὴ πολλὰ λάλει. (*xii*) πλούτει δικαίως. (*xiii*) τύχην νόμιζε. (*xiv*) ὑβριζόμενος τιμωροῦ. (*xv*) υἱοῖς μὴ καταρῶ.

2#   γύμναζε παῖδας· ἄνδρας οὐ γὰρ γυμνάσεις.

3   φοβερώτερόν ἐστι στρατόπεδον ἐλάφων ἡγουμένου λέοντος ἢ στρατόπεδον λεόντων ἡγουμένου ἐλάφου.

4#   φοβοῦ τὸ γῆρας· οὐ γὰρ ἔρχεται μόνον.

5#   καλῶς ἀκούειν μᾶλλον ἢ πλουτεῖν θέλε.

6#   ῥόδον παρελθὼν μηκέτι ζήτει πάλιν.

7   δύο ὦτα ἔχομεν, στόμα δὲ ἕν, ἵνα πλείω μὲν ἀκούωμεν, ἥττω δὲ λέγωμεν.

8   **Shorter proverbs**

(*i*) ὀξύτερον οἱ γείτονες βλέπουσι τῶν ἀλωπέκων. (*ii*) πεζῇ βαδίζων μὴ φοβοῦ τὰ κύματα. (*iii*) φαγέτω με λέων καὶ μὴ ἀλώπηξ. (*iv*) ἴσθι καὶ λέων ὅπου χρὴ καὶ πίθηκος ἐν μέρει. (*v*) ἤν τις ἔμαξε μᾶζαν, ταύτην καὶ ἐσθιέτω. (*vi*) στρατηγοῦ παρόντος πᾶσα ἀρχὴ παυσάσθω. (*vii*) ὁ πλεόνων ἐρῶν καὶ τῶν παρόντων ἀποστερεῖται. (*viii*) σιτίον εἰς ἀμίδα μὴ ἐμβάλλειν. (*ix*) ξένος ὢν ἀκολούθει τοῖς ἐπιχωρίοις νόμοις. (*x*) τὸν φίλον κακῶς μὴ λέγε, μηδ' εὖ τὸν ἐχθρόν. (*xi*) μὴ καταφρονήσῃς τοῦ πένητος εὐτυχῶν. (*xii*) μὴ κρίνετε ἵνα μὴ κριθῆτε. (*xiii*) αἱ δεύτεραί πως φροντίδες σοφώτεραι. (*xiv*) οἱ πλεῖστοι κακοί. (*xv*) ἀεὶ τὰ πέρυσι βελτίω.

9#   ἀσπίδι μὲν Σαΐων τις ἀγάλλεται, ἣν παρὰ θάμνῳ,

     ἔντος ἀμώμητον, κάλλιπον (= κατέλιπον) οὐκ ἐθέλων·

 αὐτὸς δ' ἐξέφυγον θανάτου τέλος· ἀσπὶς ἐκείνη

     ἐρρέτω· ἐξαῦτις κτήσομαι οὐ κακίω.

10   ὁ βασίλειος πῆχυς τοῦ μετρίου ἐστὶ πήχεως μείζων τρισὶ δακτύλοις.

11   The Spartans (οἱ Λάκωνες/Λακεδαιμόνιοι) were men of few words (hence our *laconic*) and had a reputation for a blunt, dry humour.

Most of the following stories are about Spartan kings.

  (*i*) Εὐδαμίδας ἰδὼν ἐν Ἀκαδαμείᾳ   Ξενοκράτη ἤδη πρεσβύτερον μετὰ τῶν μαθητῶν φιλοσοφοῦντα καὶ πυθόμενος ὅτι τὴν ἀρετὴν ζητεῖ, πότε οὖν, εἶπεν, αὐτῇ χρήσεται;

  (*ii*) Ἀργείου δέ τινος λέγοντος, ὡς φαυλότεροι γίγνονται κατὰ τὰς ἀποδημίας οἱ Λάκωνες, ἀλλ' οὐχ ὑμεῖς γε, ἔφη, εἰς τὴν Σπάρτην ἐλθόντες χείρονες ἀλλὰ βελτίονες γίγνεσθε.

  (*iii*) Ἆγις πρὸς ἄνθρωπον πονηρὸν ἐρωτῶντα τίς ἄριστος εἴη Σπαρτιάτης, εἶπεν, ὁ σοὶ ἀνομοιότατος.

  (*iv*) Ἀνταλκίδας, σοφιστοῦ μέλλοντος ἀναγιγνώσκειν ἐγκώμιον Ἡρακλέους, τίς γὰρ αὐτόν, ἔφη, ψέγει;

  (*v*) Θεαρίδας ξίφος ἀκονῶν ἠρωτήθη, εἰ ὀξύ ἐστιν, καὶ εἶπεν, ὀξύτερον διαβολῆς.

  (*vi*) Ἀρχέλαος, ἀδολέσχου κουρέως ἐρωτήσαντος αὐτόν, πῶς σε κείρω, ὦ βασιλεῦ; σιωπῶν, ἔφη.

12 ὁ Ἀριστοτέλης ἀκούσας ὑπό τινος λοιδορεῖσθαι, ἀπόντα με, ἔφη, καὶ μαστιγούτω.

13 οἱ σοφισταί, τἆλλα σοφοὶ ὄντες, τοῦτο ἄτοπον ἐργάζονται πρᾶγμα· φάσκοντες γὰρ ἀρετῆς διδάσκαλοι εἶναι πολλάκις κατηγοροῦσιν τῶν μαθητῶν ὡς ἀδικοῦσι σφᾶς, τοὺς μισθοὺς ἀποστεροῦντες καίπερ εὖ παθόντες ὑπ' αὐτῶν.

14 πολλὴ ἔχθρα καὶ μῖσος ἀλλήλων τοῖς πολίταις ἐγγίγνεται, δι' ἃ ἔγωγε μάλα φοβοῦμαι ἀεὶ μή τι μεῖζον ἢ ὥστε φέρειν κακὸν τῇ πόλει συμβῇ.

15 οἱ Λακεδαιμόνιοι ἐπρεσβεύοντο πρὸς τοὺς Ἀθηναίους ἐγκλήματα ποιούμενοι, ὅπως σφίσιν ὅτι μεγίστη πρόφασις εἴη τοῦ πολεμεῖν, ἢν (= ἐὰν) μή τι εἰσακούωσιν.

16 Κλέανδρος ἐτυράννευσε μὲν Γέλας ἑπτὰ ἔτη, ἀπέθανε δὲ ὑπὸ Σαβύλλου ἀνδρὸς Γελῴου.

17# Ἐλπὶς καὶ σὺ Τύχη, μέγα χαίρετε· τὸν λιμέν' ηὗρον·
        οὐδὲν ἐμοὶ χ' ὑμῖν· παίζετε τοὺς μετ' ἐμέ.

Notes

1 (*ii*) ἀπέχομαι is followed by the gen. (20.1/4). (*x*) Supply an imperative such as ποίει. (*xiii*) νομίζω + acc. *believe in.* (*xiv*) τῑμωροῦ < τῑμωρέου. (*xv*) καταρῶ < καταράου.

2 γάρ is here placed third word in its clause (cf. 15.3 *l*.27).

3 ἡγουμένου λέοντος and ἡγουμένου ἐλάφου are both genitive absolutes (12.1/2*b*).

8 (*iv*) ἴcθι is here the 2nd s. imp. of εἰμί (17.1/1 note 6). (*v*) ἥν ... μάζαν lit. *which bread* (ἥν is here the relative adjective, 9.1/2 note 3); ἔμαξε < μάττω. (*vi*) ἀρχή as an abstract noun can mean *magistracy* but is used here concretely in the sense *office*. (*vii*) Both ἐράω *desire* (13.1/2*a*(ii)) and ἀποcτερέομαι *be deprived of* (20.1/4) are followed by the genitive, cf. ἀπέχου in 1(*ii*) above. (*viii*) ἐμβάλλειν infinitive for imperative (17.1/1 note 5). (*xv*) Supply ἥν.

9 A poem of Archilochus (7th cent. BC), the earliest figure in Greek literature about whom we have any reliable information. *l.*2 ἔντος ἀμώμητον is in apposition to ἥν in the previous line *which, a blameless weapon,* ... *l.*3 θανάτου τέλος *[the] doom of death* (a Homeric phrase). *l.*4 κακίω f. acc. s. to agree with ἀcπίδα understood.

10 The *royal cubit* was that used by the Persians, the other was standard in the Greek world.

11 (*i*) πυθόμενος *ascertaining*; Xenocrates was *looking for virtue* in the sense that he was investigating its nature from a philosophical point of view. (*ii*) This story is also about Eudamidas, who is the subject of ἔφη; γε emphasises ὑμεῖς. (*iii*) ἄριcτος ... Cπαρτιάτης *[the] best Spartan* the article is not used with a predicate (5.1/3). (*iv*) For a down-to-earth Spartan, praising Heracles would have seemed as superfluous as praising motherhood; γάρ here introduces an ironical question *"Well, who ...?"* (*vi*) κείρω aor. subj. in a deliberative question (14.1/4*a*(ii)) *"How am I to cut ...?"*

12 After ἀκούcᾱc we have the infinitive construction for reported speech (8.1/3*a*), lit. *having heard [himself] to be abused* ...; ἀπόντα < ἄπειμι.

13 τἆλλα (= τὰ ἄλλα) adverbial accusative (20.1/5), *in other respects*; τοῦτο refers to what follows but the meaning is not *this extraordinary thing* (there is no definite article with ἄτοπον ... πρᾶγμα), but *an extraordinary thing [viz] this*; γάρ explains what precedes, but we would omit it in English; cφᾶc i.e. the sophists (9.1/4*a*); both ἀποcτεροῦντεc and παθόντεc agree with the subject of ἀδικοῦcι (3 pl. pres. ind. act., **not** a pple.), i.e. the students; αὐτῶν also refers back to the sophists and is used instead of cφῶν for variety.

14 μῖcoc ἀλλήλων *hatred of each other* (9.1/4*b*) i.e. *mutual hatred.*

15 ἐπρεcβεύοντο impf. to express repeated action (4.1/1); ποιούμενοι *making* the middle of ποιέω is used with nouns to indicate the involvement of the subject, cf. πόλεμον ποιεῖcθαι *to wage war*; εἰρήνην ποιεῖcθαι *to keep peace* but πόλεμον ποιεῖν *to cause a war* (but not necessarily be involved in it); εἰρήνην ποιεῖν *to impose peace* (on belligerents); ὅπωc (= ἵνα) + opt. to express purpose after a historic tense (14.1/4*c*(i)).

16 Γέλᾱc Doric gen. s. of Γέλᾱ.

17 χαίρετε (17.1/1 note 7) is qualified by μέγα (here an adverb), lit. *farewell greatly* (the author is pleased to be rid of them); χ᾽ ὑμῖν elision for καὶ ὑμῖν (English idiom reverses the order, *you and me*) – the clause means *there is nothing for* (i.e. *between*) *you and me*; παίζετε (here imp.) + acc. *play with.*

17.3 Extra reading

Prometheus Bound (2)

Prometheus has revealed that he alone can save Zeus from a marriage which will rob him of his divine kingship. In the scene below, Hermes, the messenger of the gods, has come to force Prometheus to disclose his secret. Shortly after, the play ends with Prometheus persisting in his refusal.

ΕΡΜΗC

cὲ τὸν cοφιcτήν, τὸν πικρῶc ὑπέρπικρον,
τὸν ἐξαμαρτόντ᾽ εἰc θεοὺc ἐφημέροιc
πορόντα τιμάc, τὸν πυρὸc κλέπτην λέγω·
πατὴρ ἄνωγέ c᾽ οὕcτιναc κομπεῖc γάμουc
αὐδᾶν, πρὸc ὦν τ᾽ ἐκεῖνοc ἐκπίπτει κράτουc·   5
καὶ ταῦτα μέντοι μηδὲν αἰνικτηρίωc,
ἀλλ᾽ αὔθ᾽ ἕκαcτα φράζε, μηδέ μοι διπλᾶc
ὁδούc, Προμηθεῦ, προcβάλῃc. ὁρᾶc δ᾽ ὅτι
Ζεὺc τοῖc τοιούτοιc οὐχὶ μαλθακίζεται.

ΠΡΟΜΗΘΕΥC

cεμνόcτομόc γε καὶ φρονήματοc πλέωc
ὁ μῦθόc ἐcτιν, ὡc θεῶν ὑπηρέτου.   10
νέον νέοι κρατεῖτε, καὶ δοκεῖτε δὴ

ναίειν ἀπενθῆ πέργαμ'· οὐκ ἐκ τῶνδ' ἐγὼ
διccοὺc τυράννουc ἐκπεcόνταc ᾐcθόμην;
τρίτον δὲ τὸν νῦν κοιρανοῦντ' ἐπόψομαι   15
αἴcχιcτα καὶ τάχιcτα. μή τί cοι δοκῶ
ταρβεῖν ὑποπτήccειν τε τοὺc νέουc θεούc;
πολλοῦ γε καὶ τοῦ παντὸc ἐλλείπω. cὺ δὲ
κέλευθον ἥνπερ ἦλθεc ἐγκόνει πάλιν·
πεύcῃ γὰρ οὐδὲν ὧν ἀνιcτορεῖc ἐμέ.   20

Notes

*l.*1 Hermes' words are aggressive and rude. This shows itself in the omission of the verb governing cέ (καλῶ *I am addressing*), trans. *you there, the clever one* ... *ll.*2f. τὸν ἐξαμαρτόντ'(α) ... πορόντα lit. *the one who offended* ... *[by] giving* (πορόντα aor. pple. of a defective verb which only exists in the aor. and perf. and is listed under the aor. ind. ἔπορον); take ἐφημέροιc with πορόντα *giving* ... *to mortals*; λέγω *I mean. l.*4 πατήρ i.e. Zeus; ἄνωγε *orders* from ἄνωγα a verb perfect in form but present in meaning (cf. 19.1/3*a*); οὕcτιναc (indirect interrogative, 10.1/2*b*) ... γάμουc plural for singular. *l.*5 πρὸc (= ὑπό) ὧν *by which*; ἐκπίπτει for vividness the present is used for the future in prophecies; κράτουc (gen.) is governed by ἐκ–. *l.*6 Understand φράζε from the next line; καὶ ... μέντοι *and indeed, and what is more*; μηδέν adverbial acc. (20.1/5) *in no way. ll.*7f. αὖθ' (= αὐτά) ἕκαcτα i.e. *each thing, every detail*; μηδέ ... προcβάλῃc negative command (17.1/1). *l.*9 τοῖc τοιούτοιc lit. *by such things* (i.e. *behaviour*). *l.*10 πλέωc 13.1/1*a*. *l.*11 ὡc *for [the talk] of a lackey,* on this restrictive use of ὡc see 21.1/1*a*(vi). *l.*12 νέον is n. acc. s. used adverbially (20.1/5) and to be taken with κρατεῖτε, lit. *you rule newly,* i.e. *you have only just come to power;* δοκεῖτε *you think, expect*; δή adds a note of sarcasm *indeed. l.*14 διccοὺc (= διττούc the non-Attic form is used in Tragedy) τυράννουc Uranus, the first king of the gods, had been dethroned by his son Cronus, who in turn was dethroned by Zeus (Prometheus sarcastically calls them τύραννοι). *l.*15 Supply ἐκπίπτοντα from ἐκπεcόνταc in the previous line; ἐπόψομαι < ἐφοράω. *l.*16 μή ... cοι δοκῶ is a question expecting a negative answer (10.1/2*a*), lit. *surely I do not seem to you* (μή here = *surely not*); τί (the accent is from the enclitic cοι, see **Appendix 8**, *d*(ix)) acc. s. n. of the indefinite τιc, here used as an adverbial acc. (20.1/5) *to some extent. l.*18 ἐλλείπω takes the gen. *I lack much* (πολλοῦ, i.e. of such behaviour), *in fact* (καί) *all* (lit. *the whole,* i.e. of such behaviour) – Prometheus is strongly emphasising that he is not frightened of the new rulers of heaven. *l*.19 κέλευθον acc. of space traversed *along the road,* after ἐγκόνει (2nd s. pres. imp. of ἐγκονέω); ἥνπερ (< ὅσπερ, i.e. ὅς + περ) is an emphatic form of the relative. *l*.20 ὧν = τούτων ἅ *of those things which* the relative pronoun has been attracted into the case of the antecedent, and the latter then omitted (9.1/2 note 2).

18 | UNIT EIGHTEEN

18.1 Grammar

18.1/1 –μι verbs

–μι verbs fall into two groups:

(*a*) The suffixless class, where the endings of the present and imperfect are added directly to the stem without any suffix or link vowel, e.g. εἰ–μί (3.1/6) and φη–μί (7.1/2). There are nine other common verbs in this class:

δίδωμι *give* and τίθημι *put, place* (18.1/2)

εἶμι *I shall go* (18.1/3; distinguish from εἰμί *I am*)

ἵστημι *make to stand* (19.1/1)

ἵημι *let go, send forth* (20.1/2)

δύναμαι *be able* and ἐπίσταμαι *know* (19.1/3*b*; the only common deponents of this type)

πίμπλημι *fill* and πίμπρημι *burn* (19.1/1 note 2)

From another such verb, ἠμί *say* (obsolescent in Attic) Plato often uses the forms ἦν *I said*, ἦ *he/she said* (13.3(i) *l*.6; both forms were originally imperfect).

(*b*) The –νῡμι class, where the stem of the present and imperfect has a νυ suffix (20.1/1).

Both classes differ from –ω verbs in the present and imperfect; of class (*a*) δίδωμι, τίθημι, ἵστημι, ἵημι also differ in the aorist active and middle (ἵστημι in the perfect and pluperfect as well). Elsewhere –μι verbs take the same suffixes and endings as –ω verbs.

18.1/2 δίδωμι *give*, τίθημι *put*, *place*

These two –μι verbs are closely parallel. In nearly all their forms an ο/ω in δίδωμι corresponds to an ε/η in τίθημι; and also οι to ει in optative forms, and ου to ει in forms other than those of the optative; the only exceptions are the 1st s. impf. act. (ἐδίδουν/ἐτίθην), the present and aorist subjunctive (see note 1) and the perfect mid./pass. (δέδομαι etc. but τέθειμαι etc.). Both verbs form their present stem by reduplication with iota (cf. γιγνώcκω); as in the perfect tense (15.1/1), an aspirated consonant is reduplicated with the corresponding non-aspirate, hence τιθη– (not θιθη–). In both, the aorist active is weak in the singular, with κ (**not** c) added to the long-vowel form of the root (δω–/θη–); in the plural the endings are added directly to the short-vowel form of the root (δο–/θε–; this is really a type of root aorist).

Their principal parts are:

PRESENT	FUTURE	AOR.ACT	PERF. ACT	PERF. MID./PASS	AOR. PASS
δίδωμι	δώcω	ἔδωκα	δέδωκα	δέδομαι	ἐδόθην
τίθημι	θήcω	ἔθηκα	τέθηκα	κεῖμαι (note 4)	ἐτέθην
				(τέθειμαι)	

The future, perfect (act. and mid./pass.), and aorist passive are regular (see above 18.1/1). The present, imperfect, and aorist active forms, which require the greatest attention and should be mastered first, are set out here. The middle and passive forms are easily recognised from their endings (for full tables see **Appendix 5**)

	PRESENT		AORIST	
INDICATIVE				
S. 1	δίδωμι	τίθημι	ἔδωκα	ἔθηκα
2	δίδωc	τίθηc	ἔδωκαc	ἔθηκαc
3	δίδωcι(ν)	τίθηcι(ν)	ἔδωκε(ν)	ἔθηκε(ν)
PL. 1	δίδομεν	τίθεμεν	ἔδομεν	ἔθεμεν
2	δίδοτε	τίθετε	ἔδοτε	ἔθετε
3	διδόαcι(ν)	τιθέαcι(ν)	ἔδοcαν	ἔθεcαν
INFINITIVE				
	διδόναι	τιθέναι	δοῦναι	θεῖναι
PARTICIPLE				
	διδούc, -όντοc	τιθείc, -έντοc	δούc, δόντοc	θείc, θέντοc
	διδοῦcα, -ούcηc	τιθεῖcα, -είcηc	δοῦcα, δούcηc	θεῖcα, θείcηc

	διδόν, -όντος	τιθέν, -έντος	δόν, δόντος	θέν, θέντος
IMPERATIVE				
s. 2	δίδου	τίθει	δός	θές
3	διδότω	τιθέτω	δότω	θέτω
PL. 2	δίδοτε	τίθετε	δότε	θέτε
3	διδόντων	τιθέντων	δόντων	θέντων
SUBJUNCTIVE (see note 1)				
s. 1	διδῶ	τιθῶ	δῶ	θῶ
2	διδῷc, etc.	τιθῇc, etc.	δῷc, etc.	θῇc, etc.
OPTATIVE				
s. 1	διδοίην	τιθείην	δοίην	θείην
2	διδοίηc	τιθείηc	δοίηc	θείηc
3	διδοίη	τιθείη	δοίη	θείη
PL. 1	διδοῖμεν	τιθεῖμεν	δοῖμεν	θεῖμεν
2	διδοῖτε	τιθεῖτε	δοῖτε	θεῖτε
3	διδοῖεν	τιθεῖεν	δοῖεν	θεῖεν

IMPERFECT ACTIVE

ἐδίδουν, ἐδίδους, ἐδίδου, ἐδίδομεν, ἐδίδοτε, ἐδίδοcαν
ἐτίθην, ἐτίθεις, ἐτίθει, ἐτίθεμεν, ἐτίθετε, ἐτίθεcαν

Notes

1   The present and aorist subjunctive active of δίδωμι have the endings
    –ῶ, –ῷc, –ῷ, –ῶμεν, –ῶτε, –ῶcι(ν) (cf. 14.1/2 note 2). τίθημι has the
    regular endings (–ῶ, –ῇc, –ῇ etc.) but in both verbs the first syllable
    of the subjunctive endings has a circumflex as a result of contraction
    (διδῶ < διδόω, τιθῶ < τιθέω).
2   The present and imperfect active of δίδωμι can also mean *offer.*
3   The aorist active also has weak forms for the 3rd pl.: ἔδωκαν (=
    ἔδοcαν), ἔθηκαν (= ἔθεcαν); weak forms may also occur in the 1st
    and 2nd pl. (ἐδώκαμεν etc.) but are rare.
4   The **present** tense of the deponent κεῖμαι *lie* (19.1/3*b*) is generally
    used instead of the **perfect passive** of τίθημι in the sense *to have
    been put, placed, established,* e.g. οἱ νόμοι οἱ ὑπὸ τῶν βαcιλέων
    κείμενοι (= τεθειμένοι) *the laws established by the kings.* Likewise
    ἐκείμην, the **imperfect** of κεῖμαι, is used for the **pluperfect passive**
    of τίθημι.

18.1/3 εἶμι *I shall come/go*

In Attic Greek prose the verb ἔρχομαι *come/go* occurs only in the present indicative. The remainder of its present tense (subjunctive, optative, imperative, infinitive, participle), and its future and imperfect are supplied by εἶμι which, though present in form, has in the indicative the future meaning *I shall come/go* (to be distinguished from εἰμί *I am*):

PESENT	IND.	SUBJ.	OPT.	IMP.	INF.	PPLE.
	ἔρχομαι	ἴω	ἴοιμι	ἴθι	ἰέναι	ἰών
	I come/go					
FUTURE	εἶμι	—	ἴοιμι	—	ἰέναι	ἰών
	I shall come/go					
IMPERFECT	ᾖα					
	I was coming/going, used to come/go					

For a complete table of forms see **Appendix 3**. Note that ἴοιμι, ἰέναι and ἰών can be either present or future (the context will normally show which tense is meant). The aorist of ἔρχομαι is ἦλθον (7.1/1 note 2), and the perfect ἐλήλυθα.

18.1/4 Other verbs with principal parts from different roots

The English verb *to be* is a combination of separate and etymologically distinct words (*be, am, was*, etc.). We have already seen the same in Greek with αἱρέω, λέγω, ὁράω, φέρω (7.1/1 note 2) as well as ἔρχομαι; other examples are ἐσθίω *eat*, πωλέω *sell*, ὠνέομαι *buy* (see **Principal parts of verbs**; the principal parts of all eight should now be learnt).

A particularly troublesome set is that associated with αἱρέω *take, capture,* whose passive is normally supplied by another verb, ἁλίσκομαι *be captured,* and whose middle αἱροῦμαι has the special sense *choose*. When used as a passive αἱροῦμαι normally means *be chosen*. These variations can be set out as follows:

PRESENT		FUTURE	AORIST	PERFECT
αἱρέω	*I take, capture*	αἱρήσω	εἶλον (stem ἑλ–)	ᾕρηκα
ἁλίσκομαι (pass.)	*I am taken, am being captured*	ἁλώσομαι	ἑάλων	ἑάλωκα
αἱροῦμαι (mid.)	*I choose*	αἱρήσομαι	εἱλόμην	ᾕρημαι
αἱροῦμαι (pass.)	*I am being chosen*	αἱρεθήσομαι	ᾑρέθην	ᾕρημαι

The moods, infinitives and participles of εἷλον *I took, captured* (stem ἑλ-, cf. 7.1/1 note 2) and of the root aorist ἑάλων *I was taken, was captured* are as follows:

IND.	SUBJ.	OPT.	IMP.	INF.	PPLE.
εἷλον	ἕλω	ἕλοιμι	ἕλε	ἑλεῖν	ἑλών
ἑάλων	ἁλῶ	ἁλοίην	ἅλωθι	ἁλῶναι	ἁλούς

ἑάλων is exactly parallel to ἔγνων (11.1/1), e.g. ind. ἑάλων, ἑάλως, ἑάλω etc.

Notes

1   Most **compounds** of λέγω have the meaning *pick up, gather,* e.g. ἐκλέγω *pick out,* cυλλέγω *collect,* καταλέγω *pick, choose* (and also *recount*). These compounds have principal parts from the stem λεγ‑ only, e.g. ἐκλέγω, ἐκλέξω, ἐξέλεξα, etc.

2   The alternative principal parts of λέγω (ἐρῶ, εἷπον etc.) are, however, used in the compounds of ἀγορεύω *speak in public,* e.g. ἀπαγορεύω *forbid* (fut. ἀπερῶ, aor. ἀπεῖπον), προαγορεύω *proclaim.*

18.1/5 Conditional sentences

Conditional sentences contain at least one main clause and one adverbial clause of condition; the latter is introduced by εἰ *if.* They fall into two clearly defined categories which, in both English and Greek, are distinguished by the form of the main clause:

Category 1

In the main clause English has the auxiliary verb *would* or *should* (or occasionally *could*), and Greek has the particle ἄν (see below). An English example is: *I would be sorry if you were not to persist with Greek.*

Category 2

In the main clause English does **not** have the auxiliary *would* or *should,* and Greek does **not** have the particle ἄν. An English example is: *I am sorry if you find Greek verbs difficult.*

There is a clear distinction between the two categories. The first is used in cases where something could have happened in the past, could be happening now, or could happen in the future. The cases covered by the second are also hypothetical (as all conditional sentences must be), but here, by not using *would* or *should* in English or ἄν in Greek, we express ourselves in a more positive and confident way.

Conditional clauses of both categories refer either to the future, present, or past. οὐ is used to negate main clauses[1] but the negative in the εἰ clause is μή. ἄν is postpositive and therefore never stands as first word in the main clause of conditional clauses of the first category.

The three time-frames of each category are given below:

CATEGORY 1	CATEGORY 2
English *would/should* in the main clause	verb without *would/should* in the main clause
Greek ἄν in the main clause	no ἄν in the main clause

FUTURE

Conditional clause

εἰ + optative (pres. or aor.)	ἐάν (see note 2) + subjunctive (pres. or aor.)

Main clause

optative (pres. or aor.) + ἄν	future indicative
εἰ τοῦτο πράξειας, ἁμάρτοις ἄν.	ἐὰν τοῦτο πράξῃς, ἁμαρτήσει.
If you were to do this, you would be wrong.	*If you do this, you will be wrong.*

PRESENT

Conditional clause

εἰ + imperfect indicative	εἰ + present indicative

Main clause

imperfect indicative + ἄν	present indicative
εἰ τοῦτο ἔπραττες, ἡμάρτανες ἄν.	εἰ τοῦτο πράττεις, ἁμαρτάνεις.
If you were [now] doing this, you would be wrong.	*If you are doing this, you are wrong.*

PAST

Conditional clause

εἰ + aorist indicative	εἰ + imperfect or aorist indicative

Main clause

aorist indicative + ἄν	imperfect or aorist indicative
εἰ τοῦτο ἔπραξας, ἥμαρτες ἄν.	εἰ τοῦτο ἔπραττες, ἡμάρτανες.
If you had done this, you would have been wrong.	*If you used to do this, you were (used to be) wrong.*
	εἰ τοῦτο ἔπραξας, ἥμαρτες.
	If you did this, you were wrong.

---

[1] Unless these are in the form of a command (17.1/1) or wish (21.1/1).

We have already seen that the particle ἄν, when used with the subjunctive in subordinate clauses (14.1/4*c*(iii)), can be represented in English by *ever.* Here, however, it has no semantic equivalent. When in English we wish to express potentiality (as in the main clause of first category conditional sentences) we use an auxiliary verb (generally *would* or *should*), e.g. *I would have liked to see you.* ἄν, however, which expresses potentiality in Greek, is an adverbial particle and modifies the verb to which it is attached: οὐκ ἐγένετο means *it did not happen*; οὐκ ἄν ἐγένετο means *it would not have happened.*

Notes

1 The meaning of εἰ ... ἔπρᾱττες/ἔπρᾱξας depends on what follows, i.e. on whether it is in a category 1 or category 2 sentence.

2 The conjunction ἐάν of the future time-frame of category 2 is a contraction of εἰ + ἄν (cf. ὅταν < ὅτε + ἄν, 14.1/4*c*(iii)). It may also be written as ἄν (to be distinguished from the particle ἄν – the latter has a short vowel) or ἤν in some dialects.

3 It is possible to combine certain time references within one sentence:

εἰ τοῦτο ἔπρᾱξας, ἐκινδύνευες ἄν.	*If you had done that, you would [now] be in danger.*
εἰ τοῦτο ἔπρᾱξας, κινδῡνεύεις.	*If you did that, you are in danger.*

4 In category 2 sentences with a future reference εἰ + fut. ind. is substituted for ἐάν + subj. where a **threat** or **warning** is implied:

ἀποκτενεῖς εἴ με γῆς ἔξω βαλεῖς.	*You will kill [me] if you throw me out of the country.*

18.1/6 ἄκρος, μέσος, ἔσχατος

These three adjectives vary in meaning according to whether they are used in the attributive or predicative position (3.1/3*b*):

τὸ ἄκρον ὄρος *the high mountain*	ἄκρον τὸ ὄρος *the top of the mountain*
τὸ μέσον ὄρος *the middle mountain*	μέσον τὸ ὄρος *the middle of the mountain*
τὸ ἔσχατον ὄρος *the furthest mountain*	ἔσχατον τὸ ὄρος *the furthest part of the mountain*

For the predicative position we may also have τὸ ὄρος ἄκρον etc.

18.2 Greek reading

1 Κυμαῖóc τιc μέλι ἐπώλει. γευcαμένου δέ τινοc καὶ εἰπόντοc, πάνυ καλόν ἐcτιν, εἰ μὴ γάρ, ἔφη, μῦc ἐνέπεcεν εἰc αὐτὸ οὐκ ἂν ἐπώλουν.

2 Λάκαινά τιc πρὸc τὸν υἱὸν λέγοντα μικρὸν ἔχειν τὸ ξίφοc εἶπε, καὶ βῆμα πρόcθεc.

3 **Proverbs**
(*i*) ἐὰν ἡ λεοντῆ μὴ ἐξίκηται, τὴν ἀλωπεκῆν πρόcαψον. (*ii*) κυνὶ δίδωc ἄχυρα, ὄνῳ δὲ ὀcτᾶ. (*iii*) ἐπ᾽ ἄκρᾳ τῇ γλώττῃ τὸ φιλεῖν ἔχειc. (*iv*) ἂν (= ἐὰν) τοὺc φίλουc μιcῶμεν, τί ποιήcομεν τοὺc μιcοῦνταc; (*v*) εἰ τυρὸν εἶχον, οὐκ ἂν ἐδεόμην ὄψου. (*vi*) # φίλον δι᾽ ὀργὴν ἐν κακοῖcι μὴ προδῷc. (*vii*) # τὸ κέρδοc ἡδύ, κἂν ἀπὸ ψευδῶν ἴῃ. (*viii*) δόc τι καὶ λαβέ τι. (*ix*) # πλάνη βίον τίθηcι cωφρονέcτερον. (*x*) αἰcχρὸν εὐεργέταc προδοῦναι. (*xi*) ἐὰν ἔχωμεν χρήματα, ἕξομεν φίλουc. (*xii*) ἴτω τὰ πράγματα ὅπῃ τῷ θεῷ φίλον.

4 # εἰc Ῥόδον εἰ πλεῖν δεῖ, τιc Ὀλυμπικὸν ἦλθεν ἐρωτῶν
  τὸν μάντιν, καὶ πῶc πλεύcεται ἀcφαλέωc·
χὠ μάντιc, πρῶτον μὲν, ἔφη, καινὴν ἔχε τὴν ναῦν,
  καὶ μὴ χειμῶνοc, τοῦ δὲ θέρουc ἀνάγου·
ταῦτα γὰρ ἦν ποιῇc, ἥξειc κἀκεῖcε καὶ ὧδε,   5
  ἢν μὴ πειρατὴc ἐν πελάγει cε λάβῃ.

5 γέρων ποτὲ ξύλα κόψαc καὶ ταῦτα φέρων πολλὴν ὁδὸν ἐβάδιζε. διὰ δὲ τὸν κόπον ἀποθέμενοc τὸ φορτίον τὸν Θάνατον ἐπεκαλεῖτο. τοῦ δε Θανάτου φανέντοc καὶ πυνθανομένου διὰ τίνα αἰτίαν ἐπεκαλεῖτο, ὁ γέρων ἔφη, ἵνα τὸ φορτίον τοῦτο ἄραc ἐπιθῇc μοι.

6 # ἅπαν διδόμενον δῶρον, ἂν καὶ μικρὸν ᾖ,
μέγιcτόν ἐcτιν, ἂν μετ᾽ εὐνοίαc δοθῇ.

7 ὄφιc, ἢν μὴ φάγῃ ὄφιν, δράκων οὐ γενήcεται.

8 # γῆc ἐπέβην γυμνόc, γυμνόc θ᾽ ὑπὸ γαῖαν ἄπειμι·
  καὶ τί μάτην μοχθῶ, γυμνὸν ὁρῶν τὸ τέλοc;

9 **More stories about Diogenes**
  (*i*) θαυμάζοντόc τινοc τὰ ἐν Cαμοθράκῃ   ἀναθήματα ἔφη, πολλῷ ἂν ἦν πλείω εἰ καὶ οἱ μὴ cωθέντεc ἀνετίθεcαν.
  (*ii*) εἰc Μύνδον ἐλθὼν καὶ θεαcάμενοc μεγάλαc τὰc πύλαc, μικρὰν δὲ τὴν πόλιν, ἄνδρεc Μύνδιοι, ἔφη, κλείcατε τὰc πύλαc μὴ ἡ πόλιc ὑμῶν ἐξέλθῃ.

(*iii*) δύσκολον ἥτει· τοῦ δ' εἰπόντος, ἐάν με πείσῃς, ἔφη, εἴ σε
ἐδυνάμην πεῖσαι, ἔπεισα ἄν σε ἀπάγξασθαι.

(*iv*) λύχνον μεθ' ἡμέραν ἅψας περιῄει λέγων, ἄνθρωπον ζητῶ.

10   In order to lure the Syracusan army away from Syracuse, the
      Athenians sent an agent who persuaded the Syracusans that they
      could surprise the Athenians at a neighbouring city, Catana. The ruse
      was totally successful. The passage is from Thucydides' account of
      the disastrous Athenian expedition to Sicily (415–413 BC).

οἱ δὲ στρατηγοὶ τῶν Συρακοσίων ἐπίστευσαν τῷ ἀνθρώπῳ πολλῷ
ἀπερισκεπτότερον, καὶ εὐθὺς ἡμέραν ξυνθέμενοι ᾗ παρέσονται
ἀπέστειλαν αὐτόν, καὶ αὐτοὶ προεῖπον πανδημεὶ πᾶσιν ἐξιέναι
Συρακοσίοις. ἐπεὶ δὲ ἑτοῖμα αὐτοῖς τὰ τῆς παρασκευῆς ἦν καὶ αἱ
ἡμέραι ἐν αἷς ξυνέθεντο ἥξειν ἐγγὺς ἦσαν, πορευόμενοι ἐπὶ 5
Κατάνης ηὐλίσαντο ἐπὶ τῷ Συμαίθῳ ποταμῷ. οἱ δ' Ἀθηναῖοι, ὡς
ᾔσθοντο αὐτοὺς προσιόντας, ἀναλαβόντες τὸ στράτευμα ἅπαν τὸ
ἑαυτῶν καὶ ἐπιβιβάσαντες ἐπὶ τὰς ναῦς καὶ τὰ πλοῖα ὑπὸ νύκτα
ἔπλεον ἐπὶ τὰς Συρακούσας.

Notes

1 γάρ *yes, for* Greek has no word which corresponds exactly to the
   English *yes* and often the assent of a speaker is implied by particles
   (24.1/1).

2 μῑκρόν is in the predicative position (3.1/3*b*), i.e. *that he had his
   sword short*, i.e. *that the sword he had was short*; καί is adverbial (*as
   well*) but need not be translated; πρόθες < προστίθημι.

3 (*i*) πρόσαψον < προσάπτω. (*iv*) ποιέω + two accusatives *do [something]
   to/with* (22.1/2*f*(ii)). (*vii*) κἄν = καὶ ἐάν; ψευδῶν < ψεῦδος. (*ix*) τίθησι
   here *render* (xi) ἕξομεν < ἔχω. (*xii*) ἴτω 3rd s. imp. of ἔρχομαι (18.1/3
   and **Appendix 3**); τῷ θεῷ φίλον (n. s.) *sc.* ἐστί *it is dear to God*.

4 *l*.1 εἰ *if* would be first word of its clause in prose. *l*.2 πλεύσεται lit.
   he will sail, but translate *he would sail*, because Greek retains the
   original tense in reported (indirect) speech (8.1/3 and 10.1/2*b*);
   ἀσφαλέως, i.e. ἀσφαλῶς the uncontracted form is Ionic (on Ionic
   forms in poetry see 1.3). *l*.3 χὠ = καὶ ὁ; καινήν predicative as in 2
   above, lit. *have the ship [which you sail in] new*, i.e. *get a new ship*.
   l.4 χειμῶνος ... θέρους gen. of time within which (7.1/7*c*). *l*.5 ἤν =
   ἐάν (also in next line and in 7 below); κἀκεῖσε (=καὶ ἐκεῖσε) καὶ
   ὧδε lit. *both thither and hither*, i.e. *both there and back*.

5 ἀποθέμενος aor. mid. pple. of ἀποτίθημι; φανέντος gen. m. s. of the
   aor. pple. of φαίνομαι; πυνθανομένου *asking*; ἄρας nom. m. s. of
   the aor. act. pple. of αἴρω; ἐπιθῇς 2nd s. aor. subj. act. of ἐπιτίθημι.
6 In both lines ἄν = ἐάν; ἐὰν (or εἰ) καί normally *although* but here
   obviously *even if* (which is usually καὶ εἰ/ἐάν); δοθῇ 3rd s. aor. subj.
   pass. of δίδωμι.
7 φάγῃ 3rd s. aor. subj. act. of ἐσθίω.
8 θ' i.e. τε.
9 (*i*) Samothrace, an island in the northern Aegean, was notorious for
   shipwrecks; the subject of ἔφη (and in (*ii*) and (*iii*)) is Diogenes;
   πολλῷ dat. of measure of difference (17.1/4*b*); take καί *also* with
   what follows; οἱ μὴ σωθέντες (aor. pass. pple. of σῴζω) the negative
   μή is used because Diogenes is referring to a general class
   (12.1/2*a*(vi)); ἀνετίθεσαν *had dedicated* the imperfect, not the
   aorist, is used because the verb refers to **repeated** action in the past.
   (*ii*) μεγάλᾱς ... μῑκρᾱ́ν both adjectives are predicative as in 2 above;
   μή introducing a negative purpose clause (14.1/4*c*(i)). (*iii*) τοῦ refers
   to the δύσκολος; ἀπάγξασθαι aor. inf. of ἀπάγχομαι (*iv*) περιῄει
   3rd s. impf. of περιέρχομαι (18.1/3); μεθ' ἡμέρᾱν *after day[break]*
   i.e. *by day,* cf. ἅμα τῇ ἡμέρᾳ.
10 *l*.1 πολλῷ (dat. of measure of difference, 17.1/4*b*) is to be taken with
   the following word. *l*.2 παρέσονται (< πάρειμι) on the future see
   note on πλεύσεται in 4 *l*.2 above (cf. ἥξειν in *l*.5). *ll*.3f. Take πᾶσιν
   ... Cυρακοσίοις with προεῖπον (< προαγορεύω,18.1/4 note 2). *l*.4 τὰ
   τῆς παρασκευῆς lit. *the [things] of their preparation* but trans. *their
   preparations. l*.6 ηὐλίσαντο < αὐλίζομαι. *l*.8 τὰ πλοῖα is acc. after
   ἐπί.

18.3 Extra reading

The sea, the sea !

The *Anabasis* of Xenophon (7.2.12) tells how an army of Greek
mercenaries, after becoming embroiled in a dispute between rivals for the
Persian throne, had to make their way back from Persia to Greece. The
following passage describes their elation when, after many months of
hardship, they finally reached the Black Sea.

καὶ ἀφικνοῦνται ἐπὶ τὸ ὄρος τῇ πέμπτῃ ἡμέρᾳ· ὄνομα δὲ τῷ ὄρει ἦν
Θήχης. ἐπεὶ δὲ οἱ πρῶτοι ἐγένοντο ἐπὶ τοῦ ὄρους καὶ κατεῖδον τὴν
θάλατταν, κραυγὴ πολλὴ ἐγένετο. ἀκούσας δὲ ὁ Ξενοφῶν καὶ οἱ
ὀπισθοφύλακες ᾠήθησαν ἔμπροσθεν ἄλλους ἐπιτίθεσθαι πολεμίους·
ἐπειδὴ δ' ἡ βοὴ πλείων τε ἐγίγνετο καὶ ἐγγύτερον καὶ οἱ ἀεὶ ἐπιόντες 5
ἔθεον δρόμῳ ἐπὶ τοὺς ἀεὶ βοῶντας καὶ πολλῷ μείζων ἐγίγνετο ἡ βοὴ
ὅσῳ δὴ πλείους ἐγίγνοντο, ἐδόκει δὴ μεῖζόν τι εἶναι τῷ Ξενοφῶντι,
καὶ ἀναβὰς ἐφ' ἵππον καὶ τοὺς ἱππέας ἀναλαβὼν παρεβοήθει· καὶ τάχα
δὴ ἀκούουσι βοώντων τῶν στρατιωτῶν, θάλαττα θάλαττα, καὶ
παρεγγυώντων. ἔνθα δὴ ἔθεον πάντες καὶ οἱ ὀπισθοφύλακες, καὶ τὰ 10
ὑποζύγια ἠλαύνετο καὶ οἱ ἵπποι. ἐπεὶ δὲ ἀφίκοντο πάντες ἐπὶ τὸ
ἄκρον, ἐνταῦθα δὴ περιέβαλλον ἀλλήλους καὶ στρατηγοὺς καὶ
λοχαγοὺς δακρύοντες.

Notes

*l.*1 ἀφικνοῦνται vivid present (see note on 7.2.13 *l.*8; cf. ἀκούουσι in *l.*9).
*l.*4 ᾠήθησαν < οἴομαι. *ll.*5f. οἱ ἀεὶ ἐπιόντες (< ἐπέρχομαι) *those who
kept coming up* refers to the different groups who went up the hill, but
τοὺς ἀεὶ βοῶντας *those who kept shouting* refers to the ever-increasing
group that could see the sea; δρόμῳ *at a run* is redundant after ἔθεον
(inceptive imperfect *began to run* 4.1/1 footnote). *l.*7 ὅσῳ etc. lit. *by how
much they became more [numerous]*; on ὅσος see 21.1/3; ἐδόκει ... τῷ
Ξενοφῶντι lit. *it seemed to Xenophon*; μεῖζόν τι *something more serious*.
*l.*8 παρεβοήθει and the imperfects in the following lines are inceptive (see
above on ἔθεον). *l.*11 ἠλαύνετο has τὰ ὑποζύγια and οἱ ἵπποι as its
subjects but it agrees with the nearer one, τὰ ὑποζύγια, which as a neuter
plural takes a singular verb (3.1/1 note 2; for another example of a double
subject see 16.2.13 *l.*1).

19 | UNIT NINETEEN

19.1 Grammar

19.1/1 ἵστημι and its compounds

ἵστημι *make to stand, set up* was originally cίcτᾱμι with a present stem of
the same formation as δίδωμι and τίθημι (i.e. reduplication with iota and
no suffix). At an early stage in the history of Greek the initial sigma
developed into a rough breathing; the resulting ἵcτᾱμι (the form in most
dialects) became ἵcτημι in Attic with the regular change of ᾱ > η.[1]
Consequently, where the alternation δω/δο occurs in δίδωμι and θη/θε in
τίθημι we have cτη/cτα in ἵcτημι; the alternation φη/φα in φημί (7.1/2) has
the same explanation (the original form of the first person singular is
φᾱμί).

The **present** and **imperfect** of ἵcτημι are almost completely parallel to
δίδωμι and τίθημι. In the active we have:

PRESENT

		IND.	IMP.	SUBJ.	OPT.
S.	1	ἵcτημι		ἱcτῶ	ἱcταίην
	2	ἵcτηc	ἵcτη	ἱcτῇc	ἱcταίηc
	3	ἵcτηcι(ν)	ἱcτάτω	ἱcτῇ	ἱcταίη
PL.	1	ἵcταμεν		ἱcτῶμεν	ἱcταῖμεν
	2	ἵcτατε	ἵcτατε	ἱcτῆτε	ἱcταῖτε
	3	ἱcτᾶcι(ν)	ἱcτάντων	ἱcτῶcι(ν)	ἱcταῖεν

INFINITIVE ἱcτάναι

PARTICIPLE ἱcτάc, ἱcτᾶcα, ἱcτάν; gen. ἱcτάντοc, ἱcτάcηc, ἱcτάντοc

IMPERFECT ἵcτην, ἵcτηc, ἵcτη, ἵcταμεν, ἵcτατε, ἵcταcαν

---

[1] This change, which occurs when ᾱ is not preceded by a vowel or ρ, is one of the more striking differences between Attic
and most other dialects.

The **future** cτήcω *I shall make to stand, shall set up* is also parallel, but we meet a divergence in the **aorist**. ἵcτημι has two sets of forms (cf. the two aorists of φύω, 11.1/1):

(*a*) A weak aorist ἔcτηcα, which is transitive and means *I made to stand, set up.*

(*b*) A root aorist ἔcτην (conjugated as ἔβην, 11.1/1), which is intransitive and means *I stood.*

Examples of these two aorists are:

ἔγχος ἔcτηcε πρὸς κίονα.	*He stood his spear against a pillar* (transitive).
Ἀλκμήνης τόκος ἔcτη cιωπῇ.	*The son of Alcmene stood in silence* (intransitive).

The two aorists have identical forms in the 3rd pl. indicative active ἔcτηcαν (ἔcτηc–αν from ἔcτηcα; ἔcτη–cαν from ἔcτην). Where this form occurs, only the context will show whether it is transitive or intransitive. ἵcτημι is also irregular in its **perfect** and **pluperfect**. Both tenses have a κ suffix in the singular of the indicative but elsewhere a stem without κ (ἑcτα–) is normally used (see below). Because these tenses are intransitive (see below) they occur only in the active voice:

PERFECT

		IND.	IMP.	SUBJ.	OPT.
S.	1	ἕcτηκα		ἑcτῶ	ἑcταίην
	2	ἕcτηκας	ἕcταθι	ἑcτῇc	ἑcταίης
	3	ἕcτηκε(ν)	ἑcτάτω	ἑcτῇ	ἑcταίη
PL.	1	ἕcταμεν		ἑcτῶμεν	ἑcταῖμεν
	2	ἕcτατε	ἕcτατε	ἑcτῆτε	ἑcταῖτε
	3	ἑcτᾶcι(ν)	ἑcτάντων	ἑcτῶcι(ν)	ἑcταῖεν

INFINITIVE ἑcτάναι

PARTICIPLES ἑcτώc, ἑcτῶcα, ἑcτόc gen. ἑcτῶτος, ἑcτώcης, ἑcτῶτος

PLUPERFECT εἱcτήκη, εἱcτήκης, εἱcτήκει(ν), ἕcταμεν, ἕcτατε, ἕcταcαν

Except for the imperative, forms with the stem ἑcτα– have alternatives in ἑcτηκ– (e.g. 3rd pl. ind. ἑcτήκᾱcι(ν), inf. ἑcτηκέναι) but these are less common.

The first syllable of the perfect stem was originally cεcτ– with reduplication of c, but, as in the present stem, the initial c developed into a rough breathing, giving ἑcτ–. Because ἑ is in fact the reduplication it is kept in **all** forms of the perfect (16.1/4). The initial εἱcτ– of the singular of the pluperfect was originally ἐϲεϲτ– with the syllabic augment and reduplication (quite irregularly the augment does not occur in the plural and hence the 1st and 2nd pl. forms are identical with those of the perfect).

Both perfect and pluperfect are intransitive and they are used as a **present** and **imperfect** tense respectively: ἕϲτηκα *I am standing* and εἱϲτήκη *I was standing*. The future perfect ἑϲτήξω *I shall stand* (cf. 16.1/4 note 2) is also intransitive.

We may summarise these forms as follows:

	Transitive		**Intransitive**
PRESENT	ἵϲτημι *I am making to stand*	PERFECT	ἕϲτηκα *I am standing*
FUTURE	ϲτήϲω *I shall make to stand*	FUT. PERF.	ἑϲτήξω *I shall stand*
IMPERFECT	ἵϲτην *I was making to stand*	PLUPERFECT	εἱϲτήκη *I was standing*
WEAK AORIST	ἕϲτηϲα *I made to stand*	ROOT AORIST	ἕϲτην *I stood*

A comprehensive table of ἵϲτημι is given in **Appendix 5**. The present middle ἵϲταμαι is intransitive and literally means *I am in the process of making myself stand*, i.e. it represents a present **act** as opposed to the perfect, which represents a present **state** (*I am in a standing position*). The imperfect middle (ἱϲτάμην) and future middle (ϲτήϲομαι) are also intransitive but the weak aorist middle (ἐϲτηϲάμην) is transitive and means *I made (something) stand for myself.*

ἵϲτημι has many compounds and these retain the same distinctions between transitive and intransitive tenses. Among the most common are:

	Transitive tenses	**Intransitive tenses**
ἀνίϲτημι (ἀνά *up*)	*raise up; restore; cause to migrate, expel, uproot*	*rise up; be expelled; migrate*
ἀφίϲτημι (ἀπό *away*)	*remove; cause to revolt*	*go away from; revolt*
καθίϲτημι (κατά *down*)	*set down; put in a certain state; appoint; establish* (laws etc.)	*settle down; come into a certain state; be appointed; be established*

The middle voice of compounds of ἵϲτημι follows the pattern of the simple verb: οἱ βάρβαροι ἀφίϲτανται *the barbarians are in [the act of] revolt* (cf. οἱ βάρβαροι ἀφεϲτᾶϲιν* (perfect) *the barbarians are in [a state of] revolt*).

Examples of the above compounds are:

ἀνέϲτηϲαν καὶ Αἰγῑνήτᾱϲ τῷ
αὐτῷ θέρει τούτῳ ἐξ
Αἰγίνηϲ ᾽Αθηναῖοι.

*In this same summer the
Athenians also expelled the
Aeginetans from Aegina.*

Βοιωτοὶ οἱ νῦν ἑξηκοϲτῷ ἔτει
μετὰ ᾽Ιλίου ἅλωϲιν ἐξ ῎Αρνηϲ
ἀναϲτάντεϲ ὑπὸ Θεϲϲαλῶν τὴν
Βοιωτίᾱν ᾤκιϲαν.

*In the sixtieth year after the
capture of Troy the present
Boeotians, after being expelled
from Arne by the Thessalians,
colonised Boeotia.*

εἰ τοὺϲ ξυμμάχουϲ αὐτῶν
ἀφιϲτάναι πειρᾱϲόμεθα,
δεήϲει καὶ τούτοιϲ ναυϲὶ
βοηθεῖν τὸ πλέον οὖϲι
νηϲιώταιϲ.

If we try (lit. *shall try) to make
their allies revolt, we shall have
to come to their assistance as
well with a fleet because they
are for the most part islanders*
(lit. *it will be necessary to assist
them also with ships, being
[for] the greater [part] islanders*).

πρῶτοι ἀπ᾽ αὐτῶν Μῆδοι ἤρξαντο
ἀφίϲταϲθαι.

*The Medes were the first to start
to revolt from them* (lit. *the
Medes first started ...*).

κατέϲτηϲε τύραννον εἶναι παῖδα
τὸν ἑαυτοῦ.

*He appointed his own son to be
tyrant.*

ἐϲ φόβον καταϲτάντων
διαφθείρονται πολλοὶ Χαόνων.

*When they were reduced to a state
of panic many of the Chaonians
were killed* (vivid present).

Notes

1   To distinguish the different forms of ἵϲτημι it is essential to remember
    that:
    (i) ἱϲτ– occurs in all forms of the present and imperfect but nowhere
        else.
    (ii) ἐϲτ– occurs only in the aorist indicative.
    (iii) ἑϲτ– occurs in all forms of the perfect and in the pluperfect
        plural but nowhere else.
    (iv) εἱϲτ– occurs only in the pluperfect singular.

2   πίμπλημι *fill* and πίμπρημι *burn* (tr.) follow ἵϲτημι in the present and
    imperfect, e.g. the pres. ind. act. of the first is: πίμπλημι, πίμπληϲ,
    πίμπληϲι(ν), πίμπλαμεν, πίμπλατε, πιμπλᾶϲι(ν).

19.1/2 Potential clauses

Potential clauses express an action or state which has or had the potentiality of happening: *I wouldn't like to meet him on a dark night*; *Alcibiades would have been a disaster at our last party*. In Greek the construction is the same as for main clauses in category 1 conditional sentences (18.1/5; for the only complication see note 1 below); and the same is true in English, which uses *would* or *could* (although other auxiliaries such as *might* are also possible). As with conditional sentences (18.1/5) we have three time-frames:

Future   The optative (present or aorist as appropriate) with ἄν: τοῦτο οὐκ ἄν γένοιτο *that would not happen*.

Present The imperfect indicative with ἄν: τοῦτο οὐκ ἄν ἐγίγνετο *that would not be happening* or *happen [now* – to make a distinction between future and present English may need to add an adverb*]*.

Past   The aorist indicative with ἄν: τοῦτο οὐκ ἄν ἐγένετο *that would not have happened*.

Notes

1   A future potential can be used as a form of politeness to make a statement or request less blunt, e.g. βουλοίμην ἄν *I should like* (cf. βούλομαι *I want*). ἐβουλόμην ἄν *I could wish* (*sc.* that something were now the case) is also frequently used with a past reference *I could have wished*; this is a relic of older use.

2   In a particular context it is sometimes possible to translate a present or future potential by *can,* instead of *could/would*; the above examples would then be translated *that can not happen/be happening*.

19.1/3 Oddities in verbs

(a) *Perfects with a present meaning*

As we have seen (15.1.1), the perfect expresses a state in the present resulting from an action in the past. The perfect of some Greek verbs is best expressed in English by the present tense of verbs which in themselves indicate a state. The most common examples are:

δέδοικα *I am afraid* (lit. *I have become alarmed*) from δείδω *be alarmed*. The aorist ἔδεισα is common and has the meaning *I was afraid*.

ἔγνωκα *I know* (lit. *I have recognised*) from γιγνώσκω *recognise*.

ἔοικα *I resemble, I seem* exists only in a few forms outside the perfect.
Poetical forms in εἰκ– occur in the infinitive (εἰκέναι, otherwise
ἐοικέναι) and participle (εἰκώς, εἰκυῖα, εἰκός, otherwise ἐοικώς etc.).

κέκτημαι,[1] lit. *I have acquired* or *I am in a state of having acquired* (<
κτάομαι *acquire*), is normally to be translated by *I possess, own*
(plpf. ἐκεκτήμην *I possessed, owned*; fut. perf. κεκτήσομαι *I shall
possess, own*).

μέμνημαι *I remember* (lit. *I have reminded myself*) from μιμνήσκομαι
remind oneself. The aorist passive ἐμνήσθην means *I remembered*
(ex. at 12.3.9 *l*.2).

οἶδα *I know* exists only in the perfect, pluperfect, and future - see
Appendix 3.

τέθνηκα *I am dead* (lit. *I have died*) from ἀποθνῄσκω *die* (the perfect
is exceptional in never having the prefix ἀπο–, whereas the other
tenses of the uncompounded verb are normally restricted to poetry).
As with the perfect of ἵστημι (19.1/1) shorter forms occur, e.g. inf.
τεθνάναι (for τεθνηκέναι), pple. τεθνεώς (for τεθνηκώς), opt.
τεθναίην.

(b) *Eccentric* –μαι *verbs*

A few deponents end in –αμαι, not –ομαι, because they belong to the –μι
class of verbs (18.1/1; cf. ἵσταμαι pres. mid./pass. of ἵστημι, 19.1/1). The
only common examples are δύναμαι *be able* and ἐπίσταμαι *know how to,
understand* (both passive deponents with a middle future – see **Principal
parts of verbs**; we have already met some forms, e.g. 10.3 *l*.5). These
differ from –ω verbs only in the present and imperfect. In these tenses
δύναμαι is conjugated:

PRESENT

INDICATIVE δύναμαι, δύνασαι, δύναται, δυνάμεθα, δύνασθε, δύνανται

INFINITIVE δύνασθαι PARTICIPLE δυνάμενος, –η, –ον

IMPERFECT

ἐδυνάμην, ἐδύνω (< –ασο), ἐδύνατο, ἐδυνάμεθα, ἐδύνασθε, ἐδύναντο.

For ἐδυν– we may also have ἠδυν–. The other moods of the present,
where they occur, follow ἵστημι (19.1/1). The forms of ἐπίσταμαι are
parallel.

---

[1] This reduplication is an exception to the rule given at 15.1/1 (we would have expected ἐκτη–).

Two similar verbs are κεῖμαι *lie, be laid down* and κάθημαι *be seated, sit*[1] which, because they both describe a continual action, exist only in the present, imperfect, and future. κεῖμαι is conjugated:

PRESENT

    INDICATIVE κεῖμαι, κεῖσαι, κεῖται, κείμεθα, κεῖσθε, κεῖνται

    INFINITIVE κεῖσθαι PARTICIPLE κείμενος, -η, -ον

IMPERFECT ἐκείμην, ἔκεισο, ἔκειτο, ἐκείμεθα, ἔκεισθε, ἔκειντο

FUTURE INDICATIVE κείσομαι, κείσῃ , etc.

The forms of κάθημαι follow the same pattern. The other moods of the present of both verbs are rare. On the use of κεῖμαι for the perfect passive of τίθημι see 18.1/2 note 4.

19.2 Greek reading

1   λέγει που Ἡράκλειτος ὅτι πάντα χωρεῖ καὶ οὐδὲν μένει, καὶ ποταμοῦ ῥοῇ ἀπεικάζων τὰ ὄντα λέγει ὡς δὶς εἰς τὸν αὐτὸν ποταμὸν οὐκ ἂν ἐμβαίης.

2# νῆφε καὶ μέμνησ' (= –σο) ἀπιστεῖν· ἄρθρα ταῦτα τῶν φρενῶν.

3   Πύρρων οὐδὲν ἔφη διαφέρειν ζῆν ἢ τεθνάναι. εἰπόντος δέ τινος, τί οὖν οὐκ ἀποθνῄσκεις; ὅτι, ἔφη, οὐδὲν διαφέρει.

4# δοκεῖτε πηδᾶν τἀδικήματ' εἰς θεοὺς
πτεροῖσι, κἄπειτ' ἐν Διὸς δέλτου πτυχαῖς
γράφειν τιν' αὐτά, Ζῆνα δ' εἰσορῶντά νιν
θνητοῖς δικάζειν; οὐδ' ὁ πᾶς ἂν οὐρανός,
Διὸς γράφοντος τὰς βροτῶν ἁμαρτίας,   5
ἐξαρκέσειεν οὐδ' ἐκεῖνος ἂν σκοπῶν
πέμπειν ἑκάστῳ ζημίαν· ἀλλ' ἡ Δίκη
ἐνταῦθά πούστιν ἐγγύς, εἰ βούλεσθ' ὁρᾶν.

5   **Proverbs and famous sayings**

(*i*) ἐὰν δύνῃ ὁδεῦσαι, μὴ πλεύσῃς. (*ii*) τοῖς σεαυτοῦ πτεροῖς ἑάλως. (*iii*) ἐκ παντὸς ξύλου Ἑρμῆς οὐκ ἂν γένοιτο. (*iv*) ὕδωρ πίνων οὐδὲν ἂν τέκοις σοφόν. (*v*)# ὁ χρήσιμ' εἰδώς, οὐχ ὁ πόλλ' εἰδώς, σοφός. (*vi*)# θεοῦ διδόντος οὐκ ἂν ἐκφύγοις κακά. (*vii*) πάντες ἄνθρωποι τοῦ εἰδέναι ὀρέγονται φύσει. (*viii*) ὅταν εὐπλοῇς, μάλιστα μέμνησο ζάλης. (*ix*) δός μοι ποῦ στῶ καὶ κινήσω τὴν γῆν. (*x*) πολυμαθίη (= –ία) νόον ἔχειν οὐ διδάσκει· Ἡσίοδον

---

[1] κάθημαι is used in prose but the uncompounded verb, ἧμαι, is found in verse (e.g. 16.3 *l*.9).

γὰρ ἂν ἐδίδαξε καὶ Πυθαγόρην (= –αν). (*xi*) τὸ φύσει πεφυκὸς οὐ
μεθίσταται. (*xii*)# κούφως φέρειν δεῖ τὰς παρεστώσας τύχας. (*xiii*)
ἀθυμοῦντες ἄνδρες οὔπω τροπαῖον ἔστησαν. (*xiv*) ἄνθρωπος ὢν
μέμνησο. (*xv*) πάγην ἱστὰς ἐν πάγῃ ληφθήςῃ. (*xvi*) πόρρω ἑστὼς ὁ
θεὸς ἐγγύθεν βλέπει. (*xvii*) ἐπὶ ξυροῦ ἵσταται.

6# ὡς τοῖς κακῶς πράςσουσιν ἡδὺ καὶ βραχὺν
χρόνον λαθέςθαι τῶν παρεστώτων κακῶν.

7 One of the most famous Spartan kings was Leonidas, who died with
three hundred Spartan soldiers at Thermopylae in an attempt to
defend the pass against the invading Persians (480 BC). The
following are stories about him:

(*i*) Λεωνίδας πρός τινα εἰπόντα, πλὴν τοῦ βασιλεύειν ἡμῶν οὐδὲν
διαφέρεις, ἀλλ' οὐκ ἄν, ἔφη, εἰ μὴ βελτίων ὑμῶν ἦν, ἐβασίλευον.
(*ii*) γενόμενος ἐν Θερμοπύλαις πρός τινα εἰπόντα, ἀπὸ τῶν
ὀϊστευμάτων τῶν βαρβάρων οὐδὲ τὸν ἥλιον ἰδεῖν ἔξεστιν, οὐκοῦν,
ἔφη, χαρίεν, εἰ ὑπὸ σκιᾷ αὐτοῖς μαχούμεθα.
(*iii*) Ξέρξου δὲ γράψαντος αὐτῷ, ἔξεστί σοι μὴ θεομαχοῦντι, μετ'
ἐμοῦ δὲ ταττομένῳ, τῆς Ἑλλάδος μοναρχεῖν, ἀντέγραψεν, εἰ τὰ
καλὰ τοῦ βίου ἐγίγνωσκες, ἀπέστης ἂν τῆς τῶν ἀλλοτρίων
ἐπιθυμίας· ἐμοὶ δὲ κρείττων ὁ ὑπὲρ τῆς Ἑλλάδος θάνατος τοῦ
μοναρχεῖν τῶν ὁμοφύλων.
(*iv*) πάλιν δὲ τοῦ Ξέρξου γράψαντος, πέμψον τὰ ὅπλα,
ἀντέγραψε, μολὼν λαβέ.

The following epitaph for Leonidas and his men was written by
Simonides:

(*v*)# ὦ ξεῖν', ἀγγέλλειν Λακεδαιμονίοις ὅτι τῇδε
κείμεθα, τοῖς κείνων ῥήμασι πειθόμενοι.

8 The normal way of publishing an official document in the Greek
world was to cut the text on stone (usually marble) and display it in
a prominent place. Many thousands of such inscriptions have
survived. The following is an extract from the record of the Athenian
settlement with the Euboean city of Chalcis after the Euboean revolt
from the Athenian empire in 446 BC, and it gives the wording of the
oath to be sworn by all adult males in Chalcis.

οὐκ ἀποστήσομαι ἀπὸ τοῦ δήμου τοῦ Ἀθηναίων οὔτε τέχνῃ οὔτε
μηχανῇ οὐδεμιᾷ οὐδ' ἔπει οὐδὲ ἔργῳ, οὐδὲ τῷ ἀφισταμένῳ
πείσομαι, καὶ ἐὰν ἀφιστῇ τις, κατερῶ Ἀθηναίοις, καὶ τὸν φόρον

208 ANCIENT GREEK

ὑποτελῶ ᾿Αθηναίοιc ὃν ἂν πείθω ᾿Αθηναίουc, καὶ ξύμμαχος
ἔcομαι οἷος ἂν δύνωμαι ἄριcτος καὶ δικαιότατος, καὶ τῷ δήμῳ 5
τῷ ᾿Αθηναίων βοηθήcω καὶ ἀμυνῶ, ἐάν τις ἀδικῇ τὸν δῆμον τὸν
᾿Αθηναίων, καὶ πείcομαι τῷ δήμῳ τῷ ᾿Αθηναίων.

Notes

1 τὰ ὄντα neuter pl., lit. *the being [things]*, i.e. *existing things*; ὡc =
   ὅτι (8.1/3*b*)
2 ταῦτα is subject and ἄρθρα predicate.
3 οὐδὲν ἔφη cf. οὐ φημί (8.1/3*a* note 4); οὐδέν *in no respect, not at all*
   (20.1/5); ζῆν and τεθνάναι (19.1/3*a*) are the subjects of διαφέρειν;
   εἰπόντος ... τινος gen. absolute (12.1/2*b*).
4 *l*.1 δοκεῖτε *do you think*; τἀδικήματ᾿(α) (= τὰ ἀδ–) is the subject of
   πηδᾶν. *l*.3 τιν᾿(α) *someone* is the subject of γράφειν and αὐτά the
   object; νιν an obsolete pronoun used solely in verse; it exists only in
   this form, which can function as the accusative of either the singular
   or plural of any gender of the 3rd person unemphatic pronoun (i.e. it
   can mean *him, her, it, them*); here it is the equivalent of αὐτά (acc.),
   i.e. the ἀδικήματα. *l*.4 Take ἄν with ἐξαρκέcειεν. *l*.6 ἐξαρκέcειεν
   (< ἐξαρκέω – the ε is not lengthened, cf. 5.1/2 note 2) is to be
   supplied after οὐδ᾿. *l*.8 ποῦcτιν crasis (11.1/5) for ποῦ ἐcτιν;
   βούλεcθ᾿ i.e. βούλεcθε.
5 (*i*) δύνῃ 2nd s. pres. subj. of δύναμαι (the subjunctive is required
   after ἐάν – 14.1/4*c*(iii)). (*ii*) ἑάλωc < ἁλίcκομαι (18.1/4). (*iii*) Not
   the god himself but a statue of him. (*iv*) ὕδωρ πῑνων is the equivalent
   of a conditional clause (*if you drink water* – 12.1/2*a*(iv)); τέκοιc 2nd
   s. aor. opt. act. of τίκτω. (*v*) εἰδώc < οἶδα (19.1/3*a* and **Appendix
   3**). (*vii*) τοῦ εἰδέναι articular infinitive (5.1/3 – other examples
   below in 7(*i*) and (*iii*)); ὀρέγομαι is followed by the genitive
   (13.1/2*a*(ii)). (*viii*) μέμνηcο cf.17.1/1 note 4. (*ix*) δόc 2nd s. aor. imp.
   act. of δίδωμι; cτῶ (1st s. intr. aor. subj. of ἵcτημι) deliberative
   subjunctive in indirect speech (14.1/4*a*(ii)), *where I am to stand*. (*x*)
   Written in Ionic (1.3); γάρ *for [otherwise]*. (*xi*) πεφῡκόc < φύω. (*xii*)
   παρεcτώcαc f. perf. pple. of παρίcτημι. (*xiii*) ἔcτηcαν gnomic aor.
   (see note on 5.2.10). (*xiv*) μέμνημαι is followed, where appropriate,
   by a participle, not an infinitive (cf. 15.1/2*a*). (*xv*) ληφθήcῃ 2nd s.
   fut. ind. pass. of λαμβάνω.
6 παρεcτώτων n. perf. pple. of παρίcτημι.

7   (*i*) Take ἡμῶν with διαφέρεις, not with βασιλεύειν. (*ii*) οὐδέ *not even*;   ἔξεστιν (also in (*iii*)) an impersonal verb meaning *it is possible* (21.1/4*a*); χαρίεν *sc*. ἔσται. (*iii*) Take ταττομένῳ (mid. of τάττω, *drawing yourself up* (*with me*)) with σοι; τοῦ μοναρχεῖν gen. of comparison (17.1/4*a*). (*iv*) μολών aor. pple. of βλώσκω. (v) ξεῖν'(ε) = ξένε; ἀγγέλλειν infinitive used as imperative (17.1/1 note 5); κείνων = ἐκείνων.

8   *ll*.1f. The first negative, οὐκ, is reinforced by οὔτε ... οὔτε ... οὐδεμιᾷ and οὐδ' ... οὐδέ, lit. *I will not ... neither in no ... nor,* etc. but trans. *I will not ... either in any ... or,* etc. (οὐδεμιᾷ goes with both τέχνῃ and μηχανῇ); the fut. mid. ἀποστήσομαι (< ἀφίστημι) is intransitive; τοῦ δήμου τοῦ ᾽Αθηναίων *the people, [i.e.] the [people] of [the] Athenians* a regular formula in inscriptions, trans. *the people of Athens*; ἔπει dat. s. of ἔπος. *ll*.3f. πείσομαι fut. of πείθομαι, not πάσχω; ἀφιστῇ   3rd s. pres. subj. act., this is a transitive tense (19.1/1) but the verb here has no object expressed – lit. *causes [others] to revolt,* i.e. *tries to stir up revolt;* κατερῶ < καταγορεύω (18.1/4 note 2); ὑποτελῶ fut. (5.1/2 note 2); τὸν φόρον ... ὃν ἂν πείθω ᾽Αθηναίους lit. *the tribute whatever I persuade the Athenians,* i.e. *whatever tribute I persuade the Athenians* (sc. *is appropriate*). *ll*.5ff. οἷος *of what sort* (21.1/3) is given a general reference (*of whatever sort*) because it is followed by ἄν and the subj. (14.1/4*c*(iii)), lit. *of whatever sort best and most just I am able [to be];* The phrase ὁ δῆμος ὁ ᾽Αθηναίων is repeated to avoid any misunderstanding whatsoever.

20 | UNIT TWENTY

20.1 Grammar

20.1/1 Verbs in –νῡμι

The –νῡμι class (18.1/1) constitutes the more numerous subdivision of –μι verbs but presents no especial difficulty. All forms of the present and imperfect contain the suffix νῡ or νῠ; the present indicative, infinitive and participle, and the imperfect have endings without the o/e characteristic of –ω verbs (cf. 2.1/5 note 3), but the present subjunctive and optative have the same endings as λύω. The other tenses, which do not keep the νῡ/νῠ suffix, are formed in the same way as those of –ω verbs. An example is δείκνῡμι *show*, which has the principal parts δείκνῡμι, fut. δείξω, aor. act. ἔδειξα, perf. act. δέδειχα, perf. mid./pass. δέδειγμαι, aor. pass. ἐδείχθην. The present and imperfect of this verb are given in full in **Appendix 6**.

Notes

1   A number of verbs in this class end in –ννῡμι rather than –νῡμι, e.g. κεράννῡμι *mix*, σκεδάννῡμι *scatter*, κρεμάννῡμι *hang* (tr.; the intransitive meaning of this verb is supplied by the passive κρέμαμαι, which is conjugated like ἵσταμαι (19.1/1)).

2   ὄλλῡμι (originally ὄλ–νῡμι) *destroy, ruin, lose* (fut. ὀλῶ) has two aorist and two perfects. The weak forms of both are transitive and the strong intransitive (cf. 15.1/1 note 2):

AORIST	(weak)	ὤλεσα	*I destroyed/ruined/lost*
	(strong)	ὠλόμην	*I perished* (middle voice, not active!)
PERFECT	(weak)	ὀλώλεκα	*I have destroyed/ruined/lost*
	(strong)	ὄλωλα	*I have perished, am ruined* or *lost*

ὄλλῡμι in its uncompounded form occurs only in verse. In prose we find the compound ἀπόλλῡμι, which has the same meaning. Cf. the use of θνήcκω in verse but ἀποθνήcκω in prose (19.1/3*a*).

20.1/2 ἵημι and its compounds

ἵημι *let go, send forth* is another –μι verb of group (*a*) (18.1/1). Its present stem was originally cιcη– (root cη/cε; cf. δίδωμι and τίθημι) but with the change of the initial sigma to a rough breathing (cf. ἵcτημι 19.1/1) and the loss of intervocal sigma (cf. 6.1/1*c*) this was reduced to ἵη– (root ἡ/ἑ).

The principal parts of ἵημι are: pres. ἵημι, fut. ἥcω, aor. act ἧκα, perf. act. εἷκα, perf. pass. εἷμαι, aor. pass. εἵθην.

As will be seen from **Appendix 5** its present and imperfect tenses are exactly parallel to those of τίθημι except in the 3rd pl. pres. ind. act., where contraction has taken place (ἱᾶcι < ἱέᾱcι). The parallelism extends to nearly every other form, although it is obscured in some cases by contraction. Note that the sing. aor. act. ind. has a κ suffix as in τίθημι.

Almost all forms of ἵημι, except those of the present and imperfect, exist only in compounds. The following are the most common:

ἀφίημι	*send forth*; *discharge*; *let go*
ἐφίημι	*send*; *set on, send against*; (mid.) *aim at, desire*
μεθίημι	*let go, release*; *give up*
παρίημι	*pass over*; *let pass*

Examples of each of these compounds are:

πρέπει cοι τὴν ὀργὴν ἀφῑέναι εἰc τὸν βλάψαντά cε.	*It is fitting for you to vent your anger on the man who harmed you.*
ἐὰν ἑλών τίc τινα ἀκουcίου φόνου καὶ cαφῶc ἐπιδείξᾱc μὴ καθαρόν, μετὰ ταῦτ᾽ αἰδέcηται καὶ ἀφῇ, οὐκέτ᾽ ἐκβαλεῖν κῡριοc τὸν αὐτόν ἐcτιν.	*If anyone convicts a man of involuntary homicide and clearly shows him to be polluted* (lit. *not pure*), *and then feels pity for him and releases him, he no longer has the power to cast the same person into exile.*
ἐφῆκε τὴν ἵππον ἐπὶ τοὺc Ἕλληναc.	*He sent the cavalry against the Greeks.*

οὐ γὰρ τοῖς ἔθνεσιν ἔχθει
ἐπίᾱσιν, ἀλλὰ τῶν ἐν τῇ
Cικελίᾳ ἀγαθῶν ἐφῑέμενοι.

*For they will not attack the races
because of hatred but because
they are aiming at the good
things of Sicily.*

ἐλευθέρᾱν δέ με, ὡc ἐλευθέρᾱ
θάνω, πρὸc θεῶν μεθέντεc
κτείνατε.

*In the name of the gods, release
me [to be] free, so that I may
die free, and [then] kill me
(a woman is speaking).*

εἰ μεθήcει τὴν ἀρχήν, ἄλλος
τιc ἀντ᾽ αὐτοῦ τύραννοc
καταcτήcεται.

*If he gives up his power, someone
else will set himself up as tyrant
in his stead.*

μὴ τοίνυν γιγνώcκοντέc γε
παρῶμεν αὐτὸ ἄρρητον.

*Let us not then, since we know
[it], pass it over unmentioned.*

χρὴ ἡμᾶc καταcκόπουc μὴ
πέμπειν μηδὲ διαμέλλειν
καιρὸν παρῑέντας.

*We ought not to send inspectors
or to delay, letting an
opportunity pass.*

20.1/3 Genitive of price or value

The genitive is used to express price or value with verbs and adjectives denoting buying, selling, valuing, and the like:

ὅταν δέῃ ἀργυρίου πρίαcθαι
ἢ ἀποδόcθαι ἵππον ...

*Whenever it is necessary to buy
or sell a horse for money ...*

τοῦτο δ᾽ ἐcτὶν ὃ τῶν
ἀναλιcκομένων χρημάτων
πάντων Φίλιπποc ὠνεῖται.

*This is what Philip is buying with
all the money which is being
spent.*

Α. πόcου διδάcκει;

A. What is his fee for teaching?
(lit. *for how much does he
teach?*)

Β. πέντε μνῶν.

B. Five minae (lit. *for five minae*).

ἡμᾶc οὐδενὸc λόγου ἀξιοῖ.

He thinks us of no account.

cμῑκρὰ καὶ ὀλίγου ἄξια ἀνερωτᾷ.

*He asks petty, insignificant
questions* (lit. *things small and
worth little*).

To value highly/little/not at all etc. is commonly expressed by ποιεῖcθαι and a genitive governed by περί: περὶ πολλοῦ (πλέονος, πλείcτου) /ὀλίγου (ἐλάττονος, ἐλαχίcτου)/ οὐδενὸc ποιεῖcθαι. Examples are:

τὰ πλείστου ἄξια περὶ ἐλαχίστου ποιεῖται, τὰ δὲ φαυλότερα περὶ πλέονος.	*He values least what is worth most, and [values] more highly what is more trivial.*
ἀναγκαῖον ἐδόκει εἶναι τὸ τοῦ θεοῦ περὶ πλείστου ποιεῖσθαι.	*It seemed essential to value most highly the god's [word].*
οὗτος ἅπαντας τοὺς πολῑ́τᾱς περὶ οὐδενὸς ἐποιήσατο.	*He valued all the citizens at nothing.*

20.1/4 Genitive of separation

The genitive is used with verbs and adjectives denoting separation, cessation, prevention, hindrance, difference, etc. It is common with verbs compounded with ἀπό and ἐκ:

ἀπέχει τῶν Ἐπιπολῶν ἐξ ἢ ἑπτὰ σταδίους.	*It is six or seven stades distant from Epipolae.*
ἔπαυσαν αὐτὸν τῆς στρατηγίᾱς.	*They deposed him from his generalship.*
ἐκώλῡον τῆς πορείᾱς αὐτόν.	*They prevented him from passing* (lit. *from the passage*).
ἐψηφίσασθε ὑμεῖς αὐτὸν εἴργεσθαι τῆς ἀγορᾶς καὶ τῶν ἱερῶν.	*You voted that he be excluded from the agora and the temples.*
οὐδὲν διοίσεις Χαιρεφῶντος.	*You will be no different from Chaerephon.*
ἔργων πονηρῶν χεῖρ' ἐλευθέρᾱν ἔχε.	*Keep your hand free from wicked deeds.*

20.1/5 Accusative of respect or specification

The accusative may be used with a verb (usually intransitive) or an adjective to denote a thing with respect to which that verb or adjective is limited. A literal translation may be obtained by employing the words *with respect to* before the noun involved, but, to produce an idiomatic translation, it will often be necessary to recast the expression somewhat in English:

| τᾱ̀ς γνάθους ἀλγήσετε. | *You will have a pain with respect to your jaws,* i.e. *you'll have sore jaws.* |
| πόδας ὠκὺς Ἀχιλλεύς. | *Swift-footed* (lit. *swift with respect to feet*) *Achilles.* |

τυφλὸς τά τ᾽ ὦτα τόν τε νοῦν   *You are blind both in (lit. with*
τά τ᾽ ὄμματ᾽ εἶ.   *respect to) ears and mind and*
                                       eyes.

τεῖχος πεντήκοντα μὲν πήχεων   *A wall fifty cubits wide and two*
τὸ εὖρος, ὕψος δὲ διᾱκοσίων   *hundred cubits high (lit. of fifty*
πήχεων.   *cubits with respect to the width,*
                                       and of two hundred with respect
                                       to height).

λέξον ὅστις εἶ γένος.   *Tell [me] who you are by race.*

Under this heading may also be included the so-called **adverbial
accusatives**, e.g. οὐδέν *in no respect, not at all*; τι *to some extent*; τί *why*
(lit. *with respect to what?*); πολύ *much, by far*; τὰ ἄλλα, τἄλλα *in other
respects*; τοῦτον τὸν τρόπον *in this way*; τίνα τρόπον... *in what way..?
how...?* Examples of these have already occurred. We have also met the
neuter accusative (both singular and plural) of adjectives employed in this
way, e.g. ὀρθὰ βαδίζειν *to walk straight* (15.2.3, see also 16.3 *l*.5, 17.3
l.12). Adjectives so used are the equivalent of adverbs.

20.2 Greek reading

1 νεανίας τίς ποτε νοσήσας εἶπε τῷ ἰατρῷ οὕτως ἀλγεῖν ὥστε μὴ
   δύνασθαι μήτε καθῆσθαι μήτε κεῖσθαι μήτε ἑστάναι · ὁ δὲ ἰατρός,
   ὦ φίλε, ἔφη, οὐδὲν ἄλλο σοι λοιπόν ἐστιν ἢ κρέμασθαι.
2# τίς δ᾽ οἶδεν εἰ ζῆν τοῦθ᾽ ὃ κέκληται θανεῖν,
   τὸ ζῆν δὲ θνήσκειν ἐστί; πλὴν ὅμως βροτῶν
   νοσοῦσιν οἱ βλέποντες, οἱ δ᾽ ὀλωλότες
   οὐδὲν νοσοῦσιν οὐδὲ κέκτηνται κακά.
3 **Proverbs and famous sayings**
   (*i*) δραχμῆς μὲν ηὔλει, τεττάρων δὲ παύεται. (*ii*) ἡ κάμηλος
   ἐπιθυμήσασα κεράτων καὶ τὰ ὦτα προσαπώλεσεν. (*iii*)# οὐκ ἔστιν
   ὅστις πάντ᾽ ἀνὴρ εὐδαιμονεῖ. (*iv*) πολλοὶ στρατηγοὶ Καρίαν
   ἀπώλεσαν. (*v*) ἀφεὶς τὰ φανερὰ μὴ δίωκε τὰ ἀφανῆ. (*vi*) χρόνος
   δίκαιον ἄνδρα δείκνυσιν μόνος. (*vii*) ἐλέφαντος διαφέρεις οὐδέν.
   (*viii*)# ἀπάτης δικαίας οὐκ ἀποστατεῖ θεός. (*ix*)# πολλῶν ἰατρῶν
   εἴσοδός μ᾽ ἀπώλεσεν. (*x*) λέων εἶ τὴν τρίχα, ὄνος δὲ τὸν βίον.
4# **An epic nose**
   τοῦ γρυποῦ Νίκωνος ὁρῶ τὴν ῥῖνα, Μένιππε,
   αὐτὸς δ᾽ οὖν μακρὰν φαίνεται εἶναι ἔτι ·

ἀλλ' ἥξει, μείνωμεν ὅμως· εἰ γὰρ πολύ, πέντε
τῆς ῥινὸς cταδίουc, οἴομαι, οὐκ ἀπέχει.
ἀλλ' αὐτὴ μέν, ὁρᾶc, προπορεύεται· ἢν δ' ἐπὶ βουνὸν   5
ὑψηλὸν cτῶμεν, καὐτὸν ἐcοψόμεθα.
5# τὴν κεφαλὴν βάπτων τιc ἀπώλεcε τὰc τρίχαc αὐτάc,
    καὶ δαcὺc ὢν λίαν ᾠὸν ἅπαc γέγονεν.

6 ἐπὶ τούτῳ Κλεάνωρ ἀνέcτη καὶ ἔλεξεν ὧδε· ἀλλ' ὁρᾶτε μέν, ὦ
ἄνδρεc, τὴν βαcιλέωc ἐπιορκίαν καὶ ἀcέβειαν, ὁρᾶτε δὲ τὴν
Τιccαφέρνουc ἀπιcτίαν, ὅcτιc, λέγων ὡc γείτων τε εἴη τῆc
Ἑλλάδαc καὶ περὶ πλείcτου ἂν ποιήcαιτο cῶcαι ἡμᾶc, καὶ ἐπὶ
τούτοιc αὐτὸc ὀμόcαc ἡμῖν, αὐτὸc δεξιὰc δούc, αὐτὸc ἐξαπατήcαc   5
cυνέλαβε τοὺc cτρατηγούc, καὶ οὐδὲ Δία ξένιον ᾐδέcθη, ἀλλὰ
Κλεάρχῳ   καὶ ὁμοτράπεζοc γενόμενοc αὐτοῖc τούτοιc
ἐξαπατήcαc τοὺc ἄνδραc ἀπολώλεκεν.
7 ἀλλ', ὦ Cώκρατεc, πειθόμενοc τοῖc νόμοιc μήτε παῖδαc περὶ
πλείονοc ποιοῦ μήτε τὸ ζῆν μήτε ἄλλο μηδὲν πρὸ τοῦ δικαίου, ἵνα
εἰc Ἅιδου ἐλθὼν ἔχῃc πάντα ταῦτα ἀπολογήcαcθαι τοῖc ἐκεῖ
ἄρχουcιν.
8 ὁ Cωκράτηc φανερὸc ἦν οὐ τῶν τὰ cώματα πρὸc ὥραν, ἀλλὰ τῶν
τὰc ψυχὰc πρὸc ἀρετὴν εὖ πεφυκότων ἐφιέμενοc.
9# γραμματικοῦ θυγάτηρ ἔτεκεν φιλότητι μιγεῖcα
    παιδίον ἀρcενικόν, θηλυκόν, οὐδέτερον.
10# Ζεὺc γὰρ τὰ μὲν μέγιcτα φροντίζει βροτῶν,
    τὰ μικρὰ δ' ἄλλοιc δαίμοcιν παρεὶc ἐᾷ.
11 οἱ δ' ἐν τῇ Χίῳ μετὰ τοῦ Ἐτεονίκου cτρατιῶται ὄντεc, ἕωc μὲν
θέροc ἦν, ἀπό τε τῆc ὥραc ἐτρέφοντο καὶ ἐργαζόμενοι μιcθοῦ
κατὰ τὴν χώραν· ἐπεὶ δὲ χειμὼν ἐγένετο καὶ τροφὴν οὐκ εἶχον
γυμνοί τε ἦcαν καὶ ἀνυπόδητοι, cυνίcταντο ἀλλήλοιc ὡc τῇ Χίῳ
ἐπιθηcόμενοι.
12# Polymnestor, who has been blinded by Hecuba, screams for
vengeance but is restrained by Agamemnon.

    ΠΟ. ὤμοι, τί λέξειc; ἦ γὰρ ἐγγύc ἐcτί που;
           cήμηνον, εἰπὲ ποῦ 'cθ', ἵν' ἁρπάcαc χεροῖν
           διαcπάcωμαι καὶ καθαιμάξω χρόα.
    ΑΓ. οὗτοc, τί πάcχειc; ΠΟ. πρὸc θεῶν cε λίccομαι,
           μέθεc μ' ἐφεῖναι τῇδε μαργῶcαν χέρα.   5
    ΑΓ. ἴcχ'· ἐκβαλὼν δὲ καρδίαc τὸ βάρβαρον
           λέγ', ὡc ἀκούcαc cοῦ τε τῇcδε τ' ἐν μέρει
           κρίνω δικαίωc ἀνθ' ὅτου πάcχειc τάδε.

Notes

1 νοσήσᾱϲ *having fallen sick* **not** *having been sick* as is shown by the context (technically called an **ingressive** aorist); μὴ δύνασθαι ... lit. *not to be able neither to ... nor to*, i.e. *not to be able either to ... or to*.

2 *l*.1 τοῦθ' (τοῦτο) is the subject of the first clause after εἰ (supply ἐστί from the next line). *l*.2 πλὴν ὅμωϲ *except however* (lit. *except nevertheless*). *l*.3 οἱ βλέποντεϲ sc. *the light of day*, a regular expression for *the living*; οἱ ὀλωλότεϲ (20.1/1 note 2) i.e. *the dead*.

3 (*i*) ηὔλει inceptive imperfect (4.1/1 footnote) *started to play the pipe*. (*ii*) καί adv. *also*. (*iii*) Lit. *there is not whatever man ...*, i.e. *there is no man who ...* (on ὅϲτιϲ, which is here used adjectivally, see 10.1/2*b* note 2). (*v*) μή negates the whole sentence, i.e. ἀφείϲ (aor. pple. of ἀφίημι) and δίωκε. (*x*) εἶ (< εἰμί) *you are*.

4 *l*.2 δ' οὖν (13.1/3*c*(ii)) introduces a contrast *but/however* (οὖν does not have its normal meaning here). *ll*.3f. μείνωμεν jussive subj. (14.1/4*a*(i)); with εἰ γὰρ πολύ supply ἀπέχει from next line, lit. *for [even] if he is far away*; πέντε ϲταδίουϲ acc. of spatial extent (7.1/7*d*); τῆϲ ῥῑνόϲ *from his nose* gen. of separation (20.1/4). *l*.5 ἤν = ἐᾱν (18.1/5 note 2), which is followed by the subj. *l*.6 ϲτῶμεν intr. aor. subj. of ἵστημι (19.1/1); καὐτόν (= καὶ αὐτόν) *him too*.

5 The participle ὤν has a concessive force *though being* (we might have expected an accompanying καίπερ (12.1/2*a*(iii)) but cf. λέγων, ὀμόσαϲ, δούϲ in the next passage, which are used in the same way); take λῑᾶν with δαϲύϲ (this unusual word order is dictated by metre).

6 *l*.1 ἀνέστη < ἀνίϲτημι. *l*.3 The indefinite relative ὅϲτιϲ (10.1/2 note 2) is also used to introduce an adjectival clause which gives a **reason**, trans. *since he*; εἴη opt. in indirect speech in historic sequence (14.1/4*d*). *l*.5 ὀμόσᾱϲ < ὄμνῡμι. *l*.6 οὐδέ *not even*; ἠδέσθη < αἰδέομαι. *l*.7 Κλεάρχῳ dat. with ὁμοτράπεζοϲ (to share a meal automatically involved permanent ties of friendship and a violation of these was an offence against Ζεὺϲ ξένιοϲ); καί *actually*; αὐτοῖϲ τούτοιϲ (instrumental dat., 11.1/2) *by these very means*.

7 μήτε ἄλλο μηδέν *nor anything else* (7.1/6); πρό lit. *in preference to* but trans. *than*; εἰϲ is used with the gen. to mean *to the place/house of* – the house of Hades is the Underworld, to which all souls (ψῡχαί) went after death; ἔχῃϲ *you may be able* (ἔχω + an infinitive means *be able*).

8 φανερὸϲ ἦν + pple. lit. *was clear(ly) ...* (cf.15.2.10); εὖ πεφῡκότων

must be taken with both phrases beginning with τῶν; εὖ πεφῡκέναι (< φύω, the pple. is used here) means *to be well endowed by nature, to be naturally sound*; τὰ cώματα and τὰς ψῡχᾱ́ς are acc. of respect (20.1/5), but trans. *in body ... in soul* and trans. πρός (lit. *towards*) by *with respect to*.

9 μιγεῖcα f. aor. pass. pple. of μείγνῡμι; the lady gave birth to triplets, whose gender reflected her father's professional interests.

10 παρείς aor. act. pple. of παρίημι.

11 ὥρᾱ *[produce of] the season*; γυμνοί lit. *naked* but here to be understood simply as *badly clothed*.

12 *l.*1 ἦ γάρ introduces a surprised question *is she really ...?* (ἦ = ἆρα). *l.*2 'cθ' i.e. ἐcτί; χεροῖν is dat. dual (24.1/4), lit. *with two hands. l.*3 καθαιμάξω aor. subj. (as is διαcπάcωμαι) after ἵνα (14.1/4c(i)); χρόα acc. s. of χρώς. *l.*4 The nom. οὗτος (which does not, in any case, have a voc.) expresses an impatient demand for the attention of the person addressed (here Polymnestor), trans. *you there!* or *what's this?*; τί πάσχεις lit. *what are you suffering?*, i.e. *what's wrong with you?. l.*5 μέθες 2nd s. aor. imp. act. of μεθίημι; ἐφεῖναι aor. inf. of ἐφίημι; *l.*6 τὸ βάρβαρον *the barbarous [element]*, i.e. *savagery*. *ll.*7f. ὡς (here = ἵνα) introduces a purpose clause (22.1/1b(ii)), and consequently κρῑ́νω is subjunctive.

21 | **UNIT TWENTY-ONE**

21.1 Grammar

21.1/1 Wishes

Like potential clauses (19.1/2) and conditional sentences (18.1/5), wishes can have reference to the present, past or future. The negative used in wishes is always μή.

(*a*) Wishes for the **future** are expressed by the optative (present or aorist, according to the aspect involved – 14.1/1) and **may** be introduced by εἴθε or εἰ γάρ (*if only ... !*):

ῡ̔μῖν θεοὶ δοῖεν ἐκπέρσαι Πριάμου πόλιν.	*May the gods grant that you sack* (lit. *give to you to sack*) *the city of Priam.*
εἴθε γράψειεν ὡς χρή.	*I wish that he would write as he should* (lit. *would that he would write as is necessary* or *if only he would ...*).

(*b*) Wishes for the **present** are expressed by the imperfect indicative and **must** be introduced by εἴθε or εἰ γάρ:

εἰ γὰρ τοσαύτην δύναμιν εἶχον.	*I wish I had so much power* (lit.*would that I had ...* or *if only I had ...*).
εἴθ᾽ εἶχες βελτῑ́ους φρένας.	*I wish you had better thoughts.*

(*c*) Wishes for the **past** are expressed by the aorist indicative, also with an obligatory εἴθε/εἰ γάρ:

εἴθ᾽ εὕρομέν σε, ὦ Ἄδμητε, μὴ λῡπούμενον.	*I wish we had not found you grieving, Admetus.*

εἴθε σοι, ὦ Περίκλεις, τότε   *I wish I had been with you then,*
συνεγενόμην.   *Pericles.*

In the nature of things only wishes for the future can be fulfilled (and then not always). Wishes for the present and past are futile protests against what is happening or has happened.

Note

A present or past wish may also be expressed by ὤφελον (the aorist of ὀφείλω *owe, be obliged to*), which has the meaning *ought*. It is followed by a present or aorist infinitive, depending on whether the wish is for the present or past. εἴθε/εἰ γάρ is optional:

ὤφελε Κῦρος ζῆν   *I wish Cyrus were alive* (lit. *Cyrus*
                      ought to be alive).

μήποτ' ὤφελον λιπεῖν τὴν   *I wish I had never left Scyrus*
Cκῦρον   (lit. *I ought never to have left ...*).

21.1/2 Further temporal conjunctions (ἕως, μέχρι, πρίν)

Each of these three words has more than one use, but all can be employed as subordinating conjunctions with the meaning *until*.

ἕως and μέχρι both take the same construction as certain other temporal conjunctions (ὅτε, ἐπειδή etc., see 14.1/4c(iii)). They are followed by the indicative when the clause they introduce refers to a definite event:

ταῦτα ἐποίουν μέχρι σκότος   *They were doing these things until*
ἐγένετο.   *darkness fell* (lit. *happened*).

When the reference is to something anticipated (but we do not know if it eventuates or not), the indefinite construction is used (14.1/4c(iii)):

περιμένετε ἕως ἂν ἔλθω.   *Wait until I come* (or *for me to*
                      come);

ἔδοξεν αὐτοῖς προϊέναι ἕως   *They decided* (lit. *it seemed good*
Κύρῳ συμμείξειαν.   *to them, 21.1/4a) to advance*
                      until they should meet Cyrus.

With these conjunctions the indefinite construction can also refer to repeated action:

περιεμένομεν ἑκάστοτε ἕως   *On each occasion we used to wait*
ἀνοιχθείη τὸ δεσμωτήριον.   *until the prison opened.*

πρίν has a wider range of constructions:

(*a*) When the main verb is **affirmative**, πρίν is followed by an infinitive (usually aorist) and has the meaning *before*:

ἐπὶ τὸ ἄκρον ἀνέβη Χειρίσοφος πρίν τινα αἰσθέσθαι τῶν πολεμίων.	*Cheirisophus went up to the peak before any of the enemy noticed.*
λέγεται Ἀλκιβιάδης, πρὶν εἴκοσιν ἐτῶν εἶναι, Περικλεῖ διαλεχθῆναι περὶ νόμων.	*Alcibiades is said to have conversed with Pericles about laws before he was twenty years old* (lit. *of twenty years*).

The rules governing the case of the subject of the infinitive are exactly the same as in the infinitive construction in indirect statement (8.1/3*a*); in the first example above, the subject (τινά) of the infinitive is not the same as the subject of the main verb and so is in the accusative.

(*b*) When the main verb is **negated** and πρίν can be translated by *until* or *before,* it has the same construction as ἕως and μέχρι:

οὐκ ἦν γένος ἀθανάτων πρὶν Ἔρως ξυνέμειξεν ἅπαντα.	*There was not a race of immortals until* (or *before*) *Love mixed everything together.*
μὴ ἀπέλθετε πρὶν ἄν μου ἀκούσητε.	*Do not go away before* (or *until*) *you hear me.*

(*c*) When the main verb is **negated** and πρίν must be translated by *before,* it has the same construction as in (*a*):

οὐδὲ πρὶν νῑκηθῆναι ἐθάρρει ὁ στρατηγός	*Not even before being defeated was the general confident* (πρίν cannot here be translated by *until*).

Notes

1 ἕως (and occasionally μέχρι) with the indicative can also mean *while, as long as*:

Κλέαρχος, ἕως πόλεμος ἦν τοῖς Λακεδαιμονίοις πρὸς τοὺς Ἀθηναίους, παρέμενεν.	*As long as the Spartans were at war* (lit. *there was war for the Spartans*) *with the Athenians, Clearchus remained loyal.*

2 μέχρι may also function as a **preposition** (+ gen.) with the meaning *until, up to, as far as* (with reference to time or space): μέχρι τοῦ γόνατος *up to the knee*; μέχρι τούτου *up to this [time].*

3 πρίν can also be used as an **adverb** meaning *before, formerly*: ἐν τῷ πρὶν χρόνῳ *in the previous time.*

4 οὐ is used to negate the indicative in the subordinate clauses described above, μή to negate the indefinite construction and also the infinitive after πρίν.

21.1/3 Further demonstrative and relative adjectives/pronouns

Greek possesses two series of adjectives, each containing a demonstrative, relative (and exclamatory), and interrogative form. One series, with the element –οc–, refers to **quantity**, the other, with the element –οι–, refers to **quality**:

DEMONSTRATIVE	RELATIVE/EXCLAMATORY	INTERROGATIVE
τοcοῦτος, τοcόcδε *so much/many*	ὅcοc *as much/many as*; *how much/many!*	πόcοc *how big?* pl. *how many?*
τοιοῦτος, τοιόcδε *of this sort, such*	οἷος *of what sort*; *what a ... !*	ποῖοc *of what sort?*

The relative/exclamatory and interrogative forms are first and second declension adjectives (3.1/3). On the declension of τοcοῦτος, τοιοῦτος see 16.1/1 note 1. τοcόcδε and τοιόcδε are compounds of τοc/τοι + οc (declined as καλός, 3.1/3) + δε. All can function as pronouns as well as adjectives.

We have already dealt with the interrogatives (10.1/2) and the use of τοcοῦτος and τοιοῦτος to anticipate an adverbial clause or phrase of result (16.1/1). We must also note that:

(*a*) τοιοῦτος is used with reference to what precedes in a narrative, τοιόcδε with reference to what follows. This is the principal use of the latter, e.g. οἱ μὲν τοιαῦτα εἶπον, οἱ δὲ 'Αθηναῖοι τοιάδε ἀπεκρίναντο *they said this* (lit. *such things as precede*) *and the Athenians replied as follows* (lit. *such things as follow*). οὗτος and ὅδε are used in the same way (9.1/1 note 1).

(*b*) τοcόcδε, like τοιόcδε, can refer to what follows but is generally the equivalent of τοcοῦτος.

(*c*) ὅσος and οἷος can introduce exclamations:

ὅσα πράγματα ἔχεις.	*How much trouble* (lit. *how many things) you have!*
οἷα δράσᾱς οἷα λαγχάνει κακά.	*After what deeds what sufferings are his!* (lit. *what things having done what evil things he obtains!*).

(*d*) πάντες ὅσοι is used in the sense *all who* (lit. *all as many as*) instead of the expected πάντες οἵ:

πάντας ἐχθαίρω θεοὺς ὅσοι κακοῦσί μ᾽ ἐκδίκως.	*I hate all the gods who unjustly wrong me.*

Very often ὅσος is used by itself in this sense:

οἱ Καδμεῖοι ὅσους κακοὺς εὗρον ...	*All the Cadmeans whom I found wicked ...* (lit. *the Cadmeans as many as I found ...*).

(*e*) τοσοῦτος/ὅσος and τοιοῦτος/οἷος are used in sentences where ὅσος and οἷος introduce a comparison. As English does not have relatives of this sort some change is needed in translation:

οἷος ὁ πατήρ ἐστιν, τοιοῦτος καὶ ὁ υἱός.	*Like father, like son* (lit. *of what sort the father is, of that sort [is] the son too*).
ἔχετε τοσούτους στρατιώτᾱς ὅσους οἱ Πέρσαι.	*You have as many soldiers as the Persians* (*sc. have*; lit. *you have so many soldiers as many as the Persians*).

The relatives alone, without the corresponding demonstratives, may be used in this way:

οὔ μοι ἡ δύναμίς ἐστιν οἵᾱ πάρος ἦν.	*I have not the same strength as I previously had* (lit. *there is not to me the strength of what sort (= of the sort which) there was previously*).

Notes

1 In verse τόσος and τοῖος often occur as the equivalents of τοσοῦτος and τοιοῦτος respectively.

2 οἷός τ' εἰμί *I am able* is a stereotyped formula (example in 13.3(ii) *l*.3); τε here is purely idiomatic and is not to be translated, and οἷος has no relative force.

21.1/4 Further impersonal verbs

Impersonal verbs have no real subject. In English they are given a grammatical subject *it,* which is purely idiomatic and does not refer to anything. In Greek impersonal verbs are simply put in the 3rd singular. We have already met δεῖ and χρή *it is necessary,* which are followed by an infinitive whose subject, if expressed, is put into the accusative (examples at 3.2.12(x), 5.2.15 etc.). Other impersonals can be classified as follows:

(*a*) *Impersonals followed by the dative and infinitive*

δοκεῖ	*it seems good*	πρέπει	*it is fitting*
ἔξεςτι	*it is allowed/possible*	προςήκει	*it concerns/is fitting*
λῡςιτελεῖ	*it is profitable*	ςυμφέρει	*it is expedient*
πάρεςτι	*it is possible*		

Examples of ἔξεςτι occur at 9.2.7 and 19.2.7(ii). Of the others we may cite:

ταῦτα πρέπει μᾶλλον βαρβάροις ποιεῖν ἢ Ἕλληςιν.	*It is more fitting for barbarians than Greeks to do these things.*
οὔ ςοι προςήκει φωνεῖν.	*You have no business speaking* (lit. *it does not concern you to speak*).

δοκεῖ is usually to be translated by *think, intend, decide,* e.g. ὡς ἐμοὶ δοκεῖ *as I think* (lit. *as it seems good to me*); δοκεῖ αὐτῷ ἀπιέναι *he intends to leave*; ἔδοξε τοῖς Ἀθηναίοις μάχεςθαι *the Athenians decided to fight* (another example at 14. 2.18 *l*.3).

Some of the above verbs can be used personally, sometimes with a different meaning, e.g. πάρειμι *I am present.*

(*b*) *Impersonals followed by the dative of the person involved and the genitive of the thing*

μέτεςτι μοι τούτου	*there is a share to me of this,* i.e. *I have a share in this*
μέλει μοι τούτου	*there is a concern to me of this,* i.e. *I am concerned about this*

μεταμέλει μοι τούτου *there is repentance to me of this,* i.e. *I repent of this*

Examples are:

τοῖc θεοῖc δίκηc μέλει.
The gods are concerned with justice.

τί τοῦδέ coι μέτεcτι πρᾱγματοc;
What concern (lit. *share*) *have you in this business?*

ῡ̔μῖν μεταμελησάτω τῶν πεπρᾱγμένων.
Repent of your deeds! (lit. *let there be repentance* [3rd s. aor. imp. act.] *to you of the things done*).

(c) Weather impersonals

The various verbs for expressing weather conditions, as ῡ̔ει *it is raining,* νείφει *it is snowing,* are not strictly impersonals because Zeus, in his capacity as sky god, is their understood subject. We should, however, translate them by the impersonal English expression.

Notes

1 ἔcτι (always so accented) is often used in the sense of ἔξεcτι (examples at 9.2.13 *l.*5 and 11.2.10 *l.*4). For other cases of this accentuation see **Appendix 8**, *d*(x).

2 πάρα, μέτα (note accent!) are often used for πάρεcτι, μέτεcτι respectively.

3 When the impersonal δεῖ means *there is need of* it takes the same construction as class (*b*) (example in 13.2.21); in the sense *it is necessary* it is always followed by the infinitive.

21.1/5 Accusative absolute

The **participle** of an impersonal verb stands in the **accusative**, in the neuter singular, in circumstances where other verbs would be placed in the genitive absolute (cf. 12.1/2*b*); it has **no** subject. Such accusative absolutes are δέον *it being necessary*; ἐξόν, παρόν, παρέχον *it being possible*; μέλον *it being a care*; προcῆκον, πρέπον *it being fitting*; δόξαν *it having been decided.* Examples are:

ἐξὸν εἰρήνην ἔχειν, αἱρεῖται πολεμεῖν.
Although he can live in peace (lit. *it being possible to have peace*), *he chooses to make war.*

δῆλον γὰρ ὅτι οἶσθα, μέλον   *For it [is] clear that you know,*
γέ cοι.   *since you are interested [in the*
    subject] (lit. *it being a care to*
    you).

cυνδόξαν τῷ πατρὶ καὶ τῇ μητρί,   *Since his father and mother*
γαμεῖ τὴν Κυαξάρου θυγατέρα.   *approved* (lit. *it having seemed*
    good also to ...) he married
    (vivid present) *the daughter of*
    Cyaxares.

The accusative absolute is also found with expressions consisting of a
neuter adjective and ὄν, such as ἀδύνατον ὄν *it being impossible*, αἰcχρὸν
ὄν *it being disgraceful*, ἄδηλον ὄν *it being unclear*, e.g.

παρεκελεύοντο ἀλλήλοιc   *They encouraged each other*
κραυγῇ οὐκ ὀλίγῃ χρώμενοι,   *with* (lit. *using) no little*
ἀδύνατον ὂν ἐν νυκτὶ ἄλλῳ τῳ   *shouting, since it was impossible*
cημῆναι.   (lit. *it being impossible) by*
    night to signal by any other
    [means].

21.2 Greek reading

1   Cπαρτιάτηc τιc εἰc Ἀθήναc ἐλθὼν καὶ ἰδὼν ἐν ἀποχωρήcει
θακοῦνταc ἐπὶ δίφρων ἀνθρώπουc, μή μοι γένοιτο, εἶπεν,
ἐνταῦθα καθίcαι ὅθεν οὐκ ἔcτιν ἐξαναcτῆναι πρεcβυτέρῳ .

2   **Proverbs**
(*i*) πρὶν τοὺc ἰχθῦc ἑλεῖν τὴν ἅλμην κυκᾷc. (*ii*) οὐ μέλει τῇ
χελώνῃ   μυιῶν. (*iii*) ἀεί με τοιοῦτοι πολέμιοι διώκοιεν. (*iv*)
προcήκει τοῖc τέκνοιc ἐντὸc θυρῶν λοιδορεῖcθαι. (*v*) οἷοc ὁ
τρόποc τοιοῦτοc ὁ λόγοc. (*vi*)# μηδένα νομίζετε εὐτυχεῖν πρὶν ἂν
θάνῃ . (*vii*)# οἷάπερ ἡ δέcποινα τοία χ ἡ κύων. (*viii*)# νέῳ δὲ cιγᾶν
μᾶλλον ἢ λαλεῖν πρέπει. (*ix*) ὦ οἵα κεφαλή, καὶ ἐγκέφαλον οὐκ
ἔχει. (*x*)# μέτεcτι τοῖc δούλοιcιν δεcποτῶν νόcου. (*xi*)# μή μοι
γένοιθ' ἃ βούλομ', ἀλλ' ἃ cυμφέρει. (*xii*) Ἅιδου πρωκτῷ
περιπέcοιc. (*xiii*)# εἴθ' ἦν ἄφωνον cπέρμα δυcτήνων βροτῶν.

3#   ὅcτιc δὲ θνητῶν θάνατον ὀρρωδεῖ λίαν,
μῶροc πέφυκε· τῇ τύχῃ τῶνδε μέλει.
ὅταν δ' ὁ καιρὸc τοῦ θανεῖν ἐλθὼν τύχῃ,
οὐδ' ἂν πρὸc αὐλὰc Ζηνὸc ἐκφύγοι μολών.

4   ὅcοι γαμοῦcι γένει κρείττους γάμους οὐκ ἐπίcτανται γαμεῖν.
5   οἴῳ   τιc ἂν τὸ πλεῖcτον τῆc ἡμέραc cυνῇ, τοιοῦτον ἀνάγκη
    γενέcθαι καὶ αὐτὸν τοὺc τρόπους.
6   ἀναcτὰc αὖθιc Θώραξ ὁ Βοιώτιοc, ὃc περὶ cτρατηγίαc Ξενοφῶντι
    ἐμάχετο, ἔφη, εἰ ἐξέλθοιεν ἐκ τοῦ Πόντου, ἔcεcθαι αὐτοῖc
    Χερρόνηcον, χώραν καλὴν καὶ εὐδαίμονα, ὥcτε ἐξεῖναι τῷ
    βουλομένῳ   ἐνοικεῖν, τῷ δὲ μὴ βουλομένῳ   ἀπιέναι οἴκαδε.
    γελοῖον δὲ εἶναι, ἐν τῇ   Ἑλλάδι οὔcηc χώραc πολλῆc καὶ 5
    ἀφθόνου, ἐν τῇ βαρβάρων μαcτεύειν. ἕωc δ᾽ ἂν, ἔφη, ἐκεῖ
    γένηcθε, κἀγὼ ὑπιcχνοῦμαι ὑμῖν τὸν μιcθόν.
7   Διογένηc ἰδών ποτε γυναῖκαc ἀπ᾽ ἐλάαc ἀπηγχονιcμέναc, εἴθε
    γάρ, ἔφη, πάντα τὰ δένδρα τοιοῦτον καρπὸν ἤνεγκεν.
8# ὅcτιc δὲ πράccει πολλά, μὴ πράccειν παρόν,
    μῶροc, παρὸν ζῆν ἡδέωc ἀπράγμονα.
9   βουλευομένοιc τοῖc cτρατιώταιc ἔδοξεν ἀποκρίναcθαι τάδε· καὶ
    ἔλεξε Χειρίcοφοc· ἡμῖν δοκεῖ, εἰ μέν τιc ἐᾷ   ἡμᾶc ἀπιέναι
    οἴκαδε, διαπορεύεcθαι τὴν χώραν ὡc ἂν δυνώμεθα ἀcινέcτατα·
    ἢν δέ τιc ἡμᾶc τῆc ὁδοῦ ἀποκωλύῃ, διαπολεμεῖν τούτῳ ὡc ἂν
    δυνώμεθα κράτιcτα.
10# Prometheus laments his lot.

    ἦ δυcπετῶc ἂν τοὺc ἐμοὺc ἄθλουc φέροιc,
    ὅτῳ   θανεῖν μέν ἐcτιν οὐ πεπρωμένον·
    αὕτη γὰρ ἦν ἂν πημάτων ἀπαλλαγή·
    νῦν δ᾽ οὐδέν ἐcτι τέρμα μοι προκείμενον
    μόχθων πρὶν ἂν Ζεὺc ἐκπέcῃ   τυραννίδοc.   5
11 καὶ ὁ Κῦροc ἀκούcαc τοῦ Γωβρύα τοιαῦτα τοιάδε πρὸc αὐτὸν
    ἔλεξεν.
12# Medea resolves to murder her children.

    εἶεν· τί δράcειc, θυμέ; βούλευcαι καλῶc
    πρὶν ἐξαμαρτεῖν καὶ τὰ προcφιλέcτατα
    ἔχθιcτα θέcθαι. ποῖ ποτ᾽ ἐξῇξαc τάλαc;
    κάτιcχε λῆμα καὶ cθένοc θεοcτυγέc.
    καὶ πρὸc τί ταῦτα δύρομαι, ψυχὴν ἐμὴν   5
    ὁρῶc᾽ ἔρημον καὶ παρημελημένην
    πρὸc ὦν ἐχρῆν ἥκιcτα; μαλθακοὶ δὲ δὴ
    τοιαῦτα γιγνόμεcθα πάcχοντεc κακά;
    οὐ μὴ προδώcειc, θυμέ, cαυτὸν ἐν κακοῖc.
    οἴμοι δέδοκται· παῖδεc, ἐκτὸc ὀμμάτων   10

ἀπέλθετ'· ἤδη γάρ με φοίνιον νέα
δέδυκε λύσσα θυμόν. ὢ χέρες χέρες,
πρὸς οἷον ἔργον ἐξοπλιζόμεσθα· φεῦ
τάλαινα τόλμης, ἢ πολὺν πόνον βραχεῖ
διαφθεροῦσα τὸν ἐμὸν ἔρχομαι χρόνῳ.   15

13 εἰς Λακεδαίμονα παραγενόμενός τις καὶ τὴν πρὸς τοὺς
πρεσβύτας τῶν νέων τιμὴν θεασάμενος, ἐν Cπάρτῃ μόνῃ, εἶπε,
λυcιτελεῖ γηράcκειν.

14# ἐχρῆν γὰρ ἡμᾶς cύλλογον ποιουμένους
τὸν φύντα θρηνεῖν εἰς ὅc' ἔρχεται κακά,
τὸν δ' αὖ θανόντα καὶ πόνων πεπαυμένον
χαίροντας εὐφημοῦντας ἐκπέμπειν δόμων.

Notes

1 The Spartans, as well as living in a primitive simplicity where a
public toilet would have been unheard of, prided themselves on old-
fashioned virtues such as respect for people older than oneself (cf. 13
below); ἔcτιν = ἔξεcτιν; ἐξαναcτῆναι intr. aor. inf. of ἐξανίcτημι.

2 (*i*) The brine is to boil the fish. (*iv*) Take τέκνοιc with λοιδορεῖcθαι,
not with προcήκει. (*v*) Supply ἐcτί with οἷοc and with τοιοῦτοc (cf.
(*vii*) below). (*vii*) χή = καὶ ἡ. (*ix*) οἶᾱ exclamatory. (*x*) Take δεcποτῶν
with νόcου, and νόcου with μέτεcτι. (*xi*) γένοιθ' = γένοιτο; βούλομ'
= βούλομαι (2.1/6*b* note); cυμφέρει is not here impersonal but has ἅ
as its subject.

3 *l*.2 τῶνδε neuter *these things*. *l*.3 ἐλθὼν τύχῃ (3rd s. aor. subj. of
τυγχάνω) *chances to come* (15.1/2*e*).

4 γένει *in race* (dat. of respect, 23.1/2*m*).

5 cυνῇ 3rd s. pres. subj. of cύνειμι, which takes a dative (here οἵῳ);
ἀνάγκη *sc.* ἐcτί; τοὺς τρόπους acc. of respect (20.1/5) with τοιοῦτον.

6 After ἔφη in *l*.2 we have a passage of indirect speech, but the last
sentence of the passage is in direct speech with an extra ἔφη inserted
(cf. 8.1/3*a* and 7.1/2 note 3). *l*.2 εἰ ἐξέλθοιεν represents in historic
sequence ἐὰν ἐξέλθωcι of the original direct speech (14.1/4*c*(iii));
ἔcεcθαι αὐτοῖc lit. *there to be going to be for them*, i.e. *they would
have*. *l*.4 τῷ ... μὴ βουλομένῳ the negative is μή because a general
class is meant (12.1/2*a*(vi)), trans. *anyone who did not [so] wish*; *ll*.6f.
ἐκεῖ γένηcθε i.e. *you get there*.

7 ἀπηγχονιcμένᾱc f. acc. pl. of the perf. pass. pple. of ἀπαγχονίζω;
εἴθε + aor. expresses a wish for the past (21.1/1*c*).

8   The old Athenian aristocratic ideal was a life of leisure. In both lines
    παρόν is an acc. absolute (21.1/5). *l.*1 μή negates πράccειν.

9   ἀπιέναι < ἀπέρχομαι (18.1/3); ὡc ... ἀcινέcτατα lit. *in whatever way*
    (ὡc ἄν) *we can most harmlessly,* i.e. *doing the least possible harm.*

10 *l.*2 ὅτῳ the relative ὅcτιc can be used to introduce an adjectival clause
    which gives a **reason** (cf. note on 20.2.6 *l.*3). *l.*3 αὕτη *this* refers to
    what has just been mentioned (i.e. death), but is attracted into the
    gender of ἀπαλλαγή. *ll.*4f. νῦν δ'(έ) *but as it is*; take μόχθων with
    τέρμα; ἐκπίπτω is here acting as the pass. of ἐκβάλλω *throw out*
    (cf.17.1/5); τυραννίδοc gen. of separation (20.1/4).

11 Take τοιαῦτα with ἀκούcαc, τοιάδε with ἔλεξεν; Γωβρύαc (1st
    declension) has the non-Attic gen. s. Γωβρύᾱ.

12 *l.*1 βούλευcαι 2nd s. aor. imp. mid. of βουλεύω. *l.*3 θέcθαι (< τίθημι)
    here *make*; ἐξῆξαc 2nd s. aor. ind. act. of ἐξαΐccω; τάλᾱc (10.1/3 note
    2) is voc. (Medea is still addressing her θῡμόc). *l.*5 πρὸc τί lit. *with a
    view to what,* i.e. *why. l.*6 ἔρημον is f. and agrees with ψῡχήν (ἔρημοc
    is one of the few two termination adjectives (3.1/3) which are not
    compounds); παρημελημένην perf. pass. pple. of παραμελέω. *ll.*7f.
    πρὸc ὦν i.e. πρὸc (= ὑπὸ) τούτων οὓc (9.1/2 note 2); δὲ δή here
    introduces an emphatic question *And so ...? Then ... ?*; when a woman
    is using the royal plural, as with γιγνόμεcθα (= –μεθα, cf. 8.2.9 and
    ἐξοπλιζόμεcθα in *l.*13 below), she refers to herself with masculine pl.
    adjectives and participles, hence μαλθακοί and πάcχοντεc; take
    τοιαῦτα ... κακά after πάcχοντεc. *l.*9 οὐ μή + fut. ind. expresses a
    strong prohibition (17.1/1). *l.*10 δέδοκται *it is decided* (i.e. *by me,* lit.
    it is in a state of seeming good [to me]) the impers. δοκεῖ (21.1/4*a*)
    is mid./pass. in the perfect; παῖδεc voc. *ll.*11f. ἀπέλθετ'(ε) 2nd pl.
    aor. imp.; με ... δέδῡκε ... θῡμόν lit. *has entered me [with respect to]
    my heart,* i.e. *has entered my heart* (acc. of respect 20.1/5). *l.*14
    τόλμηc gen. of cause (23.1/1*k*(ii)) with τάλαινα *wretched [that I am]
    because of my daring,* Medea is talking about herself; πόνον i.e. the
    labour of bearing and raising her children. *l.*15 διαφθεροῦcα fut. pple.
    to express purpose (12.1/2*a*(v)).

14 *l.*1 ἐχρῆν = ἐχρῆν ἄν a common idiom which means *it should be
    necessary,* not *it was necessary,* because it expresses something
    which should be happening now (present potential,19.1/2), trans. *we
    should ... l.*2 κακά is acc. of respect (20.1/5) after θρηνεῖν and the
    antecedent of εἰc ὅc'(α) ἔρχεται, lit. *with respect to the troubles to
    how many he is coming,* i.e. *for all the toubles he is coming to*

(21.1/3*d*). *ll.*3f. δ'(ὲ) αὖ *and in turn*; πόνων, δόμων gen. of separation (20.1/4); δόμων is also an example of the singular used for the plural, *from [his,* i.e. the dead man's*] house.*

21.3 Extra reading

Love poetry

Love poetry had a long history in Greek. The first example below is from Mimnermus (7th century BC) but the others are much later (2 and 3 are attributed to Plato, whether correctly or not we have no means of telling; the authors of 4 and 5 are unknown). All are written in elegiacs (**Appendix 9**), the metre most associated with this genre.

1 τίς δὲ βίος, τί δὲ τερπνὸν ἄτερ χρυςῆς Ἀφροδίτης;
    τεθναίην, ὅτε μοι μηκέτι ταῦτα μέλοι,
 κρυπταδίη φιλότης καὶ μείλιχα δῶρα καὶ εὐνή,
    οἷ' ἥβης ἄνθεα γίγνεται ἁρπαλέα
 ἀνδράσιν ἠδὲ γυναιξίν· ἐπεὶ δ' ὀδυνηρὸν ἐπέλθῃ   5
    γῆρας, ὅ τ' αἰςχρὸν ὁμῶς καὶ κακὸν ἄνδρα τιθεῖ,
 αἰεί μιν φρένας ἀμφὶ κακαὶ τείρουςι μέριμναι
    οὐδ' αὐγὰς προσορῶν τέρπεται ἠελίου,
 ἀλλ' ἐχθρὸς μὲν παιςίν, ἀτίμαστος δὲ γυναιξίν·
    οὕτως ἀργαλέον γῆρας ἔθηκε θεός.   10
2 ἀςτέρας εἰςαθρεῖς ἀςτὴρ ἐμός· εἴθε γενοίμην
    οὐρανός, ὡς πολλοῖς ὄμμαςιν εἰς cὲ βλέπω.
3 ἀςτὴρ πρὶν μὲν ἔλαμπες ἐνὶ ζωοῖςιν Ἑῷος·
    νῦν δὲ θανὼν λάμπεις Ἕςπερος ἐν φθιμένοις.
4 πέμπω ςοι μύρον ἡδύ, μύρῳ παρέχων χάριν, οὐ ςοί·
    αὐτὴ γὰρ μυρίςαι καὶ τὸ μύρον δύναςαι.
5 Ἠοῦς ἄγγελε, χαῖρε, Φαεςφόρε, καὶ ταχὺς ἔλθοις
    Ἕςπερος, ἣν ἀπάγεις, λάθριος αὖθις ἄγων.

Notes

1 All deviations from Attic in this poem are Ionic (1.3). *l.*2 τεθναίην the shorter form of the perf. opt. of θνήςκω (19.1/3*a*) – the opt. is used here to express a wish for the future (21.1/1*a*); ταῦτα (referring to the nouns in *l.*3) is the subject of μέλοι, which is not impersonal here and should be translated as though ind. (the verb has been assimilated to

the mood of τεθναίην). *l.*3 κρυπταδίη = –ία. *l.*4 οἶ'(α) ... γίγνεται lit. *of what sort are,* i.e. *the sorts of things which*; ἄνθεα = ἄνθη (< ἄνθος). *l.*5 ἐπεὶ ... ἐπέλθη in this indefinite construction Attic would require ἄν (14.1/4*c*(iii)). *l.*6 αἰσχρόν and κακόν (here *lowly, base*) are predicative after ἄνδρα τιθεῖ (= τίθησι), *makes a man both* (ὁμῶς) *ugly and base* – note here that we have ὁμῶς, **not** ὅμως *nevertheless.* *l.*7 φρένας ἀμφί = ἀμφὶ φρένας.

2 *l.*1 ἀστὴρ ἐμός is in apposition to *you,* the subject of εἰσαθρεῖς. *l.*2 ὡς = ἵνα (βλέπω is subj., 14.1/4*c*(i)).

3 *l.*1 πρίν here an adverb *formerly*; ἀστήρ ... Ἑῶος *the Morning Star. l.*2 Ἕσπερος *the Evening Star*; the Greeks knew that both were in fact the planet Venus (see 5 below), which makes the poet's fanciful identification of his lover with them all the more appropriate.

4 *l.*1 παρέχων χάριν *doing a favour. l.*2 καί *even* (μύρον has a very strong scent).

5 The poet, who supposes that the planet Venus in its guise as the Morning Star is taking away his girlfriend, expresses the wish that it return quickly as the Evening Star and bring her back. *l.*1 Ἠοῦς gen. of Ἠώς. *l.*2 Ἕσπερος i.e. *[as] the Evening Star*; ἣν ἀπάγει ... ἄγων *bringing [the girl] whom you are [now] leading away.*

22.1 Grammar

22.1/1 Summary of the uses of ὡc

ὡc, originally an adverb of manner meaning *in which way, how,* came to have various uses as an adverb or as a conjunction. It may also occur as a preposition.

(*a*) ὡc *as an adverb*

(i) ὡc with participles and prepositional phrases

We have already seen how ὡc is used with participles of **cause** (12.1/2*a*(ii)) and **purpose** (12.1/2*a*(v)), reflecting the attitude (thought, opinion, intention, hope) of the subject of the participle without any implication of the belief or opinion of the writer or speaker. In this use, which also occurs with phrases introduced by a preposition, ὡc expresses an alleged reason or assumed motive, and may be translated *as if, in the opinion that, under the impression that, with the (avowed) intention of,* etc.:

cυλλαμβάνει Κῦρον ὡc ἀποκτενῶν.	*He seized* (vivid present) *Cyrus with the intention of putting him to death.*
ἀγανακτοῦcιν ὡc μεγάλων τινῶν ἀπεcτερημένοι.	*They are annoyed in the belief that they have been deprived of some great [benefits].*
ἀνήγοντο ὡc ἐπὶ ναυμαχίᾱν.	*They put out to sea with the intention of fighting* (lit. *as for a sea-battle*).
ἀπέπλεον ὡc εἰc τὰc ᾿Αθήνᾱc.	*They sailed away as if for Athens.*

(ii) **ὡς exclamatory**

ὡς *how ... !* is used in exclamations with adjectives, adverbs and verbs:

ὡς ἀςτεῖος ὁ ἄνθρωπος.	*How charming the man is!*
ὡς ἀδεῶς καὶ γενναίως	*How fearlessly and nobly he*
ἐτελεύτᾱ.	*died!*
ὥς μ᾽ ἀπώλεςας, γύναι.	*How you have destroyed me,*
	woman!

(iii) **ὡς with positive adverbs**

ὡς may be used to emphasise positive adverbs: ὡς ἀληθῶς *in very truth*; ὡς ἑτέρως *quite otherwise*; ὡς αὕτως (often written ὡςαύτως) *in the same way, just so*.

Note too the common idiom where ὡς is added to the adverbs θαυμαςίως and θαυμαςτῶς (lit. *marvellously, wonderfully*) to express emphasis:

νῦν δὲ θαυμαςίως ὡς	*But now he has become*
ἄθλιος γέγονεν.	*prodigiously wretched.*
εὖ λέγει θαυμαςτῶς ὡς	*He speaks marvellously well* (lit.
ςφόδρα.	*he speaks well marvellously*
	very).

(iv) **ὡς with superlative adjectives and adverbs** (see 17.1/4*d*)

(v) **ὡς ἕκαςτος/ἑκάτερος**

ὡς is often combined with ἕκαςτος (or ἑκάτερος) in the sense *each by himself, each severally* or *individually*:

ἄλλοι παριόντες ἐγκλήματα	*Others came forward and made*
ἐποιοῦντο ὡς ἕκαςτοι.	*their separate complaints*
	(lit. *each [group] by*
	themselves).
παυςάμενοι τῆς μάχης ὡς	*They ceased from fighting and on*
ἑκάτεροι ἡςυχάςαντες τὴν	*either side* (lit. *each side by*
νύκτα ἐν φυλακῇ ἦςαν.	*themselves) remained quiet*
	[but] on guard for the night.

(vi) **ὡς restrictive**

ὡς may also be used to limit the validity of a statement, with the meaning *for*:

ἦν οὐδὲ ἀδύνατος, ὡς Λακεδαιμόνιος, εἰπεῖν.	*He was not a bad speaker* (lit. *not unable to speak*) *either, for a Spartan* (or *considering that he was a Spartan*).
μακρᾱ ὡς γέροντι ὁδός.	*A long road, for an old man.*
φρονεῖ ὡς γυνὴ μέγα.	*She has proud thoughts* (lit. *thinks big*), *for a woman.*

Restrictive ὡς is also found with the **infinitive** in certain idiomatic expressions which stand independent of the overall grammatical construction and which express some limitation or qualification of the sentence as a whole. This use is particularly common in the phrase ὡς ἔπος εἰπεῖν (or ὡς εἰπεῖν) *so to speak,* which usually modifies a sweeping statement with πᾶς or οὐδείς (or the like); occasionally it apologises for a metaphor:

ἀληθές γε ὡς ἔπος εἰπεῖν οὐδὲν εἰρήκᾱσιν.	*They have spoken virtually no word of truth* (lit. *nothing true so to speak*).
Ἱππόλυτος οὐκέτ᾽ ἐστίν, ὡς εἰπεῖν ἔπος.	*Hippolytus is as good as dead* (lit. *is no longer alive, so to speak*).
ἰδιῶται ὡς εἰπεῖν χειροτέχναις ἀνταγωνισάμενοι.	*Laymen, as it were, pitted against craftsmen* (the metaphorical use of ἀνταγωνισάμενοι is toned down).

(vii) **ὡς with numerals**

ὡς is used with numerals in the sense *about, nearly*:

διέσχον ἀλλήλων βασιλεύς τε καὶ οἱ Ἕλληνες ὡς τριάκοντα στάδια.	*The King and the Greeks were about thirty stades distant from each other.*

ὡς is similarly used in the common phrase ὡς ἐπὶ τὸ πολύ *for the most part* (lit. *nearly so far as regards the much*).

(*b*) **ὡς *as a conjunction***

(i) **in indirect speech**, *that* (see 8.1/3*b*)

(ii) **in purpose clauses**, *in order that* (see 14.1/4*c*(i))
Purpose clauses are generally introduced by ἵνα or ὅπως, but ὡς may also be used, especially in poetry and in Xenophon:

διανοεῖται τὴν γέφυραν λῦσαι ὡς μὴ διαβῆτε.	*He intends to break up the bridge in order that you may not cross.*

(iii) **in clauses of reason,** *as, since, because*

Causal clauses are regularly introduced by ὅτι, διότι *because, as,* ἐπεί, ἐπειδή *since,* but may also be introduced by ὡς. As in its use with the participle (see *a*(i) above), ὡς sometimes carries the implication that the reason given is the subjective opinion of the person described:

ἔπειτα δὲ ξύμβασιν	*Then, when they had made*
ποιησάμενοι πρὸς τὸν	*an agreement with Perdiccas*
Περδίκκᾶν, ὡς αὐτοὺς	*because (in their opinion)*
κατήπειγεν ἡ Ποτείδαια,	*[the situation in] Potidaea*
ἀπανίστανται ἐκ τῆς	*was pressing them, they*
Μακεδονίᾶς.	*withdrew* (vivid present)
	from Macedonia.

(iv) **in temporal clauses,** *when, after*

ὡς may be used like ἐπεί (cf. 14.1/4c(iii)):

ὡς ᾔσθετο Κῦρον	*When he perceived that Cyrus had*
πεπτωκότα ἔφυγεν.	*fallen, he fled.*

ὡς τάχιστα may be used for ἐπειδὴ τάχιστα in the sense *as soon as*:

ὡς τάχιστα ἤκομεν εἰς	*As soon as we had come to*
Μακεδονίᾶν, συνετάξαμεν	*Macedonia, we arranged for the*
τὸν πρεσβύτατον πρῶτον	*eldest man to speak first.*
λέγειν.	

(v) **ὡς in clauses of manner**

ὡς may be used to introduce adverbial clauses of manner in the sense *as, according as, in which way,* often coupled with οὕτω(ς) *thus, so* in the principal clause. In such clauses the verb in the subordinate clause will be in the indicative mood if the action is marked as a fact:

ἐκέλευσε τοὺς Ἕλληνας, ὡς	*He ordered the Greeks to be drawn*
νόμος αὐτοῖς ἦν εἰς	*up as was their custom for battle*
μάχην, οὕτω ταχθῆναι.	(lit. *as was their custom, so ... to*
	be drawn up).

But if the action has a future reference or is indefinite, the mood of the verb will follow the rules for indefinite clauses (cf. 14.1/4c(iii)), i.e. subjunctive with ἄν in primary sequence, optative without ἄν in historic sequence:

τὸ πέρας ὡς ἂν ὁ δαίμων	*The end of all things comes about*
βουληθῇ πάντων γίγνεται.	*in whatever way the deity wishes.*

ξυνετίθεσαν ὡc ἕκαστόν τι ξυμβαίνοι.	*They put [them] together as each [piece] fitted.*

The verb in the ὡc clause is often omitted, e.g. εἴθε πάντεc cε φιλοῖεν ὡc ἐγώ *would that all loved you as I (sc. do)*. Other examples occur at 13.2.6 and 15. ὡc is likewise frequently used to introduce clauses which are parenthetical: ὡc ἔοικε *as it seems*; ὡc ἐγῷμαι (= ἐγὼ οἶμαι) *as I think*; ὡc ἐμοὶ δοκεῖ *in my opinion* (lit. *as it seems to me*).

(*c*) **ὡc *as a preposition***

ὡc as a preposition governs the accusative case and has the sense *to, towards*. It is used only with **persons**:

ὡc Περδίκκᾱν ἔπεμψαν ἀμφότεροι πρέcβειc.	*Both sides sent ambassadors to Perdiccas.*

22.1/2 Uses of cases (1) – accusative

Apart from its use as the case of the direct object of transitive verbs (2.1/3*c*) and after certain prepositions (2.1/3*f*; 3.1/5*a*), the accusative can function in a number of ways, some of which require rephrasing to be turned into normal English.

(*a*) *Accusative and infinitive* (see 8.1/3*a*, and cf. 16.1/1)

(*b*) *Accusative to express time how long* (see 7.1/7*a*)

(*c*) *Accusative to express spatial extent* (see 7.1/7*d*)

(*d*) *Accusative of respect or specification* (see 20.1/5)

(*e*) *Accusative absolute* (see 21.1/5)

(*f*) *Verbs taking two accusatives*

These occur in Greek as in English (*we chose him leader*; *they asked us our opinion*) and can be divided into two categories:

(i) Verbs of **making, considering, naming, choosing, appointing**, etc. (factitive verbs), which take a direct object and an object complement (also called a predicate):

οἱ Θετταλοὶ καὶ οἱ Θηβαῖοι φίλον, εὐεργέτην, cωτῆρα τὸν Φίλιππον ἡγοῦντο.	*The Thessalians and Thebans considered Philip* (direct object) *a friend, benefactor and saviour* (object complement).

τρεῖς τῶν ἐμῶν ἐχθρῶν   *I shall make three of my enemies*
νεκροὺς θήσω.   *corpses.*

When such expressions are put into the passive, both accusatives
become nominative:

Λασθένης φίλος ὠνομάζετο   *Lasthenes was called the friend*
Φιλίππου.   *of Philip.*

(ii) Verbs of **asking for** (αἰτέω), **teaching** (διδάσκω), **concealing**
(κρύπτω), **depriving** (ἀποστερέω), **taking away** (ἀφαιρέομαι), and a
few others, which may take two accusatives (one accusative of the
person and the other of the thing involved). The construction of the
corresponding verbs in English is not always the same:

ὁ πόλεμος ἀείμνηστον   *The war taught them a lesson*
   παιδείᾱν αὐτοὺς ἐπαίδευσεν.   *never to be forgotten.*
ἀποστερεῖ με τὴν τῑμήν.   *He takes the honour from me.*
τὴν θυγατέρα ἔκρυπτε τὸν   *He concealed her husband's death*
   θάνατον τοῦ ἀνδρός.   *from his daughter.*

When such expressions are put into the passive, the thing involved
remains in the accusative (**retained accusative**):

ἐκεῖνοι ἵππους   *Those men have been deprived*
   ἀπεστέρηνται.   *of their horses.*
οὐδὲν ἄλλο διδάσκεται   *A man is taught nothing else*
   ἄνθρωπος ἢ ἐπιστήμην.   *except knowledge.*

Under this heading also belong the phrases ἀγαθὰ (κακά, etc.) λέγειν
τινά *to speak well* (*ill,* etc.) *of someone,* and ἀγαθὰ (κακά, etc.)
ποιεῖν τινα *to do good* (*evil,* etc.) *to someone* and the like:

τοὺς Κορινθίους πολλά τε   *He said many bad things about*
   καὶ κακὰ ἔλεγεν.   *the Corinthians.*

Instead of the neuter pl. acc. of the adjective, however, we often find
the adverbs εὖ/κακῶς, etc.:

τὸν μέντοι καὶ λόγῳ καὶ ἔργῳ   *However, I would be able neither*
   πειρώμενον ἐμὲ ἀνιᾶν οὐκ   *to speak well of nor to do good*
   ἂν δυναίμην οὔτ᾽ εὖ λέγειν   *to the man who tries to vex me*
   οὔτ᾽ εὖ ποιεῖν.   *both in word and in deed.*

For the passive of expressions using λέγω and ποιέω see 17.1/5.

(g) *Cognate accusative*

This describes an expression in which a noun and the verb (usually otherwise intransitive) by which it is governed are both derived from the same root (as in English *sing a song*): νοcεῖ νόcον ἀγρίᾱν *he is ill with a cruel disease*; ἑωρᾶτε Cωκράτη πολλὴν φλυᾱρίᾱν φλυᾱροῦντα *you used to see Socrates talking much nonsense*. Except in poetry, the cognate accusative is usually accompanied by an adjective or other attribute.

Also included under this heading are accusatives used in exactly the same way with nouns not derived from the same root as the verb: ἠcθένηcε ταύτην τὴν νόcον *he fell sick with this disease*.

Instead of a cognate noun in the accusative we may also find the neuter of an adjective used as an equivalent: Ὀλύμπια (acc. pl. n.) νῑκᾶν *to win an Olympic victory* (lit. *Olympic things*).

(h) *Accusative in oaths*

The accusative is regularly found in oaths, especially after the particles μά and νή. νή conveys strong affirmation; νὴ τὸν Δία *yes, by Zeus!*, but μά may be either affirmative or negative, the choice being determined either simply by the context (as, e.g., in 23.2.5 *l.*4) or by adding ναί or οὐ: ναὶ μὰ τὸν Δία *yes, by Zeus!*; μὰ τὸν Ἀπόλλω, οὔκ *no, by Apollo!* (cf. 24.1/1*c*).

In these expressions we must understand the verb ὄμνῡμι *swear,* which can also be used with the accusative of the god's name in the sense *I swear by*: ὄμνῡμι θεοὺς καὶ θεάς *I swear by [the] gods and goddesses.*

(i) *Accusative to express motion towards* (see 2.1/3*f*)

In poetry the accusative can be used with verbs of motion **without any preposition**:

Μήδεια πύργους γῆς ἔπλευc'   *Medea sailed to the towers of the*
Ἰωλκίᾱς.   *Iolcian land.*

22.2 Greek reading

1# cὺ δ' ὦ θεῶν τύραννε κἀνθρώπων Ἔρωc,
    ἢ μὴ δίδαcκε τὰ καλὰ φαίνεcθαι καλά,
    ἢ τοῖc ἐρῶcιν εὐτυχῶc cυνεκπόνει
    μοχθοῦcι μόχθουc ὧν cὺ δημιουργὸc εἶ.

2   ἑcπέρα μὲν γὰρ ἦν, ἧκε δ' ἀγγέλλων τιc ὡc τοὺc πρυτάνειc ὡc
    Ἐλάτεια κατείληπται. καὶ μετὰ ταῦτα οἱ μὲν εὐθὺc
    ἐξαναcτάντεc μεταξὺ δειπνοῦντεc τούc τ' ἐκ τῶν cκηνῶν τῶν

κατὰ τὴν ἀγορὰν ἐξεῖργον καὶ τὰ γέρρα ἐνεπίμπρασαν, οἱ δὲ
τοὺς στρατηγοὺς μετεπέμποντο καὶ τὸν σαλπικτὴν ἐκάλουν· καὶ 5
θορύβου πλήρης ἦν ἡ πόλις. τῇ δ᾽ ὑστεραίᾳ ἅμα τῇ ἡμέρᾳ οἱ μὲν
πρυτάνεις τὴν βουλὴν ἐκάλουν εἰς τὸ βουλευτήριον, ὑμεῖς δ᾽ εἰς
τὴν ἐκκλησίαν ἐπορεύεσθε, καί, πρὶν ἐκείνην χρηματίσαι καὶ
προβουλεῦσαι, πᾶς ὁ δῆμος ἄνω καθῆτο. καὶ μετὰ ταῦτα ὡς ἦλθεν
ἡ βουλὴ καὶ ἀπήγγειλαν οἱ πρυτάνεις τὰ προσηγγελμέν᾽ ἑαυτοῖς 10
καὶ τὸν ἥκοντα παρήγαγον κἀκεῖνος εἶπεν, ἠρώτα μὲν ὁ κῆρυξ,
τίς ἀγορεύειν βούλεται; παρῄει δ᾽ οὐδείς.

3 *In addition to translating, define each use of the accusative:*
(*i*) αἴτει καὶ τοὺς ἀνδριάντας ἄλφιτα. (*ii*) ἔςτιν τις Cωκράτης
cοφὸς ἀνήρ, τά τε μετέωρα φροντιcτὴς καὶ τὰ ὑπὸ γῆς πάντα
ἀνεζητηκώς. (*iii*) ἥκει καὶ τὰ τοῦ πάππου χρήματα ἡμᾶς
ἀποστερήcων. (*iv*)# ἦλθε πατρὸς ἀρχαῖον τάφον. (*v*)# πολλὰ
διδάcκει μ᾽ ὁ πολὺς βίοτος. (*vi*) Μέλητός με ἐγράψατο τὴν γραφὴν
ταύτην. (*vii*) ὁ Κῦρος ἦν εἶδος μὲν κάλλιcτος, ψυχὴν δὲ
φιλανθρωπότατος. (*viii*) μὰ Δία, οὐκ εἶδον ἐμαυτοῦ ἀμείνω
ὑλοτόμον. (*ix*) cπονδὰc καὶ ξυμμαχίαν ἐποιήcαντο ἑκατὸν ἔτη.
(*x*)# ὄμνυμι δ᾽ ἱερὸν αἰθέρ᾽, οἴκηcιν Διός.

4 *In addition to translating, define each use of* ὡc:
(*i*) ὡc ἡδὺ τῷ μιcοῦντι τοὺς φαύλους ἐρημία. (*ii*)# κρύπτε μηδέν,
ὡc πάνθ᾽ ὁρῶν πάντ᾽ ἀναπτύccει χρόνος. (*iii*)# τέκνα τοῦδ᾽ ἕκατι
τίκτομεν, ὡc θεῶν τε βωμοὺς πατρίδα τε ῥυώμεθα. (*iv*) κατέλαβε
τὴν ἀκρόπολιν ὡc ἐπὶ τυραννίδι. (*v*) πειρᾶcθαι δὲ χρὴ ὡc ῥᾷστα
τἀναγκαῖα (= τὰ ἀν–) τοῦ βίου φέρειν. (*vi*)# πόνος γάρ, ὡc
λέγουcιν, εὐκλείας πατήρ. (*vii*)# φεῦ, φεῦ, τὸ νικᾶν τἄνδιχ᾽ (= τὰ
ἔνδικα) ὡc καλὸν γέρας, τὰ μὴ δίκαια δ᾽ ὡc πανταχοῦ κακόν.
(*viii*)# ὡc ἡδὺς ὁ βίος, ἄν τις αὐτὸν μὴ μάθη . (*ix*)# δίδου πένηcιν
ὡc λάβῃς θεὸν δότην. (*x*)# κρίνει φίλους ὁ καιρός, ὡc χρυcὸν τὸ
πῦρ. (*xi*)# μέμνηcο νέος ὢν ὡc γέρων ἔcῃ ποτέ. (*xii*)# οὐ ζῶμεν ὡc
ἥδιcτα μὴ λυπούμενοι; (*xiii*) ἀπέπλευcαν ἐξ Ἑλληcπόντου ὡc
ἕκαcτοι κατὰ πόλεις. (*xiv*) ἄνδρες cοφοὶ ὡc ἀληθῶc.

5# ἦν Οἰδίπους τὸ πρῶτον εὐτυχὴς ἀνήρ,
εἶτ᾽ ἐγένετ᾽ αὖθις ἀθλιώτατος βροτῶν.

6# Deianeira laments the absence of her husband Heracles.

πάθη μὲν οὖν δὴ πόλλ᾽ ἔγωγ᾽ ἐκλαυcάμην·
ἐν δ᾽, οἷον οὔπω πρόcθεν, αὐτίκ᾽ ἐξερῶ.
ὁδὸν γὰρ ἦμος τὴν τελευταίαν ἄναξ

ὁρμᾶτ' ἀπ' οἴκων Ἡρακλῆς, τότ' ἐν δόμοις
λείπει παλαιὰν δέλτον ἐγγεγραμμένην 5
ξυνθήμαθ', ἁμοὶ (= ἃ ἐμοὶ) πρόςθεν οὐκ ἔτλη ποτέ,
πολλοὺς ἀγῶνας ἐξιών, οὕτω φράςαι,
ἀλλ' ὥς τι δράςων εἷρπε κοὐ θανούμενος.

7 καὶ πρῶτον πρὸς τοὺς Θρᾷκας ἐπολέμηςα, ἐκ τῆς Χερρονήςου
αὐτοὺς ἐξελαύνων βουλομένους ἀφαιρεῖςθαι τοὺς Ἕλληνας τὴν
γῆν.

8# ὦ γῆρας, οἵαν ἐλπίδ' ἡδονῆς ἔχεις,
καὶ πᾶς τις εἰς ςὲ βούλετ' ἀνθρώπων μολεῖν·
λαβὼν δὲ πεῖραν, μεταμέλειαν λαμβάνει,
ὡς οὐδέν ἐςτι χεῖρον ἐν θνητῷ γένει.

9 ἐγὼ γάρ, ὦ Κέβης, νέος ὢν θαυμαςτῶς ὡς ἐπεθύμηςα ταύτης τῆς
ςοφίας ἣν δὴ καλοῦςι περὶ φύςεως ἱςτορίαν.

Notes

1 *l.*1 κἄν- = καὶ ἀν-. *ll.*3f. ςυνεκπόνει 2nd s. pres. imp. act., as the
accent indicates (the 3rd s. pres. ind. act would be ςυνεκπονεῖ);
ἐρῶςι and μοχθοῦςι (the latter agrees with the former) are m. dat.
pl. of the pres. act. pples. of ἐράω and μοχθέω respectively.

2 A famous passage of the orator Demosthenes in which he describes
how the Athenians in 339 BC received the news that their enemy
Philip of Macedon (father of Alexander the Great) had captured a
town only three days march from Athens. *ll.*1f. ὡς τοὺς πρυτάνεις
to (22.1/1*c*) *the prytaneis* (a committee of the Council in charge of
day-to-day administration); take ὡς (= ὅτι) Ἐλάτεια κατείληπται
with ἀγγέλλων; κατείληπται 3rd s. perf. ind. pass. of καταλαμβάνω
(the tense used in the original direct speech is kept, 8.1/3). *ll.*3f.
μεταξὺ δειπνοῦντες 12.1/2*a*(i); τοὺς ἐκ τῶν ςκηνῶν lit. *those from
the stalls* but trans. *those in the stalls*; in this pregnant use of ἐκ (cf.
note on 9.2.13 *l.*13, where the use is somewhat different) the choice
of preposition has been influenced by ἐξεῖργον; the imperfect is
often used for vivid effect in narrative, hence ἐξεῖργον,
ἐνεπίμπραςαν (< ἐμπίμπρημι) etc. – trans. by the simple past
(*cleared out, set fire to*, etc.); the γέρρα (wicker-work of some kind)
were set on fire to inform the Athenians of the emergency. *l.*7 ὑμεῖς
i.e. the people (referred to as ὁ δῆμος in *l.*9). *l.*9 ἄνω *above* i.e. on
the Pnyx, a hill to the south-west of the Athenian agora which was
used for meetings of the Assembly; καθῆτο impf. (19.1/3*b*); ὡς

when (22.1/1*b*(iv)). *ll.*10f. τὰ προσηγγελμέν'(α) ἑαυτοῖc *the things reported* (perf.) *to them* (refl. because it refers back to the subject of the clause οἱ πρυτάνεις); τὸν ἥκοντα the person mentioned in the first line as having brought the message. *l.*12 παρῇει < παρέρχομαι (cf. 18.1/3).

3 (*i*) αἴτει 2nd s. pres. imp. act. (*ii*) ἔcτιν here *there is*; ἀνεζητηκώc perf. act. pple. of ἀναζητέω. (ix) Zeus dwelt in the heavens or upper air (αἰθήρ).

4 Supply ἐcτί in (*i*), (*vi*), (*vii*), (*viii*). (*ii*) πάνθ' i.e. πάντα. (*iii*) Take τοῦδ' ἕκατι together – the phrase anticipates the ὡc clause. (*vii*) δ'(έ) is placed here after the first phrase, not the first word; with τὰ μὴ δίκαια supply τὸ νῑκᾶν. (*viii*) ἄν = ἐάν. (xi) ἔcῃ 2nd s. fut. ind. of εἰμί. (*xii*) μή with a pple. to express a condition (12.1/2*a*(iv)). (*xiv*) A phrase, not a sentence.

5 τὸ πρῶτον acc. of respect (20.1/5), *with respect to the first [period]*, i.e *at first*.

6 *ll.*1f. μέν and δέ contrast πάθη ... πόλλ' (= πολλά) and ἕν (*sc.* πάθοc); οὖν δή *so then, well as you know*; with οἷον οὔπω πρόcθεν supply ἐκλαυcάμην; ἐξερῶ fut. of ἐξαγορεύω (cf. 18.1/4 note 2). *ll.*3f. γάρ begins the explanation of the previous line and need not be translated; take ὁδὸν ... τὴν τελευταίᾱν as virtual cognate acc. (22.1/2*g*) with ὡρμᾶτ'(o) *was setting out on* ...; οἴκων ... δόμοιc plural for singular (a common use in poetry). *l.*6 ξυνθήμαθ' (= -τα) a type of retained acc. (22.1/2*f*(ii)) with ἐγγεγραμμένην (*l.*5), *inscribed with signs* (ἐγγράφει ξυνθήματα δέλτῳ means *he inscribes signs on a tablet*; this can, somewhat illogically, be put into the passive δέλτοc ἐγγράφεται ξυνθήματα with the original accusative retained, but we must translate *a tablet is inscribed with signs* – this differs from the examples in 22.1/2*f*(ii) in that ἐγγράφω takes an acc. and dat., not two accusatives); ἔτλη root aor. of τλάω. *l.*7 πολλοὺc ἀγῶναc ἐξιών *going out on many exploits* virtual cognate acc. (22.1/2*g*); οὕτω *thus, like this* as Deianeira goes on to explain later. *l.*8 ὡc ... *under the impression of going to do something, as [one] going to do something* (see note on 12.3.7).

8 *l.*2 πᾶc τιc emphatic for πᾶc, lit. *every single one*; βούλετ' i.e. βούλεται *l.*4 ὡc to introduce a clause of reason (22.1/1*b*(iii)).

9 θαυμαστῶc ὡc 22.1/1*a*(iii).

22.3 Extra reading

Anacreontea

Anacreon was an Ionic poet of the sixth century BC. His personal poetry was famous but very little has survived. It attracted many imitators in antiquity and some of their poems (as 1 below) have come down under his name. The second poem is certainly genuine.

1 μακαρίζομέν σε, τέττιξ,
  ὅτε δενδρέων ἐπ' ἄκρων
  ὀλίγην δρόσον πεπωκὼς
  βασιλεὺς ὅπως ἀείδεις·
  cὰ γάρ ἐcτι κεῖνα πάντα,   5
  ὁπόcα βλέπεις ἐν ἀγροῖc,
  ὁπόcα τρέφουσιν ὗλαι.
  cὺ δὲ τίμιος βροτοῖcιν,

  θέρεος γλυκὺς προφήτης.
  φιλέουcι μέν cε Μοῦcαι,   10
  φιλέει δὲ Φοῖβος αὐτός,
  λιγυρὴν δ' ἔδωκεν οἴμην.
  τὸ δὲ γῆρας οὔ cε τείρει,
  cοφέ, γηγενέc, φίλυμνε,
  ἀπαθὴς δ', ἀναιμόcαρκε,   15
  cχεδὸν εἶ θεοῖc ὅμοιοc.

2 πολιοὶ μὲν ἡμὶν ἤδη
  κρόταφοι, κάρη τε λευκόν,
  χαρίεccα δ' οὐκέτι ἤβη
  πάρα, γηράλεοι δ' ὀδόντες.
  γλυκεροῦ δ' οὐκέτι πολλὸς   5
  βιότου χρόνος λέλειπται·

  διὰ ταῦτ' ἀναcταλύζω
  θαμὰ Τάρταρον δεδοικώς.
  Ἀΐδεω γάρ ἐcτι δεινὸc
  μυχός, ἀργαλέη δ' ἐc αὐτὸν   10
  κάθοδοc· καὶ γὰρ ἑτοῖμον
  καταβάντι μὴ ἀναβῆναι.

Notes

1 *l*.2 δενδρέων (Ionic for δένδρων, cf. 13.1/1*c*) ἐπ' ἄκρων *on the tops of trees* (18.1/6). *l*.4 βασιλεὺς ὅπως = ὅπως (*like*) βασιλεύc. *ll*.5f. πάντα, ὁπόcα (= ὅcα, as also in *l*.7) 21.1/3*d*. *l*.8 Supply εἶ (< εἰμί); βροτοῖcιν *among mortals* (dat. of reference, 23.1/2*e*). *ll*.9ff. Three examples of the use of uncontracted forms in Ionic, θέρεος (= θέρους, cf. 6.1/1*c*), φιλέουcι (= φιλοῦcι), φιλέει (= φιλεῖ). *l*.12 λιγυρήν = -άν.

2 *l*.1 Supply εἰcί; ἡμὶν (= ἡμῖν) plural for singular (the dative is one of possession, 23.1/2*c*). *l*.2 κάρη, an irregular noun, is neuter, hence λευκόν. *l*.4 πάρα = πάρεcτι (cf. 21.1/4 note 2 but here it is not used impersonally). *ll*.7f. Take θάμα with ἀναcταλύζω; δεδοικώς 19.1/3*a*. *l*.9 Ἀΐδεω = Attic Ἅιδου (gen. of Ἅιδηc), on the ending cf. 25.1/2*b*(i). *l*.10 ἀργαλέη = -έᾱ. *l*.11 ἑτοῖμον *[it is] fixed* the neuter singular adj. is used in impersonal expressions.

23.1 Grammar

23.1/1 Uses of cases (2) – genitive

Apart from its use as the case of possession (2.1/3*d*) and after certain prepositions (2.1/3*g*, 3.1/5*b*), the genitive can function in a number of ways with another noun, verb, adjective or even adverb. Although the genitive is often to be translated by *of,* in some of its uses a different rendering in English is required.

(*a*) *Possessive genitive* (see 2.1/3*d*)

In this use the genitive denotes ownership, possession or some looser association: ἡ τοῦ Δημοσθένους οἰκίᾱ *the house of Demosthenes* (or *Demosthenes' house*); οἱ Σόλωνος νόμοι *the laws of* (*made by*) *Solon*; τὰ τῆς πόλεως *the [affairs] of the city*. In certain very restricted contexts a possessive genitive qualifies a missing noun, which can easily be supplied; the most common are *wife, son/daughter* (cf. 5.1/3 note 2) and *place of abode*:

Ἀλέξανδρος ὁ Φιλίππου.	*Alexander, [son] of Philip.*
Ἄρτεμις ἡ Διός.	*Artemis, [daughter] of Zeus.*
ἐν Ἀρίφρονος.	*At Ariphron's (in [the house] of Ariphron).*
ἐν Διονῡ́σου.	*At [the shrine] of Dionysus (cf. at St. Paul's).*

(*b*) *Genitive of characteristic*

In English we may say *it is the part/duty/nature/characteristic,* etc. *of someone to do something.* In Greek this is expressed simply by the use of the third singular of εἰμί plus the genitive. In translation from Greek the appropriate English word to be supplied must be gauged from the context:

οὗτοι γυναικός ἐcτιν ἱμείρειν μάχηc.	*It is indeed not a woman's part to long for battle.*
δοκεῖ δικαίου τοῦτ᾽ εἶναι πολίτου.	*This seems to be the duty of a just citizen.*

(c) Subjective and objective genitive

An **objective** genitive stands in the same relation to a noun or adjective as an object does to a transitive verb. In *Socrates' love of the truth dominated his life,* the genitive *of the truth* is objective because the sense connection between *truth* and *love* is the same as between an object and a verb (we could say, with the same meaning, *Socrates loved the truth*; *this dominated his life*). Examples in Greek are: φόβοc τοῦ γήρωc *fear of old age,* τὸ κράτοc τῆc θαλάττηc *the command of the sea,* ἔρωc τῆc ἀρετῆc *love of virtue.* Because this use is more extensive in Greek than in English we must sometimes translate it by a different preposition: ὁ τοῦ κυνὸc λόγοc *the story about the dog,* νἵκη τῶν ἡδονῶν *victory over pleasures.* A **subjective** genitive, on the other hand, stands in the same relation to a noun as a subject does to a verb: νἵκη τῶν βαρβάρων *victory of the barbarians* (i.e. οἱ βάρβαροι νῑκῶcιν *the barbarians are victorious*). This use is only a variety of the possessive genitive.

Sometimes, however, we must decide from the context whether a genitive is subjective or objective. ὁ τῶν Ἑλλήνων φόβοc can mean *the Greeks' fear* (i.e. *the fear felt by the Greeks*) (subjective), as well as *the fear of the Greeks* (i.e. *the fear inspired by the Greeks*) (objective). A possessive adjective (9.1/5*b*) usually represents a subjective genitive, but may on occasion be the equivalent of an objective genitive: φιλίᾳ τῇ ἐμῇ can mean *through friendship for me* as well as *through my friendship.* Cf. ἐπὶ διαβολῇ τῇ ἐμῇ in 10.3 *ll.*5f.

(d) Partitive genitive

In this construction the genitive denotes the whole and the noun or pronoun on which it depends denotes a part of that whole:

μέροc τι τῶν βαρβάρων	*a part of the barbarians*
οἱ ἄδικοι τῶν ἀνθρώπων	*the unjust among men*
ὀλίγοι αὐτῶν	*few of them*
οἱ πρεcβύτατοι τῶν cτρατηγῶν	*the oldest of the generals*

The partitive genitive may also occur by itself as the object of a verb: τῆc γῆc ἔτεμον *they ravaged [part] of the land* (τὴν γῆν ἔτεμον would mean *they ravaged the [whole] land*). It can also be used predicatively:

Cόλων τῶν ἑπτὰ coφιcτῶν ἐκλήθη.	*Solon was called [one] of the Seven Sages.*

This use of the genitive also occurs in abstract nouns after the phrase εἰc τοῦτο (τοcοῦτο) ἀφικνεῖcθαι (ἥκειν etc.) *to reach this (such a) pitch/point/stage of* (cf. 16.1/1 note 3):

εἰc τοῦτο θράcουc καὶ ἀναιδείᾱc ἀφῖκετο.	*He reached such a pitch of boldness and shamelessness.*
εἰc τοῦθ᾽ ὕβρεωc ἥκει.	*He has come to such a pitch of insolence.*

Under this heading also belongs the **chorographic** genitive, or genitive of **geographic definition**:

ἔπλευcαν τῆc Ἰταλίᾱc εἰc Τάραντα	*They sailed to Tarentum in Italy* (lit. *[a part] of Italy*)
τῆc Cικελίᾱc οἱ Cυρᾱκόcιοι	*The Syracusans in Sicily*

Compare the use of the genitive with adverbs of place, e.g. εἰδέναι ὅπου γῆc ἔcτιν *to know where in the world he is* (cf. 2.2.11).

(e) *Genitive of explanation*

The genitive may be used as the equivalent of a noun in apposition which gives an explanation or definition of the preceding noun. The construction in English is generally the same:

ὦ πόλι Θηβῶν.	*O city of Thebes* (i.e. *O city,* viz *Thebes*).
τέλοc θανάτου.	*The end of death* (i.e. the end that is death).
ὕπνου δῶρον.	*The gift of sleep.*

(f) *Genitive of price or value* (see 20.1/3)

(g) *Genitive of time within which* (see 7.1/7c)

(h) *Genitive absolute* (see 12.1/2b)

(i) *Genitive of comparison* (see 17.1/4a)

(j) *Genitive of separation* (see 20.1/4)

(k) *Genitive with verbs* (see 13.1/2a)

At 13.1/2d we considered certain intransitive verbs which take the genitive. Two other groups are followed by an accusative and a genitive:

(i) Verbs of **accusing, acquitting, condemning, prosecuting** and the like are generally followed by an accusative of the person involved and a genitive of the crime or charge. Such verbs are αἰτιάομαι *accuse*, γράφομαι *indict*, διώκω *prosecute*:

ὁ Μέλητος ἀσεβείᾱς ἐμὲ ἐγράψατο.	*Meletus indicted me for impiety.*
διώξομαί σε δειλίᾱς	*I shall prosecute you for cowardice.*

However, verbs of accusing and condemning which are compounded with κατά (such as κατηγορέω *accuse*, καταγιγνώσκω *give judgement against, condemn*, κατακρῑνω *give sentence against*, καταψηφίζομαι *vote against*) reverse the normal construction, and so take a genitive of the person and an accusative of the crime or penalty:

ἐγὼ δ᾽ ὑμῶν δέομαι μὴ καταγνῶναι δωροδοκίᾱν ἐμοῦ.	*I request you not to condemn me for bribery.*
ἐμοῦ Φιλιππισμὸν κατηγορεῖ.	*He accuses me of siding with Philip.*

(ii) A genitive of **cause** can follow verbs of **emotion**. Such verbs are θαυμάζω *wonder at*, ζηλόω *admire*, οἰκτῑρω *pity*, etc.:

τούτους τῆς τόλμης θαυμάζω.	*I wonder at these men for* (or *because of*) *their boldness.*
τοῦ πάθους ᾦκτῑρεν αὐτόν.	*He pitied him for his suffering.*

A genitive of cause can also occur with adjectives: εὐδαίμων τοῦ τρόπου *happy in his way of life.*

(*l*) *Genitive of exclamation*

This genitive, which is often coupled with an interjection (φεῦ *alas* (of grief), *ah, oh* (of astonishment); οἴμοι *alas*), is akin to the genitive of cause as it gives the reason for the speaker's astonishment or grief:

οἴμοι ταλαίνης τῆσδε συμφορᾶς.	*Alas for this wretched plight!*
φεῦ φεῦ τῆς ὥρᾱς, τοῦ κάλλους.	*Ah, what youthful bloom, what beauty!*
εἶπε πρὸς αὐτόν, τῆς τύχης.	*He said to himself, "What luck!"*

23.1/2 Uses of cases (3) – dative

The Greek dative is an amalgam of three cases:

the **dative proper**, generally to be translated *to* or *for,* indicating the person (or thing) involved in an action (the recipient, the person advantaged or disadvantaged, etc.);

the old **instrumental** case, denoting that *by* which or *with* which an action is done or accompanied;

the original **locative** case, which expressed *place where* and *time when.*

Some of these uses were distinguished and made more precise by the use of prepositions (cf. 2.1/3*h*, 3.1/5).

DATIVE PROPER

(*a*) *Verbs governing the dative*

(i) Verbs followed by a direct object (accusative) and an indirect object (dative – 2.1/3*e*), such as verbs of **giving, saying, promising**: Κῦρος δίδωcιν αὐτῷ μῡρίουc δᾱρεικούc *Cyrus gives him 10,000 darics*; ὑπιcχνοῦμαί coι δέκα τάλαντα *I promise you ten talents*. However, many verbs of **reproaching, blaming** and the like, which in English take a direct object of the person involved, in Greek take a **dative** of the person and an accusative of the thing (when expressed):

μὴ πάθωμεν ὃ ἄλλοιc ἐπιτῑμῶμεν.	*Let us not get into a situation for which we censure others* (lit. *let us not experience [the thing] which we censure in others*).
αἰcχύνομαί coι τοῦτ' ὀνειδίcαι.	*I am ashamed to reproach you with this.*
τί ἄν μοι μέμφοιο;	*What would you blame me for?*

The English construction which allows the indirect object of a verb in the active voice to be made the subject of the same verb in the passive (*I was given this land*) is generally impossible in Greek. ταύτην τὴν χώρᾱν μοι ἔδωκε *he gave me this land* becomes αὕτη ἡ χώρᾱ μοι ὑπ' αὐτοῦ ἐδόθη *this land was given to me by him*. ἐδόθην would mean *I was given* in the sense *I was handed over*. For an exception see note on 22.2.6 *l*.5.

(ii) **Intransitive verbs** followed by the dative (see 13.1/2*b*)

(iii) **Impersonal verbs** followed by the dative (see 21.1/4)

(b) Dative with adjectives, adverbs and nouns

The dative is used with certain **adjectives** whose English equivalent is usually followed by *to* or *for*. These include φίλος *dear, friendly*; ἐχθρός *hateful, hostile*; ἴσος *equal*; ὅμοιος *like, resembling*; ἀνόμοιος *unlike, dissimilar*:

τύραννος ἅπᾱς ἐχθρὸς ἐλευθερίᾳ καὶ νόμοις ἐναντίος.	*Every tyrant [is] hostile to freedom and opposed to laws.*
ποιεῖτε ὅμοια τοῖς λόγοις.	*You are acting in accordance with* (lit. *doing things like*) *your words.*

Compare ὁ αὐτός with the dative *the same as* (9.1/3b).

A similar use of the dative is found after some **adverbs**:

ἀκολούθως τοῖς νόμοις	*In accordance with the laws.*
ὁμολογουμένως τῇ φύσει ζῆν	*To live in agreement with nature.*

as well as with some **nouns**, especially those related to verbs of similar meaning which take the dative:

ἐπιβουλὴ ἐμοί.	*A plot against me.*
κοινωνίᾱ τοῖς ἀνδράσι.	*Association with men.*

(c) Dative of possession

The dative is used with εἶναι (and verbs of similar meaning such as ὑπάρχειν and γίγνεσθαι) to denote the owner or possessor:

οἰκεῖοί μοί εἰσι καὶ υἱεῖς.	*I have relatives and sons* (lit. *relatives and sons are to me*);
τῷ δικαίῳ παρὰ θεῶν δῶρα γίγνεται.	*The just man has gifts* (lit. *gifts come into being for the just man*) *from the gods.*

(d) Dative of advantage and disadvantage

The dative is used to indicate the person or thing for whose advantage or disadvantage something is done: πᾶς ἀνὴρ αὐτῷ πονεῖ *every man works for himself* (advantage); ἄλλο στράτευμα αὐτῷ συνελέγετο *another army was being gathered for him* (advantage); ἥδε ἡ ἡμέρᾱ τοῖς Ἕλλησι μεγάλων κακῶν ἄρξει *this day will be the beginning of great troubles for the Greeks* (disadvantage). Sometimes this use cannot be translated by *for*: σῖτον αὐτοῖς ἀφεῖλεν *he took food away from them* (lit. *he took food away to their disadvantage*; for the other construction used with verbs meaning *take away* see 22.1/2*f*(ii)).

(e) *Dative of reference or relation*

Similarly, the dative may be used to denote a person or thing to whose case a statement is limited: τριήρει ἐστὶν εἰς Ἡράκλειαν ἡμέρᾱς μακρᾶς πλοῦς *for a trireme it is a long day's voyage to Heraclea.* This dative is often used to denote *in the eyes of* or *in the judgement of*:

ἡμῖν Ἀχιλλεὺς ἄξιος τῑμῆς.	*In our eyes* (lit. *for us*) *Achilles [is] worthy of honour.*
ἀνάξιοι πᾶσίν ἐστε δυστυχεῖν.	*In the eyes of all* (lit. *for all*) *you are unworthy to suffer misfortune.*

A participle in the dative singular is used in this way with an indefinite reference:

Ἐπίδαμνος ἐν δεξιᾷ ἐστιν εἰσπλέοντι ἐς τὸν Ἰόνιον κόλπον.	*Epidamnus is on the right as one sails into* (lit. *in relation to one sailing into*) *the Ionian Gulf.*
ἔλεγον ὅτι ἡ ὁδὸς διαβάντι τὸν ποταμὸν ἐπὶ Λῡδίᾱν φέροι.	*They said that, when one had crossed the river, the road led to Lydia.*

Compare also the phrase ὡς συνελόντι εἰπεῖν *to speak concisely, in a word* (lit. *so to speak for one having brought [the matter] together*).

(f) *Ethic dative* (a purely conventional term, with no connection with ethics)

The dative of the first or second person pronouns can be used simply to attract the attention of the person addressed. There is no grammatical connection with the surrounding words. This so-called ethic dative is usually to be represented in English by *I beg you, please, let me tell you, you know,* and the like:

καί μοι μὴ θορυβήσητε.	*And, I beg you, don't make a clamour.*
Ἀρταφέρνης ὑμῖν Ὑστάσπου ἐστὶ παῖς.	*Artaphernes, you know, is Hystaspes' son.*

(g) *Dative of the agent*

This use, replaced in most contexts by ὑπό + gen., is found with the perfect and pluperfect passive (very rarely with other tenses):

πάνθ' ἡμῖν πεποίηται. *Everything has been done by us.*

ἐπειδὴ αὐτοῖϲ παρεϲκεύαϲτο. *When they had made their preparations* (lit. *it had been prepared by them*).

For the dative of the agent with verbal adjectives, see 24.1/5*b*.

INSTRUMENTAL DATIVE

(*h*) **Dative of instrument** (see 11.1/2)

(*i*) **Dative of cause**

The dative may denote cause: ῥῑ́γει ἀπωλλύμεθα *we were perishing from* (or *because of*) *cold*. Often the noun in the dative denotes an emotional or mental condition:

ὕβρει καὶ οὐκ οἴνῳ τοῦτο ποιεῖ. *He does this through insolence and not because he is drunk* (lit. *because of wine*).

ἠπείγοντο πρὸϲ τὸν ποταμὸν τοῦ πιεῖν ἐπιθῡμίᾳ. *They were hurrying towards the river because of their desire to drink* (lit. *because of a desire for drinking*).

Occasionally cause may also be expressed by ὑπό with the genitive:

οὐκ ἐδύνατο καθεύδειν ὑπὸ λῡ́πηϲ *He could not sleep because of* (or *for*) *grief.*

(*j*) **Dative of manner and attendant circumstances**

The dative may be used to denote the manner in which something is done or the circumstances accompanying an action:

οἱ Ἀθηναῖοι παντὶ ϲθένει ἐπεκούρηϲαν. *The Athenians helped with all their strength* (manner).

ἀτελεῖ τῇ νῑ́κῃ ἀπῆλθον. *They went away with their victory incomplete* (accompanying circumstance).

Normally a noun used in this way is qualified by an adjective (as above). Some nouns, however, are regularly employed by themselves as datives of manner and are virtually the equivalent of adverbs:

βίᾳ *by force, forcibly*; δρόμῳ *at a run*; ἔργῳ *in fact, in deed*; λόγῳ *in word, in theory*; ϲιγῇ *in silence*; ϲπουδῇ *hastily*; φύϲει ... νόμῳ *by nature ... by convention*; compare also τῷ ὄντι *in reality* (see 12.1/1 note 1); τούτῳ τῷ τρόπῳ *in this way*.

Under this category are also included the datives of feminine adjectives with a noun understood: ταύτῃ *in this way*; ἰδίᾳ *privately*; δημοσίᾳ *publicly*; πεζῇ *on foot*.

(k) Dative of accompaniment

We have already met this use of the dative with αὐτός (see 9.1/3a(ii)). The dative by itself is particularly common in military contexts (the **military dative**) to denote the forces with which a journey or expedition is made:

'Αθηναῖοι ἐφ' ἡμᾶς πολλῇ   *The Athenians have made an*
στρατιᾷ ὥρμηνται   *expedition against us with a*
                            large force.

(l) Dative of measure of difference (see 17.1/4b)

(m) Dative of respect

As well as an accusative of respect (20.1/5) we may also find the dative used in a similar way:

ἀνὴρ ἡλικίᾳ ἔτι νέος *a man still young in age*; ὀνόματι σπονδαί *a truce in name [alone].*

LOCATIVE DATIVE

(n) Dative of place where

In poetry **place where** may be expressed by the dative **without a preposition**: Κρονίδης αἰθέρι ναίων *the son of Cronos living in the sky*. In Attic prose, however, a preposition is generally required (2.1/3h), except with some place names, e.g. Μαραθῶνι *at Marathon*. Traces of the old locative endings remain in such forms such as: 'Αθήνησι (= ἐν 'Αθήναις) *at Athens*; Φαληροῖ (= ἐν Φαλήρῳ) *at Phalerum*; cf. οἴκοι *at home*; these words are usually classified as adverbs.

(o) Dative of time when (see 7.1/7b)

23.2 Greek reading

1   *In addition to translating, define each use of the genitive and dative:*
    (*i*)# ὦ φίλον ὕπνου θέλγητρον, ἐπίκουρον νόσου. (*ii*) ἤθελε τῶν μενόντων εἶναι. (*iii*) ὦ Πόσειδον, τῆς τέχνης. (*iv*)# πενίαν φέρειν

οὐ παντός, ἀλλ᾽ ἀνδρὸς σοφοῦ. (ν) τούτῳ πάνυ μοι προσέχετε τὸν νοῦν. (vi) πολλαὶ θεραπεῖαι τοῖς ἰατροῖς εὕρηνται. (vii) ὕπνος πέφυκε σωμάτων σωτηρία. (viii) τὸν αὐτὸν αἰνεῖν καὶ ψέγειν ἀνδρὸς κακοῦ. (ix) τοιοῦτο ὑμῖν ἐστιν ἡ τυραννίς, ὦ Λακεδαιμόνιοι. (x)# ταῦτα Ζεὺς οἶδεν Ὀλύμπιος, αἰθέρι ναίων. (xi) αἰτιῶνται αὐτὸν κλοπῆς. (xii) οἱ ἄνθρωποι διὰ τὸ αὐτῶν δέος τοῦ θανάτου ψεύδονται. (xiii) ἐφοβοῦντο μὴ οἱ Ἀθηναῖοι μείζονι παρασκευῇ ἐπέλθωσιν. (xiv) κραυγῇ πολλῇ ἐπίασιν. (xv) ὄνομα τῷ μειρακίῳ ἦν Πλάτων. (xvi)# τέχνη ἀνάγκης ἀσθενεστέρα μακρῷ. (xvii)# ζηλῶ σε τοῦ νοῦ, τῆς δὲ δειλίας στυγῶ. (xviii) ἐγὼ τῶν κρεῶν ἔκλεπτον. (xix)# ἆρ᾽ ὑμῖν οὗτος ταῦτ᾽ ἔδρασεν ἔνδικα; (xx) θεοῖς ταῦτα ἐποίησαν. (xxi) στυγνὸς ἦν καὶ τῇ φωνῇ τραχύς. (xxii) ὁ στρατὸς ἀφίκετο τῆς Ἀττικῆς ἐς Οἰνόην. (xxiii) ὁρᾶτε τὴν βασιλέως ἐπιορκίαν. (xxiv) οὐκ εἰμὶ τοῖς πεπραγμένοις δύσθυμος.

2   ὁ Διογένης, Ἀναξιμένει τῷ ῥήτορι παχεῖ ὄντι προσελθών, ἐπίδος καὶ ἡμῖν, ἔφη, τοῖς πτωχοῖς τῆς γαστρός· καὶ γὰρ αὐτὸς κουφισθήσει καὶ ἡμᾶς ὠφελήσεις.

3#   ἦν γάρ τις αἶνος ὡς γυναιξὶ μὲν τέχναι
μέλουσι, λόγχῃ δ᾽ ἄνδρες εὐστοχώτεροι.
εἰ γὰρ δόλοισιν ἦν τὸ νικητήριον,
ἡμεῖς ἂν ἀνδρῶν εἴχομεν τυραννίδα.

4#   καὶ νῦν παραινῶ πᾶσι τοῖς νεωτέροις
μὴ πρὸς τὸ γῆρας ἀναβολὰς ποιουμένους
σχολῇ τεκνοῦσθαι παῖδας· οὐ γὰρ ἡδονή,
γυναικί τ᾽ ἐχθρὸν χρῆμα πρεσβύτης ἀνήρ·
ἀλλ᾽ ὡς τάχιστα. καὶ γὰρ ἐκτροφαὶ καλαὶ   5
καὶ συννεάζων ἡδὺ παῖς νέῳ πατρί.

5   One of the accusations brought against Socrates (10.3) was that he did not believe in the traditional gods. In the *Apology* of Plato (see 13.3), which is an account of his trial, he is represented as interrogating one of his accusers on this charge.

ΜΕΛΗΤΟΣ – ΣΩΚΡΑΤΗΣ

ΜΕ. ταῦτα λέγω, ὡς τὸ παράπαν οὐ νομίζεις θεούς.
ΣΩ. ὦ θαυμάσιε Μέλητε, τί ταῦτα λέγεις; οὐδὲ ἥλιον οὐδὲ σελήνην ἄρα νομίζω θεοὺς εἶναι, ὥσπερ οἱ ἄλλοι ἄνθρωποι;
ΜΕ. μὰ Δί᾽, ὦ ἄνδρες δικασταί, ἐπεὶ τὸν μὲν ἥλιον λίθον φησὶν εἶναι, τὴν δὲ σελήνην γῆν.   5

ΣΩ. Ἀναξαγόρου οἴει κατηγορεῖν, ὦ φίλε Μέλητε; καὶ οὕτω καταφρονεῖς τῶνδε καὶ οἴει αὐτοὺς ἀπείρους γραμμάτων εἶναι ὥστε οὐκ εἰδέναι ὅτι τὰ Ἀναξαγόρου βιβλία τοῦ Κλαζομενίου γέμει τούτων τῶν λόγων; καὶ δὴ καὶ οἱ νέοι ταῦτα παρ᾽ ἐμοῦ μανθάνουσιν, ἃ ἔξεστιν δραχμῆς ἐκ τῆς ὀρχήστρας πριαμένοις 10 Σωκράτους καταγελᾶν, ἐὰν προσποιῆται ἑαυτοῦ εἶναι, ἄλλως τε καὶ οὕτως ἄτοπα ὄντα; ἀλλ᾽, ὦ πρὸς Διός, οὑτωσί σοι δοκῶ; οὐδένα νομίζω θεὸν εἶναι;
ΜΕ. οὐ μέντοι μὰ Δία οὐδ᾽ ὁπωστιοῦν.
ΣΩ. ἄπιστός γ᾽ εἶ, ὦ Μέλητε, καὶ ταῦτα μέντοι, ὡς ἐμοὶ δοκεῖς, 15 σαυτῷ. ἐμοὶ γὰρ δοκεῖ οὑτοσί, ὦ ἄνδρες Ἀθηναῖοι, πάνυ εἶναι ὑβριστὴς καὶ ἀκόλαστος, καὶ ἀτεχνῶς τὴν γραφὴν ὕβρει τινὶ καὶ ἀκολασίᾳ καὶ νεότητι γράψασθαι. ἔοικεν γὰρ ὥσπερ αἴνιγμα συντιθέντι διαπειρωμένῳ, ἆρα γνώσεται Σωκράτης ὁ σοφὸς δὴ ἐμοῦ χαριεντιζομένου καὶ ἐναντί᾽ ἐμαυτῷ λέγοντος, ἢ ἐξαπατήσω 20 αὐτὸν καὶ τοὺς ἄλλους τοὺς ἀκούοντας; οὗτος γὰρ ἐμοὶ φαίνεται τὰ ἐναντία λέγειν αὐτὸς ἑαυτῷ ἐν τῇ γραφῇ ὥσπερ ἂν εἰ εἴποι· ἀδικεῖ Σωκράτης θεοὺς οὐ νομίζων, ἀλλὰ θεοὺς νομίζων. καίτοι τοῦτό ἐστι παίζοντος.

Notes

1 (i) ὕπνου θέλγητρον 23.1/1e. (iv) Supply ἐστί (cf. (viii) and (xvi)).
2 ἐπίδος 2nd. s. aor. imp. act. of ἐπιδίδωμι; τῆς γαστρός 23.1/1d; κουφισθήσει 2nd s. fut. ind. pass.
3 l.2 Supply εἰσί with ἄνδρες. l.3 Lit. *for if the prize of victory were through guiles* (dat. of instrument), i.e. *were [won] by guiles*.
4 ll.2f. ἀναβολὰς ποιοῦμαι (mid.) *I make delays*, i.e. for myself – the active would mean *I make delays (for others)*, cf. 8.1/1b; the middle is used in the same way with τεκνοῦσθαι; οὐ ... ἡδονή (ἐστι), i.e. in producing children in old age. l.5 ὡς τάχιστα is contrasted with σχολῇ (l.3), i.e. have children as quickly as possible; ἐκτροφαί (plural for singular) *the rearing [of children]*, i.e. *rearing children*. l.6 The neuter adj. ἡδύ is predicate *[is] a pleasant [thing]* (ἐστί is understood), cf. 5.2.5(i).
5 l.1 ταῦτα trans. *this* (the neuter plural is often used where we would have the singular in English); τὸ παράπαν οὐ *not at all*, cf. note on 11.2.12 l.3; νομίζεις *believe in*. l.2 οὐδὲ ... οὐδέ *not even ... nor* (**not neither ... nor** which is οὔτε ... οὔτε) – note that this question is **not**

marked by any introductory word (the same applies to all the questions in what Socrates says next). *l*.4 μὰ Δί'(α) here *no, by Zeus* (22.1/2h). *l*.6 Anaxagoras of Clazomenae was a philosopher of the generation before Socrates who taught that the sun and moon were material bodies suspended in the sky (the sun was a burning rock about the size of the Peloponnese); the traditional belief was that they were divinities. *ll*.7f. τῶνδε i.e. the jurymen; αὐτοὺς ... ὥστε lit. *them to be inexperienced in letters with the result ...,* i.e. *that they are [so] illiterate that ...*; οὐκ εἰδέναι an exception to the rule given at 24.1/2*d* – ὥστε + inf. is often negated by οὐ when it follows the inf. construction of indirect speech (here αὐτοὺς ... εἶναι); *ll*.10ff. ἅ is the object of πριαμένοις, lit. *which having bought ... it is allowed* (ἔξεστιν) *[to them] to mock* (καταγελᾶν)...*, i.e. *which they can buy ... and [then] laugh at ...*; δραχμῆς gen. of price (20.1/3); ἐκ τῆς ὀρχήστρᾶς lit. *from the orchestra* (a part of the Athenian agora where books were sold) but English idiom requires *in the orchestra*; ἑαυτοῦ εἶναι *[them,* i.e. the doctrines of Anaxagoras*] to be his* (lit. *of himself* possessive gen., 23.1/1*a*); ἄλλως τε καί *especially*; ἄτοπα ὄντα agrees with the understood subject of εἶναι. *l*.15 καὶ ταῦτα μέντοι *and that* (cf. note on *l*.1) *too* (ταῦτα refers to the clause ἄπιστός γ' εἰ *you are not to be believed*). *ll*.17ff. ὕβρει τινί, ἀκολασίᾳ datives of cause (23.1/2*i*); ὥσπερ (lit. *as if*) tones down the metaphor (cf. 22.1/1*a*(vi) for ὡς used in the same way) and need not be translated; αἴνιγμα object of συντιθέντι which agrees with διαπειρωμένῳ, *[a man] composing a riddle making trial [of me],* i.e. *[a man] making trial [of me] [by] composing ...* (the actual riddle is ἆρα ... ἀκούοντας); δή adds a note of sarcasm to ὁ σοφός. *l*.20 ἐμοῦ ... ἐναντί'(α) ἐμαυτῷ λέγοντος (*saying [things] opposite to myself,* i.e. *contradicting myself*) gen. absl. with two participles (*will S. realise when I ... ?*). *l*.22 ὥσπερ ἂν εἰ (= ὥσπερ εἰ) εἴποι *as if he were to say.* *l*.24 παίζοντος gen. of characteristic (23.1/1*b*).

23.3 Extra reading

Further elegiac poetry

Of the following, 1-5 are epitaphs, which were nearly always written in elegiac couplets (**Appendix 9**). Other examples of epitaphs occur at 9.2.3 and 19.2.7(*v*).

1 ναυηγοῦ τάφος εἰμί· ὁ δ' ἀντίον ἐστὶ γεωργοῦ·
   ὡς ἁλὶ καὶ γαίῃ ξυνὸς ὕπεστ' Ἀΐδης.

2 τῇδε Cάων ὁ Δίκωνος Ἀκάνθιος ἱερὸν ὕπνον
   κοιμᾶται· θνῄσκειν μὴ λέγε τοὺς ἀγαθούς.

3 δωδεκετῆ τὸν παῖδα πατὴρ ἀπέθηκε Φίλιππος
   ἐνθάδε, τὴν πολλὴν ἐλπίδα, Νικοτέλην.

4 *On the Spartans who died fighting the Persians at Plataea*
   ἄcβεστον κλέος οἵδε φίλῃ περὶ πατρίδι θέντες
   κυάνεον θανάτου ἀμφιβάλοντο νέφος·
   οὐδὲ τεθνᾶσι θανόντες, ἐπεί cφ' ἀρετὴ καθύπερθεν
   κυδαίνουc' ἀνάγει δώματος ἐξ Ἀΐδεω.

5 Αἰcχύλον Εὐφορίωνος Ἀθηναῖον τόδε κεύθει
   μνῆμα καταφθίμενον πυροφόροιο Γέλαc·
   ἀλκὴν δ' εὐδόκιμον Μαραθώνιον ἄλcος ἂν εἴποι
   καὶ βαθυχαιτήεις Μῆδος ἐπιστάμενος.

6 δάκρυα cοὶ καὶ νέρθε διὰ χθονός, Ἡλιοδώρα,
   δωροῦμαι cτοργᾶς λείψανον εἰς Ἀΐδαν,
   δάκρυα δυσδάκρυτα· πολυκλαύτῳ δ' ἐπὶ τύμβῳ
   cπένδω νᾶμα πόθων, μνᾶμα φιλοφροcύναc·
   οἰκτρὰ γὰρ οἰκτρὰ φίλαν cε καὶ ἐν φθιμένοιc Μελέαγρος   5
   αἰάζω, κενεὰν εἰς Ἀχέροντα χάριν.
   αἰαῖ, ποῦ τὸ ποθεινὸν ἐμοὶ θάλος; ἅρπαcεν Ἅιδαc,
   ἅρπαcεν, ἀκμαῖον δ' ἄνθος ἔφυρε κόνιc.
   ἀλλά cε γουνοῦμαι, γᾶ παντρόφε, τὰν πανόδυρτον
   ἠρέμα cοῖc κόλποιc, μᾶτερ, ἐναγκάλιcαι.   10

Notes

1 *l*.1 ὁ *sc.* τάφος. *l*.2 ὡς exclamatory (22.1/1*a*(ii)); ὕπεcτ'(ι) < ὕπειμι.

2 ὁ Δίκωνος 23.1/1*a*; ἱερὸν ὕπνον cognate acc. (22.1/2*g*) with
   κοιμᾶται.

3 *l*.1 ἀπέθηκε < ἀποτίθημι. *l*.2 τὴν πολλὴν ἐλπίδα is in apposition to
   παῖδα.

4 *l*.1 περὶ ... θέντεc tmesis (12.3.9 *l*.6 note) for περιθέντεc (the image
   is from putting a wreath on a person's head). *l*.2 ἀμφιβάλοντο (=
   ἀμφεβάλοντο) a Homeric form without the augment (25.1/2*d*(i)) – the
   image here is of putting on a mantle. *l*.3 τεθνᾶcι shorter form of
   τεθνήκᾱcι (19.1/3*a*); cφ'(ε) here *them*. *l*.4 κυδαίνουc'(α) f. nom.
   pple.; in prose the order of the last three words would be ἐκ δώματος
   Ἀΐδεω (= Ἅιδου, cf. 22.3.2 *l*.9 and 25.1/2*b*(i)).

5 *l.*1 Εὐφορίωνος *[son] of E.*, 23.1/1*a* (the article can be omitted). *l.*2 καταφθίμενον (Homeric aorist mid. pple.) *dead* (trans. *who died*); πῡροφόροιο (= -ου, 25.1/2*b*(ii)) Γέλᾱς Homeric use of gen. to denote place where. *ll.*3f. Μαραθώνιον ἄλσος the grove at Marathon (a village to the north of Athens) which celebrated the Athenian victory over an invading Persian force in 490 BC. Aeschylus had distinguished himself in the battle and set more value on this than on any literary achievements, if the tradition assigning the epitaph to him is correct. The subject of εἴποι is both ἄλσος and Μῆδος (with double subjects of this sort the verb may agree with the closer noun). *l.*4 ἐπιστάμενος *sc. it,* i.e. Aeschylus' ἄλκη.

6 The poem has a smattering of Doric forms, which are sometimes used in elegiac poetry; these involve ᾱ for Attic η: στοργᾶς, ᾿Αΐδᾱν (= ῞Αιδην) (*l.*2); μνᾶμα, φιλοφροσύνᾱς (*l.*4); ῞Αιδᾱς (*l.*7); γᾶ, τᾶν (*l.*9); μᾶτερ (*l.*10). *ll.*1f. Take στοργᾶς with λείψανον, which is in apposition to δάκρυα. *l.*4 μνᾶμα is in apposition to νᾶμα. *l.*5 οἰκτρὰ ... οἰκτρά n. pl. acc. used adverbially (20.1/5), *piteously.* *l.*6 κενεᾱν ... χάριν is in apposition to the whole of the preceding clause; Acheron, one of the rivers of the Underworld, is used here to mean the Underworld itself. *l.*7 ἐμοί indicates possession (23.1/2*c*); ἅρπασεν = ἥρπασεν (cf. ἀμφιβάλοντο in 4 *l.*2 above). *l.*10 ἐναγκάλισαι 2nd s. aor. imp. mid. of ἐναγκαλίζομαι.

24 UNIT TWENTY-FOUR

24.1 Grammar

24.1/1 *Yes* and *no*

Greek has four ways of answering questions where in English we would use *yes* or *no*. In answer to the question ἆρα τοῦτο εἶπας; *Did you say this?* we may have:

(*a*) the key word of the question repeated either affirmatively or negatively:

εἶπον	*yes* (lit. *I said [it]*);
οὐκ εἶπον	*no* (lit. *I did not say [it]*).

(*b*) the personal pronoun with γε:

ἔγωγε	*yes* (lit. *I at any rate [said it]*);
οὐκ ἔγωγε	*no.*

(*c*) by ναί *yes* and οὔ *no*; or by a phrase such as πάνυ μὲν οὖν *certainly*; οὐδαμῶς *certainly not.* This can take the form of an abbreviated question, e.g. πῶς γὰρ οὔ; *of course* (lit. *for how not?*); or of an oath (22.1/2h).

(*d*) a short clause such as ἀληθῆ λέγεις *you speak [the] truth* (lit. *true things*).

Sometimes one speaker in a conversation makes a comment on what the other speaker has said (which may or may not have been a question), and we must infer from his words whether he is agreeing or not:

A. σύ γ᾽ οὔπω σωφρονεῖν ἐπίστασαι.

A. *You do not yet know prudence* (lit. *how to be prudent*).

B. σὲ γὰρ προσηύδων οὐκ ἄν.

B. *[No], for I would not be speaking to you* (sc. *if I did*).

Other examples have already occurred at 13.3(ii) *l*.4 and 18.2.1.

24.1/2 Summary of uses of οὐ and μή

Both οὐ and μή are to be translated by *not*. Their uses, which involve distinctions which we do not make in English, can be classified as follows:

(*a*) In **main clauses**, οὐ is used as the negative in statements of fact and in suppositions (i.e. in the main clause of a category 1 conditional sentence (18.1/5) and in potential clauses (19.1/2)); μή is used in constructions expressing an order or desire, i.e. prohibitions (17.1/1), exhortations (14.1/4*a*(i)), and wishes (21.1/1). Also, οὐ is used in direct questions expecting the answer *yes,* μή in direct questions expecting the answer *no* (10.1/2*a*) and in deliberative questions (14.1/4*a*(ii)).

(*b*) When the verb of an **adverbial clause** is negated, μή is used in clauses of purpose (14.1/4*c*(i)), condition (18.1/5), and for indefinite adverbial clauses (14.1/4*c*(iii) and 21.1/2 note 4); elsewhere the negative is οὐ.

(*c*) When the verb of an **adjectival clause** is negated, μή is used if the clause has an indefinite or general sense whether the indefinite construction (14.1/4*c*(iii)) is used or not, e.g.

οὐ γὰρ ἃ πράττουϲιν οἱ δίκαιοι, ἀλλ᾽ ἃ μὴ πράττουϲι, ταῦτα λέγειϲ	*You are speaking not of those things which the just do, but [of those things] which they do not do.*

(*d*) οὐ is used to negate the verb of a **noun clause**, i.e. in indirect statements when expressed by a ὅτι/ὡϲ clause (8.1/3*b*), indirect questions (10.1/2*b*), and clauses following verbs of fearing (14.1/4*c*(ii)).

(*e*) **Infinitives** are always negated by μή, except in the infinitive construction for indirect statement after verbs of saying and thinking (8.1/3*a*).

(*f*) **Participles** are negated by οὐ except:
   (i) when used with the article to denote a general class (12.1/2*a*(vi)); this also applies to adjectives, e.g. οἱ μὴ ἀγαθοί *the [general class of] people who are not good,* but οἱ οὐκ ἀγαθοί *the [particular] people who are not good.*
   (ii) when used conditionally (12.1/2*a*(iv)).

(*g*) οὐ μή with the fut. ind. expresses a strong prohibition (17.1/1).

(*h*) οὐ μή with the aor. subj. expresses a strong denial:

> οὐ μὴ παύcωμαι φιλοcοφῶν. *I shall certainly not stop studying philosophy.*

(*i*) *Or not* as an alternative question in indirect speech is either ἢ οὔ or ἢ μή:

> ὑμῶν δέομαι cκοπεῖν εἰ *I ask you to examine whether I am*
> δίκαια λέγω ἢ μή (or ἢ οὔ) *speaking justly or not.*

24.1/3 Diminutives

Nouns can be modified by the addition of a suffix to indicate something smaller, e.g. *booklet* (<*book*), *islet* (< *isle*). The modified form is called a **diminutive**. Greek has a number of diminutive suffixes but the most common is –ιον, e.g. παιδίον *little child* (παῖc, stem παιδ–). All diminutives in –ιον (including those from proper names) are 2nd declension neuters, even when they denote living beings.

Very often diminutives are used to indicate affection and familiarity without any real connotation of smallness, e.g. πατρ–ίδιον *daddy* (< πατήρ with the suffix –ίδιον), Cωκρατίδιον *dear little/old Socrates.* Occasionally a diminutive has lost any special meaning and replaced the original noun, e.g. θηρίον *wild beast* (< θήρ, which has the same meaning but is used mainly in verse).

Diminutives were a feature of the colloquial language, and consequently are not found in literary genres written in an elevated style, such as tragedy. They are, however, very common in comedy, and in the dialogues of Plato, who aimed at reproducing the everyday speech of educated Athenians. An amusing example occurs in Aristophanes' *Clouds* where Strepsiades wakes his adult son by coaxing him with the diminutive of his name:

> πῶc δῆτ᾽ ἂν ἥδιcτ᾽ αὐτὸν *How could I wake him most*
> ἐπεγείραιμι; πῶc; Φειδιππίδη, *gently? How? Pheidippides,*
> Φειδιππίδιον. *dear little Pheidippides.*

24.1/4 Dual number

In addition to the singular and plural, Indo-European (1.3) also had a dual number, which was used for two persons or objects. In Homer it is still frequent, but in Attic Greek of the fifth and fourth centuries BC its use is generally confined to two persons or things closely associated or normally considered to form a pair, e.g. two brothers, sisters, hands, eyes, but even here it is optional. Its endings do not show anything like the same variety as either the singular or plural.

In **verbs** the same stems are used as elsewhere. There is **no** first person dual. In the second person the dual endings are identical for the primary and historic tenses but in the third person endings there is a distinction between primary and historic forms (cf. 4.1/1 note 1 and 8.1/1*f*) :

	ACTIVE		MIDDLE/PASSIVE	
	Primary	*Historic*	*Primary*	*Historic*
2	–τον	–τον	–cθον	–cθον
3	–τον	–την	–cθον	–cθην

In -ω verbs the link vowel (cf. 8.1/1*d*) is the same as in the singular and plural except that we have ε (not o/ε) in the present, imperfect and future. For λύω in the **indicative** we have:

		ACTIVE		MIDDLE/PASSIVE	
PRESENT	2	λύ–ετον *you two loosen*		λύ–εcθον	
	3	λύ–ετον *two (people) loosen*		λύ–εcθον	
FUTURE	2	λύc–ετον	mid.	λύc–εcθον	pass. λυθήc–εcθον
	3	λύc–ετον		λύc–εcθον	λυθήc–εcθον
IMPERFECT	2	ἐλύ–ετον		ἐλύ–εcθον	
	3	ἐλῡ–έτην		ἐλῡ–έcθην	
AORIST	2	ἐλύc–ατον	mid.	ἐλύc–αcθον	pass. ἐλύθη–τον
	3	ἐλῡc–άτην		ἐλῡc–άcθην	ἐλυθή–την
PERFECT	2	λελύκ–ατον		λέλυ–cθον	
	3	λελύκ–ατον		λέλυ–cθον	
PLUPERFECT	2	ἐλελύκ–ετον		ἐλέλυ–cθον	
	3	ἐλελυκ–έτην		ἐλελύ–cθην	

The **subjunctive** mood takes the primary endings (cf.14.1/2), giving for both second and third persons λύ–ητον (pres. act.) and λύ–ηcθον (pres. mid./pass.), etc. (the η represents the lengthening of ε in λύ–ε–τον, λύ–ε–cθον of the indicative).

The **optative** takes the historic endings (cf.14.1/3) with the same preceding diphthong as occurs in the singular and plural of the tenses which have an optative (i.e. οι/αι/ει), e.g. pres. act. 2 λῡ-οιτον, 3 λῡ-οίτην; aor. act. 2 λῦc-αιτον, 3 λῦc-αίτην; aor. pass. 2 λυθ-εῖτον, 3 λυθ-είτην.

The 2nd person dual of the **imperative** is the same as in the indicative. The 3rd person dual of the imperative is rare.

The dual endings for **nouns** and the dual forms of the **article** and **personal pronouns** are:

	NOUNS (Declension)			ARTICLE M.F.N.	PERSONAL PRONOUNS	
	1st	2nd	3rd			
N.V.A.	–ᾱ	–ω	–ε	τώ	νώ *we two*	cφώ *you two*
Gen. Dat.	–αιν	–οιν	–οιν	τοῖν	νῷν	cφῷν

The article has the same forms for all genders, and the demonstrative pronouns follow the same pattern (τούτω/τούτοιν from οὗτος; τώδε/τοῖνδε from ὅδε). In each declension **adjectives** (and αὐτός and participles) take the same endings as nouns.

Because the dual is not obligatory we often find dual and plural forms used indiscriminately:

δύο ἄνδρες προσελθόντε   *Two men came forward and* (lit.
Ἄγιδι διελεγέcθην   *having come forward) were*
                                                          talking with Agis (we might
                                                          have expected ἄνδρε instead of
                                                          δύο ἄνδρες).

24.1/5 Verbal adjectives in –τος/–τός and –τέος

(a) We have already met many verbal adjectives in –τος/–τός. Most have a prefix, in many cases the negative ἀ-/ἀν-, e.g. ἔμφυτος (ἐν + φυτος), ἄβατος (ἀ + βατος), but some have none, e.g. χυτός. They can be either:

   (i) the equivalent of a perfect passive participle, e.g. εὔγνωcτος *well-known,* ἔμφυτος *inborn,* χυτός *melted*
  (ii) the equivalent of a present participle active, e.g. ἀνόητος *stupid* (lit. *not perceiving*)
 (iii) an adjective denoting possibility, e.g. ἄβατος *impassable,* βιωτός *livable.*

Some can be either (i) or (iii), e.g. ἀόρᾱτος *unseen/invisible*.

(*b*) The verbal adjective in –τέος differs from the above in being considered a normal part of a verb, although, in its neuter singular form, it is given a separate listing in dictionaries. It is formed by replacing θη of the aorist passive stem with –τέος, e.g. φιλητέος (<φιλέω, aor. pass ἐφιλήθην), κελευστέος (<κελεύω, aor. pass. ἐκελεύσθην); and has the meaning of a present passive participle but with the added idea of necessity. The literal translation of φιλητέος εἰμί is *I am needing-to-be-loved*, i.e. *I must be loved*. The agent is expressed by the dative (23.1/2*g*), not by ὑπό + gen.:

ὁ ποταμὸς ἡμῖν ἐστι διαβατέος.	*The river is needing-to-be-* *crossed-over by us*, i.e. *we must* *cross over the river.*
ἐκείνη coι οὐ φιλητέᾱ.	*That woman [is] not needing-to-* *be-loved by you*, i.e. *you must* *not love that woman.*

The neuter singular (and occasionally the neuter plural) of the verbal adjective can be used **impersonally**: διαβατέον ἡμῖν ἐστιν *it is needing-to-be-crossed-over (there must be a crossing over) by us*, i.e. *we must cross over*. The verbal adjective of a transitive verb can, when used impersonally, take an object: τὸν ποταμὸν ἡμῖν ἐστι διαβατέον *it is needing-to-be-crossed-over the river (there must be a crossing over the river) by us*, i.e. *we must cross over the river.* There is no difference in meaning between ὁ ποταμός ἐστι διαβατέος and τὸν ποταμόν ἐστι διαβατέον.

Sometimes a literal translation of an impersonal verbal adjective is impossible:

τῷ ἀδικοῦντι δοτέον ἐστὶ δίκην	*The [person] doing wrong must* *pay the penalty* (the closest translation is *there must-be-a-* *paying of the penalty* ...).

The neuter plural of the verbal adjective has exactly the same meaning. We may equally well have τὸν ποταμόν ἐστι διαβατέα or τὸν ποταμόν ἐστι διαβατέον.

24.1/6 Verbs of precaution and striving

When these verbs, which include ἐπιμελέομαι, εὐλαβέομαι both *take care*, cπουδάζω *be eager/busy*, cκοπέω *consider, take heed*, are followed by a clause (*take care that ..., be eager that ...,* etc.), this is expressed by ὅπωc with the future indicative. The future indicative is retained even after main verbs in a historic tense. The ὅπωc clause is negated by μή:

ὅπωc ἀμυνούμεθα, οὐδεὶc παραcκευάζεται οὐδὲ ἐπιμελεῖται.	*No-one is making preparations or taking care that we should defend ourselves.*
δεῖ cκοπεῖν ὅπωc τὰ παρόντ᾽ ἐπανορθωθήcεται.	*We must take heed that the present state of affairs be remedied.*
ἐcκόπουν ὅπωc αὐτὸc ἀπολυθήcομαι τῆc ἐγγύηc.	*I was taking heed that I myself be freed from the pledge.*

Less often ὅπωc is followed by the subjunctive or optative, as in purpose clauses (14.1/4*c*(i)):

οὐ φυλάξεcθε ὅπωc μὴ δεcπότην εὕρητε;	*Will you not be on your guard that you do not find a master?*
ἐπεμελεῖτο ὁ Κῦροc ὅπωc μήποτε οἱ cτρατιῶται ἀνίδρωτοι γενόμενοι ἐπὶ τὸ ἄριcτον εἰcίοιεν.	*Cyrus took care that the soldiers should never come to breakfast without working up a sweat* (lit. *being without a sweat*).

Note

Sometimes a main verb in the imperative such as cκόπει/cκοπεῖτε *see to it* is omitted and we are left with nothing but ὅπωc and the future indicative:

ὅπωc ἔcεcθε ἄνδρεc ἄξιοι τῆc ἐλευθερίᾱc.	*[See to it] that you show yourselves* (lit. *will be*) *men worthy of freedom!*

24.1/7 Verbs of hindering, preventing, forbidding, denying

In English, verbs with these and similar meanings take various constructions (*I prevented him from entering, we forbid you to do this*). In Greek they are always followed by an infinitive which is accompanied by the negative μή; the latter is redundant from an English point of view:

εἴργω ὑμᾶϲ μὴ μάχεϲθαι *I hinder you from fighting*; ἀπαγορεύομεν αὐτὸν μὴ οἰκοδομεῖν *we forbid him to build*. When the main verb is itself negated, the infinitive is accompanied by a double redundant negative μὴ οὐ: οὐκ εἴργω ὑμᾶϲ μὴ οὐ μάχεϲθαι *I do not hinder you from fighting*. However, κωλύω *prevent* is usually followed by a simple infinitive without μή or μὴ οὐ: κωλύω αὐτὸν ἱππεύειν *I prevent him from riding*; οὐ κωλύω αὐτὸν βαδίζειν *I do not prevent him from walking*.

24.2 Greek reading

1 *In addition to translating, explain each use of a negative:*
(*i*)# ὁ μηδὲν εἰδὼϲ οὐδὲν ἐξαμαρτάνει. (*ii*) μηδένα φίλον ποιοῦ πρὶν ἂν ἐξετάϲῃϲ πῶϲ κέχρηται τοῖϲ πρότερον φίλοιϲ. (*iii*) πᾶν ποιοῦϲιν ὥϲτε μὴ δοῦναι δίκην. (*iv*) οὐδὲν ἐπράχθη διὰ τὸ μὴ τὸν ἄρχοντα παρεῖναι. (*v*) οὐκ οἶδα πότερον πορευθῶ ἢ μή. (*vi*) δέδοικα μὴ οὐχ ἱκανοὺϲ ἔχω οἷϲ τὸν χρυϲὸν δῶ. (*vii*) θάρρει, ὦ Κῦρε, οὐ μή ϲε κρύψω πρὸϲ ὅντινα βούλομαι ἀφικέϲθαι. (*viii*) οἱ δ' ἔφαϲαν ἀποδώϲειν τοὺϲ νεκροὺϲ ἐφ' ᾧ μὴ καίειν τὰϲ κώμαϲ. (*ix*)# τὸ μὴ δίκαιον ἔργον οὐ λήθει θεούϲ. (*x*) τί ἐμποδὼν μὴ οὐκ ἀποθανεῖν αὐτούϲ; (*xi*) φίλοϲ ἐβούλετο εἶναι τοῖϲ μέγιϲτα δυναμένοιϲ ἵνα ἀδικῶν μὴ διδοίη δίκην. (*xii*)# εἰ μὴ καθέξειϲ γλῶτταν, ἔϲται ϲοι κακά. (*xiii*)# οὐκ ἂν δύναιο μὴ καμὼν εὐδαιμονεῖν. (*xiv*)# οὐ μὴ δυϲμενὴϲ ἔϲει φίλοιϲ. (*xv*) εἰπὼν ἃ θέλειϲ, ἀντάκου' ἃ μὴ θέλειϲ. (*xvi*) ἢ δεῖ χελώνηϲ κρέα φαγεῖν ἢ μὴ φαγεῖν. (*xvii*) δύναϲαί μοι λέγειν εἰ διδακτὸν ἡ ἀρετὴ ἢ οὔ; (*xviii*) οὐδεὶϲ ἀπαρνήϲεται μὴ οὐχὶ ἐπίϲταϲθαι τὰ δίκαια. (*xix*) ἐφοβεῖτο μὴ οὐ δύναιτο ἐκ τῆϲ χώραϲ ἐξελθεῖν. (*xx*) μὴ ἀπέλθητε πρὶν ἂν ἀκούϲητε.

2 θεραπευτέον τοὺϲ θεούϲ, τοὺϲ φίλουϲ εὐεργετητέον, τὴν πόλιν ὠφελητέον, τὴν Ἑλλάδα πειρατέον εὖ ποιεῖν, τὴν γῆν θεραπευτέον, τῶν βοϲκημάτων ἐπιμελητέον, τὰϲ πολεμικὰϲ τέχναϲ μαθητέον.

3# ὁ φόβοϲ, ὅταν τιϲ αἵματοϲ μέλλῃ πέρι
λέγειν καταϲτὰϲ εἰϲ ἀγῶν' ἐναντίον,
τό τε ϲτόμ' εἰϲ ἔκπληξιν ἀνθρώπων ἄγει
τὸν νοῦν τ' ἀπείργει μὴ λέγειν ἃ βούλεται.

4 ὑμᾶϲ εὐλαβεῖϲθαι δεῖ ὅπωϲ μηδὲν ὧν ἰδίᾳ φυλάξαιϲθ' ἄν, τοῦτο δημοϲίᾳ ποιοῦντεϲ φανήϲεϲθε.

5   οὗτοι πάντες οἱ νόμοι κεῖνται πολὺν ἤδη χρόνον, ὦ ἄνδρες
    δικασταί, καὶ οὐδεὶς πώποτ' ἀντεῖπεν μὴ οὐ καλῶς ἔξειν αὐτούς.
6   εὐλαβοῦ μὴ φανῇς κακὸς γεγώς.
7   Socrates tells of an encounter with two sophists whom he has
    previously met (sophists were teachers who travelled about from
    one Greek city to another).

    ἠσπαζόμην οὖν αὐτῷ ἅτε διὰ χρόνου ἑωρακώς· μετὰ δὲ τοῦτο
    εἶπον πρὸς τὸν Κλεινίαν· ὦ Κλεινία, τώδε μέντοι τὼ ἄνδρε σοφώ,
    Εὐθύδημός τε καὶ Διονυσόδωρος, οὐ τὰ σμικρὰ ἀλλὰ τὰ μεγάλα·
    τὰ γὰρ περὶ τὸν πόλεμον ἐπίστασθον.
    εἰπὼν οὖν ταῦτα κατεφρονήθην ὑπ' αὐτοῖν· ἐγελασάτην οὖν ἄμφω 5
    βλέψαντε εἰς ἀλλήλω, καὶ ὁ Εὐθύδημος εἶπεν· οὗτοι ἔτι ταῦτα,
    ὦ Σώκρατες, σπουδάζομεν, ἀλλὰ παρέργοις αὐτοῖς χρώμεθα.
    κἀγὼ θαυμάσας εἶπον· καλὸν ἄν που τὸ ἔργον ὑμῶν εἴη, εἰ
    τηλικαῦτα πράγματα πάρεργα ὑμῖν τυγχάνει ὄντα, καὶ πρὸς θεῶν
    εἴπετόν μοι τί ἐστι τοῦτο τὸ καλόν;   10
    ἀρετήν, ἔφη, ὦ Σώκρατες, οἰόμεθα οἵω τ' εἶναι παραδοῦναι
    κάλλιστ' ἀνθρώπων καὶ τάχιστα.
    ὦ Ζεῦ, οἷον, ἦν δ' ἐγώ, λέγετον πρᾶγμα· πόθεν τοῦτο τὸ ἕρμαιον
    ηὕρετον; ἐγὼ δὲ περὶ ὑμῶν διενοούμην ἔτι, ὥσπερ νυνδὴ ἔλεγον,
    ὡς τὸ πολὺ τοῦτο δεινοῖν ὄντοιν, ἐν ὅπλοις μάχεσθαι, καὶ ταῦτα 15
    ἔλεγον περὶ σφῶν· ὅτε γὰρ τὸ πρότερον ἐπεδημήσατον, τοῦτο
    μέμνημαι σφὼ ἐπαγγελλομένω.
8   μετὰ τοῦτον Ξενοφῶν εἶπεν· ἐγὼ δ' οὕτω γιγνώσκω. εἰ μὲν ἀνάγκη
    μάχεσθαι, τοῦτο δεῖ παρασκευάσασθαι ὅπως ὡς κράτιστα
    μαχούμεθα. εἰ δὲ βουλόμεθα ὡς ρᾷστα ὑπερβάλλειν, τοῦτό μοι
    δοκεῖ σκεπτέον εἶναι ὅπως ὡς ἐλάχιστα μὲν τραύματα λάβωμεν,
    ὡς ἐλάχιστα δὲ σώματα ἀποβάλωμεν.
9   σκεπτέον πότερον δίκαιον ἐμὲ ἐνθένδε πειρᾶσθαι ἐξιέναι μὴ
    ἀφιέντων Ἀθηναίων ἢ οὐ δίκαιον.
10 Α. εἰπέ μοι, ἔστι σοι ἀγρός ; Β. οὐκ ἔμοιγε.
11 καὶ μὴν εἰ ὑφησόμεθα καὶ ἐπὶ βασιλεῖ γενησόμεθα, τί οἰόμεθα
    πείσεσθαι; ὃς καὶ τοῦ ὁμομητρίου ἀδελφοῦ καὶ τεθνηκότος ἤδη
    ἀποτεμὼν τὴν κεφαλὴν καὶ τὴν χεῖρα ἀνεσταύρωσεν· ἡμᾶς δέ, οἷς
    κηδεμὼν μὲν οὐδεὶς πάρεστιν, ἐστρατεύσαμεν δὲ ἐπ' αὐτὸν ὡς
    δοῦλον ἀντὶ βασιλέως ποιήσοντες καὶ ἀποκτενοῦντες εἰ 5
    δυναίμεθα, τί ἂν οἰόμεθα παθεῖν; ἆρ' οὐκ ἂν ἐπὶ πᾶν ἔλθοι ὡς
    ἡμᾶς τὰ ἔσχατα αἰκισάμενος πᾶσιν ἀνθρώποις φόβον παράσχῃ

τοῦ στρατεῦσαί ποτε ἐπ' αὐτόν; ἀλλ' ὅπως τοι μὴ ἐπ' ἐκείνῳ γενησόμεθα πάντα ποιητέον.

Notes

1 (*i*) οὐδέν adverbial acc. (20.1/5). (*ii*) ποιοῦ 2nd s. pres. imp. mid.; κέχρηται < χράομαι; πρότερον here an adverb (cf. οἱ νῦν, 5.1/3) but trans. by an adjective. (*v*) πορευθῶ (aor. subj. of πορεύομαι) deliberative subj. (14.1/4*a*(ii)) in indirect speech (cf. δῶ in (*vi*)). (*vii*) θάρρει (< θάρρε–ε) pres. imp.; κρύψω is here aor. subj. (24.1/2*h*). (*viii*) ἐφ' ᾧ 16.1/1 note 4. (*x*) ἐμποδών *sc.* ἐστί; because the construction appropriate after a negated verb of hindering, preventing etc. (μὴ οὐ) is used here, we know that the question expects the answer *nothing* and so counts as a virtual negation. (*xi*) μέγιστα adverb (17.1/2). (*xii*) καθέξεις < κατέχω. (*xiv*) οὐ μή + fut. ind., 17.1/1. (*xv*) ἀντάκου'(ε) imp. (*xvi*) κρέᾱ acc. pl. of κρέας (13.1/1*b*(iii)).

2 ἐστί is very often omitted with verbal adjectives and must be supplied with each example here.

3 A murder trial is being described. *l.*1 ὁ φόβος is the subject of ἄγει (*l.*3); take πέρι with αἵματος (see note on 11.2.4 *l.*1). *l.*2 καταστάς intr. aor. pple. of καθίστημι. *ll.*3f. Take ἀνθρώπων with στόμ'(α) and νοῦν.

4 ὅπως ... φανήσεσθε (2nd pl. fut. pass. of φαίνω) see 24.1/6; φυλάξαισθ'(ε) ἄν potential optative (19.1/2).

5 κεῖνται is used here as the perf. pass of τίθημι (18.1/2 note 4); ἕξειν fut. act. inf. of ἔχω.

6 μή = ὅπως μή.

7 The passage has many dual forms (24.1/4). *l.*1 ἑωρᾱκώς perf. act. pple. of ὁράω. *l.*2 μέντοι emphatic, not adversative (13.1/3*c*(v)). *l.*3 τὰ σμῑκρά ... τὰ μεγάλα acc. of respect with σοφώ in *l.*2 (20.1/5). *l.*7 παρέργοις here predicative with αὐτοῖς, *them* (αὐτοῖς)*[as] subordinate issues. *l.*8 θαυμάσᾱς coincidental use of the aor. pple. (12.1/1), *marvelling*; ἄν ... εἴη potential opt. (19.1/2), lit. *would be*, but trans. *must be*. *l.*10 εἵπετον 2nd dual aor. imp. act. *l.*12 κάλλιστ'(α) ἀνθρώπων καὶ τάχιστα lit. *most excellently and speedily of men*, i.e. *as excellently and speedily as is humanly possible. l.*13 οἷον exclamatory (21.1/3); ἦν δ' ἐγώ *said I* (18.1.1*a*). *l.*15 ὡς τὸ πολύ (= ὡς ἐπὶ τὸ πολύ) *for the most part*, 22.1/1*a*(vii); τοῦτο (acc. of

respect with δεινοῖν (20.1/5)) anticipates ἐν ... μάχεσθαι; δεινοῖν ὄντοιν agrees with ὑμῶν in *l.*14, although the latter is plural, not dual (note that Socrates somewhat illogically goes on to use the dual pronoun cφῶν).

8 οὕτω anticipates the following sentence, lit. *I think* (γιγνώcκω) *thus;* each τοῦτο anticipates the ὅπως clause which follows it and need not be translated; ὡc + supl. 17.1/4*d.*

9 Supply ἐcτί with both cκεπτέον (see note on 2 above) and δίκαιον; ἀφτέντων gen. pl. of the pres. act. pple. of ἀφτῆμι.

10 ἔμοιγε 24.1/1*b.*

11 *ll.*1f. καὶ μήν *and further;* ὑφηcόμεθα fut. mid. of ὑφτῆμι; τί etc. *what do we think we shall suffer* (cf. 8.1/3*a*); ὅc lit. *who* (the antecedent is βαcιλεῖ) but trans. *he* (the relative pronoun is often used to join a sentence with what precedes); καί (before τοῦ and before τεθνηκότος) *even,* but trans. the second by *and that too* for variety; take ἤδη with τεθνηκότος. *ll.*3ff. ἡμᾶc is the subject of παθεῖν in *l.*6; οἷc ... πάρεcτιν lit. *for whom there is no protector at hand;* before ἐcτρατεύcαμεν we must supply the relative οἵ from the preceding οἷc, and the two adjectival clauses can be translated *who have no protector at hand but* (δέ) *who campaigned against him* (ἐπ᾽ αὐτόν); ὡc + fut. pple. (12.1/2*a*(v)); εἰ δυναίμεθα indefinite construction in historic sequence (14.1/4*c*(iii)), lit. *if ever we could;* ἄν ... παθεῖν represents ἄν πάθοιμεν in direct speech (potential opt., 19.1/2), and the subject of the infinitive (ἡμᾶc in *l.*3) is, quite irregularly, inserted in the acc. although it is the same as the subject of οἰόμεθα – trans. *what do we think we would suffer. ll.*6ff. ἆρ᾽ οὐκ (10.1/2*a*); ἐπὶ πᾶν lit. *to everything,* i.e. *to any lengths;* ὡc introduces a purpose clause (22.1/1*b*(ii)); τὰ ἔcχατα acc. of respect (20.1/5), lit. *in respect of the worst things,* i.e. *in the worst [possible] ways;* take τοῦ cτρατεῦcαι ... as objective gen. (23.1/1*c*) with φόβον, *fear of campaigning;* the clause ὅπως ... γενηcόμεθα is governed by ποιητέον (ἐcτίν) – ὅπως + fut. is used to express purpose (the normal construction with ὅπως in this context would be the subjunctive, 14.14*c*(i)).

24.3 Extra reading

The Think Tank

Old Comedy is the term given to the form of comic drama which flourished in Athens during the fifth century BC. Two of its main characteristics, comic situations and unbridled criticism of contemporaries, can be seen in the following passage from Aristophanes' *Clouds,* which was a stinging attack on Socrates and what were popularly supposed to be his intellectual interests. In this scene Strepsiades, a stupid and uneducated Athenian of the older generation, has just gained admittance to Socrates' Φροντιστήριον (*Think Tank*) in order to improve himself.

ΣΤΡΕΨΙΑΔΗΣ – ΜΑΘΗΤΗΣ

CT. πρὸς τῶν θεῶν, τί γὰρ τάδ' ἐστί; εἰπέ μοι.

MA. ἀστρονομία μὲν αὐτηί. CT. τουτὶ δὲ τί;

MA. γεωμετρία. CT. τοῦτ' οὖν τί ἐστι χρήσιμον;

MA. γῆν ἀναμετρεῖσθαι. CT. πότερα τὴν κληρουχικήν;

MA. οὔκ, ἀλλὰ τὴν σύμπασαν. CT. ἀστεῖον λέγεις.   5
     τὸ γὰρ σόφισμα δημοτικὸν καὶ χρήσιμον.

MA. αὕτη δέ σοι γῆς περίοδος πάσης. ὁρᾷς;
     αἵδε μὲν 'Αθῆναι. CT. τί σὺ λέγεις; οὐ πείθομαι,
     ἐπεὶ δικαστὰς οὐχ ὁρῶ καθημένους.

MA. ὡς τοῦτ' ἀληθῶς 'Αττικὸν τὸ χωρίον.   10

CT. φέρε τίς γὰρ οὗτος οὑπὶ τῆς κρεμάθρας ἀνήρ;

MA. αὐτός. CT. τίς αὐτός; MA. Σωκράτης. CT. ὦ Σωκράτης.
     ἴθ' οὗτος, ἀναβόησον αὐτόν μοι μέγα.

MA. αὐτὸς μὲν οὖν σὺ κάλεσον· οὐ γάρ μοι σχολή.

CT. ὦ Σώκρατες,
     ὦ Σωκρατίδιον.

ΣΩΚΡΑΤΗΣ

                 τί με καλεῖς, ὦ 'φήμερε;   15

CT. πρῶτον μὲν ὅτι δρᾷς, ἀντιβολῶ, κάτειπέ μοι.

ΣΩ. ἀεροβατῶ καὶ περιφρονῶ τὸν ἥλιον.

CT. ἔπειτ' ἀπὸ ταρροῦ τοὺς θεοὺς ὑπερφρονεῖς,
     ἀλλ' οὐκ ἀπὸ τῆς γῆς, εἴπερ; ΣΩ. οὐ γὰρ ἄν ποτε
     ἐξηῦρον ὀρθῶς τὰ μετέωρα πράγματα,   20
     εἰ μὴ κρεμάσας τὸ νόημα καὶ τὴν φροντίδα.

Notes

The Φροντιστήριον of Aristophanes' play (he seems to have coined the word himself) was a school where various sciences were both investigated and taught. In the opening lines a pupil shows Strepsiades pieces of equipment, which, for humorous effect, are given the names of the sciences (astronomy and geometry) for which they are used. *l.*1 γάρ explains why Strepsiades has used the exclamation πρὸς τῶν θεῶν (*in the name of the gods*) but should not be translated. *l.*2 αὑτηΐ, τουτΐ emphatic forms of αὕτη, τοῦτο with the suffix ΐ, before which a final short vowel is dropped. *l.*3 οὖν *well, so*; τί lit. *in what respect. l.*4 When the pupil replies that the purpose of geometry is to measure land, Strepsiades, who is unable to rise above self-interested parochialism, asks if the land involved is for κλῆροι, which were allotments of foreign land confiscated by the state and given to poorer Athenian citizens. The term for this allocation was κληρουχίᾱ *cleruchy.* πότερα introduces alternative questions (10.1/2*a*) but the second, ἢ οὔ *or not,* is omitted; κληρουχικήν sc. γῆν *land for cleruchies. ll.*5f. Strepsiades finds the idea of measuring the whole earth attractive because he supposes that this would mean distributing it to needy Athenians. *l.*7 coi ethic dat. (23.1/2*f*). *l.*9 Large juries were a prominent feature of the Athenian legal system, which was often the butt of Aristophanes' humour. *l.*10 A main clause meaning *I assure you* must be supplied. *l.*11 At this point Socrates appears overhead suspended from the end of a crane (see note on *l.*18); φέρε 17.1/1 note 7; οὑπί = ὁ ἐπί. *l.*12 αὐτός was used to mean *the master* (cf. Irish use of *himself*); ὦ Cωκράτης (nom. **not** voc.) an exclamation *Ah, [it's] Socrates. l.*13 ἴθ'(ι) 2nd s. pres. imp. of ἔρχομαι (18.1/3); οὗτος *you there!* (see note on 20.2.12 *l.*4). *l.*15 Cωκρατίδιον 24.1/3; ὦ 'φήμερε i.e. ὦ ἐφ– (initial elision of this type (prodelision) is poetical). *l.*16 ὅτι indirect form of τί, 10.1/2*b* note 1. *ll.*17f. Socrates, who is comically represented as some sort of divine being, says he is thinking about (περιφρονῶ) the sun but Strepsiades perversely takes περιφρονῶ in its other meaning *despise* and replies with the unequivocal ὑπερφρονεῖς; ἀπὸ ταρροῦ *from your mat* although Strepsiades speaks of a basket in *l.*11 – Socrates is apparently sitting on a mat which is suspended at each corner from the gib of the crane and so resembles a basket. *l.*19 ἀλλ'(ά) trans. *and* as there is no strong contrast; εἴπερ *if indeed [that's what you're really doing]* Strepsiades expresses himself cautiously because he cannot understand what Socrates is up to; οὐ γὰρ ἄν ... lit. *for I would not* ... i.e. *yes, for I would not* ... (24.1/1). *l.*21 εἰ μὴ κρεμάcᾱc *except by* (lit. *if not*) *suspending* (εἰ is here followed by a phrase, not a clause).

25 UNIT TWENTY-FIVE

25.1 Grammar

25.1/1 Homeric Greek

The language of the *Iliad* and *Odyssey* is an older version of Ionic (1.3) with elements from other dialects. It differs to some extent from Attic in **phonology** (the individual sounds of words), **morphology** (the different forms which some words can take), and **syntax** (grammatical constructions and uses). Listed below are the main differences which occur in the passages in 25.2, together with examples from them.

A good introduction to Homer is G.S. Kirk *Homer and the Epic* (Cambridge U.P.).

25.1/2 Differences in phonology and morphology

(*a*) *Vowels and diphthongs*

(i) Contraction is not always observed, e.g. αἰδέομαι (1 *l.*3 in 25.2).

(ii) ᾱ becomes η after ε, ι and ρ, e.g. κρατερή (1 *l.*19).

(iii) Diphthongs are sometimes broken up into two vowels, e.g. ἐϋμμελίω (1 *l.*10, = εὐ–); χήτεϊ (1 *l.*24, = χήτει).

(iv) Homeric Greek sometimes has cc where the Attic has c, e.g. ὅccον (1 *l.*15)

(*b*) *Case endings*

(i) –εω, –ω (= Attic –ου) for the gen. s. of first declension masculines, e.g. ἐϋμμελίω (1 *l.*10).

(ii) –οιο (= Attic –ου) for the gen. s. of the second declension, e.g. πολέμοιο (1 *l.*4).

(iii) –άων (= Attic –ῶν) for the gen. pl. of the first declension, e.g. ῥοάων (2 *l.*8).

(iv) –εccι (= Attic –cι) for the dat. pl. of some third declension nouns, e.g. Τρώεccι (1 *l.*6).

(v) –ῃcι (= Attic –αιc) for the dat. pl. of the first declension, e.g. κονίῃcι (1 *l.*14)

(vi) πολύc has an irregular nom. pl. m. πολέεc (1 *l.*13).

(vii) The gen. s. of cύ is ceῦ (1 *l.*15).

(c) *Verbal endings*

(i) –ῃcι(ν) (= Attic –ῃ) for the 3rd s. subj. act., e.g. εἴπῃcιν (1 *l.*20).

(ii) –ατο (= Attic –ντο) for the 3rd pl. mid. and pass. of certain tenses (cf. 16.1/3 note), e.g. ἥατο (2 *l.*2).

(iii) –εν (= Attic –ηcαν) for the 3rd pl. of the aor. ind. pass. and root aorists in –ην, e.g. ἔφανεν (2 *l.*5).

(iv) –έμεν (= Attic –ειν) for the pres. (and strong aor.) inf. act., e.g. μενέμεν (4 *l.*16).

(v) The pres. inf. of εἰμί is ἔμμεναι (1 *l.* 5), not εἶναι.

(d) *Verbal stems*

(i) The augment is frequently omitted, e.g. μάθον (1 *l.*5, = ἔμαθον).

(ii) The aor. ind. stem of εἶπον (< λέγω) is given a syllabic augment, προcέειπε (1 *l.*1, = προcεῖπε).

(iii) The pres. pple. of εἰμί is ἐών, ἐοῦcα, ἐόν (see 1 *l.*17)

(e) A few words have a different form, e.g. αἰ (1 *l.*4, = εἰ *if*); ἦμαρ (1 *l.*9, = ἡμέρα).

25.1/3 Differences in syntax

(a) What became the definite article in Attic is a third person pronoun in Homer, e.g. τήν (1 *l.*1) *her* (= αὐτήν). A relic of this use survives in Attic in the idiom οἱ μὲν ... οἱ δέ (5.1/3).

(b) The future tense exists in Homer (e.g. ἔccεται 1 *l.*9), but the future can also be expressed by the subjunctive with or without ἄν or κε (an equivalent of ἄν which Homer often uses), e.g. κεν ... ἄγηται (1 *ll.*15f.) *will lead*; ἄν ὀλώλῃ (1 *l.*9) *will be destroyed* (the perfect expresses a future state, lit. *will be in a state of having perished*); εἴπῃcιν (1 *l.*20) *will say*. Further, the optative with ἄν (or κε) does not always have a strong future potential sense as in Attic, and is sometimes to be translated by a simple future, e.g. κεν ... ὑφαίνοις *you will weave* (1 *l.*17).

25.2 Readings from Homer

The Attic equivalent of certain Homeric words and endings is given in the right-hand margin. The Homeric forms so explained (e.g. τρή,1 *l.*9) are not listed separately in the vocabulary.

The Homeric poems are written in hexameters (**Appendix 9**).

1 Hector talks with his wife Andromache

τὴν δ᾽ αὖτε <u>προσέειπε</u> μέγας κορυθαίολος Ἕκτωρ·	–εῖπε
ἦ καὶ ἐμοὶ τάδε πάντα μέλει, γύναι· ἀλλὰ μάλ᾽ αἰνῶς	
αἰδέομαι Τρῶας καὶ Τρῳάδας ἑλκεσιπέπλους,	
αἴ κε κακὸς ὣς νόσφιν ἀλυσκάζω <u>πολέμοιο</u>·	–ου
οὐδέ με θυμὸς ἄνωγεν, ἐπεὶ <u>μάθον</u> <u>ἔμμεναι</u> ἐσθλὸς 5	ἔμαθον, εἶναι
αἰεὶ καὶ πρώτοισι μετὰ <u>Τρώεσσι</u> μάχεσθαι,	Τρωσί
ἀρνύμενος πατρός τε μέγα κλέος ἠδ᾽ ἐμὸν αὐτοῦ.	
εὖ γὰρ ἐγὼ τόδε οἶδα κατὰ φρένα καὶ κατὰ θυμόν·	
<u>ἔσσεται</u> ἦμαρ ὅτ᾽ ἄν ποτ᾽ ὀλώλῃ Ἴλιος <u>ἱρὴ</u>	ἔσται, ἱερή (= –ᾱ)
καὶ Πρίαμος καὶ λαὸς ἐϋμμελίω <u>Πριάμοιο</u>. 10	–ίου, –ου
ἀλλ᾽ οὔ μοι Τρώων <u>τόσσον</u> μέλει ἄλγος <u>ὀπίσσω</u>,	τόσον, ὀπίσω
οὔτ᾽ αὐτῆς Ἑκάβης οὔτε <u>Πριάμοιο</u> ἄνακτος	–ου
οὔτε κασιγνήτων, οἵ κεν <u>πολέες</u> τε καὶ ἐσθλοὶ	πολλοί
ἐν κονίῃσι πέσοιεν ὑπ᾽ ἀνδράσι <u>δυσμενέεσσιν</u>,	–ίαις, δυσμενέσιν
<u>ὅσσον</u> <u>σεῦ</u>, ὅτε κέν τις Ἀχαιῶν χαλκοχιτώνων 15	ὅσον, σοῦ
δακρυόεσσαν ἄγηται, ἐλεύθερον ἦμαρ ἀπούρας·	
καί κεν ἐν Ἄργει <u>ἐοῦσα</u> πρὸς ἄλλης ἱστὸν ὑφαίνοις,	οὖσα
καί κεν ὕδωρ <u>φορέοις</u> Μεσσηΐδος ἢ Ὑπερείης	φοροίης (= φέροις)
πόλλ᾽ ἀεκαζομένη, κρατερὴ δ᾽ ἐπικείσετ᾽ ἀνάγκη.	
καί ποτέ τις <u>εἴπῃσιν</u> ἰδὼν κατὰ δάκρυ χέουσαν· 20	εἴπῃ
Ἕκτορος ἥδε γυνή, ὃς ἀριστεύεσκε μάχεσθαι	
Τρώων ἱπποδάμων, ὅτε Ἴλιον <u>ἀμφιμάχοντο</u>.	ἀμφεμάχοντο
ὣς ποτέ τις <u>ἐρέει</u>· σοὶ δ᾽ αὖ νέον <u>ἔσσεται</u> ἄλγος	ἐρεῖ, ἔσται
χήτεϊ τοιοῦδ᾽ ἀνδρὸς ἀμύνειν δούλιον ἦμαρ.	
ἀλλά με <u>τεθνηῶτα</u> χυτὴ κατὰ γαῖα καλύπτοι, 25	τεθνεῶτα
πρίν γέ τι σῆς τε βοῆς σοῦ θ᾽ <u>ἑλκηθμοῖο</u> πυθέσθαι.	–ου

2 The Trojans camp on the the plain outside Troy

οἱ δὲ μέγα φρονέοντες ἐπὶ πτολέμοιο γεφύρας   –οῦντες, πολέμου
ἥατο παννύχιοι, πυρὰ δέ σφισι καίετο πολλά.   ἧντο, ἑκαίετο
ὡς δ' ὅτ' ἐν οὐρανῷ ἄστρα φαεινὴν ἀμφὶ σελήνην
φαίνετ' ἀριπρεπέα, ὅτε τ' ἔπλετο νήνεμος αἰθήρ·   –ῇ
ἔκ τ' ἔφανεν πᾶσαι σκοπιαὶ καὶ πρώονες ἄκροι   5   ἐφάνησαν
καὶ νάπαι· οὐρανόθεν δ' ἄρ' ὑπερράγη ἄσπετος αἰθήρ,
πάντα δὲ εἴδεται ἄστρα, γέγηθε δέ τε φρένα ποιμήν·
τόσσα μεσηγὺ νεῶν ἠδὲ Ξάνθοιο ῥοάων   τόσα, –ου, ῥοῶν
Τρώων καιόντων πυρὰ φαίνετο Ἰλιόθι πρό.   ἐφαίνετο, Ἰλίου
χίλι' ἄρ' ἐν πεδίῳ πυρὰ καίετο, πὰρ δὲ ἑκάστῳ   10   ἐκαίετο, παρά
ἥατο πεντήκοντα σέλᾳ πυρὸς αἰθομένοιο.   ἧντο, –ου
ἵπποι δὲ κρῖ λευκὸν ἐρεπτόμενοι καὶ ὀλύρας
ἑσταότες παρ' ὄχεσφιν ἐΰθρονον Ἠῶ μίμνον.   ἑστῶτες, ὄχεσιν,
     ἔμιμνον

3 The beginning of the Odyssey

ἄνδρα μοι ἔννεπε, Μοῦσα, πολύτροπον, ὃς μάλα πολλὰ
πλάγχθη, ἐπεὶ Τροίης ἱερὸν πτολίεθρον ἔπερσε·   ἐπλάγχθη, –ᾶς
πολλῶν δ' ἀνθρώπων ἴδεν ἄστεα καὶ νόον ἔγνω,   εἶδεν, ἄστη, νοῦν
πολλὰ δ' ὅ γ' ἐν πόντῳ πάθεν ἄλγεα ὃν κατὰ θυμόν,   ἔπαθεν, ἄλγη
ἀρνύμενος ἥν τε ψυχὴν καὶ νόστον ἑταίρων.   5
ἀλλ' οὐδ' ὣς ἑτάρους ἐρρύσατο, ἱέμενός περ·   καίπερ
αὐτῶν γὰρ σφετέρῃσιν ἀτασθαλίῃσιν ὄλοντο,   –αις, –αις, ὤλοντο
νήπιοι, οἳ κατὰ βοῦς Ὑπερίονος Ἠελίοιο   Ἡλίου
ἤσθιον· αὐτὰρ ὁ τοῖσιν ἀφείλετο νόστιμον ἦμαρ.

4 The Lotus-eaters

ἔνθεν δ' ἐννῆμαρ φερόμην ὀλοοῖς ἀνέμοισι   ἐφερόμην
πόντον ἐπ' ἰχθυόεντα· ἀτὰρ δεκάτῃ ἐπέβημεν
γαίης Λωτοφάγων, οἵ τ' ἄνθινον εἶδαρ ἔδουσιν.   γῆς
ἔνθα δ' ἐπ' ἠπείρου βῆμεν καὶ ἀφυσσάμεθ' ὕδωρ,   ἔβημεν, ἠφυσάμεθα
αἶψα δὲ δεῖπνον ἕλοντο θοῇς παρὰ νηυσὶν ἑταῖροι.   5   εἵλοντο, –αις,
     ναυσίν
αὐτὰρ ἐπεὶ σίτοιό τ' ἐπασσάμεθ' ἠδὲ ποτῆτος,   –ου, ἐπασάμεθα
δὴ τότ' ἐγὼν ἑτάρους προΐειν πεύθεσθαι ἰόντας
οἵτινες ἀνέρες εἶεν ἐπὶ χθονὶ σῖτον ἔδοντες,   ἄνδρες
ἄνδρε δύω κρίνας, τρίτατον κήρυχ' ἅμ' ὀπάσσας.   ὀπάσας
οἱ δ' αἶψ' οἰχόμενοι μίγεν ἀνδράσι Λωτοφάγοισιν·   10   ἐμίγησαν

οὐδ' ἄρα Λωτοφάγοι <u>μήδονθ</u>' ἑτάροισιν ὄλεθρον   ἐμήδοντο
ἡμετέροις, ἀλλά σφι <u>δόσαν</u> λωτ<u>οῖο</u> πάσασθαι.   ἔδοσαν, –οῦ
τῶν δ' ὅστις λωτ<u>οῖο</u> φάγοι <u>μελιηδέα</u> καρπόν,   –οῦ, μελιηδῆ
οὐκέτ' ἀπαγγεῖλαι πάλιν ἤθελεν οὐδὲ <u>νέεσθαι</u>,   νεῖσθαι
ἀλλ' αὐτοῦ <u>βούλοντο</u> μετ' ἀνδράσι Λωτοφάγοισι   15 ἐβούλοντο
λωτὸν ἐρεπτόμενοι <u>μενέμεν</u> νόστου τε λαθέσθαι.   μένειν
τοὺς μὲν ἐγὼν ἐπὶ νῆας <u>ἄγον</u> κλαίοντας ἀνάγκῃ,   ἦγον
<u>νηυσὶ</u> δ' ἐνὶ γλαφυρῇσιν ὑπὸ ζυγὰ <u>δῆσα</u> <u>ἐρύσσας</u>.   ναυσί, –αῖς,
    ἔδησα, ἐρύσας

αὐτὰρ τοὺς ἄλλους <u>κελόμην</u> ἐρίηρας ἑταίρους   ἐκελόμην
σπερχομένους <u>νηῶν</u> <u>ἐπιβαινέμεν</u> <u>ὠκειάων</u>,   20 νεῶν, –βαίνειν, –ῶν
μή πώς τις λωτ<u>οῖο</u> φαγὼν νόστ<u>οιο</u> λάθηται.   –οῦ, –ου
οἱ δ' αἶψ' <u>εἴσβαινον</u> καὶ ἐπὶ κληῖσι καθῖζον,   εἰσέβαινον
ἑξῆς δ' ἑζόμενοι <u>πολιὴν</u> ἅλα <u>τύπτον</u> ἐρετμοῖς.   πολιάν, ἔτυπτον

Notes

1

*l.*1 τήν = αὐτήν (25.1/3*a*). *l.*2 ἦ *indeed*; τάδε is the subject of μέλει. *l.*4 αἵ κε = ἐάν (ἀλυσκάζω is subj.); κακὸς ὡς *like a coward* (ὡς is accented when it follows the word it qualifies); take νόσφιν with πολέμοιο. *l.*5 με ... ἄνωγεν *order me [to do this]*. *l.*7 The genitives are to be translated *for*; ἐμὸν αὐτοῦ = ἐμοῦ αὐτοῦ, lit. *of me myself*. *l.*9 ὅτ'(ε) *when*; translate ἄν ... ὀλώλῃ (strong perf. subj. of ὄλλῡμι) as a future (25.1/3*b*). *l.*11 τόσσον (= normal Attic τοσοῦτο) agrees with ἄλγος (which is the subject of μέλει) and is balanced by ὅσσον in *l.*15 (21.1/3*e*). *l.*12 Ἑκάβης, Πριάμοιο (together with κασιγνήτων (*l.*13) and σεῦ (*l.*15)) are objective genitives (23.1/1*c*) with ἄλγος (*l.*11), *grief for* ... *ll.*13f. κεν ... πέσοιεν fut. potential (19.1/2) but trans. *may fall*; ὑπ'(ό) + dat. (= gen. in Attic) *by, at the hands of. ll.*15f. κεν ... ἄγηται lit. *will lead for himself* (25.1/3*b*); ἐλεύθερον ἦμαρ lit. *free day* a regular Homeric expression for *freedom*, trans. *day of liberty* (similiar expressions occur in *l.*24 below and in 3 *l.*9). *ll.*17f. The two examples of κε + opt. are potential (Hector is stating something that may possibly happen), but are better translated *will weave ... and carry* (25.1/3*b*); πρός *at the command of*; Μεσσηΐδος ἢ Ὑπερείης gen. of separation (20.1/4) *from M. or H. l.*19 πόλλ' (i.e. πολλά) adverbial acc. (20.1/5) *much*; ἐπικείσετ'(αι). *l.*20 εἴπῃσι (subj., 25.1/2*c*(i)) *will say* (25.1/3*b*); κατὰ δάκρυ χέουσαν = καταχέουσαν δάκρυ (tmesis, 12.3.9 *l.*6 note). *l.*21f. Take Τρώων ἱπποδάμων with ἀριστεύεσκε (= ἠρίστευε) *was *best of the*, etc. *l*.23 ὥc (= οὕτωc) *thus*. *l*.24 χήτεϊ (= χήτει) + gen. *because of the lack* (dat. of cause 23.1/2*i*); δούλιον ἦμαρ cf. ἐλεύθερον ἦμαρ (*l*.16). *l*.25 κατὰ ... καλύπτοι tmesis as in *l*.20 – the opt. expresses a wish for the future (21.1/1).

2

l.1 *The embankments of war* apparently means the places where battles were normally fought. *l*.2 παννύχιοι is an adj. (*staying all night*) but trans. *all night long*; cφιcι (= αὐτοῖc) is not here reflexive. *l*.3 ὡc ... ὅτ᾽(ε) *as when* introduces a simile. *ll*.4f. φαίνετ᾽(αι); aorists such as ἔπλετο and ἔφανεν are often interspersed among presents in Homeric similes and should be translated by the present; ἔκ ... ἔφανεν tmesis (see on 1 *l*.20 above). *l*.6 ὑπερράγη root aor. of ὑπορρήγνῡμι. *l*.7 τε is often used to mark similes and has no connective force; φρένα acc. of respect (20.1/5). *l*.8 τόccα agrees with πυρά (*l*.9) and brings out the point of the simile. *l*.9 Τρώων καιόντων gen. abs. (12.1/2*b*); Ἰλιόθι πρό = πρὸ Ἰλίου (the suffix –θι, which denotes *place from which*, is used as the equivalent of the genitive ending). *l*.11 cέλᾳ = cέλαι dat. s. of cέλαc (cf. 13.1/1*b*(iii)). *l*.14 The ending of ὄχεcφιν (< ὄχοc) is peculiar to Homer and is generally the equivalent of the dat. pl., as here.

3

l.1 πολλά *much* (20.1/5). *l*.2 πλάγχθη 3rd s. aor. ind. (without augment) of πλάζομαι. *l*.4 ὅ γ᾽(ε) *he* (25.1/3*a*; γε is often added to ὁ in this use and is not to be translated); ὅν **not** the relative but a 3rd person reflexive possessive adjective, ὅc, ἥ, ὅν (*his, her, its*), which did not survive in Attic – take with θῡμόν, lit. *his own heart* but trans. simply by *his heart* (but ἥν ... ψῡχήν (*l*.5) *his own life* because of the contrast with νόcτον ἑταίρων). *l*.5 ἀρνύμενοc *trying to win*. *l*.6 ὥc *so, thus* (cf. 1 *l*.23 above); ἱέμενόc (< ἵημι) περ lit. *although striving*. *l*.7 αὐτῶν ... cφετέρῃcιν *their own* (αὐτῶν lit. *of them* is added for particular emphasis); ἀταcθαλίῃcιν plural for singular. *ll*.8f. νήπιοι *fools* in apposition to the subject of ὄλοντο (*l*.7); κατὰ ... ἤcθιον tmesis; ὁ *he*, i.e. Helios; τοῖcιν (= αὐτοῖc) *from them*, dat. of disadvantage (23.1/2*d*).

4

l.2 δεκάτη *sc*. ἡμέρᾳ. *l*.3 οἵ τ᾽(ε) *who*, **not** *and who* – in Homer τε is added to the relative when the antecedent is a class (here the Lotus-eaters). *l*.5 ἕλοντο lit. *took for themselves* (the mid. of αἱρέω does not here have the meaning *choose*). *l*.6 ἐπαccάμεθ᾽(α) < πατέομαι. *l*.7 δή here not postpositive as in Attic; προΐειν 1st s. impf. ind. act. of προΐημι; ἰόντας (<εἶμι) here **fut.** pple. (18.1/3) to express purpose (12.1/2*a*(v)). *l.*8 οἵτινες indirect interrogative (10.1/2*b* note 1); εἶεν opt. in historic sequence (14.1/4*d*). *l.*9 ἄνδρε acc. dual, 24.1/4; τρίτατον κήρυχ᾽ ἅμ᾽ (= κήρυκα ἅμα) lit. *a third together* (i.e. *with them*) *[as] herald. l.*12 cφι = αὐτοῖς; λωτοῖο partitive gen. (23.1/1*d*) with δόςαν, lit. *gave of lotus,* i.e. *gave some lotus* (cf. λωτοῖο φαγών *eating some lotus l.*21 below). *l.*13 τῶν = αὐτῶν; ὅςτις ... φάγοι indefinite adj. clause (14.1/4*c*(iii)), *whoever ate. l.*15 αὐτοῦ (adv.) *there. l.*17 ἄγον ... ἀνάγκῃ *I brought by force* (the impf. here and in the following lines is used for vividness and should be translated by a simple past). *l.*21 μή πώς τις ... *lest somehow* (πως) *anyone ...*

For suggestions for further study see the Internet website
< http://tyancientgreek.org >

Appendix 1

Conjugation of λύω loosen

ACTIVE

		Pres. Indicative	Impf.	Future	Aorist	Perfect	Pluperfect
s.	1	λύ-ω	ἔλῡ-ον	λύc-ω	ἔλῡc-α	λέλυκ-α	ἐλελύκ-η
		I loosen, etc.	I was loosening, etc	I will loosen	I loosened	I have loosened	I had loosened
	2	λύ-εις	ἔλῡ-ες	λύc-εις	ἔλῡc-ας	λέλυκ-ας	ἐλελύκ-ης
	3	λύ-ει	ἔλῡ-ε(ν)	λύc-ει	ἔλῡc-ε(ν)	λέλυκ-ε(ν)	ἐλελύκ-ει(ν)
pl.	1	λύ-ομεν	ἐλύ-ομεν	λύc-ομεν	ἐλύc-αμεν	λελύκ-αμεν	ἐλελύκ-εμεν
	2	λύ-ετε	ἐλύ-ετε	λύc-ετε	ἐλύc-ατε	λελύκ-ατε	ἐλελύκ-ετε
	3	λύ-ουcι(ν)	ἔλῡ-ον	λύc-ουcι(ν)	ἔλῡc-αν	λελύκ-ᾱcι(ν)	ἐλελύκ-εcαν

Subjunctive

s.	1	λύ-ω			λύc-ω	λελύκ-ω[1]	
	2	λύ-ῃς			λύc-ῃς	λελύκ-ῃς	
	3	λύ-ῃ			λύc-ῃ	λελύκ-ῃ	
pl.	1	λύ-ωμεν			λύc-ωμεν	λελύκ-ωμεν	
	2	λύ-ητε			λύc-ητε	λελύκ-ητε	
	3	λύ-ωcι(ν)			λύc-ωcι(ν)	λελύκ-ωcι(ν)	

Optative

s.	1	λύ-οιμι		λύc-οιμι	λύc-αιμι	λελύκ-οιμι[1]	
	2	λύ-οις		λύc-οις	λύc-ειας (λύc-αις)	λελύκ-οις	
	3	λύ-οι		λύc-οι	λύc-ειε(ν) (λύc-αι)	λελύκ-οι	
pl.	1	λύ-οιμεν		λύc-οιμεν	λύc-αιμεν	λελύκ-οιμεν	
	2	λύ-οιτε		λύc-οιτε	λύc-αιτε	λελύκ-οιτε	
	3	λύ-οιεν		λύc-οιεν	λύc-ειαν (λύc-αιεν)	λελύκ-οιεν	

Imperative

s.	2	λῦ-ε			λῦc-ον	λελυκὼς ἴcθι	
	3	λῡ-έτω			λῦc-άτω	λελυκὼς ἔcτω	
pl.	2	λύ-ετε			λύc-ατε	λελυκότες ἔcτε	
	3	λῡ-όντων			λύc-άντων	λελυκότες ὄντων	

Infinitive

λύ-ειν	λύc-ειν	λῦc-αι	λελυκ-έναι

Participle

λύ-ων	λύc-ων	λύc-ᾱc	λελυκ-ώc
λύ-ουcα	λύc-ουcα	λύc-ᾱcα	λελυκ-υῖα
λῦ-ον	λύc-ον	λύc-αν	λελυκ-όc

---

[1] See also 16.1/4 note 1.

MIDDLE

		Pres.	Impf.	Future	Aorist	Perfect	Pluperfect
Indicative							
s.	1	λύ-ομαι	ἐλῡ-όμην	λύc-ομαι	ἐλῡc-άμην	λέλυ-μαι	ἐλελύ-μην
	2	λύ-ῃ (-ει)	ἐλύ-ου	λύc-ῃ (-ει)	ἐλύc-ω	λέλυ-cαι	ἐλέλυ-co
	3	λύ-εται	ἐλύ-ετο	λύc-εται	ἐλύc-ατο	λέλυ-ται	ἐλέλυ-το
pl.	1	λῡ-όμεθα	ἐλῡ-όμεθα	λῡc-όμεθα	ἐλῡc-άμεθα	λελύ-μεθα	ἐλελύ-μεθα
	2	λύ-εcθε	ἐλύ-εcθε	λύc-εcθε	ἐλύc-αcθε	λέλυ-cθε	ἐλέλυ-cθε
	3	λύ-ονται	ἐλύ-οντο	λύc-ονται	ἐλύc-αντο	λέλυ-νται	ἐλέλυ-ντο
Subjunctive							
s.	1	λύ-ωμαι			λύc-ωμαι	λελυμένος ὦ	
	2	λύ-ῃ			λύc-ῃ	λελυμένος ᾖc	
	3	λύ-ηται			λύc-ηται	λελυμένος ᾖ	
pl.	1	λῡ-ώμεθα			λῡc-ώμεθα	λελυμένοι ὦμεν	
	2	λύ-ηcθε			λύc-ηcθε	λελυμένοι ἦτε	
	3	λύ-ωνται			λύc-ωνται	λελυμένοι ὦcι(ν)	
Optative							
s.	1	λῡ-οίμην		λῡc-οίμην	λῡc-αίμην	λελυμένος εἴην	
	2	λύ-οιο		λύc-οιο	λύc-αιο	λελυμένος εἴηc	
	3	λύ-οιτο		λύc-οιτο	λύc-αιτο	λελυμένος εἴη	
pl.	1	λῡ-οίμεθα		λῡc-οίμεθα	λῡc-αίμεθα	λελυμένοι εἶμεν	
	2	λύ-οιcθε		λύc-οιcθε	λύc-αιcθε	λελυμένοι εἶτε	
	3	λύ-οιντο		λύc-οιντο	λύc-αιντο	λελυμένοι εἶεν	
Imperative							
s.	2	λύ-ου			λύc-αι	λέλυ-co	
	3	λῡ-έcθω			λῡc-άcθω	λελύ-cθω	
pl.	2	λύ-εcθε			λύc-αcθε	λέλυ-cθε	
	3	λῡ-έcθων			λῡc-άcθων	λελύ-cθων	
Infinitive							
		λύ-εcθαι		λύc-εcθαι	λύc-αcθαι	λελύ-cθαι	
Participle							
		λῡ-όμενος,		λῡc-όμενος,	λῡc-άμενος,	λελυ-μένος,	
		-ομένη,		-ομένη,	-αμένη,	-μένη,	
		-όμενον		-όμενον	-άμενον	-μένον	

Note

In all forms of the perfect which are made up of a perfect participle and εἰμί the participle must agree with the subject of the verb in number and gender.

PASSIVE

The forms for the present, imperfect, perfect and pluperfect are the same as for the middle; for the future perfect passive see 16.1/4 note 2.

Future

		Indicative	Optative		
s.	1	λυθήc–ομαι	λυθηc–οίμην		
	2	λυθήc–η (–ει)	λυθήc–οιο	**Infinitive**	λυθήc–εcθαι
	3	λυθήc–εται	λυθήc–οιτο	**Participle**	λυθηc–όμενοc,
pl.	1	λυθηc–όμεθα	λυθηc–οίμεθα		–ομένη,
	2	λυθήc–εcθε	λυθήc–οιcθε		–όμενον
	3	λυθήc–ονται	λυθήc–οιντο		

Aorist

		Indicative	Subjunctive	Optative	Imperative
s.	1	ἐλύθη–ν	λυθ–ῶ	λυθ–είην	
	2	ἐλύθη–c	λυθ–ῇc	λυθ–είηc	λύθη–τι
	3	ἐλύθη	λυθ–ῇ	λυθ–είη	λυθή–τω
pl.	1	ἐλύθη–μεν	λυθ–ῶμεν	λυθ–εῖμεν	
	2	ἐλύθη–τε	λυθ–ῆτε	λυθ–εῖτε	λύθη–τε
	3	ἐλύθη–cαν	λυθ–ῶcι(ν)	λυθ–εῖεν	λυθέ–ντων

Infinitive λυθῆ–ναι   **Participle** λυθ–είc, λυθ–εῖcα, λυθ–έν

Appendix 2

Conjugation of contracted verbs (present and imperfect)

τῑμάω *honour*

		ACTIVE		MIDDLE/PASSIVE	
		Present	**Imperfect**	**Present**	**Imperfect**
Indicative					
s.	1	τῑμῶ	ἐτῑμων	τῑμῶμαι	ἐτῑμώμην
	2	τῑμᾷς	ἐτῑμᾱς	τῑμᾷ	ἐτῑμῶ
	3	τῑμᾷ	ἐτῑμᾱ	τῑμᾶται	ἐτῑμᾶτο
pl.	1	τῑμῶμεν	ἐτῑμῶμεν	τῑμώμεθα	ἐτῑμώμεθα
	2	τῑμᾶτε	ἐτῑμᾶτε	τῑμᾶσθε	ἐτῑμᾶσθε
	3	τῑμῶσι(ν)	ἐτῑμων	τῑμῶνται	ἐτῑμῶντο
Subjunctive					
s.	1	τῑμῶ		τῑμῶμαι	
	2	τῑμᾷς		τῑμᾷ	
	3	τῑμᾷ		τῑμᾶται	
pl.	1	τῑμῶμεν		τῑμώμεθα	
	2	τῑμᾶτε		τῑμᾶσθε	
	3	τῑμῶσι(ν)		τῑμῶνται	
Optative					
s.	1	τῑμῴην		τῑμῴμην	
	2	τῑμῴης		τῑμῷο	
	3	τῑμῴη		τῑμῷτο	
pl.	1	τῑμῷμεν		τῑμῴμεθα	
	2	τῑμῷτε		τῑμῷσθε	
	3	τῑμῷεν		τῑμῷντο	
Imperative					
s.	2	τῑμᾱ		τῑμῶ	
	3	τῑμᾱτω		τῑμᾶσθω	
pl.	2	τῑμᾶτε		τῑμᾶσθε	
	3	τῑμώντων		τῑμᾶσθων	
Infinitive					
		τῑμᾶν		τῑμᾶσθαι	
Participle					
		τῑμῶν, τῑμῶσα, τῑμῶν		τῑμώμεν–ος, –η, –ον	

ποιέω *make, do*

		ACTIVE		MIDDLE/PASSIVE	
		Present	Imperfect	Present	Imperfect
Indicative					
s.	1	ποιῶ	ἐποίουν	ποιοῦμαι	ἐποιούμην
	2	ποιεῖc	ἐποίειc	ποιῇ (-εῖ)	ἐποιοῦ
	3	ποιεῖ	ἐποίει	ποιεῖται	ἐποιεῖτο
pl.	1	ποιοῦμεν	ἐποιοῦμεν	ποιούμεθα	ἐποιούμεθα
	2	ποιεῖτε	ἐποιεῖτε	ποιεῖcθε	ἐποιεῖcθε
	3	ποιοῦcι(ν)	ἐποίουν	ποιοῦνται	ἐποιοῦντο
Subjunctive					
s.	1	ποιῶ		ποιῶμαι	
	2	ποιῇc		ποιῇ	
	3	ποιῇ		ποιῆται	
pl.	1	ποιῶμεν		ποιώμεθα	
	2	ποιῆτε		ποιῆcθε	
	3	ποιῶcι(ν)		ποιῶνται	
Optative					
s.	1	ποιοίην		ποιοίμην	
	2	ποιοίηc		ποιοῖο	
	3	ποιοίη		ποιοῖτο	
pl.	1	ποιοῖμεν		ποιοίμεθα	
	2	ποιοῖτε		ποιοῖcθε	
	3	ποιοῖεν		ποιοῖντο	
Imperative					
s.	2	ποίει		ποιοῦ	
	3	ποιείτω		ποιείcθω	
pl.	2	ποιεῖτε		ποιεῖcθε	
	3	ποιούντων		ποιείcθων	
Infinitive					
		ποιεῖν		ποιεῖcθαι	
Participle					
		ποιῶν, ποιοῦcα, ποιοῦν		ποιούμεν–οc, –η, –ον	

δηλόω *make clear, show*

		ACTIVE		**MIDDLE/PASSIVE**	
		Present	**Imperfect**	**Present**	**Imperfect**
Indicative
s.	*1*	δηλῶ	ἐδήλουν	δηλοῦμαι	ἐδηλούμην
	2	δηλοῖc	ἐδήλουc	δηλοῖ	ἐδηλοῦ
	3	δηλοῖ	ἐδήλου	δηλοῦται	ἐδηλοῦτο
pl.	*1*	δηλοῦμεν	ἐδηλοῦμεν	δηλούμεθα	ἐδηλούμεθα
	2	δηλοῦτε	ἐδηλοῦτε	δηλοῦcθε	ἐδηλοῦcθε
	3	δηλοῦcι(ν)	ἐδήλουν	δηλοῦνται	ἐδηλοῦντο
Subjunctive
s.	*1*	δηλῶ		δηλῶμαι	
	2	δηλοῖc		δηλοῖ	
	3	δηλοῖ		δηλῶται	
pl.	*1*	δηλῶμεν		δηλώμεθα	
	2	δηλῶτε		δηλῶcθε	
	3	δηλῶcι(ν)		δηλῶνται	
Optative
s.	*1*	δηλοίην		δηλοίμην	
	2	δηλοίηc		δηλοῖο	
	3	δηλοίη		δηλοῖτο	
pl.	*1*	δηλοῖμεν		δηλοίμεθα	
	2	δηλοῖτε		δηλοῖcθε	
	3	δηλοῖεν		δηλοῖντο	
Imperative
s.	*2*	δήλου		δηλοῦ	
	3	δηλούτω		δηλούcθω	
pl.	*2*	δηλοῦτε		δηλοῦcθε	
	3	δηλούντων		δηλούcθων	
Infinitive
		δηλοῦν		δηλοῦcθαι	
Participle
		δηλῶν, δηλοῦcα, δηλοῦν		δηλούμεν–οc, –η, –ον	

Appendix 3

Conjugation of εἰμί *be*, ἔρχομαι (and εἶμι) *come/go*, φημί *say*, οἶδα *know*

(the last is perfect in form but present in meaning; it has been classified below according to its meaning)

		εἰμί *be*	ἔρχομαι *come/go* (18.1/3)	φημί *say*	οἶδα *know* (19.1/3a)
Present indicative					
s.	1	εἰμί	ἔρχομαι	φημί	οἶδα
	2	εἶ	ἔρχῃ (-ει)	φῇς	οἶςθα
	3	ἐcτί(ν)	ἔρχεται	φηcί(ν)	οἶδε(ν)
pl.	1	ἐcμέν	ἐρχόμεθα	φαμέν	ἴcμεν
	2	ἐcτέ	ἔρχεcθε	φατέ	ἴcτε
	3	εἰcί(ν)	ἔρχονται	φαcί(ν)	ἴcᾱcι(ν)
Present subjunctive					
s.	1	ὦ	ἴω	φῶ	εἰδῶ
	2	ᾖc	ἴῃc	φῇc	εἰδῇc
	3	ᾖ	ἴῃ	φῇ	εἰδῇ
pl.	1	ὦμεν	ἴωμεν	φῶμεν	εἰδῶμεν
	2	ἦτε	ἴητε	φῆτε	εἰδῆτε
	3	ὦcι(ν)	ἴωcι(ν)	φῶcι(ν)	εἰδῶcι(ν)
Present optative					
s.	1	εἴην	ἴοιμι	φαίην	εἰδείην
	2	εἴηc	ἴοιc	φαίηc	εἰδείηc
	3	εἴη	ἴοι	φαίη	εἰδείη
pl.	1	εἶμεν	ἴοιμεν	φαῖμεν	εἰδεῖμεν
	2	εἶτε	ἴοιτε	φαῖτε	εἰδεῖτε
	3	εἶεν	ἴοιεν	φαῖεν	εἰδεῖεν
Present imperative					
s.	2	ἴcθι	ἴθι	φαθί	ἴcθι
	3	ἔcτω	ἴτω	φάτω	ἴcτω
pl.	2	ἔcτε	ἴτε	φάτε	ἴcτε
	3	ἔcτων *or* ὄντων	ἰόντων	φάντων	ἴcτων
Present infinitive					
		εἶναι	ἰέναι	φάναι	εἰδέναι
Present participle					
		ὤν, οὖcα, ὄν	ἰών, ἰοῦcα, ἰόν	# φάc, φᾶcα, φάν	εἰδώc, εἰδυῖα, εἰδόc

Imperfect indicative

s.	1	ἦ *or* ἦν	ᾖα	ἔφην	ᾔδη
	2	ἦcθα	ᾔειcθα	ἔφηcθα *or* ἔφηc	ᾔδηcθα
	3	ἦν	ᾔει(ν)	ἔφη	ᾔδει(ν)
pl.	1	ἦμεν	ᾖμεν	ἔφαμεν	ᾖcμεν
	2	ἦτε	ᾖτε	ἔφατε	ᾖcτε
	3	ἦcαν	ᾖεcαν *or* ᾖcαν	ἔφαcαν	ᾔδεcαν *or* ᾖcαν

Future indicative

s.	1	ἔcομαι	εἶμι	φήcω	εἴcομαι
	2	ἔcῃ (-ει)	εἶ	φήcειc	εἴcῃ (-ει)
	3	ἔcται	εἶcι(ν)	φήcει	εἴcεται
pl.	1	ἐcόμεθα	ἴμεν	φήcομεν	εἰcόμεθα
	2	ἔcεcθε	ἴτε	φήcετε	εἴcεcθε
	3	ἔcονται	ἴᾱcι(ν)	φήcουcι(ν)	εἴcονται

The other parts of the future are regular. εἰμί, φημί and οἶδα do not exist in other tenses. For the other parts of ἔρχομαι see **Principal part of verbs**. The optative, infinitive and participle of εἶμι may also have a future meaning (18.1/3).

Appendix 4

Root aorists (11.1/1)

ἔβην (βαίνω) and ἔγνων (γιγνώcκω) are conjugated:

		Ind.	Subj.	Opt.	Imp.	
s.	1	ἔβην	βῶ	βαίην		**Infinitive** βῆναι
	2	ἔβηc	βῇc	βαίηc	βῆθι	
	3	ἔβη	βῇ	βαίη	βήτω	
pl.	1	ἔβημεν	βῶμεν	βαῖμεν		
	2	ἔβητε	βῆτε	βαῖτε	βῆτε	**Participle** βάc, βᾶcα, βάν
	3	ἔβηcαν	βῶcι(ν)	βαῖεν	βάντων	

s.	1	ἔγνων	γνῶ	γνοίην		
	2	ἔγνωc	γνῷc	γνοίηc	γνῶθι	**Infinitive** γνῶναι
	3	ἔγνω	γνῷ	γνοίη	γνώτω	
pl.	1	ἔγνωμεν	γνῶμεν	γνοῖμεν		
	2	ἔγνωτε	γνῶτε	γνοῖτε	γνῶτε	**Participle** γνούc,
	3	ἔγνωcαν	γνῶcι(ν)	γνοῖεν	γνόντων	γνοῦcα, γνόν

Appendix 5

Conjugation of δίδωμι *give*, τίθημι *put, place*, ἵημι *let go, send forth*, ἵστημι *make stand*

(for full details of which tenses of ἵστημι are transitive and which are intransitive see 19.1/1). Many of the forms of ἵημι occur only in compounds.

		δίδωμι	τίθημι	ἵημι	ἵστημι
				ACTIVE	

Present indicative

		δίδωμι	τίθημι	ἵημι	ἵστημι
s.	1	δίδωμι	τίθημι	ἵημι	ἵστημι
	2	δίδως	τίθης	ἵης	ἵστης
	3	δίδωσι(ν)	τίθησι(ν)	ἵησι(ν)	ἵστησι(ν)
pl.	1	δίδομεν	τίθεμεν	ἵεμεν	ἵσταμεν
	2	δίδοτε	τίθετε	ἵετε	ἵστατε
	3	διδόᾱσι(ν)	τιθέᾱσι(ν)	ἱᾶσι(ν)	ἱστᾶσι(ν)

Present subjunctive

		δίδωμι	τίθημι	ἵημι	ἵστημι
s.	1	διδῶ	τιθῶ	ἱῶ	ἱστῶ
	2	διδῷς	τιθῇς	ἱῇς	ἱστῇς
	3	διδῷ	τιθῇ	ἱῇ	ἱστῇ
pl.	1	διδῶμεν	τιθῶμεν	ἱῶμεν	ἱστῶμεν
	2	διδῶτε	τιθῆτε	ἱῆτε	ἱστῆτε
	3	διδῶσι(ν)	τιθῶσι(ν)	ἱῶσι(ν)	ἱστῶσι(ν)

Present optative

		δίδωμι	τίθημι	ἵημι	ἵστημι
s.	1	διδοίην	τιθείην	ἱείην	ἱσταίην
	2	διδοίης	τιθείης	ἱείης	ἱσταίης
	3	διδοίη	τιθείη	ἱείη	ἱσταίη
pl.	1	διδοῖμεν	τιθεῖμεν	ἱεῖμεν	ἱσταῖμεν
	2	διδοῖτε	τιθεῖτε	ἱεῖτε	ἱσταῖτε
	3	διδοῖεν	τιθεῖεν	ἱεῖεν	ἱσταῖεν

Present imperative

		δίδωμι	τίθημι	ἵημι	ἵστημι
s.	2	δίδου	τίθει	ἵει	ἵστη
	3	διδότω	τιθέτω	ἱέτω	ἱστάτω
pl.	2	δίδοτε	τίθετε	ἵετε	ἵστατε
	3	διδόντων	τιθέντων	ἱέντων	ἱστάντων

Present infinitive

	δίδωμι	τίθημι	ἵημι	ἵστημι
	διδόναι	τιθέναι	ἱέναι	ἱστάναι

Present participle

	δίδωμι	τίθημι	ἵημι	ἵστημι
	διδούς	τιθείς	ἱείς	ἱστάς
	διδοῦσα	τιθεῖσα	ἱεῖσα	ἱστᾶσα
	διδόν	τιθέν	ἱέν	ἱστάν

Imperfect indicative

s.	1	ἐδίδουν	ἐτίθην	ἵην	ἵστην
	2	ἐδίδους	ἐτίθεις	ἵεις	ἵστης
	3	ἐδίδου	ἐτίθει	ἵει	ἵστη
pl.	1	ἐδίδομεν	ἐτίθεμεν	ἵεμεν	ἵσταμεν
	2	ἐδίδοτε	ἐτίθετε	ἵετε	ἵστατε
	3	ἐδίδοσαν	ἐτίθεσαν	ἵεσαν	ἵστασαν

Future indicative

s.	1	δώσω etc.	θήσω etc.	ἥσω etc.	στήσω etc.

The other parts of the future active are formed regularly with the same stems (δωσ-, θησ-, ἡσ-, στησ-).

Aorist indicative

					Transitive	*Intransitive*
s.	1	ἔδωκα	ἔθηκα	ἧκα	ἔστησα	ἔστην
	2	ἔδωκας	ἔθηκας	ἧκας	ἔστησας	ἔστης
	3	ἔδωκε(ν)	ἔθηκε(ν)	ἧκε(ν)	ἔστησε(ν)	ἔστη
pl.	1	ἔδομεν	ἔθεμεν	εἷμεν	ἐστήσαμεν	ἔστημεν
	2	ἔδοτε	ἔθετε	εἷτε	ἐστήσατε	ἔστητε
	3	ἔδοσαν	ἔθεσαν	εἷσαν	ἔστησαν	ἔστησαν

On the alternative forms for the plural of ἔδωκα and ἔθηκα see 18.1/2 note 3.

Aorist subjunctive

s.	1	δῶ	θῶ	ὧ	στήσω	στῶ
	2	δῷς	θῇς	ἧς	στήσῃς	στῇς
	3	δῷ	θῇ	ᾗ	στήσῃ	στῇ
pl.	1	δῶμεν	θῶμεν	ὧμεν	στήσωμεν	στῶμεν
	2	δῶτε	θῆτε	ἧτε	στήσητε	στῆτε
	3	δῶσι(ν)	θῶσι(ν)	ὧσι(ν)	στήσωσι(ν)	στῶσι(ν)

Aorist optative

s.	1	δοίην	θείην	εἵην	στήσαιμι	σταίην
	2	δοίης	θείης	εἵης	στήσειας (–αις)	σταίης
	3	δοίη	θείη	εἵη	στήσειε(ν) (–αι)	σταίη
pl.	1	δοῖμεν	θεῖμεν	εἷμεν	στήσαιμεν	σταῖμεν
	2	δοῖτε	θεῖτε	εἷτε	στήσαιτε	σταῖτε
	3	δοῖεν	θεῖεν	εἷεν	στήσειαν (–αιεν)	σταῖεν

Aorist imperative

s.	2	δός	θές	ἕς	στῆσον	στῆθι
	3	δότω	θέτω	ἕτω	στησάτω	στήτω
pl.	2	δότε	θέτε	ἕτε	στήσατε	στῆτε
	3	δόντων	θέντων	ἕντων	στησάντων	στάντων

Aorist infinitive

	δοῦναι	θεῖναι	εἷναι	στῆσαι	στῆναι

Aorist participle

	δούς	θείς	εἵς	στήσᾱς	στάς
	δοῦσα	θεῖσα	εἷσα	στήσᾱσα	στᾶσα
	δόν	θέν	ἕν	στῆσαν	στάν

Perfect and pluperfect

The perfect and pluperfect active of δίδωμι, τίθημι, ἵημι are formed regularly from the stems δεδωκ, τεθηκ-, εἱκ-.
The perfect and pluperfect active of ἵστημι (which are intransitive —see 19.1/1) are conjugated as follows:

Perfect

		Indicative	Subjunctive	Optative	Imperative
s.	1	ἕστηκα	ἑστῶ	ἑσταίην	
	2	ἕστηκας	ἑστῇς	ἑσταίης	ἕσταθι
	3	ἕστηκε(ν)	ἑστῇ	ἑσταίη	ἑστάτω
pl.	1	ἕσταμεν	ἑστῶμεν	ἑσταῖμεν	
	2	ἕστατε	ἑστῆτε	ἑσταῖτε	ἕστατε
	3	ἑστᾶσι(ν)	ἑστῶσι(ν)	ἑσταῖεν	ἑστάντων

Infinitive ἑστάναι **Participle** ἑστώς, ἑστῶσα, ἑστός
On alternatives for forms in ἑστηκ– see 19.1/1

Pluperfect s. εἱστήκη *(I stood)*, εἱστήκης, εἱστήκει, pl. ἕσταμεν, ἕστατε, ἕστασαν.

MIDDLE

Present indicative

s.	1	δίδομαι	τίθεμαι	ἵεμαι	ἵσταμαι
	2	δίδοσαι	τίθεσαι	ἵεσαι	ἵστασαι
	3	δίδοται	τίθεται	ἵεται	ἵσταται
pl.	1	διδόμεθα	τιθέμεθα	ἱέμεθα	ἱστάμεθα
	2	δίδοσθε	τίθεσθε	ἵεσθε	ἵστασθε
	3	δίδονται	τίθενται	ἵενται	ἵστανται

Present subjunctive

s.	1	διδῶμαι	τιθῶμαι	ἱῶμαι	ἱστῶμαι
	2	διδῷ	τιθῇ	ἱῇ	ἱστῇ
	3	διδῶται	τιθῆται	ἱῆται	ἱστῆται
pl.	1	διδώμεθα	τιθώμεθα	ἱώμεθα	ἱστώμεθα
	2	διδῶσθε	τιθῆσθε	ἱῆσθε	ἱστῆσθε
	3	διδῶνται	τιθῶνται	ἱῶνται	ἱστῶνται

Present optative

s.	1	διδοίμην	τιθείμην	ἱείμην	ἱσταίμην
	2	διδοῖο	τιθεῖο	ἱεῖο	ἱσταῖο
	3	διδοῖτο	τιθεῖτο	ἱεῖτο	ἱσταῖτο
pl.	1	διδοίμεθα	τιθείμεθα	ἱείμεθα	ἱσταίμεθα
	2	διδοῖσθε	τιθεῖσθε	ἱεῖσθε	ἱσταῖσθε
	3	διδοῖντο	τιθεῖντο	ἱεῖντο	ἱσταῖντο

Present imperative

s.	2	δίδοσο	τίθεσο	ἵεσο	ἵστασο
	3	διδόσθω	τιθέσθω	ἱέσθω	ἱστάσθω
pl.	2	δίδοσθε	τίθεσθε	ἵεσθε	ἵστασθε
	3	διδόσθων	τιθέσθων	ἱέσθων	ἱστάσθων

Present infinitive
δίδοσθαι τίθεσθαι ἕεσθαι ἵστασθαι

Present participle
διδόμεν–ος, –η, –ον τιθέμεν–ος, –η, –ον ἱέμεν–ος, –η, –ον ἱστάμεν–ος, –η, –ον

Imperfect indicative

s.	1	ἐδιδόμην	ἐτιθέμην	ἱέμην	ἱστάμην
	2	ἐδίδοσο	ἐτίθεσο	ἵεσο	ἵστασο
	3	ἐδίδοτο	ἐτίθετο	ἵετο	ἵστατο
pl.	1	ἐδιδόμεθα	ἐτιθέμεθα	ἱέμεθα	ἱστάμεθα
	2	ἐδίδοσθε	ἐτίθεσθε	ἵεσθε	ἵστασθε
	3	ἐδίδοντο	ἐτίθεντο	ἵεντο	ἵσταντο

Future indicative

| s. | 1 | δώσομαι etc. | θήσομαι etc. | ἥσομαι etc. | στήσομαι etc. |

The other parts of the future middle are formed regularly with the same stems (δως–, θης–, ἡς–, στης–).

Aorist

The only aorist middle of ἵστημι is weak (and transitive), ἐστησάμην, conjugated in exactly the same way as ἐλυσάμην (see **Appendix 1**). The aorist middle of the other verbs are conjugated as follows:

Aorist indicative

s.	1	ἐδόμην	ἐθέμην	εἵμην
	2	ἔδου	ἔθου	εἷσο
	3	ἔδοτο	ἔθετο	εἷτο
pl.	1	ἐδόμεθα	ἐθέμεθα	εἵμεθα
	2	ἔδοσθε	ἔθεσθε	εἷσθε
	3	ἔδοντο	ἔθεντο	εἷντο

Aorist subjunctive

s.	1	δῶμαι	θῶμαι	ὧμαι
	2	δῷ	θῇ	ἧ
	3	δῶται	θῆται	ἧται
pl.	1	δώμεθα	θώμεθα	ὥμεθα
	2	δῶσθε	θῆσθε	ἧσθε
	3	δῶνται	θῶνται	ὧνται

Aorist optative

s.	1	δοίμην	θείμην	εἵμην
	2	δοῖο	θεῖο	εἷο
	3	δοῖτο	θεῖτο	εἷτο
pl.	1	δοίμεθα	θείμεθα	εἵμεθα
	2	δοῖσθε	θεῖσθε	εἷσθε
	3	δοῖντο	θεῖντο	εἷντο

Aorist imperative

s.	2	δοῦ	θοῦ	οὗ
	3	δόσθω	θέσθω	ἕσθω
pl.	2	δόσθε	θέσθε	ἕσθε
	3	δόσθων	θέσθων	ἕσθων

Aorist infinitive

δόϲθαι θέϲθαι ἕϲθαι

Aorist participle

δόμεν–οϲ, –η, –ον θέμεν–οϲ, –η, –ον ἕμεν–οϲ, –η, –ον

Perfect and pluperfect

The perfect and pluperfect middle/passive of δίδωμι and ἵημι are formed regularly from the stems δεδο– and εἱ– (e.g. perfect middle/passive indicative δέδομαι, δέδοϲαι etc., εἷμαι, εἷϲαι etc). Similar forms exist for τίθημι (τέθειμαι, τέθειϲαι etc.) but on the perfect passive of this verb see 18.1/2 note 4. The perfect middle/passive forms of ἵϲτημι are rare.

PASSIVE

As with other verbs, the forms for the present, imperfect, perfect and pluperfect are the same as for the middle. The future and aorist passive follow λύω (see **Appendix 1**):

Future indicative

δοθήϲομαι τεθήϲομαι ἑθήϲομαι ϲταθήϲομαι

Aorist indicative

ἐδόθην ἐτέθην εἵθην ἐϲτάθην

Appendix 6

Conjugation of δείκνῡμι (present and imperfect)

For the other tenses of δείκνῡμι see 20.1/1.

		ACTIVE		MIDDLE/PASSIVE	
		Present	Imperfect	Present	Imperfect
		Indicative			
s.	1	δείκνῡμι	ἐδείκνῡν	δείκνυμαι	ἐδεικνύμην
	2	δείκνῡc	ἐδείκνῡc	δείκνυcαι	ἐδείκνυcο
	3	δείκνῡcι(ν)	ἐδείκνῡ	δείκνυται	ἐδείκνυτο
pl.	1	δείκνυμεν	ἐδείκνυμεν	δεικνύμεθα	ἐδεικνύμεθα
	2	δείκνυτε	ἐδείκνυτε	δείκνυcθε	ἐδείκνυcθε
	3	δεικνύᾱcι(ν)	ἐδείκνυcαν	δείκνυνται	ἐδείκνυντο
		Subjunctive			
s.	1	δεικνύω		δεικνύωμαι	
	2	δεικνύῃc		δεικνύῃ	
	3	δεικνύῃ		δεικνύηται	
pl.	1	δεικνύωμεν		δεικνυώμεθα	
	2	δεικνύητε		δεικνύηcθε	
	3	δεικνύωcι(ν)		δεικνύωνται	
		Optative			
s.	1	δεικνύοιμι		δεικνυοίμην	
	2	δεικνύοιc		δεικνύοιο	
	3	δεικνύοι		δεικνύοιτο	
pl.	1	δεικνύοιμεν		δεικνυοίμεθα	
	2	δεικνύοιτε		δεικνύοιcθε	
	3	δεικνύοιεν		δεικνύοιντο	
		Imperative			
s.	2	δείκνῡ		δείκνυcο	
	3	δεικνύτω		δεικνύcθω	
pl.	2	δείκνυτε		δείκνυcθε	
	3	δεικνύντων		δεικνύcθων	
		Infinitive			
		δεικνύναι		δείκνυcθαι	
		Participle			
		δεικνῡc, δεικνῦcα, δεικνύν		δεικνύμεν–οc, –η, –ον	

Appendix 7

Numerals

Cardinals

For the declension of εἷς, δύο, τρεῖς, τέτταρες see 7.1/5a. διᾱκόσιοι, τριᾱκόσιοι etc. follow the plural of καλός (3.1/3).

1	εἷς	20	εἴκοσι(ν)
2	δύο	30	τριάκοντα
3	τρεῖς	40	τετταράκοντα
4	τέτταρες	50	πεντήκοντα
5	πέντε	60	ἑξήκοντα
6	ἕξ	70	ἑβδομήκοντα
7	ἑπτά	80	ὀγδοήκοντα
8	ὀκτώ	90	ἐνενήκοντα
9	ἐννέα	100	ἑκατόν
10	δέκα	200	διᾱκόσιοι
11	ἕνδεκα	300	τριᾱκόσιοι
12	δώδεκα	400	τετρακόσιοι
13	τρεῖς καὶ δέκα	500	πεντακόσιοι
14	τέτταρες καὶ δέκα	600	ἑξακόσιοι
15	πεντεκαίδεκα	700	ἑπτακόσιοι
16	ἑκκαίδεκα	800	ὀκτακόσιοι
17	ἑπτακαίδεκα	900	ἐνακόσιοι
18	ὀκτωκαίδεκα	1,000	χίλιοι
19	ἐννεακαίδεκα	10,000	μύριοι

The cardinals *two thousand, three thousand* etc. are compounds of the appropriate numeral adverbs and χίλιοι, e.g. δισχίλιοι, τρισχίλιοι etc.; likewise we have δισμύριοι *twenty thousand,* τρισμύριοι *thirty thousand* etc..

	Ordinals	Adverbs
1	πρῶτος	ἅπαξ
2	δεύτερος	δίς
3	τρίτος	τρίς
4	τέταρτος	τετράκις
5	πέμπτος	πεντάκις
6	ἕκτος	ἑξάκις
7	ἕβδομος	ἑπτάκις
8	ὄγδοος	ὀκτάκις
9	ἔνατος	ἐνάκις
10	δέκατος	δεκάκις

The ordinals are normal first and second declension adjectives (3.1/3), except that the feminine of ὄγδοος is ὀγδόη (not –ᾱ).

Appendix 8

Accentuation

The basic features of Greek accentuation are described at 1.1/2, and information given there is not repeated below.

The following terms are used to describe words according to their accent:

Oxytone - a word with an acute on its final syllable, e.g. ποταμός.

Paroxytone - a word with an acute on its penultimate (i.e. last syllable but one), e.g. λόγος.

Proparoxytone - a word with an acute on its last syllable but two, e.g. ἄνθρωπος.

Perispomenon - a word with a circumflex on its final syllable, e.g. ποταμοῦ.

Properispomenon - a word with a circumflex on its penultimate, e.g. δῶρον.

Barytone - a word with a grave on its final syllable, e.g. ποταμὸν εἶδον *I saw a river.*

These are the only places in which each accent can occur (we cannot, for example, have an acute on the last syllable but three, or a circumflex on the last syllable but two).

For purposes of accentuation a syllable is long if it contains a long vowel or diphthong (1.1./1*b,c*), and short if it contains a short vowel, except that **all endings in –αι and –οι, apart from those of the optative, are counted as short.**[1]

The length of the final syllable of a word and, to a lesser extent, of its penultimate is important for accentuation because:

- a word can only be proparoxytone if its final syllable is short, e.g. ἄνθρωπος.
- a word can only be properispomenon if its final syllable is short; as a circumflex must in any case stand on a long vowel or diphthong, a word so accented must end in – ˘ , or be a disyllable consisting of – ˘ , e.g. πολῖται, γλῶττα. Conversely, if such a word is accented on its penultimate, the accent must be a circumflex, and this is why we

---

[1] The rules in verse are different; see **Appendix 9**

get the change of accent from πολίτης to πολῖται (the reverse in γλῶττα/γλώττης).

For purposes of accentuation words are divided into five categories:

(a) Nouns, adjectives and pronouns

There are no overall rules about the position of the accent in the nominative singular of nouns or in the nominative masculine singular of adjectives and pronouns, and we must simply learn that ποταμός is oxytone but λόγος is paroxytone. There are some rules for certain small groups which can be learnt by observation, e.g. nouns in –ευς are always oxytone (as βασιλεύς); the accent of comparative and superlative adjectives is always as far from the end of the word as possible (σοφός but σοφώτερος, σοφώτατος).

Once, however, we know where a noun, adjective or pronoun is accented in the nominative (masculine) singular, it is easy to deduce how its other forms will be accented because the accent stays on the same syllable as far as this is allowed by the rules given above for proparoxytones and perispomenons. In λόγος, for example, the accent remains unchanged (λόγε, λόγον, λόγου, λόγῳ, λόγοι, λόγους, λόγων, λόγοις), but in ἄνθρωπος the accent must become paroxytone when the ending is long: ἄνθρωπε, ἄνθρωπον, ἀνθρώπου, ἀνθρώπῳ, ἄνθρωποι, ἀνθρώπους, ἀνθρώπων, ἀνθρώποις (ἄνθρωποι because –οι does **not** count as long—see above).

In many third declension nouns the genitive singular is a syllable longer than the nominative singular, e.g. σῶμα (properispomenon, not paroxytone, because it is a disyllable of the form - ˘ ; see above): σώματος, σώματι, σώματα (the accent must change to an acute because the added short syllable makes all three forms proparoxytone), σωμάτων (the added syllable is long and therefore the accent must become paroxytone), σώμασι.

We must, however, note:

(i) Where a first or second declension word has an acute on its final syllable in the nominative singular, this becomes a circumflex in the genitive and dative (in both singular and plural, cf. 2.1/2 note 3), e.g. from ποταμός we have ποταμέ, ποταμόν, ποταμοῦ, ποταμῷ, ποταμοί, ποταμούς, ποταμῶν, ποταμοῖς.[1] For an example of an adjective so accented see καλός (3.1/3).

---

[1] The Attic declension (13.1/1a) is an exception.

(ii) All first declension nouns are perispomenon in the genitive plural (2.1/2 note 4), e.g. χωρῶν (< χώρα), νεανιῶν (< νεανίᾱc). This does **not** apply to the gen. f. pl. of adjectives when this form would not otherwise differ from the masculine, e.g. μεγάλων is both gen. m. pl. and gen. f. pl. of μέγαc. Where, however, the masculine and feminine forms differ, the rule holds, e.g. χαρίειc, gen. m. pl. χαριέντων, gen. f. pl. χαριεccῶν.

(iii) In the third declension, monosyllabic nouns are accented on the final syllable of the genitive and dative, in both singular and plural, e.g. αἴξ, αἶγα, αἰγόc, αἰγί, αἶγεc, αἶγαc, αἰγῶν, αἰξί. An exception is the gen. pl. of παῖc (παίδων). Of polysyllabic nouns γυνή also follows this pattern (γυνή, γύναι (5.1/1 note 1), γυναῖκα, γυναικόc, γυναικί, γυναῖκεc, γυναῖκαc, γυναικῶν, γυναιξί), and ἀνήρ, μήτηρ and πατήρ follow it in the gen. s., dat. s., and gen. pl. (6.1/1*b*). For the accentuation of πᾶc see 10.1/3*b*.

(iv) The accent in the genitive (s. and pl.) of third declension nouns with stems in ι and of some with stems in υ (8.1/4) is quite irregular : πόλεωc, πόλεων (< πόλιc); πήχεωc, πήχεων (<πῆχυc).

(v) Contracted nouns and adjectives (6.1/2) follow the same rules as for contracted verbs (below *b*(i)).

(*b*) *Verbs*

With verbs the accent falls as far from the end of a word as possible (here too final –αι and –οι count as short, **except in optative endings**). In forms such as ἀκουετε, ἀκουουcι, κελευεcθαι, ἐκελευcαν the final short syllable shows that they must be proparoxytone: ἀκούετε, ἀκούουcι, κελεύεcθαι, ἐκέλευcαν (in disyllabic forms such as ἐλε and λῦε the accent goes back to the penultimate but becomes properispomenon in λῦε because of its long ῦ: ἔλε but λῦε). In κελευω, προφερει, ἐλυθην, where the final syllable is long, the accent is paroxytone: κελεύω, προφέρει, ἐλύθην.

We must, however, note:

(i) In the forms of contracted verbs where contraction occurs, the accent follows that of the original uncontracted form according to the following rules:

- If the accent is on neither of the syllables to be contracted it remains unchanged, e.g. ἐποίει (< ἐποίε-ε).

- If the accent is on the first of the two syllables to be contracted it becomes a circumflex on the contracted syllable, e.g. ποιεῖ (< ποιέ–ει); νῑκῶμεν (< νῑκά–ομεν).
- If the accent is on the second of the two syllables to be contracted it stays as an acute on the contracted syllable, e.g. ἐτῑμώμεθα (< ἐτῑμα–όμεθα); τῑμῷην (< τῑμα–οίην).

(ii) Certain forms of uncontracted –ω verbs and of –μι verbs are in origin contracted and for this reason the first syllable of their endings is always accented. These are:

- the aorist subjunctive passive of all verbs, e.g. λυθῶ, λυθῇς, λυθῇ, λυθῶμεν, λυθῆτε, λυθῶσι.
- the subjunctive and optative of both present (act., mid./pass.) and aorist (act., mid.) of δίδωμι, τίθημι, ἵημι and their compounds, e.g. διδῶ, διδοῖμεν, ἀποδῶ, ἀποδοῖμεν.

(iii) In all strong aorists the first syllable of the ending always carries the accent in the active participle (e.g. λαβών, λαβοῦσα, λαβόν), the active and middle infinitives (λαβεῖν, λαβέσθαι), and the 2nd s. imperative middle (λαβοῦ).

(iv) The first syllable of the ending also carries the accent in participles in –εις, –ους and –ως, e.g. λυθείς, λυθεῖσα, λυθέν; τιθείς, τιθεῖσα, τιθέν; διδούς, διδοῦσα, διδόν; λελυκώς, λελυκυῖα, λελυκός.

(v) In certain participles and infinitives the accent is always either paroxytone or properispomenon, depending on whether it stands on a short or long syllable. These are:

- infinitives in –σαι (weak aorist active), e.g. λῦσαι, νῑκῆσαι, αἰνέσαι.
- infinitives in –ναι (perf. act., aor. pass., root aor. act., and certain active infinitives of –μι verbs), e.g. λελυκέναι, λυθῆναι, γνῶναι, διδόναι.
- the infinitive and participle of the perf. mid./pass., e.g. νενῑκῆσθαι, λελυμένος.

(vi) In compound verbs the accent cannot fall further back than the augment, e.g. ἀπῆγον (< ἀπάγω), παρέσχον (< παρέχω), or the last vowel of a prepositional prefix, e.g. παράδος (< παραδίδωμι).

(c) Adverbs, conjunctions, interjections, particles, prepositions

These have only one form and therefore their accent does not vary, e.g.

σοφῶϲ *wisely,* ὅταν *whenever,* εὖ *well,* except for oxytones becoming barytones (1.1/2). A few words which would otherwise be included here are enclitic or atonic and so come under categories (*d*) or (*e*).

(*d*) *Enclitics*

An enclitic combines with the preceding word for pronunciation, and can affect its accentuation. When quoted by themselves (in paradigms, dictionaries, etc.) monosyllabic enclitics are written with no accent (e.g. γε), disyllabics as oxytone (e.g. ποτέ), except for τινῶν.

The total number of enclitics is small and consists of:

(i) The present indicative of εἰμί *I am* and φημί *say,* with the exception in both cases of the 2nd singular.

(ii) The unemphatic forms of the personal pronouns, viz με, μου, μοι; ϲε, ϲου, ϲοι; ἑ, οὑ, οἱ.

(iii) All forms of the indefinite τιϲ (10.1/1).

(iv) The indefinite adverbs ποτέ, που, πω, πωϲ.

(v) The particles γε, νυν, περ, τε.

The rules for enclitics are:

(vi) An enclitic has no accent when it follows a word accented on its final syllable, e.g. ποταμῶν τινων. If this word has a final acute (i.e. is oxytone), this accent is kept, e.g. ποταμόϲ τιϲ.

(vii) If the preceding word is paroxytone a monosyllabic enclitic has no accent but a disyllabic enclitic keeps the accent on its final syllable, e.g. ἵπποϲ τιϲ, ἵπποι τινέϲ.

(viii) If the preceding word is proparoxytone or properispomenon, an enclitic, whether monosyllabic or disyllabic, has the effect of adding an acute to the final syllable, e.g. ἄνθρωπόϲ τιϲ, ἄνθρωποί τινεϲ, δῶρόν τι, δῶρά τινα.

(ix) In groups of two or more enclitics all are accented except the last, e.g. ἡμεῖϲ γέ ποτέ πού τι εἴδομεν *we at any rate once saw something somewhere.*

(x) ἐϲτί is accented on its first syllable (ἔϲτι) when:
   it denotes existence, e.g. Ἱππόλυτοϲ οὐκέτ' ἔϲτιν *Hippolytus is no longer alive.*
   it stands for ἔξεϲτι (21.1/4 note 1)
   it follows ἀλλά, εἰ, καί, οὐκ, μή, τοῦτο, ὡϲ
   it begins a clause.

(e) *Atonics*

Atonics are monosyllables which have no accent unless followed by an enclitic. These are:

- the nom. m. and f. (s. and pl.) of the article (ὁ, ἡ, οἱ, αἱ), εἰ, οὐ, ὡc
- the prepositions εἰc, ἐκ, ἐν.

Of these, however, οὐ is accented if it occurs as last word of a clause (ex. at 5.2.21 *l.*1), and ὡc if it occurs after word it qualifies or is used in the sense of *thus* (exx. at 25.2.1 *ll.*4, 24)

Notes

1 A few words which we would expect to be properispomenon are in fact paroxytone: οὔτε, μήτε, εἴθε, ὥcτε and compound demonstratives and relatives whose second element is –δε, –περ and –τιc (οἵδε, αἵπερ, ἥτιc etc.).
2 τίc and τί never become barytone (10.1/1).
3 Certain disyllabic prepositions throw their accent back on to their first syllable when they follow the noun they govern (example at 11.2.4 *l.* 1).

Appendix 9

Greek verse

(a) *The nature of Greek verse, long and short syllables*

Greek poetry was composed on an entirely different principle from that employed in English. It was not constructed by arranging stressed syllables in patterns, nor with a system of rhymes. Greek poets employed a number of different metres, all of which consist of certain fixed arrangements of **long and short syllables.** In English verse, whether rhymed or not, the length and rhythm of a line is determined by the number and arrangement of its stressed syllables:

> They tóld me, Heraclítus, they tóld me yoú were déad;
> They broúght me bitter néws to heár and bitter teárs to shéd.
> I wépt, as I remémbered how óften yoú and I′
> Had tíred the sún with tálking and sént him down the ský.
> And nów that thou art lýing, my deár old Cárian guést,
> A hándful of gréy áshes, long lóng ago at rést,
> Stíll are thy pleásant voíces, thy níghtingales, awáke,
> For deáth he taketh áll away, but thém he cánnot táke.

In this translation of a poem of Callimachus (12.3.9) the poet, William Johnston Cary, has changed the position of stressed syllables in some lines for purposes of rhythm and emphasis. No comparable variation is possible in Greek poetry because its structure is much more formal. Every line of verse consists of a succession of long and short syllables whose number and order are prescribed by the metre used; word accent, which in any case is different from that of English (1.1/2), plays no part. To scan a line (i.e. indicate its metre) syllables are marked with a macron (‾) when long and a micron (˘) when short (to avoid a confusion, accents and breathings are omitted and capitals are not used for vowels when marking long and short syllables):

εῑπε̆ τῐc η̄ρᾱκλεῑτε̆ τε̄ο̆ν μο̆ρο̆ν ε̄c δε̆ με̆ δᾱκρῠ (first line of 12.3.9)

The rules for determining the length of syllables are:
(i) Vowels are classified as short (α, ε, ι, ο, υ) or long (ᾱ, η, ῑ, ῡ, ω).
    For metrical purposes all diphthongs are long (this is not true for accentuation – see **Appendix 8**).

(ii) A short syllable must contain a short vowel followed by either a single consonant or no consonant at all.

(iii) A syllable is long if it contains:
either a long vowel or diphthong. When, however, either occurs at the end of a word and the following word does not begin with a consonant, the long vowel or diphthong is shortened, μοῦ ἔννεπε.[1]
or a short vowel followed by two consonants (ζ, ξ, ψ count as double consonants but θ, φ, χ do not; breathings have no metrical value). When a short vowel occurs before certain combinations of two consonants where the second is λ, μ, ν, ρ, the syllable may be long or short.

(iv) In counting consonants after a final short vowel of a word no account is taken of word division, hence τεὸν μορον, τὸ σχῆμα.

(b) Metrical feet, the hexameter, pentameter and iambic trimeter

A metrical foot is made up of certain combinations of long and short syllables. Of the numerous possibilities only the following need concern us:

Dactyl	— ˘ ˘		Iamb	˘ —
Spondee	— —		Trochee	— ˘

The metre used for epic and pastoral was the hexameter; the combination of one hexameter and one pentameter forms an elegiac couplet (see below).

The **hexameter** (< ἕξ + μέτρον) consists of six feet. The first four can be either dactyls or spondees, the fifth is almost always a dactyl and the sixth can be either a spondee or trochee. This can be represented as follows:

— ˘˘ | — ˘˘ | — ˘˘ | — ˘˘ | — ˘ ˘ | — ˘

The upright lines show the syllable division between one foot and the next. They do **not** necessarily coincide with word division. The first two lines of the Odyssey (25.2.3) are scanned:

ᾱν–δρᾰ μοῐ | ἔν–νε̆–πε̆ | Μοῦ–σᾰ ‖ πο̆– | λῦτ–ρο̆–πο̆ν | ὃc μᾰ–λᾰ | πο̄λ–λᾰ
πλᾱγ–χθη ε̆– | πεῑ Τρο̄τ– | ῆc ‖ ῐ–ε̆– | ρο̄ν πτο̆–λῐ– | ε̄θ–ρο̆ν ε̆– | πε̄ρ–cĕ.

It was felt that the rhythm of a hexameter would be impaired if there were a break between words at the end of the third foot as a line so

---

[1] Epic correption (i.e. shortening). It occurs in hexameters and pentameters but is completely avoided in iambic trimeters (on these terms see below).

composed would fall into two equal halves. To avoid this, there is always a break between words (**caesura** *cut* or *break*) either (*a*) after the first syllable of the third foot (as in the second line above), or (*b*) after the second syllable of the third foot when a dactyl (as in the first line above), or (*c*) after the first syllable of the fourth foot. The caesura is marked by two vertical lines, as in the above examples.

A pentameter following a hexameter makes up an **elegiac couplet**, and is by convention indented (e.g. 12.3). It does not occur by itself. The elegiac couplet was the metre of elegiac poetry, a broad literary genre which included epigram and certain narrative, didactic, and occasional poetry. The pentameter consists of two halves of two and a half feet each; the division between the two is marked by a break between words (here called **diaeresis**, not **caesura**, because it occurs at the end, not in the middle of a metrical unit; it also is marked by two vertical lines). The metrical pattern of the **pentameter** is:

— ⏓⏓ | — ⏓⏓ | — || — ⏑ ⏑ | — ⏑ ⏑ | ⏓

Examples (from 12.3.1 and 3) are:

ο̄ν λῐ–πε̆ν | οῡχ εῡ– | ρω̄ν || η̄–ψε̆ν ο̆ν | εῡ–ρε̆ βρο̆– | χο̆ν
εῑc ᾰ–γᾰ– | θο̄c Κῐ–νῠ– | ρη̄c || καῑ Κῐ–νῠ– | ρη̄c δε̆ Κῐ– | λῑξ

The **iambic trimeter** is the chief metre used for dialogue and speeches in drama because it was considered the metre which came closest to the rhythm of normal speech. It consists of three pairs of iambs but more variation was allowed than in the hexameter or pentameter. Its basic form is:

⏓ — ⏑ — | ⏓ — ⏑ — | ⏓ — ⏑ ⏓

A caesura occurs after either the fifth or seventh syllables. Examples of iambic trimeters (from 15.2.4) are:

ᾰ–πᾱν–τε̆c ε̄c– | με̆ν || εῑc το̆ νοῡ– | θε̆–τεῑν cο̆–φοῑ
αῡ–τοῑ δ ᾰ–μᾱρ–| τᾰ–νο̄ν– τε̆c || οῡ| γῑγ–νω̄c– κο̆–με̆ν

Included in the reading are poems in some of the many other metres used by Greek poets (an example occurs at 12.2.18, which is written in anapaests).

Key to Greek Reading Exercises

Explanations and more literal interpretations are given in round brackets. Some words which have no specific equivalent in the Greek original but which must be supplied in English are enclosed in square brackets. Translations from Greek authors are generally as literal as possible and should not be taken as reflecting the style of the original.

When *God* is written with an initial capital letter, the Judeo-Christian deity should only be understood in passages from the Bible. Elswhere the Greek original (θεός) does not indicate what particular divinity is meant.

References are given for longer prose passages, for whole poems and for extracts from verse of more than two lines. In these references Roman numerals refer to books (e.g. of Thucydides), Arabic to chapters in prose works but in poetry to lines. Fragments of the Greek tragedians are given the number assigned to them in Nauck's edition (*Fragmenta Tragicorum Graecorum*). *A.P.* is the abbreviation of *Anthologia Palatina,* an enormous collection of shorter Greek poems whose present form dates from Byzantine times; it has a supplement entitled *App(endix) Plan(udea)*. In both the latter works the reference is first to book (Roman), then to poem number (Arabic).

1.2

1 Aristotelēs (Aristotle), Aristophanēs, Dēmosthenēs, Hērodotos (Herodotus), Theokritos (Theocritus), Kallimachos (Callimachus), Pindaros (Pindar), Platōn (Plato).

2 akmē, anathema, analūsis, antithesis, asbestos, automaton, aphasiā, bathos, genesis, diagnōsis, dogma, drāma, zōnē, ēthos, ēchō, ideā, kīnēma, klīmax, kosmos, krisis, kōlon, metron, miasma, nektar, nemesis, orchēstrā, pathos, skēnē, stigma, hubris, hupothesis, chaos, charaktēr, psūchē.

3 (*a*) Agamemnōn, Achilleus (Achilles), Hektōr (Hector), Helenē (Helen), Odusseus (Odysseus), Patroklos (Patroclus), Pēnelopeia (Penelope) *(all are characters in Homer)*.

(*b*) Athēnai (Athens), Argos, Thēbai (Thebes), Korinthos (Corinth), Spartē (Sparta), Krētē (Crete), Rhodos (Rhodes), Samos *(all are places in Greece)*.

2.2

(1) Odysseus has come from Troy, but Poseidon destroys his ship on (*or* at) Scheria. (2) Odysseus flees out of (*or* from) the sea and hides himself beneath [an] olive-tree near the shore. (3) In a dream Athena says to (*or* tells) the princess Nausicaa that she must (it is necessary [for her] to) wash the clothes on the shore. (4) At daybreak (*or* dawn) Nausicaa brings the clothes in [a] wagon from her house to the sea. (5) In the wagon there is also food for Nausicaa and her companions. (6) The girls quickly wash the clothes near the olive-tree where Odysseus is sleeping. (7) Then (*or* next) the girls throw the clothes on to the shore. (8) They wash themselves and eat the food which they have in the wagon. (9) While they are playing on the shore, Nausicaa throws [a] ball but the ball falls into [a] whirlpool. (10) The girls' shouts (the shouts of the girls) awaken Odysseus and frighten him. (11) Odysseus wonders where in the world he has come to, and suddenly creeps from the olive-tree. (12) He

frightens Naucisaa and her companions. (13) But Nausicaa stays on the shore because Athena puts courage into her heart. (14) Odysseus says to (or tells) Nausicaa that he has come from Ogygia. (15) Nausicaa says to (or tells) her companions that they must (it is necessary [for them] to) provide Odysseus with food and clothes (provide food and clothes to Odysseus). (16) She wishes (or is willing) to bring Odysseus to her father's house (the house of her father) but she fears (or is afraid of) the citizens' blame (the blame of the citizens) if they see her with Odysseus. (17) So Nausicaa and the girls bring the clothes back to the house in the wagon, but Odysseus waits outside.

In 2, 4 and 9 the indefinite article, which does not exist in Greek, has to be supplied in the English.

Analysis of sentence 13 (according to the steps given in 2.2)

ἀλλ᾽ ἡ Ναυσικάα ἐν τῇ ἀκτῇ ἀναμένει διότι ἡ Ἀθηνᾶ τὴν ἀνδρείᾱν εἰς τὴν καρδίᾱν εἰσβάλλει.

(*a*) ἀλλ᾽ (= ἀλλά) conjunction *but*; ἡ feminine nominative singular of the definite article (2.1/2); Ναυσικάα can be either nominative or vocative singular but, as ἡ precedes, it must be the former (the voc. would normally be preceded by ὦ (2.1/3), **never** by the article) – note that the article **must** agree in number, gender and case with the noun it qualifies (2.1/2 note 1; cf. τῇ ἀκτῇ, ἡ Ἀθηνᾶ, τὴν ἀνδρείᾱν, τὴν καρδίᾱν); ἐν preposition governing the dative *in, on, among,* and we would expect the following words to be in this case, which they are: τῇ ἀκτῇ dative singular of ἡ ἀκτή *the shore*; ἀναμένει 3rd person singular present indicative active of ἀναμένω *wait, stay* (the corresponding form of λύω would be λύει); διότι conjunction *because*; ἡ Ἀθηνᾶ nominative singular (the same reasoning applies as for ἡ Ναυσικάα); τὴν ἀνδρείᾱν accusative singular of ἡ ἀνδρείᾱ lit. *the courage*; εἰς preposition governing the accusative *to, into,* and we would expect the following words to be in this case, which they are: τὴν καρδίᾱν accusative singular of ἡ καρδίᾱ *the heart*; εἰσβάλλει 3rd person present indicative active of εἰσβάλλω *throw into, invade.*

(*b*) There are two finite verbs, ἀναμένει and εἰσβάλλει; therefore we have two clauses.

(*c*) Because ἀλλ᾽ (ά) stands as first word it must link this sentence with the previous one. As we have two clauses and διότι comes after the first finite verb, this conjunction must introduce the second clause.

(*d*) In the first clause ἡ Ναυσικάα is nominative and therefore must be the subject of ἀναμένει (we note that the verb agrees with ἡ Ναυσικάα in the way prescribed at the beginning of 2.1/4). ἐν τῇ ἀκτῇ *on the shore* (*on* seems more appropriate with *shore* than *in* or *among*) must be an adverbial phrase qualifying the verb. The clause therefore means *but Nausicaa* (the definite article can be used with proper names in Greek (2.1/2 note 1(iii)), but is never so employed in English) *stays* (or *waits*) *on the shore.* In the second clause ἡ Ἀθηνᾶ, which is nominative, must be the subject of εἰσβάλλει (note the agreement as in the previous clause). τὴν ἀνδρείᾱν is accusative and is **not** preceded by a preposition; therefore it must be the object of the verb as it can have no other grammatical function in the clause. We may translate *because Athena throws courage* (the definite article is not to be translated – 2.1/2 note 1(i)) *into*; the other meaning of εἰσβάλλω, *invade,* makes no sense in this context. εἰς τὴν καρδίᾱν *into the heart* must be an adverbial phrase qualifying the verb but we have one too many *in/into* – the problem is solved by reference to the note on (7) and we can translate *because Athena throws courage into the heart* (*to,* the other meaning of εἰς, does not seem appropriate here).

(*e*) The conjunction διότι shows that the second clause gives the reason for the first and we can put both together as *but Nausicaa stays on the shore because Athena throws courage into the heart.* English idiom requires that we specify whose heart is involved (obviously Nausicaa's, as otherwise the reason introduced by διότι would have no point – on this use of the Greek definite article see note on (1)). Also *put* seems more in accordance with English idiom than *throw* (all possible translations of some words cannot be given in either vocabularies or dictionaries). We now have: *But Nausicaa stays on the shore because Athena puts courage into her heart.*

3.2

(1) Millionaires (the very rich) are not good. (2) A large city is [a] large desert *(or* wilderness). (3) Poverty stimulates skills (*i.e.* necessity is the mother of invention). (4) [A] corpse does not bite (*i.e.* dead men tell no tales). (5) (*i*) Many [are] friends of [the] table, not of truth. (*ii*) Good fortune has many friends ([is] many-friended). (*iii*) Man [is] [a] political animal. (*iv*) Death [is] immortal *(or* deathless). (*v*) Slaves have no leisure ([there is] not leisure to/for slaves). (*vi*) Without health life [is] no life (*or* unlivable). (*vii*) Flattery [is a] disease of friendship. (*viii*) [A] wicked man [is] long-lived. (6) Fortune's great gifts involve (have) fear. (7) Wicked friends bear wicked fruit. (8) The sowing (procreation) of children is a self-inflicted (self-chosen) grief. (9) Gifts persuade [the] gods. (10) Neither [a] drinking-party without company nor wealth without virtue is pleasurable (*lit.* has pleasure). (11) For [a] human being the unexamined life [is] not worth living. (12) (*i*) A large number of (*lit.* many) frogs send messengers to the son of Cronos (*i.e.* Zeus) because they desire [a] monarch. (*ii*) The messengers say to the son of Cronos on behalf of the frogs, "Just son of Cronos, you are master of the gods. Are you willing to provide the frogs with [a] master?" (*lit.* provide [a] master to the frogs). (*iii*) The son of Cronos is very surprised and hurls [a] large log into the frogs' marsh. (*iv*) The log frightens the frogs and they quickly run away, but they begin to be suspicious, since the log does not move (*lit.* is motionless). (*v*) Later they step on to the log without fear and say "Stranger, are you [a] god or [a] human being or [an] animal?" (*vi*) Since it says nothing at all, they consider that it is despicable that they have such a master and they send messengers again to the son of Cronos about [a] new monarch. (*vii*) The messengers say to the son of Cronos, "Master, you must (it is necessary [for you] to) send the frogs (to the frogs) another monarch since the first is motionless and idle. (*viii*) The master of the gods is angry with the frogs and sends [a] great hydra. (*ix*) The hydra is pitiless and eats the frogs. (*x*) The fable makes [it] clear that one (*or* we) must (it is necessary [for one/us] to) bear (i.e. put up with) idle masters since active masters often bear (i.e. bring) hardships.

Analysis of sentence 10 (according to the steps given in 2.2)

οὔτε ϲυμπόϲιον χωρὶς ὁμῑλίᾱϲ οὔτε πλοῦτοϲ χωρὶς ἀρετῆϲ ἡδονὴν ἔχει.

(*a*) οὔτε ... οὔτε conjunctions *neither ... nor*; ϲυμπόϲιον, which is neuter, could be either nominative or accusative singular (the vocative is virtually ruled out by the meaning of the word, *drinking-party*); χωρὶς preposition governing the genitive *without*; ὁμῑλίᾱϲ could be either genitive singular or accusative plural of ὁμῑλίᾱ *company, companionship*, but as it is preceded by a preposition governing the genitive it must be the former; πλοῦτοϲ nominative singular *wealth*; χωρὶς as before; ἀρετῆϲ genitive singular of ἀρετή *courage, excellence, virtue*; ἡδονὴν accusative singular of ἡδονή *pleasure*; ἔχει 3rd person singular present indicative active of ἔχω *have*.

(*b*) and (*c*) The one finite verb, ἔχει, indicates that we have only one clause.

(*d*) and (*e*) οὔτε ... οὔτε (like *neither ... nor* in English) join elements of equal grammatical weight. Therefore, since πλοῦτος is nominative, cυμπόcιον is also nominative, and both are the subject of ἔχει (the verb is singular just as it would be in a similar construction in English, e.g. *neither my wife nor my dog was waiting for me*). As the accusative ἡδονήν is not preceded by a preposition it must be the object of ἔχει. We may now translate: *neither drinking-party without company nor wealth without virtue has pleasure* (of the possible meanings of ἀρετή *courage* and *excellence* are not appropriate as a combination of either with wealth would hardly seem to produce pleasure). English, however, would normally put the indefinite article (which does not exist in Greek) before *drinking-party*. Also, *is pleasurable* or *is enjoyable* would be more idiomatic than *has pleasure*. Our final version then could be: *neither a drinking-party without company nor wealth without virtue is pleasurable.*

4.2

(1) Pleasures [are] mortal, virtues immortal. (2) The beggar did not have bread, and was buying cheese. (3) Praise [is the] reward of virtue, and *(or* but) censure of wickedness. (4) [The] Egyptians [are] clever at contriving ways and means. (5) Necessity [is] law for slaves, but law [is] necessity for free men. (6) Once long ago [the] Milesians were brave. (7) [An] eagle does not hunt flies. (8) (*i*) You are spitting into [the] sky. (*ii*) You are plaiting [a] rope out of sand. (*iii*) You are sowing [the] sea. (*iv*) You are teaching [a] horse to run on to [a] plain. (*v*) You have come after [the] feast. (*vi*) You are whipping [a] corpse. (*vii*) You are shearing [an] ass. (*viii*) You are singing the victory-song before the victory. (*ix*) You are kicking against [the] pricks (*i.e.* of a goad). (*x*) You are bringing the war-engines after the war. (9) Croesus, the Lydian king (king of the Lydians), wanted to destroy the Persian empire (empire of the Persians). For, according to the Delphic oracle (*lit.* oracle at Delphi), he was destined to put an end to a mighty empire. But finally he put an end to his own empire, but not that (*lit.* the [empire]) of the Persians. After the Persians' victory Cyrus, the Persian king (*lit.* king of the Persians), made Croesus go up on to [a] great pyre, and Croesus began to consider the words of Solon the Athenian: no-one of men [is, *i.e.* can be considered] happy before his death. So he quietly awaited his death. But because Croesus was both pious and good, Cyrus ordered his soldiers to bring him down from the pyre and spoke as follows, "Croesus, who among (*lit.* of) men persuaded you to make an expedition [as an] enemy instead of [as a] friend against my land?" But Croesus said, "Cyrus, I (*lit.* I on the one hand) made an expedition against you, but the god (*lit.* but on the other hand the god) at Delphi persuaded me to make the expedition. For I am not foolish nor do I wish to have war instead of peace. For in peace-time the young men bury the old, but in war-time the old [bury] the young. But this was the god's pleasure (*lit.* this thing was dear to the gods)." So Cyrus set him free and made [him] sit nearby. And Croesus spoke once more, "Cyrus, what are your soldiers doing?" "They are plundering your city," said Cyrus, "and carrying off your wealth." "They are not plundering my city," said Croesus, "nor my wealth. For I have nothing (*lit.* nothing is to me). [It is] **you** [whom] they are plundering." After this he (i.e. Croesus) was dear to him; for Cyrus respected his wisdom. (Based on Herodotus i. 86-88.)

Analysis of sentence 5 (according to the steps given in 2.2) τοῖς μὲν δούλοις ἡ ἀνάγκη νόμος, τοῖς δὲ ἐλευθέροις ἀνθρώποις ὁ νόμος ἀνάγκη.

(*a*) μὲν ... δέ *on the one hand ... and/but on the other hand* indicate that we have two balanced grammatical elements (4.1/3); τοῖς ... δούλοις dative plural *to/for the slaves* (on the meaning of the dative with living things see 2.1/3*e*); ἡ ἀνάγκη nominative singular *the necessity* but to be translated *necessity* in view of 2.1/2 note 1(i); νόμος nominative singular *law*; τοῖς ... ἐλευθέροις ἀνθρώποις dative plural *to/for the free men*; ὁ νόμος nominative singular *the law*; ἀνάγκη nominative singular *necessity*.

(*b*) There are no finite verbs! However, even without the hint given in the note on (1), we learn from 3.1/3*b* and 3.1/6 that εἰμί is often omitted in clauses where something is predicated of something else. The fact that in each half of the sentence we have two nominatives suggests that this is what we have here. Since we have **two** balanced elements the appropriate part of εἰμί (viz ἐστί) is to be supplied in each. Therefore we have two clauses.

(*c*) The comma after νόμος shows the division between clauses.

(*d*) In τοῖς ... νόμος the definite article with ἀνάγκη shows that this is the subject; the absence of the definite article with νόμος shows that it is the predicate. The basic meaning (leaving aside μέν) is therefore *for the slaves* (the other meaning of the dative, *to*, is not appropriate) *necessity is law*. In τοῖς ... ἀνάγκη we realise that ὁ νόμος must be translated by *law* and not *the law* because it is parallel with ἀνάγκη and must mean the abstract concept of law, not a particular law. We then have *for the free men law is necessity*.

(*e*) We can translate μὲν ... δέ by *but* with the second clause. However, when we put both halves together we realize that we are dealing with a proverb and that the general class of slaves and the general class of free men are meant. We must, therefore, omit the definite article with each in English (2.1/2 note 1(ii)), and we have: *Necessity is law for slaves, but law is necessity for free men.*

5.2

(1) Time educates the wise. (2) Silence has many fine [points] (*i.e.* silence is golden). (3) Human beings have many troubles, strangers (*lit.* there are many troubles to human beings). (4) [One] must not (it is not necessary to) keep former evils in mind (*lit.* bear ... in memory)., (5) (*i*) Quietness *(or* peace and quiet) [is] a fine [thing]. (*ii*) Fine [things] [are] difficult. (*iii*) Moderation [is] best. (*iv*) [A] big book [is] [a] big evil. (*v*) The property (*lit.* the [things]) of friends [is] shared. (*vi*) Hermes [is] shared. (*vii*) [A] small evil [is] [a] big blessing. (*viii*) Different [things] [are] beautiful to different [people] (*i.e.* some people like one thing, others another). (*ix*) The tongue [is] [the] cause of *(or* responsible for) many troubles. (*x*) Doing [is] difficult, giving the order (*sc.* to do it) [is] easy. (*xi*) Getting drunk (*or* drunkenness) [is] [a] bad remedy for (*i.e.* way to get rid of) woe. (*xii*) One learns by experience (lit. sufferings [are] lessons). (*xiii*) [A] bad egg comes from (*lit.* [is] of) [a] bad crow. (*xiv*) Trust the land, mistrust the sea (*lit.* [the] land [is] [a] trustworthy [thing], [the] sea [an] untrustworthy [thing]). (*xv*) Even an ant can get angry (*lit.* [there is] bile (anger) even in [an] ant). 6 (*i*) One must find a wife amongst one's own class (*lit.* it is necessary [*sc.* for a person] to marry from among those who are similar. (*ii*) [A] fool speaks foolish [things]. (*iii*) You have your feet out of trouble (*lit.* foot outside mud). (*iv*) [The] pot boils, friendship lives. (*v*) You are shaving (*or* bearding) [a] lion. (*vi*) You are weeping on [your] step-mother's tomb (*i.e.* being hypocritical). (7)

Alas, alas, greatness (*lit.* great things) also suffers great evils. (8) [The] roughness of [the] road tests [the] serviceability of [the] ass. (9) Man is only (*or* nothing but) breath and shadow. (10) Fortune guides art, not art fortune. (11) Money [is] responsible for many evils for men. (12) Woman, silence is becoming (*lit.* brings decoration) for women. (13) Even for [an] old man, [it is] [a] fine [thing] to learn wisdom (*lit.* wise things). (14) The Athenians sent Thucydides the [son] of Olorus to the general of those in Thrace. (15) One should seek neither companionship (*or* company) from [a] corpse nor [a] favour from [a] miser. (16) Victory is sufficient for the free. (17) Even among rustics there is love of culture. (18) The wolf changes his coat (*lit.* hair), not his mind. (19) Money finds friends for men. (20) [A] mob [is] [a] poor judge of [a] fine matter. (21) To some of the Egyptians, therefore, crocodiles are sacred, to others [they are] not, but they treat [them] as enemies. Those around Thebes and [those around] the swamp of Moeris strongly believe that they are (*lit.* them to be) sacred. Both groups keep *(or* rear) one crocodile and train [it], and put rings made of glass in its ears and anklets round its front feet, and provide special food and offerings. So while the crocodiles are alive, they are treated very well, and after their death the Egyptians embalm them and bury them in sacred tombs. But those around the city [of] Elephantine actually eat them; for they do not consider [them] to be sacred. (Adapted from Herodotus ii.69)

6.2

From this point on the definite and indefinite articles which must be supplied for translation are no longer bracketed.

(1) (*i*) The guards guarded the Persians (φυλάττω). (*ii*) Did you hide the golden horse? (κρύπτω). (*iii*) The Athenians and the Spartans joined in an expedition (cυcτρατεύω). (*iv*) He wrote many things on the rock (ἐγγράφω). (*v*) The gods will do many great things (πράττω). (*vi*) Socrates taught us (διδάcκω). (*vii*) They damaged the house of Pericles (βλάπτω). (*viii*) We fought a sea-battle in the harbour (ναυμαχέω). (2) Bronze is the mirror of form (i.e. of the body), wine of the mind. (3) Hand washes hand, fingers [wash] fingers. (4) Speech is silver, silence is golden. (5) O God, how mortals have no escape from evils [which are] innate or (*or* and) sent by the gods! (*lit.* how there is not to mortals [an] escape...). (6) (*i*) You are writing on (*lit.* into) water. (*ii*) You are building on (*lit.* into) sand. (*iii*) [You are bringing] an owl to Athens (*cf.* coals to Newcastle). (*iv*) You are measuring the waves. (*v*) You are looking for bird's milk. (*vi*) You are teaching iron to float (*lit.* sail). (*vii*) You are lending light to the sun. (*viii*) You are pouring wine for frogs. (ix) You are beating the air. (x) He is making an elephant out of a fly (*i.e.* a mountain out of a molehill). (7) (*i*) The mind is a great check (*lit.* bit) of the soul. (*ii*) The Greeks [are] always children, an old Greek does not exist. (*iii*) For a mother (*or* for mothers) children are the anchors of [her] life. (*iv*) Lions at home, but foxes (*i.e.* cowards) in battle. (*v*) The mind sees and the mind hears. (*vi*) The arms (*lit.* hands) of tyrants [are] long. (*vii*) Ares (War) [is] a friend of falsehood *(lit.* friendly to false things). (*viii*) Athens [is] the Greece of Greece. (*ix*) You are comparing a bee with a cicada. (*x*) A daughter [is] a difficult possession. (8) The wind [kindles] fire, intimacy kindles love. (9) According to Socrates no-one errs willingly. (10) The wise man should not think after (*i.e.* repent) but before (*lit.* it is necessary for the wise man not to...). (11) The Athenian ambassadors withdrew to the army, but the generals built a wall around the Melians. Later, a small garrison of the allies remained there and continued to besiege (*lit.* was besieging) the place, while the rest

of the soldiers withdrew by land and by sea. Afterwards the Melians pulled down the Athenians' blockading wall, since not many of the guards were present. But later the Athenians sent out another army from Athens, and they now vigorously prosecuted the siege. There was treachery (*or* treachery broke out) among the Melians, and they capitulated to the Athenians. And they (*i.e.* the Athenians) killed the men among (*lit.* of) the Melians, and enslaved the women and children. And later they sent out many settlers and colonised the place. (Adapted from Thucydides v.114-116.)

7.2

(1) The proverb bids us not to move the immovable (*lit.* unmovable [things]) (2) [It is] altogether not easy to find what is right (*or* justice). (3) Ischomachus said, "Socrates, in winter a house should be well exposed to the sun, but in summer well-shaded." (4) We do not have either weapons or horses (*or* we have neither weapons nor horses). (5) No falsehood spreads for long (a length of time). (6) So for one day the Athenians encamped there. But on the following day Alcibiades called an assembly and ordered them to fight both at sea, on land and against the fortifications. "For," he said, "we have no money, whereas the enemy have plenty." (7) All human beings die (*lit.* no-one of human beings does not die). (8) (*i*) One swallow does not make a spring. (*ii*) Old men [are] children for a second time. (*iii*) You see three things in two. (*iv*) One man [is] no man. (*v*) One day does not make (a man) wise. (*vi*) The tongue leads many [people] to destruction. (*vii*) In war it is not possible to make a mistake twice. (*viii*) It is possible to recognise a lion from his claw-marks (*i.e.* to judge a person from a characteristic mark). (9) Cyrus marched forth three stages (*or* days' marches) through Lydia, [a distance of] twenty-two parasangs, to the river Maeander. Its breadth was two plethra. (10) The world [is] a stage, life an entrance: you come, you see, you depart. (11) Someone said to Socrates, "Megacles speaks ill of you." And he replied, " Yes, for he does not know how (*lit.* has not learnt) to speak well." (12) Callicratidas held the right wing of the Peloponnesians. His steersman, Hermon, said, "It is a good [idea] to retreat (*lit.* sail away); for the Athenian triremes are very strong." But Callicratidas said, "It is shameful to flee." The triremes fought [for] a long time, at first in close order, and then scattered. When Callicratidas fell overboard into the sea and was killed and Protomachus the Athenian and his men (*lit.* those with him) defeated the left wing with [their] right wing, thereupon the Peloponnesians fled (*lit.* there was a flight of...) to Chios and Phocaea, while the Athenians sailed back to Arginousae. And so of the Athenians the Spartans sank 25 triremes, whereas of the Peloponnesians the Athenians [sank] nine Laconian [triremes], and of their allies as well about 60. (Adapted from Xenophon *Hellenica* i. 6. 32.) (13) For, when Simon came to my house at night, he forced (*lit.* knocked out) the doors and entered the women's apartments, where my sister and nieces were. At first the men in the house ordered him to go away, but he refused. Then they forcibly pushed him out. But he discovered where we were dining and did a thing most extraordinary and incredible. He called me out from inside, and as soon as I had come out, he immediately attempted to strike me; and when I pushed him away, he began to pelt me with stones (*or* throw stones at me). Although he missed me, he hit Aristocritus with a stone and gashed his forehead. (Adapted from Lysias *Against Simon* 6-8.)

8.2

(1) God and Nature do nothing without reason. (2) [It is] not easy to change a wicked nature. (3) Wicked slander wipes out whole cities. (4) Jesus Christ, son of God, Saviour (*the symbol is the fish,* ἰχθύς *being an acronym of the phrase*). (5) Gold does not tarnish (*lit.* is not stained). (6) Do you think that others will save Greece, but you will run away? (7) As a result of looking at [someone] people fall in love. (8) The possession of virtue alone is secure. (9) Alas, alas, how true the old saying is: we old men are nothing but (no other thing except) noise and [outward] appearance; we creep along [as] copies of dreams; there is no sense in [us] but we think we are sane. (Euripides, fragment 25.) (10) An elephant does not bite a mouse. (11) For most people the search for truth [is pursued] without taking pains, and they turn rather to what is ready to hand. (12) The Lacedaemonians sent a herald and carried across the corpses (*or* had the corpses carried across). (13) It was wonder which made men begin to pursue philosophy both now and originally (*lit.* because of the fact of wondering men both now and at first began...). (14) The mountain laboured, and then gave birth to a mouse. (15) Hunger is (*lit.* becomes) the teacher of many [things]. (16) The Scythians do not wash with (*or* in) water. (17) (*i*) In the beginning God made the heaven and the earth. And the earth was invisible and unformed, and darkness [was] upon the abyss, and the spirit of God moved upon the water. And God said, "Let there be (*lit.* be born) light. And there was light (*lit.* light came into being). And God saw that the light was beautiful. And God made a division between the light and the darkness. And God called the light day and the darkness he called night. (*Genesis* 1.1-5.) (*ii*) I turned about and I saw beneath the sun that the race [is] not to the nimble, nor war to the strong, nor bread to the wise, nor wealth to the intelligent. (*Ecclesiastes* 9.11.) (18) Zenothemis contrived a wicked crime in collaboration with Hegestratus. They went around borrowing (*lit.* were borrowing) money in Syracuse. When they got the money, they used to send it home to Marseilles, and they loaded (*lit.* brought into) nothing on board (*lit.* into) the ship. Since the contract stipulated repayment of (*lit.* was to repay) the money after the arrival in port of the ship, they plotted to sink the ship; for they wished to defraud their creditors. Accordingly, when they were two or three days out from land (*lit.* had sailed away a voyage of ... days), Hegestratus began to cut through the bottom of the ship during the night, while Zenothemis passed the time on deck (*lit.* above) with the other passengers. But when a noise was heard (*lit.* happened), those on the ship perceived that some mischief was taking place down below, and went to the rescue. As Hegestratus was being caught and assumed that he would be badly treated, he took to his heels (*lit.* fled) and jumped into the sea. In this way then, as he deserved, a bad man, he came to a bad end (*lit.* he died badly). ([? Demosthenes] *Against Zenothemis* 4-6, slightly adapted.)

9.2

(1) Death [is] beautiful [for those] to whom life brings humiliation. (2) The wise man carries round his substance within (*lit.* in) himself. (3) Mighty in war [was] Timocritus, whose tomb this [is]; Ares spares not the brave, but the cowardly. (*A.P.* vii. 269). (4) Cleon said that not he himself but that man was general. (5) The same [people] [say] the same [remarks] about the same [subjects] to the same [people]. (6) You are telling me my [own] dream (*i.e.* nothing I don't already know). (7) Then that man said, "Well, if there is need of anything else (*lit.* another thing) in

addition to what (*lit.* these things which) Xenophon says, it will be possible to do it immediately." After this Xenophon spoke as follows: "[It is] clear that we must march where we will have supplies; and I hear that there are fine villages which are twenty stades away." (Xenophon *Anabasis* iii. 2. 33-34.) (8) A friend is another self (*or* alter ego). (9) Pythagoras was the first to name philosophy and himself a philosopher. (10) [We] must compare them with each other; for thus we will consider if they will differ from each other. (11) The Greeks mistrust each other (*lit.* are mistrustful towards themselves). (12) After dinner Cyrus asked, "Tigranes, where then is that man who used to hunt with us? You seemed to me to admire him very much." "My father here put him to death," he said. "For he said that he was corrupting me. And yet, Cyrus, he was a fine man, for even when he was about to die, he summoned me and said, 'Tigranes, you must not be angry because your father is putting me to death; for he does this not because of malice, but because of ignorance. And what (*lit.* which things) men do wrong through ignorance, I believe [they do] this against their will'." (Xenophon *Cyropaedia*, iii.1.38, adapted.) (13) Demosthenes, who saw that the Lacedaemonians intended to attack by land and by sea (*lit.* both with ships and with infantry), began to make his own preparations (*lit.* make preparations himself also), and hauled up under the fortification the triremes which remained to him, and armed the sailors from them with shields of poor quality and mostly made of osier; for it was impossible to procure arms in [this] deserted place, and even these (*sc.* which they had) they got from a thirty-oared pirate-ship and a pinnace belonging to (*lit.* of) [some] Messenians, who were there. Of these Messenians there were about forty hoplites. Accordingly, he posted the majority of his own men at the strong points of the place facing the mainland, while (*lit.* and) he himself picked out sixty hoplites and a few archers and began to go outside the wall (*sc.* of the fortification) towards the sea, [to the point] where he particularly expected the enemy (*lit.* those men) would attempt to land. So he posted his hoplites at this point right beside the sea (*lit.* towards the sea itself). (Thucydides iv. 9, adapted.)

10.2

(1) A fat belly does not generate a fine mind. (2) How sweet [it is] to look at the sea from the land. (3) Time will explain everything to posterity (*lit.* those [who come] later). (4) Happiness is an activity of the soul. (5) O Menander and life, which one of you then imitated which? (6) Who knows if life is death, and [if] down below death is considered life? (7) Life [is] short, art long (*i.e.* the art of medicine is extensive and requires a long time to master), opportunity fleeting (*lit.* swift), experiment perilous, and judgement difficult. (8) Wickedness [is] quick, virtue slow. (9) Where a man fares well, there [is his] native-land. (10) Whoever of mortals wishes to arrive at (*lit.* go/come into) hateful old age, does not reckon well; for a long life begets countless woes. (11) How sweet [it is] for slaves to get decent masters and for masters [to get] a well-disposed slave in [their] house. (12) Everything [is] burdensome except to rule over the gods. For no-one is free except Zeus. (13) Ignorant [people] are carried along in life as if on the high sea and in darkness. (14) The woman said, "My husband's virtue is sufficient adornment for me." (15) Where a man has a pain, there he applies (*lit.* has) his mind too. (16) (*i*) I hate a drinking-companion who remembers (*lit.* a mindful drinking-companion). (*ii*) Hostile [is] the eye of neighbours. (*iii*) Even a sheep bites an unlucky man. (*iv*) An unskilled man is a slave of (*lit.* to) everyone. (v) War [is] sweet to the inexperienced. (*vi*) Time decides everything (*lit.* everything is decided by time). (*vii*)

Bright in darkness, but useless in daylight. (*viii*) Hands wash each other. (*ix*) Under every stone sleeps a scorpion. (*x*) Everything [is] easy for God (*or* a god). (*xi*) Every hedgehog [is] prickly. (*xii*) The whole of time cannot whiten the man (*lit.* this [man]) whom Fate paints (*lit.* will paint) black. (17) (*i*) Diogenes was once begging [alms] from a statue. [When he was] asked why he was doing this, he said, "I am practising failure (*lit.* to fail to obtain)." (*ii*) [When he was] asked what kind of wine he liked to drink (*lit.* drank gladly), he said, "Someone else's". (*iii*) He was begging [alms] from a miser. When he hesitated (*lit.* was slow), Diogenes said, "Fellow, I'm begging [alms] from you for food, not for burial." (*iv*) [When he was] asked where he was from, he said, "[I am] a citizen of the world". (*v*) When someone said that life was bad, he said, "Not life, but a bad life".

10.3

For, gentlemen of Athens, I have this reputation for no other reason (*lit.* on account of nothing else) than a certain wisdom. What sort of wisdom [do I say] this [is]? [Just that] which is perhaps human wisdom. For in reality I am likely to be (*or* I am probably) wise in this wisdom. But these men, whom I was just now mentioning, are wise in a sort of superhuman wisdom, which I am unable to describe. For I, at any rate, do not understand it, and (*lit.* but) whoever says [that I do], is lying and speaking to arouse prejudice against me. I hope, men of Athens, that you will not interrupt me, even if I seem to you to be saying something extravagant *(lit.* big). For the story which I will tell is not mine, but I will refer [you] to someone who is worthy of credit. For I shall furnish you with the god of *(lit.* at) Delphi [as] witness of my [wisdom], [as to] whether it is actually some sort of wisdom and of what sort it is. Chaerephon was familiar to you, I think. He was a comrade of mine from youth and a partisan of the democracy. And it is well-known to you what sort [of a person] Chaerephon was, how impetuous in all respects. As a matter of fact, he actually went to Delphi once and dared to ask the oracle if anyone was wiser than I. The Pythian [priestess] answered that no-one was wiser. (Plato *Apology* 20d-21a, slightly adapted.)

11.2

From this point on the relevant part of the verb to be *which must be supplied for translation is not normally bracketed.*

(1) Tyranny is the mother of injustice. (2) The dice of Zeus always fall luckily *(lit.* well). (3) There is some degree *(lit.* measure) of pleasure even in troubles. (4) And the story is not mine, but [comes] from my mother, that heaven and earth were one shape; but when they were separated apart from each other, they brought forth everything and sent up to the light trees, winged creatures, wild beasts and [the creatures] which the sea nourishes and the race of men. (Euripides, fragment 484.) (5) Concealment (*lit.* the act of hiding) is wicked and not the mark of a well-born man. (6) Someone said to Socrates, "The Athenians condemned you to the death," and he said, "And Nature [is condemning] them [to death]." (7) The wagon pulls the ox. (8) (*i*) An old woman is dancing. (*ii*) You are graciously giving a mirror to a blind man. (*iii*) You are hunting the wind with a net. (*iv*) You are throwing stones at the sun (*lit.* pelting the sun with stones). (*v*) The/a tortoise is calling the oxen slow-footed. (*vi*) You are striking a peg with a sponge. (*vii*) You knocked out a peg with a peg (*i.e.* in solving one problem you created another). (*viii*) You are blocking

up (*i.e.* repairing) the chamber-pot with a sandal. (*ix*) You are driving out wine with wine. (*x*) You yourself are striking your own door with a stone. (9) For, for all mankind, not only for us, either straightaway or in [the course of] time, God trips up [one's] life, and no-one is happy throughout (*or* forever). (Euripides, fragment 273.) (10) For none of these things will distress me. But if you do not do this (*lit.* these things), you will inflict (*lit.* throw) grief upon all the Argives (*i.e.* Greeks). For if we do not get this man's bow (*lit.* this man's bow will not be taken), it is not possible for you to ravage the land of Dardanus. (Sophocles *Philoctetes* 66-69.) (11) Thus the venture (*lit.* things) of the Greeks came to naught (*lit.* was destroyed). And out of many a few made their way through Libya to Cyrene and were saved, but most were killed. Egypt again came (*lit.* became) under the control of the King [of Persia], except Amyrtaeus, the king in the marshes. They (*i.e.* the Persians) were unable to capture him both because of the extent of the marsh and at the same time [because] the marsh-people are particularly warlike. Inaros the Libyan king (*lit.* king of the Libyans), who had conducted (*lit.* done) the whole Egyptian venture (*lit.* everything with respect to Egypt), was captured by treachery and impaled. Fifty triremes from Athens and the rest of the confederacy sailed [as a] relieving [force] to Egypt and put in at the Mendesian arm [of the Nile]. But foot-soldiers attacked them from the land and a fleet of Phoenicians from the sea and destroyed most of the ships. So ended the great expedition (*lit.* the [things] with respect to the great expedition) of the Athenians and their allies against (*lit.* into) Egypt. (Thucydides i.110, adapted.) (12) When we had transferred to the other ship, we began to drink. It is clear that Herodes disembarked from the ship and did not re-embark (*lit.* go on board again). I did not disembark at all from the ship that night. On the following day, when the man was not to be seen, he was looked for in no way more [vigorously] by the others than by me (*i.e.* I looked for him as vigorously as anyone); and if it (his disappearance) seemed serious to any of the others, [it did so] equally to me (*i.e.* if anyone considered it a serious matter, I did). Not only (*lit.* both) was I responsible for a messenger being sent to Mytilene, but (*lit.* and), since no-one else was willing to go, either of those on (*lit.* from) the ship or of the companions of Herodes himself, I was prepared to send my own servant. But when the man did not appear either in Mytilene or anywhere else, and the wind was fair (*lit.* sailing [time] was coming into being) for us and all the other ships were putting out to sea, I too departed. (Antiphon *Murder of Herodes* 23-24, slightly adapted.)

12.2

Where participial phrases have been expanded into subordinate clauses (e.g. in 1-5; see 12.1/2a) the words added in English have not been enclosed in square brackets.

(1) The man who runs away will also fight again (*or* lives to fight another day). (2) When a bear is present (*or* around) one need not look for tracks. (3) If you love yourself too much you will not have a friend. (4) Although he does not feed himself, he feeds his dogs. (5) The person who does not marry has no troubles. (6) In trying to flee (*lit.* fleeing) the smoke you fell into the fire. (7) A man who is running away does not wait for the sound of the lyre. (8) It is said that dogs burnt just once are afraid of fire (*lit.* dogs ... are said to fear ...). (9) For I have come to bury Caesar, not to praise [him]. (10) No-one who is hungry sings sweet songs (*lit.* beautiful things). (11) Am I a bumpkin (*lit.* boorish) if I call a trough a trough? (12) The man who has been bitten by a serpent fears even a little rope. (13) The

man who is illiterate (*lit.* inexperienced in letters) sees nothing although he has sight (*lit.* does not see [although] seeing). (14) It is difficult to speak to [one's] belly, since it does not have ears. (15) Prometheus: "You behold [this] spectacle, [me] this friend of Zeus, with what woes I am bent by him." Ocean: "I see, Prometheus, and I wish to give you the best advice (*lit.* advise the best things to you), subtle (*or* ingenious) as you are (*lit.* though being)." (Aeschylus *Prometheus Bound* 304ff.) (16) From there Cyrus marched out though Lycaonia five stages, [a distance of] thirty parasangs, and he allowed the Greeks to plunder this country on the grounds that it was hostile. (17) Once when turning a book of Hesiod beneath my hands I suddenly saw Pyrrha approaching; and throwing the book to the ground with my hand I shouted this, "Why do you give me trouble, old Hesiod?" (*A.P.* ix.161.) (18) Child of Phoenician-born Europa and great Zeus, ruling over Crete of a hundred cities, I have come leaving sacred (*lit.* very holy) temples ... And we have led a chaste life since I became a mystic of Idaean Zeus,and, having conducted feasts of raw flesh as a herdsman of night-roaming Zagreus and held up torches for the mountain-wandering mother with the Curetes, I was sanctified and called an initiate of Bacchus. (Euripides, fragment 472.)

12.3

(1) A man, finding [some] gold, left a noose; but the man who did not find the gold which he had left, fastened the noose (*i.e.* to hang himself) which he had found. (*A.P.* ix.44.) (2) The Cyprian, seeing [the statue of] the Cyprian (*i.e.* of herself) in Cnidos, said, "Alas, alas, where did Praxiteles see me naked?" (*App. Plan.* 162.) (3) All Cilicians are bad men; but among the Cilicians [there is] one good man, [viz] Cinyres, but even Cinyres is Cilician. (*A.P.* xi. 236.) (4) Once Antiochus laid eyes on (*lit.* looked at) Lysimachus' cushion, and Lysimachus never again (*lit.* no longer) laid eyes on his cushion. (*A.P.* xi. 315.) (5) Although he produced twenty sons, Eutychus the painter has no likeness even among (*lit.* from) his children (*i.e.* he has as little success in producing lifelike paintings as in fathering children from a faithless wife). (*A.P.* xi. 215.) (6) You [with] the roses, you have a rosy charm. But what are you selling, yourself, or the roses, or both together? (*A.P.* v. 81.) (7) As I was kissing Agathon, I checked my soul at [my] lips; for it had come, poor wretch, with the idea of crossing over. (*A.P.* v. 78.) (8) I who laughed haughtily at Greece, I, Laïs, who kept the swarm of young lovers in [my] porch, [dedicate] [my] mirror to the Paphian; since such [as I am now] I do not wish to see myself, and such as I was formerly I am unable [to see myself]. (*A.P.* vi. 1.) (9) Someone told [me], Heraclitus, of your death, and brought tears (*lit.* a tear) to me, and I remembered how often both of us laid the sun to rest in conversation. But you, I suppose, my friend from Halicarnassus, are ashes long, long ago. But your nightingales (*i.e.* poems) live on, upon which Hades, the ravisher of all things, shall not lay his hand. (Callimachus epigram 2.)

13.2

(1) [It] is a fine [thing] indeed to be master of one's belly and one's desire[s]. (2) Both common-sense and proper deliberation (*lit.* deliberating on what it is necessary [to do]) are accustomed to accompany old age. (3) This is bravery (*lit.* the brave thing), [that is to say] forethought. (4) Everywhere the land which feeds [you is your] native-land. (5) Old age, you know, has a certain wisdom (*lit.* something

wise) indeed with respect to deliberation (*or* planning), since indeed it has seen and experienced much (*lit.* as having seen and experienced many things). (6) O unfortunate virtue, you were [a mere] word then; yet I practised you as something real (*lit.* a fact, *i.e.* as though you really existed). But you were a slave to chance after all. (7) Oedipus, the son of Laius, is my father (*lit.* father for us), and Iocaste, the daughter of Menoeceus, bore me; and the Theban people call me Polyneices. (Euripides *Phoenissae* 288-290.) (8) There is no temple of Persuasion other than speech, and her altar is in the nature of man. (9) He who chases two hares catches neither. (10) Cyrus, inasmuch as he was a child and liked elegance and distinction, was pleased with his clothes. (11) Not even the gods fight against necessity. (12) Obedience to one's stomach is a necessary evil. (13) In escaping Charybdis you have fallen into (*lit.* in with) Scylla. (14) A hungry ass pays no heed to the cudgel. (15) No-one desires life as much as the man who is growing old. (16) Death alone of the gods does not desire gifts. (17) The man who does no wrong needs no law (*sc.* to protect him). (18) Sailors (*or* those who sail) are [only] four fingers away from death. (19) You have a need of spring since you have an old cloak (*i.e.* spring [and not winter] is the right season for the threadbare cloak you are wearing). (20) The Spartan [woman] Gorgo, asked by an Attic (*i.e.* Athenian) [woman], "Why do you Spartan [women] alone rule your men (*or* husbands)?" said, "Because we alone also give birth to [real] men". (21) In reply to a certain lad who was intending to attend his classes and enquired what he needed (*lit.* of what things there is a need to him), Antisthenes the philosopher said, "A new book and a new pencil and a new writing-tablet", stressing the nous. (*The pun on* καινοῦ *and* καὶ-νοῦ *is virtually untranslatable, although in American pronunciation it comes across in 'new' and 'nous'.*) (22) The black earth drinks, and the trees drink it (*i.e.* from it); the sea drinks the streams, the sun the sea, and the moon the sun. Why do you fight with me [my] friends (*or* comrades), when I myself also wish to drink? (Anacreontea 19)

13.3

(*i*) I was making my way from the Academy straight to the Lyceum along the [road] outside the wall, close under the wall (*lit.* beneath the wall) itself. When I came to (*lit.* was in the region of) the postern gate where the spring of Panops is, there I fell in with Hippothales, the [son] of Hieronymus, and Ctesippus of Paiania, and [some] other young men [who were] with them. Seeing me approach, Hippothales said, "Socrates, where are you going and where [have you come] from?" "From the Academy," I said, "on my way (*lit.* I'm making my way) straight to the Lyceum." "[Come] over **here**," he said, "straight to us. Aren't you going to come over (*lit.* do you not come near)? Yet it's worthwhile." "Where do you mean," I said, "and who are you to whom [I am to come]?" "Over here," he said, showing me right opposite (*lit.* in the [spot] right opposite) the wall a sort of enclosure and door. "We spend our time here," he said, "both we ourselves and a lot of other fine [fellows]." "And what **is** this [place] then, and how do you spend your time (*lit.* what is [your] manner of spending time)?" "A new wrestling-school," he said. "And we usually spend our time in discussions, in which we wish you to share." "That's very kind of you (*lit.* doing well indeed)," I said. "And who teaches here?" "Your own friend," he said, "and admirer, Miccus." "My goodness (*lit.* by Zeus)," I said, "he's not unimportant (*lit.* the man [is] not insignificant), he's a competent teacher." "Well then, do you want to follow [me]," he said, "and to see those who are here?" (Plato *Lysis* 203a-204a.)

(*ii*) *Eucleides.* Just [in] from the country, Terpsion, or [did you arrive] some time ago? *Terpsion.* Quite some time ago. I was looking for you in (*lit.* throughout) the agora and was surprised that I could not find [you]. *E.* [No you couldn't], for I was not in the city. *T.* Where [were you] then? *E.* As I was going down to [the] harbour I met Theaetetus being carried to Athens from the camp at (*lit.* from) Corinth. *T.* Alive or dead? *E.* Alive, but only just (*lit.* and very hardly). For he's in a bad way actually because of some wounds, but more [than that] the disease which [has broken out] in the army is afflicting him. *T.* You don't mean dysentery, do you? *E.* Yes, I do. *T.* What a man [this is who] you say is in danger. *E.* A real gentleman (*lit.* fine and good), Terpsion, and (*lit.* since), you know, just now I was listening to some [people] singing his praises (*lit.* praising him very much) in connection with the battle. *T.* And [that's] not at all strange. But how [is it that] he did not stay (*or* lodge) here in Megara? *E.* He was hurrying [to get] home. I asked him and advised him [*sc.* to stay], but he refused. In fact, as I escorted [him home] I recalled with admiration how prophetically Socrates had spoken in particular about him (*lit.* I recalled and marvelled at Socrates how prophetically he had spoken both other things indeed and about this man). For I think that (*lit.* he seems to me to...), a little before his death, he (Socrates) met him when he was a lad, and after being with [him] and conversing [with him], greatly admired his character. (Plato *Theaetetus* 142a-c.)

14.2

The abbreviations P.S. (Primary sequence) and H.S. (Historic sequence) are used in defining the uses of the subjunctive/optative here.

(1) For there is a certain pleasure even in words, if (*lit.* whenever) they create a forgetfulness of [one's] existing troubles (*indefinite, P.S.*). (2) How then am I, a [mere] mortal (*lit.* being mortal), to fight against divine fortune (*or* fortune sent by the gods)? (*deliberative subjunctive*). (3) [It is] the mind [that one] must look at, the mind; what advantage [is there] in (*lit.* of) bodily beauty, if (*lit.* whenever) a person does not have a beautiful (*i.e.* noble) mind? (*indefinite, P.S.*). (4) Whoever is shipwrecked twice, blames Poseidon without reason (*i.e.* he should have taken Poseidon's hint the first time) (*indefinite, P. S.*). (5) Socrates said that most men live in order that they may eat, whereas he himself ate in order that he might live (*purpose, subjunctive retained in H.S.*). (6) Let us eat and drink; for tomorrow we die (*jussive subjunctive.*). (7) God plants (*lit.* produces) a fault (*lit.* blame) in mortals whenever he wishes to ruin a family completely (*indefinite, P. S.*). (8) What a charming creature (*lit.* how charming) is a man when (*lit.* whenever) he is a [real] man (*indefinite, P.S.*). (9) *A.* Who is this man? *B.* A doctor. *A.* What a bad state every doctor is in if (*lit.* if ever) no-one [else] is in a bad state! (*indefinite, P.S.*). (10) Our life is very like wine: whenever what remains (*or* the remains) is small, it becomes vinegar (*indefinite, P.S.*). (11) Those who are afraid that they may go into exile from their native-land and those who, being about to fight, are afraid that they may be defeated are not able to take (*lit.* get) either food or sleep because of their fear; but those who are already in exile or (*lit.* and) already defeated can eat and sleep even more (*or* better) than those blessed with good fortune (*fear for the future, P.S.*). (12) A monkey is a monkey even if it has golden sandals (*indefinite, P.S.*). (13) The Greeks were afraid that the Persians might advance agains the wing and, outflanking them on both sides, might cut them to pieces (*fear for the future, H.S.*). (14) When the man whom they had seized was asked from what country he

came (*lit.* was; *indirect question, H.S.*), he said that he was a Persian, and that he was proceeding from Tiribazos' army in order that he might get provisions (*purpose clause, H.S.*). (15) When Diogenes saw an archer with no natural skill, he sat down beside the target saying, "In order that I may not be hit" (*purpose clause in direct quotation, hence* **not** *H.S.*). (16) Through inexperience of death every man is afraid to leave the light of this sun (*lit.* this light of the sun). (17) A man was running so as not to get wet, and was drowned in a hole (*purpose clause, H.S.*). (18) When the generals assembled at daybreak, they were surprised that Cyrus neither sent someone else to tell [them] what to do (*lit.* it is necessary to do) nor appeared himself (*indirect statement, H.S.*). So they decided to pack up what they had and put on their full (ἐξ–) armour and move forwards. When they were already on the point of starting, at sunrise there came Procles, the ruler of Teuthrania, and Glus, the [son] of Tamos. They reported that Cyrus had been killed, but that Ariaeus was at the halting place with the rest of the barbarians and was saying that they would wait for them throughout this day (*indirect statement, H.S.*). (Xenophon *Anabasis* ii. 1. 2-3, slightly adapted.) (19) If ever he saw the soldiers going in good order, he praised [them] (*indefinite, H.S.*). (20) If you fear the law (*lit.* fearing the law) you will not be troubled by the law.

15.2

(1) [While] avoiding [the] ashes I have fallen into [the] fire (*i.e.* out of the frying-pan into the fire). (2) No-one does wicked [deeds] without the gods' knowing (*lit.* no-one escapes the notice of the gods doing wicked things). (3) A crab has not learned (*i.e.* does not know how) to walk straight. (4) We are all wise in giving warnings (*lit.* with respect to warning), but we do not realise when we ourselves make mistakes. (5) The trap has caught the mouse. (6) For the man who takes pleasure in constantly speaking does not realise (*lit.* escaped his own notice) that he is wearisome to his companions (*lit.* those who are with [him]). (7) He has eaten scorpions. (8) Whoever devises treachery (*lit.* crafty things) against another is doing this against himself unawares (*lit.* escapes [his own] notice doing this himself against himself). (9) The hoplites happened to be sleeping in the agora. (10) It was clear that Menon desired (*lit.* Menon was obvious desiring) to be exceedingly rich. (11) So they took Jesus; and carrying his own cross (*lit.* the cross for himself) he went forth to the so-called Place of a Skull, which in Hebrew is called Golgotha, where they crucified him, and with him two others one on each side (*lit.* from this side and from this side), and Jesus in the middle. Pilate also wrote a title (*or* inscription) and placed [it] on the cross, JESUS OF NAZARETH THE KING OF THE JEWS. Many of the Jews read this title, because the place where Jesus was crucified was near the city. Accordingly, the chief priests of the Jews said to Pilate, "Do not write 'The King of the Jews', but 'He claimed to be the King of the Jews' " (*lit.* but that, "he said, 'I am the King ...' "). Pilate replied, "What I have written, I have written." (John 19.16-22.) (12) For all seven days during which they were marching through [the territory of] the Kurds they continued to fight. (13) When Clearetus had encouraged his soldiers, he began to lead them against the place, but day broke while he was still marching (*lit.* day happening anticipated him marching). (14) When Archimedes was washing himself, so the story goes (*lit.* as they say), he discovered from the overflow (*sc.* of the water-level in his bath) how to measure (*lit.* the measuring of) the crown, and as if possessed or inspired (*lit.* just as from some possession or inspiration), he jumped out shouting, "I've

found [it]," and went about saying this over and over again (*lit.* often). But we have heard neither of any glutton shouting so passionately, "I have eaten," nor of any lover [shouting] "I have kissed," though countless sensualists existed in the past and [still] exist [now]. (Plutarch *Moralia* 1094C.) (15) *A.* He is married, I believe. *B.* What are you saying? Is he really married, [the man] whom I left alive and on his feet (*lit.* living and walking about)? (16) They stopped building the large wall because they feared (*lit.* fearing) that it would not be sufficient to hold out. (17) I see that for the majority of people former prosperity gives birth to insolence.

15.3

Might. We have come to [this] distant region of the earth, to [this] Scythian tract, to [this] wilderness where no men live. Hephaestus, you must concern yourself with the commands (*lit.* it is necessary that the commands be of concern to you) which the Father (*i.e.* Zeus) enjoined on you, to bind fast this wrong-doer on [these] rocks with lofty cliffs in unbreakable fetters of adamantine bonds. For [it was] your glory, the flame of fire on which all arts depend, [which] he stole and bestowed on mortals. [It is] for such a wrong, you know, [that] he must pay the penalty to the gods, in order that he may be taught (*or* learn) to accept the sovereignty of Zeus, and cease from his man-loving ways. *Hephaestus.* Might and Violence, for you two the command of Zeus has indeed fulfilment (*or* has been fulfilled) and nothing is still in [your] way, but I lack the heart to bind by force to [this] stormy ravine a god [who is my] kinsman. Yet for all that, I must (*lit.* there is necessity for me to) get the heart for this; for [it is] a grievous [matter] to disregard the words of the Father. O lofty-minded son of straight-counselling Themis, against your will and mine (*lit.* you being unwilling I being unwilling) will I fasten you in (*or* with) inextricable brazen bonds to this rock far from men, where you will perceive (*lit.* see) neither the voice nor the shape of anyone of mortals, but grilled by the sun's radiant flame you will alter the bloom of your skin; and you will be glad when (*lit.* to you being glad) night with her embroidered cloak will hide the light and [when] the sun will scatter the morning frost again; the burden of your present suffering (*lit.* the present trouble) will continually distress you; for the one who will relieve [it *or* you] is not yet born. (Aeschylus *Prometheus Bound* 1-27)

16.2

(1) When they had come to their tents, the rest (*sc.* of the soldiers) were busy about the provisions, while generals and captains met together. And at this point there was much despondency. For on one side there lay (*lit.* were) very high mountains, and on the other side the river was so deep (*lit.* of such a size) that not even their spears were above [the water] when they tested the depth. (2) When Diogenes was asked why athletes were stupid, he said, "Because they have been built up with pork and beef." (3) One must marry [only] after making a [proper] choice. (4) We are involved in constant (*lit.* we continue being in) dangers throughout all our life, so that those who talk about security do not realise (*lit.* have escaped their own notice) that they are preparing for war for the whole of time. (5) You are flaying a flayed bitch (*i.e.* you are flogging a dead horse). (6) The Potideans, waiting for the Athenians, were camped on the isthmus on the side towards Olynthus, and they had established a market outside the city. And the allies had chosen Aristeus [as] general of the whole infantry and Perdiccas of the cavalry. (7) When the barbarians

had left their land, the Athenians began to make preparations to rebuild their city. For of the houses most had collapsed, although a few survived, in which the chief men of the Persians had themselves lodged. (8) The goat has come to knives [already] sharpened (*i.e.* one is asking for trouble). (9) They passed the night there. But when day began to break, they proceeded to march in silence against the enemy, drawn up in battle-order; for a mist had also appeared, so that they came up close without being seen (*lit.* escaped notice approaching near). (10) Then an agreement was made (*lit.* comes into being (*vivid pres.*)) with respect to all those with Demosthenes as well, on condition that no-one would die either through violence (*lit.* violently) or imprisonment (*lit.* bonds) or lack of food. (11) Tiribazus said that he wished to make a treaty on condition that neither he himself would harm the Greeks nor would they burn the houses but (*lit.* and) would take the provisions that they needed. These [terms] were accepted by (*lit.* seemed good to) the generals and they made a treaty on these terms. (12) Nor is it still the time, Socrates, to be deliberating but to have finished deliberating. There is [only] one plan: all this must be completed (*or* over and done with) within this night. (13) So boldness and courage are not the same thing. Consequently the result is (*lit.* it results) that the courageous are bold but not that the bold are courageous, for boldness, like strength, comes to men from art and from anger and from madness but courage from nature and proper nurture of the soul (*lit.* souls). (14) The Spartans considered that the Athenians were first in violation of (*lit.* to be in a state of having broken) the treaty. (15) The goat has not yet given birth (*i.e.* don't count your chickens before they're hatched.) (16) Philip, the father of Alexander the Great, wanted (*lit.* wanting) to capture a strong fort. When his scouts reported that it was difficult in all respects and impregnable, he asked if it was so difficult that not even an ass carrying gold could approach [it].

16.3

I am alive and I behold what I ought to, the sky, the earth and these shafts of sun[light]. But what a terrible turmoil (*lit.* wave, surf) and confusion of mind I have fallen into (*lit.* in) and what warm breath I breathe, shallow, not steady from my lungs. Look, why am I sitting anchored like a ship with bonds on (*lit.* with respect to) my sturdy chest and arms to this stone-carved pillar (*lit.* chiselled work made of stone) broken in half, sitting next to corpses (*lit.* having a seat neighbouring corpses)? My winged weapons and bow lie scattered on the ground, which formerly shielded my arms and protected my flanks and were protected by me. Surely I have not descended back to [the house] of Hades again, having [just] completed (*lit.* having gone) the double course from Hades set by Eurystheus? But neither do I see the stone of Sisyphus or Pluto nor yet the sceptre of Demeter's daughter. I am indeed bewildered. Wherever am I in my helplessness? Help, who is there of my friends near or far who will cure my bewilderment? (Euripides *Heracles* 1089-1107.)

17.2

(1) (*i*) If (*or* when) you are wronged (*lit.* being wronged), settle your differences. (*ii*) Keep away from other people's property. (*iii*) Don't hurry when you undertake something (*lit.* undertake slowly). (*iv*) Don't rush into marriage (*lit.* delay getting married). (*v*) Know yourself (*i.e.* your human limitations). (*vi*) Respect your

parents. (*vii*) Think [only] mortal thoughts (*lit.* mortal things). (*viii*) Don't laugh over a corpse. (*ix*) Know the right moment. (*x*) Nothing in excess. (*xi*) When you drink, don't talk too much (*lit.* prattle many things). (*xii*) Use your wealth fairly (*lit.* be wealthy justly). (*xiii*) Believe in fortune. (*xiv*) If (*or* when) you are insulted, avenge yourself. (*xv*) Don't curse your sons. (2) Train your children; for you will not train [them when they are] men. (3) An army of deer led by a lion is more frightening than an army of lions led by a deer. (4) Fear old age; for it does not come alone. (5) Choose a good reputation rather than wealth (*lit.* wish to be well spoken of rather than to be rich). (6) When you have passed a rose do not seek it any longer again. (7) We have two ears but one mouth, in order that we may hear more but speak less. (8) (*i*) Neighbours have sharper eyes (*lit.* see more sharply) than foxes. (*ii*) When you are walking on foot do not fear the waves. (*iii*) Let a lion eat me, not a fox (*i.e.* if I come to grief may it be at the hands of a worthy opponent). (*iv*) Be both a lion where it is required (*lit.* necessary) and a monkey in turn (*i.e.* be prepared to assume a role suited to a particular situation). (*v*) What[ever] bread a man has kneaded, let him eat it as well. (*vi*) When the general is present, let all the officers stop (*sc.* giving orders). (*vii*) The man who desires more is also deprived of what he has (*lit.* the things which are present). (*viii*) Don't throw food into a chamberpot. (*ix*) When you are a foreigner follow the local customs. (*x*) Don't speak ill of your friend or well of your enemy. (*xi*) If (*or* when) you are prosperous, don't despise the poor. (*xii*) Judge not, that you be not judged. (*xiii*) Second thoughts are somehow wiser. (*xiv*) Most people are rogues. (*xv*) Things last year were always better. (9) One of the Saii exults in my shield, which I left unwillingly, a blameless weapon, by a thicket. But I myself escaped the doom of death; to hell with that shield; I'll get another just as good (*lit.* once more I shall obtain [one] not worse). (Archilochus 6.) (10) The royal cubit is three fingers greater (*or* longer) than the standard cubit. (11) (*i*) When Eudamidas saw Xenocrates, who was now rather old, studying philosophy in the Academy with his students and ascertained that he was searching for virtue, he said, "So when will he [be able to] use it?" (*ii*) When a certain Argive was saying that the Spartans became worse when they were abroad (*lit.* during their absences from home), he (*i.e.* Eudamidas) said, "But **you**, when you come to Sparta, do not become worse but better." (*iii*) To a wretch who was asking [him] who the best Spartan was Agis said, "The one who is most unlike you." (*iv*) When a teacher was about to read out an encomium of Heracles, Antalcidas said, "Well, who's criticising him?" (*v*) When Thearidas was sharpening a sword he was asked if it was sharp, and he said, "Sharper than slander." (*vi*) When a garrulous barber asked Archelaus, "How would you like it, your Majesty (*lit.* how am I to cut your hair, O King)?" Archelaus said, "In silence (*lit.* keeping quiet)." (12) When Aristotle heard that he was being abused by someone, he said, "Let him also whip me when I'm not there (*lit.* being absent)." (13) Although they are wise in other respects, the sophists do something extraordinary *viz* (*lit.* do an extraordinary thing [viz] this) they claim to be teachers of virtue, yet they often accuse their students of wronging them (*lit.* that they wrong them), by withholding their fees, although they have been well-treated by them (*i.e.* if the sophists had really been able to teach their students virtue, the latter would not have failed to pay their fees). (14) Much enmity and mutual hatred is innate in our citizens, on account of which I am always fearful that some disaster too great to bear may fall upon the city. (15) The Lacedaemonians kept sending embassies to the Athenians to make complaints, in order that they might have (*lit.* there might be to them) as great a pretext as possible for going to war, in case they (the Athenians) did not pay any attention. (16) Cleander was tyrant of Gela for seven years, but he was killed by Sabyllus, a man from Gela. (17) Hope and you, Luck, a long farewell; I have found the harbour. There's nothing [more] between you and me. Have your fun with those [who come] after me

17.3

Hermes. You there, the clever one, bitterly bitter to the extreme, you who offended against the gods by giving honours to mortals, you the thief of fire I mean; the Father orders you to tell [him] of the marriage of which you boast and by which he is [to be] cast out of his power. And what is more, do not [tell] it (*lit.* these things) in riddling fashion, but explain each detail as it is, and do not inflict a double journey on me, Prometheus. You see that Zeus is not softened by such behaviour. *Prometheus.* Haughty and full of arrogance is your talk, for a lackey of the gods. New you are and new your power (*lit.* you [being] new wield new power), and you think indeed that you dwell in citadels free from woe. [Yet] have I not seen two rulers cast out from them? And as the third I shall behold the present lord (*sc.* cast out) most shamefully and most speedily. You don't imagine, do you, (*lit.* surely I do not seem to you in some respect) that I am terrified and cower before these new gods? I'm far removed, indeed completely removed, from that. Hasten back along the road you came; for you will find out none of the things which you question me about. (Aeschylus *Prometheus Bound* 944-963.)

18.2

(1) A man from Cyme was selling honey. When someone tasted it and said, "It's very nice," he said, "[Yes,] for if a mouse had not fallen into it, I would not be selling it." (2) A Spartan woman, in answer to her son who was saying that the sword which he had was short, said, "Add a step" (*i.e.* take a step closer to your enemy to make up for the shortness of your sword). (3) (*i*) If the lion-skin does not suffice, put on the fox-skin (*i.e.* if behaving like a lion doesn't help, behave like a fox). (*ii*) You are giving a dog bran, and an ass bones (*i.e.* you are doing things the wrong way). (*iii*) You keep your love on the tip of your tongue. (*iv*) If we hate our friends, what shall we do to those who hate [us] ? (*v*) If I had cheese, I would not want a cooked meal (*i.e.* the small luxury of cheese would be enough—spoken of those who did not indulge themselves overmuch). (*vi*) [When] a friend [is] in trouble do not betray [him] because of anger. (*vii*) Gain is sweet, even if it comes from lies. (*viii*) Give something and take something. (*ix*) Wandering makes life more reasonable (*i.e.* travel broadens the mind). (*x*) [It is] disgraceful to betray one's benefactors. (*xi*) If we have money, we will have friends. (*xii*) Let matters proceed as God wills (*lit.* as is dear to the god). (4) A man came asking the seer Olympicus whether he should sail to Rhodes and how he would sail in safety; and the seer replied, "First, have a new ship, and put out to sea not in winter but in summer; for if you do this, you will go both there and [back} here, unless a pirate captures you at sea." (*A.P.* xi. 162.) (5) Once an old man had cut some wood and was walking a long road carrying it. Because of fatigue he laid aside the load and called upon Death. When Death appeared and asked for what reason he was calling upon him, the old man said, "So that you may lift up this load and put it on me." (6) Every gift which is given, even if it is small, is very great, if it is given with goodwill. (7) If a snake does not eat a snake, it will not become a dragon (*i.e.* to rise in the world one must be ruthless). (8) Naked I set foot upon the earth, and naked I shall

go away below the earth; and why do I vainly toil when I see the end naked? (9) (*i*) When someone was surprised at [the number of] the dedications in Samothrace, he said, "There would be far more if those who were not saved had also made dedications." (*ii*) When he came to Myndus and observed that the gates were big whereas the city was small, "Men of Myndus," he said, "Shut the gates lest your city gets out (*or* escapes)." (*iii*) He was asking a bad-tempered man [for alms]. When [the latter] said, "[Yes,] if you persuade me", [Diogenes] replied, "If I were able to persuade you, I would have persuaded you to hang yourself." (*iv*) Lighting (*lit.* having lit) a lamp in broad daylight, he used to go about saying, "I'm looking for a [genuine] human being." (10) The Syracusan generals trusted the fellow much too incautiously and immediately agreed upon a day on which they would be present and sent him back, while (*lit.* and) they themselves gave warning to the Syracusans beforehand that they would all go out in full force. When their preparations were complete and the days were at hand on which they had agreed to come, proceeding in the direction of Catana they encamped at the river Symaethus. When the Athenians perceived that they were approaching, they took all their own army and, putting it on board the ships and boats, sailed under cover of night against Syracuse. (Thucydides vi. 65, slightly adapted.)

18.3

They arrived at the mountain on the fifth day; the name of (*lit.* to) the mountain was Theches. When the vanguard got on to [the summit of] the mountain and looked down at the sea, much shouting arose. Hearing [this], Xenophon and the rearguard thought that other enemy forces were attacking up in front. But when (*or* since) the shouting was becoming greater and closer and those who kept coming up in succession were running quickly towards those who were continually shouting and the shouting became much louder in proportion as the numbers increased (*lit.* they were becoming more), it seemed to Xenophon to be something more serious. He mounted his horse and taking the cavalry set off to the rescue. And very soon they heard the soldiers shouting, "The sea, the sea!" and passing the word along. Thereupon all the rearguard also began to run, and the draught animals and the horses were driven along. When they had all arrived at the summit, they then began to embrace each other in tears, including generals and captains. (Xenophon *Anabasis* iv. 7. 21-25, slightly adapted.)

19.2

(1) Heraclitus says somewhere that everything is in motion (*or* flux) and nothing stays still, and likening existing things (*lit.* the being [things]) to the stream of a river he says that you could not (*or* cannot) step twice into the same river. (2) Keep sober and remember to distrust; these (*i.e.* sobriety and distrust) are the limbs of the mind. (3) Pyrrho said that there was no difference between life and death (*lit.* being alive or being dead differed in no way). And when someone said, "Why then do you not die?", he said, "Because it makes no difference." (4) Do you think that crimes (*or* sins) leap up with wings to the gods, and then someone writes them on the leaves of Zeus' tablet, and Zeus looks at them and gives judgements for mortals? The whole of heaven would not suffice if Zeus were writing [down] the sins of mortals nor would he (*i.e.* Zeus) examining [them] [suffice] to send a penalty to each man. No (*lit.* but), Justice is here somewhere near, if you wish to see.

(Euripides, fragment 506.) (5) (*i*) If you are able to travel (*sc.* by land), do not go by sea (*lit.* sail). (*ii*) You were caught by your own feathers (*i.e.* hoist with your own petard). (*iii*) A [statue of] Hermes cannot (*lit.* could not) be made out of every (*or* any) log. (*i.e.* you can't make a silk purse out of a sow's ear). (*iv*) If you drink water you will (*lit.* would) produce nothing wise. (*v*) The man who knows what is useful (*lit.* useful things), not the man who knows much (*lit.* many things), is wise. (*vi*) If God gives [it], you cannot (*lit.* could not) escape evil (*lit.* evil things). (*vii*) All men naturally (*or* by nature) strive after knowledge (Aristotle). (*viii*) Whenever you are having a fine voyage, be especially mindful of squalls (*lit.* a squall). (*ix*) Give me somewhere to stand (*lit.* where I am to stand) and I shall move the earth (Archimedes). (*x*) Much learning does not teach [one] to have wisdom; for (*sc.* otherwise) it would have taught Hesiod and Pythagoras (Heraclitus). (*xi*) That which exists naturally does not change. (*xii*) [One] must bear lightly [one's] present (*lit.* standing beside) fortunes. (*xiii*) Despondent men never yet (*lit.* not yet) set up a trophy. (*cf.* faint heart never won fair lady.) (*xiv*) Remember that you are a human being. (*xv*) If you set a trap, you will be caught in a trap. (*xvi*) Although he stands far off God sees from near at hand. (*xvii*) He stands on the razor['s edge] (*i.e.* he is in a difficult situation). (6) How sweet [it is] for those in distress to forget their present troubles even for a short time. (7) (*i*) To a man who said, "Except for the fact that you are King you are in no way different from us," Leonidas said, "But I wouldn't be King if I were not better than you." (*ii*) When he arrived at Thermopylae, to a man who said, "Because of the barbarians' arrows it is not even possible to see the sun," he said, "So [it will be] nice, if we fight (*lit.* will fight) them beneath the shade." (*iii*) When Xerxes wrote to him, "It is possible for you by not fighting against God but by ranging yourself with me, to be sole ruler of Greece," he wrote in reply, "If you knew (*i.e.* understood) the fine things of life, you would have refrained from the desire for other people's possessions; for me death on behalf of Greece is better than being sole ruler over my own race (*lit.* those of the same stock)." (*iv*) When Xerxes wrote again, "Send (*i.e.* surrender) your arms," he wrote in reply, "Come and get them!" (*v*) Stranger, tell the Spartans that we lie here, in obedience to (*lit.* obeying) their commands (*lit.* words). (8) I shall not revolt from the people of Athens (*lit.* of the Athenians) either in any way or means or in word or deed, nor shall I obey anyone who revolts (*lit.* the revolting man), and if anyone tries to stir up revolt, I shall denounce [him] to the Athenians; and I shall pay to the Athenians whatever tribute I persuade the Athenians [is appropriate]; and I shall be as excellent and just an ally as I am able (*lit.* I shall be an ally of whatever sort I may be able best and most just), and I shall come to the help of the people of Athens and I shall ward off anyone who (*lit.* if anyone) does wrong to the people of Athens, and I will obey the people of Athens. (*Inscriptiones Graecae* i³ 40.21-32.)

20.2

(1) Once a young man fell sick and said to his doctor that he was in such pain that he was unable either to sit or lie [down] or stand; the doctor said, "My friend, you have no alternative but (*lit.* there is no other thing left to you than) to hang". (2) Who knows if what is called death [is] life, and life is death? Except, however, [that] those of mortals who are alive (*lit.* see [*sc.* the light of day]) fall sick, whereas those who are dead never (*lit.* not at all) fall sick nor suffer ill (*lit.* possess troubles). (Euripides, fragment 833.) (3) (*i*) He started to play the flute for a drachma, and

stops (*sc.* playing it) for four. (*ii*) The camel who conceived a desire for horns lost his ears too. (*iii*) There is no man who is fortunate in all respects. (*iv*) Many generals lost Caria (*cf.* too many cooks spoil the broth). (*v*) Do not let go what is visible and choose what is invisible. (*vi*) Time alone shows a just man. (*vii*) You are in no way different from an elephant. (*viii*) God does not stand aloof from a just deceit. (*ix*) A visit from (*lit.* entrance of) many doctors destroyed me. (*x*) Your appearance is like a lion's but your life is like an ass's (*lit.* you are a lion as regards your hair, but an ass as regards your life). (4) I see the nose of hook-nosed Nico, Menippus; however, he himself seems to be still far off; but he'll come, let's wait after all. For if [he is] far [away], he is not, I suppose, five stades from (i.e. behind) his nose. But, as you see, it precedes [him] itself. If we stand on (*lit.* on to) a high mound, we'll see him too. (*A.P.* xi. 406.) (5) When he was dyeing his head (*i.e.* his hair) a man lost his hair itself, and although he was very hairy he has completely become an egg. (6) Thereupon, Cleanor stood up and spoke as follows: "Come, gentlemen, you see the perjury and impiety of the King, and you see the faithlessness of Tissaphernes, since, although he used to say that he was a neighbour of Greece and that he would consider it most important to save us, and although he himself swore an oath to us to confirm this (*lit.* upon these things) and himself gave pledges, he himself deceived and seized our generals, and he did not even respect Zeus God of Hospitality, but after actually sitting at the same table as Clearchus deceived him by these very means and has [now] destroyed the men." (Xenophon *Anabasis* iii. 2.4.) (7) Well, Socrates, obey the laws and regard (*lit.* obeying the laws, regard) neither children nor life nor anything else more highly than justice, in order that, when you go [down] to [the house] of Hades you may be able to plead all this in your defence to those who rule there. (8) Socrates manifestly longed not for those who were naturally sound in body with respect to beauty but for those who were naturally sound in soul with respect to virtue. (9) The daughter of a grammarian, after making love (*lit.* having mingled in sexual intercourse), produced a masculine child, a feminine [child], [and] a neuter [child]. (10) For Zeus gives thought to the greatest [affairs] of mortals, but leaves unimportant [matters] to other gods and lets them be. (11) While it was summer, the soldiers who were in Chios with Eteonicus supported themselves both from [the produce of] the season and by working for hire around the countryside. But when winter came on, and they had no sustenance and they were badly clothed and without shoes, they began to conspire amongst themselves (*lit.* with each other) to attack Chios. (12) *Polymnestor.* Alas, what will you say? Is she really somewhere nearby? Show [me], tell [me] where she is, in order that I may seize [her] with my hands and tear [her] apart and bloody [her] flesh. *Agamemnon.* What's this, what's wrong with you? *Po.* In the name of the gods I beseech you, let me lay my raging hand[s] on her. *Ag.* Stop; cast [this] savagery from [your] heart and speak, so that, when I have heard both you and her in turn, I may fairly decide for what reason (*lit.* in return for what thing) you are treated thus (*lit.* suffer these things). (Euripides *Hecuba* 1124-1131.)

21.2

(1) When a certain Spartan came to Athens and saw men sitting on stools in a [public] toilet, he said, "May it not happen to me to sit in a place from which (*lit.* there from where) it is not possible to rise up for (*i.e.* to give my seat to) an older man. (2) (*i*) You are stirring the brine before you catch the fish (*cf.* first catch your hare, then cook it). (*ii*) A tortoise is not concerned about flies. (*iii*) May such

enemies always pursue me. (*iv*) One should (*lit.* it is fitting to) scold children indoors. (*v*) One's speech reflects one's way of life (*lit.* of what sort [is one's] way of life, of such a sort [is one's] speech). (*vi*) Count no man fortunate (*lit.* consider no-one to be fortunate) until he dies. (*vii*) Dogs resemble their mistresses (*lit.* of what sort the mistress, of such a sort also the bitch). (*viii*) It is fitting for a child to be silent rather than to chatter. (*ix*) Oh, what a head, and it does not have a brain! (*x*) Slaves share their masters' sickness. (*xi*) May I not have (*lit.* may there not be to me) what I want but what it is advantageous (*sc.* for me to have). (*xii*) May you fall into (*lit.* in with) Hades' anus! (*i.e* may you die!) (*xiii*) Would that (*or* I wish that) the offspring of wretched men were dumb. (3) Whoever of mortals fears death too much, is by nature stupid; [for] this (*lit.* these things) is the concern of Chance. But whenever the moment of death chances to come, he could not escape [it] even if he went to the halls of Zeus. (Sophocles, fragment 865.) (4) All who marry above themselves (*lit.* as many as marry marriages better in race) do not know [how] to marry. (5) A man's character is of necessity affected by the sort of people with whom he spends most of his time (*lit.* with what sort of [a person] a man associates for the greatest part of the day, of such a sort as regards to character it is necessary for him too to become). (6) Next stood up Thorax the Boeotian, who was struggling with Xenophon about the generalship, and said that, if they got out of the Black Sea, they would have (*lit.* there would be to them) the Chersonnese, a beautiful and blessed country, so that it was possible for anyone who [so] wished to dwell there, and anyone who did not to go off home. It was ridiculous, when there was much bountiful land in Greece, to be searching for [it] in the [country] of the barbarians. "And until you get (*lit.* become) there, I too promise you pay." (Xenophon *Anabasis* v.6.25-26.) (7) Once when Diogenes saw [some] women hanging by nooses from an olive-tree, he said, "I wish that all trees had borne such a fruit." (8) Whoever does (*or* tries to do) many things if it is possible not to do [them], [is] foolish, if it is possible to live a quiet (*lit.* free from business) life pleasantly. (9) In deliberation (*lit.* deliberating) the soldiers decided to reply as follows (*lit.* the following things) and Cheirisophus was their spokesman (*lit.* spoke): "We are resolved, if we are allowed (*lit.* someone allows us) to go off home, to proceed through the country doing the least possible harm; but if anyone [tries to] hinder us from the journey, to fight it out with him as vigorously as possible." (10) Indeed [it is] with difficulty [that] you would bear **my** ordeals, to whom it is not fated to die (*or* since it is not fated for me to die); for this (*i.e.* death) would be a deliverance from [my] woes; but as it is, there is no end of toils appointed for me until Zeus is cast out from [his] sovereignty. (Aeschylus *Prometheus Bound* 752-756.) (11) When Cyrus had listened to such words from Gobryas he spoke to him as follows. (12) Well, what will you do, [my] heart? Consider well before you err and make most hateful what is [now] most dear (*lit.* the dearest things). Wherever did you rush forth, you wretch? Check [your] arrogance and strength hated of the gods. And why (*lit.* with a view to what) do I lament like this (*lit.* these things), seeing my life desolate and abandoned by those who should least (*sc.* have abandoned me)? Do we then become cowards when we suffer such evils? Do not betray yourself, [my] heart, in [the midst of] troubles. Alas, it is decided; children, go away from [my] sight (*lit.* eyes); for already a new frenzy has entered my bloody heart; O [my] hands, [my] hands, for what a [terrible] task we are preparing ourselves; alas, wretched [that I am] because of [my] daring, [I] who go to destroy in a brief moment the [product of] my great labour. (Neophron, fragment 2.) (13) When a man came to Lacedaemon and beheld the respect shown by (*lit.* of) the young towards the old, he said, "In Sparta alone it is profitable to grow old." (14) We should meet together and (*lit.* making a meeting) lament over a new-born baby (*lit.* the one [just] born) for all the troubles it is coming to, and in turn farewell with sounds of triumph the man who has died and is freed from troubles as we send him forth from his house (*lit.* farewelling [and] shouting in triumph send forth). (Euripides, fragment 449.)

21.3

(1) What life [can there be], what joy without golden Aphrodite? May I die, when these things are no longer my concern (*lit.* a care to me), [viz] secret love and gentle gifts and bed (*or* sex), the sorts of things which are the attractive flowers of youth for men and women. But when distressing old age comes on, [old age] which makes a man both ugly and base, evil cares always distress him in his heart (*or* mind), nor is he glad when he looks upon the rays of the sun, but [he is] hateful to boys and dishonoured by women. So painful did God make old age. (Mimnermus 1.) (2) You, [who are] my star, gaze at the stars. Would I might become the sky, in order that I might see you with many eyes. (3) Formerly you shone among the living [like] the Morning Star; but now you have died you shine [like] the Evening Star among the dead. (4) I am sending you sweet perfume, [thus] doing a favour to the perfume, not to you; for you yourself are able to give fragrance even to perfume. (5) Hail, Messenger of Dawn, Bringer of Light, and may you come [back] quickly [as the] Evening Star, bringing secretly back again [the girl] whom you are [now] leading away.

22.2

You, Love, ruler of gods and men, either do not teach beauty to appear beautiful or assist lovers (*lit.* those who are in love) with good fortune, as they suffer the pains of which you are the author. (Euripides, fragment 136.) (2) For it was evening, and someone had come to the prytaneis with the report (*lit.* announcing) that Elatea had been captured. After this some of them got up immediately in the middle of dinner, cleared out the people in the stalls throughout the market-place, and set fire to the wicker-work, while others sent for the generals and summoned the trumpeter. The city was filled with commotion. On the following day at dawn the prytaneis called the councillors (*lit.* the council) into the Council-chamber, while you proceeded to the Assembly, and before they dealt with the matter and framed a draft resolution the whole people was seated on the hill (*i.e.* the Pnyx; *lit.* above). After this, when the Council had arrived and the prytaneis had announced what had been reported to them and had introduced the messenger (*lit.* the one who had come) and he had spoken, the herald put the question, "Who wishes to speak?" And no-one came forward. (Demosthenes *On the Crown* 169-170.) (3) (*i*) Ask even statues for [your] daily bread (*double acc.*) (*i.e.* you're not getting anything from me!). (*ii*) There is a certain Socrates, a wise man, who speculates on (*lit.* a deep thinker about) the heavens above (*lit.* things high in the air; *accusative of respect*) and has investigated everything beneath the earth (*direct object*). (*iii*) He has come to take from us even the property of [our] grandfather (*double acc.*). (*iv*) He came to the ancient tomb of [his] father (*acc. of motion towards*). (*v*) [My] long life teaches me many things (*double acc.*). (*vi*) Meletus brought this indictment against me (*direct object*; *cognate acc.*). (*vii*) Cyrus was very handsome in appearance and very humane in spirit (*acc. of respect*). (*viii*) [No], by Zeus (*acc. in* oath), I did not see a woodcutter (*direct obj.*) better than myself. (*ix*) They made a treaty and alliance for a hundred years (*acc. to express time how long*). (*x*) I swear by the holy sky, the dwelling of Zeus (*acc. in oath*).(4) (*i*) How sweet [a thing] [is] solitude to the man who hates common people (*exclamatory adv.*). (*ii*) Hide nothing, for all-seeing (*lit.* seeing everything) time unfolds everything (*causal conjunction*). (*iii*) We bear children for this reason [viz] that we may protect the altars of the gods and [our] native land (*conjunction introducing purpose clause*). (*iv*) He seized the acropolis to gain sole power (*lit.* as for tyranny; *adv. introducing prepositional phrase*). (*v*) [We/one] must try to bear the constraints (*lit.* the necessary things) of life as lightly (*lit.* easily) as possible (ὡc+ *supl.*). (*vi*) Effort, as/so they say, is the father of fame (*conjunction introducing a parenthetical clause,* 22.1/1b(v)). (*vii*) Alas, alas, how fine a privilege is a just victory (*lit.* to win just things), but how absolutely evil is an unjust victory (*lit.* [to win] unjust things) (*exclamatory adv.*). (*viii*) How sweet is life, if a man does not understand it (*exclamatory adv.*). (*ix*) Give to the poor, in order that you find god a giver (*conjunction introducing purpose clause*). (*x*) Time judges friends as fire [judges] gold (*conjunction introducing a clause of manner*). (*xi*) When you are young remember that one day you will be old (ὡc = ὅτι, *indirect statement*). (*xii*) Do we not live as pleasantly as possible if we do not grieve? (ὡc + *supl.*). (*xiii*) They sailed away from the Hellespont separately according to their cities (22.1/1(v)). (*xiv*) Really wise men (ὡc *with positive adv.*). (5) At first Oedipus was a fortunate man, [but] then he became the most wretched of mortals. (6) Well, as you know, I have wept for many sufferings, but now I shall speak of one [suffering] such as [I have] not yet [wept for] before. When [my] lord Heracles was setting out on his last journey from home, at that time he left in the house an ancient tablet inscribed with signs, which he had never brought himself to explain to me like this before, when he went forth on [his] many exploits, but he used to go as one who was about to do something [notable] and not as one about to die. (Sophocles *Trachiniae* 153-160.) (7) I made war first against the Thracians, driving them from the Hellespont as they wanted to take the country from the Greeks. (8) O old age, what hope of pleasure you have, and every single man wishes to live through (*lit.* come) to you. But when he has made trial [of you], he regrets (*sc.* that he has; *lit.* takes regret) because there is no worse evil among the mortal race. (Euripides, fragment 1080.) (9) For I, Cebes, when young, had an enormous desire (*lit.* desired enormously) for this wisdom which they call the investigation into (*lit.* of) nature.

22.3

(*i*) We congratulate you, grasshopper, when on the tops of the trees you sing like a king, after drinking a little dew; for yours are all those things which you see in the fields, [all those things] which the woods nourish. You [are] held in honour among mortals, sweet harbinger of summer. The Muses love you, and Phoebus himself loves [you], and gave [you] a shrill power of song. Old age does not distress you, o skilful, earth-born lover of song, and since you know not suffering (*lit.* [being] unsuffering), o [creature of] bloodless flesh, you are nearly equal to the gods. (Anacreontea 34.) (*ii*) My (*lit.* to us) temples [are] now grey, and my head white, and no longer is graceful youth at hand, and my teeth are aged. No longer is there left much time of sweet life; for this reason (*lit.* on account of these things) I weep often in fear of Tartarus. For terrible is the inner chamber of Hades, and painful the path down to him; and further [it is] fixed for the man who has gone down not to come up [again]. (Anacreon 50.)

23.2

(1) (*i*) O sweet charm of sleep (*gen. of explanation*), ally against sickness (*objective gen.*). (*ii*) He wanted to be [one] of those who remained (*partitive gen.*). (*iii*) O Poseidon, what skill! (*gen. of exclamation*). (*iv*) To bear poverty is not [the nature] of everyone, but of a wise man (*gen. of characteristic*). (*v*) Pay close attention (*lit.* apply the mind very much) to this man (*dat. of indirect object*), I beg you (*ethic dat.*). (*vi*) Many treatments have been found by doctors (*dat. of agent*). (*vii*) Sleep is naturally a safeguard of the body (*lit.* of bodies; *objective gen.*). (*viii*) [It is the mark] of a wicked man to praise and blame the same person (*gen. of characteristic*). (*ix*) Such is tyranny for you, Lacedaemonians (*dat. of reference* or *ethic dat.*). (*x*) Olympian Zeus, dwelling in the sky (*dat. of place where*), knows this. (*xi*) They accuse him of theft (*verb of accusing, gen. of charge*). (*xii*) Men lie because of their own (*subjective/possessive gen.*) fear of death (*objective gen.*). (*xiii*) They were afraid that the Athenians might attack with a greater force (*military dat.*). (*xiv*) They will approach with much shouting (*dat. of manner*). (*xv*) The boy's name (*lit.* the name to the boy; *dat. of possession*) was Plato. (*xvi*) Art is weaker by far (*dat. of measure of difference*) than necessity (*gen. of comparison*). (*xvii*) I admire you for [your] intelligence, but I loathe [you] for [your] cowardice (*both gen. of cause*). (*xviii*) I tried to steal [some] of the meat (*partitive gen.*). (*xix*) In your eyes (*dat. of reference*) did this man do these things justly? *or* Did this man do these things justly for you? (*dat. of advantage*). (*xx*) They did these things for the gods (*dat. of advantage*). (*xxi*) He was loathsome and rough in his voice (*dat. of respect*). (*xxii*) The army arrived at Oenoe in Attica (*chorographic gen.*). (*xxiii*) You see the king's perjury (*subjective/possessive gen.*). (*xxiv*) I am not disheartened by what has happened (*gen. of cause*). (2) Diogenes went up to Anaximenes the orator who was fat and said, "Give [some] of your belly to us the poor too; for you will both be lightened yourself and will help us." (3) There was a saying that wiles are the concern of women, whereas men are of surer aim with the spear. For if the prize of victory were [won] by guiles, we would have sovereignty over men. (Euripides, fragment 321.) (4) And now I advise all younger [men] not to produce children tardily, making delays up to old age (*or* until they are old). For [this] (*i.e.* producing children in old age) is no pleasure, and an old man is a hateful thing to (*or* for) a woman. But [do it] as quickly as possible. For rearing [children] is beautiful and a boy sharing his youth with a youthful father is a pleasant [thing]. (Euripides, fragment 317). (5) *Meletus.* This [is what] I say, that not at all do you believe in the gods. *Socrates.* You really amaze me in speaking like this, Meletus (*lit.* o amazing Meletus, why do you say this?). Do I not even believe then that the sun or the moon are gods, as the rest of mankind [do]? *Me.* [No], by Zeus, gentlemen of the jury, since he says that the sun is a stone and the moon earth. *So.* Do you think that you are accusing Anaxagoras, my dear Meletus? And do you so despise these men and think that they are [so] illiterate (*lit.* inexperienced in letters) that they do not know that the books of Anaxagoras of Clazomenae are full of such statements? And moreover the youth learn these [doctrines], do they, from me, which they can buy for a drachma in (*lit.* from) the orchestra and [then] laugh at Socrates if he claims they are his own, especially since they are so absurd? Well, for heaven's sake (*lit.* O by Zeus), is this what you think of me (*lit.* do I seem thus to you?)? Do I not believe in any god? *Me.* No indeed, by Zeus, not in the very least. *So.* You are not to be believed, Meletus, and that too, as it seems (*lit.* you seem) to me, [even] by yourself. For this man appears to me, men of Athens, to be very violent and unrestrained, and simply to have brought this indictment through (*or* because of) violence and

lack of restraint and youthful folly. For he seems like a man making trial [of me] [by] composing a riddle: "Will Socrates the wise recognize that I am joking and contradicting myself, or shall I deceive him and the rest of those who are listening [to me]?" For he appears to me to contradict himself in the indictment, as if he were to say," Socrates is a wrong-doer [by] not believing in the gods, but by believing in the gods." And yet this is the [mark *or* conduct] of a joker (*lit.* of [someone] joking). (Plato *Apology* 26c-27a.)

23.3

(1) I am the tomb of a ship-wrecked [sailor]; and the one opposite [is the tomb] of a farmer; for Hades lies beneath, common to [both] sea and land. (2) Here Saon, the [son] of Dico, of Acanthus, slumbers in holy sleep (*lit.* sleeps a holy sleep); do not say that the good die. (3) Philip, his father, laid (*or* buried) here his twelve-year-old son, his great hope, Nicoteles. (4) These men, having invested (*lit.* placed round) their dear native-land with imperishable glory, put on the dark cloud of death; but they are not dead in death (*lit.* having died), since from above their valour glorifies them and raises them from the house of Hades. (Simonides 121 D.). (5) This monument hides Aeschylus, son of Euphorion, the Athenian, who died in wheat-bearing Gela; but of his famous valour the grove of Marathon could tell, and the long-haired Mede who knew it. (6) Tears I give to you, Heliodora, even below through the earth, a remnant of love [sent] to Hades, tears sorely wept; and on [your] much-lamented tomb I pour the stream of [my] longing, the memorial of [my] affection. Piteously, piteously I Meleager lament you, my dear (*lit.* dear you), even among the dead, an empty favour to (*or* for) Acheron. Alas, where is my flower (*lit.* shoot *or* sprout) [sorely] missed? Hades snatched [her], snatched [her], and the dust marred the flower of her youth (*lit.* the blooming flower). But I implore you, all-nurturing Earth, gently clasp her, all-lamented (*lit.* the all-lamented [girl]), to your bosom, O Mother. (Meleager *A.P.* vii.476.).

24.2

(1) *Where a negative is involved, the relevant subsection of 24.1/2 is given after the appropriate explanatory term.* (*i*) The man who knows nothing (*generic* (*f*)) makes no mistakes (*statement* (*a*)). (*ii*) Consider no-one a friend (*prohibition/negative command* (*a*)) until you examine how he has treated his previous friends. (*iii*) They do everything so as not to be punished (*infinitive* (*e*)). (*iv*) Nothing (*statement* (*a*)) was done because of the fact that the archon was not present (*infinitive* (*e*)). (*v*) I do not know (*statement* (*a*)) whether to travel (*lit.* I am to travel) or not (*deliberative question* (*a*)). (*vi*) I am afraid that I do not have (*noun clause* (*d*)) sufficient [people] to whom I am to give the gold. (*vii*) Take courage, Cyrus, I shall not hide (*strong denial* (*h*)) from you [the person] to whom I wish to go (*lit.* arrive). (*viii*) And they said that they would give back the corpses on condition that [they] did not burn (*infinitive* (*e*)) the villages. (*ix*) The deed which is not just (*generic* (*f*)) does not escape (*statement* (*a*)) the notice of the gods. (*x*) What is to prevent them from dying? (*verb of preventing is virtually negative because the answer* nothing *is expected* (24.1/7)). (*xi*) He wanted to be a friend of (*lit.* friendly to) those who were most powerful in order that, when he did wrong, he might not be punished (*purpose clause* (*b*)). (*xii*) If you don't check (*conditional clause* (*b*)) your tongue,

you will have troubles (*lit.* troubles will be to you). (*xiii*) You cannot (*lit.* could not) be prosperous if you do not toil (*participle used conditionally* (*f*)). (*xiv*) You **shall** not be hostile to your friends (*strong prohibition* (*g*)). (*xv*) If you say what you want (*sc.* to say), [then] hear in turn what you don't want (*sc.* to hear) (*general adjectival clause* (*c*)). (*xvi*) [We/one] must either eat tortoise meat or not eat [at all] (*infinitive* (*e*)). (*xvii*) Can you tell me whether virtue can be taught (*lit.* is a teachable [thing]) or not? (*alternative question* (*i*) – μή *is also possible*). (*xviii*) No-one will deny that he knows what is just (*lit.* just things) (*negated verb of denying* (24.1/7). (*xix*) He was afraid that he would not be able to go out of the country (*noun clause* (*d*)). (*xx*) Do not go away until you hear (*prohibition/negative command* (*a*)). (2) We must worship the gods, benefit our friends, help the city, try to do good to Greece, cultivate the land, look after the cattle, [and] learn the arts of war. (3) When anyone is brought to (*lit.* into) a hostile (*lit.* opposing) trial and is about to speak about bloodshed, fear brings the mouth of men to consternation and hinders the mind from saying what it wishes. (Euripides, fragment 67.) (4) You must beware not to be obviously doing publicly any of things which you would privately guard against. (5) All these laws have been in existence (*lit.* made) for a long time now, gentlemen of the jury, and no-one ever yet denied that they would be good. (6) Take care not to reveal your low birth (*lit.* lest you may appear being born lowly). (7) So I greeted the two of them, since I had not seen them for some time (*lit.* as having seen [them] after a time); and after this I said to Cleinias, "Cleinias, these two men, you know, Euthydemus and Dionysodorus, are skilled not in trivialities (*lit.* little things) but in important matters. For they know all about (*lit.* the things about) war." They despised me for saying this (*lit.* when I said this I was despised by them); so they both laughed, looking at each other, and Euthydemus said, "We do **not**, Socrates, concern ourselves with these things any longer, but deal with them [as] subordinate issues." And I said admiringly, "Your business must be a fine one, if such important matters happen to be subordinate for you; in the name of the gods, tell me what this [fine] business is." "Virtue," he said, "Socrates, [is what] we think we are able to deliver as excellently and speedily as is humanly possible." "Zeus," I said,"what a [splendid] affair. Where (*lit.* from where) did you find this treasure. I was still thinking about you, as I said just now, as for the most part being clever at this, [i.e.] fighting under arms, and this [is what] I was saying about you; for when you visited [us] before, I remember that this [is what] the pair of you professed." (Plato *Euthydemus* 273c-e.) (8) After him (*lit.* this man) Xenophon said, "And I am of the following opinion (*lit.* think thus). If it is necessary [for us] to fight, we must make preparations to fight as vigorously as possible; but if we wish to cross as easily as possible, I think we should consider how we may receive as few wounds as possible and lose as few lives as possible." (9) We must consider whether it is right or not (*lit.* just ... or not just) for me to try to leave from here without the permission of the Athenians (*lit.* the Athenians not letting [me] go). (10) *A.* Tell me, do you have a field? *B.* No, I don't. (11) And further if we submit and come into the power of the king, what do you think we shall suffer? He cut off the head and hand of even his brother by the same mother and [that too] when already dead, and impaled them. As for us, who have no protector and [who] made an expedition against him with the intention of making him a slave instead of a king and of killing him if we could, what do you think we would suffer? Surely he would go to any lengths so that, by inflicting the worst outrages on us, he might instill in all men fear of ever campaigning against him? But everything must be done so that we do not come into his power. (Xenophon *Anabasis* iii. 1.17f.)

24.3

Strepsiades. In the name of the gods, what is this (*lit.* these things)? Tell me. *Student.* This is astronomy. *Str.* And what's this? *St.* Geometry. *Str.* So what's it (*lit.* this thing) useful for? *St.* To measure out land. *Str.* [Do you mean land] for cleruchies? *St.* No, [land] as a whole. *Str.* What you say is attractive (*lit.* you say an attractive [thing]). For the device is democratic (*or* popular) and useful. *St.* And this, notice, is a map of the whole world. Do you see? Here is Athens. *Str.* What do you mean? I don't believe [you], for I cannot (*lit.* do not) see [any] jurymen sitting [there]. *St.* [I assure you] that this area is truly Attic (*or* Attica). *Str.* Come now, who's this man in the basket? *St.* The master. *Str.* Who's the master? *St.* Socrates. *Str.* Ah, [it's] Socrates. You there, go [and] call him loudly for me. *St.* No, **you** call [him] yourself. I don't have the time. *Str.* Socrates! Dear little Socrates! *Socrates.* Why do you call me, creature of a day? *Str.* In the first place, tell me, I pray, what you are doing. *So.* I tread the air and my thoughts centre round the sun (*lit.* I think about the sun). *Str.* Then you're looking down on the gods from [your] mat, and (*lit.* but) not from the earth, if [indeed that's what you're doing]. *So.* [Yes] for I would never have correctly discovered heavenly phenomena, except by suspending [my] perception and thought. (Aristophanes *Clouds* 200-209, 218-229.)

25.2

(1) Again mighty Hector of the gleaming helmet addressed her: "Indeed all this is **my** concern, [my] wife; but I am terribly afraid of the Trojans and the Trojan women with their trailing robes, if, like a coward, I shrink away far from the fighting. Nor does my spirit [so] order me, since I have learned always to be brave and to fight among the foremost [ranks of the] Trojans, winning great glory both for my father and for myself. For I know this well in my heart and in my soul: there will come (*lit.* be) a day when holy Ilium will be destroyed, and Priam and the people of Priam of the fine ash-spear. But [it is] not so much grief for the Trojans hereafter [which] troubles me, neither for Hecuba herself nor for lord Priam nor for [my] brothers, who, many and brave, may fall in the dust at the hands of the enemy (*lit.* hostile men), as [grief] for you, when one of the bronze-clad Achaeans will lead you away in tears, taking away [your] day of liberty; and living (*lit.* being) in Argos you will weave a web at the command of another [woman] (*i.e.* a mistress), and carry water from [the spring] Messeis or Hypereia, much unwilling, but strong necessity will be upon [you]. And one day a man seeing you shedding tears will say: "This is the wife of Hector, who was the best of the horse-taming Trojans at fighting [at the time] when they (*i.e.* the Greeks) besieged Ilium." Thus one day will someone speak; and for you it will be a fresh grief because of the lack of such a husband to ward off the day of slavery. But may earth heaped up cover me in death before I hear your scream when you are taken away by force (*lit.* both your scream and your being carried off)." (*Iliad* vi. 440-465.) (2) All night long they sat with high thoughts (*lit.* thinking big) along the embankments of war, and their fires blazed in great numbers (*lit.* many). Just as when in the sky the stars are seen conspicuous[ly] around the bright moon, when the air becomes windless; and there appear all the lookout-places and the tops of the headlands and the glens; and from heaven the boundless air is rent beneath, and all the stars are seen, and the shepherd rejoices in his heart. So many shone the fires as the Trojans lit [them] in front of Ilium, between the ships and the streams of Xanthus. A thousand fires

then were blazing in the plain, and beside each one sat fifty [men] in the gleam of the blazing fire. And the horses, feeding on white barley and wheat, stood beside the chariots and waited for fair-throned Dawn. (*Iliad* viii. 553-565.) (3) Tell me, Muse, of the man of many wiles, who wandered far and wide (*lit.* very much), after he had sacked the holy citadel of Troy. He saw the cities of many men and came to know [their] minds, and on the sea he suffered many griefs in his heart, striving to win his own life and the home-coming of [his] companions. But not even so did he save [his] companions, strive as he might, for they perished by their own presumptuousness, fools, who devoured the cattle of Hyperion the Sun [God]; and he took from them the day of [their] homecoming. (*Odyssey* i.1-9.) (4) From there I was carried along for nine days by baneful winds over the sea full of fish; but on the tenth [day] we stepped on to the land of the Lotus-Eaters, who feed on [that] flowery food. There we set foot on the mainland and drew water, and [my] companions quickly took their meal beside the swift ships. But when we had partaken of food and drink, then I sent ahead [some of my] companions to go and find out what sort of men were living (*lit.* eating food) in [this] land, choosing two men and sending a third with [them] as herald. They went off and quickly fell in with the Lotus-Eaters (*lit.* the Lotus-eating men]. Nor did the Lotus-Eaters plot destruction for our companions, but gave them [some] lotus to taste. Whoever of them ate the honey-sweet fruit of the lotus was no longer willing to report back [to us] or return, but wished to remain there with the Lotus-Eaters, feeding on lotus, and to forget [his] home-coming. Forcibly I brought them [back] in tears to the ships, and I dragged [them] and bound [them] under the benches in the hollowed ships. Then I ordered the rest of my trusty companions to embark with haste (*lit.* hurrying) on the swift ships, lest any of them might somehow eat of the lotus and forget their home-coming. They went quickly on board and sat down at the benches, and sitting in order they smote the grey sea with the oars. (*Odyssey* ix. 82-104.)

PRINCIPAL PARTS OF VERBS

Present	Future	Aorist	Perfect	Perfect mid. pass.	Aorist passive
ἀγγέλλω *announce*	ἀγγελῶ	ἤγγειλα	ἤγγελκα	ἤγγελμαι	ἠγγέλθην
ἄγω *lead*	ἄξω	ἤγαγον	ἦχα	ἦγμαι	ἤχθην
(ἐπ-) αἰνέω *praise*	αἰνέσομαι (αἰνέcω)	ᾔνεcα	ᾔνεκα	ᾔνημαι	ᾐνέθην
αἱρέω *take*; mid. *choose*	αἱρήcω	εἷλον	ᾕρηκα	ᾕρημαι	ᾑρέθην
αἴρω *raise*	ἀρῶ	ἦρα	ἦρκα	ἦρμαι	ἤρθην
αἰcθάνομαι *perceive*	αἰcθήcομαι	ᾐcθόμην		ᾔcθημαι	
αἰcχΰνω *dishonour*	αἰcχυνῶ	ᾔcχῡνα			ᾐcχΰνθην
ἀκούω *hear*	ἀκούcομαι	ἤκουcα	ἀκήκοα		ἠκούcθην
ἁλίcκομαι *be captured*	ἁλώcομαι	ἑάλων	ἑάλωκα		
ἁμαρτάνω *err*	ἁμαρτήcομαι	ἥμαρτον	ἡμάρτηκα	ἡμάρτημαι	ἡμαρτήθην
ἀμΰνω *ward off*	ἀμυνῶ	ἤμῡνα			
ἀνᾱλίcκω *spend*	ἀνᾱλώcω	ἀνήλωcα	ἀνήλωκα	ἀνήλωμαι	ἀνηλώθην
ἀνοίγνῡμι *open*	ἀνοίξω	ἀνέῳξα	ἀνέῳχα	ἀνέῳγμαι	ἀνεῴχθην
ἀποκρΐνομαι *answer*	ἀποκρινοῦμαι	ἀπεκρῑνάμην		ἀποκέκριμαι	
ἄρχω *begin, rule*	ἄρξω	ἦρξα		ἦργμαι	ἤρχθην
ἀφικνέομαι *arrive*	ἀφίξομαι	ἀφῑκόμην		ἀφῖγμαι	
βαίνω *go*	βήcομαι	ἔβην	βέβηκα		
βάλλω *throw*	βαλῶ	ἔβαλον	βέβληκα	βέβλημαι	ἐβλήθην

Present	Future	Aorist	Perfect	Perfect mid. pass.	Aorist passive
βλάπτω	βλάψω	ἔβλαψα	βέβλαφα	βέβλαμμαι	ἐβλάφθην
hurt, injure					ἐβλάβην
βοάω	βοήσομαι	ἐβόησα			
shout					
βούλομαι	βουλήσομαι			βεβούλημαι	ἐβουλήθην
wish					
γαμέω	γαμῶ	ἔγημα	γεγάμηκα		
marry (with man as subject)					
γαμέομαι	γαμοῦμαι	ἐγημάμην		γέγαμημαι	
marry (with woman as subject)					
γελάω	γελάσομαι	ἐγέλασα			ἐγελάσθην
laugh					
γίγνομαι	γενήσομαι	ἐγενόμην	γέγονα	γεγένημαι	
become					
γιγνώσκω	γνώσομαι	ἔγνων	ἔγνωκα	ἔγνωσμαι	ἐγνώσθην
know					
γράφω	γράψω	ἔγραψα	γέγραφα	γέγραμμαι	ἐγράφην
write					
δάκνω	δήξομαι	ἔδακον		δέδηγμαι	ἐδήχθην
bite					
δεῖ	δεήσει	ἐδέησε			
impers. *it is necessary*					
δείκνῡμι	δείξω	ἔδειξα	δέδειχα	δέδειγμαι	ἐδείχθην
show					
δέομαι	δεήσομαι			δεδέημαι	ἐδεήθην
need, ask					
δέχομαι	δέξομαι	ἐδεξάμην		δέδεγμαι	ἐδέχθην
receive, await					
δέω (A)	δεήσω	ἐδέησα			
want, lack					
δέω (B)	δήσω	ἔδησα	δέδεκα	δέδεμαι	ἐδέθην
bind					
διαλέγομαι	διαλέξομαι			διείλεγμαι	διελέχθην
converse					
διδάσκω	διδάξω	ἐδίδαξα	δεδίδαχα	δεδίδαγμαι	ἐδιδάχθην
teach					
δίδωμι	δώσω	ἔδωκα	δέδωκα	δέδομαι	ἐδόθην
give					
διώκω	διώξομαι	ἐδίωξα	δεδίωχα		ἐδιώχθην
pursue					
δοκέω	δόξω	ἔδοξα		δέδογμαι	
seem, think					
δύναμαι	δυνήσομαι			δεδύνημαι	ἐδυνήθην
be able, can					
ἐάω	ἐάσω	εἴασα	εἴακα	εἴαμαι	εἰάθην
allow, let alone					

Present	Future	Aorist	Perfect	Perfect mid. pass.	Aorist passive
ἐγείρω *arouse*	ἐγερῶ	ἤγειρα	ἐγρήγορα (intr.) *I am awake*		
ἐθέλω *wish, be willing*	ἐθελήcω	ἠθέληcα	ἠθέληκα		
εἴργω *imprison, prevent*	εἴρξω	εἶρξα		εἶργμαι	εἴρχθην
ἐλαύνω *drive*	ἐλῶ (= ἀω)	ἤλαcα	ἐλήλακα	ἐλήλαμαι	ἠλάθην
ἐλέγχω *examine, confute*	ἐλέγξω	ἤλεγξα		ἐλήλεγμαι	ἠλέγχθην
ἕλκω *drag, draw*	ἕλξω	εἵλκυcα	εἵλκυκα	εἵλκυcμαι	εἱλκύcθην
ἐπίcταμαι *understand*	ἐπιcτήcομαι				ἠπιcτήθην
ἕπομαι *follow*	ἕψομαι	ἑcπόμην			
ἐργάζομαι *work*	ἐργάcομαι	ἠργαcάμην		εἴργαcμαι	ἠργάcθην
ἔρχομαι *come, go*	εἶμι	ἦλθον	ἐλήλυθα		
ἐρωτάω *ask a question*	ἐρωτήcω ἐρήcομαι	(ἠρώτηcα) ἠρόμην	ἠρώτηκα	ἠρώτημαι	ἠρωτήθην
ἐcθίω *eat*	ἔδομαι	ἔφαγον	ἐδήδοκα	ἐδήδεcμαι	
εὑρίcκω *find*	εὑρήcω	ηὗρον	ηὕρηκα	ηὕρημαι	ηὑρέθην
ἔχω *have*	ἕξω cχήcω	ἔcχον	ἔcχηκα	ἔcχημαι	
ζάω *live*	ζήcω/ζήcομαι βιώcομαι	ἐβίων	βεβίωκα		
ἥδομαι *be pleased*	ἡcθήcομαι				ἥcθην
θάπτω *bury*	θάψω	ἔθαψα		τέθαμμαι	ἐτάφην
θαυμάζω *wonder*	θαυμάcομαι	ἐθαύμαcα	τεθαύμακα	τεθαύμαcμαι	ἐθαυμάcθην
(ἀπο–)θνήcκω *die*	θανοῦμαι	ἔθανον	τέθνηκα		
θύω *sacrifice*	θύcω	ἔθῡcα	τέθυκα	τέθυμαι	ἐτύθην
ἵημι *send*	ἥcω	ἧκα	εἷκα	εἷμαι	εἵθην
ἵcτημι *place, make stand*	cτήcω	ἔcτηcα (tr.) ἔcτην (intr.)	ἔcτηκα (intr.)	ἔcταμαι	ἐcτάθην

Present	Future	Aorist	Perfect	Perfect mid. pass.	Aorist passive
καίω *burn*	καύcω	ἔκαυcα	κέκαυκα	κέκαυμαι	ἐκαύθην
καλέω *call*	καλῶ	ἐκάλεcα	κέκληκα	κέκλημαι	ἐκλήθην
κελεύω *order, bid*	κελεύcω	ἐκέλευcα	κεκέλευκα	κεκέλευcμαι	ἐκελεύcθην
κλαίω *weep*	κλαύcομαι	ἔκλαυcα		κέκλαυμαι	
κλέπτω *steal*	κλέψω	ἔκλεψα	κέκλοφα	κέκλεμμαι	ἐκλάπην
κομίζω *convey, bring*	κομιῶ	ἐκόμιcα	κεκόμικα	κεκόμιcμαι	ἐκομίcθην
κρῑ́νω *judge*	κρινῶ	ἔκρῑνα	κέκρικα	κέκριμαι	ἐκρίθην
κτάομαι *acquire*	κτήcομαι	ἐκτηcάμην		κέκτημαι *possess*	ἐκτήθην
(ἀπο-)κτείνω *kill*	κτενῶ	ἔκτεινα	ἔκτονα		
λαγχάνω *obtain by lot*	λήξομαι	ἔλαχον	εἴληχα	εἴληγμαι	ἐλήχθην
λαμβάνω *take*	λήψομαι	ἔλαβον	εἴληφα	εἴλημμαι	ἐλήφθην
λανθάνω *escape the notice of, lie hidden* (ἐπι-)	λήcω	ἔλαθον	λέληθα		
λανθάνομαι *forget*	λήcομαι	ἐλαθόμην		λέληcμαι	
λέγω (A) *say*	λέξω / ἐρῶ	ἔλεξα / εἶπον	εἴρηκα	λέλεγμαι / εἴρημαι	ἐλέχθην / ἐρρήθην
λέγω (B) *pick up, gather*	λέξω	ἔλεξα	εἴλοχα	εἴλεγμαι (λέλεγμαι)	ἐλέγην
λείπω *leave*	λείψω	ἔλιπον	λέλοιπα	λέλειμμαι	ἐλείφθην
μανθάνω *learn*	μαθήcομαι	ἔμαθον	μεμάθηκα		
μάχομαι *fight*	μαχοῦμαι / μαχήcομαι	ἐμαχεcάμην		μεμάχημαι	
μέλει *impers. it is a care* (ἐπι-)	μελήcει	ἐμέληcε	μεμέληκε		
μελέομαι *care for*	μελήcομαι			μεμέλημαι	ἐμελήθην
μέλλω *intend*	μελλήcω	ἐμέλληcα			
μένω *remain* (ἀνα-)	μενῶ	ἔμεινα	μεμένηκα		

Present	Future	Aorist	Perfect	Perfect mid. pass.	Aorist passive
μιμνήϲκω remind	μνήϲω	ἔμνηϲα		μέμνημαι remember	ἐμνήϲθην remembered
νέω swim	νεύϲομαι	ἔνευϲα	νένευκα		
νομίζω think	νομιῶ	ἐνόμιϲα	νενόμικα	νενόμιϲμαι	ἐνομίϲθην
οἶδα know	εἴϲομαι	ᾔδη (19.1/3)			
οἴομαι (also οἶμαι) think	οἰήϲομαι				ᾠήθην
(ἀπ-) ὄλλῡμι destroy, lose	ὀλῶ	ὤλεϲα	ὀλώλεκα (tr.) ὄλωλα (intr. I am ruined)		
(ἀπ-) ὄλλυμαι be lost, perish	ὀλοῦμαι	ὠλόμην			
ὄμνῡμι swear	ὀμοῦμαι	ὤμοϲα	ὀμώμοκα	ὀμώμο(ϲ)μαι	ὠμό(ϲ)θην
ὁράω see	ὄψομαι	εἶδον	ἑόρᾱκα ἑώρᾱκα	ἑώρᾱμαι ὦμμαι	ὤφθην
ὀργίζομαι become angry	ὀργιοῦμαι			ὤργιϲμαι	ὠργίϲθην
ὀφείλω owe	ὀφειλήϲω	ὠφείληϲα ὤφελον (21.1/1)	ὠφείληκα		
πάϲχω suffer	πείϲομαι	ἔπαθον	πέπονθα		
πείθω persuade	πείϲω	ἔπειϲα	πέπεικα (tr.) πέποιθα (intr.trust)	πέπειϲμαι	ἐπείϲθην
πέμπω send	πέμψω	ἔπεμψα	πέπομφα	πέπεμμαι	ἐπέμφθην
πίμπλημι fill	πλήϲω	ἔπληϲα	πέπληκα	πέπληϲμαι	ἐπλήϲθην
πῑ́νω drink	πῑ́ομαι	ἔπιον	πέπωκα	πέπομαι	ἐπόθην
πῑ́πτω fall	πεϲοῦμαι	ἔπεϲον	πέπτωκα		
πλέω sail	πλεύϲομαι	ἔπλευϲα	πέπλευκα	πέπλευϲμαι	
πρᾱ́ττω do	πρᾱ́ξω	ἔπρᾱξα	πέπρᾱχα (tr.) πέπρᾱγα (intr. have fared)	πέπρᾱγμαι	ἐπρᾱ́χθην
πυνθάνομαι ascertain	πεύϲομαι	ἐπυθόμην		πέπυϲμαι	
πωλέω sell	ἀποδώϲομαι	ἀπεδόμην	πέπρᾱκα	πέπρᾱμαι	ἐπρᾱ́θην
ῥήγνῡμι break	ῥήξω	ἔρρηξα	ἔρρωγα (intr. am broken)		ἐρράγην
ῥῑ́πτω throw	ῥῑ́ψω	ἔρρῑψα	ἔρρῑφα	ἔρρῑμμαι	ἐρρῑ́φθην

Present	Future	Aorist	Perfect	Perfect mid. pass.	Aorist passive
σκεδάννῡμι *scatter*	σκεδῶ (= άω)	ἐσκέδασα		ἐσκέδασμαι	ἐσκεδάσθην
σπείρω *sow*	σπερῶ	ἔσπειρα	ἔσπαρκα	ἔσπαρμαι	ἐσπάρην
στέλλω *send, equip*	στελῶ	ἔστειλα	ἔσταλκα	ἔσταλμαι	ἐστάλην
σφάλλω *trip up*	σφαλῶ	ἔσφηλα		ἔσφαλμαι	ἐσφάλην
σῴζω *save*	σώσω	ἔσωσα	σέσωκα	σέσῳσμαι	ἐσώθην
τελέω *finish*	τελῶ	ἐτέλεσα	τετέλεκα	τετέλεσμαι	ἐτελέσθην
τέμνω *cut*	τεμῶ	ἔτεμον	τέτμηκα	τέτμημαι	ἐτμήθην
τίθημι *place, put*	θήσω	ἔθηκα	τέθηκα	τέθειμαι	ἐτέθην
τίκτω *beget*	τέξομαι	ἔτεκον	τέτοκα		
τιτρώσκω *wound*	τρώσω	ἔτρωσα		τέτρωμαι	ἐτρώθην
τρέπω *turn*	τρέψω	ἔτρεψα	τέτροφα	τέτραμμαι	ἐτράπην ἐτρέφθην
τρέφω *nourish*	θρέψω	ἔθρεψα	τέτροφα	τέθραμμαι	ἐτράφην ἐθρέφθην
τρέχω *run*	δραμοῦμαι	ἔδραμον	δεδράμηκα		
τυγχάνω *hit, happen*	τεύξομαι	ἔτυχον	τετύχηκα		
τύπτω *strike*	τυπτήσω	ἐτύπτησα			
ὑπισχνέομαι *promise*	ὑποσχήσομαι	ὑπεσχόμην	ὑπέσχημαι		
φαίνω *show*	φανῶ	ἔφηνα	πέφαγκα (tr. *I have shown*) πέφηνα (intr. *I have appeared*)	πέφασμαι	ἐφάνθην (*I was shown [to be]*) ἐφάνην (intr. *I appeared*)
φέρω *bring, carry*	οἴσω	ἤνεγκον	ἐνήνοχα	ἐνήνεγμαι	ἠνέχθην
φεύγω *flee*	φεύξομαι	ἔφυγον	πέφευγα		
φημί *say*	φήσω	ἔφησα (ἔφην impf.)			
φθάνω *anticipate*	φθήσομαι	ἔφθασα ἔφθην (like ἔστην)			

Present	Future	Aorist	Perfect	Perfect mid. pass.	Aorist passive
(δια-)φθείρω destroy, corrupt	φθερῶ	ἔφθειρα	ἔφθαρκα	ἔφθαρμαι	ἐφθάρην
φοβέομαι fear	φοβήσομαι			πεφόβημαι	ἐφοβήθην
φύω produce	φύσω	ἔφῡσα (tr.) ἔφῡν (intr. *grew, was*)	πέφῡκα (intr. *am by nature, am*)		
χαίρω rejoice	χαιρήσω		κεχάρηκα		ἐχάρην
χράομαι use	χρήσομαι	ἐχρησάμην		κέχρημαι	ἐχρήσθην
χρή impers. *it is necessary*	χρῆσται	χρῆν, ἐχρῆν (both impf.)			
ὠνέομαι buy	ὠνήσομαι	(ἐπριάμην)		ἐώνημαι	ἐωνήθην

VOCABULARY

In using the vocabulary the following should be noted:
(a) In addition to the abbreviations explained on p.ix the sign † is used:
   (i) **before** a simple verb whose principal parts are given on pp.330ff.
   (ii) **after** a compound verb whose simple form is included in the same list.
(b) The feminine and neuter forms of adjectives and the genitive of nouns are nearly always abbreviated and will **not** necessarily have the same accent as the form given in full, e.g. the genitive of ἄβυccoc is ἀβύccου, but these are listed below as ἄβυccoc, –ου ; in these cases the accent of the abbreviated form must be deduced from the rules for accentuation given in **Appendix 8**.
(c) The form of the article which accompanies each noun indicates its gender.

ἄβατος, –ον   *impassable*
ἄβιος, –ον   *unlivable, unsupportable*
ἄβροτος, –ον   *without men, deserted by men*
ἄβυccoc, –ου, ἡ   *abyss*
ἀγαγ– aor. stem of ἄγω
ἀγαθός, –ή, –όν   *good, noble, brave*
   ἀγαθὰ λέγω   *speak well of* (+acc., 22.1/2*f*(ii))
   ἀγαθὰ ποιέω   *do good to* (+acc., 22.1/2*f*(ii))
’Αγάθων, –ωνος, ο   *Agathon (tragic poet)*
ἀγάλλομαι   *glory, exult in* (+dat.)
ἄγαμαι (aor. ηγάcθην)   *admire*
’Αγαμέμνων, –ονος, ὁ   *Agamemnon (Greek commander at Troy)*
ἄγαν (adv.)   *too much, excessively*
ἀγανακτέω   *be annoyed*
ἀγαπάω   *love*
†ἀγγέλλω   *report, announce*
ἄγγελος, –ου, ο   *messenger*
ἄγγος, –ους, το   *vessel, urn*
’Αγις, –ιδος, ὁ   *Agis (King of Sparta)*
ἄγκῡρα, –ᾱς, ἡ   *anchor*
ἀγνοέω   *not to know, fail to understand*

ἄγνοια, –ᾱς, η   *ignorance*
ἁγνός, –ή, –όν   *chaste*
ἀγορά, –ᾱς, ἡ   *place of assembly, market-place; agora*
ἀγοράζω   *buy in the market*
ἀγορεύω   *speak* (in assembly); *proclaim*
ἄγριος, –ᾱ, –ον   *fierce, cruel*
ἄγροικος, –ον   *from the country, rustic, boorish*
ἀγρός, –οῦ, ὁ   *field, country, farm*
ἀγρυπνέω   *lie awake, pass sleepless nights*
†ἄγω   *lead, bring*
   ἄγω καὶ φέρω   *plunder*
ἀγών, –ῶνος ὁ   *contest, trial, competition, exploit*
ἀδαμάντινος, –ον   *adamantine, of steel*
ἀδελφή, –ῆς, ἡ   *sister*
ἀδελφιδῆ, –ῆς, ἡ   *niece*
ἀδελφός, –οῦ, ὁ   *brother*
ἀδεῶc (adv.)   *fearlessly*
ἄδηλος, –ον   *unclear*
ἀδικέω   *be unjust, commit a crime; wrong, injure* (+acc.)
ἀδίκημα, –ατος, τό   *crime, wrong*

ἀδικίᾱ, -ᾱc, ἡ   injustice, wrong-doing
ἄδικος, -ον   unjust, dishonest
ἀδίκως (adv.)   unjustly
Ἄδμητος, -ου, ὁ   Admetus (king of
   Pherae, husband of Alcestis)
ἀδολέσχης, -ου, ὁ   idle talker,
   babbler; (as. adj.) garrulous
ἀδύνατος -ον   impossible; incapable
ᾄδω   sing
ἀεί (adv.)   always, continually; in
   succession
ἀείδω = ᾄδω
ἀεικής, -ές   shameful
ἀείμνηςτος, -ον   not to be forgotten
#ἀεκαζόμενος, -η, -ον   unwilling(ly)
#ἀεροβατέω   tread the air
ἀετός, -οῦ, ὁ   eagle
ἀηδών, -όνος, ἡ   nightingale
ἀήρ, -έρος, ὁ   air
ἀθάνατος, -ον   immortal
Ἀθηνᾶ, -ᾶς, ἡ   Athena
Ἀθήναζε (adv.)   to   Athens
Ἀθῆναι, -ῶν, αἱ   Athens
Ἀθηναῖος, -ᾱ, -ον   Athenian
Ἀθήνηθεν (adv.)   from Athens
Ἀθήνηςι(ν) (adv.)   at Athens
ἀθλητής, -οῦ, ὁ   athlete
ἄθλιος, -ᾱ, -ον   wretched, miserable
ἆθλον, -ου, τό   prize
ἆθλος, -ου, ὁ   contest; ordeal
ἀθροίζω   gather together (tr.)
ἀθρόος, -ᾱ, -ον   all together, all at
   once, in a body
ἀθῡμέω   be despondent
#αἰ = εἰ
#αἰάζω   bewail, lament
#αἰαῖ (exclamation)   alas!
Αἴγῑνα, -ης, ἡ   Aegina (island in the
   Saronic Gulf near Athens)
Αἰγῑνήτης, -ου, ὁ   man of Aegina
Αἰγύπτιος, -ᾱ, -ον   Egyptian
Αἴγυπτος, -ου, ἡ   Egypt
αἰδέομαι   respect; feel pity for; stand
   in awe of, fear
Ἅιδης, -ου (also # Ἀΐδης), ὁ   Hades
   (god of the underworld)
εἰς Ἅιδου   to the house of Hades,
   to   the underworld (23.1/1a)
αἰδώς, -ους, ἡ   sense of shame,
   modesty, respect (13.1/1b(i))
#αἰεί = ἀεί

#αἰέν = ἀεί
αἰθήρ, -έρος, ὁ   upper air, sky
αἴθομαι   burn, blaze
αἰκίᾱ, -ᾱς, ἡ   suffering, misery
αἰκίζομαι   maltreat
αἷμα, -ατος, τό   blood; bloodshed,
   murder
Αἵμων, -ωμος, ὁ   Haemon (son of
   Creon)
†αἰνέω   praise
αἴνιγμα, -ατος, τό   riddle
αἰνικτηρίως (adv.)   riddlingly, in
   riddling fashion
αἰνίττομαι   speak in riddles
#αἶνος, -ου, ὁ   tale, story
αἰνῶς (adv.)   terribly
αἴξ, αἰγός, ὁ/ἡ   goat
#αἰπυμήτης, -ου (adj.)   with high
   thoughts, lofty-minded
αἱρέομαι   choose, elect
†αἱρέω   take, capture; convict (18.1/4)
†αἴρω   lift, raise up; set sail; exalt
†αἰσθάνομαι   perceive, notice, realise
   (+gen. or acc.,13.1/2a(iii))
Αἰσχίνης, -ου, ὁ   Aeschines
   (Athenian orator)
αἰσχρός, -ά, -όν   ugly (of people);
   base, shameful, disgraceful
   (compar. αἰσχῑ́ων, supl. αἴσχιστος)
Αἰσχύλος, -ου, ὁ   Aeschylus (tragic
   poet)
αἰσχύνη, -ης, ἡ   shame, disgrace
αἰσχῡ́νομαι   be ashamed (15.1/2c);
   feel shame before
†αἰσχῡ́νω   dishonour, disgrace
αἰτέω   ask (for) (+double acc.,
   22.1/2f(ii)); ask alms of (+acc.)
αἰτίᾱ, -ᾱς, ἡ   reason, cause;
   responsibility, blame; charge,
   accusation; fault
αἰτιάομαι   accuse
αἴτιος, -ᾱ, -ον   responsible (for),
   guilty (of) (+gen.)
#αἶψα (adv.)   quickly, forthwith
αἰών, -ῶνος, ὁ   life, lifetime; age
Ἀκαδήμεια, -ᾱς, ἡ   the Academy
   (park and gymnasium in Athens)
Ἀκάνθιος, -ᾱ, -ον   of Acanthus (city
   in Macedonia)
ἀκατασκεύαςτος, -ον   unformed
ἀκήκοα perf. ind. of ἀκούω

ἀκΐνητος, –ον motionless, immovable
#ἀκμαῖος, –ᾱ, –ον in full bloom, at the prime
ἀκμή, –ῆς, ἡ prime, zenith
ἀκολασίᾱ, –ᾱς, ἡ lack of restraint
ἀκόλαστος, –ον undisciplined, unrestrained, licentious
ἀκολουθέω follow, accompany (+dat.)
ἀκόλουθος, –ου, ὁ servant, slave
ἀκολούθως (adv.) in accordance with (+dat.)
ἀκονάω sharpen
ἄκούσιος, –ον against one's will, involuntary
†ἀκούω hear, listen (to) (+gen. of person, gen. or acc. of thing,13.1/2a(iii)); be spoken of (17.1/5)
ἀκρῑβῶς (adv.) accurately, exactly, carefully
ἄκρον, –ου, τό peak, summit
ἀκρόπολις, –εως, ἡ acropolis, citadel
ἄκρος, –ᾱ, –ον high; top of (18.1/6)
'Ακταίων, –ωνος, ὁ Actaeon (mythological character)
ἀκτή, –ῆς, ἡ shore, coast
ἄκων, ἄκουσα, ἆκον unwilling(ly)
ἀλγέω feel pain, be in pain; grieve; suffer
ἄλγος, –ους, τό grief, pain, suffering
ἀλγΰνω grieve, distress (+acc.)
'Αλέξανδρος, –ου, ὁ Alexander (the Great, of Macedon)
ἀλήθεια, –ᾱς, ἡ truth
ἀληθεύω tell the truth
ἀληθής, –ές true
τὰ ἀληθῆ (τἀληθῆ) the truth
ἀληθινῶς (adv.) truly, really
ἀληθῶς (adv.) truly, really
ὡς ἀληθῶς in very truth
'Αλικαρνασσεύς, –έως, ὁ man from Halicarnassus
†ἀλίσκομαι be caught; be convicted (18.1/4)
ἀλκή, –ῆς, ἡ valour, bravery
"Αλκηστις, –ιδος, ἡ Alcestis (wife of Admetus)
'Αλκιβιάδης, –ου, ὁ Alcibiades (Athenian general and statesman)
ἄλκιμος, –ον brave

ἀλλά (conj.) but; well, now
ἀλλάττω change
ἀλλήλους, –ᾱς, –α (reciprocal pron.) each other, one another (9.1/4b)
ἄλλοθι (adv.) elsewhere
ἄλλομαι (aor. ἡλάμην) leap
ἄλλος, –η, –ο (9.1/3) other, the rest of; as well, besides (7.2.12 l. 11)
ἄλλος . . . ἄλλον one . . . another (cf. note on 5.2.5(viii))
ἄλλοτε (adv.) at other times
ἀλλότριος, –ᾱ, –ον someone else's; alien
ἄλλως (adv.) otherwise; in vain
ἄλλως τε καί especially
ἅλμη, –ης, ἡ sea-water, brine; sea
ἄλογος, –ον speechless; irrational
ἅλς, ἁλός, ἡ sea
ἄλσος, –ους, τό grove
ἀλυσκάζω shun, shrink away
ἄλφιτα, –ων, τά barley-groats; daily-bread
ἀλωπεκῆ, –ῆς, ἡ fox-skin
ἀλώπηξ, –εκος, ἡ fox
ἅλωσις, –εως, ἡ capture
ἅμα (adv.) at the same time; (prep.+dat.) at the same time as, together with
ἅμα μέν ... ἅμα δέ partly ... partly
ἅμα ἡλίῳ ἀνέχοντι at sunrise
ἅμα (τῇ) ἡμέρᾳ at dawn
ἀμαθής, –ές ignorant
ἀμαθίᾱ, –ᾱς, ἡ ignorance, stupidity
ἅμαξα, –ης, ἡ wagon
ἅμαρτ– aor. stem of ἁμαρτάνω
ἁμαρτάνω err; do wrong; make a mistake; (+gen.,13.1/2a(iv)) miss,fail to achieve
ἁμαρτίᾱ, –ᾱς, ἡ fault, wrong, sin
ἀμείβω change, alter
ἀμείνων, –ον better (compar. of ἀγαθός)
ἀμηχανέω be at a loss/helpless
ἀμίς, –ίδος, ἡ chamber-pot
ἄμμος, –ου, ἡ sand
†ἀμΰνω keep/ward off, (acc. of person kept off and dat. of person defended); in mid., defend oneself against (+acc.)
'Αμυρταῖος, –ου, ὁ Amyrtaeus
ἀμφί (prep.+acc.) about, around

#ἀμφίαλος, -ον *sea-girt*
ἀμφιβάλλομαι† *throw around, put on*
ἀμφιδέᾱ, -ᾶς, ἡ *bracelet, anklet*
#ἀμφιμάχομαι† *besiege*
ἀμφότερος, -ᾱ, -ον *both*
ἀμφοτέρωθεν (adv.) *from/on both sides*
ἄμφω, -οιν, τώ (dual) *both*
ἀμώμητος, -ον *blameless*
ἄν untranslatable particle: in a main clause (+ind. or opt.) with a potential/conditional sense (19.1/2, 18.1/5); in a subordinate clause (+subj.) with an indef. sense (14.1/4c(iii))
ἄν = ἐάν
ἀνά (prep.+acc.) *up, up along; throughout, over*
ἀναβαίνω† *go up; come up; mount*
ἀναβιβάζω *make go up*
ἀναβοάω† *call upon*
ἀναβολή, -ῆς, ἡ *putting off, delaying*
ἀναγιγνώσκω† *read, read aloud*
ἀναγκάζω *force, compel*
ἀναγκαῖος, -ᾱ, -ον *necessary, constraining*
ἀνάγκη, -ης, ἡ *necessity, compulsion, force*
  ἀνάγκη ἐστι *it is necessary* (+dat. and inf.)
ἀνάγω† *bring up, raise;* (mid.) *set sail, put out to sea*
ἀναδίδωμι† *give forth, send up*
ἀναζητέω *investigate*
ἀνάθεμα, -ατος, τό *anything dedicated (especially to evil); an accursed thing*
ἀνάθημα, -ατος, τό *dedication*
ἀναίδεια, -ᾱς, ἡ *shamelessness*
#ἀναιμόσαρκος, -ον *with bloodless flesh*
ἀναιρέω† *pick up; give a response (of an oracle)*
ἀναίσθητος, -ον *without feeling, stupid*
ἀναίτιος, -ον *innocent*
ἀναλαμβάνω† *take up, take with one*
†ἀνᾱλίσκω *spend*
ἀνάλῡσις, -εως, ἡ *loosening, releasing; resolution* (of a problem)

ἀνάλωτος, -ον *not able to be captured, impregnable*
ἀναμένω† *wait, stay, wait for* (+acc.)
ἀναμετρέομαι *measure carefully*
ἀναμιμνῄσκω† *remind;* (pass.) *recall to mind, remember*
#ἄναξ, -ακτος, ὁ *lord, king*
Ἀναξαγόρᾱς, -ου, ὁ *Anaxagoras (philosopher of Clazomenae in Asia Minor)*
Ἀναξιμένης, -ους, ὁ *Anaximenes (early philospher)*
ἀνάξιος, -ον *unworthy*
ἀναπτύσσω *unfold, disclose*
ἀνασπάω (aor. -έσπασα) *haul up; tear up, pull down*
ἀνάσσω *rule over* (+gen., 13.1/2a(i))
#ἀνασταλύζω *weep, sob*
ἀνασταυρόω *impale*
ἀνατίθημι† *dedicate, make a dedication*
ἀναφέρω† *bring back, refer*
ἀναχωρέω *withdraw, retreat, retire*
ἀνδρ– stem of ἀνήρ
ἀνδραποδίζω *enslave*
ἀνδράποδον, -ου, τό *captive; slave*
ἀνδρείᾱ, -ᾶς, ἡ *manliness, courage*
ἀνδρεῖος, -ᾱ, -ον *manly, brave*
ἀνδριάς, -άντος, ὁ *statue*
ἄνεμος, -ου, ὁ *wind*
ἀνεξέταστος, -ον *without enquiry or investigation*
ἀνερ– = ἀνδρ–
ἀνερωτάω† *ask questions*
ἄνευ (prep.+gen.) *without*
ἀνέχω† *hold up, lift up;* intr. *rise up*
  ἅμα ἡλίῳ ἀνέχοντι *at sunrise*
ἀνήρ, ἀνδρός, ὁ *man, husband*
ἄνθινος, -η, -ον *flowery*
ἀνθίστημι† (mid. and intr. tenses of act.) *withstand, resist, oppose* (+dat.)
ἄνθος, -ους, τό *flower, bloom; glory*
ἀνθρώπινος, -η, -ον *human*
ἄνθρωπος, -ου, ὁ/ἡ *human being, person; man; fellow*
ἅνθρωπος crasis for ὁ ἄνθρωπος
ἀνιάω *distress, vex*
ἀνίδρωτος, -ον *without raising a sweat*

ἀνίϲτημι† *raise up; restore; cause to migrate, expel, uproot;* (mid. and intr. tenses of act.) *rise up, stand up; migrate, go away* (19.1/1)

ἀνιϲτορέω *make enquiry about, ask about,* (+double acc.)

ἀνόητοϲ -ον *foolish*

†ἀνοίγνῡμι *open*

ἀνοικοδομέω *build up; rebuild*

ἀνόμοιοϲ, -ον (also -ᾱ, -ον) *unlike, dissimilar* (+dat.)

ἀνταγορεύω (aor. ἀντεῖπον, 18.1/4 note 2) *speak against, deny*

ἀνταγωνίζομαι *struggle against, vie with* (+dat.)

ἀντακούω *hear in turn*

Ἀνταλκίδαϲ, -ου, ὁ *Antalcidas* (Spartan general)

ἀντεῖπον aor. of ἀνταγορεύω

ἀντέχω† *hold out, withstand*

ἀντί (prep.+gen.) *instead of, in return for*

ἀντιβολέω *entreat, beseech*

ἀντιγράφω *write in reply*

ἀντιδίδωμι† *give in return*

ἀντίθεϲιϲ, -εωϲ, ἡ *opposition, antithesis*

ἀντιλέγω† *argue against, oppose*

ἀντίον (adv.) *opposite*

Ἀντίοχοϲ, -ου, ὁ *Antiochus*

Ἀντιϲθένηϲ, -ουϲ, ὁ *Antisthenes* (philosopher)

ἀνυποδηϲίᾱ, -ᾱϲ, ἡ *going barefoot*

ἀνυπόδητοϲ, -ον *without shoes*

ἄνω (adv.) *above, up above*

#ἄνωγα (perf. with pres. sense, 19.1/3a) *command, order*

ἀνωφελήϲ, -έϲ *useless*

ἀξιόπιϲτοϲ, -ον *worthy of credit, trustworthy*

ἄξιοϲ, -ᾱ, -ον *worthy (of), deserving* (+gen.), *worthwhile*

ἀξιόω *think worthy of*

ἀόρᾱτοϲ, -ον *unseen, invisible*

ἀπαγγέλλω† *announce, report*

ἀπαγορεύω *forbid* (18.1/4 note 2)

ἀπάγχομαι *hang oneself*

ἀπαγχονίζω *hang by a noose*

ἀπάγω† *lead/take away*

ἀπαθήϲ, -έϲ *not suffering*

ἀπαίρω† *sail away, depart*

ἀπαλλαγή, -ῆϲ, ἡ *deliverance*

ἀπαλύνω *make tender/delicate*

ἀπάνθρωποϲ, -ον *far from men, desolate*

ἀπανίϲτημι† *withdraw*

ἀπαντάω *go to meet, meet* (+dat.,13.1/2b(iii))

ἅπαξ (adv.) *once only, once*

ἀπαραίτητοϲ -ον *unmoved by prayer, inexorable*

ἀπαρνέομαι *deny*

ἅπᾱϲ, ἅπᾱϲα, ἅπαν *all, the whole of*

ἀπατάω *deceive*

ἀπάτη, -ηϲ, ἡ *deceit*

ἀπέθανον aor. of ἀποθνῄϲκω

ἀπεικάζω *liken, compare*

ἀπειλέω *threaten* (+dat., 13.1/2b(i))

ἄπειμι *be absent*

ἀπείργω† *hinder, prevent*

ἀπειρίᾱ, -ᾱϲ, ἡ *inexperience*

ἄπειροϲ, -ον *ignorant of, inexperienced in* (+gen.)

ἀπείρωϲ ἔχω *be without experience*

ἀπενθήϲ, -έϲ *free from grief/woe*

ἀπεριϲκέπτωϲ (adv.) *incautiously*

ἀπέρχομαι† *go away, depart*

ἀπέχω† *be distant from* (+gen.); (mid.) *keep one's hands off, keep away from* (+gen.)

ἀπιϲτέω *distrust*

ἀπιϲτίᾱ, -ᾱϲ, ἡ *faithlessness*

ἄπιϲτοϲ, -ον *incredible; untrustworthy, not to be believed; mistrustful*

ἀπίϲτωϲ ἔχω *be mistrustful*

ἄπλετοϲ, -ον *boundless, immense*

ἅπλουϲ, -ῆ, -οῦν *simple* (6.1/2)

ἀπό (prep.+gen.) *from, away from*

ἀποβαίνω† *land*

ἀποβάλλω† *throw away, lose*

ἀποδημίᾱ, -ᾱϲ, ἡ *being abroad or away from one's country*

ἀποδιδράϲκω (fut. -δρᾱϲομαι aor. -έδρᾱν) *run away, escape, flee*

ἀποδίδωμι† *give back, return, repay;* (mid.) *sell*

ἀποθαν- aor. stem of ἀποθνῄϲκω

ἀποθνῄϲκω† *die, be killed* (17.1/5; for the perfect see 19.1/3a)

ἄποικοϲ, -ου, ὁ *settler, colonist*

†ἀποκρῑ́νομαι   answer
ἀπόκρισις, –εως, ἡ   answer, reply
ἀποκρύπτω   hide from sight; (mid.)
   conceal for one's own purposes
ἀποκτείνω†   kill
ἀποκωλύω   hinder from
ἀπολέγομαι   pick out
ἀπολεс– aor.stem of ἀπόλλῡμι
ἀπόλλῡμι†   kill, ruin, destroy, lose
   (20.1/1 note 2)
   ἀπωλόμην   I was killed
   ἀπόλωλα   I am lost/dead/ruined
Ἀπόλλων, –ωνος, ὁ   Apollo (acc.
   either –ωνα or –ω)
ἀπολογέομαι   defend oneself, speak
   in one's defence; plead in one's
   defence (+acc.)
ἀπολογίᾱ, –ᾱς, ἡ   speech in one's
   defence
ἀπολῡ́ω   free, release
ἀπομῑμέομαι   imitate, copy
ἀποπῑ́πτω†   fall overboard
ἀποπλέω†   sail away
ἀποπνῑ́γομαι   choke, suffocate, be
   drowned
ἀπορέω   be at a loss, be in difficulty
ἀπορίᾱ, –ᾱς, ἡ   lack of provisions,
   want; perplexity, difficulty
ἀποστατέω   stand aloof from (+gen.)
ἀποστέλλω†   send, send away
ἀποστερέω   deprive of, rob, defraud,
   refuse payment of
ἀποστροφή, –ῆς, ἡ   turning away
   from, escape
ἀπότακτος, –ον   set apart for special
   use
ἀποτειχίζω   wall off
ἀποτέμνω†   cut off
ἀποτίθημι†   put away, bury; (mid.)
   lay aside
ἀποτρέχω†   run away, run off
ἀποτυγχάνω†   fail to obtain
#ἀπούρας (epic aor. pple. of ἀπαυράω)
   having taken away
ἀποφαίνω†   reveal, show
ἀποφέρω†   carry away
ἀποφεύγω†   flee, run off; be acquitted
ἀποχωρέω   go away, depart
ἀποχώρησις, –εως, ἡ   privy, public
   toilet
ἀπραγμόνως (adv.)   without trouble

ἀπράγμων, –ονος   free from business,
   not meddling in public affairs
ἅπτω   fasten, fix; light (a lamp);
   (mid.) touch (+gen.)
ἀπωθέω (aor. ἀπέωσα)   push away
ἀπώλεσα aor. of ἀπόλλῡμι
ἄρα* (inferential particle)   then,
   consequently, after all
ἆρα interrog. particle (10.1/2a)
ἀργαλέος, –ᾱ, –ον   painful,
   troublesome
Ἀργεῖοι, –ων, οἱ   Argives; (poet.)
   Greeks
Ἀργεῖος, –ᾱ, –ον   Argive; (poet.)
   Greek
Ἀργινοῦσαι, –ῶν, αἱ   Arginousae
   (islands) (scene of Athenian naval
   victory)
Ἄργος, –ους, τό   Argos
ἀργός, –όν   idle, lazy
ἀργύριον, –ου, τό   silver, money
ἀργυροῦς, –ᾶ, –οῦν   made of silver,
   silver
ἀρετή, –ῆς, ἡ   courage; excellence,
   virtue
Ἄρης, –ου ὁ   Ares (god of war)
ἄρθρον, –ου, τό   joint, limb
Ἀριαῖος, –ου, ὁ   Ariaeus
ἀριθμός, –οῦ, ὁ   number, amount,
   total
#ἀριπρεπής, –ές   very bright,
   conspicuous
ἀριστάω   have breakfast
Ἀριστεύς, –έως, ὁ   Aristeus
ἀριστεύω   be best, be best at (+inf.)
Ἀριστόκριτος, –ου, ὁ   Aristocritus
ἄριστον, –ου, τό   breakfast
ἄριστος, –η, –ον   best; bravest (supl.
   of ἀγαθός)
Ἀριστοτέλης, –ους, ὁ   Aristotle
   (philosopher)
Ἀριστοφάνης, –ους, ὁ   Aristophanes
   (comic poet)
Ἀρίφρων, –ονος, ὁ   Ariphron
ἄρκτος, –ου, ἡ   bear
ἁρμόζει (impers.)   it is fitting, it
   suits
Ἄρνη, –ης, ἡ   Arne (place in
   Thessaly)
ἄρνυμαι   win
ἁρπάζω   seize, plunder, snatch

ἁρπακτής, -οῦ, ὁ robber, ravisher
#ἁρπαλέος, -ᾱ, -ον attractive,
   alluring
ἄρρηκτος, -ον unbroken,
   unbreakable
ἄρρητος, -ον unspoken, unmentioned
ἀρσενικός, -ή, -όν male, masculine
'Ἀρταφέρνης, -ους, ὁ Artaphernes
Ἄρτεμις, -ιδος, ἡ Artemis
   (goddess)
ἄρτημα, -ατος, τό ear-ring
ἄρτι (ἀρτίως) (adv.) newly, recently,
   just now
ἄρτος, -ου, ὁ bread
ἀρχαῖος, -ᾱ, -ον ancient, old;
   former
'Ἀρχέλᾱος, -ου, ὁ Archelaus (King
   of Sparta)
ἀρχή, -ῆς, ἡ beginning; rule, power;
   empire; office, magistracy, board of
   magistrates, magistrate, officer
ἀρχιερεύς, -έως, ὁ high priest
'Ἀρχιμήδης, -ους, ὁ Archimedes
   (Syracusan mathematician and
   inventor)
†ἄρχω rule, rule over, command
   (+gen., 13.1/2a(i))
   (+pple.) begin (of something
   continued by others); (mid.) begin
   (of something continued by
   oneself)
ἄρχων, -οντος, ὁ archon
   (magistrate)
ἀσαφής, -ές obscure, unclear
ἄσβεστος, -ον (also -η, -ον)
   unquenchable, inextinguishable,
   imperishable
ἀσέβεια, -ᾱς, ἡ impiety, irreverence
   (to gods)
ἀσεβέω commit impiety
ἀσθένεια, -ᾱς, ἡ weakness, illness
ἀσθενέω be weak/ill
ἀσθενής, -ές weak, ill
ἀσινέστατα (supl. adv.) most/very
   harmlessly
ἀσῑτέω be without food
ἀσκέω practise, exercise, train
ἄσμενος, -η, -ον glad, pleased
ἀσπάζομαι greet
'Ἀσπασίᾱ, -ᾱς, ἡ Aspasia (mistress
   of Pericles)

ἄσπετος, -ον enormously great,
   boundless
ἀσπίς, -ίδος, ἡ shield
ἀστεῖος, -ᾱ, -ον charming, attractive
ἀστήρ, -έρος, ὁ star
ἀστρονομίᾱ, -ᾱς, ἡ astronomy
ἄστυ, -εως, τό city, town
ἀσφάλεια, -ᾱς, ἡ safety, security
ἀσφαλής, -ές safe, secure
ἀσφαλῶς (adv.) safely
ἀταλαίπωρος, -ον without taking
   pains, not painstaking
ἀτάρ (conj.) but
ἀτασθαλίᾱ, -ᾱς, ἡ presumptuous sin,
   wickedness
ἄτε (particle) as if, as; (causal) in as
   much as, since, seeing that, because,
   as (+pple. 12.1/2a(ii))
ἀτελής, -ές incomplete
#ἄτερ (prep.+gen.) without
ἄτεχνος, -ον unskilled
ἀτεχνῶς (adv.) simply, just
ἄτη, -ης, ἡ ruin
ἀτῑμάζω dishonour
ἀτῑμαστος, -ον dishonoured
ἀτῑμίᾱ -ᾱς, ἡ dishonour; loss of
   citizen rights
ἄτῑμος, -ον dishonoured; deprived of
   citizen rights
ἄτολμος, -ον not daring, lacking the
   heart to
ἄτοπος, -ον out of place,
   extraordinary, strange, absurd
'Ἀττικός, -ή, -όν Attic, Athenian
   'Ἀττική (sc. γῆ), -ῆς Attica
ἀτυχής, -ές unlucky, unfortunate
αὖ (adv.) again, moreover
αὐγή, -ῆς, ἡ ray, beam
#αὐδάω speak, say, utter, tell
αὐθαίρετος, -ον self-chosen, self-
   inflicted
αὖθις (adv.) again; in turn, next, on
   the other hand
αὐλέω play the flute
αὐλή, -ῆς, ἡ courtyard, hall
αὐλίζομαι encamp
αὔριον (adv.) tomorrow
#αὐτάρ (conj.) but, then
αὐτάρκης, -ες sufficient
#αὖτε (adv.) again, in turn
αὐτίκα (adv.) at once, immediately

αὐτόθι (adv.) *on the spot, here*
αὐτόματον, -ου, τό *accident*
αὐτόν, -ήν, -ό (pron.) *him, her, it*
(4.1/2; 9.1/3c)
αὐτός, -ή, -ό *self* (9.1/3a)
ὁ αὐτός *the same* (9.1/3b)
αὐτός crasis for ὁ αὐτός
αὐτοῦ (adv.) *here, there, on the spot*
ἀφαιρέω† *take away (from),*
remove; (mid.) *deprive (of)* (+
double acc., 22.1/2f(ii))
ἀφανής, -ές *unseen, vanished, not to*
be seen
ἀφανίζω *make unseen, wipe out,*
destroy
ἀφασίᾱ, -ᾱς, ἡ *speechlessness*
ἀφεῖναι aor. inf. of ἀφίημι
ἄφθονος, -ον *abundant, plentiful;*
bountiful
ἀφίημι† *send forth; discharge; let go*
†ἀφικνέομαι *arrive, come*
ἀφῑκόμην aor. of ἀφικνέομαι
ἀφίστημι† *remove; make to revolt;*
(mid. and intr. tenses of act.)
withdraw; revolt (19.1/1)
Ἀφροδῑτη, -ης, ἡ *Aphrodite*
(goddess of love)
ἄφρων, -ον *senseless, foolish*
ἀφυής, -ές *without natural*
talent/skill
#ἀφύσσομαι *draw (a liquid) for*
oneself
ἄφωνος, -ον *dumb, speechless*
Ἀχαῖοι, -ων, οἱ *Achaeans, Greeks*
Ἀχέρων, -οντος, ὁ *Acheron* (river in
the underworld)
ἀχθηδών, -όνος, ἡ *burden*
ἄχθομαι *be annoyed/displeased at*
(+dat.)
Ἀχιλλεύς, -έως, ὁ *Achilles* (hero in
Iliad)
ἄχυρα, -ων, τά *chaff, bran*

βαδίζω (fut. βαδιοῦμαι) *walk, go*
βάθος, -ους, τό *depth*
βαθύς, -εῖα, -ύ *deep*
#βαθυχαιτήεις, -εσσα, -εν *long-*
haired
†βαίνω *go, come; walk*
Βάκχος, -ου, ὁ *Bacchus* (another
name for Dionysus)

#βάκχος, -ου, ὁ *person initiated into*
the rites of Bacchus
†βάλλω *throw, hit, pelt; inflict*
βάπτω *dip; dye*
βάρβαρος, -ον *barbarian, foreign*
βαρῡνομαι *be weighed down*
βαρύς, -εῖα, -ύ *heavy; wearisome*
βασίλεια, -ᾱς, ἡ *princess, queen*
βασιλείᾱ, -ᾱς, ἡ *kingship*
βασίλειος, -ᾱ, -ον *royal*
βασιλεύς, -έως, ὁ *king*
βασιλεύω *be king, rule* (+gen.,
13.1/2a(i))
#βαστάζω *lift up, carry*
βάτραχος, -ου, ὁ *frog*
βέβαιος, -ον (also -ᾱ, -ον) *secure,*
steady
βέβρωκα perf. of βιβρώσκω
βέλος, -ους, τό *missile*
βέλτιστος, -η, -ον *best* (supl. of
ἀγαθός)
βελτῑων, -ον *better* (compar. of
ἀγαθός)
βῆμα, -ατος, τό *step*
βίᾱ, -ᾱς, ἡ *force, violence*
πρὸς βίᾱν *by force*
βιάζομαι *use force, force one's way*
βιαιως (adv.) *violently*
βιβλίον, -ου, τό *book*
βίβλος, -ου, ἡ *book*
βιβρώσκω (perf. βέβρωκα) *eat*
βίος, -ου, ὁ *life; means of life;*
livelihood
#βίοτος, -ου, ὁ *life*
βιόω *live*
βιωτός, -όν *to be lived, worth living*
βλάβη, -ης, ἡ *damage*
†βλάπτω *hurt, injure; damage*
βλέπω *see, look (at); see the light of*
day, be alive
βληθείς, -εῖσα, -έν aor. pple. pass. of
βάλλω
#βλώσκω (fut. μολοῦμαι, aor. ἔμολον,
perf. μέμβλωκα) *go*
†βοάω *shout*
βόειος, -ᾱ, -ον *of beef*
βοή, -ῆς, ἡ *shout, shouting*
βοήθεια, -ᾱς, ἡ *help, aid*
βοηθέω *(run to) help* (+dat.,
13.1/2b(i))
βόθρος, -ου, ὁ *hole, pit*

Βοιωτίᾱ, -ᾱς, ἡ   Boeotia (state in north central Greece)
Βοιωτός, -οῦ, ὁ   a Boeotian
βοσκήματα, -ων, τά   cattle
βόσκω   feed, nourish
βουλευτήριον, -ου, τό   council-chamber
βουλεύω   plan, resolve, determine, deliberate; (mid.) discuss, deliberate, consider; plot
βουλή, -ῆς, ἡ   plan, counsel, advice; council
†βούλομαι   wish, want
#βουνός, -οῦ, ὁ   hill, mound
βοῦς, βοός, ὁ/ἡ   ox, bull, cow
#βούτης, -ου, ὁ   herdsman
βραδέως (adv.)   slowly
βραδΰνω   be slow, hesitate
#βραδύπους, -πουν (gen. -ποδος)   slow-footed
βραδύς, -εῖα, -ύ (compar. βραδῑ́ων, supl. βράδιστος)   slow
βραχῑ́ων, -ονος, ὁ   arm
βραχύς, -εῖα, -ύ   short, brief; small, little
βρέχω   wet (tr.)
#βροτός, -οῦ, ὁ   mortal man
βρόχος, -ου, ὁ   noose
βρῶμα, -ατος, τό   food
βωμός, -οῦ, ὁ   altar

#γαῖα, -ᾱς, ἡ = γῆ
γάλα, -ακτος, τό   milk
†γαμέω (+acc.)   marry (with the man as subject); (mid.,+dat.) marry (with the woman as subject)
γάμος, -ου, ὁ   marriage
γάρ* (connecting particle)   for, as
γαστήρ, -τρός, ἡ   stomach, belly (6.1/1b)
γαστρίμαργος, -ον   gluttonous
γε* (particle)   at least; at any rate, certainly, indeed (13.1/3b)
γεγένημαι perf. of γίγνομαι
γεγενημένα, -ων, τά   events, occurrences, the past
#γέγηθα (perf. with pres. sense, from γηθέω)   rejoice
γέγονα perf. of γίγνομαι
#γεγώς = γεγονώς (perf. pple. of γίγνομαι)

γείτων, -ονος, ὁ   neighbour; (as adj.+dat.)   neighbouring
Γέλᾱ, -ᾱς, ἡ   Gela (city in Sicily)
†γελάω   laugh
γέλοιος (also γελοῖος), -ᾱ, -ον   funny, ridiculous
Γελῷος, -ᾱ, -ον of Gela
γέλως, -ωτος, ὁ   laughter
γέμω   be full of (+gen.)
γεν- aor. stem of γίγνομαι
γένεσις, -εως, ἡ   birth, coming into being
γενναῖος, -ᾱ, -ον   noble, well-born, noble-minded
γενναίως (adv.)   nobly
γεννάω   beget, produce
γένος, -ους, τό   race; kind
γεραιός, -ά, -όν   old
γέρας, -ως, τό   prize, privilege (13.1/1 b(iii))
γέρρα, -ων, τα   wicker-work
γέρων, -οντος, ὁ   old man
γεύομαι   taste
γέφῡρα, -ᾱς, ἡ   bridge, embankment
γεωμετρίᾱ, -ᾱς, ἡ   geometry
γεωργός, -οῦ, ὁ   farmer
γῆ, -ῆς, ἡ   land, earth, ground
κατα γῆν   by land
ποῦ (τῆς) γῆς;   where on earth?
γηγενής, -ες   earth-born
γημ- aor. stem of γαμέω
#γηράλεος, -ᾱ, -ον   aged, old
γῆρας, -ως, τό   old age (13.1/1 b(iii))
γηρά́σκω   grow old
γίγᾱς, -αντος, ὁ   giant
†γίγνομαι   become, be, be born; happen, take place
†γιγνώσκω   get to know, recognise, realize; think, resolve, decide
γῑ́νομαι = γίγνομαι
Γλαῦκος, -ου, ὁ   Glaucus
γλαῦξ, -αυκός, ἡ   owl
#γλαφυρός, -ά, -όν   hollow, hollowed
Γλοῦς, -οῦ, ὁ   Glus
γλυκερός, -ά, -όν   sweet
γλυκύς, -εῖα, -ύ   sweet
γλῶττα, -ης, ἡ   tongue
γνάθος, -ου, ἡ   jaw
γνούς, γνοῦσα, γνόν aor. pple. of γιγνώσκω
γνῶθι 2nd s. imp. of ἔγνων

γνώμη, –ης, ἡ judgement, opinion,
    mind, purpose
γνώριμος, (–η), –ον well-known, familiar
γονεύς, –εως, ὁ parent
γόνυ, –ατος, τό knee (5.1/5 note 1)
Γοργώ, –οῦς, ἡ Gorgo
#γουνόομαι implore, entreat
γράμμα, –ατος, τό written character,
    letter
γραμματικός, –οῦ, ὁ grammarian
γραμματιστής, –οῦ, ὁ schoolmaster
γραῦς, γρᾱός, ἡ old woman (11.1/4)
γραφεῖον, –ου, τό pencil
γραφή, –ῆς, ἡ writing, drawing;
    indictment, charge, case
†γράφω write; draw, paint; (mid.)
    indict, charge
γρῡπός, –ή, –όν hook-nosed, aquiline
Γύλιππος, –ου, ὁ Gylippus (Spartan
    general)
γυμνάζω exercise, train
γυμνός, –ή, –όν naked; lightly/poorly
    clad
γυναικωνῖτις, –ιδος, ἡ women's
    apartments
γυνή, –αικός, ἡ woman, wife (5.1/5
    note 1)
γύψ, γῡπός, ὁ vulture
Γωβρύᾱς, –ᾱ, ὁ Gobryas (Persian
    general)

δαιμόνιος, –ᾱ –ον miraculous,
    supernatural
δαίμων, –ονος, ὁ god, deity
δαίς, δαιτός, ἡ feast
δακ– aor. stem of δάκνω
δάκνω bite; worry
δάκρυ see δάκρυον
δακρυόεις, –εσσα, –εν weeping, in
    tears
δάκρυον, –ου, τό tear (alternative
    nom. δάκρυ 13.1/1c)
δακρύω weep
δακτύλιος, –ου, ὁ ring
δάκτυλος, –ου, ὁ finger
δανείζω lend; (mid.) borrow
δανειστής, –οῦ, ὁ creditor
Δάρδανος, –ου, ὁ Dardanus
    (founder of Troy)
δᾱρεικός, –οῦ, ὁ daric (Persian gold
    coin)

δᾴς, δᾳδός, ἡ torch
δασύς, –εῖα, –ύ hairy, shaggy
δέ* (connecting particle) and, but
    δ' οὖν* be that as it may (13.1/3c)
δέδαρμαι perf. mid./pass. of δέρω
δέδοικα I fear, am afraid (19.1/3a)
#δέδορκα see, look upon (perf. of
    δέρκομαι)
†δεῖ (impers.) it is necessary
    (+acc.and infin.); there is a need of
    (+gen., 21.1/4 note 3)
#δείδω be alarmed
†δείκνῡμι show (20.1/1 and **Appendix
    6**)
δειλίᾱ, –ᾱς, ἡ cowardice
δειλός, –ή, –όν miserable, wretched,
    cowardly
δειμαίνω (+acc.) be afraid of, fear
δεινός, –ή, –όν terrible, serious,
    strange; clever at (+inf.)
δειπνέω dine, have dinner, dine on
    (+acc.)
δεῖπνον, –ου, τό dinner
δέκα (indecl. adj.) ten
δεκατός, –ή, –όν tenth
δέλτος, –ου, ἡ writing-tablet
δελφίς, –ῖνος, ὁ dolphin
Δελφοί, –ῶν, οἱ Delphi
δένδρον, –ου, τό tree (13.1/1c)
δένδρεον, –ου, τό tree
δεξιά, –ᾶς, ἡ right hand
    δεξιᾶν δίδωμι give a pledge
δεξιός, –ά, –όν on the right hand;
    clever
Δέξιππος, –ου, ὁ Dexippus
†δέομαι need, implore, ask (+gen.,
    13.1/2a(ii))
δέον (acc. absol.) it being necessary
    (21.1/5)
δέος, –ους, τό fear
#δέρκομαι see, behold
δέρω (perf. mid./pass. δέδαρμαι)
    flay
δεσμός, οῦ, ὁ (alternative pl. δεσμά,
    τά) bond
δεσμωτήριον, –ου, τό prison
δέσποινα, –ης, ἡ mistress
δεσπότης, –ου, ὁ master
δεῦρο (adv.) here, over here
δεύτερος, –ᾱ, –ον second
†δέχομαι receive

δέω (A) *need, want, lack* (+gen.)
πολλοῦ δέω *I am far from*
πολλοῦ δεῖ *far from it!*
†δέω (B) *bind, tie*
δή * (particle) *indeed, certainly*
(13.1/3*b*)
δῆλος, –η, –ον *visible, clear, obvious*
δηλόω *make clear, show, reveal*
Δημέᾱς, –ου, ὁ *Demeas*
δημηγορέω *make a public speech*
Δημήτηρ, –τρος, ἡ *Demeter* (corn-goddess, mother of Persephone)
δημιουργός, –οῦ, ὁ *craftsman; maker, author*
δῆμος, –ου, ὁ *the people; democracy; deme*
Δημοσθένης, –ους, ὁ *Demosthenes* (fifth-century Athenian general; fourth-century orator)
δημόσιος, –ᾱ, –ον *public, of the state*
δημοσίᾳ *publicly*
δημοτικός, –ή, –όν *democratic, popular*
δήξομαι fut. of δάκνω
δήπου* (particle) *I presume, I should hope, doubtless*
δῆτα* (particle) *indeed; then* (13.1/3*a*)
δηχθ– aor. pass. stem of δάκνω
Δία acc. of Ζεύς (11.1/4)
διά (prep.+acc.) *because of, on account of*; (+gen.) *through, across*
διὰ τί; *why?*
διαβαίνω† *cross, cross over*
διαβάλλω† *slander*
διαβατέον *one must cross* (24.1/5)
διαβολή, –ῆς, ἡ *slander*
διάγνωσις, –εως, ἡ *[act of] distinguishing, deciding*
διάγω† *carry over; pass, spend* (of time); *live, pass one's life*
διάδοχος, –ον *succeeding, relieving*
διαθρύπτω *enervate, pamper*
διάκειμαι (+adv.) *be in certain state/mood*
διακλέπτω† *steal and secrete, appropriate*
διακομίζομαι† *carry across*
διακόπτω *cut through*
διᾱκόσιοι, –αι, –α *200*
†διαλέγομαι *converse with* (+dat.)

διαλλάττομαι *reconcile one's differences*
διαμέλλω† *delay*
διανοέομαι *intend, plan; think, suppose*
διάνοια, –ᾱς, ἡ *intention, plan*
διαπειράομαι *make trial of*
διαπίμπλημι† *fill with* (+gen.)
διαπολεμέω *fight it out* (with someone, dat.)
διαπορεύομαι *march/proceed through* (+acc.)
διαρπάζω *plunder*
διασπάομαι (aor. –εσπασάμην) *tear apart*
διατελέω† *accomplish; continue*
διατίθημι† *dispose; put in a certain state of body or mind*
διατριβή, –ῆς, ἡ *way/manner of spending time*
διατρῑβω *pass/waste* (time)
δίαυλος, –ου, ὁ *double course* (i.e. the race up the stadium and back)
διαφέρω† *differ from* (+gen.); *make a difference; be superior to* (+gen.)
διαφθείρω† *destroy; corrupt*
διαχωρίζω *separate, divide*
διδακτός, –ή, –όν *able to be taught*
διδάσκαλος, –ου, ὁ *teacher*
†διδάσκω *teach, train*
–διδράσκω see ἀποδιδράσκω
δίδωμι *give, offer, grant* (18.1/2)
διελαύνω† *ride through*
διεξέρχομαι† *go through, relate*
διέχω† *be separated/distant from* (+gen.)
διηγέομαι *explain, relate, describe*
δικάζω *be a juror; judge, give judgement*
δίκαιος, –ᾱ, –ον *just, honest, upright*
δικαιοσύνη, –ης, ἡ *justice, honesty*
δικαίως (adv.) *justly*
δικαστήριον, –ου, τό *law-court*
δικαστης, –οῦ, ὁ *juror, dicast, judge*
δίκη, –ης, ἡ *lawsuit;* (legal) *satisfaction; justice; penalty;* (personified, with cap.) *Justice*
δίκην δίδωμι *be punished, pay the penalty*
δίκην λαμβάνω *punish, exact one's due from* (παρά+gen.)

δίκτυον, –ου, τό *net, hunting-net*
Δίκων, –ωνος, ὁ *Dico*
δΐνη, –ης, ἡ *whirlpool*
Διογένης, –ους, ὁ *Diogenes* (philosopher)
διόλλῡμι† *destroy utterly*
Διονῡσόδωρος, –ου, ὁ *Dionysodorus*
Διόνῡσος, –ου, ὁ *Dionysus* (god of wine)
διότι (conj.) *because*
διπλοῦς, –ῆ, –οῦν *double*
δίς (adv.) *twice*
διττός (διςςός), –ή, –όν *two-fold, two*
δίφρος, –ου, ὁ *stool*
δίχα (adv., or prep.+gen.) *apart, apart from*
διψάω *be thirsty* (5.1/2 note 4)
†διώκω *pursue, chase, prosecute*
#δμώς, –ωός, ὁ *slave taken in war* (13.1/1b(i))
δόγμα, –ατος, τό *opinion, belief; decision, judgement*
†δοκέω *seem, seem good; be thought; consider* (self) *to be; think;* δοκεῖ (impers., +dat. and inf.) *it seems a good idea; so* δοκεῖ μοι *I decide* (21.1/4a)
#δόλιος, –ᾱ, –ον *crafty, deceitful*
#δόλος, –ου, ὁ *trick, guile*
#δόμος, –ου, ὁ *house, home*
δόξα, –ης, ἡ *reputation, fame; opinion*
δόξαν (acc. abs.) *it having been decided* (21.1/5)
δόρυ, –ατος, τό *spear*
δοτέον *one must give* (24.1/5)
δότης, –ου, ὁ *giver*
δουλείᾱ, –ᾱς, ἡ *slavery*
δουλεύω *be a slave*
#δούλιος, –ᾱ, –ον *of slavery*
δοῦλος, –ου, ὁ *slave*
δουλόω *enslave*
δούς, δοῦσα, δόν, aor. pple. of δίδωμι
δράκων, –οντος, ὁ *dragon, serpent*
δρᾶμα, –ατος, τό *play, drama*
δραμεῖν aor. inf. of τρέχω
δραστήριος, –ον *active*
δραχμή, –ῆς, ἡ *drachma* (coin)
δράω *do, act*
δρόμος, –ου, ὁ *race;* δρόμῳ *at a run, at full speed*

δρόσος, –ου, ἡ *dew*
†δύναμαι *be able* (19.1/3b); *be powerful* μέγα δύναμαι *be very powerful*
δύναμις, –εως, ἡ *power, ability, force, strength*
δυνατός, –ή, –όν *able, possible; strong, powerful* οἱ δυνατοί *the chief men*
δύο *two* (7.1/5a)
#δύρομαι (= ὀδύρομαι) *lament*
δύςγνοια, –ᾱς, ἡ *ignorance, bewilderment*
#δυςδάκρῡτος, –ον *sorely wept*
δυςεντερίᾱ, –ᾱς, ἡ *dysentery*
δύςθῡμος, –ον *disheartened, despondent*
δύςκολος, –ον *bad-tempered*
#δύςλυτος, –ον *indissoluble, inextricable*
δυςμενής, –ές *hostile*
δυςπετῶς (adv.) *with difficulty*
δυςςεβής, –ές *impious, ungodly, profane*
#δύςτηνος, –ον *wretched*
δυςτυχέω *be unlucky/unfortunate*
δυςτυχής, –ές *unlucky, unfortunate*
δυςτυχίᾱ, –ᾱς, ἡ *misfortune*
δύςφορος, –ον *hard to bear*
δυςχείμερος, –ον *wintry, stormy*
#δυςώνυμος, –ον *having an ill name, hateful*
δύω (A) *enter, get into*
δύω (B) = δύο *two*
δώδεκα (indecl. adj.) *twelve*
#δωδεκέτης, –ου *twelve years old*
#δῶμα, –ατος, τό *house; family*
δωρέομαι *present, give*
Δωριεύς, –έως, ὁ *Dorieus* (half-brother of Spartan king Cleomenes)
δωροδοκίᾱ, –ᾱς, ἡ *bribery*
δῶρον, –ου, τό *gift, bribe*

ἑ (indir. refl. pron.) *him, her, it* (9.1/4a)
ἑάλων aor. of ἁλίσκομαι
ἐάν (conj., +subj.) *if, if ever* (14.1/4c(iii))
ἔαρ, ἦρος, τό (the season of) *spring*
ἑαυτόν, –ήν, –ό (refl. pron.) *himself, herself, itself* (9.1/4a)

†ἐάω allow, permit; let alone, let be
ἔβην aor. of βαίνω
ἑβραϊστί (adv.) in Hebrew
ἐγγελάω† laugh at (+dat.)
ἐγγίγνομαι† be born in, appear
    among
ἐγγράφω† write in/on, inscribe;
    enrol, enlist
ἐγγύη, -ης, ἡ pledge, surety
ἔγγυθεν (adv.) from nearby
ἐγγύς (adv., or prep.+gen.) near,
    nearby
†ἐγείρω arouse, awaken (perf.
    ἐγρήγορα = I am awake)
ἐγενόμην aor. of γίγνομαι
ἐγκέφαλος, -ου, ὁ brain
ἔγκλημα, -ατος, τό accusation,
    complaint
    ἔγκλημα ποιέομαι make a
    complaint
#ἐγκονέω be quick, hasten
ἐγκωμιάζω praise
ἐγκώμιον, -ου, τό encomium,
    eulogy; victory-song
ἔγνων aor. of γιγνώσκω
ἐγρήγορα perf. of ἐγείρω
ἐγχειρέω attempt, try; attack
    (+dat.)
ἔγχος, -ους, τό weapon, spear
ἐγώ (pron.) I (4.1/2)
ἔγωγε I at least; I for my part
ἐγῷμαι = ἐγὼ οἶμαι
#ἐγων = ἐγώ
ἔδαφος, -ους, τό bottom
ἐδόθην aor. pass. of δίδωμι
ἔδομαι fut. of ἐσθίω
#ἔδω eat
ἐδωδή, -ῆς, ἡ food
ἔδωκα aor. of δίδωμι
ἕζομαι seat oneself, sit
†ἐθέλω am willing, wish
ἔθηκα aor. of τίθημι
ἔθνος, -ους, τό nation, tribe, race
ἔθρεψα aor. of τρέφω
εἰ (conj.) if
    εἰ γάρ or εἴθε would that, I wish
      that (to introduce wishes, 21.1/1)
    εἰ δὲ μή but if not, otherwise
εἶ 2nd s. of εἰμί be or εἶμι shall
    come/go
εἴᾱσα aor. of ἐάω

#εἶδαρ, -ατος, τό food
εἰδείην opt. of οἶδα
εἰδέναι inf. of οἶδα
#εἴδομαι be seen, appear
εἶδον aor. of ὁράω
εἶδος, -ους, τό form, shape,
    appearance; beauty
εἰδώς, εἰδυῖα, εἰδός knowing (pple.
    of οἶδα)
εἶεν (particle) well, well then
εἴθε see εἰ
εἴκοσι(ν) (indecl. adj.) twenty
εἴκω give way, yield
    (+dat.,13.1/2b(ii))
εἰκώς, -υῖα, -ός like, resembling
    (+dat.,19.1/3a)
εἴληφα perf. of λαμβάνω
εἱλόμην aor. of αἱρέομαι
εἷλον aor. of αἱρέω
εἰμί be (3.1/6 and **Appendix 3**)
εἶμι shall come/go (inf. ἰέναι; impf.
    ᾖα, 18.1/3 and **Appendix 3**)
#εἰν = ἐν
εἶναι to be (inf. of εἰμί)
εἰπ– aor. act./mid. stem of λέγω or of
    ἀγορεύω in compounds
εἴπερ (strengthened form of εἰ) if
    indeed
εἶπον aor. of λέγω and of ἀγορεύω in
    compounds (18.1/4 note 2)
†εἴργω shut up, imprison; prevent,
    hinder, exclude
εἴρηκα perf. act. of λέγω
εἴρημαι perf. mid./pass. of λέγω
εἰρήνη, -ης, ἡ peace
    εἰρήνην ἄγω live in/be at peace
    εἰρήνην ποιέομαι make peace
εἰς (prep.+acc.) to, into, on to; with
    regard to, in relation to
    εἰς τοσοῦτο/τοῦτο (+gen., 23.1/1d)
    to such a pitch/point/degree of
εἷς, μίᾱ, ἕν one (7.1/5a)
#εἷς 2nd s. of εἰμί or εἶμι
εἰσάγω† introduce
#εἰσαθρέω look/gaze at
εἰσακούω† give ear, pay attention
εἰσβαίνω† go into, go on board
εἰσβάλλω† throw into; invade
εἰσβολή, -ῆς, ἡ invasion
εἰσέρχομαι† enter, go inside
εἴσοδος, -ου, ἡ entrance; visit

εἴcομαι fut. of οἶδα

εἰcοράω† *behold, look at*

εἰcπλέω† *sail in*

εἰcφέρω† *bring/carry into*

εἶτα (adv.) *then, next*

εἴτε ... εἴτε *whether ... or*

εἶχον impf. of ἔχω

εἴωθα *I am accustomed*

εἰωθώc, -υῖα, -όc *customary, usual*

ἐκ (prep.+gen.; before vowel ἐξ) *out of, from*

Ἑκάβη, -ηc, ἡ *Hecuba* (wife of Priam)

ἕκαcτοc, -η, -ον *each, every*
  ὡc ἕκαcτοc *each individually* (22.1/1*a*(v))

ἑκάcτοτε (adv.) *on each occasion*

ἑκάτεροc, -ᾱ -ον *each (of two)*
  ὡc ἑκάτεροc *each (of two) individually* (22.1/1*a*(v))

#ἕκατι (prep.+gen.) *on account of,for the sake of* (usually comes after word it governs)

#ἑκατομπτολίεθροc, -ον *with a hundred cities*

ἑκατόν (indecl. adj.) *100*

ἐκβαίνω† *step out, go forth; disembark*

ἐκβάλλω† *throw out, expel* (into exile)

#ἐκδίκωc (adv.) *unjustly*

ἐκεῖ (adv.) *there*

ἐκεῖθεν (adv.) *from there*

ἐκεῖνοc, -η, -ο (pron. and adj. 9.1/1) *that*

ἐκεῖcε (adv.) *(to) there*

ἐκκαίω† *kindle*

ἐκκαλέω† *call* (someone) *out*

ἐκκληcίᾱ, -ᾱc, ἡ *assembly*

ἐκκόπτω *knock out*

ἐκκρούω *knock out*

ἐκλέγω *pick out* (18.1/4 note 1)

ἐκμανθάνω† *learn thoroughly*

ἑκουcίωc (adv.) *willingly*

ἐκπέμπω† *send out*

#ἐκπέρθω *destroy utterly*

ἐκπῑπτω† *fall out; be thrown out; be banished, be sent into exile* (17.1/5)

ἐκπλέω† *sail out/off*

ἔκπληξιc, -εωc, ἡ *panic, consternation*

ἐκπλήττω *strike with panic, frighten; amaze*

ἐκπρᾱττω† *bring to pass, accomplish*

ἐκτόc (adv., and prep.+gen.) *outside*

ἐκτροφή, -ῆc, ἡ *bringing up, rearing*

Ἕκτωρ, -οροc, ὁ *Hector* (Trojan hero in *Iliad*)

ἐκφαίνομαι† *appear, shine out/forth*

ἐκφέρω† *carry out*

ἐκφεύγω† *escape*

ἑκών, -οῦcα, -όν *willing(ly), wittingly*

ἐλ- aor. act./mid. stem of αἱρέω

ἐλάᾱ, -ᾱc, ἡ *olive-tree*

ἔλαβον aor. of λαμβάνω

ἔλαθον aor. of λανθάνω

Ἐλάτεια, -ᾱc, ἡ *Elatea* (town in Phocis)

ἐλάττων, -ον *smaller; fewer; less*

†ἐλαύνω *drive* (tr. and intr.); *drive out; march*

ἔλαφοc, -ου, ὁ/ἡ *deer*

ἐλάχιcτοc, -η, -ον *smallest, least; fewest*

ἔλαχον aor. of λαγχάνω

ἐλέγχω *test, examine*

ἑλεῖν aor. inf. act. of αἱρέω

ἕλειοc, -ον *living in the marshes*

Ἑλένη, -ηc, ἡ *Helen*

ἐλευθερίᾱ, -ᾱc, ἡ *freedom*

ἐλεύθεροc, -ᾱ, -ον *free*

ἐλευθερόω *set free*

Ἐλεφαντίνη, -ηc, ἡ *Elephantine* (city in Egypt)

ἐλεφᾱc, -αντοc, ὁ *elephant*

ἐλήλυθα perf. of ἔρχομαι

ἐλήφθην aor. pass. of λαμβάνω

ἐλθ- aor. stem of ἔρχομαι

ἔλιπον aor. of λείπω

ἑλίccω *turn*

#ἑλκεcίπεπλοc, -ον *with trailing robes*

#ἑλκηθμόc, -οῦ, ὁ *[act of] being carried off, seizure*

†ἕλκω *pull, drag*

Ἑλλάc, -άδοc, ἡ *Greece*

ἐλλείπω† *be lacking in, fall short of* (+gen.)

Ἕλλην, -ηνοc, ὁ *a Greek*

Ἑλληνικόc, -ή, -όν *Greek*

Ἑλλήcποντοc, -ου, ὁ *the Hellespont*

ἕλος, -ουc, τό *marsh*
ἐλπίζω *hope, expect*
ἐλπίς, -ίδος, ἡ *hope*
ἔμαθον aor. of μανθάνω
ἐμαυτόν, -ήν (refl. pron.) *myself*
  (9.1/4*a*)
ἐμβαίνω† *step on/into, embark,*
  board
ἐμβάλλω† *throw in, put in*
ἔμολον aor. of βλώcκω
ἐμός, -ή, -όν (poss. adj.) *my, mine*
ἔμπειρος, -ον *experienced, skilled*
ἐμπίμπλημι† *fill*
ἐμπίμπρημι *burn, set on fire*
ἐμπίπτω† *fall into/on/upon*
ἔμπνους, -ουν *alive*
ἐμποδών (adv.) *in the way* (+dat.)
ἔμπροcθεν (adv.) *in front, ahead*
ἐμπρόcθιος, -ον *in front, fore*
ἐμφανής, -έc *open, obvious*
ἔμφυτος, -ον *inborn, innate*
ἐν (prep.+dat.) *in, on, among*
  ἐν τούτῳ *meanwhile*
ἐναγκαλίζομαι *take in one's arms,*
  clasp
ἐναντίον (+gen.) *opposite, facing;*
  (as adv.) *face to a face*
ἐναντιόομαι *oppose, withstand*
  (+dat.)
ἐναντίος, -ᾱ, -ον *opposite, facing,*
  opposed to
ἐνδεεcτέρωc (compar. adv.) *in a*
  more/rather deficient/inadequate
  way
ἔνδεια, -ᾱc, ἡ *lack*
ἐνδίδωμι† *give in, surrender*
ἔνδικος, -ον *just, legitimate*
ἔνδοθεν (adv.) *from inside*
ἔνδον (adv.) *inside*
#ἔνδυτα, -ων, τά *clothes*
ἐνεγκ- aor. act./mid. stem of φέρω
ἐνεδρεύω *lie in ambush*
ἔνειμι *be in* (+dat.)
  ἔνεcτι (impers.) *it is possible*
  (+dat.)
ἕνεκα (prep.+gen.) *because of, for*
  the sake of (usually follows its
  noun)
ἐνέργεια, -ᾱc, ἡ *activity, operation*
ἔνθα (adv.) *thereupon*
ἐνθάδε (adv.) *here*

ἔνθεν (adv.) *from there; thereafter;*
  ἔνθεν μέν . . . ἔνθεν δέ *on one side*
  . . . on the other
#ἐνί = ἐν
ἐννέα (indecl. adj.) *nine*
#ἐννέπω (and ἐνέπω) *tell, tell of*
#ἐννῆμαρ (adv.) *for nine days*
ἐννοέω *consider, understand;*
  discover
ἐνοικέω *dwell in, inhabit*
ἐνταῦθα (adv.) *here, there, at this*
  point
ἐντεῦθεν (adv.) *from then; from*
  here/there, thereupon
ἐντολή, -ῆc, ἡ *order, command*
ἐντόc (prep.+gen.) *within, inside*
#ἔντος, -ουc, τό *weapon*
ἐντυγχάνω† *fall in with, meet with,*
  come upon (+dat.,13.1/2*b*(iii))
ἐξ = ἐκ
ἕξ (indecl. adj.) *six*
ἐξαγορεύω (fut. ἐξερῶ, 18.1/4 note 2)
  make known, speak of; speak out,
  utter aloud
ἐξάγω† *lead, bring out*
ἐξαιρέω† *take out, remove*
ἐξαΐccω *rush forth*
ἐξαίφνης (adv.) *suddenly*
ἐξακόcιοι, -αι, -α *600*
ἐξάλλομαι (aor. ἐξηλάμην) *jump out*
ἐξαμαρτάνω† *make a mistake; do*
  wrong against (εἰc+acc.)
ἐξανίcτημι† (mid. and intr. tenses of
  act.) *stand up from, get up from* (a
  table)
ἐξαπατάω *deceive, trick*
ἐξαπίνης (adv.) *suddenly*
ἐξαρκέω *be quite enough, suffice*
#ἐξαῦτιc (adv.) *once more, anew*
ἐξείργω† *shut out from, drive out*
ἐξελαύνω† *drive out, expel, exile;*
  (intr.) *march out*
ἐξέρχομαι† *go out, come out*
#ἐξερῶ fut. of ἐξαγορεύω
ἔξεcτι (impers.) *it is*
  allowed/possible (+dat. and inf.,
  21.1/4*a*)
ἐξετάζω *examine*
ἐξευρίcκω† *find out, discover*
ἑξήκοντα (indecl. adj.) *60*
ἑξηκοcτόc, -ή, -όν *sixtieth*

ἐξηλάμην aor. of ἐξάλλομαι
ἑξῆc (adv.)   in order, in a row
ἐξικνέομαι (principal parts as for
    ἀφικνέομαι)   suffice
ἐξόν (acc. absol.)   it being
    permitted/possible (21.1/5)
ἐξοπλίζομαι   arm oneself completely
ἔξω (+gen.)   outside
ἔξω fut. of ἔχω
ἐξωθέω   push out
ἔοικα   resemble, seem
    (+dat.,13.1/2b(iv)) (19.1/3a)
    ἔοικε (impers.)   it seems
ἑορτή, -ῆc, ἡ   feast, festival
ἐπαγγέλλομαι†   profess, make
    profession of
ἔπαθον aor. of πάcχω
ἐπαινέτης, -ου, ὁ   admirer
ἐπαινέω†   praise, commend
ἔπαινος, -ου, ὁ   praise
ἐπανέρχομαι†   return
ἐπανορθόω   remedy (a situation)
ἐπάνω (prep.+gen.)   upon
ἐπαχθής, -έc   burdensome
ἐπεγείρω†   awaken, rouse up
ἐπεί (conj.)   since, when
ἐπείγομαι   hurry, hasten; be eager
ἐπειδάν (conj.+subj.)   when (ever)
ἐπειδή (conj.)   when, since, because
    ἐπειδὴ τάχιστα   as soon as
ἔπειμι†   be upon
ἔπειτα (adv.)   then, next
ἐπεξάγω†   lead out against
ἐπέρχομαι†   go against, attack
    (+dat.); come on, approach
ἐπερωτάω†   ask (a question)
ἐπέχω†   hold back, check
ἐπί (prep.) (+acc.)   on to, to, against;
    (+gen.) on; in the direction of; in
    the time of; (+dat.) at, on, upon;
    with a view to; in the power of
ἐπιβαίνω†   step on to (+gen. or dat.)
ἐπιβάλλω†   throw upon, impose
    upon
ἐπιβάτης, -ου, ὁ   passenger
ἐπιβιβάζω   put on board
ἐπιβουλεύω   plot against
ἐπιβουλή, -ῆc, ἡ   plot
ἐπιγίγνομαι†   come after
Ἐπίδαμνος, -ου, ἡ   Epidamnus (town
    on the east coast of Adriatic)

Ἐπίδαυρος, -ου, ἡ   Epidaurus (town
    in southern Greece)
ἐπιδείκνῡμι†   prove, show,
    demonstrate; exhibit, display
ἐπιδημέω   come to stay in a place,
    visit
ἐπιδίδωμι†   give in addition
ἐπιεικής, -έc   reasonable, moderate,
    fair
ἐπιεικῶc (adv.)   fairly, quite
ἐπιθόμην aor. of πείθομαι
ἐπιθῡμέω   desire, yearn for
    (+gen.,13.1/2a(ii))
ἐπιθῡμίᾱ, -ᾱc, ἡ   desire, passion
ἐπικαλέομαι†   call upon, summon
ἐπίκειμαι   lie upon, be upon
ἐπικουρέω   help, remedy (+dat.)
ἐπίκουρος, -ου, ὁ   helper, ally; (pl.)
    mercenaries
ἐπιλανθάνομαι†   forget (+acc. or
    gen.,13.1/2a(iii))
ἐπιμέλεια, -ᾱc, ἡ   concern, care
†ἐπιμελέομαι   care for
    (+gen.,13.1/2a(ii)), take care
ἐπιμελητέον   one must take care of
    (+gen.) (24.1/5)
ἐπιορκίᾱ, -ᾱc, ἡ   perjury
ἐπιπῑπτω†   fall upon, attack (+dat.)
ἐπίπνοια, -ᾱc, ἡ   inspiration
Ἐπιπολαί, -ῶν, αἱ   Epipolae (plateau
    above Syracuse)
ἐπιπονέω   labour on
ἐπισκοπέω   inspect, examine, observe
†ἐπίσταμαι   know how to; understand
    (19.1/3b)
ἐπιστέλλω†   send to
ἐπιστήμη, -ης, ἡ   understanding,
    knowledge
ἐπιστολή, -ῆc, ἡ   order, command;
    (pl.) letter, epistle
ἐπιστρέφω†   turn about
ἐπιτήδεια, -ων, τά   necessities of life,
    provisions
ἐπιτήδειος, -ᾱ, -ον   suitable, useful
    for; friendly
ἐπιτίθημι†   put/place upon (+dat.);
    (mid.) attack (+dat.)
ἐπιτῑμάω   censure (+dat.)
ἐπιτρέπω†   entrust; allow (+dat.)
ἐπιτρέχω†   overrun
ἐπιφέρομαι†   move (intr.)

ἐπίφθονος, -ον burdensome
ἐπιφράττω block up
ἐπιχαίρω† rejoice at (+dat.)
ἐπιχειρέω attempt, take in hand
  (+dat.,13.1/2b(iii))
ἐπιχώριος, -ον (also -ᾱ, -ον) of the
  country, local
#ἔπλετο 3rd s. aor. of πέλομαι
ἕπομαι follow (+dat., 13.1/2b(iii))
#ἔπορον (aor., no pres. exists) give,
  furnish
ἔπος, -ουc, τό word
  ὡς ἔπος εἰπεῖν so to speak
  (22.1/1a(vi))
ἐπριάμην aor. of ὠνέομαι
ἑπτά (indecl. adj.) seven
ἐραστής, -οῦ, ὁ lover
ἐράω love, desire passionately
  (+gen.,13.1/2a(ii))
†ἐργάζομαι work, perform, do
ἔργον, -ου, τό task, labour, job,
  deed, action; fact, achievement;
  field
  ἔργῳ in fact, indeed
  ἔργα παρέχω give trouble
#ἐρέπτομαι feed on (+acc.)
#ἐρετμόν, οῦ, τό oar
ἐρέω fut. of λέγω
ἐρημίᾱ, -ᾱς, ἡ solitude, desert,
  wilderness
ἔρημος (also ἐρῆμος), -ον empty,
  deserted, desolate, devoid
#ἐρίηρος, -ον (m. pl. nom. ἐρίηρες,
  acc. ἐρίηρας) trusty, faithful
ἔρις, -ιδος, ἡ strife (acc. ἔριν)
ἑρμαῖον, -ου, τό godsend, windfall,
  treasure
ἑρμηνεύς, -έως, ὁ interpreter
Ἑρμῆς, -οῦ, ὁ Hermes
Ἕρμων, -ωνος, ὁ Hermon
ἕρπω creep, crawl; move about,
  spread; go
ἔρρω go to one's harm, go to hell
#ἐρύω drag
†ἔρχομαι come, go (18.1/3 and
  Appendix 3)
ἔρως, -ωτος, ὁ love, desire;
  (personified, with cap.) Love
†ἐρωτάω ask (aor. ἠρόμην)
ἐρωτικός, -ή, -όν amorous, in love
ἐς = εἰς

ἐσθίω eat
#ἐσθλός, -ή, -όν brave
ἑσμός, -οῦ, ὁ swarm
ἔσομαι fut. of εἰμί (be) (3rd s.
  ἔσται)
ἐσοράω see εἰσοράω
ἔσπαρμαι perf. mid./pass. of σπείρω
ἑσπέρᾱ, -ᾱς, ἡ evening
ἕσπερος, -ον of/at evening; (as m.
  noun with cap.) the Evening Star
ἑσπόμην aor. of ἕπομαι
ἔσται 3rd s. fut. of εἰμί (be)
ἑστηκώς, -υῖα, -ός standing (perf.
  pple. of ἵσταμαι) (or ἑστώς, -ῶσα,
  -ός) (19.1/1)
ἔστι it is possible (21.1/4 note1);
  there is
ἔσχατος, -η, -ον furthest, last; worst
  (18.1/6)
ἔσχον aor. of ἔχω
ἑταίρᾱ, -ᾱς, ἡ female companion;
  prostitute, courtesan
ἑταῖρος (epic also ἕταρος), -ου, ὁ
  companion, comrade
Ἐτεόνῑκος, -ου, ὁ Eteonicus
  (Spartan commander)
ἕτερος, -ᾱ -ον (pron. and adj.) one
  or the other of two
ἑτέρως (adv.) in the other way
  ὡς ἑτέρως quite otherwise
ἔτι (adv.) still, yet; further
  ἔτι καὶ νῦν even now
ἑτοιμάζω get ready, prepare
ἕτοιμος, -η, -ον ready, ready to
  hand, prepared; fixed, certain
ἔτος, -ουc, τό year
ἐτραπόμην aor. of τρέπομαι
ἔτυχον aor. of τυγχάνω
εὖ (adv.) well
  εὖ λέγω speak well of (+acc.,
  22.1/2f(ii))
  εὖ ποιέω treat well, do good to
  (+acc., 22.1/2f(ii))
  εὖ πράττω fare well, be prosperous
εὐγενής, -ές noble, well-born;
  generous
εὔγνωστος, -ον well-known
εὐδαιμονέω prosper, thrive; be
  happy
εὐδαιμονίᾱ, -ᾱς, ἡ prosperity,
  happiness

εὐδαίμων, –ον *blessed with good fortune; happy; rich*
Εὐδᾱμίδᾱς, –ου, ὁ *Eudamidas*
εὐδόκιμος, –ον *famous, glorious*
εὕδω *sleep*
εὔελπις, –ι *hopeful* (stem εὐελπιδ–)
εὐεργεσίᾱ, –ᾱς, ἡ *kindness, service*
εὐεργετέω *do good to, benefit*
εὐεργέτης, –ου, ὁ *benefactor*
εὐεργετητέον *one must benefit* (24.1/5)
εὐήλιος, –ον *sunny, with a sunny aspect*
#εὔθρονος (epic ἐΰ–), –ον *fair-throned*
εὐθύ (+gen.) *straight towards*
Εὐθύδημος, –ου, ὁ *Euthydemus*
εὐθύς (adv.) *at once, straightaway*
εὔκλεια, –ᾱς, ἡ *fame, glory*
Εὐκλείδης, –ου, ὁ *Eucleides*
εὐλαβέομαι *be cautious, beware, take care*
εὔλογος, –ον *reasonable, sensible*
εὐμενής, –ές *well-disposed, kindly, favourable*
#εὐμμελίης (epic ἐΰ–), –ου *armed with a good ash spear*
εὐμορφίᾱ, –ᾱς, ἡ *beauty of form or body*
εὐνή, –ῆς, ἡ *bed; marriage; sex*
εὔνοια, –ᾱς ἡ *good will*
εὔνους, –ουν *well-disposed*
#εὐπλοέω *have a fine voyage*
εὐπορίᾱ, –ᾱς, ἡ *abundance, means*
εὐπρᾱξίᾱ, –ᾱς, ἡ *prosperity*
εὑρ– aor. act./mid. stem of εὑρίσκω
εὕρηκα perf. of εὑρίσκω
Εὐρῑπίδης, –ου, ὁ *Euripides* (tragic poet)
†εὑρίσκω *find; get; invent*
εὖρος, –ους, τό *breadth*
εὐρύς, –εῖα, –ύ *broad, wide*
Εὐρυσθεύς, –έως, ὁ *Eurystheus* (King of Mycenae)
Εὐρώπη, –ης, ἡ *Europa* (character in mythology)
εὔσκιος, –ον *well-shaded*
εὔστοχος, –ον *aiming well*
εὐτάκτως (adv.) *in good order*
εὐτροφίᾱ, –ᾱς, ἡ *proper nurture*
εὐτυχέω *be fortunate/lucky*

εὐτυχής, –ές *fortunate, lucky*
εὐτυχίᾱ, –ᾱς, ἡ *good fortune*
Εὔτυχος, –ου, ὁ *Eutychus*
εὐτυχῶς (adv.) *with good fortune*
εὐφημέω *shout in triumph*
Εὐφορίων, –ωνος, ὁ *Euphorion* (father of Aeschylus)
εὔχαρις, –ι *charming* (stem εὐχαριτ–)
εὐχή, –ῆς, ἡ *prayer*
εὔχομαι *pray*
εὐώνυμος, –ον *of good name or omen; euphemistically for left, on the left hand* (the side of a bad omen)
#εὐωριάζω *disregard, neglect*
εὐωχέομαι *have a feast/party*
ἐφ' = ἐπί
  ἐφ' ᾧτε *on condition that* (+inf. or fut. ind., 16.1/1 note 4)
ἐφάνην aor. of φαίνομαι
ἐφήμερος, –ον *living but a day; mortal*
ἔφην impf. of φημί (7.1/2)
ἐφῑημι† *send; set on, send against; allow;* (mid.) *aim at, long for, desire* (+gen.)
ἐφίστημι† *set over, appoint*
ἐφοράω† *oversee, observe, watch*
ἔφυγον aor. of φεύγω
ἔφῡν *be naturally, was naturally* (see φύω)
#ἐχθαίρω *hate*
ἐχθές (adv.) *yesterday*
ἔχθιστος supl. of ἐχθρός
ἔχθος, –ους, τό *hatred*
ἔχθρᾱ, –ᾱς, ἡ *enmity, hostility*
ἐχθρός, –ά –ον *hostile* (supl. ἔχθιστος)
ἐχθρός, –οῦ, ὁ *(personal) enemy*
ἐχῖνος, –ου, ὁ *hedgehog*
ἐχρῆν impf. of χρή
ἐχυρός, –ά, –όν *strong, secure*
†ἔχω *have, hold, check;* (intr.) *land, put in;* (+adv.) *be in a certain condition;* (+inf.) *be able*
ἑῷος, –ᾱ, –ον *of the morning*
ἑώρᾱκα perf. of ὁράω
ἑώρων impf. of ὁράω
ἕως (conj.) (+ἄν-subj.) *until;* (+opt.) *until;* (+ind.) *while, until* (21.1/2)

ἕως, ἕω (acc. ἕω), ἡ   dawn (13.1/1*a*)

Ζαγρεύς, -έως, ὁ   *Zagreus* (another name of Dionysus)
#ζάθεος, -ᾱ, -ον   *very holy, sacred*
ζάλη, -ης, ἡ   *squall, storm*
†ζάω   *be alive, live, pass one's life*
ζεύγνῡμι   *yoke, bind, join*
Ζεύς, Διός, ὁ   *Zeus* (poetical also Ζῆνα, Ζηνός, Ζηνί)
ζέω   *boil*
ζηλόω   *admire, envy, emulate*
ζημίᾱ, -ᾱς, ἡ   *fine, penalty, loss*
ζημιόω   *fine, punish*
Ζηνόθεμις, -ιδος, ὁ   *Zenothemis*
ζητέω   *look for, seek* (+acc.)
ζήτησις, -εως, ἡ   *search, inquiry, investigation*
ζυγόν, -οῦ, τό   *yoke; bench* (of ship)
ζωγράφος, -ου, ὁ   *painter*
ζωγρέω   *take prisoners* (alive)
ζώνη, -ῆς, ἡ   *belt, girdle*
ζῷον, -ου, τό   *animal, creature*
ζωός, -ή, -όν   *alive, living*
ζώω = ζάω   *live, pass one's life*

ἤ   *or; than*
ἦ   (particle)   *indeed, really*
ἦ   1st s. impf. of εἰμί (*be*)
ἦ δ᾽ ὅς   *said he* (see note on 13.3(i) *l.* 7)
ᾗ   (adv.)   *where*
ᾖα   impf. of ἔρχομαι/εἶμι
ἡβάω   *be a young man*
ἥβη, -ης, ἡ   *youth*
ἤγαγον   aor. of ἄγω
ἡγεμών, -όνος, ὁ   *leader, guide*
ἡγέομαι   *lead* (+dat.); *think, consider*
Ἡγέστρατος, -ου, ὁ   *Hegestratus*
#ἠδέ   (conj.)   *and*
ᾔδει   3rd s. past of οἶδα (19.1/3 and **Appendix 3**)
ᾔδεσαν   3rd pl. past of οἶδα (19.1/3 and **Appendix 3**)
ἡδέως   (adv.)   *with pleasure, gladly, sweetly, pleasantly*
ἤδη   (adv.)   *(by) now, already, from now on*
ᾔδη   1st s. past of οἶδα (19.1/3 and **Appendix 3**)
†ἥδομαι   *enjoy, be pleased with* (+dat.)
ἡδονή, -ῆς, ἡ   *pleasure*

ἡδύς, -εῖα, -ύ   *sweet, pleasant, enjoyable* (supl. ἥδιστος) (10.1/3*a*)
ἠέ (= ἤ)   *or*
#ἠέλιος = ἥλιος
ἦθος, -ους, τό   *custom, usage, character;* (in pl.) *manners, customs*
ἥκιστα (adv.)   *least of all, no, not at all*
ἠκονημένος, -η, -ον   perf. mid./pass. pple. of ἀκονάω
ἥκω   *have come* (fut. ἥξω *will come*)
ἦλθον   aor. of ἔρχομαι/εἶμι
ἡλικίᾱ, -ᾱς, ἡ   *time of life, age*
Ἡλιοδώρᾱ, -ᾱς, ἡ   *Heliodora*
ἥλιος, -ου, ὁ   *sun;* (personified, with cap.) *Sun-god*
ἧμαι   *be seated, sit*
#ἦμαρ, -ατος, τό   *day*
ἡμεῖς (pron.)   *we* (4.1/2)
ἡμέρᾱ, -ᾱς, ἡ   *day*
   ἅμα (τῇ) ἡμέρᾳ   *at dawn*
   καθ᾽ ἡμέρᾱν   *daily, by day*
ἡμέτερος, -ᾱ, -ον (poss. adj.)   *our*
#ἡμίθραυστος, -ον   *half-broken, broken in half*
ἥμισυς, -εια, -υ   *half*
#ἦμος (conj.)   *when*
ἤν = ἐάν
ἦν   3rd s. impf. of εἰμί   *be*
ἦν δ᾽ ἐγώ   *said I* (see note on 13.3(i) *l.* 6)
ἤνεγκον   aor. of φέρω
ἧπαρ, -ατος, τό   *liver*
ἤπειρος, -ου, ἡ   *mainland; continent*
ἠπιστάμην   impf. of ἐπίσταμαι
Ἥρᾱ, -ᾱς, ἡ   *Hera* (consort of Zeus)
Ἡράκλεια, -ᾱς, ἡ   *Heraclea* (town on Black Sea)
Ἡράκλειτος, -ου, ὁ   *Heraclitus*
Ἡρακλῆς, -κλέους, ὁ   *Heracles* (=*Hercules*)
ἠρέμα (adv.)   *gently, softly*
Ἡρόδοτος, -ου, ὁ   *Herodotus* (historian)
ἠρόμην   aor. of ἐρωτάω
Ἡρώδης, -ου, ὁ   *Herodes*
ἥρως, -ωος, ὁ   *hero* (13.1/1*b*(i))
ἦσαν   3rd pl. impf. of εἰμί   *be*
ἦσθα   2nd s. impf. of εἰμί   *be*
ᾔσθην   aor. of ἥδομαι
ᾐσθόμην   aor. of αἰσθάνομαι

Ἡσίοδος, -ου, ὁ   Hesiod (early
  Greek poet)
ἡcυχάζω be quiet, keep quiet
ἡcυχῇ   quietly, gently
ἡcυχιᾱ, -ᾱc, ἡ   peace, quiet
ἥcυχος, -η, -ον   quiet, peaceful
ἥττάομαι   be defeated
ἥττων, ἧττον (compar. adj.)   lesser,
  weaker, inferior (17.1/2 note 3)
ηὗρον aor. of εὑρίcκω
Ἥφαιcτος, -ου, ὁ   Hephaestus (god
  of fire)
ἠχώ, -οῦc, ἡ   echo (13.1/1b(ii))
#ἠώc, ἠοῦc, ἡ   dawn; (personified,
  with cap.) Dawn

θᾱκέω   sit
θᾶκος, -ου, ὁ   seat
θάλαττα, -ης, ἡ (Ionic θάλαcca)   sea
Θαλῆc, -οῦ, ὁ   Thales (philosopher
  from Miletus)
#θάλος, -ουc, τό   shoot, sprout
θαμά (adv.)   often
θάμνος, -ου, ὁ   bush, thicket
θαν- aor. stem of θνῇcκω
θάνατος, -ου, ὁ   death
†θάπτω   bury, honour with funeral rites
θαρράλεος, -ᾱ, -ον   bold
θαρρέω   be of good courage, take
  courage, be confident
θάρcος (Attic θάρρος), -ουc, τό
  boldness
θάτερος, -ᾱ, -ον = ὁ ἕτερος
θάττων, θᾶττον   quicker (compar. of
  ταχύc,17.1/2b)
θαῦμα, -ατος, τό   wonder, marvel;
  astonishment
†θαυμάζω   wonder,marvel at (+gen.);
  be surprised; admire (+acc.)
θαυμάcιος, -ᾱ -ον   wonderful,
  strange; extraordinary
θαυμαcίωc (adv.)   marvellously,
  wonderfully
  θαυμαcίωc ὡc   exceedingly,
  prodigiously (22.1/1a(iii))
θαυμαcτῶc (adv.)   marvellously,
  wonderfully
  θαυμαcτῶc ὡc   marvellously
  (22.1/1a(iii))
θε- aor. act./mid. stem of τίθημι
θέᾱ, -ᾱc, ἡ   sight

θεά, -ᾶc, ἡ   goddess
Θεαίτητος, -ου, ὁ   Theaetetus
θέᾱμα, -ατος, τό   sight, spectacle
θεᾱομαι   watch, gaze at, look at,
  observe
Θεαρίδᾱc, -ου, ὁ   Thearidas
θεᾱτής, -οῦ, ὁ   spectator
θεήλατος, -ον   sent by the gods
θεῖοc, -ᾱ, -ον   divine, of the gods
θέλγητρον, -ου, τό   charm, spell
θέλω   wish, be willing (Ionic for
  ἐθέλω)
θέμενος, -η, -ον aor. pple. of τίθεμαι
θέμις, -ιδος, ἡ   that which is meet
  and right; justice; right
  θέμιc ἐcτί   it is right
Θέμις, -ιδος, ἡ   Themis (mother of
  Prometheus)
Θεμιστοκλῆc, -κλέουc, ὁ
  Themistocles (Athenian statesman)
Θεόκριτος, -ου, ὁ   Theocritus
  (pastoral poet)
θεομαχέω   fight against (a) god
θεός, -οῦ, ὁ/ἡ   god(dess)
  πρὸc θεῶν   in the name of the gods
#θεοcτυγής, -ές   hated by the gods
θεραπεῖᾱ, -ᾱc, ἡ   service, treatment
θεραπευτέον   one must look
  after/worship (24.1/5)
θεραπεύω   look after, tend; look
  after the interests of, protect
#θεράπων, -οντος, ὁ   servant
Θερμοπύλαι, -ῶν, αἱ   Thermopylae
θερμός, -ή, -όν   hot
θέρος, -ουc, τό   summer
θέc   place! put! (2nd s. aor. imp. act.
  of τίθημι)
θέcθαι aor. inf. of τίθεμαι
Θετταλός, -οῦ, ὁ   a Thessalian
θέω   run
Θῆβαι, -ῶν, αἱ   Thebes
Θηβαῖοι, -ων, οἱ   Thebans
Θηβαῖοc, -ᾱ, -ον   of Thebes, Theban
θήκη, -ηc, ἡ   tomb
θηλυκός, -ή, -όν   female, feminine
θῆλυς, -εια, -υ   female
θήρ, θηρός, ὁ   wild beast
θηράω   hunt
θηρεύω   hunt
θηρίον, -ου, τό   wild beast
Θήχης, -ου, ὁ   (Mt.) Theches

†θνῄσκω *die*
θνητός, -ή, -όν *mortal*
θοἰμάτιον crasis for τὸ ἱμάτιον
#θοός, -ή, -όν *quick, swift*
θορυβέω *make a disturbance/din*
θόρυβος, -ου, ὁ *noise, din, clamour, commotion*
Θουκῡδίδης, -ου, ὁ *Thucydides (historian)*
Θρᾴκη, -ης, ἡ *Thrace*
Θρᾷξ, Θρᾳκός, ὁ *Thracian*
θράσος, -ους, τό *boldness*
θρασύς, -εῖα, -ύ *bold, brave*
θρεψ- aor. act./mid. stem of τρέφω
θρηνέω *bewail, lament over*
θρίξ, τριχός, ἡ *hair* (5.1/5 note 1)
θῡμός, -οῦ, ὁ *spirit, heart; anger*
θύρᾱ, -ᾱς, ἡ *door*
θυσίᾱ, -ᾱς, ἡ *sacrifice*
†θύω (A) *sacrifice*
θύω (B) *rage*
θώραξ, -ᾱκος, ὁ *trunk, chest (of body)*
Θώραξ, -ᾱκος, ὁ *Thorax (a Boeotian)*

ἰᾱομαι *heal, cure*
ἰᾱτρός, -οῦ, ὁ *doctor, healer*
ἰδ- aor. act./mid. stem of ὁράω
Ἰδαῖος, -ᾱ, -ον *of Mt. Ida (in Crete), Idaean*
ἰδέᾱ, -ᾱς, ἡ *form, shape, type*
ἰδίᾳ (adv.) *privately*
ἴδιος, -ᾱ, -ον *private, personal, one's own*
ἰδιώτης, -ου, ὁ *private individual; layman*
ἰδού (adv.) *look! here! hey!*
ἰέναι inf. of ἔρχομαι/εἶμι (18.1/3 and **Appendix 3**)
ἱερά, -ῶν, τά *rites, sacrifices*
ἱερεῖα, -ων, τά *offerings*
ἱερεύς, -έως, ὁ *priest*
ἱερόν, -οῦ, τό *temple, sanctuary*
ἱερός, -ά, -όν *sacred, holy*
Ἱερώνυμος, -ου, ὁ *Hieronymus*
†ἵημι *let go, launch, send forth* (20.1/2); (mid., poet.) *be eager, strive*
Ἰησοῦς, -οῦ, ὁ *Jesus*

Ἰθάκη, -ης, ἡ *Ithaca (island home of Odysseus)*
ἴθι 2nd s. imp. of ἔρχομαι/εἶμι (18.1/3 and **Appendix 3**)
ἱκανός, -ή, -όν *sufficient; competent, capable* (+inf.)
ἱκετεύω *beg, supplicate*
ἱκέτης, -ου, ὁ *suppliant*
ἵλεως, -ων *propitious* (13.1/1a)
Ἰλιάς, -άδος, ἡ *Iliad (epic poem by Homer)*
#Ἰλιόθι epic equivalent of gen. of Ἴλιος/Ἴλιον
Ἴλιον, -ου, τό *Ilium, Troy*
Ἴλιος, -ου, ἡ *Ilium, Troy*
ἱμάτιον, -ου, τό *cloak;* (pl.) *clothes*
#ἱμείρω *long for, desire* (+gen.)
ἵνα (conj.) (+subj. or opt.) *in order that, to* (14.1/4c(i)); (+ind.) *where*
Ἴναρως, -ω, ὁ *Inaros (King of Libya)*
Ἰοκάστη, -ης, ἡ *Iocasta (mother and wife of Oedipus)*
Ἰόνιος, -ᾱ, -ον *Ionic, Ionian*
Ἰουδαῖος, -ου, ὁ *Jew*
ἱππεύς, -έως, ὁ *horseman, cavalry; rider*
ἱππεύω *ride*
#ἱππόδαμος, -ον *horse-taming*
Ἱπποθάλης, -ους, ὁ *Hippothales*
Ἱπποκράτης, -ους, ὁ *Hippocrates*
Ἱππόλυτος, -ου, ὁ *Hippolytus*
Ἱππόνῑκος, -ου, ὁ *Hipponicus*
ἱπποπόταμος, -ου, ὁ *hippopotamus*
ἵππος, -ου, ὁ *horse;* ἡ *cavalry*
ἀπὸ (ἀφ') ἵππου *from horseback*
ἴσᾱσι 3rd pl. of οἶδα (**Appendix 3**)
ἴσθι 2nd s. imp. of εἰμί and οἶδα (**Appendix 3**)
ἰσθμος, οῦ, ὁ *isthmus*
ἴσμεν 1st pl. of οἶδα (**Appendix 3**)
ἴσος, -η, -ον *equal to* (+dat.)
†ἵστημι *make to stand;* (mid. and intr. tenses of act.) *stand* (19.1/1)
ἱστορίᾱ, -ᾱς, ἡ *enquiry, investigation*
ἱστός, -οῦ, ὁ *loom; web*
Ἴστρος, -ου, ὁ *Danube*
#ἴσχε (2nd s. imp. of ἴσχω, a form of ἔχω) *stop!*
Ἰσχόμαχος, -ου, ὁ *Ischomachus*
ἰσχῡρός, -ά, -όν *powerful, strong*

ἰϲχῡρῶϲ (ad.)   *very much, exceedingly*
ἴϲωϲ (adv.)   *perhaps*
Ἰταλίᾱ, -ᾱϲ, ἡ   *Italy*
#ἰχθυόειϲ, -εϲϲα, -εν   *full of fish*
ἰχθῦϲ, -ύοϲ, ὁ   *fish*
ἴχνοϲ, -ουϲ, τό   *track, footstep*
ἴω subj. of ἔρχομαι/εἶμι (**Appendix 3**)
Ἰώλκιοϲ, -ᾱ, -ον   *of Iolcus* (city at east of Thessaly)
ἰών, ἰοῦϲα, ἰόν pple. of ἔρχομαι/εἶμι (**Appendix 3**)

κἀγώ crasis for καὶ ἐγώ
Καδμεῖοϲ, -ᾱ, -ον   *Cadmean* (i.e. Theban)
καθαιμάττω   *make bloody, stain with blood*
καθαιρέω†   *take down, destroy*
καθαίρω†   *cleanse, purify*
καθαρόϲ, -ᾱ́, -όν   *free from guilt/defilement, pure*
καθεύδω   *sleep*
κάθημαι   *be seated* (19.1/3*b*)
καθίζω   *sit down* (tr. and intr.); (mid.) *sit down* (intr.)
καθίϲτημι†   *set down; put in a certain state; appoint; establish;* (mid. and intr.tenses of act.) *settle down; come into a certain state; be appointed; be established*
κάθοδοϲ, -ου, ἡ   *way down*
καθοράω†   *see, catch sight of, look down on*
καθύπερθεν (adv.)   *from above*
καί (conj.)   *and;* (adv.) *also; even; actually, in fact*
  καὶ . . . καί   *both . . . and*
  τε* . . . καί   *both . . . and*
  καὶ γάρ   *in fact; yes, certainly*
  καὶ δή   *and really, moreover; as a matter of fact; look!; let us suppose* (13.1/3*c*)
  καὶ δὴ καί   *and especially, and in particular*
  καὶ μήν   *what's more; look!*
καινόϲ, -ή, -όν   *fresh, new, novel*
καίπερ   *although* (+pple. 12.1/2*a*(iii))
καιρόϲ, -οῦ, ὁ   *right time; opportunity; time; crisis*

Καῖϲαρ, -αροϲ, ὁ   *Caesar*
καίτοι (particle)   *and yet, however* (13.1/3*c*(iv))
†καίω   *burn, kindle, set fire to*
κακηγορίᾱ, -ᾱϲ, ἡ   *slander*
κακίᾱ, -ᾱϲ, ἡ   *wickedness*
κακίζω   *abuse*
κακίων, -ον   *worse* (compar. of κακόϲ)
κακοδαίμων, -ον   *unlucky, unfortunate*
κακονοια, -ᾱϲ, ἡ   *malice*
κακόϲ, -ή, -όν   *bad, evil, wicked; cowardly; mean, lowly;* (neuter used as noun) *trouble*
  κακὰ (κακῶϲ) λέγω   *speak ill of* (+acc., 22.1/2*f*(ii))
  κακὰ (κακῶϲ) ποιέω   *treat badly; do harm to* (+acc., 22.1/2*f*(ii))
κακόω   *ruin; wrong, maltreat*
κακῶϲ (adv.)   *badly, wickedly*
  κακῶϲ ἔχω   *be in a bad state/condition*
καλεϲ- aor. act./mid. stem of καλέω
καλέω   *call, summon; name*
Καλλικρατίδᾱϲ, -ου, ὁ   *Callicratidas*
Καλλίμαχοϲ, -ου, ὁ   *Callimachus* (Alexandrian poet)
κάλλιϲτοϲ, -η, -ον   *most beautiful* (supl. of καλόϲ)
καλλῑ́ων, -ον   *more beautiful* (compar. of καλόϲ)
κάλλοϲ, -ουϲ, τό   *beauty*
καλόϲ, -ή, -όν   *beautiful, good, fine; honourable*
Καλυψώ, -οῦϲ, ἡ   *Calypso* (nymph who detained Odysseus on the island Ogygia) (13.1/1*b*(ii))
καλῶϲ (adv.)   *well, rightly*
  καλῶϲ ἔχω   *be in a good state/condition*
κάμηλοϲ, -ου, ὁ/ἡ   *camel*
κάμνω (aor. ἔκαμον)   *toil, labour*
κάμπτω   *bend*
κἄν crasis for καὶ ἄν and καὶ ἐάν
κἄν crasis for καὶ ἐν
καπνόϲ, -οῦ, ὁ   *smoke*
καρδίᾱ, -ᾱϲ, ἡ   *heart*
Καρδοῦχοι, -ων, οἱ   *Kurds*
#κάρη, -ητοϲ, τό   *head*

Κᾱρίᾱ, -ᾱς, ἡ   Caria (region in S.W. Asia Minor)

καρκίνος, -ου, ὁ   crab

καρπός, -οῦ, ὁ   fruits, harvest

καρτερός, -ά, -όν   strong, mighty

#κασίγνητος, -ου, ὁ   brother

κατά (prep.) (+acc.)   in, on, at; in the region of; by, according to; down, throughout, during; in relation to, with respect to
   κατὰ γῆν καὶ κατὰ θάλατταν   by land and by sea
   (+gen.) below, down from; against

καταβαίνω†   go down, come down

καταβιβάζω   make go down, bring down

καταγελάω†   laugh at, mock (+gen.)

καταγιγνώσκω†   condemn (acc.of the charge, gen. of the person, 23.1/1k(i))

καταγορεύω (fut. κατερῶ, 18.1/4 note 2)   denounce

κατάγω†   take/lead down; bring back/restore (from exile)

καταδουλόω   enslave

καταδύω   make to sink, lay to rest

#καταθνῄσκω†   die

κατακαλύπτω   cover over

κατάκειμαι   lie down

κατακόπτω   cut to pieces

κατακρῑνω†   give sentence against (acc. of penalty, gen. of person, 23.1/1k(i))

καταλαμβάνω†   overtake, come across; seize, catch, capture

καταλέγω   pick, choose; recount (18.1/4 note 1)

καταλείπω†   leave behind, bequeath

κατάλυσις, -εως, ἡ   overthrow, destruction

καταλύω   bring to an end, destroy; finish; (intr.) stay, lodge

καταμείγνῡμι†   mix in, combine

Κατάνη, -ης, ἡ   Catana (city in Sicily)

καταντικρύ (prep.+gen.)   right opposite

καταπαύω   put an end to (+acc.)

καταπῑπτω†   fall down

καταπλέω†   sail down/back

κατάπλους, -ου, ὁ   arrival in port

καταράομαι   call down curses on (+dat.)

κατασκευάζω   prepare, arrange

κατάσκοπος, -ου, ὁ   scout, spy; inspector

καταστρέφομαι   subdue, subject to oneself

καταστροφή, -ῆς, ἡ   overthrowing; conclusion

#καταφθίμενος, -η, -ον   dead

καταφρονέω   despise, look down on (+gen.)

καταχέω   pour down, shed

καταψηφίζομαι   vote against (acc. of penalty, gen. of person, 23.1/1k(i))

κατέλιπον aor. of καταλείπω

κατεπείγω   press hard

κατέρχομαι†   go down/back; return from exile

κατεσθίω†   eat up, devour

κατέχω†   hold back, check

κατηγορέω   accuse (acc. of charge, gen. of person, 23.1/1k(i))

κατίσχω   hold back, check

κατόπιν (adv., and prep.+gen.)   after

κάτοπτρον, -ου, τό   mirror

κατοχή, -ῆς, ἡ   possession (by a spirit)

κάτω (adv.)   below, down

καυσ- fut. and aor. act./mid. stem of καίω

#κε(ν) = ἄν

Κέβης, -ητος, ὁ   Cebes

κεῖμαι   lie; be placed (19.1/3b)

κεῖνος, -η, -ο = ἐκεῖνος

κείρω   cut (the hair), shear

κεῖσε = ἐκεῖσε

κέκρικα perf. of κρῑνω

κέκτημαι   own, possess (perf. of κτάομαι 19.1/3a)

#κέλευθος, -ου, ἡ   road, path

κελευστέον   one must order (24.1/5)

†κελεύω   order, urge, tell . . . to, bid

κέλης, -ητος, ὁ   fast-sailing ship, pinnace

#κέλομαι   urge, order, command

#κενεός, -ά, -όν = κενός

κενός, -ή, -όν   empty

κέντρον, -ου, τό   goad

κεράννῡμι   mix

κέρας, -ατος, τό horn; branch (of a river); with gen. κέρως, wing of an army/fleet (13.1/b(iii))

κέρδος, -ους, τό gain; profit

#κεύθω hide, conceal

κεφαλή, -ῆς, ἡ head

κηδεμών, -όνος, ὁ protector

κῆρυξ, -υκος, ὁ herald

Κίλιξ, -ικος, ὁ a Cilician

κινδυνεύω be in danger, run a risk; be likely to (+inf.)

κίνδῡνος, -ου, ὁ danger

κῑνέω move

κῑνημα, -ατος, τό movement

Κινύρης, -ου, ὁ Cinyres

Κίρκη, -ης, ἡ Circe (enchantress in Odyssey on island Aeaea)

κῑων, -ονος, ἡ pillar

Κλαζομένιος, -ᾱ, -ον of/from Clazomenae

†κλαίω weep; weep for, lament; (mid.) bewail to oneself

κλαυσ- aor. act./mid. stem of κλαίω

Κλέανδρος, -ου, ὁ Cleander

Κλεάνωρ, -ορος, ὁ Cleanor

Κλεάρετος, -ου, ὁ Clearetus

Κλέαρχος, -ου, ὁ Clearchus

Κλεινιᾱς, -ου, ὁ Cleinias

κλείω close, shut

κλέος, -ους, τό glory

κλέπτης -ου, ὁ thief

†κλέπτω steal

Κλέων, -ωνος, ὁ Cleon (Athenian politician)

κληθείς, -εῖσα, -έν aor. pass. pple. of καλέω

#κληΐς, -ΐδος, ἡ rowing-bench

κληρουχικός, -ή, -όν belonging to a cleruchy

κλῖμαξ, -ακος, ἡ ladder, stairway

κλοπή, -ῆς, ἡ theft

κλύδων, -ωνος, ὁ wave, surf; turmoil

κλωπεύω steal

Κνίδος, -ου, ἡ Cnidos (city in Asia Minor)

κοιμάομαι sleep, slumber

κοινῇ (adv.) in common

κοινός, -ή, -όν common, shared, public

κοινωνίᾱ, -ᾱς, ἡ association, intercourse

κοινωνός, -οῦ, ὁ partner

#κοιρανέω be lord/master of, rule over (+gen.)

κολάζω punish

κολακείᾱ, -ᾱς, ἡ flattery

κόλπος, -ου, ὁ bosom; gulf

†κομίζω carry, convey, bring; (mid.) acquire, recover

κομπέω boast of

#κονίᾱ, -ᾱς, ἡ dust

#κόνις, -εως, ἡ dust

Κόνων, -ωνος, ὁ Conon (Athenian admiral)

κόπος, -ου, ὁ exertion, fatigue

κόπτω cut; knock on

κόραξ, -ακος, ὁ crow

κόρη, -ης, ἡ maiden, girl

Κορίνθιοι, -ων, οἱ Corinthians

Κορίνθιος, -ᾱ, -ον from Corinth

Κόρινθος, -ου, ἡ Corinth

#κορυθαίολος, -ον with gleaming helmet

κοσμοπολῑτης, -ου, ὁ citizen of the world

κόσμος, -ου, ὁ decoration, ornament; order; universe; world

κοὐ(κ) crasis for καὶ οὐ(κ)

κουρεύς, -έως, ὁ barber

Κουρῆτες, -ων, οἱ Curetes (minor divinities associated with orgiastic rites)

κουφίζω lighten, make light

κοῦφος, -η, -ον light, nimble

κούφως (adv.) lightly

κρᾱνίον, -ου, τό skull

#κρατερός, -ά, -όν hard, strong

κρατέω hold sway/power over, rule, control; defeat (+gen., 13.1/2a(i))

κρᾱτήρ, -ῆρος, ὁ mixing-bowl

κράτιστος, -η, -ον best, strongest (supl. of ἀγαθός, κρείττων)

κράτος -ους, τό strength, power; supremacy; (personified) Might

κατὰ κράτος vigorously

κρατύνω strengthen

κραυγή, -ῆς, ἡ shouting, din

κρέας, -ως, τό meat (13.1/1b(iii))

κρείττων, -ον stronger, greater; better (compar. of ἀγαθός)

κρεμάθρᾱ, -ᾱς, ἡ hanging basket

κρεμάννῡμι *hang* (tr.); (mid.
κρέμαμαι) *hang* (intr.)
κρήνη, -ης, ἡ *spring*
Κρήτη, -ης, ἡ *Crete*
#κρῖ (nom. and acc. s. only), τό
barley
†κρῑνω *judge, decide; select, choose*
κρίcιc, -εως, ἡ *judgement; decision;
dispute; trial*
κριτης, -οῦ, ὁ *judge*
Κροῖcοc, -ου, ὁ *Croesus* (King of
Lydia)
κροκόδῑλοc, -ου, ὁ *crocodile*
Κρονίδης, -ου, ὁ *son of Cronos* (i.e.
Zeus)
κρόταφοι, -ων, οἱ *temples* (of
forehead)
#κρουνόc, -οῦ, ὁ *spring, stream*
κρούω *strike, knock*
#κρυπτάδιοc, -ᾱ, -ον *secret,
clandestine*
κρύπτω *keep secret, hide; bury; cover*
†κτάομαι *acquire, get;* (perf.) *own,
possess* (19.1/3*a*)
†κτείνω *kill*
κτῆμα, -ατος, τό *(a) possession*
Κτηcιπποc, -ου, ὁ *Ctesippus*
κτῆcιc, -εως, ἡ *possession*
κτίζω *found, build*
κτύποc, -ου, ὁ *din, noise*
κυάνεοc, -ᾱ, -ον *dark, black*
Κυαξάρης, -ου, ὁ *Cyaxares* (uncle
of Cyrus)
κυβερνήτης, -ου, ὁ *helmsman,
captain*
κύβοc, -ου, ὁ *(a) die;* (mostly in pl.)
dice
#κῡδαίνω *glorify*
κυκάω *stir*
κῦμα, -ατος, τό *wave*
Κυμαῖοc, -ᾱ, -ον *of or from Cyme*
(city in Asia Minor)
Κύπριc, -ιδοc, ἡ *the Cyprian
(goddess), Cypris* (a name of
Aphrodite, from the island of
Cyprus)
Κῡρήνη, -ης, ἡ *Cyrene* (city in N.
Africa)
κύριοc, -ᾱ, -ον *having
power/authority*
Κῦροc, -ου, ὁ *Cyrus* (1. founder of

the Persian empire; 2. younger son
of Darius II)
κύων, κυνόc, ὁ/ἡ *dog*
κῶλον, -ου, τό *limb*
κωλύω *prevent, stop* (+acc. and inf.,
24.1/7)
κώμη, -ης, ἡ *village*

λαβ– aor. act./mid. stem of λαμβάνω
λαγχάνω *obtain by lot; win as a
portion, get* (+gen.)
λαγώc, -ώ, ὁ *hare* (13.1/1*a*)
λαθ– aor. act./mid. stem of λανθάνω
λάθρᾳ (adv.) *secretly*
#λάθριοc, -ον *secret, secretly*
#λάϊνοc, -η, -ον *of stone*
Λάϊοc, -ου, ὁ *Laius* (father of
Oedipus)
Λάϊc, -ΐδοc, ἡ *Lais*
Λάκαινα, -ης, ἡ *Laconian
(Spartan) woman*
Λακεδαιμόνιοc, -ου, ὁ
Lacedaemonian, Spartan
Λακεδαίμων, -ονοc, ἡ *Lacedaemon,
Sparta*
λακτίζω *kick*
Λάκων, -ωνοc, ὁ *Laconian, Spartan*
Λακωνικόc, -ή, -όν *Laconian,
Spartan*
λαλέω *talk, prattle, chatter*
†λαμβάνω *take, get, capture*
δίκην λαμβάνω *punish, exact
one's due from* (παρά+gen.)
λαμπρόc, -ᾱ, -όν *bright, brilliant,
famous*
λάμπω *shine*
†λανθάνω *escape notice of* (15.1/2*f*);
(mid.) *forget*
#λᾱόc, -οῦ, ὁ *people*
Λαcθένηc, -ουc, ὁ *Lasthenes*
λαχ– aor. act./mid. stem of λαγχάνω
λέγω *speak, say, tell, mean*
οὐδὲν λέγω *speak/talk nonsense*
λείβω *pour; let flow, shed*
†λείπω *leave, abandon*
λείψανον, -ου, τό *remnant*
λέληθα perf. of λανθάνω
λεοντῆ, -ῆc, ἡ *lion-skin*
λεπτόc, -ή, -όν *subtle, fine; delicate,
thin*
λέcχη, -ης, ἡ *conversation*

λευκαίνω (aor. ἐλεύκανα) *make white, whiten*
λευκός, -ή, -όν *white*
#λεύccω *look upon, behold*
λέων, -οντος, ὁ *lion*
Λεωνίδᾱς, -ου, ὁ *Leonidas* (Spartan king)
λεωργός, -όν *villainous*; (as noun) *wrong-doer*
#λεώς, -ώ, ὁ *people* (13.1/1a)
λήθη, -ης, ἡ *forgetfulness*
λήθω = λανθάνω
ληκύθιον, -ου, τό *little oil-flask*
#λῆμα, -ατος, τό *arrogance, audacity*
ληcτρικός, -ή, -όν *belonging to pirates*
ληφθ– aor. pass. stem of λαμβάνω
λήψομαι fut. of λαμβάνω
λῑ́ᾱν (adv.) *very, exceedingly; too much*
Λιβύη, -ης, ἡ *Libya*
Λίβυc, -υος, ὁ *a Libyan*
λιγυρός, -ά, -όν *clear, shrill*
λίθινος, -η, -ον *made of stone* (see also χυτός)
λίθος, -ου, ὁ *stone*
λιμήν, -ένος, ὁ *harbour*
λίμνη, -ης, ἡ *lake* (especially marshy)
λῑμός, -οῦ, ὁ *hunger, famine*
#λίccομαι *beg, beseech*
λογίζομαι *calculate, reckon, consider*
λόγος, -ου, ὁ *speech, tale, word, account; argument; reason, explanation*
λόγχη, -ης, ἡ *spear, javelin*
λοιδορέω *abuse, revile;* (mid., +dat.) *abuse, scold*
λοιπός, -ή, -όν *left, remaining*
λούω *wash (the body)*; (mid.) *wash oneself*
λόφος, -ου, ὁ *hill*
λοχᾱγός, -οῦ, ὁ *company commander, captain*
Λῡδίᾱ, -ᾱc, ἡ *Lydia* (territory in west of Asia Minor)
Λῡδός, -οῦ, ὁ *Lydian*
Λυκαονίᾱ, -ᾱc, ἡ *Lycaonia* (country in Asia Minor)

Λύκειον, -ου, τό *the Lyceum* (park and gymnasium in Athens)
Λύκιος, -ου, ὁ *Lycius*
λύκος, -ου, ὁ *wolf*
Λυκοῦργος, -ου, ὁ *Lycurgus* (traditional Spartan legislator)
λῡπέω *cause distress to, annoy, grieve;* (mid.) *be distressed, grieve*
λῡ́πη, -ης, ἡ *pain, grief*
λύρᾱ, -ᾱc, ἡ *lyre*
Λῡcίμαχος, -ου, ὁ *Lysimachus*
λῡcιτελεῖ (impers.) *it is profitable* (+dat. and inf., 21.1/4a)
#λύccα, ης, ἡ *frenzy, raging madness*
λυτήριον, -ου, τό *remedy, deliverance*
λύχνος, -ου, ὁ *lamp*
λύω *loosen, release; break up;* (mid.) *ransom*
λῷcτος, -η, -ον (supl. adj.) *best*
λωτός, -οῦ, ὁ *lotus*
Λωτοφάγοι, -ων, οἱ *Lotus-Eaters*
λωφάω *lighten, relieve*

μά (particle of asseveration, affirmative or negative) *yes by ..., no by ... !* (+acc., 22.1/2h))
μᾶζα, -ης, ἡ *barley bread*
μαθ– aor. act./mid. stem of μανθάνω
μάθημα, -ατος, τό *lesson*
μαθήcομαι fut. of μανθάνω
μαθητέον *one must learn* (24.1/5)
μαθητής, -οῦ, ὁ *student*
Μαίανδρος, -ου, ὁ *Maeander* (river in Phrygia)
μαίνομαι *rage, be furious, be mad*
μακαρίζω *congratulate*
μακάριος, -ᾱ, -ον *blessed, happy*
Μακεδονίᾱ, -ᾱc, ἡ *Macedonia*
μακρόβιος, -ον *long-lived*
μακρός, -ά, -όν *long, large, big*
μακρᾱ́ν (adv. acc.) *far off*
μακρῷ *by far*
μάλα (adv.) *very; quite*
μαλθακίζομαι *be softened*
μαλθακός, -ή, -όν *faint-hearted, cowardly*
μάλιcτα (supl. of μάλα) *especially, particularly; yes*
μᾶλλον (compar. of μάλα) *more; rather*

†μανθάνω   learn, understand; (+inf.)
  learn how to
μανίᾱ, -ᾱς, ἡ   madness
μαντεύομαι   consult an oracle
μαντικῶς (adv.)   prophetically
μάντις, -εως, ὁ   seer, prophet
Μαραθών, -ῶνος, ὁ   Marathon (in
  Attica)
  Μαραθῶνι   at Marathon
  Μαραθώνιος, -ᾱ, -ον   of Marathon
#μαργῶν, -ῶσα, -ῶν (pple. of μαργάω)
  raging
#μάρπτω   take hold of, seize
μαρτυρέω   give evidence, bear
  witness
μαρτυρίᾱ, -ᾱς, ἡ   evidence, testimony
μάρτυς, -υρος, ὁ/ἡ   witness
Μασσαλίᾱ, -ᾱς, ἡ   Marseilles
μαστεύω   seek, search after
μαστῑγοφόρος, -ου, ὁ   whip-bearer
μαστῑγόω   whip, flog
μαστίζω   whip, flog
μάτην (adv.)   in vain; without reason
μά̄τηρ = μήτηρ
μάττω   knead
μάχαιρα, -ᾱς, ἡ   knife
μάχη, -ης, ἡ   battle, fight
μάχιμος, -η, -ον   warlike
†μάχομαι   fight (+dat., 13.1/2b(iii))
Μεγακλῆς, -έους, ὁ   Megacles
Μεγαροῖ (adv.)   in/at Megara
μέγας, μεγάλη, μέγα (stem μεγαλ-;
  3.1/3)   great, big; tall; important;
  loud
μέγεθος, -ους, τό   size
μέγιστος, -η, -ον   greatest (supl. of
  μέγας)
μεθῑ́ημι†   let go, release; give up;
  allow
μεθίστημι† (mid. and intr. tenses of
  act.)   change, alter (intr.)
μεθύω   be drunk
μείγνῡμι (also μῑγ-, aor. pass.
  ἐμίγην)   mix, join; (pass.) be
  joined, mix with, have sexual
  intercourse with (+dat.)
Μειδίᾱς, -ου, ὁ   Meidias
μείζων, -ον   greater (compar. of
  μέγας)
#μείλιχος, -ον   gentle, kind
μειράκιον, -ου, τό   lad, boy

μέλας, -αινα, -αν   black (10.1/3 note
  2)
Μελέαγρος, -ου, ὁ   Meleager (poet
  and philosopher)
†μέλει (impers.)   there is a
  care/concern (+dat. of pers. and
  gen. of thing, 21.1/4b)
μελετάω   practise
Μέλητος, -ου, ὁ   Meletus (accuser of
  Socrates)
μέλι, -ιτος, τό   honey
#μελιηδής, -ές   honey-sweet
μέλιττα, -ης, ἡ   bee
†μέλλω   be destined to; be about to, be
  going to; intend; hesitate
μέλον (acc. absol.)   it being a care
  (21.1/5)
#μέλω (for principal parts see under
  μέλει)   be of concern
μέμνημαι (perf.)   remember (+gen.,
  13.1/2a(iii)) (19.1/3a)
μέμφομαι   blame, criticise, find fault
  with (+dat. or acc.)
μέν* . . . δέ*   on the one hand . . .
  and/but on the other (4.1/3)
μὲν οὖν   no, on the contrary
  (13.1/3c(iii))
Μένανδρος, -ου, ὁ   Menander
  (writer of New Comedy)
Μενδήσιος, -ᾱ, -ον   of Mendes (a
  town in the Nile Delta), Mendesian
Μενέλᾱος, -ου, ὁ   Menelaus
  (brother of Agamemmon, husband
  of Helen)
Μενέλεως, -ω, ὁ   Menelaus (13.1/1a)
Μένιππος, -ου, ὁ   Menippus
Μενοικεύς, -έως, ὁ   Menoeceus
μέντοι* (particle)   really, you know;
  however, yet (13.1/3c(v))
†μένω   remain, stay, wait (for); be at
  rest, be still
Μένων, -ωνος, ὁ   Meno
μέριμνα, -ης, ἡ   care
μέρος, -ους, τό   share, part
  ἐν μέρει   in turn
#μεσηγύ (adv., and prep.+gen.)
  between
μέσος, -η, -ον   middle (of), in the
  middle (18.1/6)
Μεσσηΐς, -ΐδος, ἡ   Messeis (a
  spring)

Μεccήνιοc, -ᾱ, -ον *Messenian*
μέτα = μέτεcτι (21.1/4 note 2)
μετά (prep.) (+acc.) *after*; (+gen.)
 with; (+dat., poetic*)* *among*
μεταβάλλω† *change, alter* (tr. and intr.)
μεταβολή, -ῆc, ἡ *change*
μεταγιγνώcκω† *change one's mind*;
 repent (of)
μεταδίδωμι† *give a share of* (+dat.
 of pers. and gen. of thing)
μεταμέλει† (impers.) *there is
 repentance* (+dat. of pers. and gen.
 of thing, 21.1/4*b*)
μεταμέλεια, -ᾱc, ἡ *regret*
μετανοέω *think afterwards, change
 one's mind, repent*
μεταξύ (adv.) *in the middle*; (+pple.)
 in the middle of doing something
 (12.1/2*a*(i))
μεταπέμπομαι† *summon, send for*
μετάρcιοc, -ον *superficial, shallow*
μετεκβαίνω† *go from one place into
 another, transfer*
μέτεcτι (impers.) *there is a share*
 (+dat. of pers. and gen. of thing,
 21.1/4*b*)
μετέχω† *share in* (+gen., 13.1/2*a*(v))
μετέωροc, -ον *high in the air*
 τὰ μετέωρα *things in the heaven
 above, astronomical phenomena*
μετρέω *measure*
μέτρηcιc, -εωc, ἡ *measurement*
μέτριοc, -ᾱ, -ον *moderate,
 reasonable, fair, average; standard*
μετρίωc (adv.) *in moderation*
μέτρον, -ου, τό *measure, due
 measure, moderation*
μέτωπον, -ου, τό *forehead*
μέχρι (prep.+gen.) *until, up to, as
 far as;*
 μέχρι οὗ *until;* (conj.) *until* (21.1/2)
μή *no(t)*; (+imp. or aor. subj.) *don't*
 (17.1/1); (+subj.) *lest*; inviting a
 neg. answer (10.1/2*a*); (on other
 uses see 24.1/2)
μηδαμῶc (adv.) *not at all, in no way*
μηδέ (conj.and adv.) *nor, not even*
Μήδεια, -ᾱc, ἡ *Medea* (wife of
 Jason)
μηδείc, μηδεμίᾱ, μηδέν *no, no-one,
 nothing*

Μηδικόc, -ή, -όν *of the Medes*
 τὰ Μηδικά (*sc.* πράγματα) *the
 Persian Wars*
#μήδομαι *plot, plan, devise*
Μῆδοc, -ου, ὁ *Mede; Persian*
μηκέτι (adv.) *no longer*
μῆκοc, -ουc, τό *length*
Μήλιοι, -ων, οἱ *Melians*
μῆλον, -ου, τό *apple*
μήν * (particle) *then, indeed; further*
 (13.1/3*a*)
 τί μήν; *of course*
μήν, -όc, ὁ *month*
μηνῡτήc, -οῦ, ὁ *informer*
μηνύω *give information*
μήποτε (adv.) *never*
μήπω (adv.) *not yet*
μήτε . . . μήτε *neither . . . nor*
μήτηρ, -τρόc, ἡ *mother* (6.1/1*b*)
μητρυιά, -ᾶc, ἡ *step-mother*
μηχανάομαι *devise, contrive; procure
 for oneself*
μηχανεύομαι = μηχανάομαι
μηχανή, -ῆc, ἡ *device, plan; means;
 engine of war*
μιαίνω *stain, pollute*
μίαcμα, -ατοc, τό *stain, pollution*
Μίκκροc, -ου, ὁ *Miccus*
μῑκρόc, -ᾱ́, -όν *small, short, little,
 petty*
Μῑλήcιοc, -ᾱ, -ον *of Miletus,
 Milesian*
Μιλτιάδηc, -ου, ὁ *Miltiades*
 (Athenian general)
μῑμημα, -ατοc, τό *imitation*
μιμνήcκομαι *remind oneself*
μίμνω = μένω
#μιν (acc. s. pron. of 3rd pers.) *him,
 her, it*
μῑcέω *hate*
μιcθόομαι *hire*
μιcθόc, -οῦ, ὁ *hire, pay, reward*
μιcθωτόc, -οῦ, ὁ *hireling, hired
 servant*
μῖcοc, -ουc, τό *hatred*
μνᾶ, μνᾶc, ἡ *mina* (100 drachmas)
μνᾶμα = μνῆμα
μνῆμα, -ατοc, τό *monument, tomb;
 memorial*
μνήμη, -ηc, ἡ *remembrance, memory*
μνήμων, -ονοc *mindful, unforgetting*

μοῖρα, -ᾱς, ἡ *fate, lot, destiny; death*
Μοῖρις, -εως, ἡ *Moeris (lake in Egypt)*
μόλις (adv.) *hardly, scarcely, with difficulty*
#μολών, -οῦσα, -όν *having come/gone* (aor. pple. of βλώσκω)
μοναρχέω *be sole ruler over* (+gen.)
μοναρχίᾱ, -ᾱς, ἡ *monarchy*
μόναρχος, -ου, ὁ *monarch*
μόνον (adv.) *only, merely*
οὐ μόνον ... ἀλλὰ καί *not only ... but also*
μόνος, -η, -ον *alone, only*
#μόρος, -ου, ὁ *fate, destiny, doom; death*
μορφή, -ῆς, ἡ *shape, form*
Μοῦσα, -ης, ἡ *Muse*
μουσική, -ῆς, ἡ *music* (including poetry)
μοχθέω *labour, toil*
μόχθος, -ου, ὁ *toil, hardship*
μῦθος, -ου, ὁ *story, fable*
μυῖα, -ᾱς, ἡ *fly*
Μυκῆναι, -ῶν, αἱ *Mycenae* (city in S. Greece)
Μύνδιος, -ᾱ, -ον *Myndian*
Μύνδος, -ου, ὁ *Myndus* (city in Caria)
μυρίζω *make fragrant*
μύριοι, -αι, -α *10,000*
μῡρίος, -ᾱ, -ον *numberless, countless*
μύρμηξ, -ηκος, ὁ *ant*
μύρον, -ου, τό *perfume*
μῦς, μυός, ὁ *mouse*
μύστης, -ου, ὁ *initiate*
Μυτιλήνη, -ης, ἡ *Mytilene* (chief city of Lesbos)
μυχός, -οῦ, ὁ *inner chamber*
μῶν; (adv.) *surely not?* (10.1/2a)
μῶρος, -ᾱ, -ον *stupid, foolish*

Ναζωραῖος, -ᾱ, -ον *of Nazareth*
ναί (particle) *yes* (22.1/2h, 24.1/1)
ναίω *dwell, abide*
νᾶμα, -ατος, τό *stream*
νᾱός, -οῦ, ὁ *temple*
νάπη, -ης, ἡ *glen*
ναυᾱγέω *suffer shipwreck*
ναυηγός, -όν *ship-wrecked*

ναυμαχέω *fight a sea battle*
ναυμαχίᾱ, -ᾱς, ἡ *naval battle*
ναῦς, νεώς, ἡ *ship* (11.1/4)
Ναυσικάᾱ, -ᾱς, ἡ *Nausicaa* (daughter of Alcinous, King of Phaeacians)
ναύτης, -ου, ὁ *sailor*
ναυτικόν, -οῦ, τό *fleet*
ναυτικός, -ή, -όν *naval*
νεᾱνίᾱς, -ου, ὁ *young man*
νεᾱνίσκος, -ου, ὁ *young man*
νείφει (impers.) *it is snowing* (21.1/4c)
νεκρός, -οῦ, ὁ *corpse*
νέκταρ, -αρος, τό *nectar*
νέμεσις, -εως, ἡ *retribution*
νέμω *distribute, apportion, allot, assign*
#νέομαι *go back, return*
νέος, -ᾱ, -ον *young; new; strange, unexpected*
ἐκ νέου *from childhood*
νεότης, -ητος, ἡ *youthfulness, youthful folly*
#νέρθε (adv.) *beneath, below*
νέφος, -ους, τό *cloud*
†νέω *swim*
νεώς, -ώ, ὁ *temple* (13.1/1a)
νή (particle of asseveration) *yes by ... !* (+acc.; 22.1/2h)
νήνεμος, -ον *windless, calm*
νήπιος, -ᾱ, -ον *childish, foolish*
νησιώτης, -ου, ὁ *islander*
νῆσος, -ου, ἡ *island*
νήφω *be sober* (literally or metaphorically)
νῑκάω *win, defeat*
νίκη, -ης, ἡ *victory, conquest*
νῑκητήριον, -ου, τό *prize of victory*
Νῑκίᾱς, ου, ὁ *Nicias*
Νῑκοτέλης, -ους, ὁ *Nicoteles*
Νίκων, -ωνος, ὁ *Nico*
#νιν* (acc.) *him, her, it, them*
νίπτω *wash*
νοέω *perceive*
νόημα, -ατος, τό *thought, perception*
†νομίζω *acknowledge, think, believe (in); treat as customary; (of a legislator) enact*
νόμος, -ου, ὁ *law, convention, observance*

νόος = νοῦς

νοσέω   be sick/ill

νόσημα, –ατος, τό   a disease, illness, plague

νόσος, –ου, ἡ   disease, illness

νοστέω   return

#νόστιμος, –ον   belonging to one's return/homecoming

#νόστος, –ου, ὁ   homecoming

#νόσφι(ν) (adv., and prep.+gen.)   afar off, away from

νουθετέω   warn, rebuke

νοῦς (νόος), νοῦ, ὁ   mind, sense, intelligence (6.1/2)

ἐν νῷ ἔχω   have in mind, intend

#νυκτιπόλος, –ον   night-roaming

νῦν (adv.)   now, at present

νυν*   well then; now then

νυνδή (adv.; strengthened form of νῦν)   just now

νύξ, νυκτός, ἡ   night, darkness

ὑπὸ νύκτα   under cover of night

Ξανθίππη, –ης, ἡ   Xanthippe

Ξάνθος, –ου, ὁ   Xanthus (another name for river Scamander at Troy)

ξεῖνος = ξένος

ξένιος, –ᾱ, –ον   belonging to friendship and hospitality (used as a title of Zeus, as god of hospitality)

Ξενοκράτης, –ους, ὁ   Xenocrates

ξένος, –ου, ὁ   foreigner, alien, stranger; guest; host

Ξενοφῶν, –ῶντος, ὁ   Xenophon (Athenian historian and general)

Ξέρξης, –ου, ὁ   Xerxes (Persian king)

ξίφος, –ους, τό   sword

ξυγ– = συγ–

ξύλον, –ου, τό   (piece of) wood, log

ξυμ– = συμ–

ξύν = σύν

ξυν– = συν–

ξῡνός, –ή, –όν   common

ξυρέω   shave

ξυρόν, –οῦ, τό   razor

ὁ, ἡ, τό   the (2.1/2, 3.1/1)

ὁ μὲν ... ὁ δέ   the one ... the other, one man ... another (5.1/3)

οἱ μὲν ... οἱ δέ   some ... others (5.1/3)

ὁ δέ   and/but he (5.1/3)

ὅδε, ἥδε, τόδε   this (pron. and adj., 9.1/1)

ὁδεύω   travel (by land)

ὁδός, –οῦ, ἡ   road, way, journey

ὀδούς, –όντος, ὁ   tooth

ὀδυνηρός, –ά, –όν   painful

ὀδύρομαι   lament

Ὀδυσσεύς, –έως, ὁ   Odysseus (hero of the Odyssey)

ὅθεν (rel. adv.)   from where

οἷ (rel. adv.)   (to) where

οἱ see ἑ (9.1/4a)

†οἶδα   know (19.1/3 and **Appendix 3**)

χάριν οἶδα   be grateful to (+dat.)

Οἰδίπους, –ποδος, ὁ   Oedipus (son of Laius, king of Thebes)

οἴκαδε (adv.)   homewards

οἰκεῖος, –ᾱ, –ον   related, domestic; private; one's own

οἰκεῖος, –ου, ὁ   relative

οἰκέτης, –ου, ὁ   house-slave

οἰκέω   dwell (in), live, inhabit

οἴκημα, –ατος, τό   room

οἴκησις, –εως, ἡ   dwelling

οἰκίᾱ, –ᾱς, ἡ   house

οἰκίζω   colonise

οἰκοδομέω   build a house

οἰκοδόμημα, –ατος, τό   building, structure

οἰκοδομίᾱ, –ᾱς, ἡ   building, structure

οἴκοθεν (adv.)   from home

οἴκοι (adv.)   at home

οἶκος, –ου, ὁ   house, home

οἰκτίρω   pity

οἰκτρός, –ά, –όν   piteous

†οἶμαι, οἴομαι   think

#οἴμη, –ης, ἡ   way/power of song

οἴμοι (interjection)   alas! oh dear!

#οἶμος, –ου, ὁ   tract, strip of land

Οἰνόη, –ης, ἡ   Oenoë (town in Attica)

οἶνος, –ου, ὁ   wine

οἰνοχοέω   pour wine

οἴομαι see οἶμαι

οἷον   as, just as

#οἶος, –ᾱ, –ον (note smooth breathing)   alone

οἷος, –ᾱ, –ον   what a ...!

(exclamation); *of what sort, of the kind which* (21.1/3)
οἷός τ' εἰμί *be able to* (+inf., 21.1/3 note 2)
οἷοσπερ strengthened form of οἷος
οἰc– fut. stem of φέρω
οἴcτευμα, –ατος, τό *arrow*
οἰcυΐνος, –η, –ον *made of osier/wickerwork*
οἴχομαι *be off, depart, be gone*
ὀκτώ (indecl. adj.) *eight*
ὀλ– aor. stem of ὄλλυμαι
ὄλβιος, –ᾱ, –ον *happy, blessed*
ὄλεθρος, –ου, ὁ *destruction*
ὀλεc– aor. stem of ὄλλῡμι
ὀλιγαρχίᾱ, –ᾱc, ἡ *oligarchy*
ὀλίγος, –η, –ον *small, few, little*
†ὄλλῡμι *destroy, kill, lose* (20.1/1 note 2)
#ὀλοός, –ή, –όν *destructive, baneful*
Ὄλορος, –ου, ὁ *Olorus* (father of Thucydides)
ὅλος, –η, –ον *whole, complete*
Ὀλυμπικός, –οῦ, ὁ *Olympicus* (name of a seer)
Ὀλύμπιος, –ᾱ, –ον *Olympian*
Ὀλύμπια νῑκάω *win an Olympic victory* (22.1/2g)
Ὄλυνθος, –ου, ἡ *Olynthus*
ὄλυραι, –ῶν, αἱ *a one-seeded wheat* (used as fodder for horses)
#ὁμαρτέω *accompany* (+dat.)
Ὅμηρος, –ου, ὁ *Homer* (author of *Iliad* and *Odyssey*)
ὁμῑλέω *be in company with, associate with* (+dat.)
ὁμῑλίᾱ, –ᾱc, ἡ *company, companionship*
ὁμίχλη, –ηc, ἡ *mist, fog*
#ὄμμα, –ατος, τό *eye*
†ὄμνῡμι *swear, swear by* (+acc., 22.1/2h)
ὁμοιόομαι *be like, resemble* (+dat., 13.1/2b(iv))
ὅμοιος, –ᾱ, –ον *like, similar to* (+dat.)
ὁμοίωc (adv.) *in the same way, likewise*
ὁμολογέω *agree*
ὁμολογίᾱ, –ᾱc, ἡ *agreement*
ὁμολογουμένωc (adv.) *in agreement/conformity with* (+dat.)

ὁμομήτριος, –ᾱ, –ον *born of the same mother*
ὁμόνοια, –ᾱc, ἡ *agreement, harmony*
ὁμοτράπεζος, –ον *eating at the same table with* (+dat.)
ὁμοῦ (adv.) *together (with)* (+dat.)
ὁμόφῡλος, –ον *of the same race* or *stock*
ὅμωc (adv.) *nevertheless, however*
#ὁμῶc (adv., accompanying two words joined by καί) *both*
ὄν see ὤν
ὄναρ (nom. and acc. only), τό *dream;* (as adv.) *in a dream*
ὀνειδίζω *reproach, chide, insult* (+dat.)
ὄνειδος, –ουc, τό *insult, rebuke*
ὄνειρος, –ου, ὁ (also ὄνειρον, –ου, τό) *dream*
ὄνομα, –ατος, τό *name, reputation*
ὀνόματι *in/by name*
ὀνομάζω *call, name*
ὄνος, –ου, ὁ/ἡ *ass*
ὄνυξ, –υχος, ὁ *claw, nail*
ὄξος, –ουc, τό *vinegar*
ὀξύς, –εῖα, –ύ *sharp, keen; quick, swift*
#ὀπάζω *give, bestow; make to follow*
ὅπῃ (adv.) *in what way, how, as*
ὄπιcθε (adv.) *behind*
ὀπιcθοφύλαξ, –ακοc, ὁ *member of rear-guard*
#ὀπίcω (adv.) *hereafter*
ὅπλα, –ων, τά *weapons, arms*
ἐν ὅπλοιc *under arms*
ὁπλίζω *equip, arm*
ὁπλίτης, –ου, ὁ *hoplite*
ὁπόθεν (rel. adv.) *from where*
ὅποι (rel. adv.) *to where*
ὁποῖος, –ᾱ, –ον *of what kind* (10.1/2b)
ὁπόσος, –η, –ον *how big, how much;* (pl.) *how many* (10.1/2b)
ὁπόταν (conj.+subj.) *whenever* (14.1/4c(iii))
ὁπότε (conj.) *when;* (+opt.) *whenever* (14.1/4c(iii))
ὅπου (rel. adv.) *where, wherever;* (indir. interrog.) *where*
ὅπωc (adv.) *how* (in answer to πῶc;); *how;* (poet.) *like, as;* (conj.+subj.)

or opt.) *in order that, to* (14.1/4*c*(i))

ὁπωcτιοῦν (adv.) *in any way whatever*

†ὁράω *see, look at*

ὀργή, -ῆc, ἡ *temperament; anger*
  ἐν ὀργῇ ἔχω *be angry with* (+acc.)

†ὀργίζομαι (aor. ὠργίcθην) *become angry with* (+dat., 13.1/2*b*(i))

ὀρέγομαι *strive after* (+gen.)

ὄρειοc, -ᾱ, -ον *of the mountains, mountain-wandering*

Ὀρέcτηc, -ου, ὁ *Orestes* (son of Agamemnon)

#ὀρθόβουλοc, -ον *straight-counselling, wise*

ὀρθόc, -ή, -όν *straight; correct; right*

ὀρθόω *set upright; guide aright*

ὀρθῶc (adv.) *correctly*

ὅρκοc, -ου, ὁ *oath*

ὁρμάομαι *set off, start out; make an expedition*

ὁρμή, -ῆc, ἡ *setting oneself in motion*
  ἐν ὁρμῇ εἰμί *be on the point of starting*

ὁρμίζω *moor, anchor*

ὄρνῑc, -ῑθοc (acc. ὄρνιν, 5.1/1 note 2), ὁ/ἡ *bird*

ὄροc, -ουc, τό *mountain*

ὅροc, -ου, ὁ *boundary*

ὀρρωδέω *fear, dread*

ὀρχήcτρᾱ, -ᾱc, ἡ *orchestra* (the dancing-space in the theatre and also a section of the agora where books were sold)

ὅc, ἥ, ὅ (rel. pron., 9.1/2) *who, which*

#ὅc, ἥ, ὅν (refl. poss. adj.) *his, her, its*

ὅcιοc, -ᾱ, -ον *holy, sacred; pious, devout*

ὁcιόω *sanctify*

ὅcοc, -η, -ον *how much/many/great!* (exclamation); *as much/many as* (21.1/3)

ὅcοcπερ, ὅcηπερ, ὅcονπερ *as great as, as many as*

ὅcπερ, ἥπερ, ὅπερ (rel. pron.) *the very one who/which*

#ὁccάκιc (interrog. adv.) *how often*

ὅcτιc, ἥτιc, ὅτι (indef. rel. pron. and

indir. interrog., 10.1/2*b*) *who(ever), which(ever), what(ever)*

ὀcτοῦν, -οῦ, τό *bone*

ὅcῳ (+compar.) *the more* (lit. *by how much*)

ὅταν (conj.+subj.) *whenever* (14.1/4*c*(iii))

ὅτε (conj.) *when*

ὅτι (A) (conj.) *that; because* (+supl.) *as ... as possible* (17.1/4*d*)

ὅτι (B) neuter nom./acc. s. of ὅcτιc

ὅτου = οὗτινοc

ὅτῳ = ᾧτινι

οὐ (οὐκ, οὐχ) *no(t)*
  οὐ μόνον ... ἀλλὰ καί *not only ... but also*

οὐ see ἕ (9.1/4*a*)

οὗ (rel. adv.) *where*

οὐδαμοῦ (adv.) *nowhere*

οὐδαμῶc (adv.) *in no way; not at all*

οὐδέ (conj.) *and not, nor*; (adv.) *not even*

οὐδείc, οὐδεμίᾱ, οὐδέν *no, no-one, nothing*

οὐδέν (adverbial acc.) *in no respect, not at all*

οὐδέποτε (adv.) *never*

οὐδέπω (adv.) *not yet*

οὐδέτεροc, -ᾱ, -ον *neither of two; neuter* (of gender)

οὐκ = οὐ

οὐκέτι (adv.) *no longer*

οὔκουν (particle) *not ... therefore* (13.1/3*c*(i))

οὐκοῦν (particle) *therefore, accordingly* (13.1/3*c*(i))

οὖν* (particle) *therefore, so, then*
  οὖν δή *well, as you know*

οὖν crasis for ὁ ἐν

οὕνεκα = ἕνεκα

οὔποτε (adv.) *never*

οὔπω (adv.) *not yet*

#οὐρανόθεν (adv.) *from heaven*

οὐρανόc, -οῦ, ὁ *sky, heaven*; (personified, with cap.) *Uranus*

οὖc, ὠτόc, τό *ear*

οὐcίᾱ, -ᾱc, ἡ *property, wealth, substance, means*

οὔτε ... οὔτε *neither ... nor*

οὔτιc, οὔτινοc *no-one*

οὔτοι (adv.) *indeed not*

οὗτος, αὕτη, τοῦτο (pron. and adj., 9.1/1) *this*; οὗτος can express *you there!*

οὑτοςί (strengthened form) *this man here*

οὕτω(ς) (adv.) *thus, so, in this way; to such an extent, so much*

οὑτωςί strengthened form of οὕτως

οὐχ = οὐ

οὐχί emphatic form of οὐ

ὀφείλω *owe; be bound, ought* (see 21.1/1 note)

ὄφελος, -ους, τό *help, use, advantage*

ὀφθαλμός, -οῦ, ὁ *eye*

ὄφις, -εως, ὁ *serpent*

ὄχλος, -ου, ὁ *crowd, mob*

#ὀχμάζω *bind fast*

#ὄχος, -ους, τό *chariot*

ὀχυρός, -ά, -όν *strong, secure*

ὀψέ (adv.) *late*

ὄψις, -εως, ἡ *vision, sight*

ὄψομαι fut. of ὁράω

ὄψον, -ου, τό *cooked food, a made dish; delicacies*

πάγη, -ης, ἡ *trap, snare*

#παγίς, -ίδος, ἡ *trap, snare*

πάγος, -ου, ὁ *crag, rock; frost*

παθ- aor. stem of πάσχω

πάθημα, -ατος, τό *suffering, misfortune*

πάθος, -ους, τό *suffering, experience*

Παιανιεύς, -έως, ὁ *of the deme Paeania*

παιδαγωγός, -οῦ, ὁ *tutor*

παιδειά, -ᾶς, ἡ *education, teaching,lesson; culture; childhood*

παιδεύω *train, teach, educate*

παιδίον, -ου, τό *child; slave*

παίζω *play, make sport of* (+acc.), *joke at* (πρός+acc.)

παῖς, παιδός, ὁ/ἡ *child, boy, girl; slave*

πάλαι (adv.) *long ago*

παλαιός, -ά, -όν *ancient, (of) old*

παλαίστρᾱ, -ᾶς, ἡ *wrestling-school, palaestra*

παλαίτατος, -η, -ον supl. of παλαιός

πάλιν (adv.) *back again, again*

παμπήδην (adv.) *entirely, completely*

παμπλούςιος, -ον *very rich*

πανδημεί (adv.) *in a body, in full force*

παννύχιος, -ον *all night long*

#πανόδυρτος, -ον *all-lamented*

Πάνοψ, -οπος, ὁ *Panops*

παντάπᾱςι(ν) (adv.) *in every respect*

πανταχόθεν (adv.) *from all directions*

πανταχοῦ (adv.) *everywhere; absolutely, altogether*

πανταχῶς (adv.) *in all ways, altogether*

παντελῶς (adv.) *completely, outright*

#πάντεχνος, -ον *assisting all the arts*

πάντοθεν (adv.) *from every side*

#παντρόφος, -ον *all-nurturing*

πάντως (adv.) *in all ways, especially*

πάνυ (adv.) *very (much)*

πάνυ γε, πάνυ μὲν οὖν *certainly, of course* (13.1/3c(iii))

πάππος, -ου, ὁ *grandfather*

#πάρ = παρά

πάρα = πάρεςτι (21.1/4 note 2)

παρά (prep.) (+acc.) *along, beside; against, contrary to; compared with;* (+gen.) *from;* (+dat.) *with, beside, in the presence of*

παραβαίνω† *transgress*

παραβάλλω† *compare* (+παρά and acc.); (intr.) *come near, approach*

παραβοηθέω *come to help* (+dat.); *assist*

παραγγέλλω† *give an order*

παραγίγνομαι† *be present; come to, arrive at*

παράγω† *bring forward, introduce*

παραδίδωμι† *hand over, deliver*

παραδως- fut. act./mid. stem of παραδίδωμι

παραινέω† *advise* (+dat., 13.1/2b(i))

παρακαλέω† *summon; invite; encourage*

παράκειμαι *lie/be placed beside* (+dat.)

παρακελεύομαι† *exhort, encourage* (+dat.)

παραλαμβάνω† *take/receive from*

παραμελέω (< παρά+ἀμελέω) *disregard, pay no heed to*

παραμένω† *remain; remain loyal*

παράπαν (adv.) *altogether,*
absolutely (also τὸ παράπαν)
παραπλέω† *sail by, sail close to*
παραπλήσιος, (-ᾱ), -ον *very similar*
to (+dat. or καί)
παρασάγγης, -ου, ὁ *parasang* (a
Persian measure of distance of
about 30 stades)
παρασκευάζω *prepare, equip;* (mid.)
make one's preparations
παρασκευή, -ῆς, ἡ *preparation,*
equipping; force
παρασπίζω *bear a shield beside,*
shield (+dat.)
παραυτίκα (adv.) *immediately,*
straight away
παρεγγυάω *pass (the word) along*
πάρειμι *be at hand; be present; be*
near (+dat.)
  πάρεστι (impers.) *it is possible for*
  (+dat. and inf., 21.1/4a)
παρελαύνω† *drive past*
παρεμφαίνω† *emphasise*
πάρεργον, -ου, τό *subordinate issue*
παρέρχομαι† *pass, go by; come*
forward
παρέχον (acc. abs.) *it being*
possible/allowed (21.1/5)
παρέχω† *give to, provide; offer,*
furnish, cause
  πράγματα παρέχω *cause trouble*
  παρέχει (impers.) *it is*
  possible/allowed (+dat. and inf.)
παρθένος, -ου, ἡ *girl, maiden*
παρίημι† *pass over; let pass;*
leave, allow, admit
παρίστημι† (mid. and intr. tenses of
act.) *stand beside, be near/at hand*
παριών, -οῦσα, -όν pple. of
παρέρχομαι
πάροδος, -ου, ἡ *passage, entrance*
πάροιθε (adv.) *formerly*
παροιμιᾱ, -ᾱς, ἡ *proverb*
παρόν (acc. absol.) *it being possible*
(21.1/5)
πάρος (adv.) *previously; before* (=
πρίν)
παρών, -οῦσα, -όν pple. of πάρειμι
be present
πᾶς, πᾶσα, πᾶν (10.1/3b) *all, every*
  ὁ πᾶς *the whole*

†πάσχω *undergo; experience; suffer*
  εὖ/κακῶς πασχω *be well/badly*
  treated (17.1/5)
#πατέομαι (aor. ἐπασάμην) *eat of,*
partake of (+gen.)
πατήρ, -τρός, ὁ *father* (6.1/1b)
πατρίδιον, -ου, τό *daddy*
πατρίς, -ίδος, ἡ *fatherland, native*
land
Πάτροκλος, -ου, ὁ *Patroclus* (friend
of Achilles)
πάτταλος, -ου, ὁ *peg*
παύω (tr.) *stop; depose;* (mid., intr.)
stop, cease from (+gen. or pple.)
Πάφιος, -ᾱ, -ον *from Paphos,*
Paphian; (as fem. noun) *the*
Paphian (sc. goddess, a name of
Aphrodite derived from Paphos in
Cyprus)
πάχνη, -ης, ἡ *hoar-frost*
παχύς, -εῖα, -ύ *thick, stout, fat*
πέδη, -ης, ἡ *fetter*
πεδίον, -ου, τό *plain*
πέδον, -ου, τό *ground, land, region*
πεζομαχέω *fight on foot/land*
πεζός, -ή, -όν *on foot*
  πεζοί *foot soldiers, infantry*
  πεζῇ *on foot*
†πείθω *persuade;* (mid.) *believe, trust,*
obey (+dat., 13.1/2b(ii))
πειθώ, -οῦς, ἡ *persuasion; obedience*
(13.1/1b(ii))
πεινάω *be hungry* (5.1/2 note 4)
πεῖρα, -ᾱς, ἡ *attempt, experiment,*
trial
Πειραιεύς (acc. -αιᾶ, gen. -αιῶς, dat.
-αιεῖ), ὁ *Piraeus* (port of Athens)
πειράομαι *try; test* (+gen.)
πειρατέον *one must try* (24.1/5)
πειρᾱτής, -οῦ, ὁ *pirate*
πείσομαι fut. of πασχω or πείθομαι
πέλαγος, -ους, τό *sea, high sea*
πέλας (adv.+gen.) *near; nearby*
Πελασγοί, -ῶν, οἱ *Pelasgians*
#πέλομαι (ἔπλετο 3rd s. strong aor.)
be
Πελοποννήσιοι, -ων, οἱ
Peloponnesians
Πελοπόννησος, -ου, ἡ *Peloponnese*
πέμπτος, -η, -ον *fifth*
†πέμπω *send*

πένης, -ητος   poor (man)
πένθος, -ους, τό   grief, sorrow, mourning
πενίᾱ, -ᾱς, ἡ   poverty
πέντε (indecl. adj.)   five
πεντήκοντα (indecl. adj.)   fifty
πέποιθα (strong perf. of πείθω) trust, rely on (+dat.)
πέπονθα perf. of πάσχω
πεπρωμένος, -η, -ον   destined, fated
πέπτωκα perf. of πίπτω
πέπυσμαι perf. of πυνθάνομαι
πέπωκα perf. of πῑ́νω
περ* = καίπερ; –περ at the end of a word (e.g. ὅσπερ) is emphatic
πέρας, -ατος, τό   end
#πέργαμα, -ων, τά   citadel, acropolis
Περδίκκᾱς, -ου, ὁ   Perdiccas
#πέρθω   ravage, destroy, sack
περί (prep.) (+acc.)   about, around; (+gen.) about, concerning; (+dat.) in, on, about
περὶ (+acc.) εἰμί   be busy with
περὶ πολλοῦ ποιέομαι   value highly (+acc.) (20.1/3)
περιάγω†   lead round
περιβάλλω†   throw round; embrace
περίβολος, -ου, ὁ   enclosure
περιγίγνομαι†   remain over; excel
περίειμι   survive, remain
περιέπω†   treat
περιεργάζομαι†   waste one's labour
περιέρχομαι†   go round, walk round
Περικλῆς, -κλέους, ὁ   Pericles (Athenian statesman)
περιμένω†   wait, wait for (+acc.)
περίοδος, -ου, ἡ   chart, map
περιοράω†   overlook, allow
περιπαθῶς (adv.)   passionately
περιπατέω   walk around
περιπῑ́πτω†   fall in with, encounter (+dat.)
περίπλους, -ου, ὁ   circumnavigation
περιπτύσσω   outflank
περιτειχίζω   build a wall round
περιτείχισμα, -ατος, τό   wall of circumvallation, blockading wall
περιτίθημι†   put around, bestow on
περιφέρω†   carry round
περιφρονέω   think about/around; despise

Πέρσης, -ου, ὁ   Persian
πέρυσι (adv.)   last year
πεσ- aor. stem of πίπτω
#πετεινός, -ή, -όν   winged
πέτομαι   fly
πέτρᾱ, -ᾱς, ἡ   rock, cliff
πέτρος, -ου, ὁ   stone, boulder
πεύθομαι = πυνθάνομαι
πεύσομαι fut. of πυνθάνομαι
πέφῡκα   be by nature, be naturally (see φύω)
πῇ (interrog. particle)   where? how?
πηδάω   leap, jump
πηλός, -οῦ, ὁ   mud
#πῆμα, -ατος, τό   woe, misery, calamity
#πημονή, -ῆς, ἡ   woe, misery
Πηνελόπεια, -ᾱς, ἡ   Penelope (wife of Odysseus)
πῆχυς, -εως, ὁ   forearm; cubit
πιέζομαι   be oppressed/distressed
πιθ- aor. act./mid. stem of πείθομαι
πιθανός, -ή, -όν   persuasive
πίθηκος, -ου, ὁ   monkey
πικρός, -ά, -όν   bitter, harsh, severe
πικρῶς (adv.)   bitterly
Πιλᾶτος, -ου, ὁ   (Pontius) Pilate
†πίμπλημι   fill with (+gen. or dat.) (19.1/1 note 2)
πίμπρημι   burn (tr.) (19.1/1 note 2)
πινακίδιον, -ου, τό   writing-tablet
Πίνδαρος, -ου, ὁ   Pindar (lyric poet)
†πῑ́νω   drink
†πῑ́πτω   fall
πιστεύω   trust (+dat., 13.1/2b(ii))
πίστις, -εως, ἡ   pledge, assurance; good faith; trust
πιστός, -ή, -όν   reliable, trustworthy, faithful
#πλάζομαι (aor. ἐπλάγχθην)   wander
πλανάομαι   wander
πλάνη, -ης, ἡ   wandering
Πλάτων, -ωνος, ὁ   Plato (philosopher)
πλέθρον, -ου, τό   plethron (c. 30 metres)
πλεῖστος, -η, -ον   most (supl. of πολύς)
πλείων, πλέον   more (compar. of πολύς, 17.1/2b)
πλέκω   plait; devise, contrive

πλέον (adv.)   *more*
πλεύμων, -ονος, ὁ   *lung*
πλευρά, -ᾶς, ἡ   *rib, flank*
πλεύϲομαι fut. of πλέω
πλέω   *sail*
πλέωϲ, -ᾱ, -ων   *full of* (+gen.)
   (13.1/1*a*)
πληγή, -ῆϲ, ἡ   *blow, stroke, lash*
πλῆθοϲ, -ουϲ, τό   *number, crowd; the*
   people
πλήν (adv.)   *but, except;* (also
   prep.+gen.) *except, except for*
πλήρηϲ, -εϲ   *full*
πληϲιάζω   *approach* (+dat.,
   13.1/2*b*(iii))
πληϲίοϲ, -ᾱ, -ον   *near, close to*
   (+gen.)
πληϲμονή, -ῆϲ, ἡ   *repletion*
πλήττω   *strike, hit*
πλοῖον, -ου, τό   *vessel, ship, boat*
πλοῦϲ (πλόοϲ), -οῦ, ὁ   *sailing,*
   voyage; time for sailing (6.1/2)
πλούϲιοϲ, -ᾱ, -ον   *rich, wealthy*
πλουτέω   *be rich*
πλοῦτοϲ, -ου, ὁ   *wealth*
Πλούτων, -ωνοϲ, ὁ   *Pluto* (god of
   the underworld)
πλύνω   *wash* (clothes)
πνεῦμα, -ατοϲ, τό   *breath*
πνέω (aor. ἔπνευϲα)   *breathe*
πνῑγω   *choke, strangle*
   ἐπνίγην (root aor.) *choked* (intr.)
πνοή, -ῆϲ, ὁ   *breath*
ποδαπόϲ, -ή, -όν   *from what country?*
ποθεινόϲ, -η, -όν   *longed for, desired*
πόθεν (interrog. adv.)   *from where?*
πόθοϲ, -ου, ὁ   *longing, desire*
ποῖ (interrog. adv.)   *to where?*
   ποῖ τῆϲ γῆϲ   *to where in the world?*
ποιέω   *make, do;* (mid.) *make, think,*
   consider
   ἀγαθὰ (εὖ) ποιέω   *treat well, do*
      good to (+acc., 22.1/2*f*(ii))
   κακὰ (κακῶϲ) ποιέω   *treat badly,*
      harm (+acc., 22.1/2*f*(ii))
ποιητέον   *one must make/do* (24.1/5)
ποιητήϲ, -οῦ, ὁ   *poet*
#ποικιλείμων, -ον   *with embroidered*
   coat
ποικίλοϲ, -η, -ον   *many-coloured;*
   subtle, ingenious

ποιμήν, -ένοϲ, ὁ   *shepherd*
ποῖοϲ, -ᾱ, -ον;   *of what sort?*
πολεμέω   *make war*
πολεμικόϲ, -ή, -όν   *military, martial*
πολέμιοι, -ων, οἱ   *the enemy*
πολέμιοϲ, -ᾱ, -ον   *hostile, enemy*
πόλεμοϲ, -ου, ὁ   *war*
πολιορκέω   *besiege*
#πολιόϲ, -ά, -όν   *grey*
πόλιϲ, -εωϲ, ἡ   *city, city-state*
πολῑτείᾱ, -ᾱϲ, ἡ   *citizenship;*
   constitution
πολῑτεύομαι   *be a citizen*
πολῑτηϲ, -ου, ὁ   *citizen*
πολῑτικόϲ, -ή, -όν   *political*
πολλάκιϲ (adv.)   *often*
πολλόϲ Ionic for πολύϲ
#πολύκλαυτοϲ, -ον   *much lamented*
πολύλογοϲ, -ον   *talkative*
πολυμαθίᾱ, -ᾱϲ, ἡ   *much learning*
Πολυνείκηϲ, -ουϲ, ὁ   *Polynices* (son
   of Oedipus)
πολύϲ, πολλή, πολύ (stem πολλ-;
   3.1/3)   *much* (pl. *many*); *long*
   πολλοῦ δεῖ   *far from it!*
   πολλοῦ δέω   *I am far from*
   πολλῷ   *by far*
   πολύ (adv. acc.)   *very, much*
   οἱ πολλοί   *the majority; the mob*
   ὡϲ ἐπὶ τὸ πολύ   *for the most part*
      (22.1/1*a*(vii))
#πολύτροποϲ, -ον   *of many wiles* (or
   much travelled)
πολύφιλοϲ, -ον   *having many*
   friends
πονέω   *toil, labour*
πονηρίᾱ, -ᾱϲ, ἡ   *wickedness*
πονηρόϲ, -ά, -όν   *wicked, bad; of*
   poor quality; wretched
πόνοϲ, -ου, ὁ   *toil, labour; distress,*
   trouble, stress, suffering
πόντοϲ, -ου, ὁ   *sea;* (with cap.) *the*
   Black Sea
πορείᾱ, -ᾱϲ, ἡ   *course, passage*
πορεύομαι   *march, journey, travel*
πορθέω   *destroy, plunder, sack*
πορίζομαι   *procure*
πόρρω (adv.)   *far away*
πορών pple. of ἔπορον
Ποϲειδῶν, -ῶνοϲ, ὁ   *Poseidon* (god
   of the sea) (acc. Ποϲειδῶ)

πόcoc, -η, -ον;   how big?, how much?;
pl. how many?
ποταμός, -οῦ, ὁ   river
ποτέ*   once, ever
πότε; (interrog. adv.)   when?
Ποτείδαια, -ᾱς, ἡ   Potidea (city in
northen Greece)
Ποτειδεᾶται, -ῶν, οἱ   Potideans
πότερα = πότερον (introducing
alternative questions, 10.1/2a)
πότερον ... ἤ ...   whether ... or ..?
πότερος, -ᾱ, -ον;   which (of two)?
#ποτής, -ῆτος, ἡ   drink
#πότμος, -ου, ὁ   fate
που*   somewhere, anywhere; I
suppose
ποῦ; (adv.)   where?
πούς, ποδός, ὁ   foot
πρᾶγμα, -ατος, τό   thing; business,
negotiation; affair; (in pl.) trouble
πράγματα παρέχω   cause trouble
Πραξιτέλης, -ουc, ὁ   Praxiteles
(sculptor)
πρᾱ́ccω = πρᾱ́ττω
πρᾱ́ττω   do, carry out, get on, fare
εὖ (or καλῶc) πρᾱ́ττω   fare well,
be prosperous
κακῶc πρᾱ́ττω   fare badly, be in
distress
πρέπει (impers.)   it befits, it is proper
for (+dat., 21.1/4a)
πρέπον (acc. absol.)   it being fitting
(21.1/5)
πρέcβειc, -εων, οἱ   ambassadors
(8.1/4 note)
πρεcβεύομαι   send an embassy
πρεcβευτής, -οῦ, ὁ   ambassador
πρεcβύτεροc, -ᾱ, -ον   older, rather
old
Πρίαμος, -ου, ὁ   Priam (King of
Troy)
πρίαcθαι aor. inf. of ὠνέομαι
πρίν (adv.)   before, formerly; (conj.)
before, until (21.1/2)
πρό (prep.+gen.)   before, in front of
πρὸ τοῦ   previously
προαγορεύω (aor. προεῖπον, 18.1/4
note 2)   proclaim
προάγω†   lead on/forward
προαιρέομαι†   choose in preference
προαιcθάνομαι†   perceive beforehand

προβάλλω†   put forward; expose
πρόβατον, -ου, τό   sheep
προβουλεύω   make a preliminary
resolution (of the Council, for
referral to the Assembly)
πρόγονος, -ου, ὁ   forebear, ancestor
προδίδωμι†   betray
προδοcίᾱ, -ᾱς, ἡ   treachery
προεῖπον aor. of προαγορεύω
προέρχομαι†   go forward, advance
προθῡμέομαι   be ready, eager
προθῡμίᾱ, -ᾱς, ἡ   desire, eagerness,
goodwill
πρόθῡμος, -ον   ready, eager, willing
πρόθυρον, -ου, τό   porch, front door
προΐημι†   send forth
προκείμενος, -η, -ον   proposed,
appointed
Προκλῆς, -έουc, ὁ   Procles
προλείπω†   leave, abandon
προμάχομαι†   fight in defence of
Προμηθεύς, -έωc, ὁ   Prometheus
(giver of fire to mortals)
προμηθίᾱ, -ᾱς, ἡ   forethought
προνοέω   think beforehand
πρόνοια, -ᾱς, ἡ   foresight, providence
προπέμπω†   escort
προπορεύομαι   go in front, precede
πρός (prep.) (+acc.)   to, towards;
(+gen.) in name of, by; under
protection of, at the command of;
suiting, befitting, the mark of;
(poet.) by (= ὑπό), on the side of,
towards; (+dat.) near, in addition to
προcαγγέλλω†   report to
προcαγορεύω (aor. προcεῖπον, 18.1/4
note 2)   address
προcάγω†   bring towards/forward;
(intr.) advance
προcαπόλλῡμι†   lose in addition
προcάπτω   fasten on, put on
προcαυδάω   speak to, address
προcβάλλω†   attack, assault (+dat.)
προcβλέπω   look at
προcδέομαι†   be in want/need of
besides
προcδέχομαι†   await, wait for, expect
προcδίδωμι†   give in addition
προcεθίζομαι   accustom oneself
πρόcειμι   be present/at hand
προcεῖπον aor. of προcαγορεύω

προςέρχομαι† go/come towards, advance, approach

προςέχω† bring near, apply to
προςέχω τὸν νοῦν pay attention to (+dat.)

προςήκει (impers.) it concerns, it is fitting (+dat. and inf., 24.1/4a)
προςῆκον (acc. absol.) it being fitting (21.1/5)

πρόςθε(ν) (adv.) previously; before; (+gen.) in front of

προςκαλέω† summon

προςοράω† look at

προςπαςςαλεύω nail fast to, fasten

προςπίπτω† fall upon; meet; attack (+dat.)

προςποιέομαι claim, pretend

προςτάττω assign to

προςτίθημι† put to, add

προςτρέχω† run towards

προςφερής, -ές similar, like (+dat.)

προςφιλής, -ές dear, beloved

πρόςω (adv.) far off

πρότερον (adv.) formerly, previously

πρότερος, -ᾱ, -ον first (of two); previous

προτίθημι† set before

προτρέπω† urge on, impel

πρόφαςις, -εως, ἡ pretext, excuse

προφέρω† bring forward

προφήτης, -ου, ὁ harbinger

πρόχειρος, -ον ready to hand

πρυτάνεις, -εων, οἱ prytaneis (the 50 members of the tribe presiding in the Council or Assembly)

πρωκτός, -οῦ, ὁ anus

#πρών, -ῶνος (epic nom. pl. πρώονες), ὁ headland

Πρωτόμαχος, -ου, ὁ Protomachus

πρῶτον (adv., also τὸ πρῶτον) first, at first

πρῶτος, -η, -ον first

πτερόν, -οῦ, τό wing

πτερωτός, -ή, -όν winged

#πτολίερθρον, -ου, τό citadel

πτυχή, -ῆς, ἡ leaf (of book)

πτύω spit

πτωχός, -οῦ, ὁ beggar

πυθ- aor. stem of πυνθάνομαι

Πῡθαγόρᾱς, -ου, ὁ Pythagoras (philosopher)

Πῡθίᾱ, -ᾱς, ἡ the Pythia (the priestess of Pythian Apollo at Delphi)

πυκνός, -ή, -όν thick, dense

πύλη, -ης, ἡ gate

πυλίς, -ιδος, ἡ postern gate

†πυνθάνομαι inquire, ascertain, learn (+acc. and gen., 13.1/2a(iii))

πῦρ, πυρός, τό fire; (pl. πυρα, 13.1/1c) watch-fires, beacons, fire-signals

πυρά, -ᾶς, ἡ funeral pyre

πύργος, -ου, ὁ tower

#πῡροφόρος, -ον wheat-bearing

Πύρρη, -ης, ἡ Pyrrha (woman's name)

Πύρρων, -ωνος, ὁ Pyrrho (philosopher of Elis)

πω* yet

πωλέω* sell

πώποτε* ever yet

πως* somehow

πῶς; how?

πῶς γὰρ οὔ; of course

ῥᾴδιος, -ᾱ, -ον easy

ῥᾳδίως (adv.) easily, lightly

ῥᾷστος, -η, -ον easiest, very easy (supl. of ῥᾴδιος)

ῥᾴων, -ον easier (compar. of ῥᾴδιος)

ῥέω flow; fall/drop off

†ῥήγνῡμι break, shatter, burst

ῥῆμα, -ατος, τό word

ῥήτωρ, -ορος, ὁ orator, politician

ῥῖγος, -ους, τό frost, cold

†ῥῑπτω throw

ῥῑς, ῥῑνός, ἡ nose

#ῥοδόεις, -εςςα, -εν rosy

ῥόδον, -ου, τό rose

Ῥόδος, -ου, ἡ Rhodes

ῥοή, -ῆς, ἡ stream

ῥόπαλον, -ου, τό club, cudgel

ῥοῦς (ῥόος), -οῦ, ὁ stream (6.1/2)

ῥυθμος, -οῦ, ὁ rhythm

#ῥύομαι (aor. ἐρρυςάμην) save, rescue

Ῥωμαῖος, -ου, ὁ Roman

Ῥώμη, -ης, ἡ Rome

ῥώμη, -ης, ἡ strength, force

Cάβυλλος, –ου, ὁ   Sabyllus
Cάϊοι, –ων, οἱ   Saii (Thracian tribe)
cαλπικτής (and cαλπιγκτής), –οῦ, ὁ
    trumpeter
Cαμοθρᾴκη, –ης, ἡ   Samothrace
    (island in Aegean)
Cάμος, –ου, ἡ   Samos (island in
    Aegean)
cάνδαλον, –ου, τό   sandal
Cαπφώ, –οῦς, ἡ   Sappho (poetess of
    Lesbos) (13.1/1b(ii))
cατράπης, –ου, ὁ   satrap (Persian
    governor)
cαφηνίζω   make clear, explain
cαφής, –ές   clear, plain, true
    τὸ cαφές   the truth
cαφῶς (adv.)   clearly
Cάων, –ωνος, ὁ   Saon
cεαυτόν, –ήν (also cαυτ–; reflex.
    pron.)   yourself (9.1/4a)
cέβομαι   revere, worship
cειcμός, –οῦ, ὁ   earthquake
cέλας, –ως, τό   flame, gleam
cελήνη, –ης, ἡ   moon
cεμνός, –ή, –όν   revered, holy;
    august, majestic
#cεμνόcτομος, –ον   haughty
cῆμα, –ατος, τό   mound, tomb
cημαίνω   signal, indicate, show
cημεῖον, –ου, τό   signal, sign
cθένος, –ους, τό   strength, might
cῑγάω   be quiet, keep silent
cῑγή, –ῆς, ἡ   silence
cίδηρος, –ου, ὁ   iron
Cικελίᾱ, –ᾱς, ἡ   Sicily
Cίκελοι, –ων, οἱ   Sicels (indigenous
    Sicilians)
Cίμων, –ωνος, ὁ   Simon
#Cιcύφειος, –ᾱ, –ον   of Sisyphus
cῑτία, –ων, τά   provisions, food
cῖτος, –ου, ὁ   food (pl. τὰ cῖτα
    (13.1/1c))
cιωπάω   be silent
cιωπή, –ῆς, ἡ   silence
cκαιός, –ά, –όν   clumsy, stupid
cκάφη, –ης, ἡ   trough, tub, bowl
†cκεδάννῡμι (fut. cκεδῶ[–άω])   scatter
cκεπτέον   one must consider (24.1/5)
cκέπτομαι   examine, look carefully
    at, consider
cκεύη, –ῶν, τά   gear, furniture

cκηνή, –ῆς, ἡ   tent; stage (in theatre);
    stall, booth
cκηνόω   lodge, take up one's abode
cκῆπτρον, –ου, τό   sceptre, staff
cκιᾱ́, –ᾶς, ἡ   shadow, shade
cκοπέω   consider, examine, take heed
cκοπιᾱ́, –ᾶς, ἡ   lookout-place
cκοπός, –οῦ, ὁ   mark (at which one
    aims), target
cκορπίος, –ου, ὁ   scorpion
cκότος, –ου, ὁ (also –ους, τό)
    darkness
Cκύθης, –ου, ὁ   Scythian (also as
    adj. in poetry)
Cκύλλα, –ης, ἡ   Scylla (a sea-
    monster)
Cκῦρος, –ου, ἡ   Scyrus (island in
    Aegean)
cμῑκρός, –ά, –όν   small, short, little
cοβαρός, –ά, –όν   pompous, haughty
Cόλων, –ωνος, ὁ   Solon (Athenian
    statesman and poet)
cός, cή, cόν (poss. adj.)   your (s.)
cοφίᾱ, –ᾱς, ἡ   wisdom
cόφιcμα, –ατος, τό   clever device
cοφιcτής, –οῦ, ὁ   sophist, thinker,
    teacher, sage
cοφός, –ή, –όν   wise, clever, brilliant,
    accomplished
Cπάρτη, –ης, ἡ   the city of Sparta
Cπαρτιᾱ́της, –ου, ὁ   Spartiate (a full
    citizen of Sparta)
Cπάρτωλος, –ου, ἡ   Spartolus (city)
†cπείρω   sow (with seed), engender,
    scatter
cπείcαcθαι aor. inf. of cπένδομαι
cπένδω   pour (a drink offering);
    (mid.) pour libations; make a treaty
cπέρμα, –ατος, τό   seed; offspring
#cπέρχομαι   hurry, hasten
cπόγγος, –ου, ὁ   sponge
cποδιᾱ́, –ᾶς, ἡ   heap of ashes, ashes
cποδός, –οῦ, ἡ   ashes, embers
cπονδή, –ῆς, ἡ   libation; (pl.) treaty,
    truce
cπορᾱ́, –ᾶς, ἡ   sowing; begetting
cποράς, –άδος (adj.)   scattered
cπουδάζω   be busy about, concern
    oneself about (+acc.)
cπουδή, –ῆς, ἡ   zeal, haste,
    seriousness

cτάδιον, –ου, τό (plur. –α and –οι) stade (c. 200 metres)

#cταθευτόc, –ή, –όν scorched, grilled

cταθμόc, –οῦ, ὁ station, halting-place; stage, day's march

cτᾶc, cτᾶcα, cτάν (root aor. pple. of ἵcτημι)

cτάcιc, –εωc, ἡ faction, sedition, discord

cταυρόc, –οῦ, ὁ stake; cross (for crucifixion)

cταυρόω crucify

cτέγω contain, hold

†cτέλλω send; equip

cτενάζω groan

cτένω groan

cτέργω love; be content with, accept

cτέφανοc, –ου, ὁ crown, wreath, garland

cτίγμα, –ατοc, τό tattoo-mark

cτολή, –ῆc, ἡ clothing, clothes

cτόμα, –ατοc, τό mouth

#cτοργή, –ῆc, ἡ love

cτρατειά, –ᾶc, ἡ expedition, campaign

cτράτευμα, –ατοc, τό army; expedition, campaign

cτρατεύομαι advance with an army or fleet; wage war

cτρατεύω serve in war; send a force, make an expedition

cτρατηγέω be general

cτρατηγιᾱ, –ᾶc, ἡ generalship

cτρατηγόc, –οῦ, ὁ general, commander

cτρατιᾱ, –ᾶc, ἡ army

cτρατιώτηc, –ου, ὁ soldier

cτρατοπεδεύω make camp, encamp (also mid.)

cτρατόπεδον, –ου, τό camp, army

cτρατόc, –οῦ, ὁ army

cτρεπτόc, –οῦ, ὁ collar

Cτρεψιάδηc, –ου, ὁ Strepsiades

cτυγέω loathe, hate

cτυγνόc, –ή, –όν hateful, loathsome

cύ (pron.) you (s.) (4.1/2)

cυγγενήc, –έc related to, relative

cυγγενήc, –οῦc, ὁ relation, kinsman

cυγγίγνομαι† be with, have intercourse with, have dealings with (+dat.)

cυγγιγνώcκω† pardon, forgive (+dat.)

cυγγνώμη, –ηc, ἡ pardon, forgiveness cυγγνώμην ἔχω forgive, pardon

cυγγραφαί, –ῶν, αἱ contract, bond

cυγκομίζω† bring/gather together

cυγκρῑνω† compare (something with something, acc. and dat.)

cυγχωρέω agree to/with; concede, admit; yield to (+dat.)

cυλλαμβάνω† collect; understand; seize, arrest

cυλλέγω† collect, gather

cύλλογοc, –ου, ὁ meeting

Cυμαῖθοc, –ου, ὁ Symaethus (river in Sicily)

cυμβαίνω† happen, occur, result; correspond with, fit

cύμβαcιc, –εωc, ἡ agreement, arrangement

cυμβουλεύω advise, give advice (+dat. and inf.); (mid.) consult, discuss with (+dat.)

cυμμαχίᾱ, –ᾶc, ἡ alliance

cυμμαχιc, –ίδοc, ἡ alliance, confederacy

cύμμαχοc, –ου, ὁ ally

cυμμείγνῡμι mix together; (intr.) meet with (+dat.)

cυμπάρειμι be present together

cύμπᾶc, cύμπᾶcα, cύμπαν (= πᾶc) all, all together, the whole

cυμπληρόω fill up

cυμπορεύομαι march in company with

cυμπόcιον, –ου, τό drinking-party, symposium

cυμπότηc, –ου, ὁ drinking-companion

cυμφέρει (impers.) it is useful/expedient (+dat. and inf., 21.1/4a)

cυμφορά, –ᾶc, ἡ event; disaster, mishap

cύν (prep.+dat.) together with; with the help of

cυναγορεύω (aor. cυνεῖπον, 18.1/4 note 2) advocate (a course of action) with (someone)

cυναιρέω† to bring together ὡc cυνελόντι εἰπεῖν to speak concisely, in a word

cυναμφότεροc, –ᾱ, –ον both together

cυνδόξαν (acc. absol.) *it having seemed good also* (21.1/5)
cύνειμι *be with, be joined with* (+dat.)
cυνεκπονέω *assist* (+dat.)
cυνελών see cυναιρέω
cυνέρχομαι† *come together, assemble*
cυνετός, -ή, -όν *intelligent*
cυνήθεια, -ᾱc, ἡ *acquaintance, intimacy*
cύνθημα, -ατοc, τό *sign*
cυνθηράω *hunt with* (+dat.)
cυντ́ημι† *understand*
cυνίcτημι† (mid. and intr. tenses of act.) *conspire* (+dat.)
#cυννεάζω *be young with* (+dat.)
cυντάττω *arrange, draw up in battle-order*
cυντίθημι† *put together*; (mid.) *arrange, agree upon*
cύντομος, -ον *concise, brief*
cυντρῑβω *smash, gash*
cυντυγχάνω† *meet with* (+dat.)
Cυρᾱκόcιοc, -ᾱ, -ον *Syracusan*
Cυρᾱκοῦcαι, -ῶν, αἱ *Syracuse*
cυcκευάζομαι *pack up; contrive, concoct*
cύcταcιc, -εωc, ἡ *composition, constitution*
cυcτρατεύω *join an expedition, fight alongside*
cφαγή, -ῆc, ἡ *slaughter, slaughtering*
cφάζω *slaughter, sacrifice*
cφαῖρα, -ᾱc, ἡ *ball*
cφαλερός, -ά, -όν *perilous, precarious*
†cφάλλω *trip up, make to fall;* (pass.) *be tripped up, stumble, fall; be baffled /disappointed*
cφᾶc (cφῶν, cφίcι) see ἑ (9.1/4a)
#cφε (dat. cφι(ν)) (pron. acc. s. or pl.) *him, her, them*
cφέτεροc, -ᾱ, -ον (poss. adj., strengthened by αὐτῶν, 25.2.3 l. 7) *their own*
cφόδρα (adv.) *very much, exceedingly*
cφοδρός, -ά, -όν *impetuous*
cφώ, cφῷν (pron.) *you two* (dual of cύ, 24.1/4)

cχ- aor. act./mid. stem of ἔχω
cχεδόν (adv.) *nearly, near, almost*
#cχεθεῖν poet. aor. act. inf. of ἔχω
Cχερίᾱ, -ᾱc, ἡ *Scheria* (land of the Phaeacians)
cχῆμα, -ατοc, τό *form, shape, appearance; character*
cχήcω fut. of ἔχω
cχοινίον, -ου, τό *little rope*
cχολή, -ῆc, ἡ *leisure, rest*
cχολῇ *in a leisurely way, tardily*
†cῴζω *save, keep safe*
Cωκράτηc, -ουc, ὁ *Socrates* (philosopher)
Cωκρατίδιον, -ου, τό (diminutive) *dear little Socrates*
cῶμα, -ατοc, τό *body, person*
Cωcιγένηc, -ουc, ὁ *Sosigenes*
cωτήρ, -ῆροc, ὁ *saviour*
cωτηρίᾱ, -ᾱc, ἡ *safety*
cωφρονέω *be discreet/prudent*
cωφροcύνη, -ηc, ἡ *good sense, moderation*
cώφρων, -ον *sensible, temperate, reasonable, moderate, discreet*

ταλαιπωρίᾱ, -ᾱc, ἡ *hardship, distress*
τάλαντον, -ου, τό *talent* (= 6,000 drachmas)
#τάλᾱc, -αινα, -αν *miserable, wretched, unhappy* (10.1/3 note 2)
τἆλλα (or τἄλλα) crasis for τὰ ἄλλα
ταμιεῖον, -ου, τό *storeroom*
Ταμώc, -ῶ, ὁ *Tamos* (13.1/1a)
ταξίαρχοc, -ου, ὁ *taxiarch, brigadier*
τάξιc, -εωc, ἡ *arrangement, rank, battle-array*
#τάραγμα, -ατοc, τό *confusion*
Τάρᾱc, -αντοc, ὁ *Tarentum* (town in southern Italy)
ταράττω *trouble, disturb*
ταρβέω *be terrified*
ταριχεύω *embalm, mummify*
ταρρόc, -οῦ, ὁ *mat*
#Τάρταροc, -ου, ὁ *Tartarus; the underworld*
τάττω *station, draw up; appoint, place in order; order, instruct*
ταύτῃ *here; by this route; in this way*
ταφή, -ῆc, ἡ *burial*
τάφοc, -ου, ὁ *grave, tomb*

τάχα (adv.) *quickly*
ταχέως (adv.) *quickly, soon*
τάχιστος, -η, -ον *quickest* (supl. of ταχύς)
  τὴν ταχίστην *the quickest way*
  ἐπειδὴ τάχιστα *as soon as*
τάχος, -ους, τό *speed*
ταχύς, -εῖα, -ύ *quick, fast*
τε* *and*
τε* ... καί/τε* *both ... and*
τέθνηκα *I am dead* (perf. of [ἀπο]θνῄσκω 19.1/3*a*)
τείνω *stretch; lead* (a life)
#τείρω *oppress, distress*
τείχισμα, -ατος, τό *wall, fort*
τειχομαχέω *fight against walls/fortifications*
τεῖχος, -ους, τό *wall*
τεκ- aor. stem of τίκτω
τεκμαίρομαι *conclude, infer*
τεκμήριον, -ου, τό *evidence, proof*
τέκνον, -ου, τό *child*
τεκνόομαι *beget, produce*
τελευταῖος, -ᾱ, -ον *last*
τελευτάω *end, finish; die*
τελευτή, -ῆς, ἡ *end, death*
†τελέω *accomplish, fulfil, complete; conduct*
τέλος, -ους, τό *end, consummation, fulfilment*
  τέλος (adv. acc., 20.1/5) *in the end, finally*
  διὰ τέλους *through to the end, throughout*
†τέμνω *cut; ravage*
#τέος = σός
#τέρμα, -ατος, τό *end*
τερπνός, -ή, -όν *delightful, pleasant*
τέρπομαι *enjoy oneself*
Τερψίων, -ωνος, ὁ *Terpsion*
τέταρτος, -η, -ον *fourth*
τέτοκα perf. of τίκτω
#τετράπαλαι (adv.) *long, long ago*
τετταράκοντα (indecl. numeral) *forty*
τέτταρες, -α *four* (7.1/5)
τέττιξ, -ῑγος, ὁ *cicada, grasshopper*
Τευθρανίᾱ, -ᾱς, ἡ *Teuthrania*
τέχνη, -ης, ἡ *skill, art, expertise; way, manner, means; trick, wile*
τῇδε (adv.) *here*

τηλικοῦτος, -αύτη, -οῦτον *so great, so important*
#τηλουρός, -όν *distant*
τήμερον (adv.) *today*
τηρέω *watch, guard; watch for, observe*
τί; *what? why?* (10.1/1 note 1); *in what respect?*
Τιγράνης, -ου, ὁ *Tigranes*
†τίθημι *put, place; make, render* (act. and mid.) (18.1/2)
  νόμους τίθημι *lay down laws*
  νόμους τίθεμαι *make/adopt laws*
†τίκτω *bear, beget, give birth to*
τῑμάω *honour; value, reckon;* (+dat.) *fine*
τῑμή, -ῆς, ἡ *honour, privilege, respect*
  ἐν τῑμῇ ἔχω *respect, honour*
τίμιος, -ᾱ, -ον *held in honour*
Τῑμόκριτος, -ου, ὁ *Timocritus*
τῑμωρέω *avenge* (+dat.); (act. and mid.) *take vengeance on, punish* (+acc.)
τῑμωρίᾱ, -ᾱς, ἡ *revenge, vengeance*
Τιρίβαζος, -ου, ὁ *Tiribazus*
τις, τι* (indef. pron.) *a certain, someone, something* (10.1/1)
  τι (adv. acc., 20.1/5) *to some extent*
τίς; τί; (interrog. pron.) *who? which? what?* (10.1/1)
Τισσαφέρνης, -ους, ὁ *Tissaphernes* (Persian satrap)
τίτλος, -ου, ὁ *title, inscription*
†τιτρώσκω *wound*
#τλάω (aor. ἔτλην) *venture, bring oneself to do something*
τλήμων, -ον *wretched, unfortunate; patient, resolute*
τοι* (particle) *in truth, be assured*
τοίνυν* (particle) *now then, well now* (13.1/3*a*)
#τοῖος, -ᾱ, -ον = τοιοῦτος
τοιόσδε, -άδε, -όνδε *of this sort, of such a sort, such* (21.1/3)
τοιοῦτος, -αύτη, -οῦτο(ν) *of this sort, of such a sort* (21.1/3)
τόκος, -ου, ὁ *offspring*
τόλμα, -ης, ἡ *daring*
τολμάω *dare, be daring; undertake*
τόξον, -ου, τό *bow* (also in plur.

τόξα, *bow [and arrows]*); (poetry)
ray/shaft (of sunshine)
τοξότης, –ου, ὁ *archer*
τόπος, –ου, ὁ *place, region; topic*
#τόςος, –η, –ον = τοςοῦτος
τοςόςδε, –ήδε, –όνδε *so much, so
large, so great* (pl. *so many*)
(21.1/3)
τοςοῦτος, –αύτη, –οῦτο(ν) *so much,
so large, so great* (pl. *so many*)
(21.1/3)
τότε (adv.) *then, at that time*
του = τινος *of someone/something*
τοῦ can = τίνος; *of whom/what?*
τοὔνομα crasis for τὸ ὄνομα
τούτῳ dat.of οὗτος
    ἐν τούτῳ *meanwhile*
τράπεζα, –ης, ἡ *table; bank*
τραῦμα, –ατος, τό *wound*
τράχηλος, –ου, ὁ *neck, throat*
τραχύς, –εῖα, –ύ *rough, prickly*
τραχύτης, –ητος, ἡ *roughness*
τρεῖς, τρία *three* (7.1/5)
†τρέπω *cause to turn, put to flight*
†τρέφω *rear, raise, feed, nourish*
†τρέχω *run*
τριάκοντα (indecl. numeral) *thirty*
τριάκόντερος, –ου, ἡ (*sc.* ναῦς)
    thirty-oared ship
τριάκόσιοι, –αι, –α *300*
τρῖβω *rub*
τριηραρχέω *serve as trierarch*
τριήραρχος, –ου, ὁ *trierarch*
τριήρης, –ους, ἡ *trireme*
τρίς (adv.) *three times*
τριςχῑλιοι, –αι, –α *3,000*
#τρίτατος = τρίτος
τρίτος, –η, –ον *third*
τρίχες, αἱ nom. pl. of θρίξ
Τροιᾱ, –ᾱς, ἡ *Troy*
τροπαῖον, –ου, τό *trophy*
τρόπος, –ου, ὁ *way, manner, way of
life;* (in pl.) *ways, habits, character*
    τίνα τρόπον ; (adv. acc., 20.1/5) *in
    what way?, how?*
    τοῦτον τὸν τρόπον (adv. acc.) *in
    this way*
    τούτῳ τῷ τρόπῳ *in this way*
τροφή, –ῆς, ἡ *food, nourishment*
τρύω *wear out, distress*
Τρῳάς, –άδος, ἡ *Trojan woman*

Τρῶες, –ων, οἱ *Trojans* (13.1/1b(i))
Τρωικός, –ή, –όν *Trojan*
    τὰ Τρωικά (*sc.* πράγματα) *the
    Trojan War*
†τυγχάνω (+gen., 13.1/2a(iv)) *hit* (the
    mark), *succeed; chance/happen
    upon, obtain;* (+pple.) *happen to -,
    be actually -* (15.1/2e)
#τύκιςμα, –ατος, τό *working* or
    chiselling in stone
τύλη, –ης, ἡ *cushion*
τύμβος, –ου, ὁ *tomb*
τυπείς aor. pass. pple. of τύπτω
τύπτω *strike, hit, beat*
τυραννεύω *be tyrant*
τυραννίς, –ίδος, ἡ *sovereignty;
    tyranny*
τύραννος, –ου, ὁ *absolute ruler,
    sovereign; tyrant*
τῡρός, –οῦ, ὁ *cheese*
τυφλός, –ή, –όν *blind*
τυχ– aor. stem of τυγχάνω
τύχη, –ης, ἡ *chance, luck, good* or
    bad fortune; (personified, with
    cap.) *Chance, Fortune*
τῳ = τινι *to/for someone/something*
τῷ can = τίνι; *to/for whom/what?*
τῷ ὄντι *in fact, really*

ὑβρίζω *treat violently/ disgracefully;
    humiliate*
ὕβρις, –εως, ἡ *aggression, violence,
    insolence, insult, humiliation*
ὑβριστής, –οῦ, ὁ *violent/ insolent
    person*
ὑγιεια, –ᾱς, ἡ *health*
ὕδρᾱ, –ᾱς, ἡ *hydra* (water serpent)
ὕδωρ, –ατος, τό *water*
ὕει (impers.) *it is raining* (21.1/4c)
ὕειος, –ᾱ, –ον *of pigs, pork*
υἱός, –οῦ, ὁ *son* (13.1/1c)
ὕλη, –ης, ἡ *wood, forest*
ὑλοτόμος, –ου, ὁ *woodcutter*
ὑμεῖς (pron.) *you* (pl., 4.1/2)
ὑμέτερος, –ᾱ, –ον (poss. adj.) *your* (pl.)
ὑπάρχω† *be; begin* (+gen.)
ὕπειμι *be beneath* (+dat.)
ὑπέρ (prep.) (+acc.) *beyond;* (+gen.)
    for, on behalf of
ὑπερβαίνω† *step over, cross*
    (mountains)

ὑπερβάλλω† *pass over, cross*

Ὑπέρεια, -ᾱς, ἡ *Hypereia* (a spring)

ὑπερέχω† *be above, stick out above*

Ὑπερίων, -ωνος, ὁ *Hyperion* (the Sun-god)

#ὑπερμαχέω *fight for*

#ὑπέρπικρος, -ον *exceedingly bitter*

ὑπερύψηλος, -ον *very high*

ὑπερφρονέω *be overproud, look down on*

ὑπέρχυσις, -εως, ἡ *overflow*

ὑπηρετέω *perform a service*

ὑπηρέτης, -ου, ὁ *servant*

†ὑπισχνέομαι *promise*

ὕπνος, -ου, ὁ *sleep*

ὑπό (prep.) (+acc.) *under, along under, up under*; (+gen.) *from under; by, at the hand of*; (+dat.) *under, beneath*; (Homeric) *at the hand(s) of*

ὑπόδημα, -ατος, τό *sandal*

ὑποζύγιον, -ου, τό *beast of burden, draught animal*

ὑπόθεσις, -εως, ἡ *proposal, supposition*

ὑποκαταβαίνω† *descend gradually*

ὑπολαμβάνω† *take up, answer, reply; assume*

ὑπολείπω† *leave behind*

ὑπόλοιπος, -ον *remaining*

ὑποπέμπω† *send secretly*

ὑποπτεύω *suspect, be suspicious*

ὑποπτήττω *cower before* (+acc.)

#ὑπορρήγνῡμι† *burst beneath*

ὑποτελέω† *pay* (tribute)

ὑποτίθημι† *place under*

ὑποφαίνω† *dawn, begin to break*

ὗς, ὑός, ὁ/ἡ *pig*

Ὑστάσπης, -ου, ὁ *Hystaspes*

ὑστεραῖος, -ᾱ, -ον *following, next*
τῇ ὑστεραίᾳ *on the following day*

ὕστερον (adv.) *later, afterwards*

ὕστερος, -ᾱ, -ον *later, last* (of two)

ὑφ' = ὑπό

ὑφαίνω *weave*

ὑφαιρέομαι† (aor. act./ mid. stem ὑφελ-) *steal, take by stealth*

ὑφῑημι† *send;* (mid. and intr. tenses of act.) *submit, yield*

#ὑψηλόκρημνος, -ον *with lofty cliffs*

ὑψηλός, -ή, -όν *high*

ὕψος, -ους, τό *height,*

φαγ– aor. stem of ἐσθίω

#φαεινός, -ή, -όν *shining, radiant, bright*

φαεσφόρος, -ον *light-bringing;* (personified, with cap.) *the Light-Bringer,* i.e *the Morning Star*

†φαίνω *reveal, declare;* (pass.) *appear, be seen, seem;* (+pple.) *obviously be;* (+inf.) *seem to be* (15.1/2d)

Φάληρον, -ου, τό *Phalerum* (a port of Athens)

Φαληροῖ *at Phalerum*

φάναι inf. of φημί

φανερός, -ά, -όν *clear, obvious, visible*

φάος, -ους, τό *light, daylight*

φάραγξ, -αγγος, ἡ *chasm, ravine*

φάρμακον, -ου, τό *poison; drug; remedy; potion*

φάσκω *allege, state, declare, claim*

φαῦλος, -ον (also –η, –ον) *mean, poor, low; trivial, ordinary, indifferent, cheap*

Φειδιππίδης, -ου, ὁ *Pheidippides*

Φειδιππίδιον, -ου, τό (diminutive) *dear little Pheidippides*

φείδομαι *spare* (+gen.)

φέρε (2nd s. imp. of φέρω) *come!*

†φέρω *carry, bring; bear, endure; produce; lead* (of a road)
ἄγω καὶ φέρω *plunder*
χαλεπῶς φερω *be annoyed at* (+acc.)

φεῦ (interjection) *alas!;* (+gen.) *alas for*

†φεύγω *flee, flee from, escape* (+acc.); *be a defendant, be on trial; be proscribed, be banished, be in exile* (17.1/5)

†φημί *say* (7.1/2)

†φθάνω *anticipate* (15.1/2f)

φθέγγομαι *speak, say, utter*

†φθείρω *destroy, ruin*

#φθίμενος, -η, -ον *dead*

φθονέω *feel ill-will/envy/jealousy against, grudge* (+dat.,13.1/2b(i))

φθόνος, -ου, ὁ *envy, jealousy*

φιλάνθρωπος, -ον *loving mankind, man-loving, humane*

φιλάργυρος, -ον *avaricious, miserly*
φιλέω *love, like, be a friend of; kiss;*
be accustomed to (+inf.)
φιλητέον *one must love* (24.1/5)
φιλίᾱ, -ᾱς, ἡ *friendship*
Φιλιππισμός, -οῦ, ὁ *siding with*
Philip
Φίλιππος, -ου, ὁ *Philip* (father of
Alexander the Great)
φιλόκαλος, -ον *loving beauty, fond*
of elegance
Φιλοκράτης, -ους, ὁ *Philocrates*
φίλος, -η, -ον *dear, friendly;*
pleasing to (+dat.)
φίλος, -ου, ὁ *friend*
φιλοσοφέω *pursue/study philosophy*
φιλοσοφίᾱ, -ᾱς, ἡ *philosophy*
φιλόσοφος, -ου, ὁ *philosopher*
φιλότης, -ητος, ἡ *love, friendship;*
sexual intercourse
φιλότῑμος, -ον *loving distinction,*
ambitious
φιλοφροσύνη, -ης, ἡ *love, affection*
φίλτατος, -η, -ον *most dear* (supl. of
φίλος)
#φίλυμνος, -ον *loving song*
φλόξ, -ογός, ἡ *flame*
φλυᾱρέω *talk nonsense*
φλυᾱρίᾱ, -ᾱς, ἡ *nonsense*
†φοβέομαι *fear, be afraid of*
φοβέομαι μή *fear lest/that*
(14.1/4c(ii))
φοβερός, -ά, -όν *terrible, frightening*
φόβος, -ου, ὁ *fear, panic*
#φοῖβος, -η, -ον *pure, bright, radiant*
Φοῖβος, -ου, ὁ *Phoebus* (Apollo)
#Φοινικογενής, -ές *Phoenician-born*
Φοῖνιξ, -ικος, ὁ *Phoenician*
#φοίνιος, -ᾱ, -ον *bloody*
φοιτάω *go regularly to, frequent,*
resort to (a person as a teacher)
φονεύς, -έως, ὁ *murderer*
φονεύω *murder, slay*
φόνος, -ου, ὁ *murder, slaughter,*
homicide
φορέω *carry, bring*
φορος, -ου, ὁ *tribute*
φορτίον, -ου, τό *load, burden*
φράζω *explain, tell, declare*
#φρήν, φρενός, ἡ *heart, mind* (pl. is
used in the same sense)

φρονέω *think, consider; be wise,*
sensible
εὖ φρονέω *be sane*
μέγα φρονέω *be proud, have high*
thoughts
φρόνημα, -ατος, τό *arrogance, pride*
φρόνιμος, -ον *sensible, wise*
φροντίζω *think, ponder, consider,*
worry; pay heed to (+gen.)
φροντίς, -ίδος, ἡ *thought, care,*
concern
Φροντιστήριον, -ου, τό *Think Tank,*
Thinking shop
φροντιστής, -οῦ, ὁ *deep thinker*
φρούριον, -ου, τό *fort*
φρύγανα, -ων, τά *dry wood, firewood*
φυγάς, -άδος, ὁ *exile; runaway;*
fugitive
φυγή, -ῆς, ἡ *flight*
φυλακή, -ῆς, ἡ *guard, guarding,*
garrison
ἐν φυλακῇ εἰμι *be on guard*
φύλαξ, -ακος, ὁ *guard*
φυλάττω (perf. πεφύλαχα) *guard,*
watch; (mid.) *take care, be on one's*
guard against (+acc.)
φῡρω *spoil, defile, mar*
φύσις, -εως, ἡ *nature, character,*
temperament
†φῡω *cause to grow, produce*
ἔφῡν *was born; am naturally*
πέφῡκα *am naturally, am inclined*
by nature
Φώκαια, -ᾱς, ἡ *Phocaea* (city in
Asia Minor)
φωνέω *speak*
φωνή, -ῆς, ἡ *voice, language,*
speech
φῶς, φωτός, τό *light*

Χαιρεφῶν, -ῶντος, ὁ *Chaerephon*
(disciple of Socrates)
†χαίρω *rejoice*
χαῖρε *greetings! hello! farewell!*
(17.1/1 note 7)
χαλεπαίνω *be angry/annoyed at*
(+dat.)
χαλεπός, -ή, -όν *difficult, hard*
χαλεπῶς ἔχω *be in a bad way*
χαλεπῶς φερω *be angry/displeased*
at (+acc.)

χαλινός, –οῦ, ὁ   bit (for a horse's bridle)

#χάλκευμα, –ατος, τό   anything bronze; (pl.) brazen bonds

χαλκός, –οῦ, ὁ   bronze

χαλκοῦς, –ῆ, –οῦν   of bronze

#χαλκοχίτων, –ωνος   bronze-clad

Χάονες, –ων, οἱ   the Chaonians (tribe in Epirus)

χάος, –ους, τό   chaos

χαρακτήρ, –ῆρος, ὁ   engraved mark; characteristic, character

χαρίεις, –εσσα, –εν   graceful, elegant, charming, nice

χαριεντίζομαι   jest, joke

χαρίζομαι   oblige, do a favour to (+dat.); give graciously

χάρις, –ιτος (acc. χάριν), ἡ   grace, charm; favour; recompense, thanks

χάριν οἶδα / ἔχω   be grateful to (+dat.)

Χάρυβδις, –εως, ἡ   Charybdis (a whirlpool)

χεῖλος, –ους, τό   lip

χειμών, –ῶνος, ὁ   storm; winter

χείρ, χειρός, ἡ   hand

Χειρίσοφος, ου, ὁ   Cheirisophus (Lacedaemonian general of Cyrus)

χείριστος, –η, –ον   worst (supl. of κακός)

χειροτέχνης, –ου, ὁ   craftsman

χείρων, –ον   worse (compar. of κακός)

χελῑδών, –όνος, ἡ   swallow

χελώνη, –ης, ἡ   tortoise

Χερρόνησος, –ου, ἡ   the Chersonese (the Gallipoli peninsula)

χἠ crasis for καὶ ἡ

χῆτος, –ους, τό   want, lack, need

χθές   yesterday

#χθών, χθονός, ἡ   earth, land

χίλιοι, –αι, –α   thousand

Χίος, –ου, ἡ   Chios (island and city in the Aegean)

χιτών, –ῶνος, ὁ   tunic, shirt

χιών, –όνος, ἡ   snow

χολή, –ῆς, ἡ   bile, gall; anger

χορεύω   dance

†χράομαι   deal with, associate with, treat, use (+dat., 13.1/2b(iii))

χρεία, –ᾱς, ἡ   use, serviceability

†χρή   it is necessary (+acc. and inf.)

χρῄζω   desire, want, need (+gen.)

χρῆμα, –ατος, τό   thing; (pl.) money, goods

χρηματίζω   deal with business (in the Council or Assembly)

χρῆσθαι inf. of χράομαι

χρήσιμος, –η, –ον   profitable, useful

χρησμός, –οῦ, ὁ   oracle

χρηστήριον, –ου, τό   oracle

χρηστός, –ή, –όν   good, fine, serviceable

χρῆται 3rd s. pres. of χράομαι

χρῑστός, –ή, –ον   anointed

χροιά, –ᾶς, ἡ   skin

χρόνος, –ου, ὁ   time

διὰ χρόνου   after a time

χρῡσίον, –ου, τό   a piece of gold, gold

χρῡσός, –οῦ, ὁ   gold

χρῡσοῦς, –ῆ, –οῦν   golden

#χρώς, –ωτός (also χρόα, χροός, χροΐ), ὁ   skin, flesh

χυτός, –ή, –όν   poured; melted (with λίθινος, made of glass); piled, heaped up

χύτρᾱ, –ᾱς, ἡ   pot

χὠ crasis for καὶ ὁ

χώρᾱ, –ᾱς, ἡ   land, country

χωρέω   go, come; be in motion

χωρίζω   separate

χωρίον, –ου, τό   place, space; region; farm

χωρίς   without, apart, separately (from) (+gen.)

ψάλια, –ων, τά   curb-chain of bridle, bridle

ψάμμος, –ου, ἡ   sand

ψέγω   blame, censure

ψευδής, –ές   false, lying

ψεύδομαι   lie, tell lies; cheat, deceive

ψεῦδος, –ους, τό   falsehood, lie

ψευδῶς (adv.)   falsely

ψηφίζομαι   vote

ψήφισμα, –ατος, τό   decree

ψῆφος, –ου, ἡ   voting-pebble, vote

ψῑλοί, –ῶν, οἱ   light-armed troops

ψόγος, –ου, ὁ   blame

ψόφος, –ου, ὁ   noise

ψύλλα, –ης, ἡ   flea

ψῡχή, -ῆς, ἡ   soul, life, spirit
ψῦχος, -ους, τό   cold, period of cold
   weather
ψῡχρός, ᾱ, -όν   cold

ὤ   what! (+gen.)
ὦ   O (addressing someone);   ah!
   (exclamation of surprise)
Ὠγυγίᾱ, -ᾱς, ἡ   Ogygia (island of
   Calypso)
ὧδε (adv.)   thus, as follows; (poet.) to
   here, hither
ὠδῑνω   be in labour (of childbirth)
ὠή (exclamation)   help!
Ὠκεανός, -οῦ, ὁ   Ocean (son of
   Heaven and Earth)
#ὠκύς, -εῖα, -ύ   swift, quick
ὠλόμην aor. of ὄλλυμαι
ᾤμην impf. of οἶμαι
ὤμοι (exclamation)   ah me, woe is
   me, alas
#ὠμοφάγος, -ον   eating raw flesh,
   where raw flesh is eaten
ὤν, οὖσα, ὄν pres. pple. of εἰμί
   τὸ ὄν   reality
   τῷ ὄντι   in fact, really
†ὠνέομαι (aor. ἐπριάμην)   buy
ᾠόν, -οῦ, τό   egg
ὥρᾱ, -ᾱς, ἡ   season (of the year);
   time; beauty
ὡρμισμένος, -η, -ον perf. mid./pass.
   pple. of ὁρμίζω

ὡς (for a summary of uses see 22.1/1)
   (adv.)   as; like
   (exclamatory)   how! (+adj. or
      adv.)
   (+numerals)   about, nearly
   (+pples.)   on the grounds that,
      under the impression that; with
      the intention of (fut. pple.)
      (12.1/2a(ii) and (v))
   (restrictive)   for, considering
      that
   (+supl.)   as . . . as possible
   (conj.)   that (= ὅτι); in order that
      (= ἵνα, ὅπως); when, as (ὡς
      τάχιστα as soon as, lit. when
      quickest, but if this expression is
      used adverbially it means as
      quickly as possible, 17.1/4d);
      since
   (prep.)   to, towards, to the house of
ὥς (adv.)   thus, so
ὡσαύτως (also ὡς αὔτως) (adv.)   in
   the same way, just so
ὥσπερ (adv./conj.)   like, as, as if
ὥστε (conj.)   so that, that, with the
   result that, consequently (+inf. or
   ind., 16.1/1)
ὠτ- stem of οὖς   ear
ᾦτε see ἐφ᾽
ὠφελέω   help, assist, be of use to,
   benefit
ὠφελητέον   one must help (24.1/5)

Index